An Investment Perspective on
Global Value Chains

An Investment Perspective on Global Value Chains

Christine Zhenwei Qiang | Yan Liu |
Victor Steenbergen

 WORLD BANK GROUP

Contents

Boxes

Figures

Maps

Tables

Foreword

Global value chains (GVCs) have played a critical role in transforming business sectors in many developing countries by allowing specialization in certain activities and stages of production. Participation in GVCs is often associated with a faster pace of industrialization, improving both firm productivity and new job creation.

However, GVC formation has stagnated in the past decade, possibly because of factors such as market saturation, geopolitics, automation, and increasing local capacity. The COVID-19 (coronavirus) pandemic has magnified the impact of a wide range of dynamic factors on GVCs. For example, new technologies have been altering the way products and services are designed, produced, distributed, and sold. The need for social distancing and restrictions on travel have accelerated investment in some of these technologies. In parallel, economic nationalism and policy uncertainty are tilting firms' investment decisions and the geographical distribution of GVCs. Growing awareness of climate change and the push for sustainability are speeding up the adoption of clean technology and the implementation of new rules, regulations, and standards. Increasing investment originating from developing countries is adding new dynamics in shaping future GVCs.

Against this background, this report investigates several pertinent questions: What are the main drivers of GVCs? Will COVID-19 lead to a significant reconfiguration of GVCs? What can developing countries do to maximize their opportunities for GVC integration?

To answer these questions, the report focuses on how multinational corporations (MNCs) shape GVCs and highlights the role of their relationships with domestic firms. It documents that MNCs were instrumental in the rapid rise of GVCs during the 1990s and 2000s. These firms are the architects of many GVCs, and their business decisions often have implications for the evolution of GVCs over time. To facilitate sectoral transformation through GVCs, policy makers in developing countries need to better understand MNCs' business strategies, further integrate domestic firms into global markets, and ensure their policies create a favorable environment for these firms.

Part I of the report presents a comprehensive review of industrial organization theories and empirical evidence to illustrate the mutually reinforcing relationship between foreign direct investment (FDI) and GVC participation. MNCs can reduce costs, mitigate risks, and increase their market power when organizing their global production networks. Domestic firms can internationalize and participate in GVCs through four main pathways: supplier linkages with international firms, strategic alliances with international firms, direct exporting, and outward FDI. The most powerful engine of productivity and competitiveness appears to lie in firm-to-firm interactions. In light of this evidence, the report identifies strategies that policy makers can adopt to stimulate GVC participation by attracting MNCs and linking them to domestic firms.

Part II consists of case studies examining the approaches of developing countries in leveraging FDI to stimulate and facilitate GVC participation and upgrading. In each of its examples—Kenya (horticulture), Honduras (apparel), Malaysia (electronics), Mauritius (tourism), and the Republic of Korea, India, and China (digital economy)—the report studies how countries' comparative advantages, as well as the specific roles of MNCs and domestic firms, differ. It describes the specific strategies and the mix of policy instruments used to strengthen a country's participation in the target GVC. Finally, a quantitative case study (Rwanda and West Bengal, in India) using firm- and transaction-level data provides new insights into the dynamics between MNCs and domestic firms in selected GVCs.

The report also discusses the potential impact of COVID-19 on FDI flows and GVCs. The pandemic has posed unprecedented challenges to GVCs worldwide, with an estimated 9.5 percent decline in global trade and a 42 percent decline in FDI in 2020. It has triggered new questions about GVCs and accelerated precrisis global trends such as digitalization and the drive for sustainability—in nature, health, and development. How MNCs and their supplier firms respond to the supply and demand shocks, as well as the policy uncertainty, will play a critical role in shaping the future of GVCs.

The pandemic has powerfully displayed the complex interdependence of firms and economies around the world. Maintaining an open trading system and improving investment competitiveness are key to global economic recovery. Practical policy advice presented in this report is critical to upgrading GVCs by attracting FDI and helping domestic firms internationalize. This advice is more valuable now than ever to strengthen growth and create jobs, and to formulate strategies for green, inclusive, and resilient development.

M. Ayhan Kose
Acting Vice President
Equitable Growth, Finance and
Institutions Practice Group

Acknowledgments

This report, *An Investment Perspective on Global Value Chains*, was authored by Christine Zhenwei Qiang, Practice Manager, and Yan Liu and Victor Steenbergen, both Economists, of the Global Investment Climate Unit at the World Bank Group.

Key inputs were provided by Maximilian Philip Eltgen, Ulla Heher, Ryan Chia Kuo, Tushar Nandi, Monica Paganini, Jakob Rauschendorfer, Anna Twum, Di Yang, and Xiaoou Zhu. Aarushi Sinha provided invaluable support in the production process. Special thanks also to Gerlin May Catangui, Xavier Forneris, Armando E. Heilbron, Priyanka Kher, Hania Kronfol, Peter Kusek, Yue Li, Graciela Miralles Murciego, Ivan Anton Nimac, Georgiana Pop, Abhishek Saurav, and Douglas Zhihua Zeng for their invaluable comments and suggestions. The authors particularly appreciate the guidance and support of Caroline Freund, Global Director of Trade, Investment and Competitiveness at the World Bank.

The team thanks the following programs and donors for making this report possible through their financial contributions: the Improving Business Environment for Prosperity (IBEP) program, with support from the UK Prosperity Fund managed by the Foreign, Commonwealth and Development Office (FCDO); and the Competitive Industries and Innovation Program (CIIP), with support from the European Union and the governments of Austria, Norway, and Switzerland.

The team is also grateful to the many reviewers who provided thoughtful insights and guidance at both the concept and decision stages. External peer reviewers include Bernard Hoekman (European University Institute), Bert Hofman (National University of Singapore), Richard Newfarmer (International Growth Centre), and James Zhan (United Nations Conference on Trade and Development). Reviewers internal to the World Bank were Thomas Farole, Hiau Looi Kee, and the Prospects Group (through Franziska Ohnsorge, Temel Taskin, and Shu Yu). Additional invaluable comments were provided by Francisco Campos, Alejandro Cedeño, Paolo Correa, Poonam Gupta, Lars Johannes, Nicholas Andrew Keyes, Hans Peter Lankes, Liane Lohde, Martin Raiser, Susan Starnes, Erik von Uexkull, and Deborah Winkler.

Amy Lynn Grossman was the production editor for the report. The cover was designed by Sergio Andrés Moreno. Production and logistics support was provided by Jewel McFadden. The communications efforts were led by Elizabeth Price and Inae Riveras.

Finally, the team thanks any individuals or organizations that contributed to this report but that were inadvertently omitted from these acknowledgments.

Abbreviations

¥	Chinese yuan
3D	three-dimensional
ABCD	Archer Daniels Midland, Bunge, Cargill, and Louis Dreyfus
AHM	Asociación Hondureña de Maquiladores
AI	artificial intelligence
AMNE	Activity of Multinational Enterprises
ASEAN	Association of Southeast Asian Nations
BAT	Baidu, Alibaba, and Tencent
BIT	bilateral investment treaty
BPM	business process management
CBI	Caribbean Basin Initiative
CBTPA	Caribbean Basin Trade Partnership Act
DCK	Dansk Chrysanthemum and Kultur
DMC	destination management company
E&E	electrical and electronics
EAP	East Asia and Pacific
EBIT	earnings before interest and taxes
EPZ	export processing zone
EU	European Union
F&V	fruits and vegetables
FDI	foreign direct investment
fintech	financial technology
FPEAK	Fresh Produce Exporters Association of Kenya
GDP	gross domestic product
GIC	Global Investment Competitiveness
GVC	global value chain
HCDA	Horticultural Crops Development Authority
HS	Harmonized System
IIoT	industrial internet of things
IC	integrated circuit
ICT	information and communication technology
IIA	international investment agreement
IoT	internet of things
IP	intellectual property
IPA	investment promotion agency
IPR	intellectual property rights
IT	information technology

JV	joint venture
KePHIS	Kenya Plant Health Inspectorate Service
KFC	Kenya Flower Council
M&A	mergers and acquisitions
MCO	movement control order
MIC	middle-income country
MICE	meetings, incentives, conferences, and events
MIDA	Malaysian Investment Development Authority
MLP	Medium- to Long-Term Strategic Plan (China)
MNC	multinational corporation
MOFCOM	Ministry of Commerce
MUR	Mauritian rupee
NDRC	National Development and Reform Commission
NEM	nonequity mode
OECD	Organisation for Economic Co-operation and Development
OFDI	outward foreign direct investment
P2P	peer-to-peer
PAC	Penang Automation Cluster
PC	personal computer
PPE	personal protective equipment
PRT	property rights theory
PSDC	Penang State Development Corporation
PTA	preferential trade agreement
R&D	research and development
RF	Rwanda franc
RM	Malaysian ringgit
S&E	science and engineering
SDP	supplier development program
SDP	state domestic product
SEZ	special economic zone
SKU	stock-keeping unit
SMEs	small and medium enterprises
SPE	special purpose entity
STI	science, technology, and innovation
TCE	transaction cost economics
UNCTAD	United Nations Conference on Trade and Development
US$	United States dollar
VAT	value added tax
VC	venture capital
WTO	World Trade Organization

Overview

Summary

The benefits of global value chain (GVC) participation have been extensively documented in the literature (Constantinescu, Mattoo, and Ruta 2018; Rocha and Winkler 2019; World Bank 2020a). *World Development Report 2020: Trading for Development in the Age of Global Value Chains* defines two features of GVCs—hyperspecialization in specific tasks and durable firm-to-firm relationships (figure O.1)—that distinguish them from traditional trade. Hyperspecialization by firms at different stages of value chains enhances efficiency and productivity, and durable firm-to-firm relationships foster technology transfer and access to capital and inputs along value chains. The result is increased productivity and income growth—more so than what countries achieve through domestic production but also than what they achieve through trade in finished goods (World Bank 2020a).

To better understand GVCs, it is essential to appreciate the role of multinational corporations (MNCs), which are at the heart of most GVCs. The emergence and evolution of GVCs are actually the result of MNCs' investment and trade decisions as MNCs have relocated their production activities worldwide. GVCs involve cross-border flows of all factors of production: capital, goods, services, people, technology, and knowledge.

Countries' GVC entry and upgrading are aggregate outcomes of their domestic firms' internationalization pathways. Integrating the domestic economy into MNCs' production networks opens up new opportunities for local firms, which no longer have to wait for the emergence of an in-country industrial base or the upstream capabilities formerly required to compete internationally. This can ultimately help developing countries industrialize more rapidly.

This report takes a close look at GVCs from an investment perspective. It summarizes the latest theories and the literature surrounding MNCs' and domestic firms' strategies and approaches, and the relationships, interactions, and dynamics among these firms along the various GVCs. The underlying analyses combine global foreign direct investment (FDI) data, trade data, and novel firm-level and transaction-level data to uncover the dynamics between investment and GVCs. The report also features six case studies analyzing the horticulture GVC in Kenya; tourism GVC in Mauritius; apparel GVC in Honduras; electrical and electronics GVC in Malaysia; and digital economy GVC in the Republic of Korea, India, and China; and providing a comparative analysis of GVC participation by Rwanda and West Bengal (India). These case studies were based in part on interviews the authors conducted between January and March 2020 with representatives of multinational corporations,

FIGURE O.1 Hyperspecialization and firm-to-firm relationships increasingly define global value chains

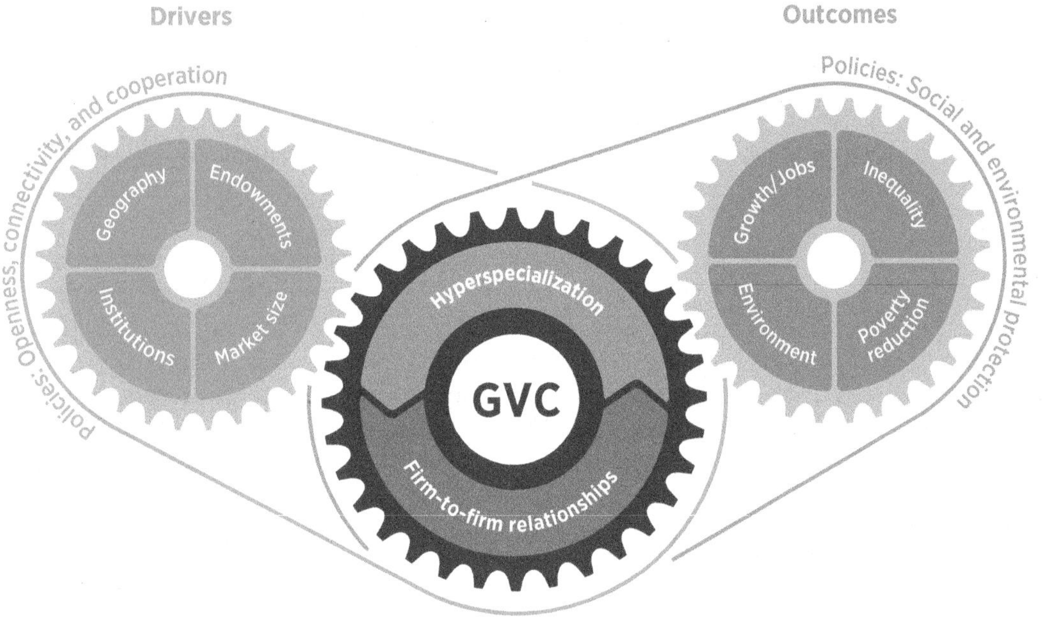

Drivers   Outcomes

Policies: Openness, connectivity, and cooperation

Geography
Endowments
Institutions
Market size

Hyperspecialization

GVC

Firm-to-firm relationships

Policies: Social and environmental protection

Growth/Jobs
Inequality
Environment
Poverty reduction

Source: World Bank 2020a.
Note: GVC = global value chain.

domestic firms, and government officials. The six case studies—and many other examples throughout the report—aim to provide practical insights for developing countries in different contexts on how they can develop strategies and approaches that leverage FDI to strengthen their GVC participation and upgrading.

The recent COVID-19 (coronavirus) pandemic brings added context to this report. The outbreak has triggered new questions about GVCs and has accelerated precrisis global trends. How MNCs and their supplier firms respond to the supply and demand shocks as well as policy uncertainties will play a critical role in crisis responses and recovery. The resilience of the GVCs during the first year of the pandemic signified the strong firm-to-firm relationships and networks.

The report concludes that participation in GVCs can confer considerable benefits on domestic firms because firms can learn from MNCs through investment, partnerships, and trade. The knowledge and experiences they gain through these interactions can raise firms' productivity and help them obtain the necessary production capabilities and foreign market knowledge to compete in international markets and to upgrade their roles in GVCs.

Even as new technologies, the drive for sustainability, and the changing origin of MNCs play an increasing role in shaping future GVCs, the pandemic has further revealed the complex interdependence of firms and economies around the world. GVCs are always evolving, and the search for diversification, resilience, and sustainability continues for both economic and political reasons. This report calls for global leaders to resist the lure of protectionist policies and work together to restore investor confidence and secure the hard-earned gains derived from GVCs.

Technology and hyperspecialization stimulated multinational activities in global value chain expansions

A primary impetus for GVC expansion in the past three decades came from MNCs, which were enabled by dramatically reduced communications and trade costs and have moved their operations to the global arena through production fragmentation, offshoring, and outsourcing.

Intensified multinational activities led to a period of hyperglobalization characterized by a surge in FDI as well as rapid increases in the share of trade in world gross domestic product and share of GVC trade in total trade. This rising importance of FDI and GVCs has provided new opportunities for many firms to participate in GVCs through a wide variety of investment, trade, contractual, and partnership arrangements. Until recently, most countries were excluded from participating in the production of complex products such as autos and electronics because of the required capital investments and technological knowledge. Now it is possible to specialize in a narrow stage of production, enabling more countries to participate.

Although all countries participate in GVCs, they have different comparative advantages and specialize in different sectors and segments of production. This report classifies sectors into six broad GVC archetypes in order of ascending average product complexity: commodities, labor-intensive services, labor-intensive goods, regional processing, knowledge-intensive services, and knowledge-intensive goods, as adapted from MGI (2019). These archetypes are used as an organizing framework in most chapters of this report to analyze how specific GVCs affect MNCs' strategies, domestic firms' internationalization pathways, and government policies intended to encourage GVC integration. At the same time, the report recognizes the high degree of heterogeneity within individual sectors and archetypes, as reflected in different stages of production, product differentiation, and differences in production technologies, and includes caveats, limitations, and examples to avoid overgeneralization.

Commodity exporters are most common in Sub-Saharan Africa and the Middle East. Labor-intensive services (such as tourism and transport) are the biggest GVC archetype for many small African, Caribbean, and Pacific countries. Countries specializing in labor-intensive goods (textiles, apparel, and leather products) are scattered around the world, and include Benin, Cambodia, Pakistan, and El Salvador. Regional processing (such as food processing) is the dominant GVC archetype for many countries in Sub-Saharan Africa and Latin America. A handful of countries, largely in North America, Western Europe, and the East Asia and Pacific region, participate primarily in knowledge-intensive goods GVCs (such as electronics and cars). Although no country has knowledge-intensive services as its dominant GVC archetype, such services are usually only second to knowledge-intensive goods GVCs in value in many advanced economies, notably Singapore, the United Kingdom, and the United States. See table O.1.

Foreign direct investment and global value chain participation are mutually reinforcing

There are mutually reinforcing dynamics between FDI and GVCs. Trade with foreign markets induces initial FDI from the lead firm by lowering its entry costs into the

TABLE O.1   **Key players in the six archetypes of global value chains, 2019**

GVC archetype	Commodities or sectors used for illustration	Top five exporters	Top five countries with the highest RCA
Commodities	Mineral fuels and oils (HS2 code: 27)	Russian Federation, United States, Saudi Arabia, Canada, Iraq	Kuwait, Brunei Darussalam, Azerbaijan, Republic of Congo, United Arab Emirates
Labor-intensive services	Transportation, hotels, tourism, and restaurants	China, United States, Germany, Japan, United Kingdom	Bermuda, Cayman Islands, Aruba, Georgia, Botswana
Labor-intensive goods	Textiles and clothing (HS2 code: 50–63)	China, Bangladesh, Vietnam, Germany, Italy	Pakistan, Cambodia, Benin, El Salvador, Mauritius
Regional processing	Food and beverage products (HS2 code: 16–24)	Germany, United States, Netherlands, France, China	Malawi, Cabo Verde, Seychelles, Belize, Côte d'Ivoire
Knowledge-intensive services	Professional services, computer and IT services, R&D	United States, Germany, Japan, United Kingdom, France	United States, Japan, Germany, France, United Kingdom
Knowledge-intensive goods	Transportation equipment (HS2 code: 86–89)	Germany, United States, Japan, Mexico, France	Slovak Republic, Japan, Czech Republic, Germany, France

Sources: United Nations Comtrade; United Nations Conference on Trade and Development–Eora Global Value Chain database; World Bank calculations.
Note: This table shows the top five exporters and top five countries with the highest RCA in selected products across the six GVC archetypes in 2019 (or 2015 for services). GVC = global value chain; HS2 = 2-digit Harmonized System codes; IT = information technology; RCA = revealed comparative advantage; R&D = research and development.

host country; lower entry costs and high switching costs encourage the lead firm to bring its GVC partners into the host country as well, and a herd effect triggers subsequent FDI. Finally, FDI stimulates further GVC entry and upgrading through spillovers and agglomeration effects. As a result, GVC expansion has mirrored the growth of MNCs' investments to unbundle production processes and relocate them worldwide.

Both FDI and GVC network analyses were conducted for this report to reveal the interrelationship between investment, trade, and GVCs in greater detail, and to depict the relationships among various actors and how they influence each other. GVCs are complex and multifaceted networks encompassing flows of people, capital, goods, services, information, and ideas. Each actor's own characteristics are only half the story in a globally interconnected world.

Countries' importance in the global FDI network is highly correlated with their importance in GVC network (figure O.2, panel a). Although countries take different development paths, their growing importance in the GVC network is often preceded by increasing FDI links with the rest of the world. FDI and GVC participation are concentrated in three regions, each with a central node (figure O.2, panel b): Western Europe (Germany), East Asia and Pacific (China, which replaced Japan since 2011), and North America (United States). Many countries in these three regions are both FDI hubs and GVC hubs. A few countries in Sub-Saharan Africa and Latin America have relatively high FDI and GVC centrality, such as Brazil, Mauritius, Mexico, Nigeria, and South Africa. But most other developing countries are marginal nodes in both the FDI and the GVC networks.

FIGURE O.2 Global value chain network and correlation with foreign direct investment network

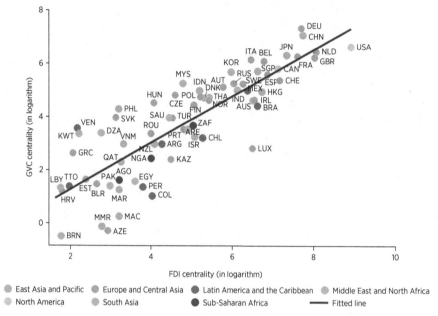

a. Countries that are central in global value chain networks are also central in global foreign direct investment networks, 2017

Source: World Bank calculations based on United Nations Conference on Trade and Development–Eora Global Value Chain database and International Monetary Fund bilateral foreign direct investment database.
Note: The x axis shows countries' weighted degree in the 2017 adjusted foreign direct investment network in natural logarithm. The y axis shows each country's weighted degree in the 2017 global value chain network in natural logarithm.

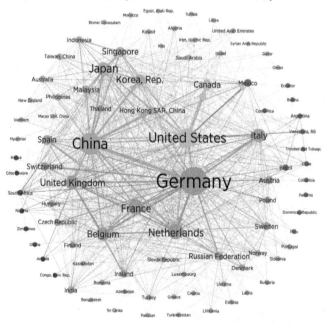

b. Germany, China, and the United States are the central nodes in global value chain trade networks, 2019

Sources: United Nations Conference on Trade and Development–Eora Global Value Chain database.
Note: The size of each node represents its weighted degree, which measures the corresponding economy's centrality to global value chains. Data for 2018 and 2019 are forecast based on the International Monetary Fund *World Economic Outlook*.

Foreign direct investment accompanied countries' upgrading into new global value chains

Almost all countries that have upgraded into new GVC archetypes in the past three decades have benefited from strong FDI inflows in related sectors. The most remarkable examples of countries' upgrading journeys include Costa Rica, which has successfully transformed its export composition from primary products to high-tech manufacturing and knowledge-intensive services industries thanks to a robust inflow of FDI in the past decades. FDI also played an indispensable role in China's move from labor-intensive goods to knowledge-intensive goods during the same period. China's FDI liberalization in 1992 generated a large influx of FDI. As of 2001, about 400 of the world's 500 largest MNCs had entered China. From 2001 to 2010, China's knowledge-intensive goods exports jumped by 700 percent, and the country become the world's second-largest GVC hub since 2011.

Other changes over the same period include Guatemala and Indonesia upgrading from commodities to regional processing, and Albania and Papua New Guinea joining labor-intensive services GVCs. Several countries also changed their export baskets noticeably, driven by increasing FDI inflows in more recent years, including Ethiopia and Vietnam, though they have not completely changed their dominant GVC archetypes. In contrast, a few other countries, such as Azerbaijan, the Democratic Republic of Congo, Iraq, and the Kyrgyz Republic, which previously specialized in labor-intensive services, have downgraded to become heavily reliant on commodity exports.

This report brings together the three key stakeholders in GVCs from an investment perspective: MNCs, domestic firms, and policy makers (figure O.3). To stimulate economic transformation through GVCs, policy makers in developing countries need to better understand MNCs' business strategies and support domestic firms' internationalization pathways.

Multinational corporations are the main architects of global value chains

MNCs are firms that operate direct business activities and own assets in at least two countries. Early MNCs invested abroad primarily to seek raw materials from developing countries. After World War II, many MNCs began operating in manufacturing, and the past three decades have seen more geographically fragmented activities in both manufacturing and services. MNCs increasingly outsource and develop business activities with a variety of external partners, ranging from subcontractors to suppliers to partners in research and development (R&D) or production activities. New structures have been developed to account both for these external networks and for networks of affiliates internal to the companies (Dietrich and Krafft 2012).

FIGURE O.3 A unifying framework for the three key players in global value chains: Multinational corporations, domestic firms, and policy makers

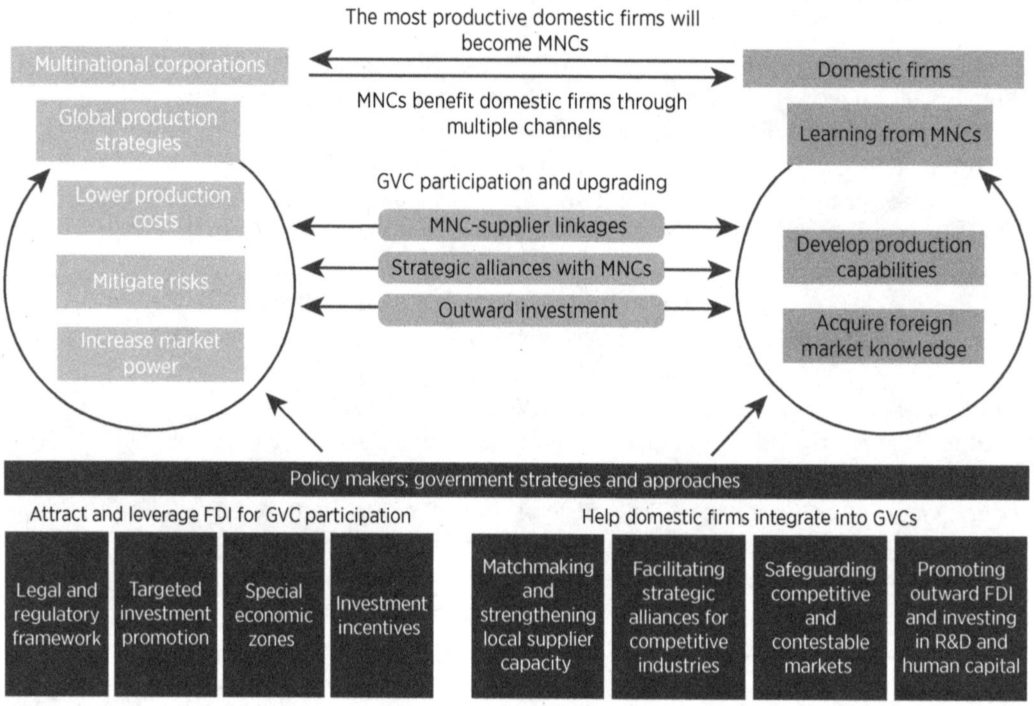

Source: World Bank.
Note: FDI = foreign direct investment; GVC = global value chain; MNC = multinational corporation; R&D = research and development.

MNCs have proliferated since the 1970s. Global estimates indicate that there were roughly 7,000 parent MNCs in 1970; this number had jumped to 38,000 by 2000 (OECD 2018) and was estimated at more than 100,000 in 2011 (UNCTAD 2011). Together, these MNCs had close to 900,000 affiliates in foreign countries.

MNCs account for a significant share of global output and trade in most sectors. According to the Organisation for Economic Co-operation and Development's Analytical Activities of MNEs (multinational enterprises) database, MNCs and their affiliates accounted for 36 percent of global output in 2016, including about two-thirds of global exports and more than half of imports. Their contribution is especially pronounced in knowledge-intensive goods sectors and in regional processing sectors (figure O.4). Motor vehicle manufacturing is the most internationalized sector: MNCs make up 90 percent of its exports. Regional processing is the second–most traded product group, and MNCs are responsible for about 70 percent of exports within it. Given the bulky or perishable nature of these products, most of the trade in this group happens in regional rather than global value chains.

FIGURE O.4 Multinational corporations' contributions to global exports rise with average product complexity

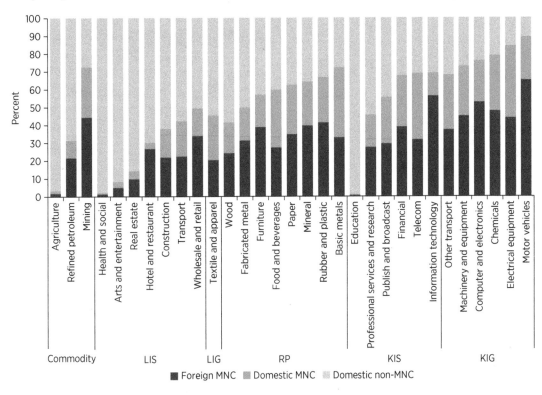

Source: World Bank calculations based on the Organisation for Economic Co-operation and Development's Analytical Activities of MNEs (multinational enterprises) database.
Note: Data are averaged from 2008 to 2016. KIG = knowledge-intensive goods; KIS = knowledge-intensive services; LIG = labor-intensive goods; LIS = labor-intensive services; MNC = multinational corporation; RP = regional processing.

Multinational corporations' business decisions aim to lower costs, mitigate risks, and increase market power

GVCs encompass a myriad of firm-to-firm relationships and the full range of activities required to bring a product or service from conception to its end use. These activities must be managed and coordinated. MNCs organize their international production networks through investment, trade, people, and information flows. Their objectives and business decisions have profound implications for the global economy (Buckley 2009, 2010; Buckley, Driffield, and Kim, forthcoming; Buckley and Strange 2011). Understanding GVCs is impossible without understanding how MNCs make their global production decisions.

MNCs have three main objectives in organizing their global production: lowering production costs, mitigating risks, and increasing market power (figure O.5). These three objectives are rooted in the theory of firms, industrial organization, and international trade and investment. MNCs balance rewards and risks in all these decisions, and they leverage their market power to raise their markups or negotiate

FIGURE O.5 Multinational corporations balance three interconnected objectives in organizing their global production

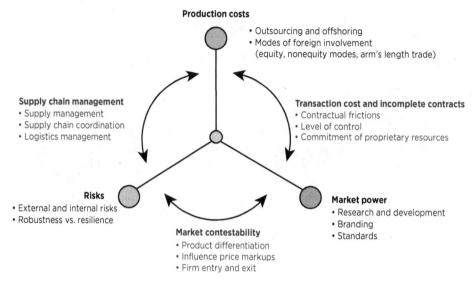

Production costs
- Outsourcing and offshoring
- Modes of foreign involvement
  (equity, nonequity modes, arm's length trade)

Supply chain management
- Supply management
- Supply chain coordination
- Logistics management

Transaction cost and incomplete contracts
- Contractual frictions
- Level of control
- Commitment of proprietary resources

Risks
- External and internal risks
- Robustness vs. resilience

Market power
- Research and development
- Branding
- Standards

Market contestability
- Product differentiation
- Influence price markups
- Firm entry and exit

Source: World Bank.

better terms of trade with suppliers. MNCs' "make or buy" decisions define the firms' boundaries. Their choices about which markets to serve, where to operate plants, what products to export, and which countries to source inputs from are interdependent (Bernard et al. 2018). These decisions affect variable production costs and prices and influence exports of products to markets and imports of inputs from source countries.

Despite their unrelenting quest for efficiency, MNCs also try to minimize and mitigate value chain risks by reducing production length, diversifying suppliers, and increasing supply chain visibility. However, the relationship between risks and all these measures is complicated and depends on the GVC archetype and its network structure. MNCs are increasingly willing to trade efficiency for risk mitigation as they grapple with increasing geopolitical tensions, environmental concerns, natural disasters, and volatile demand. Increasing uncertainty calls for more rigorous risk management.

MNCs are generally the largest and most productive firms in their respective markets. They use their market power to charge higher markups and improve their terms of trade with suppliers and customers. MNCs gain market power through a combination of strategies in addition to firm-specific assets. Some sectors (such as utilities and digital services) tend to be natural monopolies because of economies of scale and network effects. MNCs in such sectors benefit hugely from first-mover advantages. In many sectors, MNCs also gain market power through intangibles such as branding, design, and technology. They tend to invest aggressively in R&D, patenting, and marketing to establish their dominance. Most MNCs adopt multiple strategies that allow them to benefit disproportionally from GVCs.

The three objectives and MNCs' business strategies are inherently interconnected—MNCs often make purchasing, production, and selling decisions simultaneously. Their business strategies affect the gains that GVCs bring with respect to the distribution of value added, linkages to domestic firms, knowledge spillovers, allocation of resources, and consumer welfare. By understanding MNC objectives and strategies, developing countries can better stimulate their integration into GVCs and increase the development benefits from MNC activities in their economies.

Domestic firms' internationalization is a learning process through interactions with multinational corporations

Although GVCs are dominated by MNCs, studies often underestimate the importance of smaller firms in GVCs and the extent to which they participate in them. For example, Slaughter (2013) finds that the typical US MNC buys more than US$3 billion in inputs from more than 6,000 US small and medium enterprises (SMEs)—about 25 percent of all inputs the MNC purchases. One concept to correct is that GVC participation does not always require that a firm directly export goods or services. Instead, firms may be integrated into GVCs indirectly by producing and supplying intermediates to exporting firms or by offshoring part of their production facilities (Cusolito, Safadi, and Taglioni 2016).

Domestic firms internationalize, and thus participate in GVCs, through four main pathways: supplier linkages in a GVC network, strategic alliances with MNCs, direct exporting, and outward FDI (figure O.6). Supplier linkages depend on the presence of an international partner (possibly an MNC or domestic exporter) that is willing and able to source local inputs, together with capable domestic firms that are able to produce these inputs according to the appropriate production specifications. Strategic alliances rely on the complementary capacities and market knowledge of a domestic firm and an MNC. Direct exporting requires that domestic firms have both the minimum production capabilities and the overseas market knowledge to compete internationally. Outward FDI is a pathway for only a small number of domestic firms that meet the minimum firm scale and financial solvency requirements to be able to afford investing abroad.

In practice, these pathways are not mutually exclusive and can build on each other to help firms gain the technical and commercial knowledge to internationalize. Companies generally undertake the internationalization process as a cautious, stepwise progression and choose the pathways that appear more familiar and less risky (de Caldas Lima 2008). Firms that are successful in one area (for example, supplier linkages) also become increasingly likely to extend their involvement in other global production networks (for example, by coproducing with MNCs, direct exporting to international markets, or possibly shifting production processes or sales affiliates abroad) (Alcacer and Oxley 2014).

This report's quantitative case study from Rwanda and West Bengal, India (chapter 11), finds that all pathways of entry into GVCs raise the probability that a firm will become a direct exporter (figure O.7). Domestic firms were also found

FIGURE O.6 Domestic firms can improve their competitiveness by participating in global value chains and interacting with multinational corporations

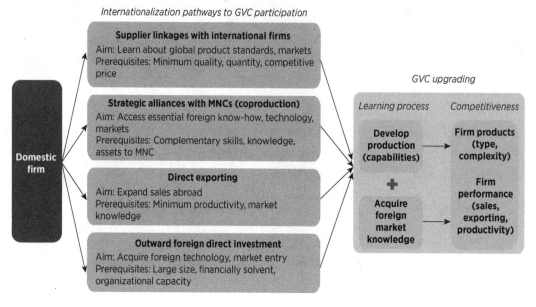

Internationalization pathways to GVC participation

Supplier linkages with international firms
Aim: Learn about global product standards, markets
Prerequisites: Minimum quality, quantity, competitive price

Strategic alliances with MNCs (coproduction)
Aim: Access essential foreign know-how, technology, markets
Prerequisites: Complementary skills, knowledge, assets to MNC

Direct exporting
Aim: Expand sales abroad
Prerequisites: Minimum productivity, market knowledge

Outward foreign direct investment
Aim: Acquire foreign technology, market entry
Prerequisites: Large size, financially solvent, organizational capacity

Domestic firm

GVC upgrading

Learning process   *Competitiveness*

Develop production (capabilities) → Firm products (type, complexity)

＋

Acquire foreign market knowledge → Firm performance (sales, exporting, productivity)

Source: World Bank.
Note: GVC = global value chain; MNC = multinational corporation.

FIGURE O.7 The more closely domestic firms interact with multinational corporations, the higher their probability of becoming direct exporters themselves

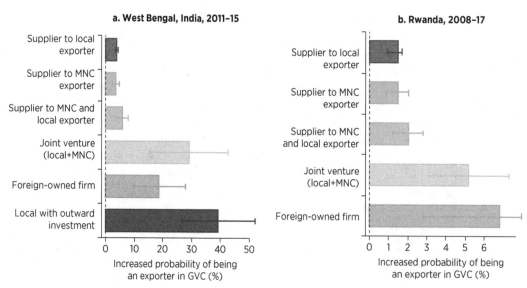

a. West Bengal, India, 2011–15

- Supplier to local exporter
- Supplier to MNC exporter
- Supplier to MNC and local exporter
- Joint venture (local+MNC)
- Foreign-owned firm
- Local with outward investment

Increased probability of being an exporter in GVC (%)

b. Rwanda, 2008–17

- Supplier to local exporter
- Supplier to MNC exporter
- Supplier to MNC and local exporter
- Joint venture (local+MNC)
- Foreign-owned firm

Increased probability of being an exporter in GVC (%)

Source: World Bank calculations; see chapter 11 of this report.
Note: GVC = global value chain; MNC = multinational corporation.

to engage in more than one pathway to GVC entry (for example, supplying some MNCs while engaged in a joint venture with another MNC). The more closely domestic firms interact with international firms, the more likely they will start exporting themselves. As such, investment-based GVC participation (that is, joint ventures and outward FDI) is a stronger predictor of becoming an exporter than supplier linkages. These observations further illustrate that the most powerful engine of capacity building lies in firm-to-firm interactions (Sutton 2014) and that firms move into deeper levels of the pathways to GVC entry when they feel more confident and ready.

Domestic firms can achieve GVC upgrading by increasing their interactions with MNCs and by continuing to learn from them. This way, domestic firms can obtain the necessary production capabilities and foreign market knowledge to directly compete in international markets. Increased interactions strengthen firms' ability to produce more, or more complex, products, or with better quality, and in turn, improve overall firm performance. An event study of MNC suppliers in Costa Rica (Alfaro-Ureña, Manelici, and Vasquez 2019) uses firm-to-firm transaction data and finds that becoming a supplier to an MNC resulted in strong and persistent improvement in performance, including a 20 percent expansion of sales to non-MNC buyers, a 26 percent expansion in firms' workforces, and a 6–9 percent increase in total factor productivity four years after becoming a supplier. Similar evidence comes from a study in the Czech Republic (Javorcik and Spatareanu 2009) as well as from surveys of MNCs in which multinationals reported that between 35 percent and 50 percent of their suppliers had increased their technological competence because of continued engagement through supplier links (Ivarsson and Alvstam 2005, 2011).

Although foreign firms can spur productivity spillovers to domestic firms (Havránek and Irsova 2010), it is important to remember that MNCs are not actively trying to foster technological development in their suppliers and partners. When technological development and upgrading do occur, domestic firms are often the main instigators, constantly adapting their operations to better suit the global production networks established by MNCs (Calof and Beamish 1995) and respond to opportunities that they identify in the GVCs in which they participate (Jordaan, Douw, and Qiang 2020). For supplier linkages, firms should focus on the three L's: labeling, linking, and learning. For strategic alliances, they should aim to absorb the technical know-how within the alliance for their own competitive advantage. For outward FDI, firms become MNCs and need to develop their own GVC strategies. In many cases, firms make use of multiple strategies to increase their competitiveness in the international market.

Government policies can help integrate countries into global value chains through strong economic fundamentals and "light-handed" industrial policies

Governments have often played key roles in promoting GVC participation in the past decades. Governments shape key elements of GVCs through their macroeconomic policies, infrastructure building, enabling regulatory environment, and human capital development (World Bank 2020a). These government policies and actions constitute a set of necessary minimum conditions for investment attraction and GVC partici-pation. In some cases, governments have played a more direct role, in what some describe as "soft" or "light-handed" industrial policies (Harrison and Rodríguez-Clare 2010; Taglioni and Winkler 2016). These descriptors refer to government policy mak-ing at the micro level, aimed at solving specific sectors' market failures caused by externalities, imperfect information, and coordination problems.

Policy makers can help improve and showcase a country's comparative advan-tages to attract and link MNCs. Investment policies aim to solve specific market or government failures aligned with common determinants of FDI and trade within a country. These policies may focus on regulatory reforms to reduce restrictions or pro-cedural burdens on investors. Or they may aim to provide public goods (for example, high-quality infrastructure) to MNCs within a special economic zone. In other cases, foreign investors may simply be made aware of a country's endowments through its investment promotion agencies. Governments also use investment incentives to tilt MNCs' decisions to locate to a new country.

Government policies can assist domestic firms with internationalizing and inte-grating into GVCs through continuous learning from engagements with foreign firms. Successful support programs tend to combine information provision (increasing expo-sure), matchmaking (overcoming coordination failures), and temporary subsidies (to compensate for expected social benefits from these interactions) to address specific market failures and stimulate positive externalities. They may combine matchmak-ing with support for strengthening local supplier capacity, facilitate strategic alliances building on competitive industries, safeguard competitive and contestable markets, and remove outward FDI restrictions and invest in R&D and human capital.

Successful integration of developing countries into GVCs requires that reforms be implemented as coherent packages. Individually such policies are likely to have a marginal effect, only partially addressing existing market or government failures. A combined approach, however, can be influential in shaping the behavior of both MNCs and domestic firms (Akileswaran, Calabrese, and Said 2018). For a combi-nation of methods to work, a sustained, coordinated, and long-term approach is required, based on incentive mechanisms that are tailored to the specific needs of the countries, types of firms, and value chains in question (Cusolito, Safadi, and Taglioni 2016).

There is no "blueprint" for strengthening GVC integration; different countries have adopted different approaches to leveraging FDI according to their own comparative advantages and target GVCs. The choice of sector is not about "picking winners." Through GVCs, firms in developing countries enter foreign markets at lower costs, benefit from specialization in niche tasks, and gain access to larger markets for their output. Such specialization is often the result of a country's long-term involvement in a specific sector that takes advantage of and builds on the country's unique combina-tion of factor endowments and firm capacity.

This report identifies examples in which packages of policies were successfully used to improve the investment climate, link up with global lead firms, and make it less costly to produce and trade products in a GVC sector or segment (box O.1). Part II of this report provides more details on each of these case studies. The efficacy of specific approaches is partly based on GVC characteristics and a country's income level. For example, strengthening MNC-supplier linkages can be especially effective for GVCs that are simpler and whose inputs can be supplied at arm's length, whereas targeted investment promotion may be more influential in GVCs that are dominated by a few global lead firms. From left to right in figure BO1.1 in box O.1, the sectors become more complex and increasingly demanding on domestic firms that participate in GVCs. Sectoral complexity and firm capabilities are both correlated with country income level (Bloom and Van Reenen 2010; McMillan, Rodrik, and Verduzco-Gallo 2014).

BOX O.1 **Examples of approaches for leveraging foreign direct investment to integrate into global value chains by combining policy instruments**

This box summarizes some examples where countries successfully used a package of policies to integrate into specific global value chains (GVCs) by linking up with global lead firms. The usefulness of the various approaches is partly based on GVC characteristics and partly the general capacity that exists within domestic institutions and local firms (figure BO.1.1).

FIGURE BO.1.1 **Global value chain characteristics and capacity levels help identify suitable approach**

GVC characteristics	GVCs with simpler inputs that can be supplied at arm's length but need to meet stringent global requirements set by lead firms	GVCs with many low-margin, distributed suppliers with highly competitive production and trade costs to supply global MNCs	GVCs dominated by a few global lead firms with expansive supply networks and distinct requirements to avoid supply chain disruptions	GVCs that rely on intangible assets (brands, management practices, production techniques) that can be codified and protected	GVCs that rely on intangible assets that are highly specialized and difficult to protect from competitors
Strategic approach	Use MNC-supplier linkages to help local firms meet global product standards	Invest in SEZs, and use trade and investment agreements to attract export-processing FDI	Use targeted investment promotion, incentives, and facilitation to attract global lead firms	Partner with foreign firms to help expand and upgrade an existing, viable industry	Promote outward FDI and invest in human capital and R&D capacity to help domestic firms develop and compete globally
Examples	Rwanda (coffee) Kenya (horticulture)	Honduras (textiles) Ethiopia (textiles)	Malaysia (electronics) Costa Rica (electronics)	Mauritius (tourism) India (BPO to fintech)	Korea Rep., India, and China (digital economy)
Common GVC type	Regional processing and commodities	Labor-intensive goods	Knowledge-intensive goods	Labor- and knowledge-intensive services	Knowledge-intensive goods and services

Lower-income countries → *Higher-income countries*

Prevalence of use, based on country's income level

Source: World Bank.
Note: BPO = business process outsourcing; FDI = foreign direct investment; fintech = financial technology; GVC = global value chain; MNC = multinational corporation; R&D = research and development; SEZ = special economic zone.

Continued on next page ›

BOX O.1 Examples of approaches for leveraging foreign direct investment to integrate into global value chains by combining policy instruments (*continued*)

- *Using linkages between multinational corporations (MNCs) and suppliers to help local firms meet global product standards.* In many cases, the fastest way to integrate existing local firms into GVCs is to create pathways into international markets for them. Supplier linkages to foreign firms help local firms meet global product standards by stimulating the three L's: linking (providing local firms with supply channels and necessary information on global standards), learning (supporting them as they train to meet those standards), and labeling (facilitating the process of certifying their ability to meet the standards). Examples of this approach are found in Kenya's horticulture industry (English, Jaffee, and Okello 2004) and Rwanda's coffee industry (Morjaria and Steenbergen 2017).

- *Investing in special economic zones and using trade and investment agreements to attract export-processing foreign direct investment (FDI).* Countries can jump-start GVC participation by attracting low-cost, low-margin export-processing MNCs. To lower operating costs for such firms, governments can concentrate scarce public funding on building up certain areas (known as special economic zones) with higher-quality infrastructure and regulatory flexibility. These islands of excellence only work, however, when they address key market failures—such as access to land, high administrative costs, inconsistent electricity, and access to imported inputs—that discouraged foreign entry. To complement this public investment, governments can use bilateral investment treaties and trade agreements to lower investors' risks and trade costs. Examples of this approach were identified in the garment industry in Ethiopia (Oqubay 2015) and Honduras (Farole and Akinci 2011).

- *Using targeted investment promotion, incentives, and facilitation to attract global lead firms.* A government may also target specific global lead firms in a select GVC and use promotion efforts to attract them to the country. The government sometimes may offer these "superstar" firms temporary tax incentives and firm-specific support (such as vocational training, purpose-built infrastructure, and customs support) to entice them to come. Such lead firms can help establish a new GVC cluster in the country that will help upgrade domestic suppliers and attract additional FDI over time. Examples of this approach are found in the electronics industries in Costa Rica and Malaysia (Freund and Moran 2017).

- *Partnering with foreign firms to help expand and upgrade an existing, viable industry.* Another approach aims to expand and upgrade an existing, viable industry into a higher-value GVC segment. Local firms may seek out partnerships with foreign firms to access their technology, international brands, and managerial techniques. MNCs may choose to partner with such local firms to access their complementary capacities and knowledge of the domestic market. Facilitating such collaborations (through joint ventures, franchising, or licensing) can help a country's existing industries shift into higher-value tasks and segments within their GVCs. Examples of this approach can be found in India's shift from business processing to financial technology (Fernandez-Stark, Bamber, and Gereffi 2011) and Mauritius's tourism industry (Cattaneo 2009).

- *Promoting outward FDI and investing in human capital and research and development to help domestic firms develop and compete globally.* A final approach is for large, competitive domestic firms to develop their own global production and sales networks by investing overseas. Governments may support this development by building human capital and helping firms to invest in research and development. Outward FDI can be stimulated by liberalizing outward investment regulation and through proactive promotion using a combination of financial and fiscal measures, information provision, development assistance programs, and international investment agreements. Prominent examples of this approach are found in the Republic of Korea, India, and China related to the digital economy (see chapter 10 of this report).

Source: Summary from the case studies in part II (chapters 6 to 11) of this report.

COVID-19 has triggered new challenges for global value chains

The COVID-19 pandemic has posed unprecedented challenges to GVCs worldwide. Global trade is projected to fall by 9.5 percent in 2020, a 10.6-percentage-point decrease from 2019 (World Bank 2021). Although trade is expected to recover in 2021, the timing of this recovery depends on the duration of the outbreak and the effectiveness of policy responses to it (WTO 2020). FDI, which was already in decline before the pandemic, fell by 42 percent in 2020 (UNCTAD 2021). This stark drop in trade and FDI reflects the confluence of pandemic-induced supply and demand shocks and policy and geopolitical uncertainties (figure O.8). COVID-19's impact on FDI may persist longer than that on trade as MNCs wait to make investment plans, given current weak demand and the tremendous uncertainty in the global economy.

Although declines in GVC activities are evident across nearly all sectors, certain sectors have experienced more severe supply disruptions or larger drops in demand than others. From a supply perspective, sectors whose supply chains are more concentrated in areas heavily afflicted by the pandemic and those whose supply chains are longer or more complex have felt greater supply chain pressure. On the demand side, the direct effect of lockdowns and travel bans has been greater for sectors that rely on in-person spending, such as hotels and accommodations. In addition, certain sectors, such as energy and financial services, are more procyclical than others, making them more vulnerable to the general decline in economic activity caused by the pandemic.

The adverse effects of the COVID-19 pandemic on GVCs translate into impacts on the firms involved in GVCs, which range from MNCs and other large corporations to small local suppliers and customers. The chief executives of the large firms and MNCs that anchor many GVCs generally believe that it will take years for business activities to return to precrisis levels (Murray 2020). A World Bank Group survey (Saurav et al. 2020a) of MNC affiliates in 34 low- and middle-income countries finds similar results: 97 percent of respondents have experienced some adverse impacts since the

FIGURE O.8 **COVID-19 (coronavirus) affects global value chains through a combination of supply, demand, and policy shocks**

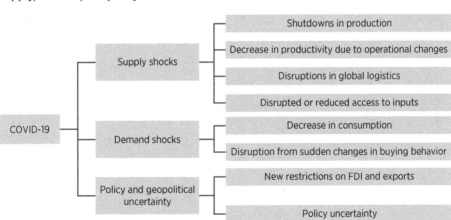

Source: World Bank 2020b.
Note: FDI = foreign direct investment.

pandemic began. The most substantial impacts resulted from weak demand, reduced worker productivity, and reduced investment. Business performance improved in the third quarter of 2020, but nearly 60 percent of survey respondents still expected income and revenue to be down in the fourth quarter compared with the same period in 2019 (figure O.9), highlighting that the effects of the crisis are likely to remain widespread.

In turn, suppliers to MNCs, many of which are SMEs, are in turn facing pressure. They are exposed to ripple effects from both demand and supply shocks. SMEs are more financially fragile than larger firms and may lack the capacity to adjust their business models in light of the COVID-19 pandemic. The pandemic has thus far exacerbated preexisting credit and liquidity constraints among SMEs and posed an existential threat to many suppliers and SMEs.

Although the Schumpeterian view postulates that crises can have a cleansing effect and increase long-term productivity by eliminating inefficient firms, these firms, integrated into GVCs, are normally the most productive ones in their sectors. However, in the wake of COVID-19, they are also facing severe shocks. Losing this part of the economy would slow each country's recovery and depress overall productivity. In addition, protracted crises destroy entrepreneurial knowledge and have negative consequences for long-term growth.

FIGURE O.9 **COVID-19 (coronavirus) has had adverse impacts on most multinational corporations since its outbreak, with some easing expected in the fourth quarter of 2020**

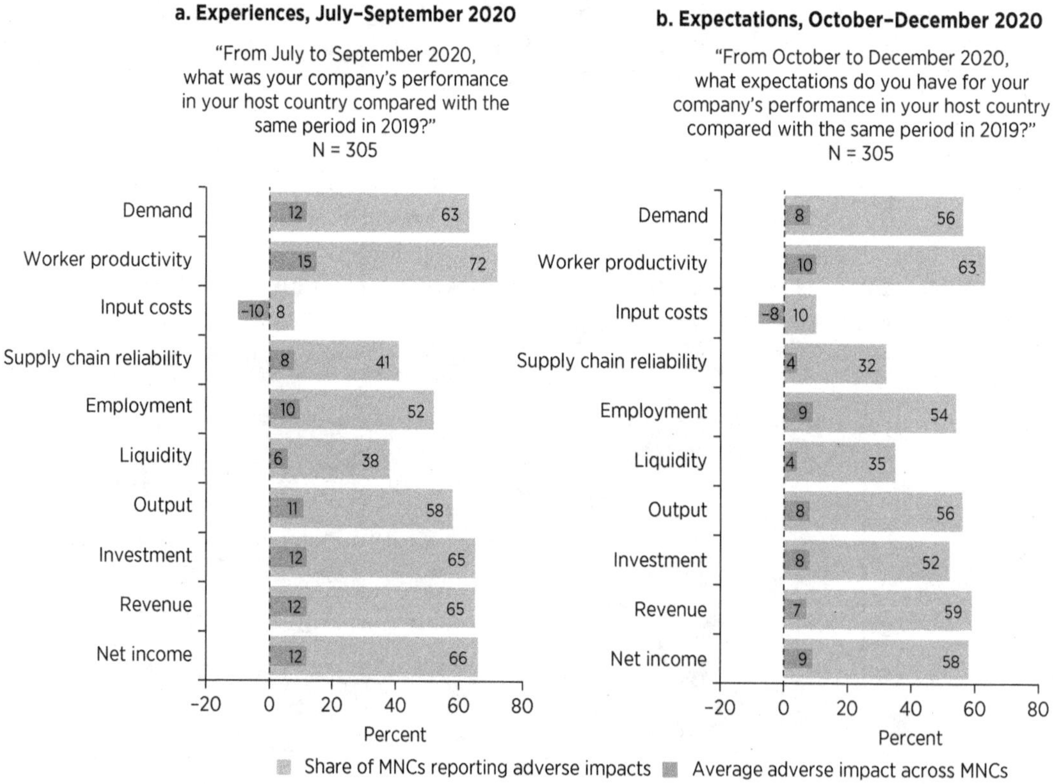

a. Experiences, July–September 2020

"From July to September 2020, what was your company's performance in your host country compared with the same period in 2019?"
N = 305

b. Expectations, October–December 2020

"From October to December 2020, what expectations do you have for your company's performance in your host country compared with the same period in 2019?"
N = 305

Share of MNCs reporting adverse impacts ■ Average adverse impact across MNCs

Sources: Saurav et al. 2020a, 2020b.
Note: MNC = multinational corporation.

Firms take various measures to survive the crisis, enhance agility, and speed up business transformation

Firms have taken various measures to survive the crisis, such as furloughing employees, repurposing production lines, and adopting new technologies. Some of these measures were taken at the start of the outbreak to keep businesses afloat, whereas other measures are intertwined with long-term megatrends and will take time to materialize. Shrinking market demand and disruptions to supply chains push firms to aggressively reduce their expenditures. However, cost-cutting is less likely to occur in areas that are perceived to be critical to sustaining growth in the midst of the pandemic, such as digital transformation, customer experience management, and cybersecurity (Edwards 2020). In contrast to the cuts they have made to labor costs, firms are seizing the opportunity to roll out new technologies in these areas and to speed up their digital transformations.

Several businesses, across industries and countries, are repurposing their production lines and R&D capabilities to supply critical materials for the fight against COVID-19 or are pivoting to new ways to generate revenue. For example, textile companies are making hygienic masks and medical robes, cosmetics companies are making hand sanitizer, hotels have become quarantine centers, and automotive companies are evaluating their options to produce urgently needed medical devices such as ventilators. Repurposing can simultaneously serve the greater good, help businesses keep their production lines up and running in times of low demand, generate moderate revenue, and positively affect businesses' reputations (Qiang et al. 2020).

It might be premature to conclude that firms should or will shift gears from "just-in-time" GVCs to "just-in-case" GVCs. Shorter GVCs and localized production are not necessarily less vulnerable to shocks. Supplier diversification and relocation can be costly and impractical for complex products. And holding more inventory and building redundant capacity would create inefficiencies in many industries.

Eventually firms' supply chain strategies should adhere to the same principles as ever: assess costs, take risk-based precautions, and build tools to enhance agility and flexibility. Mapping supply chains, investing in digital technologies to monitor risks and make timely adjustments, standardizing inputs to facilitate replacement, stockpiling strategically important inputs, building extra capacity (in low–risk tolerance businesses), and rationalizing production lines are all options. As business leaders struggle to guide their firms through the COVID-19 crisis and to plan for the long term, decisions ranging from where to sell to how to manage supply chains will ultimately hinge on business rationales as well as expectations about the future of globalization.

COVID-19 is unlikely to significantly change global value chains

Debate continues about whether COVID-19 will significantly change GVCs. Some economists foresee little significant change and predict that adjustments will be concentrated in health-related industries because the economic rationales for most GVCs continue to hold. Others believe that COVID-19 has become a wake-up call for a new risk-reward balance for GVCs (Baldwin and Evenett 2020) because pandemics, climate change, natural disasters, and human-caused crises may expose the world to more frequent shocks.

Indeed, the pandemic has highlighted the importance of supply chain robustness and resilience, and reopened the question of reshoring, nearshoring, and regionalization of value chains. Some economists foresee more unexpected shocks and argue for an increasing emphasis on holding more inventory, diversifying suppliers, and shortening supply chains (Javorcik 2020). Others recommend that firms "aggressively evaluate near-shore options and increase proximity to customers" (Betti and Hong 2020). Some policy makers are even calling for their countries' manufacturers to bring their production back home for self-reliance.

Many business executives find that these prescriptions oversimplify the problem or are driven by other motives. The presence of extensive supply chain networks with diversified and geographically dispersed suppliers is actually the rescue in the pandemic rather than the problem. GVCs have proven their resilience during the pandemic by adjusting better and contributing to firms' speedy recovery. Those calls for reshoring may be just wishful thinking: Incentives provided by a small number of governments (Japan, for instance) are too small to cover the costs of moving, let alone the continuing burden of a higher cost base (Beattie 2020). A World Bank survey of MNCs found that 37 percent and 18 percent were diversifying their sourcing and production bases, respectively, in response to COVID-19, but only a relatively small portion (14 percent) were considering nearshoring or reshoring (Saurav et al. 2020a).

Regional value chains are likely to intensify in the future, driven by new technologies and shifting global economic governance. Additive manufacturing, automation, and 3D (three-dimensional) printing could result in more integrated production processes, making nearshoring and onshoring more feasible and appealing, as companies start manufacturing goods closer to markets with higher levels of customization (UNCTAD 2020b; Zhan 2021). New production technologies such as 3D printing and others could lead to unbundling. Global economic governance is also shifting away from multilateral to regional and bilateral policy frameworks (UNCTAD 2020b). The Regional Economic Partnership Agreement signed in November 2020, for example, will further deepen investment and trade relations between member countries in Asia (Cali 2020).

However, GVCs remain critical given that the largest trading economies are located in different regions. The recently signed European Union–Vietnam free trade agreement and the European Union–China Comprehensive Agreement on Investment will further enhance integration between Europe and the East Asia and Pacific region. Other regions, including Latin America and the Caribbean, South Asia, and Sub-Saharan Africa have always relied more heavily on GVCs than on regional value chains because of limited intraregional specialization, and these regions continue to deepen their integration with global partners.

In addition, highly complex products, servicification of manufacturing, and potential services offshoring could intensify global fragmentation. High-tech sectors, for example, require a wide spectrum of knowledge and know-how that involves many countries scattered around the world (World Bank et al. 2019). More advanced production methods increasingly require embedding various digital and information and communication technology services within the manufacturing process or as new services added to final products (such as software upgrades for cars and washing machines). These changes can lead to a hybrid, highly fragmented environment in which manufacturing activities are increasingly integrated with digital services (Bolwijn, Casella, and Zhan 2018; UNCTAD 2020a). Complex tasks in services sectors that can be performed remotely—which likely increased substantially as a by-product of the pandemic—may build up a new "frontier" of offshoring (Zhan 2020).

New technologies, market concentration, economic nationalism, drive for sustainability, and multinational corporations from the developing world will play an increasing role in shaping future global value chains

Five trends that began before the COVID-19 outbreak have been amplified or accelerated as a result of this crisis:

Technology adoption. COVID-19 has been an unexpected catalyst for technology adoption across the world. When the outbreak and lockdown measures snarled GVCs, firms realized the importance of value chain visibility and risk management, as they have in previous crises. Because of this heightened understanding, 88 percent of MNCs surveyed by the World Bank in the third quarter of 2020 reported increasing their use of digital supply chain management technologies. The pandemic drove a rapid migration to online settings across every domain, and many of those changes are here to stay. At present, many firms have to serve their customers through online channels and allow employees to work remotely whenever possible, which has created a boom for video conferencing, online shopping, contactless payment, and delivery services. The COVID-19 lockdowns have also increased interest in robotics adoption and 3D printing.

Concentration of market power in some major industries was already an emerging policy concern before COVID-19. In digital markets, network externalities associated with platform-based business models have led to winner-takes-all outcomes. COVID-19 could cause a further rise in corporations' market power because large corporations are in the best position to withstand the economic downturn and deploy new technologies. Digital platform businesses have been among the few to experience soaring demand at a time when the rest of the economy was shutting down. History suggests that economic slowdowns widen existing divisions between companies. The same divergence has been evident since the start of the COVID-19 outbreak (Aviva Investors 2020). Moreover, there has already been a wave of business bankruptcies (Mathurin, Aliaj, and Fontanella-Khan 2020) and permanent closures since the pandemic began, and the wave is expected to grow. Increasing corporate market power could lower consumer well-being, decrease demand for labor, and dampen investment in capital, eventually distorting the distribution of economic rents and discouraging innovation.

Economic nationalism was on the rise even before the COVID-19 crisis, and it has gained further momentum since the outbreak began. Defensive nationalism—closing borders, building walls, imposing tariffs, and cutting back on migration—was a defining feature of the past decade (Bush 2020). It began in developed economies, stemming from their domestic backdrops of disappointing economic performance since the global financial crisis, rising inequality and political polarization. The pandemic has reinforced recent trends toward restrictive investment and trade policies and economic nationalism. Many countries have already adopted more stringent approaches to screening foreign investment to protect domestic businesses and industrial actors. The most common measure introduced since March 2020 has been increasing screening (29 countries), followed by restrictions on hiring foreign workers (7 countries), and tightening regulations on land ownership (1 country) (figure O.10, panel a). Some countries are also emphasizing self-reliance and taking an inward-looking stance on both economic and foreign policy (Baldwin and Evenett 2020). As a result, the global economic policy uncertain index reached a historical peak in March 2020 (figure O.10, panel b).

Awareness of and push for sustainability. The COVID-19 crisis has raised critical awareness of the links between nature, health, and sustainable development. Increased caution and scrutiny from regulatory authorities, consumers, investors, business partners, insurers, banks, and financial markets could all push firms to be more environmentally responsible and identify synergies between sustainability and business rationale. A rising number of MNCs have already pledged to work only with suppliers that adhere to their social and environmental standards (Villena and Gioia 2020). Sustainability trends are likely to accelerate and will play a bigger role in influencing the future development of GVCs, although it is important to recognize the costs associated with building up green production networks and to develop collective approaches to addressing externalities and sharing the costs and responsibilities. By transforming private sector activity through sustainable investment, countries can accelerate their recoveries and stimulate resilient growth.

More top MNCs are from developing countries and are state-owned enterprises. Many competitive firms have sprung up in developing countries amid rapid economic growth and deepening global integration in the past decade. By 2019, outward FDI flows

FIGURE O.10 **The pandemic reinforced economic nationalism and escalated policy uncertainty**

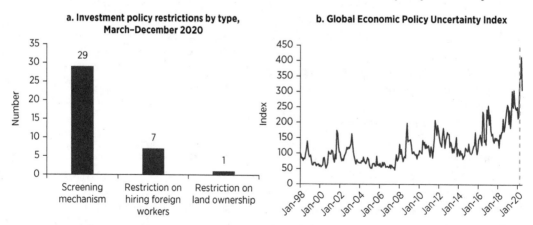

Source: World Bank calculations based on Forneris and de Bonneval, forthcoming; Global Economic Policy Uncertainty Index constructed by Baker, Bloom, and Davis (https://www.policyuncertainty.com/about.html).
Note: Updated January 18, 2021.

from developing countries were the equivalent of more than 40 percent of that from developed countries (figure O.11, panel a). A few large developing countries made up the bulk of the developing-country outward FDI stock (figure O.11, panel b). In 2020, 158 of the Fortune 500 companies were from developing countries, more than double the 76 in 2010.[1] State-owned enterprises are also growing cross-border market players—their share among the world's 2,000 largest firms doubled to 20 percent in the past two decades, driven by state-owned enterprises in developing markets (Qiang and Pop 2020). Outward FDI from middle-income countries increasingly aims to gain access to strategic assets such as cutting-edge technology, globally recognized brand names, and established customer networks. On the other hand, country-of-origin effects or state ownership may create a disadvantageous image among potential clients (Bilkey and Nes 1982; OECD 2016). In any event, MNCs from developing countries will play an increasing role in shaping future GVCs, and the new dynamics and impact are yet to be seen, which may have important implications for global policy coherence and coordination.

Maintaining an open system and improving countries' investment competitiveness are key to global economic recovery

It is far too early to declare the end of GVCs and globalization, as some are doing. The COVID-19 outbreak is a stress test for globalization. This pandemic has revealed the complex interdependence of economies around the world. For years to come, many will likely cite this crisis as one of the inflection points calling for a reevaluation

FIGURE O.11 Outward foreign direct investment flows and stock

a. OFDI flows have increasingly originated from developing economies since 2005

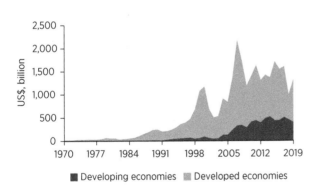

■ Developing economies   ▨ Developed economies

b. BRICS countries account for 40 percent of OFDI stock from the developing world in 2019, with a leading role by China (OFDI stock, US$, billion)

Source: World Bank calculations based on data from United Nations Conference on Trade and Development (https://unctadstat.unctad.org/EN/).
Note: BRICS = Brazil, Russian Federation, India, China, and South Africa; FDI = foreign direct investment; OFDI = outward foreign direct investment.

of collective attitudes toward globalization. Protectionism and nationalism, like the world's other preexisting conditions, started before the COVID-19 crisis. It is not surprising to see heightened consideration for national security (in areas such as health, food, information, and technology) and environmental sustainability in light of the outbreak. But some of the new restrictions on investment and trade are not necessarily meant to increase productivity.

Policy makers need effective strategies to preserve and improve countries' investment climate through the COVID-19 pandemic and to expand the private sector's role in driving productive jobs and economic transformation during the recovery. The crisis is disrupting the pathways by which countries achieve productivity growth—and, by extension, job and wage growth—by threatening spatial integration (by disrupting international production), reallocation (by reducing competitive pressure), and technological upgrading (by reducing cross-border investment). However, the crisis also provides opportunities for deep structural changes and for rebuilding systems better than they were before.

GVCs will continue to evolve. Financial incentives, as well as considerations of national security and environmental sustainability, will affect the geographic configuration of some GVCs and locational decisions within them. Potential GVC reconfigurations could create opportunities for some developing countries that are close to major markets, benefiting from possible nearshoring, and that have both comparative advantages in relevant sectors and business environments that are open and conducive to GVC entry.

Should new investment opportunities emerge, they will require new priorities for investment policies and investment promotion reforms. Policy makers should reflect on the market's possible shifts and let business realities guide their policy responses, building on economic fundamentals. This will entail realigning investment incentive regimes to the new national development priorities likely to emerge after COVID-19. Governments should also resist protectionist policies. Crisis-related investment screening and approval mechanisms should be limited and phased out to allow FDI to resume normal entry.

Tackling the complex challenges presented by the current global environment will require global leadership and cooperation. The pandemic has illustrated the shared public health and economic vulnerabilities that countries face. It has also highlighted the critical importance of exchanging data, sharing information on good practices, and strengthening collaboration. The magnitude and scale of the current crisis require policy makers to deploy their full set of policy tools to improve business confidence and boost countries' investment competitiveness. Global policy coordination has become even more important given that multilateralism has been challenged on several fronts. Maintaining an open system, solidifying trust among countries, and ensuring shared benefits from FDI and GVC participation are key to the world's future economic growth.

Note

1. For more information, see Fortune 500 (https://fortune.com/global500/2020/search/).

References

Akileswaran, Kartik, Linda Calabrese, and Jonathan Said. 2018. "Missing Links for Economic Transformation: Securing Policy Coherence in Eastern Africa." Tony Blair Institute for Global Change and Overseas Development Institute, London.

Alcacer, J., and J. Oxley. 2014. "Learning by Supplying." *Strategic Management Journal* 35 (2): 204–23.

Alfaro-Ureña, A., I. Manelici, and J. P. Vasquez. 2019. "The Effects of Joining Multinational Supply Chains: New Evidence from Firm-to-Firm Linkages." Working Paper. https://papers.ssrn.com/sol3/papers.cfm?abstract_id=3376129.

Aviva Investors. 2020. "Size Matters: Will COVID-19 Concentrate Corporate Power?" July 21, 2020. https://www.avivainvestors.com/en-us/views/aiq-investment-thinking/2020/04/will-covid-19-concentrate-corporate-power/.

Baldwin, R., and S. J. Evenett, eds. 2020. *COVID-19 and Trade Policy: Why Turning Inward Won't Work*. London: CEPR Press.

Beattie, A. 2020. "Will Coronavirus Pandemic Finally Kill off Global Supply Chains?" *Financial Times*, May 28, 2020. https://www.ft.com/content/4ee0817a-809f-11ea-b0fb-13524ae1056b.

Bernard, A. B., J. B. Jensen, S. J. Redding, and P. K. Schott. 2018. "Global Firms." *Journal of Economic Literature* 56 (2): 565–619.

Betti, Francisco, and Per Kristian Hong. 2020. "Coronavirus Is Disrupting Global Value Chains. Here's How Companies Can Respond." World Economic Forum, February 27, 2020. https://www.weforum.org/agenda/2020/02/how-coronavirus-disrupts-global-value-chains/.

Bilkey, W. J., and E. Nes. 1982. "Country-of-Origin Effects on Product Evaluations." *Journal of International Business Studies* 13 (1): 89–100.

Bloom, Nicholas, and John Van Reenen. 2010. "Why Do Management Practices Differ across Firms and Countries?" *Journal of Economic Perspectives* 24 (1): 203–24.

Bolwijn, R., B. Casella, and J. Zhan. 2018. "International Production and the Digital Economy." Chapter 2 in *International Business in the Information and Digital Age*, edited by R. Van Tulder, A. Verbeke, and L. Piscitello, 39–64. Bingley, U.K.: Emerald Publishing Limited. https://www.emerald.com/insight/content/doi/10.1108/S1745-886220180000013003/full/html.

Buckley, P. J. 2009. "Internalisation Thinking: From the Multinational Enterprise to the Global Factory." *International Business Review* 18 (3): 224–35.

Buckley, P. J. 2010. "The Role of Headquarters in the Global Factory." In *Managing the Contemporary Multinational*, edited by A. Ulf and H. Ulf, 60–84. Cheltenham, U.K.: Edward Elgar.

Buckley, P. J., N. Driffield, and Kim Jae-Yeon. Forthcoming. "The Role of Outward FDI in Creating Korean Global Factories." Warwick Business School, Coventry, U.K.

Buckley, P. J., and Roger Strange. 2011. "The Governance of the Multinational Enterprise: Insights from Internalization Theory." *Journal of Management Studies* 48 (2): 460–70.

Bush, Stephen. 2020. "Gordon Brown: 'The Solution to This Crisis Is Still Global.'" *New Statesman*, April 22, 2020. https://www.newstatesman.com/politics/uk/2020/04/gordon-brown-solution-crisis-still-global.

Cali, M. 2020. "The Significance of the Regional Economic Partnership Agreement." *Future Development* (blog), November 20, 2020. https://www.brookings.edu/blog/future-development/2020/11/20/the-significance-of-the-regional-economic-partnership-agreement/.

Calof, Jonathan L., and Paul W. Beamish. 1995. "Adapting to Foreign Markets: Explaining Internationalization." *International Business Review* 4 (2): 115–31.

Cattaneo, O. 2009. "Tourism as a Strategy to Diversify Exports: Lessons from Mauritius." In *Breaking into New Markets: Emerging Lessons for Export Diversification*, edited by Richard Newfarmer, William Shaw, and Peter Walkenhorst, 183–96. Washington, DC: World Bank.

Constantinescu, C., A. Mattoo, and M. Ruta. 2018. "Trade in Developing East Asia: How It Has Changed and Why It Matters." Policy Research Working Paper 8533, World Bank, Washington, DC.

Cusolito, Ana Paula, Raed Safadi, and Daria Taglioni. 2016. *Inclusive Global Value Chains: Policy Options for Small and Medium Enterprises and Low-Income Countries*. Directions in Development Series. Washington, DC: World Bank.

de Caldas Lima, J. M. 2008. *Patterns of Internationalization for Developing Country Enterprises: Alliances and Joint Ventures*. Vienna: United Nations Industrial Development Organization.

Dietrich, Michael, and Jackie Krafft. 2012. "The Economics and Theory of the Firm." In *Handbook on the Economics and Theory of the Firm*, edited by Michael Dietrich and Jackie Krafft, 3–26. Cheltenham, U.K.: Edward Elgar Publishing.

Edwards, Neil. 2020. "Two New COVID-19 Studies Reveal CFO's Focus on Workplace Reboot, Revenue, and Cost Cutting." *Forbes*, April 27, 2020. https://www.forbes.com/sites/neiledwards/2020/04/27/two-new-covid-19-studies-reveal-cfos-focus-on-workplace-reboot-revenue-and-cost-cutting/#4b14221e65b6.

English, P., S. Jaffee, and J. Okello. 2004. "Exporting out of Africa – Kenya's Horticulture Success Story." Case study for Scaling Up Poverty Reduction: A Global Learning Process and Conference, Shanghai, May 25–27.

Farole, T., and G. Akinci, eds. 2011. *Special Economic Zones. Progress, Emerging Challenges, and Future Directions*. Directions in Development Series. Washington, DC: World Bank.

Fernandez-Stark, K., P. Bamber, and G. Gereffi. 2011. "The Offshore Services Value Chain: Upgrading Trajectories in Developing Countries." *International Journal of Technological Learning, Innovation and Development* 4 (1): 206–34.

Forneris, Xavier, and Philippe de Bonneval. Forthcoming. "FDI Entry Measures and COVID-19." World Bank Group, Washington, DC.

Freund, C., and T. Moran. 2017. "Multinational Investors as Export Superstars: How Emerging-Market Governments Can Reshape Comparative Advantage." PIIE Working Paper 17-1, Peterson Institute for International Economics, Washington, DC.

Harrison, Ann, and Andrés Rodríguez-Clare. 2010. "Trade, Foreign Investment, and Industrial Policy for Developing Countries." Chapter 63 in *Handbook of Development Economics*, Vol. 5, edited by Dani Rodrik and Mark Rosenzweig, 4039–214. Oxford, U.K.: Elsevier.

Havranek, Tomas, and Zuzana Irsova. 2010. "Meta-Analysis of Intra-Industry FDI Spillovers: Updated Evidence." *Czech Journal of Economics and Finance* 60 (2): 151–74.

Ivarsson, I., and C. G. Alvstam. 2005. "Technology Transfer from TNCs to Local Suppliers in Developing Countries: A Study of AB Volvo's Truck and Bus Plants in Brazil, China, India, and Mexico." *World Development* 33 (8): 1325–44.

Ivarsson, I., and C. G. Alvstam. 2011. "Upgrading in Global Value-Chains: A Case Study of Technology-Learning among IKEA-Suppliers in China and Southeast Asia." *Journal of Economic Geography* 11 (4): 731–52.

Javorcik, Beata. 2020. "Global Supply Chains Will Not Be the Same in the Post-COVID-19 World." Chapter 8 in *COVID-19 and Trade Policy: Why Turning Inward Won't Work*, edited by R. Baldwin and B. W. di Mauro, 111–16. London: CEPR Press.

Javorcik, Beata Smarzynska, and Mariana Spatareanu. 2009. "Tough Love: Do Czech Suppliers Learn from Their Relationships with Multinationals?" LICOS Discussion Paper 249/2009, Centre for Institutions and Economic Performance, Leuven, Belgium.

Jordaan, J., W. Douw, and C. Z. Qiang. 2020. "Foreign Direct Investment, Backward Linkages, and Productivity Spillovers." In Focus Note, World Bank, Washington, DC.

Kim, June-Dong, and In-Soo Rang. 1997. "Outward FDI and Exports: The Case of South Korea and Japan." *Journal of Asian Economics* 8 (1): 39–50.

Mathurin, P., O. Aliaj, and J. Fontanella-Khan. 2020. "Pandemic Triggers Wave of Billion-Dollar US Bankruptcies." *Financial Times*, August 21, 2020. https://www.ft.com/content/277dc354-a870-4160-9117-b5b0dece5360.

McMillan, M., D. Rodrik, and I. Verduzco-Gallo. 2014. "Globalization, Structural Change, and Productivity Growth, with an Update on Africa." *World Development* 63: 11–32.

MGI (McKinsey Global Institute). 2019. "Globalization in Transition: The Future of Trade and Value Chains." Report, McKinsey & Company. https://www.mckinsey.com/~/media/McKinsey/Featured%20Insights/Innovation/Globalization%20in%20transition%20The%20future%20of%20trade%20and%20value%20chains/MGI-Globalization%20in%20transition-The-future-of-trade-and-value-chains-Full-report.pdf.

Morjaria, A., and V. Steenbergen. 2017. "Understanding Constraints to Value Addition in Rwanda's Coffee Sector." IGC Policy Brief, International Growth Centre, London.

Murray, Alan. 2020. "Fortune 500 CEO Survey: How Are America's Biggest Companies Dealing with the Coronavirus Pandemic?" *Fortune*, May 14, 2020. https://fortune.com/2020/05/14 /fortune-500-ceo-survey-coronavirus-pandemic-predictions/.

OECD (Organisation for Economic Co-operation and Development). 2016. *State-Owned Enterprises as Global Competitors: A Challenge or an Opportunity?* Paris: OECD Publishing.

OECD (Organisation for Economic Co-operation and Development). 2018. "Multinational Enterprises in the Global Economy: Heavily Debated but Hardly Measured." Policy Note, OECD, Paris. https://www.oecd.org/industry/ind/MNEs-in-the-global-economy -policy-note.pdf.

Oqubay, Arkebe. 2015. *Made in Africa: Industrial Policy in Ethiopia*. Oxford, U.K.: Oxford University Press.

Qiang, Christine Zhenwei, Yue Li, Yan Liu, Monica Paganini, and Victor Steenbergen. 2020. "Foreign Direct Investment and Global Value Chains in the Wake of COVID-19: Lead Firms of GVC." *Private Sector Development Blog*, World Bank, May 21, 2020. https://blogs. worldbank.org/psd/foreign-direct-investment-and-global-value-chains-wake-covid-19-lead -firms-gvc.

Qiang, Christine Zhenwei, and Georgiana Pop. 2020. "State-Owned Enterprises and COVID-19." *Private Sector Development Blog*, July 28, 2020. World Bank, Washington, DC. https://blogs. worldbank.org/psd/state-owned-enterprises-and-covid-19.

Rocha, Nadia, and Deborah E. Winkler. 2019. "Trade and Female Labor Participation: Stylized Facts Using a Global Dataset." Policy Research Working Paper 9098, World Bank, Washington, DC.

Saurav, Abhishek, Peter Kusek, Ryan Kuo, and Brody Viney. 2020a. "The Impact of COVID-19 on Foreign Investors: Evidence from the Quarterly Global MNE Pulse Survey for the Third Quarter of 2020." World Bank Group, Washington, DC.

Saurav, Abhishek, Peter Kusek, Ryan Kuo, and Brody Viney. 2020b. "The Impact of COVID-19 on Foreign Investors: Evidence from the Second Round of a Global Pulse Survey." *Private Sector Development Blog*, October 6, 2020. https://blogs.worldbank.org/psd /impact-covid-19-foreign-investors-evidence-second-round-global-pulse-survey.

Slaughter, M. J. 2013. "American Companies and Global Supply Networks: Driving U.S. Economic Growth and Jobs by Connecting with the World." Business Roundtable, United States Council for International Business, and United States Council Foundation.

Stephenson, Matthew Hector Travis Millan. 2018. "Investment as a Two-Way Street: How China Used Inward and Outward Investment Policy for Structural Transformation, and How this Paradigm Can Be Useful for Other Emerging Economies." PhD thesis, Graduate Institute of International and Development Studies, Geneva. https://repository.graduateinstitute.ch /record/295767.

Sutton, J. 2014. *An Enterprise Map of Mozambique*. London: International Growth Centre.

Taglioni, Daria, and Deborah Winkler. 2016. *Making Global Value Chains Work for Development*. Washington, DC: World Bank.

UNCTAD (United Nations Conference on Trade and Development). 2011. *World Investment Report 2011: Non-equity Modes of International Production and Development*. Geneva: United Nations.

UNCTAD (United Nations Conference on Trade and Development). 2020a. "Investment Promotion Agencies: Striving to Overcome the Covid-19 Challenge." IPA Observer Special Issue 8, United Nations, Geneva.

UNCTAD (United Nations Conference on Trade and Development). 2020b. *World Investment Report 2020: International Production beyond the Pandemic*. Geneva: United Nations.

UNCTAD (United Nations Conference on Trade and Development). 2021. *Investment Trends Monitor*, No. 38. United Nations, Geneva. https://unctad.org/system/files/official-document /diaeiainf2021d1_en.pdf.

Villena, V. H., and D. A. Gioia. 2020. "A More Sustainable Supply Chain." *Harvard Business Review*, March–April. https://hbr.org/2020/03/a-more-sustainable-supply-chain.

World Bank. 2020a. *World Development Report 2020: Trading for Development in the Age of Global Value Chains*. Washington, DC: World Bank.

World Bank. 2020b. "Supporting Businesses and Investors: A Phased Approach of Investment Climate Policy Responses to COVID-19." Unpublished, Investment Climate Unit, World Bank, Washington, DC.

World Bank. 2021. *Global Economic Prospects, January 2021*. Washington, DC: World Bank.

World Bank, Institute of Developing Economies, Organisation for Economic Co-operation and Development, Research Center of Global Value Chains at the University of International Business and Economics, and World Trade Organization. 2019. *Global Value Chain Development Report 2019: Technical Innovation, Supply Chain Trade, and Workers in a Globalized World*. Washington, DC: World Bank.

WTO (World Trade Organization). 2020. "Trade Shows Signs of Rebound from COVID-19, Recovery Still Uncertain." Press Release 862, October 6, 2020. https://www.wto.org/english/news_e/pres20_e/pr862_e.htm.

Zhan, J. 2020. "The WIR@30: Paradigm Shift and a New Research Agenda for the 2020s." *AIB Insights* 20 (4). https://insights.aib.world/article/18045-the-_wir_-30-paradigm-shift-and-a-new-research-agenda-for-the-2020s.

Zhan, J. 2021. "GVC Transformation and a New Investment Landscape in the 2020s: Driving Forces, Directions, and a Forward-Looking Research and Policy Agenda." *Journal of International Business Policy* (forthcoming).

PART I

Chapter 1

Foreign Direct Investment and Global Value Chains

Key findings

- Foreign direct investment (FDI) has been the primary driver of global value chain (GVC) expansion in the past several decades. Mutually reinforcing dynamics occur between FDI and GVC participation. Trade with foreign markets could induce initial FDI from lead firms by lowering entry costs; lead firms tend to bring their suppliers with them, and a herd effect triggers more FDI inflows; and FDI stimulates further GVC entry and upgrading through spillovers and agglomeration effects.

- Firms' production and trade decisions are interdependent. The more recent industrial organization literature emphasizes firms' choices between domestic and foreign markets and between integration and outsourcing simultaneously in the context of heterogeneous, within-sector productivity, and further adds the role of ex ante network embeddedness in facilitating firms' entry into foreign markets.

- The geographic distribution of GVC and FDI is unequal: only three regions—East Asia and Pacific, Western Europe, and North America—are highly integrated into global production networks. Other regions rely largely on commodity exports; investment and trade ties within those regions are relatively sparse.

- Although countries take different paths, the growing importance of each country in the GVC network is often preceded by its increasing FDI linkages with the rest of the world.

- Countries have different comparative advantages and specialize in different sectors or segments of production. Almost all countries that have successfully upgraded their dominant archetypes of GVCs during the past three decades have benefited from strong FDI inflows in related sectors.

Global value chains: Definition, measurement, and archetypes

A global value chain (GVC) consists of a series of stages involved in producing a good or service, with each stage adding value and with at least two stages produced in different countries (World Bank 2020). There is no consensus on the definition of the term GVC—the concept encompasses a myriad of interactions between firms around the world through the flows of goods, services, people, funds, information, and knowledge. Table 1.1 lists the definitions of some of the most common measures of GVCs used in the literature and in this report.

Most GVC-related studies use aggregate trade data and intercountry input-output tables to depict the intercountry and interindustry flow of goods (Antràs 2020; Antràs et al. 2012, Antràs and Chor 2013; Hummels, Ishii, and Yi 2001; Johnson and Noguera 2012; Koopman, Wang, and Wei 2014). This macro-level approach is widely used to estimate the factor content of trade, value added exchange rates, international inflation spillovers, and business cycle synchronization. However, these aggregate data lack detailed information on intraindustry trade, leaving the true structure and complexity of GVCs obscured. This approach also relies on many strong assumptions to back out certain bilateral intermediate input trade flows that are not available in either customs data or national input-output tables.

A growing body of literature now tries to map GVCs by firm business records and customs or transaction-level data (Dedrick, Kraemer, and Linden 2011; Xing and Detert 2010). This micro-level approach accurately shows the structure of GVCs, but it is often limited to a small number of firms, and it cannot reflect the aggregate GVC participation of a country or industry. However, as customs data and transaction-level data have become increasingly available, recent research has shed new light on how multinational corporations (MNCs) organize their global production and sourcing (Alfaro et al. 2019; Bernard et al. 2018) and how domestic firms benefit from joining the supply networks of MNCs (Alfaro-Ureña, Manelici, and Vasquez 2019).

More notably, most existing studies on GVCs—using either macro- or microeconomic approaches—fail to consider their multidimensional nature. Current studies

TABLE 1.1 Definitions of global value chain measures

Backward GVC participation	Backward GVC participation involves importing foreign inputs to produce goods and services for export. It is measured as the foreign content of exports (foreign value added, or FVA).
Forward GVC participation	Forward GVC participation involves exporting goods and services that become inputs in the exports of other countries. It comprises transactions in which a country's exports are not consumed in the importing country but are instead reexported by that country as part of a good or service (indirect value added, or DVX) to a third country.
Total GVC participation	Total GVC participation is the sum of the foreign value added and the indirect value added in an export to a third country (FVA + DVX).
GVC intensity	GVC intensity is a country's total GVC participation as a share of its total trade. GVC intensity = (FVA + DVX)/(exports + imports).

Source: World Bank summary based on Antràs 2020 and World Bank 2020.
Note: DVX = indirect value added (domestic value added in another country's exports); FVA = foreign value added; GVC = global value chain.

often dissect GVCs from only a trade perspective because trade data are most available, but GVCs involve the cross-border flows of all production factors: funds, goods, services, people, information, and knowledge. Firms, especially multinational firms, are the architects of GVCs through their unbundling, outsourcing, and offshoring production processes, which they undertake to balance risks and rewards.

GVC intensity—or the share of GVC trade in a country's total trade—expanded rapidly in the 1990s as information and communication technologies (ICTs) dramatically reduced communication costs and stimulated multinational activities (Amador and Cabral 2016). This intensity dropped following the global financial crisis of 2007–09; it later recovered somewhat, but never to the precrisis level. More recently, GVC intensity (for both simple and complex GVCs) has been flat or even trending downward. The global fragmentation of production has also declined since 2011 (Timmer et al. 2016), mirroring a slowdown in foreign direct investment (FDI).

There are many explanations for the stagnation of GVCs, including the saturation of possibilities for unbundling production, increasing geopolitical risks and costs associated with trade and investment, increasing local capacity and local sourcing in some developing countries, automation-induced reshoring and nearshoring, and a global shift in demand away from goods toward services.

Measurement issues may also explain the recent stagnation of GVC intensity. Global flows of data, information, and people are intensifying; and the world is becoming more linked than ever. However, trade in services and information is still not fully captured in world input-output tables, resulting in low numbers for GVC intensity.

This report classifies GVCs into six archetypes (table 1.2). These archetypes provide a broad sectoral classification to frame the report's analyses, with the caveat that the business activities involved in each archetype and sector are heterogeneous. To complement this analysis, the report also includes in-depth country case studies that give more nuanced pictures of specific GVCs.

TABLE 1.2   **The six archetypes of global value chains**

GVC archetypes	Sectors	Tradability	Labor intensity	Knowledge intensity
Commodities	Agriculture, fuel, minerals	High	Low	Low
Labor-intensive services	Wholesale and retail, transportation and storage, tourism, health and social services, personal services, leasing, other services	Low	High	Low
Labor-intensive goods	Textiles, apparel, toys, leather products	High	High	Low
Regional processing	Food and beverages, fabricated metal products, rubber and plastics, glass, cement and ceramics, furniture	Low	Low	Low
Knowledge-intensive services	Research and development, IT services, professional services, education	Low	Low	High
Knowledge-intensive goods	Automobiles, transportation equipment, computers and electronics, electrical machinery and equipment, chemicals and pharmaceuticals	High	Low	High

Source: World Bank adaptation of MGI 2019.
Note: GVC archetypes are in ascending order of average product complexity. "High" and "Low" are assigned based on average level across sectors in each archetype, which could mask huge variations across sectors. GVC = global value chain; IT = information technology.

Foreign direct investment and global value chains are mutually reinforcing

FDI has been the primary driver of GVC expansion in the past several decades. The emergence and evolution of GVCs have mirrored MNCs' investment and trade decisions as they have relocated their production activities worldwide. The surge in FDI after the 1990s reflects these decisions and accelerated the expansion of GVCs. In contrast, the past 10 years have witnessed a slowdown of GVC expansion, also in tandem with decreasing global FDI flows. However, despite this connection, theories and empirical studies on the relationship between FDI and GVCs have gained attention in the literature only in recent years. These theories show a mutually reinforcing dynamic between FDI and GVC participation.

Initial empirical research has established a series of stylized facts: only some firms export, exporters are more productive than nonexporters, and trade liberalization is accompanied by an increase in aggregate industrial productivity. Recent evidence has shown that global trade is concentrated in a few importing-exporting firms. These firms, many of which are MNCs, constitute 15 percent of all traders (World Bank 2020) yet account for about 80 percent of total trade (UNCTAD 2013).

Early trade theories did not establish a direct relationship between FDI and trade because factors of production were often assumed to be internationally immobile. However, some scholars did discuss whether FDI substitutes for or complements international trade. Mundell (1957) argues that the two are complete substitutes for each other under the identical production function assumption, which is characterized by the Heckscher-Ohlin-Samuelson theory of trade. Later, Schmitz and Helmberger (1970) and Purvis (1972) show that foreign investment may complement international trade if production functions vary between the two trading countries. Kojima (1975) further illustrates that FDI can improve productivity and expand production possibilities in the host country through the transfer of technology and managerial skills, therefore creating more trade. FDI can also substitute for trade if it shifts demand for a product in the same direction in the two countries. These early discussions were based on a model with two countries, two final goods, and two homogeneous factors of production. Although powerful in highlighting the differences in the two countries' factor endowments and the two products' factor intensities, that model was oversimplified and included many restrictive assumptions.

Since the 1980s, several prominent studies have modeled the firm behaviors that give rise to GVCs. These studies build on the industrial organization literature, such as Williamson (1985) and Grossman and Hart (1986). Grossman and Helpman (2002) formulate firms' choice between integration and outsourcing. Their model emphasizes the trade-off between the costs of running a large and less specialized organization and the costs arising from search friction, relationship-specific investment, and imperfect contracting. Helpman, Melitz, and Yeaple (2004) analyze firms' decisions on whether to serve foreign markets through arm's length trade or through investment. They focus on the trade-off between trade costs and the costs of investing in foreign markets and on within-sector productivity heterogeneity. Antràs and Helpman (2004) combine these two strands of modeling frameworks and study firms' choices between domestic and foreign markets and between integration and outsourcing simultaneously in the context of heterogeneous within-sector productivity.

Among many theories on FDI and GVCs, Melitz (2003) and Helpman, Melitz, and Yeaple (2004) establish a microeconomic theoretical framework from an entry cost perspective to explore the factors determining firms' internationalization choices between FDI and trade. The framework concludes that the entry cost required for FDI is higher than that required for exporting. Thus, only the most productive firms would incur the former costs and engage in FDI; less productive firms would export, and the least productive firms would merely serve the domestic market. Many empirical studies have confirmed this finding (Kimura and Kiyota 2006; Lee 2010; Wagner 2006).

Recent studies extend this model by emphasizing the role of ex ante network embeddedness in facilitating firms' entry into foreign markets (Kimura and Kiyota 2006 [for Japan]; Koenig 2009; Kumar 2008 [for India]; Singh 2011). Bernard et al. (2018) further develop a theoretical framework that allows firms to have large market shares and to decide simultaneously on their sets of production locations, export markets, input sources, products to export, and inputs to import. Their model suggests that firms' importing, exporting, and production decisions are interdependent. Evidence from US firms and trade transaction data support the main predictions of their theory: MNCs (referred to as "global firms" in their paper) participate in GVCs more intensively than other firms and magnify the impact of underlying differences in firm characteristics, increasing their share of aggregate trade.

There are multiple mutually reinforcing dynamics between FDI and GVC participation:

- Trade could induce initial FDI from the lead firm by lowering its entry costs.

- Lower entry costs and high switching costs encourage the lead firm to bring its GVC partners into the host country as well, and a herd effect triggers subsequent FDI.

- FDI stimulates further GVC entry and upgrading in the host country through spillovers and agglomeration effects.

Trade could induce initial FDI by lowering entry costs into a market for foreign firms (Kathuria and Yatawara 2020). This possibility is most relevant for market-seeking FDI. Before a firm invests abroad, it must weigh the costs and benefits of entering a new market. Entry costs include sunk costs before entry, fixed entry costs, and variable entry costs. The sunk costs before entry consist of information acquisition, due diligence, regulatory research, costs of matching up with partners, and contracting costs, all of which cannot be recovered if the firm eventually decides not to enter. Fixed entry costs include building plants and buying equipment and vary by entry mode. If the firm starts operating in the foreign market, it will also bear variable costs such as material costs, labor costs, transportation costs, and tariffs. However, previous trade with firms in the destination country offers access to information, a peer support network, and experience-based trust, which can help reduce the fixed costs of entry.

Once a lead firm sets up affiliates in a host country, it often brings its suppliers to the same location (Baldwin and Venables 2010). This phenomenon is described as "sticky buyer-seller relationships" in the GVC literature: high matching costs encourage relationship-specific investment, leading to high switching costs and a "lock-in" effect, especially in new markets (World Bank 2020). The initial wave of FDI inflow also generates a herd effect known as FDI clustering. Firms will learn from the behavior of other firms because a firm's location decisions reflect the information that guided its choices. If enough firms favor a destination, other firms will be tempted to copy their moves to the same destination, even if they possess information that suggests they should move elsewhere.

Finally, the proximity of foreign firms will benefit domestic firms through various types of spillovers, which will stimulate domestic firms to enter into and upgrade in GVCs themselves. FDI spillovers can happen through direct linkages, indirect demonstration effects, supplier sharing, labor mobility, or resource reallocation. FDI spillovers will enable more domestic firms to enter GVCs, ultimately expanding GVC participation and upgrading in the host country.

Numerous studies have empirically tested the relationship between FDI and GVC participation. Buelens and Tirpák (2017) use an augmented gravity model to demonstrate a positive association between bilateral FDI stock and both gross bilateral trade and the bilateral import content of exports. World Bank (2020) finds that FDI inflows play a strong role in the extent of backward GVC participation shares and levels, driven by GVC integration of the manufacturing sector. The lack of foreign-owned firms in manufacturing is an important reason for low backward GVC participation in Sub-Saharan Africa. Countries attracting FDI in manufacturing may also reduce their exports of raw agricultural goods and intermediate services embodied in exports of resource-intensive goods, thereby lowering their forward GVC participation (World Bank 2020). FDI not only contributes to countries' GVC participation directly by integrating local firms into global production networks, but can also provide higher-quality inputs and services to local firms, generating widespread positive spillovers that expand host countries' GVC participation indirectly (World Bank 2020). GVC participation in turn stimulates FDI flows. Martínez-Galán and Fontoura (2019) show that a country's degree of GVC participation contributed positively to bilateral inward FDI stocks in the 2000s.

International production networks

Network analysis offers important new tools with which to consider the interrelationship between investment, trade, and GVCs in greater detail. Network analysis is a set of integrated techniques to depict relations among various actors to analyze the structure of these links (Chiesi 2001). It thus highlights relations *between* actors in addition to individual actors' attributes. In a globally interconnected world, each actor's own characteristics are only half the story because people, businesses, and countries are interdependent. GVCs are complex and multifaceted networks encompassing flows of people, capital, goods, services, information, and ideas. Thus, network analysis could fittingly depict the ties among these many players and how the players influence each other. Table 1.3 explains the basic concepts of network analysis used in this report.

TABLE 1.3 **Basic concepts of network analysis**

Node	Each actor in a network is represented as a node. For example, a node can denote a person, a firm, a sector, or a country.
Directed and undirected relations	• Directed relations have a clear source and destination and thus a clear direction (for example, firm A sells to firm B). • Undirected relations are symmetric and do not have a direction (for example, firm A and firm B have the same owner).
Degree	• In-degree: The number of linkages that point to a given node as a destination, or the number of incoming interactions the node receives. • Out-degree: The number of linkages that go out from a given node as a source, or the number of outgoing interactions the node initiates. • Degree: The sum of a node's in-degree and out-degree. In unidirectional networks, the degree is the number of linkages each node is adjacent to.
Strength of a link	Values can be attached to linkages to represent an attribute of the link (for example, the strength of a relationship, the information capacity of a linkage, the distance between nodes, or the frequency of interaction between nodes).
Weighted degree	The degree of a node weighted by the strength of its linkages. This chapter uses weighted degree to measure a node's centrality to the network.
Average degree	The average number of linkages for each node.
Network diameter	The shortest distance between the two most distant nodes in the network.
Graph density	The number of existing relationships in a network relative to the maximum possible number of relationships. Dense networks indicate highly integrated markets with many transactions among different countries.
Average path length	The average length of the shortest paths between each pair of nodes.

Source: World Bank summary based on Wasserman and Faust 1994.

China's rise to prominence in the global production network may be the most noteworthy GVC trend of the past three decades. In 1990, Germany, the United States, and Japan were the three central nodes connecting cross-continent trade flows. China was a tiny dot with very low participation in GVCs, both backward and forward. However, by 2019 China had replaced Japan as the central node in Asia and replaced the United States as the second-largest GVC hub globally (figure 1.1). Although China has moved into knowledge-intensive manufacturing GVCs, textiles and apparel remain the second-largest source of value added in China's GVC participation. Germany remains the global leading player with the highest GVC participation. As the world's knowledge-intensive manufacturing powerhouse, Germany makes heavy use of many other countries' value added in its exports, especially electrical machinery, transportation equipment, and chemicals. The United States is the third-largest GVC hub in the world, and its GVC participation is dominated by forward linkages. The United States' value added is concentrated in machinery, transportation equipment, financial services, and pharmaceuticals. Western Europe, North America, and East Asia and Pacific are the three regions most integrated into GVCs, as shown by the density of their networks and their average node sizes. GVC participation is limited in Latin America and the Caribbean, South Asia, and Sub-Saharan Africa, especially in low-income countries.

FDI statistics are notoriously inconsistent because of varying statistical approaches and the existence of phantom FDI for tax avoidance purposes.[1] With or without adjusting for special purpose entities[2] (SPEs) and the ultimate recipients of investments, FDI

FIGURE 1.1 **Global value chain participation network, 1990 and 2019**

a. 1990

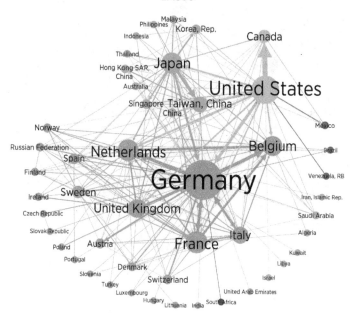

b. 2019

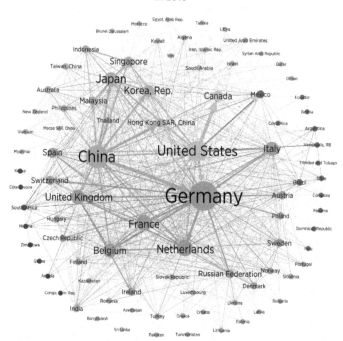

Source: World Bank calculations based on United Nations Conference on Trade and Development–Eora Global Value Chain database.
Note: These two panels are based on the country-to-country value added matrixes for 1990 and 2019, which include 189 economies and a "rest of the world" group. For each exporting economy, the matrixes show the value added contributed by all other economies in the world. In the two panels, each node stands for an economy, and the thickness of each link reflects the source economy's value added in the destination economy's exports. The panels display only linkages that are worth at least US$500 million. Nodes are colored by World Bank region. The size of each node represents its weighted degree, which measures the corresponding economy's centrality to global value chains. Data for 2019 are forecast on the basis of the International Monetary Fund World Economic Outlook database.

networks vary significantly. The unadjusted FDI stock network shows the Netherlands and Luxembourg as the first- and third-biggest nodes, respectively, which is disproportionate to their market size (figure 1.2). Major pass-through economies—such as Bermuda; the British Virgin Islands; the Cayman Islands; Hong Kong SAR, China; Ireland; Luxembourg; the Netherlands; and Singapore—host more than 85 percent of the world's SPEs (Damgaard, Elkjaer, and Johannesen 2019). When the FDI network is adjusted for SPEs and the ultimate recipients of investments, Luxembourg and the Netherlands become much less central, and China, France, Germany, and the United Kingdom emerge as major nodes. Brazil, India, Israel, and South Africa also show up as the FDI hubs in their respective regions.

Overall, countries' adjusted FDI centrality is highly correlated with their GVC centrality (figure 1.3). A 1 percent increase in a countries' adjusted FDI centrality is associated with a 0.87 percent increase in its GVC centrality. The positive correlation remains highly significant at the 0.10 percent level even when total population and gross domestic product (GDP) are controlled for.

Countries that maintain a relatively high share of manufacturing value added in GDP (usually more than 20 percent), such as China, Germany, major economies in the Association of Southeast Asian Nations, and some Eastern European countries, are more central in the GVC network than in the FDI network. These include advanced economies that specialize in knowledge-intensive manufacturing and innovative activities, such as Germany, Japan, the Republic of Korea, and many emerging markets that successfully joined labor-intensive manufacturing, as well as knowledge-intensive manufacturing GVCs, such as China, the Czech Republic, Malaysia, the Philippines, and the Slovak Republic. A few countries that rely heavily on commodity exports, such as Algeria, Kuwait, and República Bolivariana de Venezuela, are also more central in the GVC network than in the FDI network. These countries participate in GVCs primarily by supplying raw materials that are used in other countries' exports, which does not require high levels of FDI.

Countries that have low shares of manufacturing value added in GDP (typically less than 12 percent), such as Azerbaijan; Colombia; Luxembourg; Macao SAR, China; the Netherlands; the United Kingdom; and the United States, tend to be more central in the FDI network than in the GVC network. Advanced economies such as Luxembourg, the Netherlands, the United Kingdom, and the United States started deindustrialization several decades ago by outsourcing and offshoring manufacturing activities to cheaper locations; these countries now specialize in upstream innovative activities as well as financial services and other downstream services. Developing countries such as Azerbaijan, Colombia, the Arab Republic of Egypt, Myanmar, and Peru underperform in GVC participation relative to their FDI centrality because these economies have a weak manufacturing base while FDI inflows are concentrated in nonmanufacturing sectors. Many other developing countries are marginal nodes in both the FDI and the GVC networks.

For many countries, joining regional value chains is the stepping-stone to GVC participation, especially for developing countries in Europe and Central Asia, East Asia and Pacific, and North America. Regional value chains are subsets of GVCs. Neighboring countries and economies within the same region are often each other's primary value chain and FDI sources and destinations. An analysis of the value chains

FIGURE 1.2 Global foreign direct investment stock network, 2017

a. Unadjusted

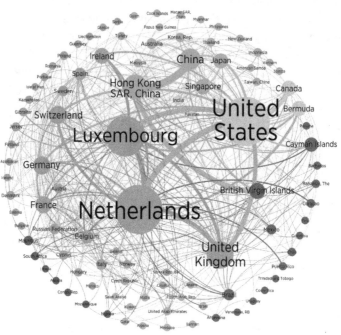

b. Adjusted

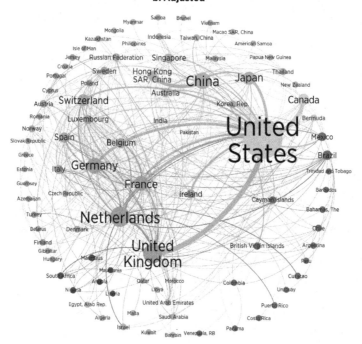

Source: World Bank calculations based on International Monetary Fund bilateral foreign direct investment database, 2019.
Note: These two panels are undirected networks. The size of each node represents the weighted degree of its corresponding economy (the total inward and outward foreign direct investment [FDI] stock into and from all other economies in the network). The thickness of the linkages represents the sum of the inward and outward FDI stocks between the two linked economies. Only bilateral linkages worth at least US$5 billion are included in the network analysis. Nodes are colored by World Bank region.

FIGURE 1.3 High correlation between countries' foreign direct investment centrality and global value chain centrality, 2017

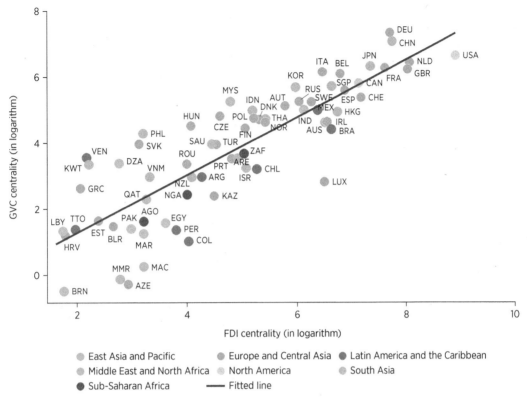

Source: World Bank calculations based on United Nations Conference on Trade and Development–Eora Global Value Chain database and International Monetary Fund bilateral foreign direct investment database.
Note: The x axis shows each country's weighted degree in the 2017 adjusted FDI network in natural logarithm. The y axis shows each country's weighted degree in the 2017 GVC network in natural logarithm. FDI = foreign direct investment; GVC = global value chain.

within each region reveals more nuanced dynamics. In the network analyses, higher average degree, average weighted degree and graph density, and lower average path length indicate more within-region connections.

The Europe and Central Asia region has by far the densest regional value chain and FDI network, followed by the East Asia and Pacific region. On average, each country in the Europe and Central Asia region has 37 inward and outward linkages in the regional trade network and 14 linkages in the regional FDI network, which is more than twice the level in East Asia and Pacific and much higher than the three other regions. This density occurs partly because there are more countries in the Europe and Central Asia region. East Asia and Pacific has the second-highest average degree and average weighted degree in both networks. Latin America and the Caribbean and the Middle East and North Africa have fewer regional value chains and FDI connections because of their limited intraregion specialization. The Middle East and North Africa region has relatively high graph density in the GVC network, but intraregion investment is much weaker. The Sub-Saharan Africa region is the least integrated into global networks, and it has the sparsest regional value chains and FDI networks (table 1.4).

TABLE 1.4 **Statistics of regional value chain and foreign direct investment networks**

	Regional value chain network, 2019				Adjusted FDI network, 2017			
Region	Average degree	Average weighted degree (US$, billion)	Graph density	Average path length	Average degree	Average weighted degree (US$, billion)	Graph density	Average path length
SSA	3.8	0.1	0.10	2.1	2.3	1.4	0.08	2.3
MENA	13.1	0.4	0.69	1.3	2.4	3.8	0.14	2.2
LAC	11.2	1.0	0.36	1.7	4.8	8.0	0.17	2.1
EAP	16.2	34.8	0.65	1.3	5.1	80.2	0.21	1.9
ECA	37.3	46.8	0.73	1.3	13.7	107.1	0.24	1.9

Source: World Bank calculations based on United Nations Conference on Trade and Development–Eora Global Value Chain database and International Monetary Fund bilateral FDI database.
Note: EAP = East Asia and Pacific; ECA = Europe and Central Asia; FDI = foreign direct investment; LAC = Latin America and the Caribbean; MENA = Middle East and North Africa; SSA = Sub-Saharan Africa.

The regional value chain network figures in this chapter use the United Nations Conference on Trade and Development (UNCTAD)-Eora country-to-country input-output table from 2019. A link from country A to country B indicates A's value added in B's exports. Only edges weighted at more than US$1 million are displayed. The regional FDI networks use bilateral FDI positions data for 2017 from the International Monetary Fund. Only edges weighted at more than US$1 billion are displayed. The size of each node represents the corresponding economy's weighted degree, and the color represents the scale of the weighted degree.

Europe and Central Asia's regional value chain and FDI networks are very dense, with many sophisticated participants and the shortest average path length in the world (figure 1.4). Germany is the regional GVC hub, whereas the Netherlands is the FDI hub; they are surrounded by Belgium, France, the United Kingdom, and other countries. These countries are involved in knowledge-intensive manufacturing and knowledge-intensive services GVCs. Each country specializes in specific segments, and all are closely connected by trade and FDI given their complementary capabilities. Central and Eastern European countries are less connected than those of Western Europe—the former countries are mostly involved in regional processing and tourism GVCs, given their proximity to the consumer markets of the European Union (EU).

The East Asia and Pacific region is also highly integrated into regional value chains and FDI networks (figure 1.5). The region is home to about 30 percent of the world's population, as of 2019, and it is becoming the world's biggest consumer market. China is the regional hub, and it has strong trade and FDI linkages with Hong Kong SAR, China; Japan; Korea; Malaysia; Singapore; and Thailand. Most countries and economies that have upgraded from commodity or labor-intensive goods GVCs to knowledge-intensive goods or services GVCs come from East Asia and Pacific. Hong Kong SAR, China; Japan; Korea; Taiwan, China; and Singapore have successfully upgraded into advanced economies, and China, Malaysia, Thailand, and Vietnam are rising in global and regional networks.

Brazil is the largest regional GVC and FDI hub in Latin America and the Caribbean, followed by Argentina, Chile, and Mexico (figure 1.6). Mexico is more integrated in

FIGURE 1.4 **Regional value chain and foreign direct investment networks in Europe and Central Asia**

a. Regional value chain network, 2019

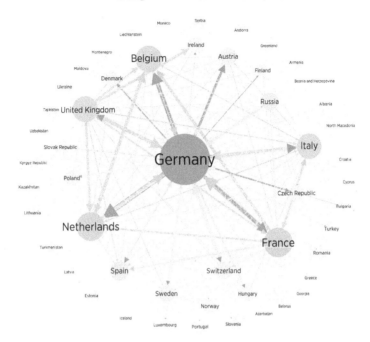

b. Foreign direct investment network, 2017

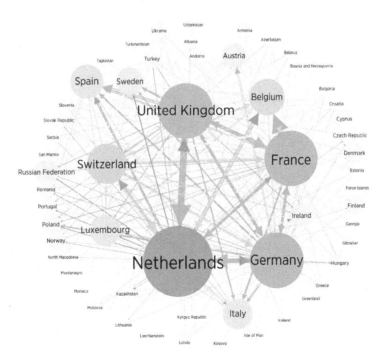

Source: World Bank calculations using United Nations Conference on Trade and Development–Eora Global Value Chain database and International Monetary Fund bilateral foreign direct investment database.

FIGURE 1.5 **Regional value chain and foreign direct investment networks in East Asia and Pacific**

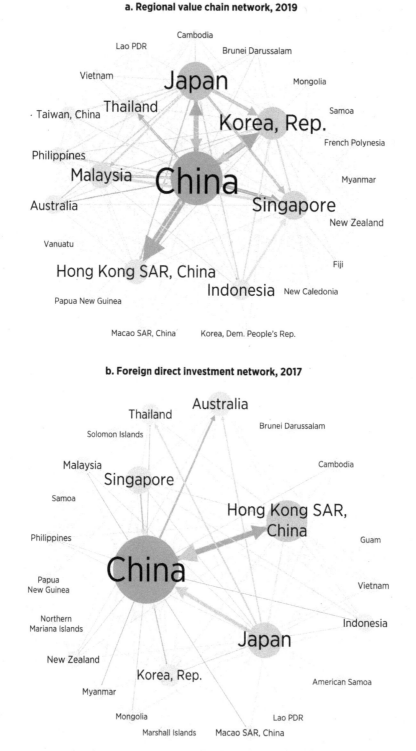

a. Regional value chain network, 2019

b. Foreign direct investment network, 2017

Source: World Bank calculations using United Nations Conference on Trade and Development–Eora Global Value Chain database and International Monetary Fund bilateral foreign direct investment database.

FIGURE 1.6 Regional value chain and foreign direct investment networks in Latin America and the Caribbean

a. Regional value chain network, 2019

b. Foreign direct investment network, 2017

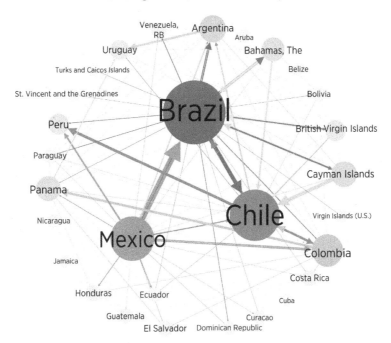

Source: World Bank calculations using United Nations Conference on Trade and Development–Eora Global Value Chain database and International Monetary Fund bilateral foreign direct investment database.

FIGURE 1.7 **Regional value chain and foreign direct investment networks in Sub-Saharan Africa**

a. Regional value chain network, 2019

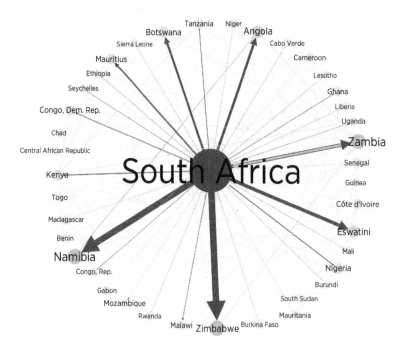

b. Foreign direct investment network, 2017

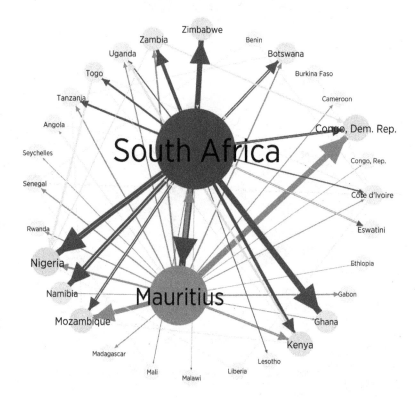

Source: World Bank calculations using United Nations Conference on Trade and Development–Eora Global Value Chain database and International Monetary Fund bilateral foreign direct investment database.

the North America regional value chain. Most countries in Latin America and the Caribbean remain commodity exporters or engage in regional processing. Even the region's major GVC hubs, Argentina, Brazil, and Chile, obtain 40–50 percent of their value added in exports from regional processing. Mexico was the only country in the region specializing in knowledge-intensive goods GVCs in 1990, and Costa Rica is among the few countries in Latin America and the Caribbean that have transformed from commodity exporters into knowledge-intensive goods exporters.

South Africa is the prominent central node in Sub-Saharan Africa's regional value chains, and connections between other countries are very sparse (figure 1.7). For many countries in this region, such as Burundi, the Central African Republic, Eritrea, São Tomé and Príncipe, and Sierra Leone, the only way to participate in GVCs is through South Africa. Countries in Sub-Saharan Africa generally participate in commodities or labor-intensive services GVCs. The dominant GVC archetypes in the region remained almost the same from 1990 to 2015, with very few exceptions. Ethiopia moved from commodities to labor-intensive services, but the Democratic Republic of Congo and Uganda moved in the opposite direction. The region's FDI network looks slightly different in 2015, with Mauritius as a major FDI investor and recipient. Once an economy known for sugar plantations, textiles, and tourism, Mauritius has transformed into a middle-income country and the financial hub of the continent. However, its exorbitantly high FDI figures suggest round-tripping at a large scale.[3]

Recent research shows more complex value chains often have stronger regional linkages. Although GVCs expanded both globally and regionally in the past three decades, different trends emerged across regions. Value chains in East Asia and Pacific and Europe and Central Asia are more focused on trade within the region, even though GVC integration in other regions has been mostly global and is continuing in that direction (World Bank 2020). Global policy coordination has become even more important as multilateralism has been challenged on several fronts. Maintaining an open system, solidifying trust among countries, and ensuring shared benefits from FDI and GVC participation are key to ensuring sustainable economic growth and shared prosperity in the future.

Hyperspecialization

Countries have different comparative advantages and specialize in different sectors and segments of production. This section uses trade and GVC participation data to illustrate selected value chains in the six archetypes to identify the key players in those value chains.[4] Global GVC and FDI hubs are almost always present as top exporters in at least one of the archetypes. Top exporting countries already show some specialization: the Russian Federation and some Middle Eastern countries are top oil exporters; Bangladesh, China, India, and Vietnam have clear comparative advantages in labor-intensive goods; and Germany, Japan, and the United States specialize in knowledge-intensive goods and knowledge-intensive services.

To illustrate specialization, table 1.5 lists the top five exporters with the highest revealed comparative advantage for sample sectors in each archetype. Kuwait, Brunei Darussalam, Azerbaijan, the Republic of Congo, and the United Arab Emirates rely

TABLE 1.5   **Key players in the six archetypes of global value chains, 2019**

GVC archetype	Commodities or sectors used for illustration	Top five exporters	Top five countries with highest RCA
Commodities	Mineral fuels and oils (HS2 code: 27)	Russian Federation, United States, Saudi Arabia, Canada, Iraq	Kuwait, Brunei Darussalam, Azerbaijan, Republic of Congo, United Arab Emirates
Labor-intensive services	Transportation, hotels, tourism, and restaurants	China, United States, Germany, Japan, United Kingdom	Bermuda, Cayman Islands, Aruba, Georgia, Botswana
Labor-intensive goods	Textiles and clothing (HS2 code: 50–63)	China, Bangladesh, Vietnam, Germany, Italy	Pakistan, Cambodia, Benin, El Salvador, Mauritius
Regional processing	Food and beverage products (HS2 code: 16–24)	Germany, United States, Netherlands, France, China	Malawi, Cabo Verde, Seychelles, Belize, Côte d'Ivoire
Knowledge-intensive services	Professional services, computer and IT services, R&D	United States, Germany, Japan, United Kingdom, France	United States, Japan, Germany, France, United Kingdom
Knowledge-intensive goods	Transportation equipment (HS2 code: 86–89)	Germany, United States, Japan, Mexico, France	Slovak Republic, Japan, Czech Republic, Germany, France

Sources: United Nations Comtrade; United Nations Conference on Trade and Development–Eora Global Value Chain database; and World Bank calculations.
Note: This table shows the top five exporters and top five countries with the highest RCA in selected products across the six GVC archetypes in 2019 (or 2015 for services). GVC = global value chain; HS2 = 2-digit Harmonized System codes; IT = information technology; RCA = revealed comparative advantage; R&D = research and development.

heavily on fuel exports, which make up more than 80 percent of total goods exports in these countries. Tourism accounted for more than 20 percent of total value added in exports in Bermuda, Cayman Islands, Aruba, Georgia, and Botswana in 2015. Pakistan, Cambodia, Benin, El Salvador, and Mauritius saw more than 30 percent of their goods exports from textiles and clothing. Malawi and several Sub-Saharan African countries are highly dependent on food exports; a few Eastern European countries specialize in transport equipment, including the Slovak Republic and the Czech Republic. All five countries with the highest revealed comparative advantage in information technology (IT) services, professional services, and research and development (R&D) are advanced economies.

Russia, the United States, and Saudi Arabia were the top three oil exporters in 2019 (figure 1.8). Russia serves primarily the European and Asian markets; Saudi Arabia's top export destination is Asia; and the United States exports mainly to Latin America. The United States' shale oil technology has made great strides in recent years, transforming the global oil market. Other Middle Eastern countries also have a strong presence in the oil value chain, and a few Sub-Saharan African countries, such as Nigeria, Angola, and Gabon, are also major oil exporters.

Most oil exporters, regardless of income level, have yet to diversify their export portfolios and are heavily reliant on oil rents. For example, oil exports made up an average of 84 percent of total merchandise exports in Organization of the Petroleum Exporting Countries from 2014 to 2018. These countries are vulnerable to oil price fluctuations and tend to suffer from the "resource curse." The resource curse is the observation that countries endowed with rich natural resources can struggle to make effective use of these resources and often end up poorer and have less economic growth than countries with fewer natural resources. It is crucial for oil exporters to spread the benefits of oil wealth among their population and to invest in other industries so that they can have more balanced and stable growth.

FIGURE 1.8 Commodity trade network: Mineral fuels and oils, 2018

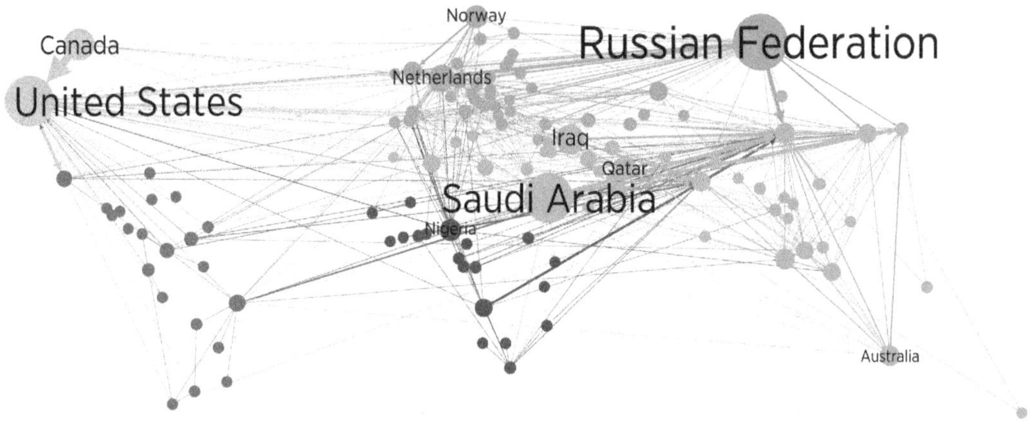

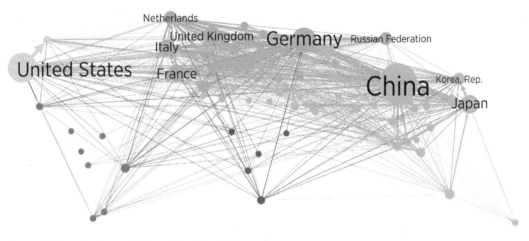

Source: United Nations Comtrade database, 2019.
Note: Figure uses Harmonized System (HS) code 27 for mineral fuels and oils. Only linkages worth at least US$500 million are included. The top 10 exporters are labeled.

FIGURE 1.9 Labor-intensive services trade network: Transportation, hotels, tourism, and restaurants, 2015

Source: Data from the Eora sector-to-country matrix, 2015.
Note: Each source node represents the origin of the value added in the selected sector; each destination node represents the country exporting that added value. Only linkages worth at least US$50 million are included.

Global tourism has surged since the 1950s, consistently outpacing global GDP growth. Intraregional trade dominates the transportation and tourism value chains (figure 1.9). According to the United Nations World Tourism Organization, four-fifths of tourists travel within their own region. Tourism connections among EU countries are very dense because the region is highly integrated and people can move freely across borders within the EU. With a population of more than 1.4 billion and growing demand for international travel, China accounts for a large share of global tourism GDP. The United States is the second-largest source country for travel and tourism, and its close ties with Europe make the Europe and Central Asia region its top destination.

As disposable income rose rapidly in developing countries and the world's appetite for travel grew, the global tourism industry was flourishing before the COVID-19 (coronavirus) crisis. China's international departures reached almost 150 million in 2018, about 40 percent higher than Germany's 108 million. Tourism was also playing an increasingly large role in the global economy. Travel and tourism generated 10.3 percent of global GDP in 2019 and employed 330 million people.[5] Tourism is the main pillar of the economy in many small island states and Oceanian countries. However, overreliance on tourism increases economic vulnerability, as the catastrophic impact of the COVID-19 outbreak on the industry showed in 2020.

The global textile and apparel value chain is largely centered around China (figure 1.10). Some apparel manufacturers have left China for lower-cost places, including Bangladesh, Ethiopia, and Vietnam. However, most firms that have exited China physically are still entangled in its supply networks. As a result, China actually increased its share of textile exports from 2008 to 2019. Chinese fabrics are produced by highly automated processes and then shipped to Bangladesh, Vietnam, and other countries for labor-intensive cutting and sewing. These countries also import sewing machines, zippers, fasteners, and labels from China before the finished clothing is exported to the United States and Europe. Most textile and apparel exports from China do not carry Chinese brands because many of the big Chinese exporting firms are original equipment manufacturers for global brands. However, as the quality of their products improves, some Chinese producers are aiming to make their own brands more appealing to final consumers worldwide and are moving into new segments of the clothing value chain, such as design and marketing.

Europe and Central Asia, North America, and East Asia and Pacific are the three top sources and destinations for prepared food exports (figure 1.11). Germany became the largest food exporter in 2019; its food exports range from chocolates, baked goods, and cheese to pork, wine, and other produce. The United States was the second-largest food exporter, and it is the world's largest corn producer and among the largest producers of oats, tomatoes, soybeans, and spices. The Netherlands is another major

FIGURE 1.10 **Labor-intensive goods trade network: Textiles and clothing, 2019**

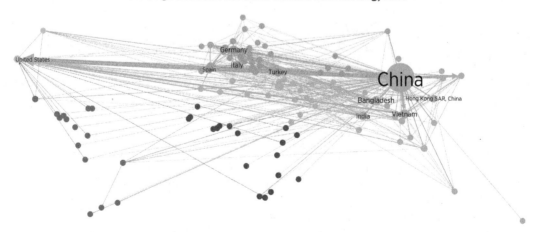

Source: United Nations Comtrade database, 2019.
Note: Figure uses Harmonized System (HS) code 50–63 for textiles and clothing. Only linkages worth at least US$200 million are included. The top 10 exporters are labeled.

FIGURE 1.11 **Regional processing trade network: Food and beverage products, 2018**

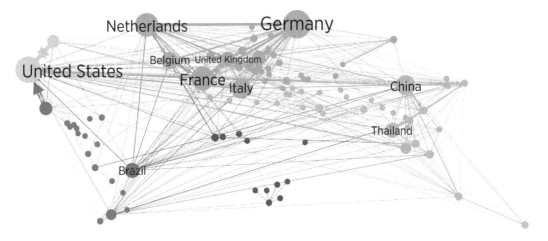

Source: United Nations Comtrade database, 2019.
Note: Figure uses Harmonized System (HS) code 16–24 for food and beverage products. Only linkages worth at least US$200 million are included. The top 10 exporters are labeled.

food exporter, with dairy, eggs, meat, and vegetables making up the bulk of Dutch food exports. France is the world's largest wine-exporting country by value; its wine exports exceeded US$11 billion in 2018, far ahead of its nearest rival, Italy.

Many developing countries are highly involved in the food and beverage value chain, but they are often involved only as agricultural commodity exporters. Brazil is the largest producer of sugarcane, oranges, and coffee; and it is also among the top-ranked producers of corn, soybeans, chicken, beef, and various fruits. Indonesia exports about half of the world's supply of palm oil, and Thailand contributes a third of global rice exports. Coffee and tea are many African countries' main exports. Africa accounted for 20 percent of global tea exports in 2015–17, and Kenya is by far its leading tea exporter (and the third-largest tea exporter in the world). The global food and beverage industry is projected to grow steadily over the next few decades, with an increasing focus on quality, traceability, sustainability, and convenience. This growth will create new opportunities for developing countries to expand and upgrade their food production and their ability to add value.

The United States is the dominant player in many knowledge-intensive services value chains, ranging from ICT services and R&D to all sorts of professional services (figure 1.12). Of the top 100 digital MNCs by sales or operating revenues, 67 are US firms, 23 are European, and 4 are Japanese (UNCTAD 2017). The ICT sector has led the way in technological breakthroughs over the past several decades and is anticipated to bring about the next industrial revolution. ICTs have become highly integrated with a large share of economic activities, and they are profoundly transforming the ways people live and work. Some ICT services are altering the distribution of value within existing GVCs: many manufactured products embody them, and they account for a significant share of those products' value. For example, the design of the iPhone and the operating system it runs on are worth much more than the iPhone's hardware. Other ICT services have created new industries and new stages of

FIGURE 1.12 **Knowledge-intensive services trade network: Professional services, computer and information technology services, and research and development, 2015**

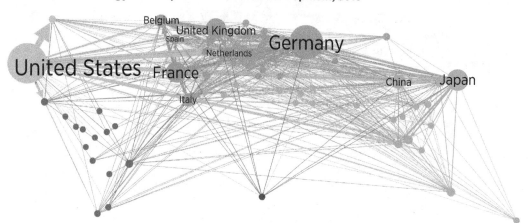

Source: Data from the Eora sector-to-country matrix, 2015.
Note: Each source node represents the origin of the value added in the selected sector; each destination node represents the country exporting that added value. Only linkages worth at least US$50 million are included. The top 10 exporters are labeled.

production in GVCs. In the data-driven global economy, talent, data, and algorithms have become key ingredients for success. Although competition for these ingredients is intense, companies can also expand their value creation through collaborative eco-systems built around ICTs (Frederick, Bamber, and Cho 2018).

Famous for its car brands, Germany has solidified its leading position in the transportation equipment value chain over the past several decades (figure 1.13). The United States was the largest car manufacturer in the world until recently; Chrysler, Ford, and General Motors are known as the "Big Three" US automakers and are among the largest global auto exporters. Japan is the world's second-largest auto exporter; its automotive industry took off in the 1970s and overtook that of the United States after the 1980s. Japan and Germany are also among the biggest rail equipment exporters. Japan launched the first class of bullet trains in 1964 and has continuously advanced its rail technology. It boasts some of the most important train manufacturers in the world, including Hitachi, Kawasaki, and Mitsubishi. Germany also plays a central role in international rail markets; Siemens and other German firms are known for their innovative capacity and intelligent traffic systems. The United States has the largest aerospace sector in the world, and it is the main supplier of both military and civilian aerospace hardware to the rest of the world.

Mexico emerged as the fourth-largest auto exporter and a major aerospace parts exporter by attracting FDI. Unlike Germany, Japan, and the United States, Mexico does not have its own world-famous car brands; instead, it developed its automotive industry by attracting foreign firms such as Chrysler, Ford, General Motors, and Volkswagen. Mexico's aerospace exports also surged in recent years by virtue of a large influx of FDI into its aerospace sector. Aerospace exports from Mexico reached US$8.4 billion in 2019, a 17 percent increase over the previous year, and FDI in the industry is estimated to have reached US$13 billion in 2019, of which 75 percent will originate in North America and the rest in Europe (TECMA Communications 2019).

FIGURE 1.13 **Knowledge-intensive goods trade network: Transportation equipment, 2019**

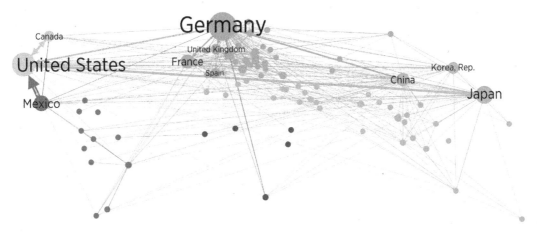

Source: United Nations Comtrade database, 2019.
Note: Figure uses Harmonized System (HS) code 86–89 for transportation equipment. Only linkages worth at least US$500 million are included. The top 10 exporters are labeled.

Leveraging foreign direct investment to upgrade into new global value chain archetypes

Over the past three decades, some countries have upgraded into new dominant archetypes of GVCs (table 1.6). Using sector-level value added data from the UNCTAD-Eora Global Value Chain database, this report maps each country to a dominant GVC archetype. The most remarkable examples of countries' upgrading journeys include those of Costa Rica, which transformed from a commodity exporter in 1990 to a knowledge-intensive goods exporter in 2015, and China, which moved from labor-intensive goods to knowledge-intensive goods during the same period. Other changes over that period include Guatemala and Indonesia upgrading from commodities to regional processing and Albania and Papua New Guinea joining labor-intensive services GVCs. However, a few other countries, such as Azerbaijan, the Democratic Republic of Congo, Iraq, and the Kyrgyz Republic, formerly specialized in labor-intensive services but have downgraded to become heavily reliant on commodity exports.

Overall, most countries have maintained their dominant GVC archetype over the past three decades, and labor-intensive services have been the biggest source of value added in many countries' exports. Transportation, hotels and restaurants, entertainment, and personal services make up the bulk of these countries' value added in exports, especially for small African, Caribbean, and Pacific countries.

Almost all countries that have upgraded into new archetypes have benefited from strong FDI inflows in related sectors. Below are four noteworthy examples of how developing countries have joined, or upgraded their roles in, GVCs with the help of FDI. China's and Costa Rica's transformations started a few decades ago, whereas Ethiopia's and Vietnam's cases are more recent. Additional examples can be found in part II of this report.

TABLE 1.6 **Economies that changed their dominant global value chain archetype, 1990–2015**

Dominant GVC archetype, 1990	Dominant GVC archetype, 2015	Economies
Upgraded		
Commodities	Regional processing	Guatemala, Indonesia
Commodities	Labor-intensive services	Albania, Papua New Guinea
Commodities	Knowledge-intensive goods	Costa Rica
Labor-intensive services	Labor-intensive goods	Cambodia, El Salvador
Labor-intensive services	Knowledge-intensive goods	Philippines, Singapore
Labor-intensive goods	Knowledge-intensive goods	China; Hong Kong SAR, China
Downgraded		
Regional processing	Commodities	Bolivia, Kenya, Lao PDR, Paraguay
Labor-intensive services	Commodities	Azerbaijan; Congo, Dem. Rep.; Iraq; Kyrgyz Republic; Mongolia; Trinidad and Tobago; Uganda

Source: World Bank calculations based on the United Nations Conference on Trade and Development–Eora Global Value Chain database as revised by the *World Development Report 2020* team.
Note: "Dominant GVC archetype" refers to the archetype that has the highest share in an economy's total value added to exports in the specified year. GVC = global value chain; PDR = People's Democratic Republic; SAR = special administrative region.

Costa Rica

FDI has profoundly changed Costa Rica's export specialization and has significantly propelled its integration into GVCs. Despite the small size of Costa Rica's economy, the country has successfully transformed its export composition from primary products to high-tech manufacturing and value added service industries thanks to a robust inflow of FDI over the past decades. In the early 1980s, Costa Rica was exporting undifferentiated and unprocessed agricultural products such as coffee, bananas, and sugar. The Costa Rican government decided to adopt an export-oriented growth strategy, including trade liberalization and the promotion of export-led FDI, to create employment, diversify exports, and boost the country's productivity. Generous investment incentives and proactive investment promotion were key factors that attracted lead firms into Costa Rica. Following the arrival of the world-leading technology company Intel in the late 1990s, more and more MNCs started to invest and set up shop in Costa Rica, gradually diversifying and upgrading the country's production base and exports. The country's FDI volume grew from US$340 million in 1995 to more than US$2.9 billion in 2014 (figure 1.14).

More recently, foreign companies have upgraded their operations in Costa Rica toward more knowledge-intensive activities, including software design and R&D. Along with this trend, the Costa Rican government has shifted toward a more selective approach to attracting FDI, focusing on companies that operate in knowledge-intensive sectors such as knowledge-processing services, medical devices and the life sciences, and clean technologies. In general, FDI has been a key factor in the transformation of Costa Rica's economy, and it has been pivotal to diversifying the country's exports, boosting economic growth, and generating skilled jobs.

FIGURE 1.14 **Costa Rica's foreign direct investment inflows and export growth, 1994–2018**

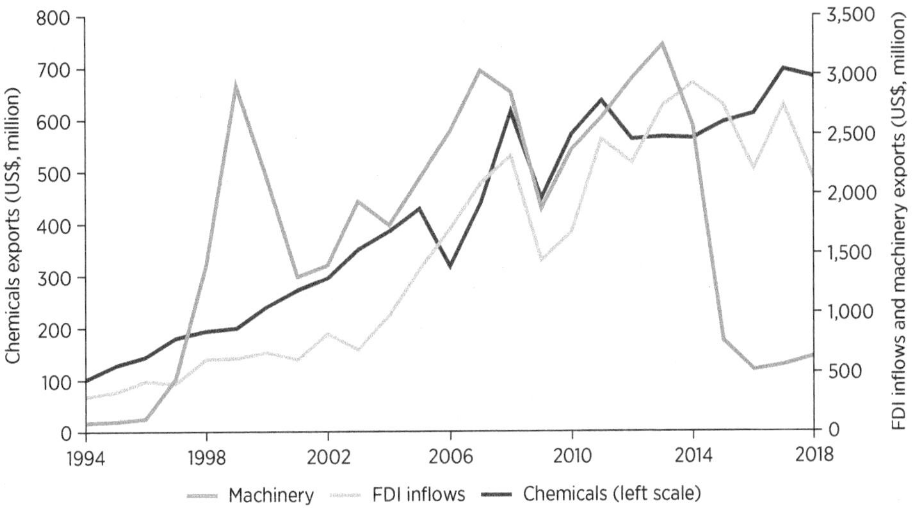

Source: World Bank calculations based on data from United Nations Conference on Trade and Development and United Nations Comtrade database.
Note: FDI = foreign direct investment.

China

FDI has played a critical role in China's economic transformation and enduring growth. China's FDI inflows followed three main stages: the FDI spurt in the 1990s that jump-started China's export growth; the wave of FDI in the 2000s that further accelerated China's economic transformation; and more diverse FDI inflows since 2010 that have increasingly focused on knowledge-intensive goods and services.

China's "Reform and Opening Up" policy began in 1978, but until the 1990s FDI inflows into China remained negligible. In the spring of 1992, Deng Xiaoping delivered his famous speech on deepening reforms and opening up by attracting foreign investment. The Chinese government subsequently made a series of major policy reforms to improve the country's investment climate, with a focus on attracting FDI in infrastructure and manufacturing that would boost exports. China saw a large influx of FDI immediately in 1992: close to 50,000 new foreign enterprises were established in the country, and the actual use of foreign capital reached US$11 billion, a 150 percent jump from the previous year (China, MOFCOM 2019). FDI continued to surge in the following years as more and more MNCs accelerated their investment in China. As of 2001, about 400 of the world's 500 largest MNCs had entered China. Most of these firms, including Ericsson, General Motors, Motorola, Nokia, Siemens, and Volkswagen, are in capital- and technology-intensive industries. The advanced technologies, knowledge, equipment, and products brought by foreign firms greatly accelerated domestic firms' development. From 1992 to 2000, China's textile and footwear exports more than doubled, and the country's knowledge-intensive goods exports increased by more than 400 percent (figure 1.15).

Upon its accession to the World Trade Organization in 2001, China's internationalization reached a new level. The Chinese government proactively sought to attract

FIGURE 1.15 **China's foreign direct investment inflows and export growth, 1982–2018**

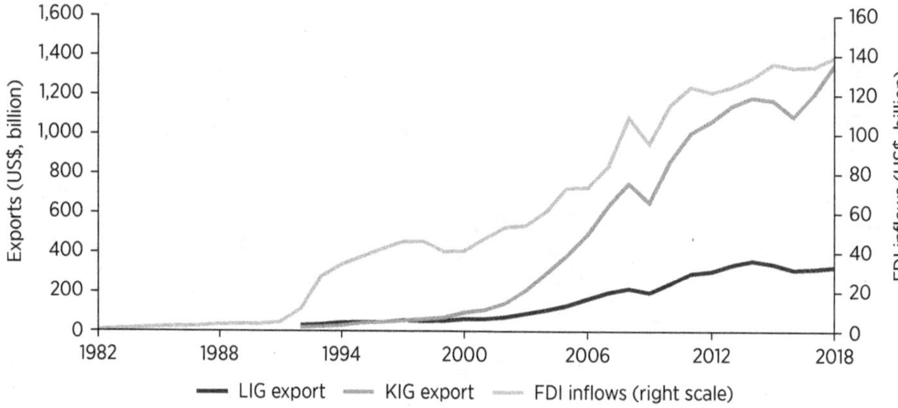

Source: World Bank calculations based on data from United Nations Conference on Trade and Development and United Nations Comtrade database.
Note: FDI = foreign direct investment; KIG = knowledge-intensive goods; LIG = labor-intensive goods.

high-quality FDI to align with the transformation of the domestic economy. From 2001 to 2007, China opened 100 of the country's 160 services sectors and revised its laws and regulations to create an encouraging business environment for MNCs. Sole proprietorship became MNCs' most popular mode of entry into the country.[6] China also promoted FDI in its central and western regions to narrow regional gaps in economic development. From 2001 to 2010, China's knowledge-intensive goods exports jumped by 700 percent, and the country became the world's second-largest GVC hub.

Global FDI flows into China have slowed since the global financial crisis of 2007–09, but China has stepped up its efforts to attract and retain FDI and to maximize the development benefits it brings. These efforts revolve around three goals: continuing to reduce FDI entry restrictions, promoting investment facilitation, and creating a transparent and predictable business environment (China, MOFCOM 2019). Despite the stagnation of worldwide FDI flows, China remains one of the world's top investment destinations. Its FDI inflows increased steadily from US$115 billion in 2010 to US$140 billion in 2018. In the meantime, China's knowledge-intensive goods exports continued to expand rapidly, from US$860 billion in 2010 to US$1,350 billion in 2018.

Ethiopia

Over the past decade, Ethiopia has emerged as one of the largest foreign investment hubs in Africa. The expansion of the country's textile and garment sector since 2006 is an illustration of how a surge of inward FDI has transformed the country's domestic economy. Ethiopia's garment sector has been expanding at an annual rate of more than 50 percent, and it currently hosts about 65 international investment projects. Although Ethiopia's first textile factories can be traced back to the mid-1940s, the sector took off only after this rise in FDI inflows. From 2009 to 2017, Ethiopia's total apparel exports to the rest of the world grew from about US$33 million to more than US$151 million, roughly coinciding with an increase in FDI from about US$220 million to US$4 billion (figure 1.16).

FIGURE 1.16 **Ethiopia's foreign direct investment inflows and export growth, 2006–18**

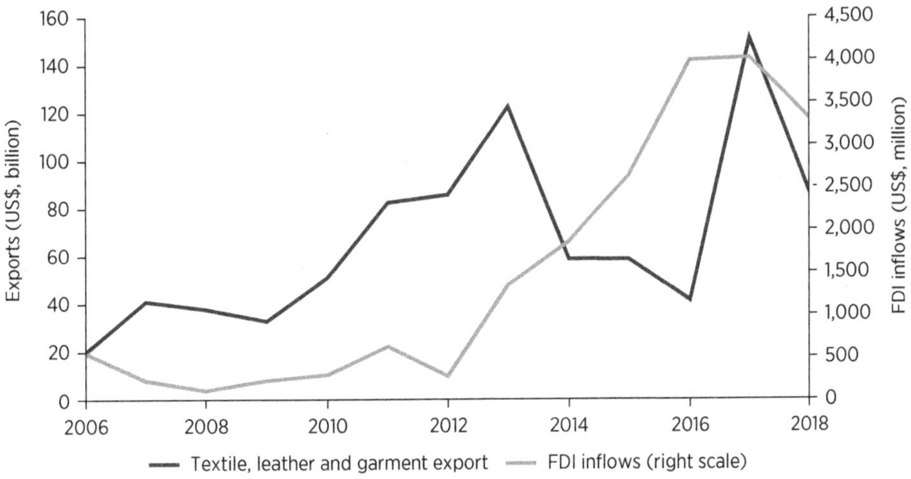

Source: World Bank calculations based on data from United Nations Conference on Trade and Development and United Nations Comtrade.
Note: FDI = foreign direct investment.

The significant flow of foreign investment into Ethiopia's textile and garment sector has occurred alongside the government's state-driven industrialization strategy for attracting FDI. In the early 2000s, the Ethiopian government planned to rely on domestic investment to spur textile and garment production for export. At that time, the country's inward FDI was very small and came only from individual investors. However, the government soon realized the limited effectiveness of local investment and shifted its industrialization strategy toward attracting and harnessing foreign investment. To provide incentives to prospective foreign investors, the government has implemented a series of policies since 2012, including removing sectoral restrictions on FDI and exempting foreign investors from customs duties and income taxes. The arrival of Turkish textile giants in 2008 was an important milestone because they not only established factories and created thousands of jobs locally but also started to move Ethiopia into GVCs by attracting additional investors. Facilitated by the government's efforts to improve Ethiopia's infrastructure and establish specialized industrial parks, a significant number of transnational garment manufacturers, mostly from Asia (particularly Bangladesh, China, and India), arrived after 2013 to cluster in those parks and invest in production bases (Balchin and Calabrese 2019). Some Western brands, such as PVH, also began to source from Ethiopia in the mid- to late 2010s.

The Ethiopian government continues to work toward its vision of building the country into the manufacturing powerhouse of Africa, and it aims for Ethiopia's textile and garment exports to reach US$300 billion by 2025. Though the evidence that it has spurred backward linkages and local ownership currently remains relatively weak, the textile and garment sector in Ethiopia has already achieved noticeable growth in a short period, and the country has great potential to become the next global garment manufacturing hub.

Vietnam

Vietnam's is another success story of achieving rapid growth by taking advantage of FDI. Since passage of the Law on Foreign Investment in 1987 during the period of Doi Moi (Renovation) reforms, the Vietnamese government has made great efforts to harness FDI to boost economic growth and to transform the country into one of the world's most favorable destinations for foreign investment. Over the past 30 years, FDI from 160 countries, mostly from East Asia, has poured into 68 provinces and cities in Vietnam. These investments have occurred in a wide range of high-tech industries, such as telecommunications, oil and gas, electronics, chemicals, steel, automobile and motorbike manufacturing, and IT, as well as in some traditional manufacturing sectors, such as garments and textiles, footwear, and agricultural product processing (figure 1.17). By the end of 2016, more than 20,000 projects were in operation with total registered capital of more than US$290 billion (Hanh et al. 2017). Foreign-invested projects are estimated to account for about a quarter of Vietnam's total socioeconomic capital and about two-thirds of the country's total exports (Hanh et al. 2017).

FDI has played an indispensable role in Vietnam's integration into GVCs by increasing domestic competition, providing incentives for innovation and technology transfer, promoting production efficiency, and developing supporting industries (Focus Economics 2018). In recent years, the government has also increased its efforts to enforce the connection between FDI and domestic businesses to keep pace with technological advances in manufacturing production around the globe. Local firms have been encouraged to innovate and enhance their technologies and management practices to supply MNCs and to perform competitively in the international market.

FIGURE 1.17 Vietnam's foreign direct investment inflows and export growth, 2000–18

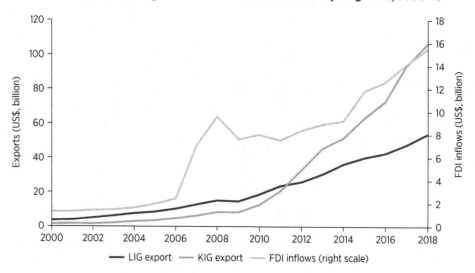

Source: World Bank calculations based on data from United Nations Conference on Trade and Development and United Nations Comtrade.
Note: FDI = foreign direct investment; KIG = knowledge-intensive goods; LIG = labor-intensive goods.

Notes

1. Bilateral FDI data between home and host countries often exhibit large discrepancies. The statistical methodology for measuring FDI also varies vastly across countries. One methodology is the fair market valuation approach, which adds up the market value of all the foreign equity of listed enterprises in the country. However, this value is subject to stock market fluctuations and does not include any unlisted FDI equity, which can amount to 22–156 percent of the host country's gross domestic product (GDP) (Damgaard and Elkjaer 2014). The most common FDI valuation method—own funds at book value—promotes cross-country comparability but hugely distorts FDI assets and liabilities by measuring them at outdated historical cost and often fails to capture the growing importance of intangibles (Lipsey 2010). More important, FDI statistics do not always reflect real economic activity. Nearly 40 percent of global FDI flows in 2017 was funneled to special purpose entities and offshore financial centers for tax purposes, obscuring the true "brick and mortar" investments that have real economic impacts on host countries (Damgaard, Elkjaer, and Johannesen 2019). Moreover, modern MNCs have increasingly complex ownership structures: an investment often travels through a chain of entities before reaching its final recipient. Tracing the initial investor and the ultimate destination and use of funds has become extremely difficult.
2. An SPE is a separate legal entity created by an organization. The SPE is a distinct company with its own assets and liabilities as well as its own legal status. SPEs are usually created for a specific objective, often to isolate financial risk.
3. Round-tripping refers to the channeling of domestic funds through offshore centers and then back to the local economy in the form of FDI (Aykut, Sanghi, and Kosmidou 2017).
4. For goods-producing GVCs (commodities, labor-intensive goods, regional processing, and knowledge-intensive goods), this section uses bilateral trade data from the United Nations Comtrade database because those data are more up to date and more granular. However, export data do not reflect real value added captured by these countries and hence may not always reflect countries' true positions in GVCs.
5. Based on 2020 data from the World Travel and Tourism Council (https://wttc.org/).
6. "China and the WTO" (http://www.xinhuanet.com/2018-06/28/c_1123050189.htm).

References

Alfaro, L., D. Chor, P. Antràs, and P. Conconi. 2019. "Internalizing Global Value Chains: A Firm-Level Analysis." *Journal of Political Economy* 127 (2): 508–59.

Alfaro-Ureña, A., I. Manelici, and J. P. Vasquez. 2019. "The Effects of Joining Multinational Supply Chains: New Evidence from Firm-to-Firm Linkages." Working Paper. https://papers.ssrn.com/sol3/papers.cfm?abstract_id=3376129.

Amador, J., and S. Cabral. 2016. "Global Value Chains: A Survey of Drivers and Measures." *Journal of Economic Surveys* 30 (2): 278–301.

Antràs, P. 2020. "Conceptual Aspects of Global Value Chains." Background paper, *World Development Report 2020: Trading for Development in the Age of Global Value Chains*, World Bank, Washington, DC.

Antràs, P., and D. Chor. 2013. "Organizing the Global Value Chain." *Econometrica* 81 (6): 2127–204.

Antràs, P., D. Chor, T. Fally, and R. Hillberry. 2012. "Measuring the Upstreamness of Production and Trade Flows." *American Economic Review* 102 (3): 412–16.

Antràs, P., and E. Helpman. 2004. "Global Sourcing." *Journal of Political Economy* 112 (3): 552–80.

Aykut, D., A. Sanghi, and G. Kosmidou. 2017. "What to Do When Foreign Direct Investment Is Not Direct or Foreign: FDI Round Tripping." Policy Research Working Paper 8046, World Bank, Washington, DC.

Balchin, Neil, and Linda Calabrese. 2019. "Comparative Country Study of the Development of Textile and Garment Sectors: Lessons for Tanzania." Overseas Development Institute, London.

Baldwin, R., and A. J. Venables. 2010. "Relocating the Value Chain: Off-Shoring and Agglomeration in the Global Economy." CEPR Discussion Paper 8163, Center for Economic Policy Research, London.

Bernard, A. B., J. B. Jensen, S. J. Redding, and P. K. Schott. 2018. "Global Firms." *Journal of Economic Literature* 56 (2): 565–619.

Buelens, C., and M. Tirpák. 2017. "Reading the Footprints: How Foreign Investors Shape Countries' Participation in Global Value Chains." *Comparative Economic Studies* 59 (4): 561–84.

Chiesi A. M. 2001. "Network Analysis." In *International Encyclopedia of the Social & Behavioral Sciences*, edited by Neil J. Smelser and Paul B. Baltes, 10499–502. Oxford, U.K.: Elsevier Science Ltd.

China, MOFCOM (Ministry of Commerce). 2019. "History of China's FDI Utilization." Ministry of Commerce of the People's Republic of China, Beijing. http://history.mofcom.gov.cn/?specialthree=ggkfzqdlywzgz.

Damgaard, J., and T. Elkjaer. 2014. "Foreign Direct Investment and the External Wealth of Nations: How Important Is Valuation?" *Review of Income and Wealth* 60 (2): 245–60.

Damgaard, J., T. Elkjaer, and N. Johannesen. 2019. *What Is Real and What Is Not in the Global FDI Network?* Washington, DC: International Monetary Fund.

Dedrick, J., K. L. Kraemer, and G. Linden. 2011. "The Distribution of Value in the Mobile Phone Supply Chain." *Telecommunications Policy* 35 (6): 505–21.

Focus Economics. 2018. "The Role of FDI in Vietnam's Socio-economic Development." *Focus Economics* (blog), January 3, 2018. https://www.focus-economics.com/blog/the-role-of-fdi-in-vietnams-socio-economic-development.

Frederick, S., P. Bamber, and J. Cho. 2018. "The Digital Economy, Global Value Chains and Asia." Joint report, Duke University Global Value Chains Center and Korea Institute for Industrial Economics & Trade. https://gvcc.duke.edu/wp-content/uploads/DigitalEconomyGVCsAsia2018.pdf.

Grossman, G. M., and E. Helpman. 2002. "Integration versus Outsourcing in Industry Equilibrium." *Quarterly Journal of Economics* 117 (1): 85–120.

Grossman, S. J., and O. D. Hart. 1986. "The Costs and Benefits of Ownership: A Theory of Vertical and Lateral Integration." *Journal of Political Economy* 94 (4): 691–719.

Hanh, N. P., D. V. Hung, N. T. Hoat, and D. T. T. Trang. 2017. "Improving Quality of Foreign Direct Investment Attraction in Vietnam." *International Journal of Quality Innovation* 3 (1).

Helpman, E., M. J. Melitz, and S. R. Yeaple. 2004. "Export versus FDI with Heterogeneous Firms." *American Economic Review* 94 (1): 300–16.

Hummels, D., J. Ishii, and K. M. Yi. 2001. "The Nature and Growth of Vertical Specialization in World Trade." *Journal of International Economics* 54 (1): 75–96.

Johnson, R. C., and G. Noguera. 2012. "Proximity and Production Fragmentation." *American Economic Review* 102 (3): 407–11.

Kathuria, S., and R. A. Yatawara. 2020. *Regional Investment Pioneers in South Asia: The Payoff of Knowing Your Neighbors.* Washington, DC: World Bank Group.

Kimura, F., and K. Kiyota. 2006. "Exports, FDI, and Productivity: Dynamic Evidence from Japanese Firms." *Review of World Economics* 142 (4): 695–719.

Koenig, P. 2009. "Agglomeration and the Export Decisions of French Firms." *Journal of Urban Economics* 66 (3): 186–95.

Kojima, K. 1975. "International Trade and Foreign Investment: Substitutes or Complements." *Hitotsubashi Journal of Economics* 16 (1): 1–12.

Koopman, R., Z. Wang, and S. J. Wei. 2014. "Tracing Value-Added and Double Counting in Gross Exports." *American Economic Review* 104 (2): 459–94.

Kumar, N. 2008. "Internationalization of Indian Enterprises: Patterns, Strategies, Ownership Advantages, and Implications." *Asian Economic Policy Review* 3 (2): 242–61.

Lee, H. 2010. "The Destination of Outward FDI and the Performance of South Korean Multinationals." *Emerging Markets Finance and Trade* 46 (3): 59–66.

Lipsey, R. E. 2010. "Measuring the Location of Production in a World of Intangible Productive Assets, FDI, and Intrafirm Trade." *Review of Income and Wealth* 56 (S1): S99–S110.

Martínez-Galán, E., and M. P. Fontoura. 2019. "Global Value Chains and Inward Foreign Direct Investment in the 2000s." *World Economy* 42 (1): 175–96.

Melitz, M. J. 2003. "The Impact of Trade on Intra-industry Reallocations and Aggregate Industry Productivity." *Econometrica* 71 (6): 1695–725.

MGI (McKinsey Global Institute). 2019. "Globalization in Transition: The Future of Trade and Value Chains." Report, McKinsey & Company. https://www.mckinsey.com/~/media /McKinsey/Featured%20Insights/Innovation/Globalization%20in%20transition%20 The%20future%20of%20trade%20and%20value%20chains/MGI-Globalization%20 in%20transition-The-future-of-trade-and-value-chains-Full-report.pdf.

Mundell, R. A. 1957. "International Trade and Factor Mobility." *American Economic Review* 47 (3): 321–35.

Purvis, D. D. 1972. "Technology, Trade and Factor Mobility." *Economic Journal* 82 (327): 991–99.

Schmitz, A., and P. Helmberger. 1970. "Factor Mobility and International Trade: The Case of Complementarity." *American Economic Review* 60 (4): 761–67.

Singh, N. 2011. "Emerging Economy Multinationals: The Role of Business Groups." *Economics, Management, and Financial Markets* 6 (1): 142–81.

TECMA Communications. 2019. "The Aerospace Industry in Mexico in 2019: An Overview." *Made in Mexico* (blog), August 18, 2019. (https://www.madeinmexicoinc.com /the-aerospace-industry-in-mexico-in-2019/).

Timmer, M., B. Los, R. Stehrer, and G. de Vries. 2016. "An Anatomy of the Global Trade Slowdown Based on the WIOD 2016 Release." GGDC Research Memorandum GD-162, Groningen Growth and Development Centre, University of Groningen.

UNCTAD (United Nations Conference on Trade and Development). 2013. *World Investment Report 2013: Global Value Chains: Investment and Trade for Development*. Geneva: United Nations.

UNCTAD (United Nations Conference on Trade and Development). 2017. *World Investment Report 2017: Investment and the Digital Economy*. Geneva: United Nations.

Wagner, Joachim. 2006. "Exports, Foreign Direct Investment, and Productivity: Evidence from German Firm Level Data." *Applied Economics Letters* 13 (6): 347–49.

Wasserman, S., and K. Faust. 1994. *Social Network Analysis: Methods and Applications*. Structural Analysis in the Social Sciences, Vol. 8. Cambridge, U.K.: Cambridge University Press.

Williamson, Oliver E. 1985. *The Economic Institutions of Capitalism*. New York: Simon and Schuster.

World Bank. 2018. *Global Investment Competitiveness Report 2017/2018: Foreign Investor Perspectives and Policy Implications*. Washington, DC: World Bank.

World Bank. 2020. *World Development Report 2020: Trading for Development in the Age of Global Value Chains*. Washington, DC: World Bank.

Xing, Y., and N. C. Detert. 2010. "How the iPhone Widens the United States Trade Deficit with the People's Republic of China." ADBI Working Paper 257, Asian Development Bank Institute, Tokyo.

Chapter 2

Multinational Corporations Shape Global Value Chain Development

Key findings

- Global value chains (GVCs) encompass a myriad of firm-to-firm relationships and the full range of activities required to bring a product or service from conception to its end use. These activities are managed and coordinated by multinational corporations (MNCs) via investment, trade, people, technology, and information flows. Their business decisions have profound implications for the global economy.

- It is impossible to understand GVCs without understanding how MNCs make their global production decisions. By understanding the objectives and strategies of MNCs, developing countries can better stimulate their entry into GVCs and increase the development benefits from MNC activities in their economies.

- MNCs have proliferated since the 1970s. They and their affiliates contributed 36 percent of global output in 2016, including around two-thirds of global exports and more than half of imports. Countries that are major global exporters all benefit from a strong presence of MNCs.

- Three objectives dominate the production decisions of MNCs: lowering production costs, mitigating risks, and increasing market power. MNCs balance their level of control, their commitment of proprietary resources, the type and level of risks they take, and the costs and returns of various transaction modes to organize their global production networks.

- The business strategies MNCs use to pursue each of their objectives are inextricably intertwined with the structural characteristics of the specific GVCs they operate within.

- The rise of superstar firms and their increased market concentration have a dual impact on growth and distribution. MNCs' business strategies affect the gains that foreign direct investment and GVCs bring in knowledge spillovers, resources, consumer welfare, and the distribution of value added in the supply chains.

Multinational corporations are the drivers of global value chains

Multinational corporations (MNCs) are firms that conduct direct business activities and own assets in at least two countries (Dietrich and Krafft 2012). Although cross-border direct business activities date back a long time (for example, the British East India Company began its operations in the early seventeenth century), the real forerunners of MNCs were the nineteenth century's joint stock companies. Early MNCs invested abroad primarily to seek raw materials from developing countries. After World War II, many MNCs began operating in manufacturing, and the past three decades have seen more geographically fragmented activities in both manufacturing and services.

The internal organizational structure of companies evolved alongside developments in their activities and geographic scope as well as progress in communication and transportation technologies. Most early companies operated in a single sector with a functional structure. The multidivisional form, in which divisions are established along product lines, emerged only in the twentieth century. A further development, the matrix structure, allowed product lines and geographic lines to be considered simultaneously. Advances in information and communication technologies (ICTs) greatly reduced communication costs; transportation costs also fell dramatically in the past few decades, spurring a wave of globalization. MNCs increasingly outsource to and develop business activities with a variety of external partners, ranging from subcontractors to suppliers to partners in research and development (R&D) or production activities. New structures have been developed to account for these external networks as well as for networks of affiliates internal to the companies (Dietrich and Krafft 2012).

Because of these developments, MNCs have proliferated since the 1970s. Global estimates indicate that there were roughly 7,000 parent MNCs in 1970; this number had jumped to 38,000 by 2000 (OECD 2018) and was estimated at more than 100,000 in 2011 (UNCTAD 2011). Together, these MNCs had close to 900,000 affiliates in foreign countries. Most MNCs originated in developed countries (70 percent according to UNCTAD [2011]), although more and more MNCs are headquartered in developing countries, and those MNCs are growing rapidly. In 2019, 12 companies headquartered in developing countries were among the world's top 100 nonfinancial MNCs as ranked by foreign assets, compared with only 2 such companies in 2003 (UNCTAD 2005, 2020).

Foreign direct investment (FDI) is the primary form of global expansion for MNCs, and until recently it was their defining type of investment. The IMF (1977) sets a threshold of 10 percent as the minimum equity ownership necessary for a parent company to be considered to have a controlling interest in a foreign affiliate. Foreign investment involving a lower percentage of equity is classified as portfolio investment.[1] FDI flows consist of equity capital (assets and liabilities), reinvested earnings (net), and other capital (such as intercompany loans). A direct investment enterprise may be (a) a subsidiary (an enterprise of which more than 50 percent is owned by a nonresident investor), (b) an associate (an enterprise of which 10 percent to 50 percent is owned by a nonresident investor), or (c) a branch (an unincorporated enterprise wholly or jointly owned by a non-resident) (OECD 2010).

The use of nonequity modes (NEMs) by MNCs in international production has increased rapidly over the past two decades, outpacing the growth of FDI (figure 2.1). NEMs are contractual agreements, such as licensing, franchising, or management contracts. Global FDI flows have shown anemic growth since 2008; net of one-off factors such as tax reforms, megadeals, and volatile financial flows, FDI has averaged only 1 percent growth per year for the past decade, compared with 8 percent from 2000 to 2007 and more than 20 percent before 2000 (UNCTAD 2020). Much of the continued expansion of international production has been driven by intangibles, such as royalties, licensing fees, and service exports. NEMs have been growing faster than FDI since 2000. They have also expanded fastest in the sectors in which they were most prevalent, as is evident in the relative growth rates of royalties, licensing fees, and trade in services (UNCTAD 2011, 2020). Compared with FDI, NEMs have lower up-front capital requirements, less exposure to risk, and greater flexibility to adapt to change, all of which have become critical so that MNCs can be agile in an ever-evolving market.

Asset-light forms of investment also increased in the past decade because of digitalization and the new business models it made feasible. Top technology MNCs, such as Facebook and Google, can reach markets worldwide through digital channels without a significant physical presence. New business models, such as the sharing economy, allow MNCs such as Airbnb and Uber to enter foreign markets by building peer-to-peer networks and without owning physical assets themselves (UNCTAD 2020).

There is a large body of literature studying the motivation and entry mode of MNCs (Antràs and Yeaple 2014; Helpman, Melitz, and Yeaple 2004; Melitz 2003). Various FDI taxonomies have been developed in different periods with diverse focus (box 2.1). These taxonomies, however, have many overlapping elements given that

FIGURE 2.1 Indicators of international production, by tangibility

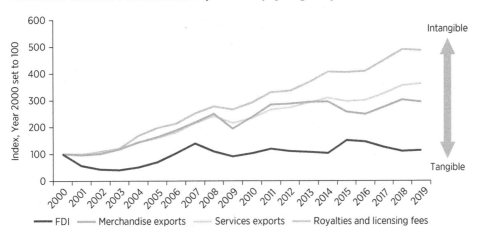

Source: From UNCTAD 2020, © United Nations. Reprinted with the permission of the United Nations.
Note: FDI = foreign direct investment.

BOX 2.1 Motivations for and modes of foreign direct investment

Dunning's framework

In 1977, Dunning first established the OLI (ownership, location, internalization) paradigm of why (ownership advantages), where (location advantages), and how (internalization advantages) a firm decides to invest abroad. He identified four types of foreign direct investment (FDI) motives: resource seeking, efficiency seeking, strategic asset seeking, and market seeking. These types are cross-cutting with horizontal and vertical FDI. The potential limitation of this widely accepted taxonomy is that this theory was established before the rapid rise of global value chains (GVCs), and thus tended to pay little attention to the role of GVC network coordination on firms' outward investment motivation.

In addition to Dunning's framework, FDI is commonly categorized as being horizontal or vertical.

Horizontal FDI

Horizontal FDI occurs when multinationals undertake the same production activities in multiple countries. Horizontal FDI with a market-seeking motive is one of the earliest and most established types of FDI. This type of FDI is often associated with trade, that is, investment substitution. The reasons behind horizontal FDI include, among others, proximity to consumers, adaptation to local needs, tax planning, and sometimes tariff jumping. Japanese firms have been very active in using this strategy in the auto industry and electronics in US and European Union markets (Belderbos and Sleuwaegen 1998; Head and Ries 2003). Greenfield FDI and mergers and acquisitions are both common modes of horizontal FDI.

Vertical FDI

Vertical FDI takes place when firms fragment production processes and locate each stage in the country where it can be performed at the least cost. The conventional interpretation for the motivation is factor cost differences, that is, efficiency-seeking FDI (Aizenman and Marion 2004). An increasing portion of the literature also suggests that vertical FDI also entails the strategic asset–seeking motivation to augment firm capacities. Strategic assets can include technology, production processes, management skills, networks, and more (Amann and Virmani 2015; Driffield and Love 2003).

In addition, vertical FDI is used as an organizational format to minimize transaction costs. In a GVC network, market-based cross-border transactions may suffer from high transaction costs because of the absence of strong legal systems. Also, the increasing organizational complexity and growing length and layers of GVCs create additional transaction costs. Firms are therefore motivated to vertically integrate to avoid contract hazards and deficiencies (Antràs 2019; World Bank et al. 2017).

Agglomeration FDI

FDI might also be attracted by location-specific spillovers. Production-unbundling costs associated with cross-border management, coordination, and logistics might outweigh the benefits of reduced factor costs. In such case, a firm may choose to move along with its GVC partners to new locations against its own comparative advantage (Baldwin and Venables 2010). For firms hoping to join new value chains through outward investment, location-specific externalities, such as pooled markets of skilled labor, availability of specialized inputs and services, and benefits of technological spillovers, become attractive conditions. For example, Japanese firms tend to be in proximity to other Japanese firms in the United States to access trained Japanese workers in the cluster (Head, Ries, and Swenson 1995). Also, outward investors from Belgium, Germany, Italy, Japan, the Netherlands, Switzerland, the

Continued on next page ›

BOX 2.1 **Motivations for and modes of foreign direct investment (FDI) (*continued*)**

United Kingdom, and the United States have demonstrated a positive correlation between locating investment in France with the proximity of nonhome foreign firms. It is possible that new firms use the experience and performance of other foreign firms as an Indicator of the business climate at that location (Crozet, Mayer, and Mucchielli 2004).

The significant contributions of multinational corporations to global output and trade

The production and business strategies developed by MNCs to fragment, outsource, and offshore various activities gave rise to global value chains (GVCs). The internationalization of knowledge, technical and commercial alike, benefits both MNCs and the wider economies in their home and host countries. It is impossible to understand GVCs without understanding how MNCs make their global production decisions. As microeconomic data have become increasingly available, research has changed dramatically over the past 20 years: attention has shifted from countries and industries toward firms that engage in international production, investment, and trade.

Data on MNCs' activities and performance are scattered among different sources and are rarely comparable across countries.[2] This report uses a new database developed by the Organisation for Economic Co-operation and Development (OECD) to shed light on the overall contributions of MNCs to the global economy. This Analytical Activities of MNEs (multinational enterprises) (AMNE) database contains official data collected and published by national statistics offices along with estimates made using various statistical methods. It covers 59 countries and a "rest of the world" group and provides disaggregated data for 34 sectors. Gross output, value added, exports, and imports from 2005 to 2016 are broken down into foreign firms (defined as having at least 50 percent foreign ownership) and domestic firms. The database further distinguishes (from 2008 onward) between domestically owned MNCs and firms that operate only domestically.

MNCs, both domestic and foreign, account for a significant share of exports in most sectors (figure 2.2). According to the OECD AMNE database, MNCs and their affiliates contributed 36 percent of global output in 2016, including about two-thirds of global exports and more than half of imports. Their contribution is especially pronounced in knowledge-intensive goods, knowledge-intensive services, and regional processing sectors. Motor vehicle manufacturing is the most internationalized sector: MNCs make up 90 percent of the sector's exports. In general, foreign

FIGURE 2.2 **Multinational corporations' contribution to global exports, by sector**

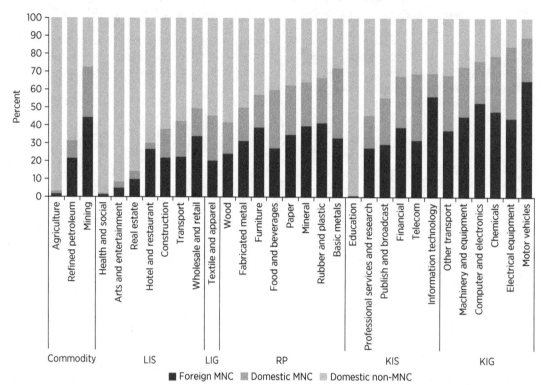

Source: Calculations based on Organisation for Economic Co-operation and Development Analytical Activities of MNEs (multinational enterprises) database.
Note: Data are averaged from 2008 to 2016. KIG = knowledge-intensive goods; KIS = knowledge-intensive services; LIG = labor-intensive goods; LIS = labor-intensive services; MNC = multinational corporation; RP = regional processing.

MNCs represent a larger share of output and exports than domestic MNCs, but the opposite holds in a few sectors, such as textiles and apparel, telecommunications, and basic metals.

Positive correlation between the importance of multinational corporations and trade value across sectors and countries

Countries that are major global exporters all benefit from a strong presence of MNCs. Panel a of figure 2.3 shows a positive correlation between a country's total exports and the share of exports contributed by MNCs. The breakdown between foreign and domestic MNCs in panel b of figure 2.3 reveals a more nuanced picture: the relationship between countries' total exports and foreign MNCs' share in those exports is bell-shaped. In other words, the role of foreign MNCs in exports increases first, then declines when a country's exports exceed a certain level. However, the slope of the polynomial line of best fit for domestic MNCs and exports is positive: exports by these

FIGURE 2.3 **Multinational corporations' share of exports**

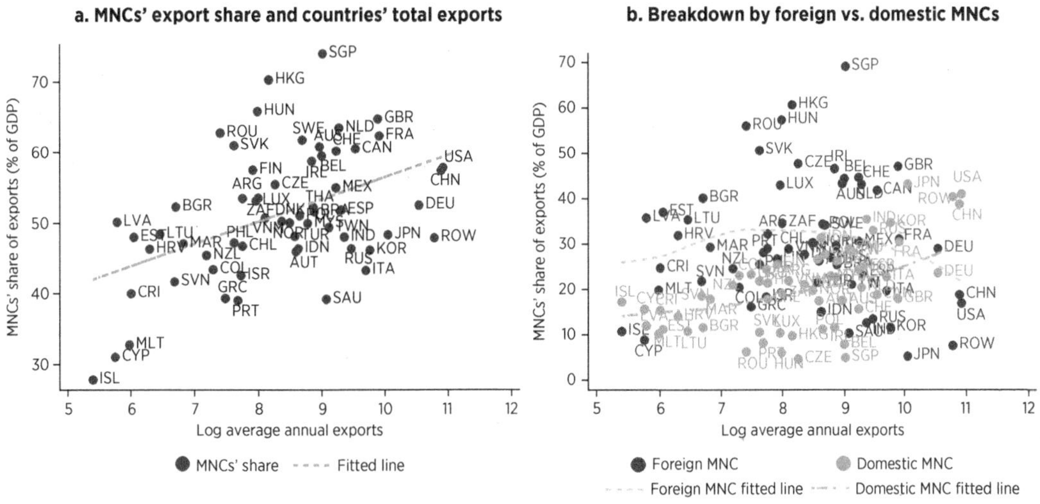

a. MNCs' export share and countries' total exports

b. Breakdown by foreign vs. domestic MNCs

Source: Calculations based on Organisation for Economic Co-operation and Development Analytical Activities of MNEs (multinational enterprises) database, 2008–16 average.
Note: MNC = multinational corporation.

MNCs increase with their countries' total exports. As countries learn through exporting and as their economies grow, their own firms begin to internationalize. These domestic MNCs then play an important role in export expansion. For example, in China, Japan, and the United States, domestic MNCs contribute more than 40 percent of exports, twice as much as foreign MNCs contribute. However, foreign MNCs still act as primary exporters for many small economies with highly liberalized trade and FDI. For example, foreign MNCs' contribution to exports is as high as 70 percent in Singapore.

The contribution of foreign firms to exports in 2016 was highest in Sub-Saharan Africa, having increased from 2005 to 2016 as FDI liberalization attracted more foreign investment and domestic firm capability remained weak (figure 2.4). Some countries in the Europe and Central Asia region also experienced increases in the export share of foreign firms because of the European Union's enlargement and the further integration of Europe's economies. For instance, foreign firms' export share increased by 18 percentage points in Romania. The Czech Republic, Hungary, and the Netherlands also saw increases of about 10 percentage points. In contrast, countries in East Asia, including China, the Republic of Korea, Malaysia, the Philippines, Singapore, Thailand, and Vietnam, generally experienced a decrease in foreign firms' export share: foreign firms' exports in these countries are still growing but were overtaken by those of domestic firms. Foreign firms' contributions in Latin America and the Caribbean remain relatively low and declined from 2005 to 2016. And, last, foreign firms' contribution is the lowest in South Asia despite modest growth.

The dominance of MNCs increases with total sectoral exports in the manufacturing sector (figure 2.5). Knowledge-intensive goods made up more than half of the global goods trade in 2018; international cooperation is crucial to producing these

FIGURE 2.4 Foreign firms' share of exports, by region, 2005 and 2016

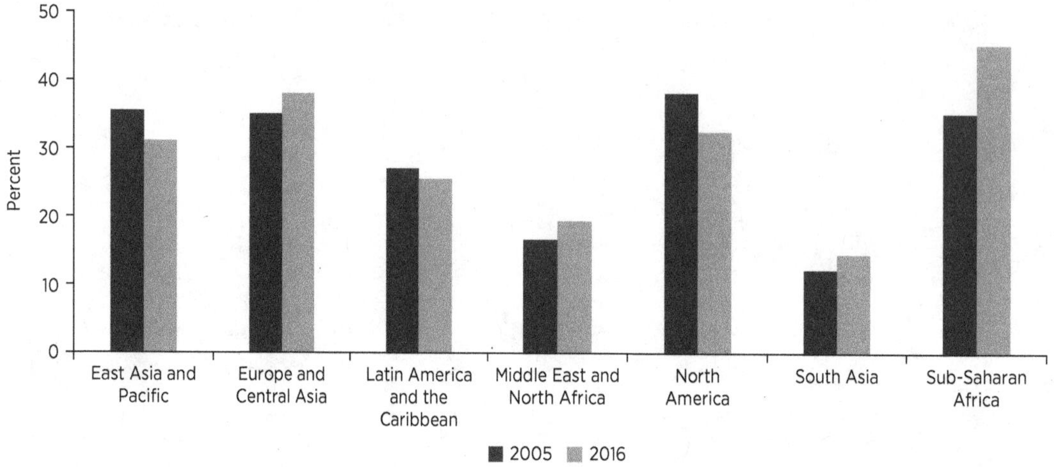

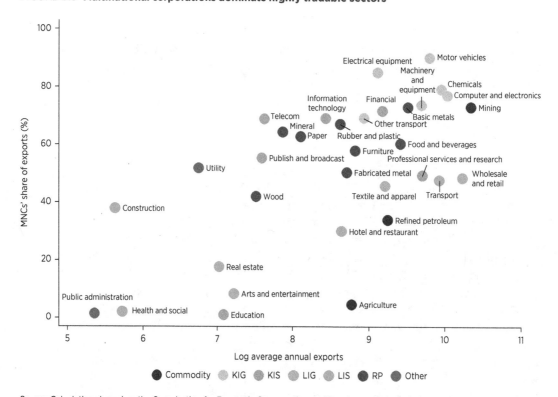

Source: Calculations based on the Organisation for Economic Co-operation and Development Analytical Activities of MNEs (multinational enterprises) database.

FIGURE 2.5 Multinational corporations dominate highly tradable sectors

Source: Calculations based on the Organisation for Economic Co-operation and Development Analytical Activities of MNEs (multinational enterprises) database.
Note: This figure shows average annual global exports from 2008 to 2016 and the share of MNCs (both foreign and domestic) in total sectoral exports. KIG = knowledge-intensive goods; KIS = knowledge-intensive services; LIG = labor-intensive goods; LIS = labor-intensive services; MNC = multinational corporation; RP = regional processing.

products, given their complexity. MNCs contribute about 80 percent of exports in these sectors. Regional processing is the second most highly traded product group, and MNCs contribute about 70 percent of exports within it. Given the bulky or perishable nature of these products, most of the trade in this group happens in regional rather than global value chains. Labor-intensive goods have a much lower total trade value than knowledge-intensive goods because their unit prices tend to be very low, but MNCs still play a leading role in the GVCs of these goods, especially textile and apparel.

The contribution of MNCs increases with tradability in the service sector. Among labor-intensive services, transportation and wholesale and retail are the most tradable: transportation directly moves goods and people across borders, and retail firms deliver goods to final consumers. MNCs account for about half of global exports in these sectors. For knowledge-intensive services, financial services, information technology, and telecommunications are the top three traded sectors. MNCs contribute about 70 percent of these sectors' global exports. Publishing and broadcasting, professional services, and research activities are also highly tradable, and MNCs' shares in these sectors are greater than 50 percent. Among all the service sectors, education, health and social services, and public administration are the least tradable and are almost entirely dominated by domestic, non-MNC firms.

Multinational corporations' objectives and strategies in global value chains

The business objectives and strategies of MNCs shape the development of GVCs. GVCs encompass a myriad of firm-to-firm relationships and the full range of activities required to bring a product or service from conception to its end use. These activities must be managed and coordinated. MNCs organize their international production networks via investment, trade, people, and information flows. Their production decisions have profound implications for the global economy and for the development of its subunits (Buckley 2009, 2010; Buckley, Driffield, and Kim, forthcoming; Buckley and Strange 2011).

MNCs have three main objectives in organizing their global production: lowering production costs, mitigating risks, and enhancing market power (figure 2.6). These three objectives are rooted in the theory of firms, industrial organizations, and international trade and investment. The "make or buy" decisions of MNCs define the firms' boundaries; their "where and how to make" decisions determine their geographic distribution (in the form of FDI or NEM); and their "where and how to buy" decisions link suppliers from multiple locations into their global production networks with varying coordination intensity. MNCs balance rewards and risks in all these decisions, and they leverage their market power to raise their markups or negotiate better terms of trade with suppliers. These three objectives, and MNCs' business strategies, are inherently interconnected—MNCs often make purchasing, production, and selling decisions simultaneously. This chapter focuses on the purchasing and production decisions and strategies because these decisions are most relevant for GVCs.

FIGURE 2.6 Multinational corporations' three objectives in organizing their global production

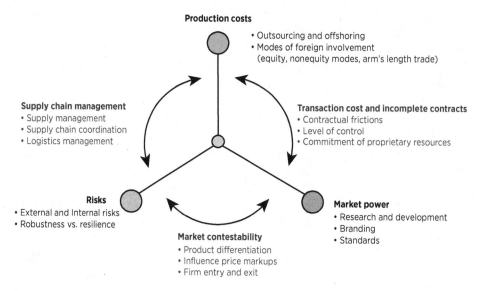

Source: World Bank.

Lowering production costs

MNCs spread their production networks across the globe to benefit from factor cost arbitrage and economies of scale. To lower their production costs, MNCs segment their stages of production and assign each stage to the internal or external units that can perform it most cost-effectively. This process is characterized by the "smile curve" of GVCs, in which the two ends of the value chain, typically conception and marketing, add more value to the product than the middle—manufacturing—part of the chain (figure 2.7). From R&D and product design to marketing and sales, the MNC-led high-value-adding activities mostly concern intangibles, such as technology and branding, which constitute the core proprietary resources that enabled the MNC's growth and global expansion in the first place. Labor-intensive production is usually offshored to lower-cost locations.

Production segmentation, outsourcing, and offshoring are the most important distinguishing features of contemporary globalization (Arndt and Kierzkowski 2001). Production segmentation is usually the precondition for outsourcing. Both outsourcing and offshoring can increase production length, defined in this report as the number of firms (including cross-border intrafirm trade) a product or service must go through before reaching its final customer (Fally 2012; Wang et al. 2017). Production length captures the degree of specialization and complexity involved in the production process (Antràs et al. 2012; Wang et al. 2017).

Offshoring and outsourcing define not only a firm's boundary but also its geographic footprint. Offshoring lengthens production through cross-border intrafirm or interfirm trade, whereas outsourcing lengthens production through domestic or international interfirm trade (table 2.1). MNCs can set up their own subsidiaries or

FIGURE 2.7 **Smile curve of value-adding activities in global value chains**

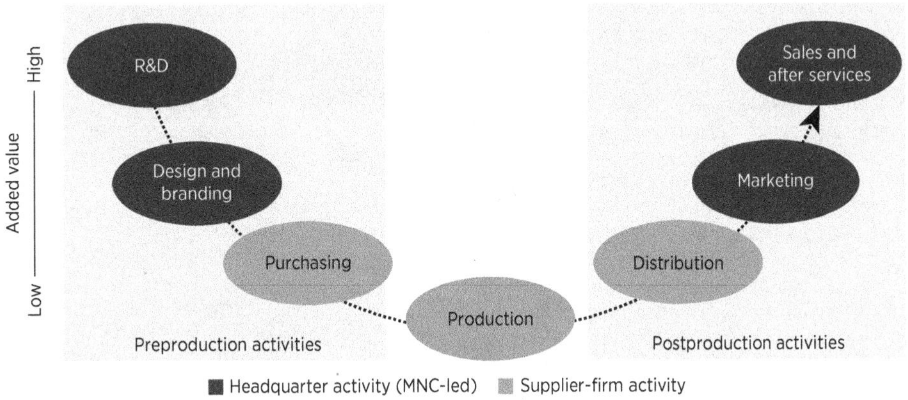

Source: World Bank.
Note: The base price is the factory price or production cost, in contrast to the retail price, which adds in shipping and insurance costs, tariffs, sales taxes, and various markups. MNC = multinational corporation; R&D = research and development.

TABLE 2.1 **How offshoring and outsourcing affect production length**

Production strategy	Offshoring	Outsourcing	Impact on production length
Fully in-house production: Lead firm carries out the whole production process by itself in its home country (internalized production kept in-house)	No	No	No GVC involved, no impact on production length
Offshore in-sourcing: Lead firm sets up its own subsidiary in another country to carry out certain stages of production (internalized production done by foreign affiliates)	Yes	No	Lengthens production through intrafirm trade
Domestic outsourcing: Lead firm hands over some production stages to another firm in the same country (externalized production at home)	No	Yes	Lengthens production through domestic interfirm trade
Offshore outsourcing: Lead firm uses overseas suppliers to supply inputs or carry out certain tasks (externalized production abroad)	Yes	Yes	Lengthens production through international interfirm trade

Source: Adaptation of Radlo 2016 and UNCTAD 2004.
Note: GVC = global value chain.

entities offshore to benefit from cheaper labor costs while ensuring better control over quality and intellectual property. This strategy is called offshore in-sourcing. Firms can also outsource and offshore at the same time, known as offshore outsourcing, if they use foreign suppliers for certain inputs and tasks. Outsourcing and offshoring have resulted in longer GVCs, which offer both advantages and disadvantages for MNCs (figure 2.8).

FIGURE 2.8 **Advantages and disadvantages of outsourcing and offshoring**

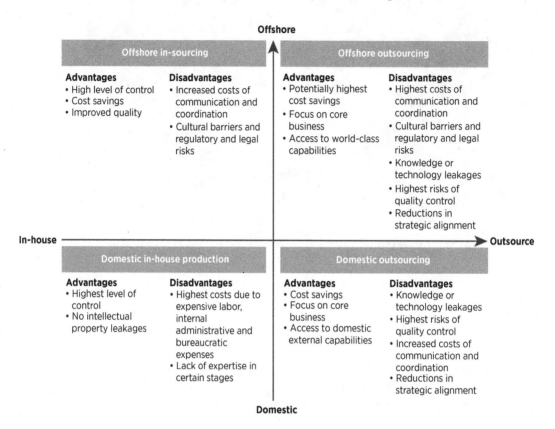

Source: Summary of Inman and Helms 2005 and Radlo 2016.

Economists have developed two main theories to explain firms' boundary decisions (what to outsource and what to keep in house): transaction cost economics (TCE; pioneered by Klein, Crawford, and Alchian [1978] and Williamson [1973, 1975, 1985]) and property rights theory (PRT; pioneered by Grossman and Hart [1986] and Hart and Moore [1990]). TCE assumes that market transactions are plagued by incomplete contracts and locking-in among trading partners. Locking-in usually happens when relationship-specific investment in the trading partner is required. Locking-in leads the value of the partners' relationship to exceed the value of the trading partners' outside alternatives, creating "quasi-rents." Firms decide what to own and what to outsource by comparing the efficiencies of the available transaction modes. TCE thus predicts that MNCs tend to integrate transactions for which there are high levels of quasi-rents and incompleteness in contracts. The PRT theory, in contrast, focuses on distortions in ex ante investments rather than in the ex post haggling costs central to TCE. When one external supplier is acquired by another, the supplier has less incentive to invest in the quality of its products because its profits are shared with the parent firm. The PRT theory predicts that MNCs outsource the production of key inputs to limit underinvestment in these crucial inputs. Recent empirical studies confirm that TCE and PRT forces jointly shape MNCs' outsourcing patterns (Alfaro et al. 2019; Berlingieri, Pisch, and Steinwender 2018).

Theories and empirical studies also abound regarding firms' offshoring behavior and choice of locations (Alfaro and Charlton 2009; Blonigen 2005; Du, Lu, and Tao 2008; Head, Ries, and Swenson 1995; Helpman 1984; Makino, Lau, and Yeh 2002; Osnago, Rocha, and Ruta 2017). Helpman (1984) developed a general equilibrium model of international trade in which MNCs choose where to locate their product lines to minimize costs. Several economists then developed the "new trade theory of the MNC" on the basis of assumptions of increasing returns to scale and firm profit maximization modeling (Helpman 1985; Helpman and Krugman 1985; Markusen 1984, 1995, 1998). MNCs have developed multitiered, complex offshore outsourcing and in-sourcing strategies that are based on the integration and coordination of materials, processes, tasks, designs, technologies, and suppliers (Monczka and Trent 1991).

There is a tension between cost differences that create incentives to offshore production and colocation or agglomeration forces that bind stages of production together. Reductions in international friction facilitate the relocation of production to align with comparative costs, but this relocation is not necessarily continuous or monotonic (Baldwin and Venables 2010). Geographic proximity to major markets, availability of cheap labor, local industrial agglomeration, supportive business environments, good infrastructure, and open trade and investment policies are the common determinants—along with many other factors, such as international trade and investment agreements and cultural factors—for both offshore outsourcing (trade) and vertical FDI.

Core questions in MNCs' outsourcing and offshoring decisions are how much proprietary resources the MNCs wish to commit to their relationships, what level of control they demand, what type and degree of costs and risks they are willing to bear, and what return on investment they require (McDonald, Burton, and Dowling 2002). MNCs use firm-specific ownership advantages (in R&D, management, or marketing and distribution) as inputs that can serve product lines in multiple locations (Helpman 1984). They manage GVCs through both internalization (ownership) and externalization (NEMs, arm's length trade). FDI thus occurs when a firm can increase its value by internalizing markets for its intangible assets.[3] Ownership also offers the benefits of a higher level of control of assets, employees, products, and prices. However, MNCs do not expand their business activities indefinitely because the internal administrative costs of ownership will eventually outweigh its benefits.

MNCs use different transaction modes to balance cost, risk, and control in their interfirm relationships when outsourcing or offshoring business activities. MNCs organize their production networks using three main modes: equity investment (FDI), NEMs, and arm's length trade. Equity investment includes mainly wholly owned subsidiaries and joint ventures. NEMs include, among others, licensing, franchising, and management contracts. Arm's length trade refers to imports, exports, and subcontracting with unrelated parties. Equity investment generally requires higher costs, entails more risks, and promises greater returns than NEMs and arm's length trade. Equity investment also allows a higher degree of control over assets, employees, and operations and is less likely to leak proprietary knowledge. NEMs offer a mode in between equity investment and arm's length trade. They generally have lower entry costs than equity investment and allow firms to quickly expand into new markets without much risk or large capital investments. NEMs also give firms greater flexibility in adapting to change. Arm's length trade has the lowest setup costs and lowest risks, but MNCs pursuing this approach have little control over their import suppliers and limited access to foreign markets through exports for certain goods and services. Arm's length trade and NEMs can either pave the way for future FDI or serve as substitutes for FDI, depending on the specific motivations of the MNCs in question. There is high heterogeneity in firms' configurations of investment and trade and the range of nonequity, contract-based partnerships in GVCs across sectors and markets (Andrenelli et al. 2019).

Which mode of foreign involvement an MNC chooses often hinges on the host country's context, especially its trade, investment, and competition policies. Many countries still impose caps on foreign equity shares and limit FDI in certain industries. Tariff jumping is another key motivation for MNCs to set up production facilities abroad to serve local customers: MNCs can avoid tariffs imposed by the host country by establishing local production capacity. Foreign acquisitions can alter the domestic and global competitive landscapes for the host country; host countries tend to use competition policy to regulate foreign takeovers to ensure market contestability. MNCs constantly adapt their transaction modes to reflect their host countries' regulations and business environments.

FDI, NEMs, and arm's length trade have different implications for development, depending on the specific sector involved and the stage of production in a GVC where they take place. All three modes have made significant contributions to employment worldwide. NEMs can drive export growth, transfer intellectual property, improve labor skills, and foster local entrepreneurship. They encourage domestic enterprise development and investment in productive assets. Eventually, NEM activities can enhance the productive capabilities of developing countries and deepen those countries' integration into GVCs. FDI generates productivity spillovers in host countries through the demonstration and linkage effects (Alfaro et al. 2004; Barba Navaretti and Venables 2004; Du, Harrison, and Jefferson 2011; Farole and Winkler 2014; Javorcik, Lo Turco, and Maggioni 2017; Javorcik and Spatareanu 2009; Lipsey 2004). FDI can also improve resource allocation by pushing out the host countries' least productive firms (Alfaro and Chen 2018), but doing so requires an ecosystem of good institutions, a deep talent pool, quality infrastructure, and other complementary factors to attract FDI in the first place and to spread its benefits throughout the host country's wider economy.

Once MNCs have set up their global production networks, supply chain management becomes pivotal to increasing their efficiency and reducing waste. As different parts of the world have become more connected and MNCs' supply chains have grown longer, the need for better supply chain management has intensified. MNCs leverage their worldwide purchasing power, production capacity, and distribution channels to reduce material inventories, eliminate waste, and improve efficiency.

Supplier selection, supply chain coordination, and logistics management are key elements in MNCs' supply chain management (Tomas and Hult 2003). Once an MNC determines its needs, it identifies a pool of suppliers capable of fulfilling them. It then evaluates each potential supplier on the basis of a set of criteria and finally contracts with the suppliers it selects. MNCs often have hundreds or even thousands of suppliers. Coordination is therefore crucial to improving supply chain performance by aligning the plans and objectives of MNCs and their suppliers. Supply chain coordination usually focuses on inventory management and ordering decisions in distributed intercompany settings (Kumar 1992). Logistics management is also central to inventory management and ordering decisions because access to efficient and reliable transportation, warehousing, and distribution can be a core advantage for MNCs over their competition. This global supply chain management affects all functions of an organization. Successful global supply chain management requires focused efforts across the entire company and collaboration with all outside suppliers and service providers.

Ultimately, MNCs' choices as to which markets to serve, where to operate plants, what products to export, and which countries to source inputs from are interdependent (Bernard et al. 2018). These decisions affect variable production costs and prices and influence exports of products to markets and imports of inputs from source countries. Incurring the fixed costs of sourcing inputs from one country can give a firm access to lower-cost suppliers, reducing its production costs and prices while increasing its profits. This effect in turn allows the firm to increase its scale of operation, making it more likely that the firm will find it profitable to incur the fixed costs of outsourcing (Antràs, Fort, and Tintelnot 2017; Tintelnot 2017). Exporting and importing decisions are also interdependent. More productive firms lower their production costs by sourcing inputs from more countries. They also expand their scale of operation by both exporting more products to each market and exporting to more markets overall.

Mitigating risks

In their unrelenting quest for efficiency, MNCs also try to minimize and mitigate value chain risks. Such risks stem from multiple sources, both external (such as macroeconomic, social, health, environmental, political, and regulatory risks) and internal (such as operational, process, financial, personnel, management, planning, and control risks) (Calatayud and Ketterer 2016). The trade-off between production efficiency and value chain robustness has been a perennial challenge for MNCs.

Supply chain risks are affected not only by production length but also by several other factors. MNCs tend to face growing risks as their global supply chains lengthen, their tiers of suppliers multiply, and their overall complexity increases. However, the relationship between supply chain risks and production length is complicated. For example, geographically dispersed production networks may be more prone to disruption, but they also diversify locational risks. Idiosyncratic shocks to any individual firm could propagate though the entire network and lead to aggregate fluctuations; how risk affects upstream and downstream firms depends on the network's structure and input specificity, among other factors. (Acemoglu et al. 2012; Barrot and Sauvagnat 2016).

Supplier diversification is a key strategy for mitigating supply chain risks. For each specific need, a firm chooses between single sourcing and multiple sourcing on the basis of input specificity, supplier capability, and a range of other factors. MNCs often source the same inputs from multiple locations and multiple suppliers. This multiple sourcing often promotes innovation and competition among suppliers, giving MNCs access to better prices and higher quality. Multiple sourcing also helps MNCs maintain their supply chains' agility and thus reduces their risks.

However, supplier diversification could result in high costs because identifying potential suppliers and building stable relationships requires significant investment and effort. Diversification is also not always an option: capable suppliers that can deliver products or services with the required quality, timeliness, and volume can be rare in highly specialized segments. Complex products often require special machinery and customized components, requiring relationship-specific investments in suppliers and stable, long-term contracts. Additionally, although single sourcing may seem more risky than multiple sourcing, it requires much less work to initiate and maintain, particularly when it comes to qualifying suppliers. Single sourcing also maximizes an MNC's volume leverage over its chosen supplier's prices and allows it to maintain a stronger relationship with the supplier, which can result in better terms and more stability in the long term (table 2.2).

Increasing supply chain visibility is another frequently cited strategy for MNCs to map and manage risks. MNCs with very complex global supply chains have realized the importance of end-to-end visibility as they face more frequent supply chain disruptions. They work to increase transparency throughout their multitier supply chains, constructing databases with information on the location, performance, audit results, and risk factors of both direct and indirect suppliers. MNCs also work closely with key suppliers to monitor the most relevant risks, define possible scenarios and assess their impacts, and develop response strategies.

As with supplier diversification, gaining end-to-end supply chain visibility is easier said than done. The weak links in a supply chain often purposefully conceal their weaknesses; uncovering them can be quite challenging. Studies show that business risks increase with the tier of a supplier: second-tier suppliers often have many

TABLE 2.2   Pros and cons of single- versus multiple-sourcing strategies

Sourcing strategy	Pros	Cons
Single sourcing	• Less work to qualify the source and less administrative effort involved, which can be a significant advantage when dealing with highly technical materials • Maximizes leverage based on total quantity; firms more likely to negotiate a volume-based price • Stronger relationships that may offer better terms in the long term	• Potential loss of market-competitive pricing • Difficult to find alternative suppliers during supply shortages • High risk of product unavailability, with possible catastrophic loss of customer goodwill, should the supplier's operations be interrupted
Multiple sourcing	• Diversified suppliers act as safety net to ensure products' availability • Could promote innovation and competition among suppliers, leaving the MNC more likely to get better prices and quality • Supply chain agility maintained by developing a database of qualified suppliers, enabling opportunities in a variety of scenarios	• More costly to build and maintain relationships with multiple suppliers; high administrative costs • Loss of the volume leverage that can help MNCs obtain attractive pricing

Source: Blome, Constantin, and Michael Henke 2009. Burke, Carillo and Vakharia 2007.
Note: MNC = multinational corporation.

more risk issues than first-tier suppliers, and so on. The criticality of risk issues also increases further down the supply chain, with third-tier suppliers showing on average more critical issues than second- and first-tier suppliers (DeAngelis 2015). To detect such risks, MNCs need in-depth and proactive supply chain management that can monitor and analyze many more variables than would seem humanly possible. Big data and new technologies are making supply chain visibility much more effective and affordable.

MNCs are increasingly willing to trade efficiency for risk mitigation as they grapple with increasing geopolitical tensions, environmental concerns, natural disasters, and volatile demand. Increasing uncertainty calls for more rigorous risk management. MNCs thus need to invest more time and resources into building risk management capability, assembling dedicated teams for risk management, and embedding risk management processes into their operations and decision-making processes.

Enhancing market power

MNCs are generally the largest and most productive firms in their respective markets. They often use their market power to charge higher markups and improve their terms of trade with suppliers and customers. The textbook definition of market power is a firm's ability to influence the price at which it sells its products (Syverson 2019). Using this definition, the magnitude of a firm's market power is tied to the size of the gap between price and marginal cost at its profit-maximizing level of output.

Decades of microeconomic study have built a sound knowledge base for market power analysis. The structure-conduct-performance paradigm describes how market structure affects economic performance through firm conduct (Boner and Krueger 1991). Market structure, as captured mainly by the number of sellers and buyers in a market, their relative negotiation strength as measured by their ability to set prices, the degree of concentration among sellers and buyers, the degree of differentiation and uniqueness of products, and barriers to entry and exit, is the primary determinant of both firm conduct and firm performance. At one extreme—perfect competition (a market with very many sellers and buyers and no barriers to entry or exit, among other conditions)—no seller or buyer has the power to influence, on his or her own, the price (or terms) at which a product is sold or purchased. At the other extreme—a monopoly or monopsony—the seller or buyer has the power to set the price (or terms) most advantageous for him or her. The great majority of markets fall between these two scenarios and involve imperfect competition.

Markups are difficult to measure directly because doing so requires information on not just prices but also hard-to-observe marginal costs (Syverson 2019). As a result, many alternative metrics have been used in economic research, such as the number of competitors (actual or potential), profit rates, the costs of market entry, market shares, and market concentration (Aghion et al. 2005; Autor et al. 2020; Collins and Preston 1969; De Loecker, Eeckhout, and Mongey 2018; De Loecker, Eeckhout, and Unger 2020; De Loecker and Warzynski 2012). The two most common concentration measures are the Herfindahl-Hirschman index, which is the sum of firms' squared market shares, and C_n, which is the combined market share of the largest n firms.

For lack of data measuring market power through price markups, this chapter uses the total sales, market shares, gross margins, and earnings before interest and taxes (EBIT) margins of lead firms to proxy their market power.[4]

MNCs gain market power through firm-specific assets as well as a combination of strategies. Some sectors tend to have natural monopolies because of economies of scale and network effects. MNCs in such sectors benefit hugely from first-mover advantages. In many sectors, MNCs also gain market power through intangibles, such as branding, design, and technology. They tend to invest aggressively in R&D, patenting, and marketing to establish their dominance. Table 2.3 summarizes some common strategies MNCs adopt to maximize their market power. Most MNCs implement multiple strategies, and the importance of each strategy varies from one MNC to another.

The market power MNCs possess allows them to benefit disproportionally from GVCs. Although most existing research on market power focuses on product market power, firms can also have market power in factor markets. MNCs can require a monopsony markdown on the prices they pay their suppliers, employees, and capital service providers. As a result, consumers may have to pay a much higher price than they would in a perfectly competitive market, and suppliers may get only a fraction of the value they add (figure 2.9). For example, in the coffee value chain, large roasters and retailers like Nestle and Starbucks are estimated to capture 85 percent of the retail

TABLE 2.3   Multinational corporations' strategies to increase market power

Strategy	Description
Branding	Construct an entry barrier by establishing a brand. This strategy tilts the bargaining power in production to the firm that holds the brand. Branding promotes recognition among customers, helps set a firm apart from its competitors, and lets customers know what to expect from the brand.
Undertaking R&D and innovation	Invest aggressively in R&D and patenting to ensure a firm's technological lead, and protect its proprietary assets through patents, trademarks, and other forms of intellectual property protections to reduce the potential for technology leaks.
Setting standards	Set, monitor, and facilitate compliance among actors within the value chain with rules covering a range of parameters (such as the resolution, display type, and picture mode of a television) and standards. Setting and enforcing industry standards gives the lead firm a powerful edge with which to entrench its first-mover advantage and market dominance.
Engaging in mergers and acquisitions	Acquire competitors to increase market share and consolidate resources.
Strengthening customer relationships	Increase switching costs and gain customer loyalty by strengthening customer relationships. This strategy not only helps retain existing customers but also can attract new customers.
Segmenting the market and catering to niche audiences	Identify a market segment that has the greatest need or want for a firm's products or services and tailor the firm's message to that market. This strategy works best when the firm targets a highly specific, clearly defined customer demographic.
Exploiting network effects and building ecosystems	Incur large up-front costs to develop a product or service, race to the market, and entice new users to reach a critical mass. Once the number of users hits a critical mass, network effects induce a virtuous cycle because the product or service becomes more valuable as more people use it. Develop an ecosystem of products or services. This ecosystem further increases switching costs for users, and lead firms can collect multifaceted user data to strengthen their dominant positions.

Source: World Bank summary based on Boston Consulting Group 2020; Clifton 2009; Dalgic 2006; Hill 1997.
Note: R&D = research and development.

FIGURE 2.9 **Value chain cost breakdown for selected products**

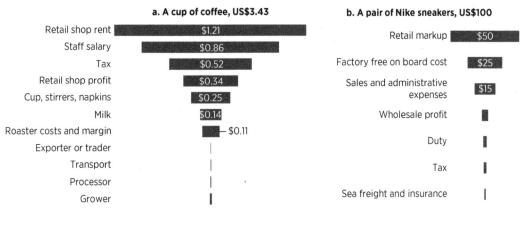

a. A cup of coffee, US$3.43

Retail shop rent	$1.21
Staff salary	$0.86
Tax	$0.52
Retail shop profit	$0.34
Cup, stirrers, napkins	$0.25
Milk	$0.14
Roaster costs and margin	$0.11
Exporter or trader	
Transport	
Processor	
Grower	

b. A pair of Nike sneakers, US$100

Retail markup	$50
Factory free on board cost	$25
Sales and administrative expenses	$15
Wholesale profit	
Duty	
Tax	
Sea freight and insurance	

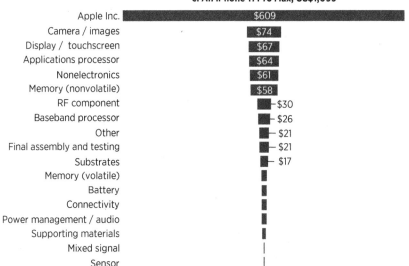

c. An iPhone 11 Pro Max, US$1,099

Apple Inc.	$609
Camera / images	$74
Display / touchscreen	$67
Applications processor	$64
Nonelectronics	$61
Memory (nonvolatile)	$58
RF component	$30
Baseband processor	$26
Other	$21
Final assembly and testing	$21
Substrates	$17
Memory (volatile)	
Battery	
Connectivity	
Power management / audio	
Supporting materials	
Mixed signal	
Sensor	

Source: World Bank illustrations based on news reports.
Note: RF = radio frequency. All dollar amounts are US dollars.

value of a US$3.43 cup of coffee. Coffee growers get only one cent, or 0.4 percent of the final retail price (Bruce-Lockhart and Terazono 2019). For a pair of Nike sneakers sold at US$100, the factory free on board cost is only US$25; Nike is estimated to capture US$21.50 of the value added, and the retail shop charges another 100 percent markup (Kish 2014). A breakdown of the iPhone 11 Pro Max by Tech Insights (Yang, Wegner, and Cowsky 2019) reveals that the total cost to produce an iPhone that sells for US$1,099 is US$490.50. Apple keeps US$609, or more than 55 percent of the sales price, far greater than the amount received by any other firm in the supply chain. MNCs in service sectors sometimes have even higher profit rates. For example, Microsoft's gross margin exceeded 63 percent in 2019.[5] MNCs then reinvest the huge profits they make from GVCs into R&D, marketing, expansion, and innovation to maintain their leading positions.

Bringing it together: Global value chain archetypes and multinational corporations' business strategies

The previous section of this chapter introduces a general framework for MNCs' objectives and business strategies; this section explores how these strategies interact with the characteristics of different GVC archetypes (table 2.4). Note that sectors within a given archetype still have very different characteristics—this table covers only the most common characteristics and MNCs' business strategies.

Structural characteristics of global value chains across six archetypes

This report classifies sectors into six archetypes. This section elaborates on the structural characteristics of each of the six GVC archetypes and how these characteristics influence the business strategies of MNCs. There is still vast heterogeneity across sectors, segments, and tasks within each GVC archetype; this section focuses on the most salient features of each archetype and explains how sectors within an archetype can differ.

Commodities are natural resources, such as agricultural products, energy, or metals, that have a global market. Commodity markets are characterized by nearly homogeneous products and high fungibility. Still, different types of commodity producers have distinct characteristics and can vary vastly in production organization, supply chain management, and market power. For agricultural commodities, MNCs' level of control is very low, their production length is short, and their suppliers are extremely diversified. As the most ancient industry, agriculture has very low barriers to entry and remains the only source of livelihood in many low-income areas. The four major agricultural commodity traders, Archer Daniels Midland, Bunge, Cargill, and Louis Dreyfus, collectively known as the "ABCD" companies, share a significant presence in many agricultural commodities; for example, they control as much as 90 percent of the global grain trade (Murphy, Burch, and Clapp 2012). Their main suppliers are numerous farmers, together with seed, fertilizer, agrochemical, and agricultural machinery companies. They sell agricultural products to all sorts of downstream buyers and final consumers. Despite their high market share, the lead firms have relatively low market power. The gross margin for the ABCD firms averages about 6 percent, and their average EBIT margin was only 2.3 percent in 2018.

In contrast to agricultural commodities, energy and metal GVCs are capital and knowledge intensive but do not create as many jobs. MNCs tend to have higher levels of control in these sectors, and equity investment is the most common mode by which they enter foreign markets. Production length is relatively short, and lead firms enjoy high market power and profitability because of the nonrenewable nature of the commodities and the high barriers to enter the market (for example, high sunk costs). Most commodities have inelastic supply in the short term: tiny changes in demand result in huge price fluctuations (Caldara, Cavallo, and Iacoviello 2016). Inelastic demand and supply often subject both commodity exporters and major commodity importers to magnified shocks.

Labor-intensive services encompass a hodgepodge of activities that have absorbed most unskilled labor in recent years. These industries include retail, wholesale,

TABLE 2.4 **Global value chain characteristics and multinational corporations' business strategies**

GVC archetype	Sectors	GVC characteristics	Strategies		
			Lower production costs	Mitigate risks	Increase market power
Commodities	Agriculture, fuel, minerals	Nearly homogeneous products and high fungibility, inelastic supply and demand, high price fluctuations	Arm's length trade, contract farming; short value chains	Multiple sourcing, usually extremely diverse suppliers, various strategies to hedge commodity price risk	Economies of scale
Labor-intensive services	Wholesale and retail, transportation and storage, tourism, health and social services, personal services, leasing, other services	Labor intensive, low entry barriers, some sectors less tradable	NEMs (for example, management contracts, franchising); short value chains	Multiple sourcing, improving logistics, demand forecasting, data sharing with suppliers for inventory management	Branding
Labor-intensive goods	Textiles, apparel, toys, leather products, footwear	Production requires human dexterity, highly differentiated products with short lifespans, highly tradable	Contract manufacturing; long value chains	Multiple sourcing to diversify risks, trend analysis and prediction, agile supply chain management and small-batch production, supply chain visibility	Branding
Regional processing	Food and beverages, fabricated metal products, rubber and plastics, glass, cement and ceramics, furniture	Perishable, fragile, or bulky products; high transportation and storage costs; relatively low entry barriers; highly differentiated products	Arm's length trade, contract manufacturing, FDI; short to medium value chains	Multiple sourcing to diversify risks	Economies of scale, branding
Knowledge-intensive services	Research and development, IT services, professional services, education	Knowledge intensive, tradability varies across sectors	FDI; short value chains	Limited outsourcing, intellectual property protection	R&D, network effects, setting standards
Knowledge-intensive goods	Automobiles, transportation equipment, computers and electronics, electrical machinery and equipment, chemicals and pharmaceuticals	Highly sophisticated products, high level of specialization, high switching costs, highly tradable	Contract manufacturing and FDI; extremely long and complex value chains	Likely single sourcing for key components, strong ties with suppliers, intense supply chain coordination, supply chain visibility	R&D, branding, setting standards

Source: World Bank.
Note: FDI = foreign direct investment; GVC = global value chain; IT = information technology; NEMs = nonequity modes; R&D = research and development.

transportation, real estate, health and social services, food and accommodations, and personal services. Service value chains are very different from value chains for goods: some services link different stages of goods production, such as transportation, wholesale, and retail; other services are stand-alone, such as health and social services. Franchising and management contracts are most common in fast food, retail, and hotel chains, although equity investment coexists with this model. Both labor-intensive and knowledge-intensive services value chains tend to be short, usually even shorter than commodity value chains. Entry barriers for labor-intensive services are very low. Most small enterprises and microenterprises operate in labor-intensive services. Establishing a brand, acquiring competitors, and catering to niche markets are among the most common strategies lead firms in these industries use to maximize their market power.

Textiles, clothing, footwear, and toys are typical labor-intensive goods that are highly tradable and employ many unskilled manufacturing workers. The garment and footwear sectors have many different segments serving a range of consumers who differ in demographics, location, purchasing power, and fashion taste. MNCs' control remains low to moderate. Big-brand companies work on design and marketing and outsource manufacturing to contractors who often operate multiple factories in Asia and Sub-Saharan Africa. Textiles, apparel, and footwear value chains are long and global; suppliers are well diversified to reduce their risks. For example, Nike, the world's top sportswear company, outsources production to 42 countries, and its 567 independent factories employ more than 1 million workers. The largest single footwear factory accounted for only 5 percent of Nike's total footwear production, and the largest single apparel factory accounted for 7 percent of Nike-brand apparel production. MNCs in these sectors enjoy high market power from their branding and sales channels. Nike's gross margin was 43.8 percent, and its EBIT margin was 12.2 percent in 2018, whereas the average gross margin of its top five direct suppliers was 23 percent and their average EBIT margin was 6.3 percent.

Regional processing sectors feature perishable, fragile, or bulky products that have high transportation and storage costs. Food and beverages, wood and furniture, and metal and mineral products fall into this archetype. Firms in these sectors face intense competition globally and locally; most small and medium-size firms earn only marginal returns. MNCs' mode of involvement in GVCs of this archetype varies by sector and segment, ranging from contract manufacturing to wholly owned subsidiaries. Regional processing sectors have, on average, slightly longer production length than commodities, with diversified suppliers. These sectors' lead firms enjoy economies of scale and highlight product differentiation to persuade buyers that their offerings are better, faster, and safer than those of their competitors. Sales, marketing, and logistics thus play an important role in these sectors. PepsiCo, for example, spent US$2.6 billion—4 percent of its total revenue—on marketing in 2018, and it pales in comparison with its rival Coca-Cola, which spent US$5.8 billion on global advertising. Lead firms capture a high share of value added along these value chains. Nestle, PepsiCo, and Coca-Cola, the three lead firms in food and beverages, earned an average gross margin of 58 percent and an EBIT margin of almost 20 percent in 2018.

Knowledge-intensive services include professional services, education, scientific research, and ICT. Some knowledge-intensive services, such as ICT and R&D, are highly tradable and generate huge spillovers for the entire economy. The network effect is a prominent feature of digital services, and it has created superstar firms in the ICT sector. Technology has advanced rapidly in the ICT sector, and major players generally spend as much as 10–20 percent of their revenue on R&D. Talent, data, and algorithms are the most valuable assets in this industry, and firms need a whole eco-system of digital hardware and software to operate. These firms tend to set up wholly owned subsidiaries to expand into foreign markets without risking data or technology leaks. Concerns have grown around concentration in the digital market: a handful of "gatekeepers" have come to control key arteries of online commerce, content, and communications. Google, for example, both dominates the search engine market with a market share of 90 percent (Desjardins 2018) and offers a wide array of digital services, such as email, maps, translation, and cloud services, that permeate every nook and corner of modern life. Another leading firm, Microsoft, dominates the personal computer operating system market and leads the market for software products.

Knowledge-intensive goods include chemicals, pharmaceuticals, electrical machinery and equipment, and transportation equipment. These products are highly complex and require hyperspecialization in hundreds of different inputs. Their production is truly global because no country or firm can efficiently produce every part by itself. Many parts and components have special configurations, and capable suppliers of key components are often scarce, resulting in extremely high switching costs. In consumer electronics, MNCs generally use contract manufacturing to assemble the final product, whereas equity investment is more common in automobiles and sophisticated machinery and equipment. The leading firms still capture a dominant share of profits in this GVC archetype, although specialization allows key suppliers to negotiate and achieve high profit margins. Knowledge-intensive goods require close interaction among large groups of trained professionals with a wide spectrum of knowledge.

Production length

Outsourcing and offshoring are most common in manufacturing GVCs, although ICTs have enabled a remarkable increase in services offshoring. MNCs headquartered in advanced economies now use lower-cost countries for product manufacturing, technical support, customer service, claims processing, and data entry activities. Recent empirical studies reveal that MNCs in manufacturing GVCs tend to outsource the inputs that are less technologically important (Berlingieri, Pisch, and Steinwender 2018). Whether a multinational firm outsources the production of a given input also depends on the elasticity of demand it faces, the relative contractibility of stages along its value chain, and its own productivity (Alfaro et al. 2019; Del Prete and Rungi 2017; Luck 2019). MNCs in services GVCs initially used offshore outsourcing mainly for basic services. More recently, direct offshore subsidiaries have been increasingly used to organize complex services (Nieto and Rodriguez 2011).

The level of control held by MNCs tends to be higher in industries that feature high entry barriers, large economies of scale, and differentiated, technology-intensive products. In commodity and regional processing industries, MNCs usually purchase raw materials through arm's length trade, such as direct or indirect exports or contract farming (as does the Cargill company in the food GVC). In labor-intensive goods, MNCs use contract manufacturing to outsource the production stage (for example, Nike uses contract manufacturing for its sportswear and shoes). In labor-intensive services, MNCs often use franchising or management contracts to expand their global footprint (for example, Shangri-La's hotel chains). In knowledge-intensive goods, MNCs either outsource manufacturing to third parties (for example, Apple) or set up joint ventures or wholly owned subsidiaries to manufacture the final product (for example, Toyota or General Motors). And, in knowledge-intensive services, MNCs tend to set up wholly owned subsidiaries to access foreign markets without leaking their intellectual property (for example, Google or Microsoft). To compare the degree of outsourcing and offshoring in various GVCs, this chapter estimates production length at the sectoral level using global input-output tables. All economic activities are linked together, making it almost impossible to calculate production length accurately. However, researchers have come up with various methods for estimating the length of forward and backward linkages by industry. This report adopts the method proposed by Wang et al. (2017) and defines industry-level production length as the number of firms involved in backward linkages. Using the World Input-Output Database, production length was calculated for 55 industries in 2014. Manufacturing of electrical equipment, base metals, motor vehicles, and electronics had the longest production length, whereas real estate activities, household activities, education, and financial services had the shortest production length. This result is largely consistent with the literature (De Backer and Miroudot 2013; Fally 2012; Wang et al. 2017) and a separate estimation using the OECD TiVA (Trade in Value Added) database. Compared with previous estimates that were based on data from 2008, these results suggest that manufacturing of electrical equipment, chemicals, and chemical products has become more fragmented over time.

Goods GVCs tend to have greater production length than services GVCs, and, overall, production length is positively correlated with product complexity (table 2.5).[6] Product complexity measures the diversity and sophistication of the knowledge needed to produce a product. Producing complex products could lead to economic upgrading and sustainable growth (Hausmann et al. 2014; Hidalgo and Hausmann 2009). Knowledge-intensive goods GVCs generally have the longest production

TABLE 2.5   **Production length, by global value chain archetype**

Broad sector	Archetype	Production length	Average product complexity index
Goods GVCs	Knowledge-intensive goods	3.0	0.63
	Regional processing	2.9	−0.06
	Labor-intensive goods	2.8	−0.53
	Commodities	2.2	−1.06
Services GVCs	Labor-intensive services	2.1	−0.62
	Knowledge-intensive services	1.9	0.31

Source: World Bank calculation based on 2014 data from the World Input-Output Database (http://www.wiod.org /home).
Note: Archetypes are in descending order of average production length. The production length of final goods is based on backward linkages. The numbers provided are index scores; higher values mean longer production length. The product complexity index is from the Atlas of Economic Complexity (https://atlas.cid.harvard.edu/) and is based on 2017 data. GVCs = global value chains.

length because they involve many intricate parts produced by specialized suppliers. Services GVCs typically have shorter production length because of their limited potential for geographic fragmentation and the cultural, legal, and regulatory barriers they face to offshore activities. Knowledge-intensive services are an exception to the production length–product complexity trend: although their production length is the shortest among all six GVC archetypes, their product complexity is second only to knowledge-intensive goods. Most professional services, such as law, accounting, translation, and consulting, require highly skilled labor and do not generate many backward linkages.

Evidence from firm transactional data largely confirms the macro-level production lengths calculated from input-output tables. Using value added tax data, customs transaction data, and firm registration data from Rwanda in 2017, this analysis found that production length is longer in goods GVCs than in services GVCs and that production length increases from commodities to knowledge-intensive goods. Similar results were also found using value added tax data from West Bengal, India (see chapter 11 of this report).

Outsourcing and offshoring decisions in turn affect the long-term development of MNCs. These firms stand to gain substantially from global sourcing because it will let them purchase inputs from wherever the price is lowest. Global sourcing also allows lead firms to focus their valuable time on the most rewarding tasks. But too much outsourcing and offshoring could put a firm's future at risk even though it makes sense from a short-term financial point of view (box 2.2).

The past decade has seen both increases and decreases in production length across archetypes. On one hand, there has been a trend toward outsourcing activities that can be performed more cost-effectively by specialized actors. This trend has been particularly evident in labor-intensive services such as logistics (especially transportation and distribution) and customer support, which can be provided at lower operational costs, at higher levels of efficiency (particularly in logistics), and with greater flexibility (such as by handling customer support through call centers) by specialists. On the other hand, progress has been made toward the vertical integration of key activities, often in knowledge-intensive goods and services archetypes, such as R&D, to add value and improve firms' competitive edge by establishing specialized departments to encourage process innovation and reduce technology leaks.

Disruptive technologies and new business models have had a noteworthy impact on production length. New technologies such as the Internet of Things (IoT), big data analytics, 3D (three-dimensional) printing, autonomous robotics, smart sensors, and artificial intelligence simplify production processes and weaken the advantage of low labor costs, thereby not only shortening production chains but also enabling nearshoring or reshoring (Dachs, Kinkel, and Jäger 2017). Furthermore, the rise of platform firms and the sharing economy allows producers and service providers to match directly to final users, making production length even shorter. However, new technologies also reduce transaction and communication costs and make production unbundling and offshoring more appealing (Ferrantino and Koten 2019). In particular, the IoT, big data, and cloud computing greatly reduce the costs of tracking and monitoring production across different locations and increase the efficiency of complex coordination and collaboration.

BOX 2.2 **Boeing: Aerospace giant hobbled by ill-planned outsourcing**

Boeing is among the largest global aerospace manufacturers, as is its European rival Airbus. It is the fourth-largest employer in the US manufacturing sector and employs 153,000 people worldwide (Peterson 2011). It maintained a leading role in commercial airplane production for more than 80 years, led by an expert group of engineers and builders who always worked in proximity to each other. Its executives held patents, designed wings, and spoke the language of engineering and safety as a mother tongue (Useem 2019).

This culture began to change after Boeing bought its rival McDonnell Douglas in 1997. The Mc-Donnell executives ended up in charge of the combined entity, and a stock price–focused culture ascended. Boeing started outsourcing and offshoring on a large scale as a way of lowering costs and accelerating development (Denning 2013). It relied on a complex web of suppliers worldwide to manufacture its planes. In-house labor was replaced with outside partners who did not possess the required skill sets. And, through all these changes, employees' voices went unheard (Denning 2013).

After losing market share to Airbus in the early 2000s, Boeing decided to design a new aircraft that would not only lower costs for airlines but also improve the flight experience for passengers. The 787 Dreamliner program was launched in 2004, targeting a 2008 introduction. Unlike in earlier programs, when Boeing kept design, engineering, and manufacturing in-house as much as possible and subcontracted components only on a strict build-to-print basis, more than 90 percent of the parts for the 787 Dreamliner were outsourced. Furthermore, the contracts for these parts were based on perverse incentives to work at the speed of the slowest supplier. They imposed penalties for delays but no rewards for timely delivery, contributing to a slow and uncoordinated supply chain.

The project's new technology coupled with this new supply chain exceeded Boeing's ability to manage and coordinate effectively. Additional costs also arose because of cultural and language differences and physical distances between suppliers in the supply chain. These factors impeded much-needed communication.

Boeing's tiered outsourcing approach aggravated the project's risks. Boeing established partnerships with about 50 tier-one strategic suppliers, who served as integrators that assembled different parts and subsystems produced by tier-two and tier-three suppliers. However, some tier-one suppliers lacked the ability to develop various sections of the aircraft, and some lacked the experience to manage their tier-two suppliers.

This strategy of delegating engineering and procurement to subcontractors had tremendous consequences. Boeing ended up outsourcing major technological innovations (including new electrical systems, power systems, and distribution panels) that were unproven in any airplane and were introduced simultaneously. This outsourcing increased delays and costs in coordinating the application of the new technologies. The 787 Dreamliner project finally finished in September 2011, three years later than originally planned and with much higher costs.

A corporate culture centered on cost cutting coupled with technical miscalculations and management misjudgments eventually culminated in two fatal crashes that killed 346 people in 2018 and 2019. Boeing continued to outsource work to low-paid contractors and subcontractors for

Continued on next page ›

> **BOX 2.2 Boeing: Aerospace giant hobbled by ill-planned outsourcing (continued)**
>
> its other plane models. It laid off experienced engineers and pressed suppliers to cut costs for the software for the 737 Max. Experienced Boeing engineers confirmed that the 737 Max crashes were caused by the outsourcing of some software-development tasks to recent college graduates earning as little as US$9 per hour who were employed by an Indian subcontractor (Robinson 2019). The Boeing employees were also driven by pressure to get the new planes to customers quickly and without requiring their pilots to undergo extensive retraining (Duncan, Laris, and Aratini 2020).
>
> Taken together, overreliance on outsourcing and offshoring without sufficient up-front effort to define products and assess costs and risks eventually hurt Boeing's prospects and cost hundreds of lives.

Supply chain management and risk mitigation

Different products and services demand distinct supply chain management practices and risk mitigation measures. In the manufacturing sectors, supply chain management involves literally moving objects from one place to another. Transportation and warehousing costs are based on the size, weight, perishability, and fragility of goods. Risks arise at every step: conceiving of the product, securing raw materials, having parts and components manufactured and delivered on time from multitiered suppliers, assembling the product, and storing and shipping it. In service sectors, however, the flow of information matters more. Production is often inseparable from consumption, and hence risks are more likely to stem from the demand side or from internal administration.

Supplier diversification is especially common in commodities, regional processing, and labor-intensive goods and services. Coca-Cola, Gap, Nike, and PepsiCo all adopt this strategy so that no single supplier contributes a significant share of their inputs or sales. Single sourcing is more common in knowledge-intensive sectors, where capable suppliers for crucial inputs are often rare and the costs to identify and evaluate potential suppliers can outweigh the benefits of diversification. Apple (box 2.3) is one such case.

GVCs for knowledge-intensive goods require the most intense supply chain coordination among lead firms and suppliers. These products vary vastly in the type and number of raw materials, parts, and components required. A mobile phone may have hundreds of parts; a single car has about 30,000 parts; and an airplane can have millions of parts. The more parts a product has, the longer its supply chain becomes, and the more supply chain coordination matters in its production. MNCs in knowledge-intensive goods GVCs have gone to great lengths to map their production networks, improve efficiency, and minimize risks (box 2.4).

BOX 2.3 Input specificity limits Apple's choice of suppliers for key components

Apple is one of the most valuable companies to date, with a market capitalization of more than US$1 billion. It purchases key components and outsources assembly from more than 200 direct suppliers worldwide. A highly profitable company, Apple's gross margin was more than 40 percent in 2019. Owing to its agile supply chain management strategy, Apple churns out hundreds of millions of units without owning any factories.

Apple has long adopted a supply chain strategy of using multiple suppliers for the same components whenever possible. Multiple sourcing helps Apple mitigate supply chain disruptions and maintain its high gross margin. Apple constantly adjusts its ordering ratios with existing suppliers to minimize the risk of third-party issues associated with volume dependency. Apple also has exclusive long-term agreements with its key suppliers and uses prepayments to negotiate favorable pricing terms, secure strategic raw materials, and guarantee high volumes of production.

However, because Apple's key components are highly sophisticated products and are often custom made, it has to single source some components. According to the firm's annual report, several components of Apple's products are currently obtained from single or limited sources. In addition, Apple competes for various components with other players in the mobile communication, media device, and personal computer markets. Many components are subject to industrywide shortages and significant price fluctuations that can materially affect Apple's financial condition and operating results. Apple also uses some custom components that are not commonly used by its competitors, and its new products often use other custom components available from only one source. This hyperspecialized electronics value chain allows both key suppliers and the lead firm to earn high returns (table B2.3.1).

TABLE B2.3.1 **Apple and key suppliers' financial performance**

Firm	Components supplied for Apple, Inc.	Sales (US$, billion)	Gross profits (US$, billion)	Gross margin (%)	EBIT margin (%)	R&D and sales (%)
Apple Inc.		260.0	111.0	42.6	24.6	6.2
Samsung Electronics Co., Ltd.	DRAM, flash memory, application processors, OLED screens	199.0	72.0	36.1	12.1	8.6
Micron Technology	DRAM, other memory modules	23.4	16.1	68.9	31.4	10.4
Qualcomm	Baseband processors, power management modules, GSM/CDMA receivers and transceivers	19.6	12.4	63.2	16.6	27.6

Continued on next page ›

BOX 2.3 Input specificity limits Apple's choice of suppliers for key components
(continued)

TABLE B2.3.1 **Apple and key suppliers' financial performance** *(continued)*

Firm	Components supplied for Apple, Inc.	Sales (US$, billion)	Gross profits (US$, billion)	Gross margin (%)	EBIT margin (%)	R&D and sales (%)
Analog Devices	Capacitive touchscreen controllers	6.0	4.4	73.4	30.2	18.9
Texas Instruments	Touchscreen controllers	14.4	9.9	69.0	39.7	10.7
Broadcom	Chips	22.6	16.5	72.9	18.8	20.8
Skyworks Solutions	Chips	3.4	2.0	57.8	28.4	12.6
Intel	Chips	72.0	53.0	73.3	31.2	18.6
Infineon	Chips	9.0	3.0	37.7	14.1	11.8

Source: Orbis database.
Note: CDMA = code-division multiple access; DRAM = dynamic random-access memory; EBIT = earnings before interest and taxes; GSM = global system for mobile communications; OLED = organic light-emitting diode; R&D = research and development.

BOX 2.4 Toyota's global supply chain management

Toyota Motor Corporation is a model of successful supply chain management. As the world's second-largest car manufacturer, Toyota has a diverse supply chain distributed around the world. Toyota outsources about 70 percent of its vehicles to a trusted group of partner firms, which has enabled Toyota to develop new cars faster than other market players (Liker and Choi 2004). The firm's Japanese plant buys about 150,000 types of inputs from 200 direct suppliers in Japan and dozens of direct suppliers in other countries. Every vehicle the plant makes requires assembling thousands of parts seamlessly. Toyota's widely lauded supply chain practices adapt to the latest trends and have gone through different phases. Toyota's three most renowned strategies are building reliable relationships with suppliers, manufacturing components just in time, and increasing the visibility of its supply chain.

Maintaining strong ties with key suppliers has been a top priority for Toyota since its founding. Managing a large global supply network requires close collaboration with suppliers at every link of the chain. Toyota has in-house and outside departments that assist suppliers in implementing product and process improvements and in aligning business objectives and supply chain functions. To ensure quality, Toyota maintains tight control of the overall design and engineering of its vehicles and sources only from suppliers that have proven their ability to deliver with the required timeliness, quality, low costs, and continuous innovation. Toyota hands out awards yearly to suppliers that exceed their targets to encourage good performance and innovation.

Toyota is perhaps best known for its just-in-time (JIT) manufacturing system, also known as the Toyota Production System. Toyota has used JIT manufacturing since 1938, but it only realized the true potential of this strategy when the company integrated JIT with the Toyota Production System in the

Continued on next page >

BOX 2.4 **Toyota's global supply chain management** *(continued)*

1970s (Ohno 1988). After World War II, Japanese automakers faced a sharp decline in demand and high costs of production. Japan's lack of space to build big factories and the country's shortage of natural resources further prompted its firms to improve the efficiency of their production processes. Against this backdrop, Toyota adopted JIT manufacturing and produced its vehicles according to the orders it received through its dealers. In JIT manufacturing, the company uses its supply chain in such a manner that parts are received only as they are needed to manufacture ordered vehicles. Thus, the manufacturing and transportation of parts take place simultaneously, which allows Toyota to minimize its inventory of vehicle parts. JIT manufacturing also emphasizes the importance of efficiency. According to Toyota's website, the "use of JIT within the Toyota Production System means that individual cars can be built to order and that every component has to fit perfectly [the] first time because there are no alternatives available." The Toyota Production System has been crucial to Toyota's enduring success and has become very popular globally. Several multinational corporations in global value chains for knowledge-intensive goods have embraced this strategy, including General Electric, Hewlett-Packard, and Motorola (Plenert 2007).

However, the devastating earthquake that struck northern Japan in March 2011 alerted Toyota that natural disasters can wreak havoc on even perfectly functioning global supply chains. Because many of Toyota's components were single sourced, the earthquake caused a widespread shortage of parts that persisted for several months. As a result, Toyota had to throttle back its production by 30 percent (Marchese and Lam 2014). Stung by the experience, Toyota has made serious efforts to strengthen the resilience of its supply chain. It developed a RESCUE (REinforce Supply Chain Under Emergency) system by establishing a database of supplier information that identifies the vulnerabilities and parts information of more than 650,000 supplier sites. It then worked internally with its engineers, technologists, and business leaders and externally with its suppliers to address the vulnerabilities this database exposed. As a result, Toyota now has a more forward-looking, flexible, and resilient supply chain.

New technologies are dramatically transforming supply chain management and risk mitigation. MNCs across industries are experimenting with a variety of digital and data-enabled tools to improve how they plan, source, make, and deliver. These innovations are making supply chains smarter by increasing their predictability, transparency, and speed of delivery. In particular, the IoT, big data analytics, and artificial intelligence (AI) have automated a broad range of activities that were traditionally performed by skilled workers and have unearthed patterns that have helped firms achieve greater efficiency, minimize waste, and increase growth. They allow firms to view their entire supply networks so that they can effectively monitor and respond in real time to any problems. They can also speed up the flow of goods by tracking shipments and routing delivery trucks on the basis of current road conditions. More important, big data and AI can anticipate and prevent supply chain disruptions more efficiently than older methods. For example, Morrisons, a British grocery chain, reduced its incidence of out-of-stock items by 30 percent and cut its inventory needs by several days by replacing manual stock planning with an AI system for demand forecasting and replenishment. Orsay, a German fashion retailer, used a self-teaching algorithm to make 112,000 autonomous pricing decisions. And Intel, a leading manufacturer of computer chips, estimates that it has saved US$58 million with better forecast modeling through AI (*Economist* 2019).

Market power

MNCs' strategies to increase their market power hinge primarily on the nature of their products and the characteristics of their customers. Although branding, R&D, standards setting, and mergers and acquisitions are common across sectors, these techniques are used with different intensity across different sectors. The characteristics of GVCs affect which strategies MNCs' pursue to increase their market power.

Branding is a key strategy in industries with standardized production technology and highly differentiated products and services. Such industries include food and beverages, furniture, apparel, footwear, airlines, consumer electronics, and automobiles. According to the accounting firm Deloitte's summary of listed companies, consumer packaged goods firms spend on average almost a quarter of their revenue on marketing, twice the all-industry average share (figure 2.10). Technology, software, and consumer services firms spend the second-highest share of revenue on marketing (15 percent). Branding not only makes a memorable impression on consumers but also builds an expectation of standard, high-quality products, which is crucial to retaining customer loyalty and creating barriers to entry for competitors. Lead firms can increase their market share and charge higher prices by establishing a successful brand, which will allow them to maintain their long-term profitability and gain bargaining power over their suppliers (Porter 1979).

Investing in R&D and in minimizing technology leaks via patenting is key to protecting firms' core competencies in knowledge-intensive goods and knowledge-intensive services sectors. Today's top technology firms all spend billions of dollars each year to spearhead cutting-edge research. In 2019, Amazon spent US$36 billion on R&D, more than any other firm in the world that publishes R&D spending, and Alphabet and Samsung rounded out the top three with R&D expenses of US$26 billion and

FIGURE 2.10 Marketing budgets by sector

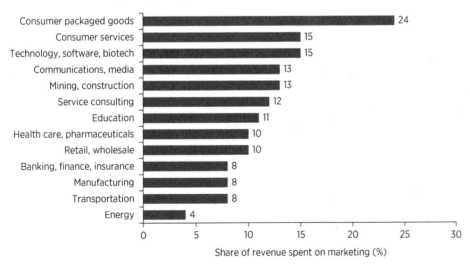

Source: Deloitte 2017 Chief Marketing Officer survey (https://deloitte.wsj.com/cmo/2017/01/24/who-has-the-biggest-marketing-budgets/).

US$17 billion, respectively. And, with regard to R&D intensity, smaller firms dwarf these technology giants—small firms often spend more than 40 percent of their revenue on R&D (table 2.6). Chen (2018) estimates that intangible capital investment, including R&D, has also been on the rise in developing countries.

Setting industry standards

MNCs sometimes coordinate activities in GVCs by setting and enforcing product and process parameters. Government agencies and international organizations often help set these parameters because they are concerned with quality, labor rights, sanitary conditions, health, or environmental impact. However, MNCs are the drivers of GVCs, and thus they hold great sway during parameter-setting processes. They set

TABLE 2.6 **Top 10 research and development spenders, 2019**

		By R&D amount		
Rank	Company	Country of incorporation (ISO code)	R&D expenses (US$, billion)	R&D expenses/ sales (%)
1	Amazon.com, Inc.	USA	36	12.8
2	Alphabet, Inc.	USA	26	16.1
3	Samsung Electronics Co., Ltd.	KOR	17	8.6
4	Microsoft Corporation	USA	17	13.4
5	Apple Inc.	USA	16	6.2
6	Facebook, Inc.	USA	14	19.2
7	Intel Corporation	USA	13	18.6
8	Johnson & Johnson	USA	11	13.8
9	Merck & Co., Inc.	USA	10	20.7
10	Gilead Sciences, Inc.	USA	9	39.8

		By R&D intensity		
Rank	Company	Country of incorporation (ISO code)	R&D expenses (US$, billion)	R&D expenses/ sales (%)
1	BeiGene, Ltd.	CYM	0.9	216.6
2	Pinterest, Inc.	USA	1.2	105.6
3	United Therapeutics Corporation	USA	1.2	81.0
4	Incyte Corporation	USA	1.2	53.5
5	Snap, Inc.	USA	0.9	49.6
6	Workday, Inc.	USA	1.2	42.9
7	Vertex Pharmaceuticals, Inc.	USA	1.8	42.2
8	Lyft, Inc.	USA	1.5	41.6
9	Cadence Design Systems, Inc.	USA	0.9	40.1
10	Gilead Sciences, Inc.	USA	8.9	39.8

Source: Orbis database.
Note: ISO = International Organization for Standardization; R&D = research and development.

parameters to operate more efficiently and sustainably and to minimize the risk of product failure.

These parameters are often turned into industry standards, a battlefield where many MNCs fiercely compete. Such competition has always been intense, especially in high-tech industries. The first-mover advantage that comes from setting rules and standards can give a company a powerful edge (box 2.5). Many lead firms make aggressive moves to extend their influence by pushing their standards globally, often working in close alliance with governments.

BOX 2.5 Microsoft and Intel: How the Wintel standard ruled the personal computer industry

Establishing its technology as an industry standard is one critical way for a firm to achieve long-term competitiveness. The success of Microsoft and Intel, which still dominate today's personal computer (PC) industry, can be attributed largely to their ownership of the industry's standards (the so-called Wintel standard).

Before the 1980s, the early microcomputer market was rife with chaos and incompatibility (Casadesus-Masanell and Yoffie 2005). Over time, a small number of de facto industry standards emerged, including the S-100 bus, the CP/M (Control Program for Microcomputers) operating system, the Apple II computer, Microsoft BASIC in read-only memory, and the 5¼ inch floppy drive. No single firm controlled the industry, and fierce competition spurred innovation in both hardware and software.

But gradually Microsoft and Intel processors gained ascendance. The two companies had been collaborating since before IBM introduced its first PC in 1981, a machine that used Microsoft's DOS (disk operating system) and the Intel chip design known as x86. Their continuing alliance gave them market dominance and shaped the PC business by defining the standard by which software developers created applications.

The power to decide the shape of the PC rested firmly with IBM in the early 1980s. The IBM PC with the DOS operating system and the x86 chipset soon became the best-selling PC in the world, and a major part of the market began to use the same exact hardware (or a clone of it) to take advantage of the hardware-specific features offered by IBM. However, this group's power to set industry standards began to shift in the late 1980s. Some major PC manufacturers, known as the Gang of Nine, decided to develop a bus type that would be open to all manufacturers, run as fast as or faster than IBM's, and yet retain backward compatibility.

About the same time, Microsoft's Windows operating environment started to gain popularity. IBM planned to replace DOS with the vastly superior OS/2 (originally an IBM-Microsoft joint venture), but instead Microsoft pushed the industry standards in the direction of its own product, Windows. The Wintel alliance became particularly lucrative after Microsoft's easier-to-use Windows software helped make the PC a mainstay in homes and companies. For the many competing computer manufacturers, the only common factors providing joint technical leadership were the operating system from Microsoft and CPUs (central processing units) from Intel.

Over the following years, both firms in the Wintel partnership attempted to extend their monopolies (Wingfield and Clark 2011). Intel made a successful major push into the motherboard and chipset markets—at one point it was the largest motherboard manufacturer in the world and almost the only chipset manufacturer. Microsoft had two competitors in its core market in 1990 but none by 1996.[a] It pursued a policy of insisting on per-processor royalties instead of per-install royalties.

Continued on next page ›

BOX 2.5 **Microsoft and Intel: How the Wintel standard ruled the personal computer industry** *(continued)*

Computer manufacturers had to pay a royalty for every computer they shipped (because each computer has a CPU), regardless of whether the machine was preloaded with Microsoft's operating system. If a computer manufacturer shipped a machine with a competing operating system, it still needed to pay the same royalty to Microsoft and an additional royalty to the operating system producer, making competing operating systems unattractive to computer manufacturers (Baseman, Warren-Boulton, and Woroch 1995). Microsoft also integrated DOS into Windows 95 to freeze out other operating system vendors and charged a higher price. The firm was also able to take over most of the networking market with Windows NT and the business application market with Microsoft Office (Kennedy 2008).

By establishing the computer industry's standards, Microsoft and Intel gained the high market power that they maintain to this day. Although MacOS, Linux, and other operating systems have chipped away at Microsoft's lead, Windows remains the front-runner, with a market share of more than three-quarters of desktop PCs as of January 2020.[b]

a. "Deal clears deck for Novell DOS 7.0," *Personal Computer World*, October 1994.
b. "Global market share held by operating systems for desktop PCs, from January 2013 to July 2020," Statista (https://www.statista.com/statistics/218089/global-market-share-of-windows-7/#:~:text=Microsoft%20Windows%20became%20and%20stayed,trailing%20as%20a%20distant%20second).

Standards tend to look back to validate and document what has worked well over a certain period. A consensus must be reached about them, so they usually capture only mainstream positions or conclusions. Promoting innovation is not an objective of the standards process; in contrast, standards tend to promote the status quo.

Using network effects and creating ecosystems

The most successful companies and products of the internet era have been predicated on the concept and ever-increasing value of network effects. Network effects are key for technology giants like Amazon and Google as well as for open-source projects like Wikipedia. The theory behind network effects is that platforms and products with these effects get better as they get bigger—not just increasing their value to users but also accruing more resources to improve themselves, thus strengthening their advantages (Coolican and Jin 2018).

Platforms can offer multiple players a powerful way to build new revenue streams from products and services that they could not develop and bring to market on their own (Meyer et al. 2018). For example, Alibaba's platform provides a range of services for its users: travel, entertainment, gaming, finance, transportation, and e-commerce. It is an eclectic mix, and it generates a wide-ranging array of data. By capturing and analyzing data from multiple sources, Alibaba can tailor individualized offers to its users—targeting and timing the offers for maximum effectiveness—and provide tools that help its online sellers enhance their respective businesses. The sellers' results, in turn, provide more data to the platform. This cycle reinforces the lead firm's market power by increasing user retention and amassing user data on many fronts.

Data ecosystems will play a critical role in defining the future of competition, particularly in business-to-business industries, because they enable companies to enhance their market power through data monopolies. New data-driven products and services deliver unique value propositions that extend beyond a company's traditional hardware products, deepening customer relationships and creating competitive advantage. They thus generate recurring high-margin revenue streams and raise barriers to entry by others. They also help firms build highly defensible positions rooted in economies of scale and scope, similar to positions based on proprietary intellectual property or trade secrets (Ringel, Baeza, and Manly 2019).

Superstar firms and the impacts on growth and distribution

Increased concentration is seen across industries, signaling the greater market power of global lead firms. One category of interest is "superstar" firms, that is, firms that have high sales, market capitalization, and employment. These firms are typically the largest MNCs. A growing body of literature about these firms has emerged (Choi, Lou, and Mukherjee 2018; David et al. 2017; Freund and Pierola 2015; Osgood et al. 2017; Van Reenen 2018; Vavoura 2017). Although the definition of superstar firms varies slightly in different contexts, these firms share common attributes such as higher efficiency, greater profits, higher levels of digitalization, and higher skill and innovation intensity relative to their peers.

Superstar firms capture a higher share of industry output than do other firms (Autor et al. 2020). They lead the way in R&D and in intangible investments, global trade, and productivity. They also shape their home countries' export patterns (Freund and Pierola 2015). Among 32 developing countries studied,[7] the country's top firm on average accounts for 14 percent of its total nonoil exports, the country's top five firms make up an average of 30 percent of nonoil exports, and the country's revealed comparative advantage can be created by a single firm.

The market power of superstar firms has increased significantly in the past two decades. The most prominent explanations for this increase seem to be technological advancements and changes in market structures (De Loecker, Eeckhout, and Mongey 2018). Technology adoption and innovation can be prohibitively expensive for many small firms, whereas large firms are not constrained by domestic inputs and domestic demand, which helps them grow and realize economies of scale (World Bank 2020). This strength allows large firms to invest billions of dollars to develop cutting-edge technology that further reinforces their market power. The decline in antitrust enforcement also played a role (Gutierrez and Philippon 2018). Superstar firms outperform their peers by using their market power to create various barriers to entry that protect their positions (Autor et al. 2020). Established firms may also lobby for regulatory barriers that complicate market entry or expansion for new and small firms and thus allow incumbent firms higher monopolistic gains (Autor et al. 2020). There is some evidence that markups grow in sectors with rising superstar firm intensity (Hall 2018).

FIGURE 2.11 Sectoral distribution of superstar firms

a. 1995–97

- Natural resources, 6%
- Insurance, 2%
- Automobiles, 6%
- Internet and media, 7%
- Machinery, 7%
- Electronics, 9%
- Telecom, 11%
- Banking, 25%
- Food and beverage, 14%
- Pharmaceuticals, 13%

b. 2014–16

- Machinery, 3%
- Retail, 3%
- Automobiles, 3%
- Telecom, 4%
- Other, 5%
- Food and beverage, 8%
- Banking, 12%
- Pharmaceuticals, 19%
- Electronics, 23%
- Internet and media, 20%

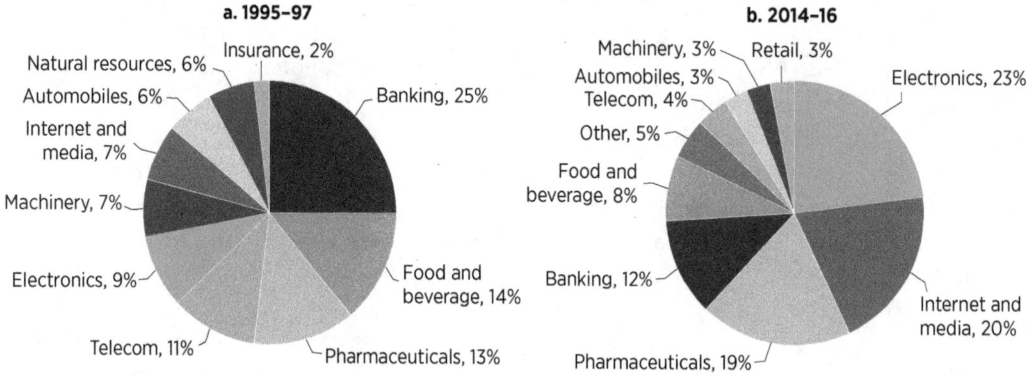

Source: Manyika et al. 2018.
Note: The panels show sectoral distribution of the top 1 percent of economic profit. Economic profit is calculated as a firm's invested capital times its return above the cost of capital. The sample includes nearly 6,000 of the world's largest public and private firms whose annual revenues are greater than $1 billion. These firms together make up 65 percent of global corporate pretax earnings.

Continuous adoption of new technologies strengthens network effects and favors firms that can more readily adapt to new modes of production (Autor et al. 2020). Two decades ago, banking and food and beverages accounted for nearly 40 percent of superstar firms. By 2016, electronics and internet and media represented 43 percent of superstar firms (figure 2.11). These new superstar firms include internet and technology giants such as Alibaba, Apple, Facebook, and Oracle. Superstar firms come disproportionately from the world's largest economies, with more than 95 percent hailing from Group of 20 countries.[8] However, superstar firms are more diverse with regard to source country and sector today than they were 20 years ago. US firms represented 38 percent of superstar firms in 2016, compared with 45 percent two decades ago. Companies headquartered in Asian economies (China, India, Japan, and Korea) make up 27 percent of the top 10 percent of superstar firms. Superstar firms are distributed across various sectors such as electronics, internet and media, pharmaceuticals and medical products, banking and insurance, food and beverages, apparel and luxury goods, automobiles, machinery, and retail.

The rise of superstar firms and increased market concentration have a dual impact on growth. On one hand, superstar firms are more productive and efficient than other firms; they promote productivity growth and innovation. On the other hand, the gains of such firms may be distributed unequally across locations, between capital and labor, and among different firms and workers (World Bank 2020; World Bank et al. 2017, 2019). At the geographic level, urban agglomeration of superstar firms causes unequal distribution of income between urban and rural areas. This division is particularly evident in developing countries where labor is not perfectly mobile.

In the labor market, increasing skill premiums and heightened competition have widened income gaps between workers. Firm size and the skilled worker share are strongly correlated (Akerman 2018). Increasing demand for skilled workers has boosted the skill premium in both developed and developing countries, while labor-saving technologies have displaced many unskilled workers in developed countries (World Bank 2020).

The emergence of superstar firms has also exacerbated income and wealth inequality between capital owners and workers (Autor et al. 2020; Kehrig and Vincent 2020). Technological change and higher markups reallocate value added from labor to capital—many developed countries experience a declining labor income share (Dorn et al. 2017).

The increased market power of superstar firms could also induce resource misallocation by reducing labor force participation, delaying variable input adjustments, and generating negative effects on market entry and innovation (De Loecker, Eeckhout, and Mongey 2018). Gutierrez and Philippon (2017) find that increased industry concentration is mainly driven by a decrease in domestic competition, which in turn leads to a decrease in firm-level investment, particularly in intangible assets by industry leaders. De Loecker, Eeckhout, and Unger (2020) find similar results.

Notes

1. Portfolio investments include equity securities and debt securities in the form of bonds, notes, or money market instruments. When the equity securities held by foreign investors account for less than 10 percent of an enterprise's capital, the investment is classified as a portfolio investment (OECD 2010).
2. Despite the indispensable role of MNCs in GVCs, evidence on their contribution to global trade and value added is scant. FDI data are often used to study MNCs across sectors and countries, but FDI and MNC activities are different concepts. FDI reflects only the value of financial transactions (flows and positions) between direct investors and investment enterprises. FDI data provide no information on how these funds are being used and what outcomes they achieve. Sometimes large amounts of money go through various shell companies in offshore financial centers before being used productively somewhere else. Tracking such money's real investors and recipients is challenging. Because of these characteristics, aggregate FDI statistics provide only a limited understanding of how MNCs operate in GVCs (Beugelsdijk et al. 2010; Blanchard and Acalin 2016; Cadestin et al. 2018; Leino and Ali-Yrkkö 2014).
3. Such intangibles cannot be exchanged through arm's length trade because of their nonrivalrous and nonexcludable features.
4. However, these alternative measures are one step removed from a firm's ability to raise prices above marginal costs, and they each have various caveats. Market share and market concentration can be noisy barometers of market power. High market concentration itself is not necessarily a problem if markets remain open to competition, including from imports and from other domestic and foreign firms. Even highly concentrated markets will be forced to price "competitively" if the potential exists for "hit and run" entry (Baumol, Panzar, and Willig 1982). In addition, intense competition could result in high concentration if less competitive firms are forced out of the market.
5. See Microsoft's 2019 annual report (https://www.microsoft.com/investor/reports/ar19/index.html).
6. Note that production length as measured by industry input-output tables significantly underestimates production length for complex products. Ideally, if a firm-to-firm input-output table for all firms in the world existed, the same method could be used to calculate the true production length from the number of firms a product goes through. However, existing global input-output tables aggregate activities at the industry level, obscuring all intraindustry transactions.

7. These countries are Albania, Bangladesh, Botswana, Bulgaria, Burkina Faso, Cambodia, Cameroon, Chile, Colombia, Costa Rica, the Dominican Republic, Ecuador, the Arab Republic of Egypt, Guatemala, the Islamic Republic of Iran, Jordan, Kenya, Lebanon, Malawi, Mauritius, Mexico, Morocco, Nicaragua, Niger, North Macedonia, Pakistan, Peru, Senegal, South Africa, Tanzania, Uganda, and the Republic of Yemen.

8. Group of 20 members comprise Argentina, Australia, Brazil, Canada, China, France, Germany, India, Indonesia, Italy, Japan, the Republic of Korea, Mexico, the Russian Federation, Saudi Arabia, South Africa, Turkey, the United Kingdom, the United States, and the European Union.

References

Acemoglu, D., V. M. Carvalho, A. Ozdaglar, and A. Tahbaz-Salehi. 2012. "The Network Origins of Aggregate Fluctuations." *Econometrica* 80 (5): 1977–2016.

Aghion, Philippe, Nick Bloom, Richard Blundell, Rachel Griffith, and Peter Howitt. 2005. "Competition and Innovation: An Inverted-U Relationship." *Quarterly Journal of Economics* 120 (2): 701–28.

Aizenman, J., and N. Marion. 2004. "The Merits of Horizontal versus Vertical FDI in the Presence of Uncertainty." *Journal of International Economics* 62 (1): 125–48.

Akerman, A. 2018. "The Relative Skill Demand of Superstar Firms and Aggregate Implications." Research Papers in Economics 2018: 2, Department of Economics, Stockholm University.

Alfaro, L., and A. Charlton. 2009. "Intra-industry Foreign Direct Investment." *American Economic Review* 99 (5): 2096–119.

Alfaro, L., and M. X. Chen. 2018. "Selection and Market Reallocation: Productivity Gains from Multinational Production." *American Economic Journal: Economic Policy* 10 (2): 1–38.

Alfaro, L., D. Chor, P. Antràs, and P. Conconi. 2019. "Internalizing Global Value Chains: A Firm-Level Analysis." *Journal of Political Economy* 127 (2): 508–59.

Alfaro, Laura, Andrés Rodríguez-Clare, Gordon H. Hanson, and Claudio Bravo-Ortega. 2004. "Multinationals and Linkages: An Empirical Investigation." *Economia* 4 (2): 113–69.

Amann, E., and S. Virmani. 2015. "Foreign Direct Investment and Reverse Technology Spillovers: The Effect on Total Factor Productivity." *OECD Journal: Economic Studies* 2014: 129–53.

Andrenelli, Andrea, Iza Lejárraga, Sébastien Miroudot, and Letizia Montinari. 2019. "Micro-Evidence on Corporate Relationships in Global Value Chains: The Role of Trade, FDI and Strategic Partnerships." OECD Trade Policy Papers 227, OECD Publishing, Paris.

Antràs, P. 2019. "Global Value Chains: The Economics of Spiders and Snakes." Keynote speech at 2019 IEFS-EAER Conference, Seoul National University, June 5. https://www.eaerweb.org/j_data/JE0002/2019/20194/JE0002_2019_20194_30.pdf.

Antràs, Pol, D. Chor, T. Fally, and R. Hillberry. 2012. "Measuring the Upstreamness of Production and Trade Flows." *American Economic Review* 102 (3): 412–16.

Antràs, Pol, Teresa C. Fort, and Felix Tintelnot. 2014. "The Margins of Global Sourcing: Theory and Evidence from U.S. Firms." NBER Working Paper 20772, National Bureau of Economic Research, Cambridge, MA.

Antràs, Pol, Teresa C. Fort, and Felix Tintelnot. 2017. "The Margins of Global Sourcing: Theory and Evidence from US Firms." *American Economic Review* 107 (9): 2514–64.

Antràs, Pol, and S. R. Yeaple. 2014. "Multinational Firms and the Structure of International Trade." In *Handbook of International Economics*, Vol. 4, edited by G. Gopinath, E. Helpman, and K. Rogoff, 55–130. Oxford, U.K.: North-Holland.

Arndt, Sven W., and Henryk Kierzkowski, eds. 2001. *Fragmentation: New Production Patterns in the World Economy*. Oxford, U.K.: Oxford University Press.

Autor, D., D. Dorn, L. F. Katz, C. Patterson, and J. Van Reenen. 2020. "The Fall of the Labor Share and the Rise of Superstar Firms." *Quarterly Journal of Economics* 135 (2): 645–709.

Baldwin, R., and A. J. Venables. 2010. "Relocating the Value Chain: Off-Shoring and Agglomeration in the Global Economy." CEPR Discussion Paper 8163, Center for Economic Policy Research, London.

Barba Navaretti, Giorgio, and Anthony Venables. 2004. *Multinational Firms in the World Economy*. Princeton, NJ: Princeton University Press.

Barrot, J. N., and J. Sauvagnat. 2016. "Input Specificity and the Propagation of Idiosyncratic Shocks in Production Networks." *Quarterly Journal of Economics* 131 (3): 1543–92.

Baseman, K. C., F. R. Warren-Boulton, and G. A. Woroch. 1995. "Microsoft Plays Hardball: The Use of Exclusionary Pricing and Technical Incompatibility to Maintain Monopoly Power in Markets for the Operating System Software." *Antitrust Bulletin* 40 (2): 265–315.

Baumol, W. J., J. Panzar, and R. Willig. 1982. *Contestable Markets and the Theory of Industrial Structure*. New York: Harcourt Brace Jovanovich.

Belderbos, R., and L. Sleuwaegen. 1998. "Tariff Jumping DFI and Export Substitution: Japanese Electronics Firms in Europe." *International Journal of Industrial Organization* 16 (5): 601–38.

Berlingieri, G., F. Pisch, and C. Steinwender. 2018. "Organizing Global Supply Chains: Input Cost Shares and Vertical Integration." NBER Working Paper 25286, National Bureau of Economic Research, Cambridge, MA.

Bernard, A. B., J. B. Jensen, S. J. Redding, and P. K. Schott. 2018. "Global Firms." *Journal of Economic Literature* 56 (2): 565–619.

Beugelsdijk, S., J. F. Hennart, R. Smeets, and A. H. L. Slangen. 2010. "Why and How FDI Stocks Are a Biased Measure of MNE Affiliate Activity." *Journal of International Business Studies* 41: 1444–59.

Blanchard, Olivier, and Julien Acalin. 2016. "What Does Measured FDI Actually Measure?" PIIE Policy Brief 16-17, Peterson Institute for International Economics, Washington, DC.

Blome C., and M. Henke. 2009. "Single Versus Multiple Sourcing: A Supply Risk Management Perspective." In *Supply Chain Risk. International Series in Operations Research & Management Science*, vol. 124, edited by G. A. Zsidisin and B. Ritchie. Boston, MA: Springer.

Blonigen, B. A. 2005. "A Review of the Empirical Literature on FDI Determinants." *Atlantic Economic Journal* 33 (4): 383–403.

Boner, R. A., and R. Krueger. 1991. "The Basics of Antitrust Policy: A Review of Ten Nations and the European Communities." Technical Paper 160, World Bank, Washington, DC.

Bruce-Lockhart, C., and E. Terazono. 2019. "From Bean to Cup, What Goes into the Cost of Your Coffee?" *Financial Times*, June 3, 2019. https://www.ft.com/content/44bd6a8e-83a5-11e9-9935-ad75bb96c849.

Buckley, P. J. 2009. "Internalisation Thinking: From the Multinational Enterprise to the Global Factory." *International Business Review* 18 (3): 224–35.

Buckley, P. J. 2010. "The Role of Headquarters in the Global Factory." In *Managing the Contemporary Multinational*, edited by A. Ulf and H. Ulf, 60–84. Cheltenham, U.K.: Edward Elgar.

Buckley, P. J., N. Driffield, and Kim Jae-Yeon. Forthcoming. "The Role of Outward FDI in Creating Korean Global Factories."

Buckley, P. J., and Roger Strange. 2011. "The Governance of the Multinational Enterprise: Insights from Internalization Theory." *Journal of Management Studies* 48 (2): 460–70.

Burke, Gerard J., Janice E. Carrillo, and Asoo J. Vakharia. 2007. "Single versus Multiple Supplier Sourcing Strategies." *European Journal of Operational Research* 182 (1): 95–112.

Cadestin, C., K. De Backer, I. Desnoyers-James, S. Miroudot, D. Rigo, and M. Ye. 2018. "Multinational Enterprises and Global Value Chains: The OECD Analytical AMNE Database." OECD Trade Policy Papers 211, OECD Publishing, Paris.

Calatayud, Agustina, and Juan Antonia Ketterer. 2016. "Integrated Value Chain Risk Management." IDB Technical Note 922, Inter-American Development Bank, Washington, DC.

Caldara, Dario, Michele Cavallo, and Matteo Iacoviello. 2016. "Oil Price Elasticities and Oil Price Fluctuations." International Finance Discussion Paper 1173, Board of Governors of the Federal Reserve System, Washington, DC.

Casadesus-Masanell, R., and D. B. Yoffie. 2005. "Wintel: Cooperation or Conflict." HBS Working Paper 05-083, Harvard Business School, Boston, MA.

Chen, W. 2018. "Cross-Country Income Differences Revisited: Accounting for the Role of Intangible Capital." *Review of Income and Wealth* 64 (3): 626–48.

Choi, D., D. Lou, and A. Mukherjee. 2018. "The Effect of Superstar Firms on College Major Choice." In *9th Miami Behavioral Finance Conference eJournal.* https://www.ssrn.com/index .cfm/en/fen/ads/04172019ann002/.

Clifton, Rita, and Sameena Ahmad. 2009. *Brands and Branding.* New York: Bloomberg Press.

Collins, Norman, and Lee Preston. 1969. *Concentration and Price-Cost Margins in Manufacturing Industries.* Berkeley: University of California Press.

Coolican, D'Arcy, and Li Jin. 2018. "The Dynamics of Network Effects." Andreessen Horowitz, Menlo Park, CA. https://a16z.com/2018/12/13/network-effects-dynamics-in-practice/.

Crozet, M., T. Mayer, and J. L. Mucchielli. 2004. "How Do Firms Agglomerate? A Study of FDI in France." *Regional Science and Urban Economics* 34 (1): 27–54.

Dachs, Bernhard, Steffen Kinkel, and Angela Jäger. 2017. "Bringing It All Back Home? Backshoring of Manufacturing Activities and the Adoption of Industry 4.0 Technologies." MPRA Paper 83167. https://mpra.ub.uni-muenchen.de/83167/1/MPRA_paper_83167.pdf.

David, H., D. Dorn, L. F. Katz, C. Petterson, and J. Van Reenen. 2017. "Concentrating on the Fall of the Labor Share." *American Economic Review: Papers & Proceedings* 107 (5): 180–85.

Dalgic, Tevfik, ed. 2006. *Handbook of Niche Marketing: Principles and Practice.* Binghamton, NY: The Haworth Press.

DeAngelis, S. F. 2015. "Supply Chain Risk Management: Dealing with Length & Depth." Supply Chain Minded. https://supplychainminded.com/supply-chain-risk-management -dealing-length-depth/.

De Backer, Koen, and Sébastien Miroudot. 2013. "Mapping Global Value Chains." OECD Trade Policy Paper 159, OECD Publishing, Paris.

De Loecker, J., J. Eeckhout, and S. Mongey. 2018. "Quantifying Market Power." Unpublished.

De Loecker, J., J. Eeckhout, and G. Unger. 2020. "The Rise of Market Power and the Macroeconomic Implications." *Quarterly Journal of Economics* 135 (2): 561–644.

De Loecker, Jan, and Frederic Warzynski. 2012. "Markups and Firm-Level Export Status." *American Economic Review* 102 (6): 2437–71.

Del Prete, D., and A. Rungi. 2017. "Organizing the Global Value Chain: A Firm-Level Test." *Journal of International Economics* 109 (November): 16–30.

Denning, Steve. 2013. "What Went Wrong at Boeing?" *Forbes,* January 21, 2013. https://www .forbes.com/sites/stevedenning/2013/01/21/what-went-wrong-at-boeing/#b72e3e7b1b7b.

Desjardins, Jeff. 2018. "How Google Retains More Than 90% of Market Share." *Business Insider,* April 23, 2018. https://www.businessinsider.com/how-google-retains-more-than-90 -of-market-share-2018-4.

Dietrich, Michael, and Jackie Krafft. 2012. "The Economics and Theory of the Firm." In *Handbook on the Economics and Theory of the Firm,* edited by Michael Dietrich and Jackie Krafft, 3–26. Cheltenham, U.K.: Edward Elgar Publishing.

Dorn, D., L. F. Katz, C. Patterson, and J. Van Reenen. 2017. "Concentrating on the Fall of the Labor Share." *American Economic Review* 107 (5): 180–85.

Driffield, N., and J. H. Love. 2003. "Foreign Direct Investment, Technology Sourcing and Reverse Spillovers." *The Manchester School* 71 (6): 659–72.

Driffield, N., and J. H. Love. 2007. "Linking FDI Motivation and Host Economy Productivity Effects: Conceptual and Empirical Analysis." *Journal of International Business Studies* 38 (3): 460–73.

Du, J., Y. Lu, and Z. Tao. 2008. "Economic Institutions and FDI Location Choice: Evidence from US Multinationals in China." *Journal of Comparative Economics* 36 (3): 412–29.

Du, L., A. Harrison, and G. Jefferson. 2011. "Do Institutions Matter for FDI Spillovers? The Implications of China's 'Special Characteristics.'" Policy Research Working Paper 5757, World Bank, Washington, DC.

Duncan, Ian, Michael Laris, and Lori Aratini. 2020. "Boeing 737 Max Crashes Were 'Horrific Culmination' of Errors, Investigators Say." *Washington Post,* September 16, 2020. https:// www.washingtonpost.com/local/trafficandcommuting/boeing-737-max-crashes-were-horr ific-culmination-of-errors-investigators-say/2020/09/16/72e5d226-f761-11ea-89e3-4b9efa 36dc64_story.html.

Dunning, J. H. 1977. "Trade, Location of Economic Activity and the MNE: A Search for an Eclectic Approach." In *The International Allocation of Economic Activity: Proceedings of a Nobel Symposium Held at Stockholm*, edited by B. Ohlin, P.-O. Hesselborn, and P. M. Wijkman, 395–418. London: Palgrave Macmillan.

Dunning, J. H., ed. 1985. *Multinational Enterprises, Economic Structure, and International Competitiveness*. Hoboken, NJ: John Wiley & Sons Inc.

Economist. 2019. "Digitisation Is Helping to Deliver Goods Faster." July 11, 2019. https://www.economist.com/special-report/2019/07/11/digitisation-is-helping-to-deliver-goods-faster.

Fally, Thibault. 2012. "Production Staging: Measurement and Facts." Unpublished. https://www2.gwu.edu/~iiep/assets/docs/fally_productionstaging.pdf.

Farole, T., and D. Winkler, eds. 2014. *Making Foreign Direct Investment Work for Sub-Saharan Africa: Local Spillovers and Competitiveness in Global Value Chains*. Washington, DC: World Bank.

Ferrantino, M. J., and E. E. Koten. 2019. "Understanding Supply Chain 4.0 and Its Potential Impact on Global Value Chains." Chapter 5 in *Global Value Chain Development Report 2019: Technological Innovation, Supply Chain Trade, and Workers in a Globalized World*, 103–20. Geneva: World Trade Organization.

Freund, Caroline, and Martha Denisse Pierola. 2015. "Export Superstars." *Review of Economics and Statistics* 97 (5): 1023–32.

Grossman, S. J., and O. D. Hart. 1986. "The Costs and Benefits of Ownership: A Theory of Vertical and Lateral Integration." *Journal of Political Economy* 94 (4): 691–719.

Gutiérrez, G., and T. Philippon. 2017. "Declining Competition and Investment in the US." NBER Working Paper 23583, National Bureau of Economic Research, Cambridge, MA.

Gutiérrez, G., and T. Philippon. 2018. "How EU Markets Became More Competitive than US Markets: A Study of Institutional Drift." NBER Working Paper 24700, National Bureau of Economic Research, Cambridge, MA.

Hall, Robert. 2018. "New Evidence on the Markup of Prices over Marginal Costs and the Role of Mega-Firms in the US Economy." NBER Working Paper 24574, National Bureau of Economic Research, Cambridge, MA.

Hart, O., and J. Moore. 1990. "Property Rights and the Nature of the Firm." *Journal of Political Economy* 98 (6): 1119–58.

Hausmann, R., C. A. Hidalgo, D. P. Stock, and M. A. Yildirim. 2014. "Implied Comparative Advantage." Harvard Kennedy School Working Paper RWP14-003, Harvard Kennedy School, Cambridge, MA.

Head, K., and J. Ries. 2003. "Heterogeneity and the FDI versus Export Decision of Japanese Manufacturers." *Journal of the Japanese and International Economies* 17 (4): 448–67.

Head, K., J. Ries, and D. Swenson. 1995. "Agglomeration Benefits and Location Choice: Evidence from Japanese Manufacturing Investments in the United States." *Journal of International Economics* 3 (3–4): 223–47.

Helpman, E. 1984. "A Simple Theory of Trade with Multinational Corporations." *Journal of Political Economy* 92 (3): 451–71.

Helpman, E. 1985. "Multinational Corporations and Trade Structure." *Review of Economic Studies* 52 (3): 443–57.

Helpman, E., and P. Krugman. 1985. *Market Structure and Foreign Trade: Increasing Returns, Imperfect Competition, and the International Economy*. Cambridge, MA: MIT Press.

Helpman, E., M. J. Melitz, and S. R. Yeaple. 2004. "Export versus FDI with Heterogeneous Firms." *American Economic Review* 94 (1): 300–16.

Hidalgo, Cesar A., and Ricardo Hausmann. 2009. "The Building Blocks of Economic Complexity." *Proceedings of the National Academy of Sciences of the United States of America* 106 (26): 10570–75.

Hill, C.W. 1997. "Establishing a Standard: Competitive Strategy and Technological Standards in Winner-Take-All Industries." *Academy of Management Perspectives* 11 (2): 7–25.

IMF (International Monetary Fund). 1977. *Balance of Payments Manual, Fourth Edition*. Washington, DC: International Monetary Fund.

Inman, R. A., and M. M. Helms. 2005. "Outsourcing and Offshoring." In *Encyclopedia of Management, 5th edition*. Farmington Hills, MI: Thomson Gale.

Javorcik, Beata Smarzynska, Alessia Lo Turco, and Daniela Maggioni. 2017. "New and Improved: Does FDI Boost Production Complexity in Host Countries?" CEPR Discussion Paper 11942, Center for Economic Policy Research, London.

Javorcik, Beata Smarzynska, and Mariana Spatareanu. 2009. "Tough Love: Do Czech Suppliers Learn from Their Relationships with Multinationals?" LICOS Discussion Paper 249/2009, Centre for Institutions and Economic Performance, Leuven.

Kehrig, M., and N. Vincent. 2020. "The Micro-Level Anatomy of the Labor Share Decline." CES Working Paper 20-12, Center for Economic Studies, US Census Bureau.

Kennedy, R. C. 2008. "Fat, Fatter, Fattest: Microsoft's Kings of Bloat." *InfoWorld*, April 14, 2008. https://www.infoworld.com/article/2650502/fat--fatter--fattest--microsoft-s-kings-of-bloat.html.

Kish, Matthew. 2014. "The Cost Breakdown of a $100 Pair of Sneakers." *Portland Business Journal*, December 16, 2014. https://www.bizjournals.com/portland/blog/threads_and_laces/2014/12/the-cost-breakdown-of-a-100-pair-of-sneakers.html.

Klein, B., R. G. Crawford, and A. A. Alchian. 1978. "Vertical Integration, Appropriable Rents, and the Competitive Contracting Process." *Journal of Law and Economics* 21 (2): 297–326.

Kumar, A. 1992. "Supply Contracts and Manufacturing Decisions." PhD thesis, Graduate School of Industrial Administration, Carnegie Mellon University, Pittsburgh.

Lang, Nikolaus, Christoph Lechner, Charline Wurzer, and Maximilian Dexheimer. 2020. "Four Strategies to Orchestrate a Digital Ecosystem." Boston Consulting Group, September 9, 2020. https://www.bcg.com/publications/2020/four-strategies-to-orchestrate-digital-ecosystem.

Leino, Topias, and Jyrki Ali-Yrkkö. 2014. "How Does Foreign Direct Investment Measure Real Investment by Foreign-Owned Companies? Firm-Level Analysis." ETLA Reports 27, The Research Institute of the Finnish Economy, Helsinki.

Liker, J., and T. Y. Choi. 2004. "Building Deep Supplier Relationships." *Harvard Business Review*, December 2004. https://hbr.org/2004/12/building-deep-supplier-relationships.

Lipsey, Robert. 2004. "Home- and Host-Country Effects of Foreign Direct Investment." In *Challenges to Globalization: Analyzing the Economics*, edited by Robert E. Baldwin and L. Alan Winters, 333–82. University of Chicago Press, Chicago, IL.

Luck, P. 2019. "Global Supply Chains, Firm Scope and Vertical Integration: Evidence from China." *Journal of Economic Geography* 19 (1): 173–98.

Makino, S., C. M. Lau, and R. S. Yeh. 2002. "Asset-Exploitation versus Asset-Seeking: Implications for Location Choice of Foreign Direct Investment from Newly Industrialized Economies." *Journal of International Business Studies* 33 (3): 403–21.

Manyika, J., S. Ramaswamy, J. Bughin, J. Woetzel, M. Birshan, and Z. Nagpal. 2018. "Superstars: The Dynamics of Firms, Sectors, and Cities Leading the Global Economy." Discussion paper, McKinsey & Company. https://www.mckinsey.com/~/media/McKinsey/Featured%20Insights/Innovation/Superstars%20The%20dynamics%20of%20firms%20sectors%20and%20cities%20leading%20the%20global%20economy/MGI_Superstars_Discussion%20paper_Oct%202018-v2.pdf.

Marchese, Kelly, and Bill Lam. 2014. "Toyota Pioneers New Global Supply Chains." *Wall Street Journal*, August 12, 2014. https://deloitte.wsj.com/cio/2014/08/12/toyota-pioneers-new-global-supply-chains/.

Markusen, J. R. 1984. "Multinationals, Multi-Plant Economies, and the Gains from Trade." *Journal of International Economics* 16 (3–4): 205–26.

Markusen, J. R. 1995. "The Boundaries of Multinational Enterprises and the Theory of International Trade." *Journal of Economic Perspectives* 9 (2): 169–89.

Markusen, J. R. 1998. "Multinational Firms, Location and Trade." *World Economy* 21 (6): 733–56.

McDonald, F., F. Burton, and P. Dowling. 2002. *International Business*. High Holborn, U.K.: Thomson.

Melitz, M. J. 2003. "The Impact of Trade on Intra-Industry Reallocations and Aggregate Industry Productivity." *Econometrica* 71 (6): 1695–725.

Meyer, M., N. Lang, N. Baise, K. Maggard, G. Hill, J. Wong, H. Maher, S. Verma, E. León, and B. Tanson. 2018. "Digital Innovation on the World Stage." Excerpt from *2018 BCG*

Global Challengers: Digital Leapfrogs. Boston, MA: Boston Consulting Group. https://www
.bcg.com/publications/2018/global-challengers-2018-digital-innovation-world-stage.

Monczka, R. M., and R. J. Trent. 1991. "Global Sourcing: A Development Approach."
International Journal of Purchasing and Materials Management 27 (2): 2–8.

Murphy, Sophia, David Burch, and Jennifer Clapp. 2012. *Cereal Secrets: The World's Largest Grain
Traders and Global Agriculture*. Oxfam Research Reports. Oxford, U.K.: Oxfam International.

Nieto, M. J., and A. Rodríguez. 2011. "Offshoring of R&D: Looking Abroad to Improve
Innovation Performance." *Journal of International Business Studies* 42 (3): 345–61.

OECD (Organisation for Economic Co-operation and Development). 2010. *Measuring
Globalization. OECD Economic Globalization Indicators 2010*. Paris: OECD Publishing.

OECD (Organisation for Economic Co-operation and Development). 2018. "Multinational
Enterprises in the Global Economy: Heavily Debated but Hardly Measured." Policy Note,
OECD, Paris. https://www.oecd.org/industry/ind/MNEs-in-the-global-economy-policy
-note.pdf.

Ohno, T. 1988. *Toyota Production System: Beyond Large-Scale Production*. Boca Raton, FL: CRC Press.

Osgood, Iain, Dustin Tingley, Thomas Bernauer, In Song Kim, Helen V. Milner, and Gabriele
Spilker. 2017. "The Charmed Life of Superstar Exporters: Survey Evidence on Firms and
Trade Policy." *Journal of Politics* 79 (1): 133–52.

Osnago, A., N. Rocha, and M. Ruta. 2017. "Do Deep Trade Agreements Boost Vertical FDI?"
World Bank Economic Review 30 (Supplement 1): S119–25.

Peterson, Kyle. 2011. "Special Report: A Wing and a Prayer: Outsourcing at Boeing." Reuters,
January 20, 2011. https://www.reuters.com/article/us-boeing-dreamliner/special-report-a
-wing-and-a-prayer-outsourcing-at-boeing-idUSTRE70J2UX20110120.

Plenert, G. 2007. *Reinventing Lean: Introducing Lean Management into the Supply Chain*. Oxford,
U.K.: Butterworth-Heinemann.

Porter, M. E. 1979. "How Competitive Forces Shape Strategy." *Harvard Business Review* 57: 137–45.

Radlo, M. J. 2016. "Offshoring, Outsourcing, Production Fragmentation: Definitions, Measures
and Origin of the Research." In *Offshoring, Outsourcing and Production Fragmentation*, 8–40.
London: Palgrave Macmillan.

Ringel, M., R. Baeza, and J. Manly. 2019. "How Collaborative Platforms and Ecosystems
Are Changing Innovation." Chapter 3 in *The Most Innovative Companies 2019: The Rise of AI,
Platforms, and Ecosystems*. Boston, MA: Boston Consulting Group.

Robinson, P. 2019. "Boeing's 737 Max Software Outsourced to $9-an-Hour Engineers."
Bloomberg, June 28, 2019. https://www.bloomberg.com/news/articles/2019-06-28
/boeing-s-737-max-software-outsourced-to-9-an-hour-engineers.

Syverson, C. 2019. "Macroeconomics and Market Power: Context, Implications, and Open
Questions." *Journal of Economic Perspectives* 33 (3): 23–43.

Tintelnot, Felix. 2017. "Global Production with Export Platforms." *Quarterly Journal of Economics*
132 (1): 157–209.

Tomas, G., and M. Hult. 2003. "Global Supply Chain Management: An Integration of Scholarly
Thoughts." *Industrial Marketing Management* 33 (1): 3–5.

UNCTAD (United Nations Conference on Trade and Development). 2004. *World Investment
Report 2004: The Shift towards Services*. Geneva: United Nations.

UNCTAD (United Nations Conference on Trade and Development). 2005. *World Investment Report
2005: Transnational Corporations and the Internationalization of R&D*. Geneva: United Nations.

UNCTAD (United Nations Conference on Trade and Development). 2011. *World Investment Report
2011: Non-equity Modes of International Production and Development*. Geneva: United Nations.

UNCTAD (United Nations Conference on Trade and Development). 2020. *World Investment
Report 2020: International Production beyond the Pandemic*. Geneva: United Nations.

Useem, J. 2019. "The Long-Forgotten Flight That Sent Boeing Off Course." *Atlantic*,
November 20, 2019. https://www.theatlantic.com/ideas/archive/2019/11/how-boeing
-lost-its-bearings/602188/.

Van Reenen, John. 2018. "Increasing Differences between Firms: Market Power and the Macro-
Economy." CEP Discussion Paper 1576, Centre for Economic Performance, London School
of Economics and Political Science.

Vavoura, C. 2017. "Liberalising Trade in the Shadow of Superstar Firms." Unpublished, Department of Economics, University of Nottingham.

Wang, Z., S. J. Wei, X. Yu, and K. Zhu. 2017. "Characterizing Global Value Chains: Production Length and Upstreamness." NBER Working Paper 23261, National Bureau of Economic Research, Cambridge, MA.

Williamson, Oliver E. 1973. "Markets and Hierarchies: Some Elementary Considerations." *American Economic Review: Papers and Proceedings of the Eighty-fifth Annual Meeting of the American Economic Association* 63 (2): 315–25

Williamson, Oliver E. 1975. *Markets and Hierarchies: Analysis and Antitrust Implications: A Study in the Economics of Internal Organization.* New York: The Free Press.

Williamson, Oliver E. 1985. *The Economic Institutions of Capitalism.* New York: Simon and Schuster.

Wingfield, Nick, and Don Clark. 2011. "Microsoft Alliance with Intel Shows Age." *Wall Street Journal*, January 4, 2011. https://www.wsj.com/articles/SB1000142405274870380870457 6062073117494078.

World Bank. 2020. *World Development Report 2020: Trading for Development in the Age of Global Value Chains.* Washington, DC: World Bank.

World Bank, Institute of Developing Economies, Organisation for Economic Co-operation and Development, Research Center of Global Value Chains at the University of International Business and Economics, and World Trade Organization. 2017. *Global Value Chain Development Report 2017: Measuring and Analyzing the Impact of GVCs on Economic Development.* Washington, DC: World Bank.

World Bank, Institute of Developing Economies, Organisation for Economic Co-operation and Development, Research Center of Global Value Chains at the University of International Business and Economics, and World Trade Organization. 2019. *Global Value Chain Development Report 2019: Technical Innovation, Supply Chain Trade, and Workers in a Globalized World.* Washington, DC: World Bank.

Yang, Daniel, Stacy Wegner, and Albert Cowsky. 2019. "Apple iPhone 11 Pro Max Teardown." *Tech Insights*, September 23, 2019. https://www.techinsights.com/blog/apple-iphone-11-pro-max-teardown.

Chapter 3
The Internationalization of Domestic Firms

Key findings

- Participation in global value chains (GVCs) can bring considerable benefits to domestic firms because they can learn from multinational corporations through investment, partnerships, or trade. The knowledge they gain can raise their productivity and help them obtain the necessary production capabilities and foreign market knowledge to directly compete in international markets and to upgrade their roles in GVCs.

- By assimilating offshore supply chain links, firms can specialize in specific tasks and functions to support niches or segments of GVCs led and organized by firms in other countries. Local firms no longer have to wait for the emergence of an in-country industrial base or the upstream capabilities formerly required to compete internationally.

- The acceleration effect from GVC participation provides a powerful case for looking into internationalization and upgrading among domestic firms. Stimulating firms to begin participating in GVCs or to upgrade their participation in them can ultimately have considerable macroeconomic effects by helping developing countries industrialize more rapidly.

- Domestic firms can internationalize and participate in GVCs through four main pathways: supplier linkages with international firms, strategic alliances with international firms, direct exporting, and outward foreign direct investment. The most powerful engine of capacity building lies in firm-to-firm interactions.

- Opportunities for GVC participation do not present themselves equally to all firms. It can be a difficult and risky experience, at least initially, for firms to shift their production focus or sales from domestic to international markets. There are a number of firm-level prerequisites for GVC participation. There is also a relationship between a given GVC's characteristics and the likely pathways by which firms will enter it.

- Although foreign firms can stimulate productivity spillovers to domestic firms, it is important to remember that, where technological development and upgrading do occur, domestic firms are often their main instigators, responding to opportunities that they identify in the GVCs in which they participate. Thus, domestic firms need to constantly adapt their operations (strategy, structure, and resources) and strengthen their capabilities to better suit global production networks.

Domestic firm participation in global value chains: Pathways

A firm is a participant in a global value chain (GVC) if it produces at least one stage in the value chain (Antràs 2020). Although GVCs are dominated by multinational corporations (MNCs) (see chapter 2), studies often underestimate the importance of smaller firms in GVCs and the extent to which they participate in them.[1] Part of this misconception derives from how GVC participation is often defined at the country-industry level using world input-output tables (see chapter 1). This perspective ignores the roles of individual firms in global production networks. Even studies that consider firm-level GVC participation often limit their definition of participation to only firms that both import and export (Antràs 2020; Johnson 2018; and the Activites of MNEs [multinational enterprises] database referenced in chapter 2). However, GVC participation does not always require that a firm directly exports goods or services. Instead, firms may be integrated into GVCs indirectly by producing and supplying intermediate elements to exporting firms or by offshoring part of their production facilities (Cusolito, Safadi, and Taglioni 2016). Therefore, to get the most accurate representation of GVC participation, it is important to use a broader definition of the term and to consider the wide variety of firms engaged in global production networks.

Firms internationalize and participate in GVCs through different pathways. To begin participating in GVCs, firms need to gradually shift their production or sales focus from domestic to international markets. This process is known as "internationalization" (Welch and Luostarinen 1988). This chapter identifies four main ways, or "internationalization pathways," by which firms can participate in GVCs (figure 3.1), each with its own prerequisites (see the following section on prerequisites to internationalization):

1. *Supplier linkages with international firms.* Firms can domestically produce and supply goods or services to international firms (such as MNCs or domestic exporters), which will in turn export those products on the international market.
2. *Strategic alliances with MNCs* (coproduction). Firms can coproduce goods or services together with MNCs, which will then use those inputs in their global production networks.
3. *Direct exporting.*[2] Firms can domestically produce goods or services and sell them directly on the international market.
4. *Outward foreign direct investment (OFDI).* Firms can use OFDI to move part of their production facilities abroad or to establish an overseas sales affiliate, thereby internationalizing their production and most likely their sales.

In practice, many firms participate in GVCs in more than one way. As shown in the rest of this chapter, the various types of GVC participation complement each other in important ways. Firms that are successful along one pathway (for example, supplier linkages) become increasingly likely to extend their involvement in global production networks along others (for example, by coproducing with MNCs [strategic alliances], starting to sell on the international market [direct exporting], or shifting production processes or sales affiliates abroad [OFDI]) (Alcacer and Oxley 2014).

FIGURE 3.1 Global value chain participation and internationalization

Internationalization pathways to GVC participation

Domestic firm

Supplier linkages with international firms
Aim: Learn about global product standards, markets
Prerequisites: Minimum quality, quantity, competitive price

Strategic alliances with MNCs (coproduction)
Aim: Access essential foreign know-how, technology, markets
Prerequisites: Complementary skills, knowledge, assets to MNC

Direct exporting
Aim: Expand sales abroad
Prerequisites: Minimum productivity, market knowledge

Outward foreign direct investment
Aim: Acquire foreign technology, market entry
Prerequisites: Large size, financially solvent, organizational capacity

GVC upgrading

Learning process   *Competitiveness*

Develop production (capabilities) → **Firm products (type, complexity)**

+

Acquire foreign market knowledge → **Firm performance (sales, exporting, productivity)**

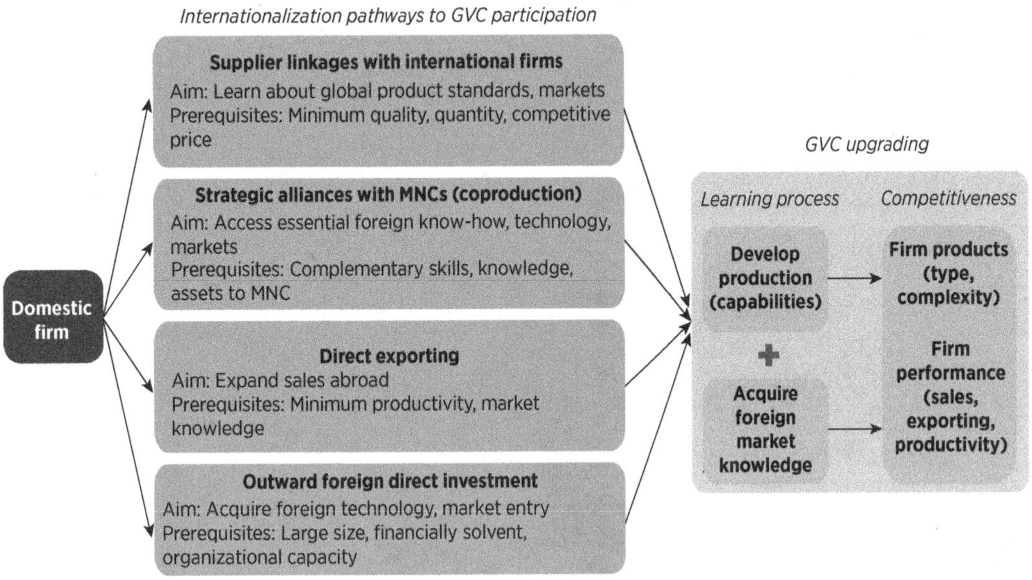

Source: World Bank elaboration of the literature.
Note: GVC = global value chain; MNC = multinational corporation.

Companies generally internationalize in a cautious, stepwise process involving strategic planning and risk minimization. In general, companies will choose the pathways that appear more familiar and less risky and will gradually move into deeper levels of participation as they gain experience and confidence in their production capabilities and foreign market knowledge (de Caldas Lima 2008).

Participation in a GVC can offer important learning opportunities to domestic firms. A wide set of literature, ranging from international economics to business to development, has emphasized the benefits that participation in GVCs can have on the performance of firms in emerging market economies (Alcacer and Oxley 2014; Gereffi et al. 2001; Gereffi, Humphrey, and Sturgeon 2005; Meyer and Sinani 2009). A key reason for these benefits is that GVC participation opens up firms to new levels of competition. International buyers typically have stronger preferences for product quality than domestic ones, which forces GVC firms to upgrade their production and managerial practices to satisfy client demands (Atkin et al. 2017; Khandelwal and Teachout 2016; Newman et al. 2016). To remain competitive, firms need to learn two types of skills and knowledge. The first is *essential production capabilities*. Firms need to prepare themselves to compete technologically, to meet the necessary quality standards for the products they produce, and to be productive enough to compete internationally (Pedersen and Petersen 1998). The second is *foreign market knowledge*. Firms need to learn the specific details of the overseas markets they enter, such as their business climates, cultural patterns, market structures, and consumer characteristics (Johanson and Vahlne 1977).

Firms that manage to enter GVCs tend to become more productive and improve their competitiveness. The firms that successfully compete internationally often use their new skills and knowledge to further strengthen their performance. GVC participation provides firms with opportunities to obtain managerial expertise, technical knowledge, the fruits of innovation, and access to new markets, thereby allowing these firms to more efficiently allocate their resources and to enhance their productivity (Montalbano, Nenci, and Pietrobelli 2018; see also Agostino et al. 2015; Gereffi 1999; Giovannetti, Marvasi, and Sanfilippo 2015; Morrison, Pietrobelli, and Rabellotti 2008; Theyel 2013; Woldesenbet, Ram, and Jones 2012; Wynarczyk and Watson 2005). Entering GVCs is also found to improve export diversification by enabling firms to enter new product lines (Goldberg et al. 2010). Internationalized firms exploit their productivity gains to outcompete their domestic rivals on price or to distinguish themselves through higher-quality products. This success, in turn, can increase their firm-level market power and allow them to increase their profit margins.

GVC participation can thus help transform firms from being "opportunity and cost oriented" to being "strategy and value oriented," allowing them to shape their competitive advantage (Xiao and Liu 2015). Evidence for the productivity gains caused by GVC participation is presented in figure 3.2, which shows the productivity of Japanese firms that started exporting (panel a) and those that started to invest abroad (panel b). In both cases, the initial labor productivity of these firms was higher than that of firms that remained domestic. However, once these firms internationalized in 2001, the gap in labor productivity between the "switchers" and the "nonswitchers" expanded (Wakasugi 2014). This continuous improvement helped the switching firms compete internationally and deepen their GVC participation.

This report's quantitative case study finds similar evidence for firms' improvements in competitiveness after starting to participate in GVCs. In both Rwanda (figure 3.3) and West Bengal, firms that began exporting for international markets often became larger and more productive. They also became more dependent on higher-complexity imports either directly preceding or following their internationalization, suggesting that they were sourcing capital equipment rather than raw inputs. GVC participation also has a significant effect on firms' employment dynamics, often leading to a steep

FIGURE 3.2 **The effect of global value chain participation on firm productivity in Japan, 2000–05**

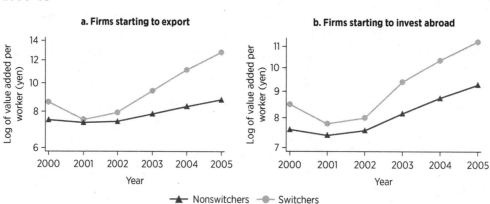

Source: Wakasugi 2014.

FIGURE 3.3 **The effect of global value chain participation (direct exporting) on firm imports and employment in Rwanda, 2008–17**

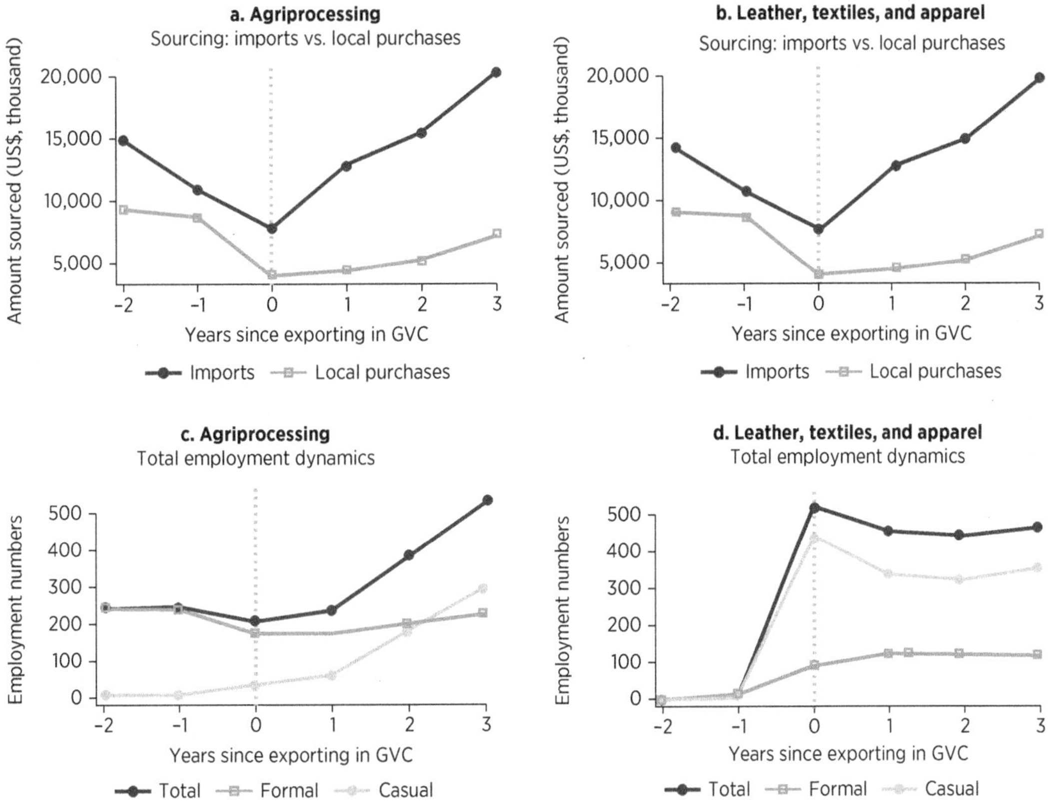

Source: World Bank calculations; see chapter 11 of this report.
Note: GVC = global value chain.

rise in employment.[3] Overall, these dynamics suggest that recently internationalized firms tend to upgrade their essential production capabilities (for example, their capital, skill, and research and development [R&D] intensity) to meet more demanding global product requirements.

Stimulating firms to begin participating in GVCs or to upgrade their participation in them can ultimately have considerable macroeconomic effects by helping developing countries to industrialize more rapidly (Balié et al. 2017; Greenville, Kawasaki, and Beaujeu 2017; Kowalski et al. 2015; Taglioni and Winkler 2016). Although firm-level improvements to competitiveness from GVC participation and upgrading may be small in scale, these changes can quickly add up to significant sectoral and ultimately macroeconomic productivity gains and growth. Moreover, by assimilating offshore supply chain linkages, firms can specialize in specific tasks and functions to support specific niches or segments of GVCs led and organized by firms in other countries. Local firms no longer have to wait for the emergence of an in-country industrial base or the upstream capabilities formerly required to compete internationally (IMF 2015). This acceleration effect provides a powerful case for looking into internationalization, GVC participation, and upgrading among domestic firms.

Prerequisites to firm internationalization and global value chain participation

Opportunities for GVC participation do not present themselves equally to all firms. Shifting production focus or sales from domestic to international markets can be a difficult and risky experience, at least initially, for firms. These challenges lead to a number of firm-level prerequisites for GVC participation. A given GVC's characteristics are also related to the likely pathways by which firms will participate in it.

Firm-level prerequisites

Only the most productive firms manage to internationalize, and their pathways to doing so are influenced by their productivity levels. A consistent finding in the literature is that high-productivity firms self-select into producing for international markets, whereas less productive firms keep producing for their domestic market or are forced to close (Melitz 2003). Only the most productive firms are able to overcome the costs, both tangible (such as production requirements, tariffs, and transportation) and intangible (such as host-country market information), necessary to compete abroad (for exports) or to locate and produce abroad (for OFDI) (Helpman, Melitz, and Yeaple 2004). Firms that choose to invest abroad need to overcome even larger fixed costs than exporters, and therefore they tend to be the most productive (Melitz 2003). Evidence for this ordering is found in studies of both high-income countries (figure 3.4, featuring the Netherlands) and developing countries (figure 3.5, featuring Rwanda). In both cases, average productivity increases as firms internationalize. Domestic firms tend to be the least productive, followed by firms that supply exporters and then by the exporting firms themselves. Multinational firms that both export and engage in FDI are, on average, the most productive.[4]

In addition to productivity thresholds, there are also specific firm-level prerequisites for each of the pathways to internationalization. These requirements depend largely on a firm's initial production capabilities, market knowledge, and size, as summarized in table 3.1; and they are important determinants of firms' entry into GVCs.

Supplier linkages depend on the presence of both an international partner (possibly an MNC or a domestic exporter) that is willing and able to source local inputs and domestic firms that are capable of producing those inputs to the appropriate production specifications. Domestic firms need to be able to produce goods according to the standards required by the international firm and to offer a reliable and timely supply at a competitive price (Farole and Winkler 2014). Affiliates of MNCs, in particular, often use screening, testing programs, or, where relevant, international certifications to ensure that they select domestic firms that are able to provide high-quality and cost-effective inputs, possibly with the aid of the affiliates (Jordaan, Douw, and Qiang 2020). Domestic firms that succeed as suppliers to MNCs therefore tend to have relatively high skills and technological capabilities (Jordaan, Douw, and Qiang 2020). For example, evidence in Turkey's manufacturing industry found that MNC suppliers were considerably more likely to be exporters themselves, to have higher R&D

FIGURE 3.4 Productivity distribution of Dutch manufacturers and services, 2010–16

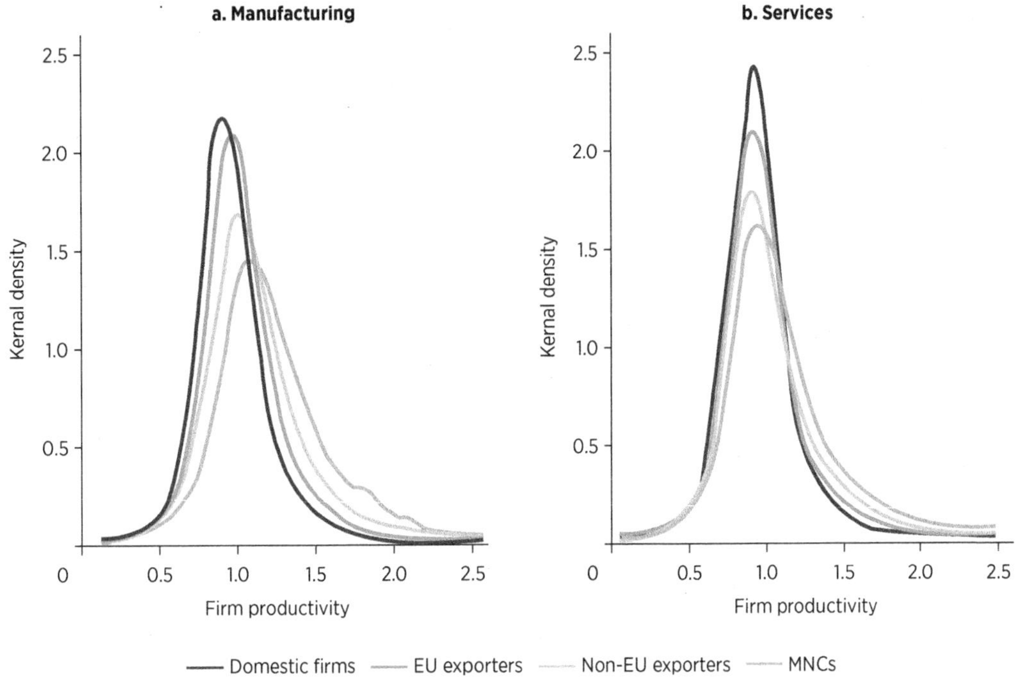

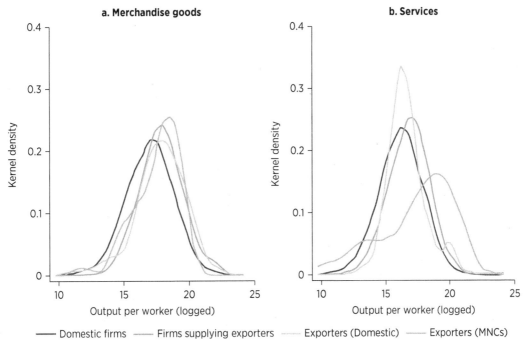

a. Manufacturing
b. Services
Kernal density
2.5
2.0
1.5
1.0
0.5
0
0.5
1.0
1.5
2.0
2.5
Firm productivity
Domestic firms
EU exporters
Non-EU exporters
MNCs

Source: Brakman et al. 2020.
Note: EU = European Union; MNC = multinational corporation

FIGURE 3.5 Productivity distribution of Rwandan goods and services, 2008–17

a. Merchandise goods
b. Services
Kernel density
0.4
0.3
0.2
0.1
0
10
15
20
25
Output per worker (logged)
Domestic firms
Firms supplying exporters
Exporters (Domestic)
Exporters (MNCs)

Source: World Bank calculations; see chapter 11 of this report.
Note: MNC = multinational corporation.

capability (as measured by the number of patent applications), to be larger in size, and to be foreign owned (Heher, Steenbergen, and Thoma 2019).

Strategic alliances rely on the complementary capacities and market knowledge possessed by a domestic firm and an MNC. Alliances are built around general complementarities in firms' interests and capabilities. An MNC may wish to partner with local firms in its target country because those firms have greater knowledge of the domestic market and are better placed to handle the local regulatory environment (de Caldas Lima 2008). An alliance may also lower the MNC's entry risk and capital requirements by allowing it to use the local partners' assets. In certain sectors, full ownership by foreign nationals is prohibited, and thus joint ventures are the only legal way to gain market access. MNCs tend to look for local partners that are generally more profitable, more productive, and larger than the average domestic firm, with high initial export participation and many patents (Jiang et al. 2018).

Direct exporting requires that domestic firms have both the minimum production capabilities and sufficient overseas market knowledge to compete internationally. Pedersen and Petersen (1998) suggest that firms move into the export market by first learning how to confront the international competition in local markets and then gradually expanding their sales overseas. This learning process includes two main components. It first requires that firms acquire the minimum production capabilities to be technologically competitive, meet the necessary quality standards of the sector, and be sufficiently productive to compete internationally (Pedersen and

TABLE 3.1 Firm-level prerequisites across internationalization pathways

Internationalization pathways	Prerequisites
Supplier linkages with international firms	• An international partner (possibly an MNC or domestic exporter) to source local inputs for export-oriented production. • A domestic firm with the ability to produce goods or services that meet the standards required by the partner (possibly verified through international certification) with a reliable and timely supply available at a competitive price (Farole and Winkler 2014; Jordaan, Douw, and Qiang 2020).
Strategic alliances with MNCs	• An MNC that is willing to establish a new affiliation with a local partner and to share part of its technological knowledge. • A domestic firm with proven experience in production for the domestic market, knowledge of local institutional and regulatory mechanisms, and the capacity and willingness to engage with a foreign partner to upgrade and expand its business (de Caldas Lima 2008; Jiang et al. 2018).
Direct exporting	A domestic firm that has the minimum production capabilities (productivity and quality) to compete internationally and sufficient overseas market knowledge (of factors such as consumer characteristics) to tailor products for and supply them to foreign markets (Johanson and Vahlne 1977; Pedersen and Petersen 1998).
Outward foreign direct investment	A domestic firm that meets the minimum scale, productivity, market experience, and financial solvency requirements to afford internationalization via OFDI. Such firms also need the capacity to develop and manage outward expansion and to establish a foreign subsidiary (Brakman et al. 2020; El-Sahli, Gullstrand, and Olofsdotter 2018; Thomas and Narayanan 2017).

Source: World Bank summary of the literature.
Note: MNC = multinational corporation; OFDI = outward foreign direct investment.

Petersen 1998). Second, these firms must learn the details of the overseas markets they wish to enter, such as the business climate, cultural patterns, market structures, and consumer characteristics (Johanson and Vahlne 1977).

OFDI is a pathway to internationalization for only the small number of domestic firms that are sufficiently large and financially solvent to afford to invest abroad. Firms that engage in OFDI are consistently larger, more productive, and more R&D-intensive than firms that do not invest abroad. Larger firm sizes may be necessary to attain the minimum financial solvency to afford this internationalization strategy. Other major requirements include having the capacity to develop and manage outward expansion and to establish a foreign subsidiary (Brakman et al. 2020; El-Sahli, Gullstrand, and Olofsdotter 2018; Thomas and Narayanan 2017).

These internationalization pathways build on each other to enable firms to enter and participate in GVCs. In other words, different internationalization pathways can be important complements. For example, a domestic firm may start as a supplier to a particular MNC, thereby establishing an interfirm relationship in which trust and confidence can develop. This relationship, in turn, may evolve to the point at which the local firm licenses the MNC's technology or the two firms decide to engage in a joint venture (both of which are forms of strategic alliances) (de Caldas Lima 2008). Similarly, a strategic alliance can build up a domestic firm's size, profitability, and organizational capacity, which can help prepare it to engage in OFDI. Finally, the increased exposure to international markets that firms gain through all these pathways makes the firms more likely to export directly.

Global value chain–specific factors

There is also a relationship between a GVC's characteristics and the likely pathways by which firms will enter it. As illustrated in chapter 2, GVCs' characteristics and MNCs' outsourcing or offshoring decisions are interdependent. MNCs balance their level of control, the commitment of proprietary resources, the type and level of risks involved, and the costs and returns of various transaction modes when organizing their global production networks. As a result, various GVC inputs (parts, components, and services) differ in whether they are sourced via arms length trade (direct exports) or contract manufacturing (supplier linkages), coproduced by firms under the MNCs' direct oversight (strategic alliances), or produced in house by the MNCs (OFDI).

These characteristics also shape the likelihood that domestic firms will engage in a certain type of GVC participation. Whereas direct exporting is common across all GVCs, the other three pathways to participation differ significantly in their prevalence. In particular, three main elements help shape which type of participation is dominant in a given GVC: (a) the importance of intangible assets (such as technology, brands, and managerial techniques) in production; (b) the degree to which production inputs are standardized, specialized, or unique; and (c) the ease with which any embodied intellectual property can be effectively codified or protected (such as through licensing, franchising, or patents).

Supplier linkages are more likely to occur in simpler GVCs that rely more on standardized, physical inputs and involve few intangible assets. The inputs sourced by international firms (such as MNCs) in these GVCs are highly standardized and bear little proprietary information. As a result, codifying or protecting any embodied intellectual property within the supply chain is likely unnecessary. MNCs can specify their requirements and receive their inputs through arm's length procurement. A good example of this type of GVC is horticulture (see box 3.1). The GVC's lead firms (large supermarket chains) stipulate the standards for each type of produce (including its expected size and the appropriate use of fertilizers and pesticides in growing it), but this information is nonproprietary. As a result, the lead firms can have many individual suppliers that each deliver some of the produce.

Strategic alliances are more frequent in medium-complexity GVCs in which some intangible assets (such as technologies or brands) influence production. The inputs used by MNCs in these GVCs are often specialized and embody some proprietary information (such as purpose-built machinery or a special way to manage operations). However, MNCs do not mind sharing this intellectual property with their suppliers because they can effectively codify and protect it (such as through licensing agreements, franchising, or patents). One such GVC is tourism (see box 3.2), in which large hotel chains share their brand and management techniques with local partners in return for management contracts.

OFDI takes place most often in high-complexity GVCs in which intangible assets make up a large share of the production process.[5] In these GVCs, all inputs tend to be unique and to embody a high level of proprietary information, and firms may have weak ability to codify or protect this intellectual property. This type of GVC is exemplified by the software industry, in which the source code essentially is the product. This input tends to be unique to each application and very difficult to protect from abuse by suppliers (because they could simply cut and paste lines of code from a program and use them for other applications). In such cases, outsourcing production (to either a supplier or a joint venture) tends to be too risky, and internal expansion through a foreign subsidiary is often the best way to scale up production.

These patterns are largely in line with the internalization theory, the imperfect contracting theory, and the property rights theory (Benito, Petersen, and Welch 2019; Gereffi, Humphrey, and Sturgeon 2005; UNCTAD 2020), as well as with global sectoral data. Table 3.2 considers the relative shares of different internationalization

TABLE 3.2   The importance of internationalization pathways across global value chain archetypes

GVC archetype	Supplier links (Share of contract farming or manufacturing in total sales)	Strategic alliances (Share of joint ventures, franchises, or management contracts in total sales)	OFDI (Ratio of total FDI to total trade per sector)
Commodities	Low	Low	High
Regional processing	Medium	Low	Low
Labor-intensive goods	High	Low	Low
Knowledge-intensive goods	High	High	Medium
Labor-intensive services	Low	High	High
Knowledge-intensive services	Low	Medium	High

Source: World Bank estimates using UNCTAD 2011 for supplier linkages, Kang and Sakai 2000 and UNCTAD 2011 for strategic alliances, and UNCTAD 2020 for OFDI.
Note: Sectoral performance is aggregated into the six GVC archetypes and then ranked into the bottom third ("low"), the middle third ("medium"), and the top third ("high"). FDI = foreign direct investment; GVC = global value chain; OFDI = outward foreign direct investment.

FIGURE 3.6 **Internationalization pathways followed by domestic firms in case studies included in this report**

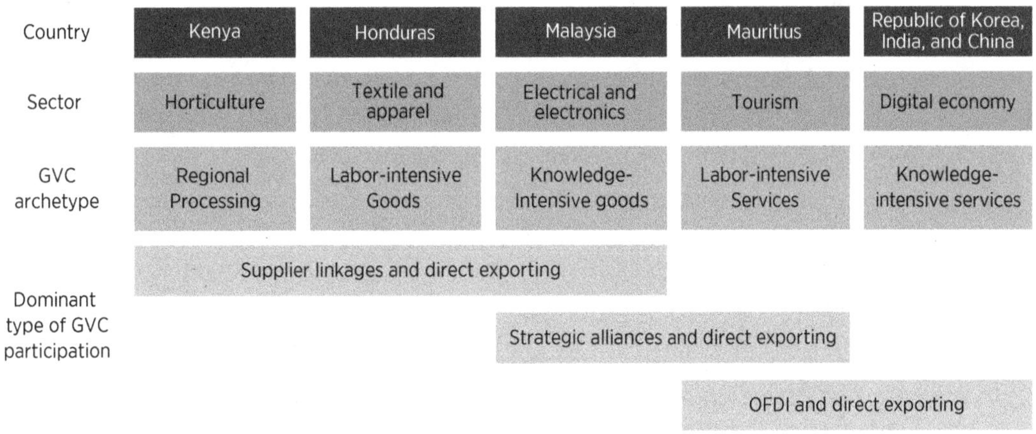

Country	Kenya	Honduras	Malaysia	Mauritius	Republic of Korea, India, and China
Sector	Horticulture	Textile and apparel	Electrical and electronics	Tourism	Digital economy
GVC archetype	Regional Processing	Labor-intensive Goods	Knowledge-Intensive goods	Labor-intensive Services	Knowledge-intensive services

Dominant type of GVC participation	Supplier linkages and direct exporting				
			Strategic alliances and direct exporting		
					OFDI and direct exporting

Source: World Bank elaborations based on chapters 6 to 11 of this report.
Note: GVC = global value chain; OFDI = outward foreign direct investment.

pathways across GVC archetypes using global sectoral data from the United Nations Conference on Trade and Development (UNCTAD 2011, 2020) and Kang and Sakai (2000). These data show that opportunities for internationalization differ across GVC archetypes and that each archetype tends to source its inputs in one or two dominant ways.

Supplier linkages appear most important for labor- and knowledge-intensive goods GVCs, followed by those in regional processing. Strategic alliances are most prevalent in knowledge-intensive goods and labor-intensive services and are also used to a lesser extent in knowledge-intensive services. OFDI is most important for labor- and knowledge-intensive services as well as for commodities.

This report's case studies further illustrate the comparative potential of developing countries' firm internationalization across GVCs. Five qualitative case studies were conducted, each reflecting a different GVC archetype. Each case study finds examples of firms internationalizing through one or more of the three indirect pathways, all combined with direct exporting (figure 3.6). The patterns observed are in line with those described in table 3.2.

- In regional processing GVCs (Kenya, horticulture) and labor-intensive goods GVCs (Honduras, textiles and apparel), firms depend most strongly on supply linkages to internationalize. These GVCs' products have the lowest share of intangible assets and standardized inputs, and thus they are the best suited to arm's length transactions.

- In knowledge-intensive goods GVCs (Malaysia, electronics), firms use both supply linkages and strategic alliances to internationalize. This variety is explained by how electronics supplies range from standardized, low-complexity inputs (such as assembly of consumer goods) to more complicated inputs that use proprietary machinery (such as the production of microchips).

- In labor-intensive services GVCs (Mauritius, tourism), firms have used both strategic alliances and OFDI to internationalize. Export-oriented services tend to be high quality and to rely in large part on specialized management techniques and brand recognition. Such high degrees of intangible assets can be partially supported through strategic alliances (such as management contracts). However, as firms develop their own brands, they increasingly rely on direct outward investment to internationalize.

- In knowledge-intensive services GVCs (Republic of Korea, India, and China; digital economy), firms frequently internationalize using OFDI because their inputs are dominated by intangible assets. In such cases, outsourcing production (to either a supplier or a joint venture) tends to be too risky, and internal expansion through a fully owned foreign subsidiary is often the most feasible way to scale up production.

Global value chain upgrading: A learning process to improve competitiveness

This report's quantitative case study from West Bengal, India, and from Rwanda finds that firms' competitiveness increases as they interact more closely with international firms. The case study combined firm- and transaction-level data sets to obtain information on firms' sectors and ownership, firm-to-firm linkages, and trade.[6] From these data, three types of suppliers to exporters were identified: those that supply local exporters, those that supply MNC exporters, and those that supply both. In addition, the study identified firms that are engaged in joint ventures with MNCs, that are fully foreign owned, or (in the case of West Bengal) that are engaged in OFDI. This information was used in a firm-level regression analysis to see how such types of GVC participation relate to the firms' likelihood of becoming direct exporters (as a proxy for international competitiveness).

Results from both countries (figure 3.7) suggest that all pathways of entry into GVCs raise the probability that a firm will become a direct exporter. The more closely domestic firms interact with international firms, the more likely they will start exporting. Thus, investment-based GVC participation (joint ventures and OFDI) is a stronger predictor of becoming an exporter than supplier linkages. In many cases, domestic firms were also found to engage in more than one pathway to GVC entry (for example, supplying some MNCs while engaged in a joint venture with another MNC). All these observations further illustrate that the most powerful engine of capacity building lies in firm-to-firm interactions (Sutton 2014) and that firms move along the pathways to GVC entry when they are ready in the learning process.

Domestic firms can achieve GVC upgrading by increasing their interactions with MNCs and by learning from them. The pathways to GVC participation described above often rely on domestic firms learning from MNCs through either supplier relationships, partnerships, or investment. However, although foreign firms can stimulate productivity spillovers to domestic firms (Havránek and Irsova 2010), it is important to remember that MNCs are not actively trying to foster technological development among their suppliers or partners. Where technological development and upgrading do occur, domestic firms are often the main instigators, responding to opportunities

FIGURE 3.7 **The comparative impact of different types of global value chain participation on the probability of a firm becoming a direct exporter in select value chains**

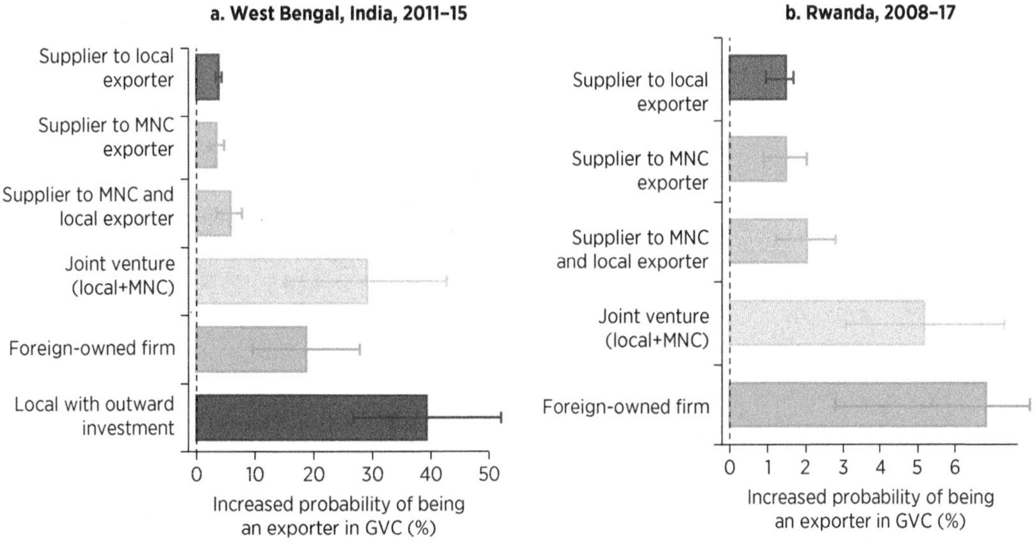

a. West Bengal, India, 2011–15

b. Rwanda, 2008–17

Source: World Bank calculations; see chapter 11 of this report.
Note: West Bengal's foreign firms were identified using Orbis data only, and therefore they represent only a small number of large, publicly listed firms in the region. The ownership of Rwandan firms was determined using data from the national investment promotion agency (the Rwanda Development Board). All regressions include sector and year fixed effects and robust standard errors. Joint ventures are defined as any firms in which a foreign partner has an equity stake between 10 and 50 percent. Foreign-owned firms are firms in which a foreign partner has an equity stake of 51 percent or more. Local firms with outward investment are defined as firms that are headquartered in the country and have one or more foreign subsidiaries. GVC = global value chain; MNC = multinational corporation.

that they identify in the GVCs in which they participate (Jordaan, Douw, and Qiang 2020). Thus, domestic firms need to actively adapt their operations (strategy, structure, and resources) to better suit the production networks set out by MNCs (Calof and Beamish 1995). The rest of this section summarizes the empirical evidence on the impact of GVC participation on firm competitiveness and behavior and presents ways in which firms can achieve GVC upgrading along specific internationalization pathways.

Supplier linkages with international firms: Learning by supplying

Firms can learn about global product standards and foreign markets through supplier linkages. Domestic firms may know how to produce specific goods for their domestic markets, but, if they seek to expand their sales abroad, they might struggle at first for lack of exposure to global markets or product standards. As an interim step, a firm may choose to first supply foreign firms with inputs. MNCs tend to have demanding product requirements for their customers in international markets, so a domestic supplier will need to learn to produce higher-quality goods in line with global product standards (Bastos and Verhoogen 2018; Kugler and Verhoogen 2012). The domestic firm could learn even more about the overseas market by engaging with the initial MNC's network of suppliers and traders. Eventually, the firm could follow the

MNC to other production locations, build on its new knowledge and experience to expand its clients beyond the MNC, or even start exporting directly (Conconi, Sapir, and Zanardi 2010; Dunning 1993; Xiao and Liu 2015).

Empirical evidence supports the positive impact of learning through supplier linkages on overall firm performance. Alfaro-Ureña, Manelici, and Vasquez (2019) use firm-to-firm transaction data to conduct an event study of MNC suppliers in Costa Rica. They find that becoming a supplier to an MNC resulted in strong and persistent improvement in performance, including a 20 percent expansion of sales to non-MNC buyers, a 26 percent expansion in firms' workforces, and a 6–9 percent increase in total factor productivity four years after becoming a supplier (figure 3.8). In a follow-up survey, suppliers noted that their interactions with MNCs helped them learn about new technologies and management practices, expand their production capacity, use more high-skilled workers, and produce higher-quality and more cost-effective products. This improvement, in turn, had a statistically significant impact on the firms' probability of exporting. The survey results confirmed that many firms saw supplying to MNCs as a stepping-stone to direct exporting. Similar evidence comes from a study in the Czech Republic (Javorcik and Spatareanu 2009) as well as surveys of MNCs in which multinationals reported that between 35 and 50 percent of their suppliers had increased their technological competence because of continued engagement through supplier linkages (Ivarsson and Alvstam 2005, 2011).

MNC linkages can also expand the types and complexity of products made by local suppliers. Javorcik, Lo Turco, and Maggioni (2018), for example, find that Turkish firms in sectors and regions more likely to supply foreign affiliates gradually began

FIGURE 3.8 Domestic firms in Costa Rica increase their scale and productivity after starting to supply multinational corporations

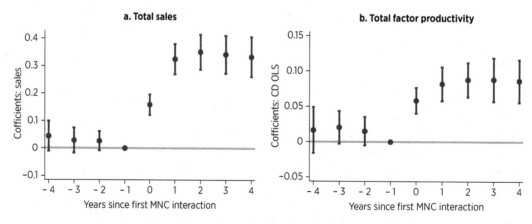

Source: Alfaro-Ureña, Manelici, and Vasquez 2019.
Note: This figure presents the results of an event study in Costa Rica that compared suppliers to MNCs with other domestic firms. Panel a shows normalized firm-level sales on the y axis; panel b shows normalized firm TFP on the y axis estimated using a Cobb-Douglas ordinary least squares (CD OLS) production function. In both cases, MNC suppliers initially had sales and productivity comparable with other domestic firms. However, once these firms started interacting with MNCs, both their sales and their TFP increased significantly compared with the domestic firms. MNC = multinational corporation; TFP = total factor productivity.

producing more complex products (as defined by Hidalgo and Hausmann's [2009] product complexity index). An increase in the presence of MNCs in the Polish automotive sector also resulted in domestic suppliers developing new products (Gentile-Lüdecke and Giroud 2012).

However, not all firms manage to enhance their productivity or internationalize via MNC supply linkages. For example, firm-level studies in China, India, and Vietnam find a clear, positive connection between MNC supplier linkages and domestic firm performance in China, but that the connection was much weaker for Indian and Vietnamese firms (UNIDO 2018). Another study finds that supplier linkages led to firm upgrading in fewer than 20 percent of the cases examined (Pipkin and Fuentes 2017).

The absorptive capacity of local suppliers is key to their learning and upgrading process. To realize spillovers, domestic firms must possess sufficient capacity to absorb technologies and other knowledge from their foreign-owned client firms. A study of domestic firms in 122 developing countries finds that only the more economically dynamic domestic firms—as measured by relative employment growth—experienced positive backward spillovers (World Bank 2018). Other domestic firm characteristics that are found to have a positive effect on knowledge spillovers to suppliers include the firms' size, their level of human capital, whether they have experience producing for international markets, and whether they are involved in R&D activities (Jordaan, Douw, and Qiang 2020).

The intensity of the MNC-supplier relationship is also critical to whether linkages stimulate spillovers and upgrading. Alcacer and Oxley (2014) find that who a firm supplies to and what kind of involvement the firm has also matter. Learning by supplying is positively related to both the duration and the extent of supply activities. This finding is supported by Gentile-Lüdecke and Giroud (2012), who note that only firms that were actively facilitating knowledge exchanges with their MNC clients experienced production improvements and created new products, services, or technologies. Cajal Grossi, Macchiavello, and Noguera (2019) set out this effect more explicitly for the Bangladeshi garment industry. They compare *spot procurement*, in which MNCs pay for each order without any explicit or implicit agreement regarding future trade, with *relational sourcing*, in which MNCs use an ongoing relationship to provide incentives to suppliers to undertake noncontractible actions such as guaranteeing reliable and on-time delivery. They find that, on average, relational suppliers receive approximately 10 percent greater markups than do spot suppliers. Relational suppliers use these higher markups to invest more in their products and production processes, which helps them upgrade their firms.

This report's quantitative case study (see chapter 11) finds similar evidence for the importance of relational MNC-supplier linkages. In Rwanda, MNC-supplier linkages had the highest probability of helping firms begin producing for international markets and exporting directly in GVCs with higher complexity. In these GVCs, including textiles and chemicals, MNCs are more likely to pursue relational ties with their suppliers, providing the suppliers with opportunities to produce to higher product standards. In contrast, firms that supplied MNCs with inputs that did not require close supplier relationships (such as coffee and tea or agriprocessing) were less likely to internationalize as a result of their supplier linkages. And, in West Bengal, the effect of MNC-supplier linkages on firms' probability of internationalizing was smallest in sectors in which many small firms sell individual inputs to MNCs (such as leather, textiles, and apparel). In contrast, in the food product sector, in which a small number of firms supply a range of inputs to specific MNCs, firms had a higher probability of starting to produce for international markets and export directly.

To foster technological development, firms may want to underscore the three L's: labeling, linking, and learning (UNIDO 2002):

1. *Labeling* refers to the process of exposing domestic firms to the product standards and certifications that MNCs and governments use to ensure compliance with global product requirements. These codified market criteria support the upgrading of local suppliers and are a key tool for improving productivity.

2. *Linking* relates to the longevity and strength of the relational tie between a domestic firm and an MNC's supply network, which affects the intensity of the spillover between them (Manyati 2014). Domestic firms should aim to use the client MNC's production network to connect with outsiders to acquire needed technologies and skills. It is important for domestic firms to go beyond arm's length transactions (such as spot procurement) and develop lasting relationships that build trust and interbusiness commitment so as to facilitate steady knowledge transfers between the firms.

3. *Learning* captures the process by which firms are able to master newly required processes and technologies. The acquisition, accumulation, and appropriation of tacit and explicit knowledge are an integral part of firm upgrading through supply linkages (Abrol and Gupta 2014; Manyati 2014).

Box 3.1 provides an example from this report's qualitative case study of Kenya's horticulture firms of how these firms applied the three L's to help themselves internationalize and upgrade.

Strategic alliances with multinational corporations

Domestic firms can access essential foreign knowledge, technology, and markets through strategic alliances with MNCs. Some domestic firms lack access to specific types of technology or intellectual property (such as production methods, international brands, or managerial techniques) that they would need to competitively produce for an international market. In such cases, establishing a strategic alliance with an MNC will allow the domestic firm to quickly obtain the knowledge and expertise it lacks. Strategic alliances can take various forms; they include any interbusiness arrangement in which there is some sharing of intangible assets (such as intellectual property or management practices) or equity participation (investment) (UNCTAD 2002). The new alliance may start exporting immediately, or the domestic firm's parent company may use the newly acquired technology to gradually expand its export processes (de Caldas Lima 2008).

Strategic alliances can improve domestic firms' productivity and technology upgrading. Jiang et al. (2018) use administrative data to analyze the firm-level effects of all joint ventures taking place in China from 1998 to 2007—roughly a quarter of all international joint ventures in the world. They find that joint ventures lead

BOX 3.1 **How the three L's (labeling, linking, and learning) helped Kenya's horticulture firms internationalize**

About 50 percent of Kenyan horticulture firms indicate that they became exporters after first supplying a multinational corporation (MNC) in-country (Kaiser Associates Economic Development Partners 2014). One important reason for this trend is that both MNCs and these domestic firms managed to stimulate spillovers by fostering the three L's: labeling, linking, and learning (Krishnan and Foster 2017).

Labeling. Pietrobelli and Rabellotti (2011) find that, in general, supplying to MNCs is an important impetus for domestic firms to innovate and enter global value chains because doing so forces them to adhere to more complex standards and requirements to access international markets. This dynamic was also important in Kenya (Kaiser Associates Economic Development Partners 2014).

Linking. In Kenya, local suppliers were able to leverage their foreign direct investment relationships to access new customers (often through referrals) or new export markets. Labor market linkages further helped diffuse new skills, expertise, and business networks across the sector. Individual employees who have worked for foreign companies in-country have started new operations or switched to working with local firms. Kenya's survey results highlight that, on average, more than 80 percent of skilled staff at MNC affiliates (such as managers, supervisors, and those in technical positions) are locals, reflecting the long tradition and international exposure of the country's horticulture sector. Furthermore, about 10 percent of all employees at Kenyan horticulture firms have previous experience in foreign operations. An interviewee further observed that "product or process improvements trickle down as farmers observe what their neighbors are doing."

Learning. Survey results have shown that 100 percent of Kenya's foreign-owned agricultural investors and 88 percent of the country's foreign-owned suppliers provided some level of assistance to local firms. Such assistance includes agricultural inputs and materials, advance payments and access to finance, worker training, and support for quality assurance and health, safety, and environmental standards. This assistance led to improved production techniques, the use of higher-quality inputs, and improved operational processes (such as postharvest handling, transportation, and storage) (Kaiser Associates Economic Development Partners 2014).

Source: Chapter 6 of this report.

to substantial technology transfers, which increase total factor productivity, patent applications, and the introduction of new products. Firms that participated in these ventures also tended to become larger than other local firms and to have higher export shares. These positive externalities appear to be about twice as large as any demonstration-based productivity spillovers domestic firms experience by learning from foreign-owned firms operating in the same industry (Jiang et al. 2018). Bai et al. (2019) focus on the Chinese auto industry and find that firms that engage in joint ventures see sharper increases in both sales value and sales quantity than domestic firms and that the gaps widen over time (figure 3.9).

Domestic firms that are acquired by foreign investors become more competitive and are more likely to internationalize. Ragoussis (2020) compares the performance of firms that were acquired by MNCs with that of domestically owned firms

FIGURE 3.9 **The performance of joint ventures and domestic firms in the Chinese auto industry**

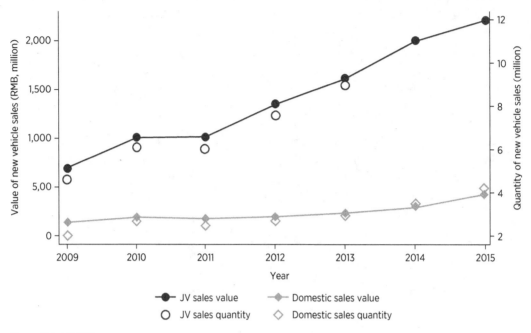

Source: Bai et al. 2019.
Note: JV = joint venture; RMB = renminbi.

in six developing countries—China, Côte d'Ivoire, Indonesia, Moldova, Serbia, and Vietnam. He finds that firms acquired by MNCs not only performed better than the average domestic firm at the time of the acquisition but also improved their performance after acquisition faster than did local firms. Employment also tended to grow faster in newly acquired firms than in domestic firms with similar characteristics, at approximately 4.0 percent versus 1.5 percent after two years, and acquired firms paid wages 40–50 percent higher than did other domestic firms. In addition, foreign acquisition may help domestic firms internationalize because such firms are 70–100 percent more likely to begin exporting over their first five years of operation than are other domestic firms (figure 3.10, panel a). Such firms were also considerably more likely to innovate and to diversify their products (figure 3.10, panel b).

Equity-type alliances, such as joint ventures and mergers and acquisitions, can be transformational, but their effects depend strongly on the firms in question possessing complementary capabilities. Such an alliance results in a new enterprise in which each party contributes assets, participates in equity, and shares risk. Because both parties are willing to share their intangible assets, this type of strategic alliance is often the most transformational. For example, Havránek and Irsova (2012) conduct a large meta-analysis of FDI spillovers, finding that the largest firm-level productivity gains came from joint ventures between MNCs and domestic firms. However, these alliances are difficult to establish because the two firms must first have useful complementarities in their interests and capabilities. Local firms often provide local market intelligence, production facilities, and possibly favorable relationships with the government, especially in highly regulated sectors (Balsvik and Haller 2010; Curran, Lv,

FIGURE 3.10 **Firms are more likely to export and to diversify their products after acquisition by foreign investors**

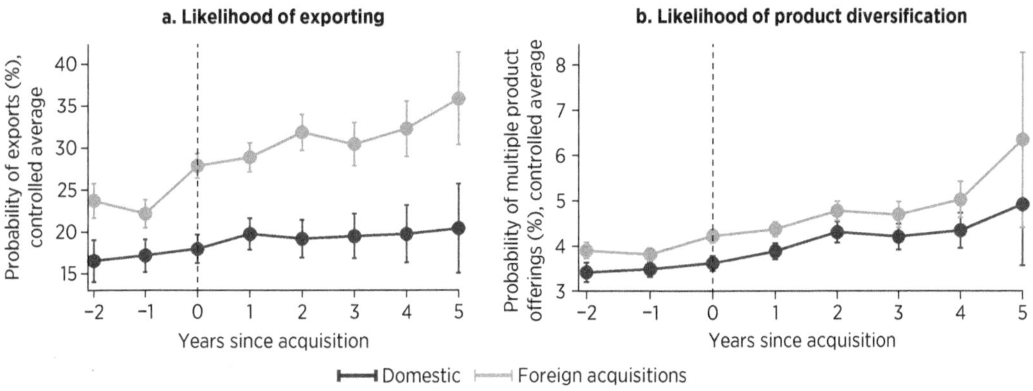

a. Likelihood of exporting

b. Likelihood of product diversification

■—■ Domestic   ├———┤ Foreign acquisitions

Source: Ragoussis 2020.

and Spigarelli 2017; Davies, Desbordes, and Ray 2018). To leverage such qualities, foreign investors tend to cherry-pick the more successful, productive, and profitable domestic firms that suit their plans (Almeida 2007; Balsvik and Haller 2010; Bertrand et al. 2012; Guadalupe, Kuzmina, and Thomas 2012). These requirements mean that domestic firms must clear a high bar of entry to engage in such structural alliances.

Evidence from this report's Rwanda case study also suggests that equity-type alliances benefit foreign investors through their local partners' knowledge of local languages and the domestic regulatory environment. Two sectors stood out in Rwanda for their high shares of joint ventures: agriprocessing and professional services. In both sectors, Rwandan firms offer key complementarities to foreign firms—either the ability to engage with suppliers who speak only the local language (agriprocessing) or the ability to manage a complex regulatory environment (professional services). In both cases, engagement in FDI-type alliances was found to be an important predictor of becoming a producer and exporter for international markets (see chapter 11 of this report).

Nonequity mode (NEM) alliances (licensing, franchising, and management contracts)[7] provide another way for domestic firms to obtain new technologies, but they are often more restricted in scope or more highly regulated than other strategic alliances. NEM arrangements foster knowledge and technology transfers to domestic companies through contractual relationships with foreign firms in return for fees or profit sharing. Although NEMs can be both financially rewarding and educational for both parties, they are not without risk or effort. In many cases, domestic firms are required to invest their own funds in acquiring new machinery, redesigning their production processes, and modifying their working conditions as part of the contractual arrangement, alongside any up-front fees or training costs and ongoing royalties (UNCTAD 2011). Domestic firms would only consider such contracts if they saw them as opportunities for learning, in the hope that eventually local capacity could be built up and the use of MNC-specific technology, branding, or standards could be partially or totally phased out (de Caldas Lima 2008). However, firms often face strict contracts meant to prevent them from using such information outside the NEM framework, whether by shifting away from the brand or by applying the concepts to the parent company's other affiliate firms.

MNCs, though not risking capital in NEM relationships, still take a risk when establishing them because the knowledge and proprietary rights the MNCs transfer to their partners are the very foundation of their competitive advantage. An untrustworthy partner could cause business or reputational damage to the MNC or become a competitor in the future. As a result, NEMs have been restricted in scope, especially for newly established alliances. This characteristic can limit their usefulness for teaching the domestic firm (de Caldas Lima 2008).

To maintain a strategic alliance, domestic firms should focus on increasing their relevance and power within it. In many cases, domestic firms are more dependent on the alliance than the MNCs they work with, which can erode the benefits of the alliance over time. For that reason, domestic firms must develop strengths that can be used to keep and, over time, increase their relevance within a strategic alliance. This effort requires a deliberate strategy to build power, a continuing assessment of their strengths and weaknesses in the alliance's balance of power (including over such determinants as technology, brand ownership, or local relationships), and proactively sustaining and increasing their strength. De Caldas Lima (2008) notes four examples of sources of power that domestic firms can nurture and that may not easily be challenged by the foreign partner, at least in the short term:

1. Overall knowledge of the domestic business environment and relationships with government
2. Ownership of local brands that can command recognition and consumer preference (see box 3.2)
3. Control over distribution and technical and marketing assistance to dealers and customers
4. Proprietary assets that allow the domestic firm to control inputs that are needed by the strategic alliance

Outward foreign direct investment

Firms with sufficient capital may choose to invest abroad directly to upgrade their products or expand their market access. They often seek to directly acquire cutting-edge foreign technology or R&D facilities to help the firm's outward expansion (Amann and Virmani 2015; Child and Rodrigues 2005; Pedersen and Petersen 1998). Alternatively, they may choose to establish a subsidiary in a foreign country to obtain direct knowledge of foreign markets and thus to facilitate or accelerate the firm's ability to access and compete in the new markets (Ahmad, Draz, and Yang 2016; Amann and Virmani 2015; Pedersen and Petersen 1998).

Among India's manufacturing firms, for example, OFDI is one of the strongest predictors that a firm will become an exporter (Thomas and Narayanan 2017). Similarly, Ahmad, Draz, and Yang (2016) find that firms in Southeast Asia used OFDI to leapfrog into exports. From 1981 to 2013, a 1 percent increase in OFDI led to a US$750 million

BOX 3.2 **Brand development helped domestic tourism firms in Mauritius reach new export markets**

To reach new export markets (foreign tourists), tourism firms in Mauritius have increasingly focused on branding. A strong global brand and marketing strategy are seen as essential to competing for customers who have a variety of options because many of them tend to decide on the basis of brand recognition.

A large domestic hotel group in Mauritius engaged in a strategic alliance with multinational corporations (MNCs) to leverage their brands. The group acknowledged the increased importance of branding but concluded that it did not possess the necessary capital, human resources, and expertise to build its own brand and manage it successfully. Instead, it chose to partner and learn from existing brands under varying arrangements depending on each MNC's preferences. In some cases, the MNC acquired a minority interest in the hotel; in others, a pure management contract was used. The domestic group preferred the acquisition option because it better aligned with the firms' interests. Under a pure management contract, the MNC might focus more on developing its own brand than on acting in the firms' joint interests.

Partnering with MNCs has helped the hotel group learn about brand management and increase its reach among new foreign tourists. With the help of the MNCs, the domestic hotel group is developing an online travel agency strategy and extending its digital marketing. According to an executive, working with the MNCs has brought multiple benefits. The domestic firms have learned about the MNCs' brands, how the MNCs organize themselves, and their sales and marketing strategies. They also learned about the MNCs' guest-centric culture and were provided with useful technology, including a customer-response app.

Working with the MNCs also enabled the domestic hotel group to attract different types of customers and to learn about distribution channels other than tour operators. For example, one of the partner brands was particularly savvy at attracting high–net worth Chinese customers, whereas the hotel group had previously attracted mainly middle-class customers. Ultimately, this hotel group aims to create its own brand—partnering with MNCs is just one step along the way.

Source: Chapter 9 of this report.

rise in exports for the Philippines, a US$72 million rise for Singapore, a US$41 million rise for Thailand, and a US$31 million rise for Malaysia.

OFDI serves as a learning mechanism, either as a springboard or as a stepping-stone depending on the type of country it targets (Perea and Stephenson 2018). In high-income markets, firms from developing countries use OFDI as a springboard to acquire new capabilities (Luo and Tung 2007), in contrast to developed-country firms, which generally exploit existing capabilities when investing in foreign countries. For example, Chen, Li, and Shapiro (2012) examine OFDI from 20 developing countries from 2000 to 2008 and find that OFDI from developing countries into high-income countries is particularly R&D-oriented given that these ventures increase both R&D employment and R&D expenditure in host economies.

However, when firms from developing countries target other *developing* markets, OFDI can be used in a stepping-stone internationalization strategy in which firms first enter smaller, closer, and more similar economies (Arita 2013). This strategy works in part because developing-country firms may have an institutional advantage in other developing countries, given their experience operating in uncertain and untrustworthy investment climates (Cuervo-Cazurra and Genc 2008).

Firms that engage in OFDI can do so via various modalities, each with its own advantages and disadvantages. In general, firms choose among three main modalities: they can establish a fully new operation in the host country (greenfield investment), engage in a new partnership with an existing company (a joint venture), or acquire an existing firm (through a merger or acquisition) in the host country (figure 3.11).

Greenfield investment has the advantage that parent firms retain full control of the investment process, including over the subsidiary's location and operational scale. It also allows firms to maintain tight oversight of their management techniques, technology, and patents (that is, it minimizes the risk of proprietary information leaking to competitors). However, there is significant cost and risk to setting up operations in a foreign country without knowing the host country's culture, business environment, and institutional setting (Buckley and Ghauri 2004; Cooke 2013; de Caldas Lima 2008). This type of investment also exposes the parent firm to the most intense competition because it will have to acquire market share from other companies; such projects are thus the least likely to survive the early stage. The experience of firms

FIGURE 3.11 Advantages and disadvantages of different outward foreign direct investment modalities

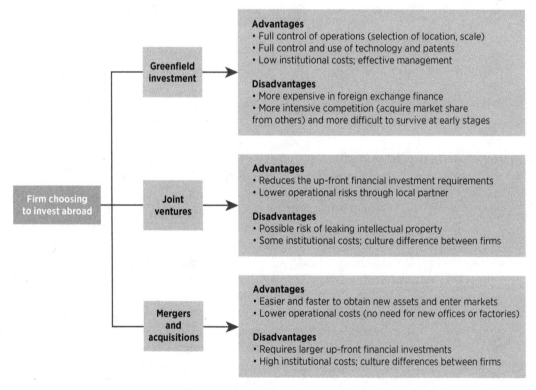

Source: World Bank elaborations on de Caldas Lima 2008 and Xiao and Liu 2015.

BOX 3.3 **Republic of Korea: Internationalization through greenfield outward foreign direct investment**

The Republic of Korea provides an appealing example of how emerging market economies can use outward foreign direct investment (OFDI) to upgrade—in Korea's case, from a clothing exporter to a leading player in high-tech products such as electronics and semiconductors. Prompted by rising labor costs, a small domestic market, and aspirations to move up the value chain, Korean firms began to expand their operations overseas in the 1970s. They proactively engaged in strategic, asset-seeking OFDI by setting up research centers in advanced economies to acquire cutting-edge technology.

With strong encouragement from the Korean government through incentives and investment promotion, Korean firms started investing heavily abroad. From 1980 to 2016, the country's large domestic champions invested more than US$78 billion in foreign projects, and by 2016 the number of companies in the United States affiliated with Korean firms grew to exceed 13,000. These companies accounted for more than 20 percent of Korea's worldwide OFDI. Samsung Electronics, one of the most recognized Korean electronics brands, initially invested in the United States to take advantage of the development of dynamic random-access memory, a type of digital memory used in many electronic devices. Once Samsung acquired this technology, it established production plants in low-cost countries to exploit their cost advantage (Kim, Driffield, and Love 2018). OFDI thus played an increasingly important role in driving Korea's industry upgrading (Bhaumik, Driffield, and Zhou 2016; Driffield and Love 2003).

Note: See chapter 10 of this report for more details on how outward investment, human capital, and research and development helped the development of the digital economy in Korea, India, and China.

from Korea provides a good example of how firms in emerging market economies can use greenfield OFDI to internationalize (box 3.3).

A joint venture allows a firm to partner with a local company in the host country, reducing the firm's up-front cash input and overall operational risk. However, this arrangement does involve additional risks, including unauthorized use or theft of intellectual property by the host-country firm's parent company (Xiao and Liu 2015). Joint ventures also may result in management friction because firms may struggle to bring together two distinct office cultures (Barkema and Vermeulen 1998; de Caldas Lima 2008; Larimo 2003).

Mergers and acquisitions have the advantage of allowing firms to quickly obtain new assets and enter new markets. They also have lower operational costs than greenfield investment because there is less need to construct new offices or factories (which the foreign company will already have). However, mergers and acquisitions come with their own particular cost: the large up-front financial investment to acquire a foreign firm. They also come with increased risk of management friction if the two firms have different office cultures (Barkema and Vermeulen 1998; Larimo 2003) This modality was the least commonly used among Chinese firms engaged in OFDI; only 16 percent of firms used it (Xiao and Liu 2015).

The case of Lenovo shows how firms can develop using joint ventures or acquisitions. Lenovo relied on acquiring foreign firms and entering into joint ventures with foreign firms to gain access to strategic assets such as proprietary technology, globally recognized brand names, and established customer networks and sales channels (see box 3.4).

BOX 3.4 Lenovo: Internationalization through joint ventures and acquisition

Since its inception in 1984, Lenovo has grown into one of the world's major information and communication technology manufacturing players. It started producing personal computers (PCs) in 1991, and, through collaborations with well-established software and hardware firms such as Microsoft and Intel, it grew into China's leading PC maker (as measured by number of PCs shipped) in 1996 and attained 17.9 percent of China's PC market. In 1999, it became the largest PC seller in the Asia-Pacific region (excluding Japan); however, it was still focused exclusively on the domestic market.

In 2004, Lenovo began its first successful internationalization effort when it acquired IBM's PC division. Lenovo had been feeling pressure to internationalize because of potential threats in its home market, particularly since China's accession to the World Trade Organization in 2001, and it had tried to sell its PCs outside of China without success. In late 2004, the company decided to acquire IBM's PC division, which tripled its worldwide share in the PC market and made it the third-largest PC maker in the world. Importantly, Lenovo acquired IBM's successful "Think" brand and gained access to a huge distribution network spanning 150 countries. As part of the transaction, IBM and Lenovo entered a strategic alliance that specified IBM as the preferred provider of leasing, financing, and after-sales services for Lenovo products. In return, IBM granted Lenovo exclusive access to its distribution network; in other words, it agreed to supply Lenovo PCs exclusively throughout its boundary-crossing network of 150 countries and 30,000 employees. Acquiring IBM's PC division gave Lenovo a head start at positioning itself globally, both in establishing a global distribution network and in gaining rapid brand awareness.

From 2005 to 2015, Lenovo chose repeatedly to grow via acquisitions, joint ventures, and alliances. This growth enabled it to become the largest PC maker in the world and to achieve a global market share of nearly 17 percent. In 2011, it formed a strategic alliance and joint venture with the Japanese electronics giant NEC. Through the partnership, NEC intended to benefit from Lenovo's considerable buying power and efficient global supply chain and to greatly expand its product lines and market access. Lenovo, for its part, gained extended access to Japan's highly isolated PC market. As part of the strategic alliance, NEC and Lenovo founded a joint venture called NEC Lenovo Japan Group in which Lenovo holds a majority stake of 51 percent. In the same year, Lenovo acquired the German PC maker Medion with the aim of rebalancing its business and reducing its overreliance on its home market. The acquisition united Medion's expertise in marketing, sales, service, and retail activities with Lenovo's manufacturing and supply chain capabilities.

After a successful internationalization process, Lenovo now designs, develops, manufactures, and sells PCs, tablet computers, smartphones, workstations, servers, electronic storage devices, information technology management software, and smart televisions; and it remains the world's largest PC vendor by unit sales.

Source: Adapted from Schmid and Polat 2018.
Note: See chapter 10 of this report for more details on how outward investment and research and development helped the development of the digital economy in the Republic of Korea, India, and China.

This chapter illustrates the various ways in which firms participate in GVCs, explores which firms manage to internationalize, and discusses the effect GVC participation has on firm learning and competitiveness. It finds that MNCs are critical to helping firms in developing countries access GVCs, exposing these firms to more advanced technologies and production processes (which may foster technological upgrading), and ultimately helping encourage them to produce and sell internationally. Four pathways to internationalization stand out: supply linkages with international firms, strategic alliances between domestic firms and MNCs, direct exporting, and OFDI. However, these paths do not present themselves equally to all firms. Firms' capability to produce according to MNCs' production specifications, to provide complementary capabilities and market knowledge to MNCs, and to amass enough capital to afford investing abroad all vary considerably. In addition, firms' internationalization pathways are related to the type of GVC inputs they produce: the importance of intangible assets in their GVC's production, the degree to which these production inputs are standardized, and the ability of the GVC's parent firms to effectively codify or protect intellectual property all affect the likelihood of a firm engaging in a particular pathway.

Finally, this chapter illustrates the impact that GVC participation can have on upgrading. Participating in a GVC is a learning process by which firms can develop production capabilities and acquire foreign market knowledge. This knowledge, in turn, can help improve firms' ability to produce more, or more complex, products. In addition, it may help firms raise their total sales, exports, and productivity. To make the most of GVC-related opportunities, domestic firms must constantly adapt their operations (their strategy, structure, and resources) to better suit global production networks. For supplier linkages, firms should focus on the three L's: labeling, linking, and learning. For strategic alliances, they should absorb the technical knowledge within the alliance and use it to their own competitive advantage. In OFDI, the firms themselves become MNCs and must develop their own GVC strategies (as described in chapter 2). In many cases, these pathways to internationalization are complementary, and firms often use multiple strategies to increase their competitiveness in the international market. A powerful example of this last point comes from Zhongxing Telecom Equipment, a Chinese firm that started as a supplier, increasingly engaged in strategic alliances with MNCs, and finally used OFDI to acquire cutting-edge technology. Through this process, it grew from a medium-size domestic Chinese firm into one of the largest telecommunications equipment providers in the world (see box 3.5).

BOX 3.5 **Zhongxing Telecom Equipment's internationalization and upgrading journey**

Zhongxing Telecom Equipment (ZTE) Corporation is a telecommunications equipment and network solutions provider. Established in 1985, ZTE's product range has expanded over time to include virtually every sector of the wireline, wireless, terminal, and service markets.

From 1995 to 2004, ZTE served other developing countries as a telecommunications equipment supplier, and it used those experiences to learn and grow. A relative latecomer to the telecommunications market, it faced fierce competition from established multinational vendors in China. As a result, ZTE found that overseas markets (especially developing countries) were more lucrative places to sell its products and services. By successfully exploiting its relatively low costs, the company could

Continued on next page ›

BOX 3.5 Zhongxing Telecom Equipment's internationalization and upgrading journey *(continued)*

quickly meet the demand for telecommunications equipment in several developing countries and replicate its business model in others. ZTE's share of overseas revenue in its total revenue rose from 4 percent in 2001 to 22 percent in 2004. The firm's market share in Africa expanded especially rapidly: after winning a contract to build a mobile phone network in Algeria in 2004, ZTE struck similar deals in Angola, Ethiopia, Ghana, Lesotho, and Tunisia.

In the following years, ZTE began to target high-income markets and set up research and development (R&D) centers and strategic alliances as springboards to obtain cutting-edge technological knowledge. Having officially declared 2005 its "internationalization year," ZTE set up 15 branches offering marketing, technological support, service, and maintenance in Europe that year. It also began to dedicate more than a third of its workforce and at least 10 percent of its resources to R&D, and it created 18 overseas R&D centers, including 5 in the United States and 2 in Europe. ZTE also invested significantly in training local staff and forging links with local academic and research institutions in the countries where it operated. In 2013, it also established cross-licensing agreements with various other telecommunications firms, which allowed ZTE to use other companies' technologies and bandwidth in return for sharing some of its licensed technology.

Along its internationalization path from being a supplier to engaging in strategic alliances and outward foreign direct investment, ZTE managed to become a global leader in the telecommunications equipment manufacturing industry. In 2011 and 2012, ZTE was ranked first in international patent applications by the World Intellectual Property Organization. ZTE managed to both grow its overseas market (which accounted for 55.7 percent of its income in 2011) and, at the same time, gain significant market share in the Chinese market. In 2011, ZTE replaced Apple as the world's fourth-largest handset vendor, and, in 2013, it became the fifth-largest smartphone company in the world, a position it maintains to this day. In addition, ZTE is currently the largest provider of optical networks (such as 5G) in the world.

Source: Adapted from Baskaran 2017 and OECD 2008.
Note: See chapter 10 of this report for more details on how outward investment, human capital, and R&D helped the development of the digital economy in the Republic of Korea, India, and China.

Notes

1. For example, Slaughter (2013) finds that the typical US MNC buys more than US$3 billion in inputs from more than 6,000 US small and medium enterprises—about 25 percent of all inputs each MNC purchases.
2. Although direct exporting is an important way for domestic firms to internationalize, not all types of direct exporting constitute GVC participation (for example, cross-border trade of simple crafts is not GVC-based trade).
3. Whether this employment is formal or informal depends on the skill intensity of the firms' specific sectors.
4. The literature agrees that internationalized firms are generally more productive in both the manufacturing and service sectors. Manufacturing firms that engage in FDI are also more productive than those that merely export (Helpman, Melitz, and Yeaple 2004). However, there is ongoing discussion over whether this distribution also holds for the service sector. Services exhibit relatively high intangible requirements for entry (such as social capital, information, and trust). The most productive firms are able to absorb these intangible costs remotely and may thus directly export (Bhattacharya, Patnaik, and Shah 2012; Foster-McGregor, Isaksson, and Kaulich 2015; Wagner 2014).

5. This analysis of OFDI focuses on internationalizing firms from developing countries because MNCs from developed countries have different strategies (described in chapter 2).

6. For the Rwanda case study, this classification was based on national data sets only (taxpayer registration, corporate tax data, value added tax data, and customs declarations, together with the national investment promotion agency's information on firm ownership). For the case study on West Bengal, India, national data sets (taxpayer registration and value added tax declarations) were combined with firm ownership data from the data collection company Bureau van Dijk's global Orbis firm database.

7. Licensing is a contractual relationship in which an international firm grants a host-country firm the right to use intellectual property (such as copyrights, trademarks, patents, branding, industrial design rights, or trade secrets) in exchange for payment (royalties). Franchising permits a franchisee to run a business modeled on the systems developed by the franchisor in exchange for an initial fee or a markup on goods (that is, a training fee or royalties). Management contracts provide operational control of an asset to an international firm, which manages the asset in return for a fee. The management provided often entails the technical operation of a production facility, the management of personnel, accounting, marketing services, or training (de Caldas Lima 2008; UNCTAD 2011).

References

Abrol, Dinesh, and Ankush Gupta. 2014. "Understanding the Diffusion Modes of Grassroots Innovations in India: A Study of Honey Bee Network Supported Innovators." *African Journal of Science, Technology, Innovation and Development* 6 (6): 541–52.

Agostino, M., A. Giunta, D. Scalera, and F. Trivieri. 2015. "Italian Firms in Global Value Chains: Updating our Knowledge." In *Global Value Chains, Trade Networks and Firm Performance: International Evidence and the Italian Case*, edited by Stefano Manzocchi and Gianmarco I. P. Ottaviano. Serra.

Ahmad, F., M. U. Draz, and S. C. Yang. 2016. "A Novel Study on OFDI and Home Country Exports: Implications for the ASEAN Region." *Journal of Chinese Economic and Foreign Trade Studies* 9 (2): 131–45.

Alcacer, J., and J. Oxley. 2014. "Learning by Supplying." *Strategic Management Journal* 35 (2): 204–23.

Alfaro-Ureña, A., I. Manelici, and J. P. Vasquez. 2019. "The Effects of Joining Multinational Supply Chains: New Evidence from Firm-to-Firm Linkages." Working Paper.

Almeida, Rita. 2007. "The Labor Market Effects of Foreign-Owned Firms." *Journal of International Economics* 72 (1): 75–96.

Amann, E., and S. Virmani. 2015. "Foreign Direct Investment and Reverse Technology Spillovers: The Effect on Total Factor Productivity." *OECD Journal: Economic Studies* 2014: 129–53.

Antràs, P. 2020. "Conceptual Aspects of Global Value Chains." Background paper, *World Development Report 2020: Trading for Development in the Age of Global Value Chains*, World Bank, Washington, DC.

Arita, S. 2013. "Do Emerging Multinational Enterprises Possess South-South FDI Advantages?" *International Journal of Emerging Markets* 8 (4): 329–53.

Atkin, David, Azam Chaudhry, Shamyla Chaudry, Amit K. Khandelwal, and Eric Verhoogen. 2017. "Organizational Barriers to Technology Adoption: Evidence from Soccer-Ball Producers in Pakistan." *Quarterly Journal of Economics* 132 (3): 1101–64.

Bai, J., P. Barwick, S. Cao, and S. Li. 2019. "Quid Pro Quo, Knowledge Spillover and Industrial Quality Upgrading." CID Working Paper 368, Center for International Development, Harvard University, Cambridge, MA.

Balié, Jean, Davide Del Prete, Emiliano Magrini, Pierluigi Montalbano, and Silvia Nenci. 2017. "Agriculture and Food Global Value Chains in Sub-Saharan Africa: Does Bilateral Trade Policy Impact on Backward and Forward Participation?" Working Paper 4/17, Sapienza University of Rome, DISS.

Balsvik, Ragnhild, and Stefanie A. Haller. 2010. "Picking 'Lemons' or Picking 'Cherries'? Domestic and Foreign Acquisitions in Norwegian Manufacturing." *Scandinavian Journal of Economics* 112 (2): 361–87.

Barkema, H. G., and F. Vermeulen. 1998. "International Expansion through Start-Up or Acquisition: A Learning Perspective." *Academy of Management Journal* 41 (1): 7–26.

Baskaran, A., J. Liu, H. Yan, and M. Muchie, 2017. "Outward Foreign Direct Investment and Knowledge Flow in the Context of Emerging MNEs: Cases from China, India and South Africa." *African Journal of Science, Technology, Innovation and Development* 9 (5): 539–55.

Bastos, S., and E. Verhoogen. 2018. "Export Destinations and Input Prices." *American Economic Review* 108 (2): 353–92.

Benito, G. R., B. Petersen, and L. S. Welch. 2019. "The Global Value Chain and Internalization Theory." *Journal of International Business Studies* 50 (8): 1414–23.

Bertrand, Olivier, Katariina Nilsson Hakkala, Pehr-Johan Norbäck, and Lars Persson. 2012. "Should Countries Block Foreign Takeovers of R&D Champions and Promote Greenfield Entry?" *Canadian Journal of Economics* 45 (3): 1083–124.

Bhattacharya, R., I. Patnaik, and A. Shah. 2012. "Export versus FDI in Services." *World Economy* 35 (1): 61–78.

Bhaumik, S. K., N. Driffield, and Y. Zhou. 2016. "Country Specific Advantage, Firm Specific Advantage and Multinationality—Sources of Competitive Advantage in Emerging Markets: Evidence from the Electronics Industry in China." *International Business Review* 25 (1): 165–76.

Brakman, S., H. Garretsen, R. van Maarseveen, and P. Zwaneveld. 2020. "Firm Heterogeneity and Exports in the Netherlands: Identifying Export Potential beyond Firm Productivity." *Journal of International Trade & Economic Development* 29 (1): 36–68.

Buckley, P., and P. Ghauri. 2004. "Globalisation, Economic Geography and the Strategy of Multinational Enterprises." *Journal of International Business Studies* 35 (2): 81.

Cajal Grossi, J. C., R. Macchiavello, and G. Noguera. 2019. "International Buyers' Sourcing and Suppliers' Markups in Bangladeshi Garments." IGC Working Paper F-37119-PAK-2, International Growth Center, London. https://www.theigc.org/wp-content /uploads/2019/01/Grossi-et-al-2019-Working-paper.pdf.

Calof, Jonathan L., and Paul W. Beamish. 1995. "Adapting to Foreign Markets: Explaining Internationalization." *International Business Review* 4 (2): 115–31.

Chen, V. Z., J. Li, and D. M. Shapiro. 2012. "International Reverse Spillover Effects on Parent Firms: Evidences from Emerging Market MNEs in Developed Markets." *European Management Journal* 30 (3): 204–18.

Child, J., and S. B. Rodrigues. 2005. "The Internationalization of Chinese Firms: A Case for Theoretical Extension?" *Management and Organization Review* 1 (3): 381–410.

Conconi, Paola, André Sapir, and Maurizio Zanardi. 2010. "The Internationalization Process of Firms: From Exports to FDI?" NBB Working Paper 198, National Bank of Belgium, Brussels.

Cooke, P. 2013. *Complex Adaptive Innovation Systems: Relatedness and Transversality in the Evolving Region.* Abingdon, U.K.: Routledge.

Cuervo-Cazurra, A., and M. Genc. 2008. "Transforming Disadvantages into Advantages: Developing-Country MNEs in the Least Developed Countries." *Journal of International Business Studies* 39 (6): 957–79.

Curran, Louise, Ping Lv, and Francesa Spigarelli. 2017. "Chinese Investment in the EU Renewable Energy Sector: Motives, Synergies and Policy Implications." *Energy Policy* 101 (February): 670–82.

Cusolito, Ana Paula, Raed Safadi, and Daria Taglioni. 2016. *Inclusive Global Value Chains: Policy Options for Small and Medium Enterprises and Low-Income Countries.* Directions in Development Series. Washington, DC: World Bank.

Davies, Ronald B., Rodolphe Desbordes, and Anna Ray. 2018. "Greenfield versus Merger and Acquisition FDI: Same Wine, Different Bottles?" *Canadian Journal of Economics* 51 (4): 1151–90.

de Caldas Lima, J. M. 2008. *Patterns of Internationalization for Developing Country Enterprises: Alliances and Joint Ventures.* Vienna: United Nations Industrial Development Organization.

Driffield, N., and J. H. Love. 2003. "Foreign Direct Investment, Technology Sourcing and Reverse Spillovers." *The Manchester School* 71 (6): 659–72.

Dunning, J. 1993. *Multinational Enterprises and the Global Economy.* Reading, MA: Addison Wesley.

El-Sahli, Z., J. Gullstrand, and K. Olofsdotter. 2018. "Exploring Outward FDI and the Choice of Destination: Evidence from Swedish Firm-Level Data." *Applied Economics Letters* 25 (17): 1222–25.

Farole, T., and D. Winkler, eds. 2014. *Making Foreign Direct Investment Work for Sub-Saharan Africa: Local Spillovers and Competitiveness in Global Value Chains.* Washington, DC: World Bank.

Foster-McGregor, Neil, Anders Isaksson, and Florian Kaulich. 2015. "Foreign Ownership and Performance in Sub-Saharan African Manufacturing and Services." *Journal of International Development* 27 (7): 1197–222.

Gentile-Lüdecke, S., and A. Giroud. 2012. "Knowledge Transfer from TNCs and Upgrading of Domestic Firms: The Polish Automotive Sector." *World Development* 40 (4): 796–807.

Gereffi, G. 1999. "International Trade and Industrial Upgrading in the Apparel Commodity Chain." *Journal of International Economics* 48 (1): 37–70.

Gereffi, G., J. Humphrey, R. Kaplinsky, and T. J. Sturgeon. 2001. "Introduction: Globalisation, Value Chains and Development." *IDS Bulletin* 32 (3): 1–8.

Gereffi, G., J. Humphrey, and T. Sturgeon. 2005. "The Governance of Global Value Chains." *Review of International Political Economy* 12 (1): 78–104.

Giovannetti, G., E. Marvasi, and M. Sanfilippo. 2015. "Supply Chains and the Internationalization of Small Firms." *Small Business Economics* 44: 845–65.

Goldberg, P. K., A. K. Khandelwal, N. Pavcnik, and P. Topalova. 2010. "Imported Intermediate Inputs and Domestic Product Growth: Evidence from India." *Quarterly Journal of Economics* 125 (4): 1727–67.

Greenville, J., K. Kawasaki, and R. Beaujeu. 2017. "How Policies Shape Global Food and Agriculture Value Chains." OECD Food, Agriculture and Fisheries Papers 100, OECD Publishing, Paris.

Guadalupe, Maria, Olga Kuzmina, and Catherine Thomas. 2012. "Innovation and Foreign Ownership." *American Economic Review* 102 (7): 3594–627.

Havránek, Tomas, and Zuzana Irsova. 2010. "Meta-Analysis of Intra-Industry FDI Spillovers: Updated Evidence." *Czech Journal of Economics and Finance* 60 (2): 151–74.

Heher, U, V. Steenbergen, and F. Thoma. 2019. "Promoting FDI Linkages in Turkey: Demand-Supply Gap Analysis." Unpublished, World Bank, Washington, DC.

Helpman, E., M. J. Melitz, and S. R. Yeaple. 2004. "Export versus FDI with Heterogeneous Firms." *American Economic Review* 94 (1): 300–16.

Hidalgo, Cesar A., and Ricardo Hausmann. 2009. "The Building Blocks of Economic Complexity." *Proceedings of the National Academy of Sciences of the United States of America* 106 (26): 10570–75.

IMF (International Monetary Fund). 2015. *Regional Economic Outlook. Sub-Saharan Africa.* Washington, DC: IMF.

Ivarsson, I., and C. G. Alvstam. 2005. "Technology Transfer from TNCs to Local Suppliers in Developing Countries: A Study of AB Volvo's Truck and Bus Plants in Brazil, China, India, and Mexico." *World Development* 33 (8): 1325–44.

Ivarsson, I., and C. G. Alvstam. 2011. "Upgrading in Global Value-Chains: A Case Study of Technology-Learning among IKEA-Suppliers in China and Southeast Asia." *Journal of Economic Geography* 11 (4): 731–52.

Javorcik, Beata Smarzynska, Alessia Lo Turco, and Daniela Maggioni. 2018. "New and Improved: Does FDI Boost Production Complexity in Host Countries?" *Economic Journal* 128 (614): 2507–37.

Javorcik, Beata Smarzynska, and Mariana Spatareanu. 2009. "Tough Love: Do Czech Suppliers Learn from Their Relationships with Multinationals?" LICOS Discussion Paper 249/2009, Centre for Institutions and Economic Performance, Leuven.

Jiang, K., W. Keller, L. D. Qiu, and W. Ridley. 2018. "International Joint Ventures and Internal vs. External Technology Transfer: Evidence from China." NBER Working Paper 24455, National Bureau of Economic Research, Cambridge, MA.

Johanson, J., and J.-E. Vahlne. 1977. "The Internationalization Process of the Firm: A Model of Knowledge Development and Increasing Foreign Market Commitments." *Journal of International Business Studies* 8 (1): 23–32.

Johnson, R. 2018. "Measuring Global Value Chains." *Annual Review of Economics* 10: 207–36.

Jordaan, J., W. Douw, and C. Z. Qiang. 2020. "Foreign Direct Investment, Backward Linkages, and Productivity Spillovers." In Focus Note, World Bank, Washington, DC.

Kaiser Associates Economic Development Partners. 2014. "Sector Case Study Agribusiness." Chapter 6 in *Making Foreign Direct Investment Work for Sub-Saharan Africa: Local Spillovers and Competitiveness in Global Value Chains*, edited by T. Farole and D. Winkler, 163–207. Washington, DC: World Bank.

Kang, N., and K. Sakai. 2000. "International Strategic Alliances: Their Role in Industrial Globalisation." OECD Science, Technology and Industry Working Papers 2000/5, OECD Publishing, Paris.

Khandelwal, A. K., and M. Teachout. 2016. "Special Economic Zones for Myanmar." IGC Policy Note, International Growth Centre, London.

Kim, J.-Y., N. Driffield, and J. Love. 2018. "Outward FDI from South Korea: The Relationship between National Investment Position and Location Choice." In *Contemporary Issues in International Business*, edited by D. Castellani, R. Narula, Q. T. K. Nguyen, I. Surdu, and J. Walker. Academy of International Business. Cham, Switzerland: Springer Nature.

Kowalski, P., J. L. Gonzalez, A. Ragoussis, and C. Ugarte. 2015. "Participation of Developing Countries in Global Value Chains: Implications for Trade and Trade-Related Policies." OECD Trade Policy Paper 179, OECD Publishing, Paris.

Krishnan, Aarti, and Christopher Foster. 2017. "A Quantitative Approach to Innovation in Agricultural Value Chains: Evidence from Kenyan Horticulture." *European Journal of Development Research* 30 (1): 108–35.

Kugler, K., and E. Verhoogen. 2012. "Prices, Plant Size, and Product Quality." *Review of Economic Studies* 79 (1): 307–39.

Larimo, J. 2003. "Form of Investment by Nordic Firms in World Markets." *Journal of Business Research* 56 (10): 791–803.

Luo, Y., and R. Tung. 2007. "International Expansion of Emerging Market Enterprises: A Springboard Perspective." *Journal of International Business Studies* 38 (4): 481–98.

Manyati, T. 2014. "Agro-Based Technological Innovation: A Critical Analysis of the Determinants of Innovation in the Informal Sector in Harare, Zimbabwe." *African Journal of Science, Technology, Innovation and Development* 6 (6): 553–61.

Melitz, M. J. 2003. "The Impact of Trade on Intra-Industry Reallocations and Aggregate Industry Productivity." *Econometrica* 71 (6): 1695–725.

Meyer, Klaus, and Evis Sinani. 2009. "When and Where Does Foreign Direct Investment Generate Positive Spillovers? A Meta-Analysis." *Journal of International Business Studies* 40 (7): 1075–94.

Montalbano, P., S. Nenci, and C. Pietrobelli. 2018. "Opening and Linking Up: Firms, GVCs, and Productivity in Latin America." *Small Business Economics* 50: 917–35.

Morrison, Andrea, Carlo Pietrobelli, and Roberta Rabellotti. 2008. "Global Value Chains and Technological Capabilities: A Framework to Study Learning and Innovation in Developing Countries." *Oxford Development Studies* 36 (1): 39–58.

Newman, Carol, John Page, John Rand, Abebe Shimeles, Mans Soderbom, and Finn Tarp. 2016. *Made in Africa: Learning to Compete in Industry*. Washington, DC: Brookings Institution.

OECD (Organisation for Economic Co-operation and Development). 2008. "China 2008: Encouraging Responsible Business Conduct." OECD Investment Policy Review, OECD Publishing, Paris.

Pedersen, T., and B. Petersen. 1998. "Explaining Gradually Increasing Resource Commitment to a Foreign Market." *International Business Review* 7 (5): 483–501.

Perea, Jose Ramon, and Matthew Stephenson. 2018. "Outward FDI from Developing Countries." In *Global Investment Competitiveness Report 2017/2018: Foreign Investor Perspectives and Policy Implications*, 101–34. Washington, DC: World Bank Group.

Pietrobelli, Carlo, and Roberta Rabellotti. 2011. "Global Value Chains Meet Innovation Systems: Are There Learning Opportunities for Developing Countries?" *World Development* 39 (7): 1261–69.

Pipkin, Seth, and Alberto Fuentes. 2017. "Spurred to Upgrade: A Review of Triggers and Consequences of Industrial Upgrading in the Global Value Chain Literature." *World Development* 98 (C): 536–54.

Ragoussis, Alexandros. 2020. "How Beneficial Are Foreign Acquisitions of Firms in Developing Countries? Evidence from Six Countries." Chapter 2 in *Global Investment Competitiveness Report 2019/20: Rebuilding Investor Confidence in Times of Uncertainty*. Washington, DC: World Bank.

Schmid, Stefan, and Cigdem Polat. 2018. "Lenovo: From Chinese Origins to a Global Player." *Internationalization of Business: Cases on Strategy Formulation and Implementation*, edited by Stefan Schmid, 125–54. New York: Springer.

Slaughter, M. J. 2013. "American Companies and Global Supply Networks: Driving U.S. Economic Growth and Jobs by Connecting with the World." Business Roundtable, United States Council for International Business, and United States Council Foundation.

Sutton, J. 2014. *An Enterprise Map of Mozambique*. London: International Growth Centre.

Taglioni, Daria, and Deborah Winkler. 2016. *Making Global Value Chains Work for Development*. Washington, DC: World Bank.

Theyel, Nelli. 2013. "Extending Open Innovation throughout the Value Chain by Small and Medium-Sized Manufacturers." *International Small Business Journal* 31 (3): 256–74.

Thomas, R., and K. Narayanan. 2017. "Determinants of Outward Foreign Direct Investment: A Study of Indian Manufacturing Firms." *Transnational Corporations* 24 (1): 9–26.

UNCTAD (United Nations Conference on Trade and Development). 2002. *World Investment Report 2002: Transnational Corporations and Export Competitiveness*. Geneva: United Nations.

UNCTAD (United Nations Conference on Trade and Development). 2011. *World Investment Report 2011: Non-equity Modes of International Production and Development*. Geneva: United Nations.

UNCTAD (United Nations Conference on Trade and Development). 2020. *World Investment Report 2020: International Production beyond the Pandemic*. Geneva: United Nations.

UNIDO (United Nations Industrial Development Organization). 2002. *Industrial Development Report 2002/2003: Competing through Innovation and Learning*. Vienna: UNIDO.

UNIDO (United Nations Industrial Development Organization). 2018. "Global Value Chains and Industrial Development: Lessons from China, South-East and South Asia." UNIDO, Vienna.

Wagner, Joachim. 2014. "Low-Productive Exporters Are High-Quality Exporters. Evidence from Germany." *Economics Bulletin* 34 (2): 745–56.

Wakasugi, Ryuhei, ed. 2014. *Internationalization of Japanese Firms: Evidence from Firm-Level Data*. Cham, Switzerland: Springer.

Welch, Lawrence, and Reijo Luostarinen. 1988. "Internationalization: Evolution of a Concept." *Journal of General Management* 14 (2): 155–71.

Woldesenbet, K., M. Ram, and T. Jones. 2012. "Supplying Large Firms: The Role of Entrepreneurial and Dynamic Capabilities in Small Businesses." *International Small Business Journal* 30 (5): 493–512.

World Bank. 2018. *Global Investment Competitiveness Report 2017/2018: Foreign Investor Perspectives and Policy Implications*. Washington, DC: World Bank.

Wynarczyk, Pooran, and Robert Watson. 2005. "Firm Growth and Supply Chain Partnerships: An Empirical Analysis of U.K. SME Subcontractors." *Small Business Economics* 24 (1): 39–51.

Xiao, Wen, and Liyun Liu. 2015. *Internationalization of China's Privately Owned Enterprises. Determinants and Pattern Selection*. Singapore: World Scientific.

Chapter 4

Using Investment Policies to Stimulate Global Value Chain Participation

Key findings

- In the past decades, there have been many cases in which governments have played key roles in promoting global value chain (GVC) participation. Sound macroeconomic policy, infrastructure building, an enabling regulatory environment, and human capital development constitute a set of necessary minimum conditions for any country to be considered an attractive investment destination and to participate in GVCs.

- In some cases, governments have played a more direct role in solving specific sectors' market failures caused by externalities, imperfect information, and coordination problems, in what some describe as "soft" or "light-handed" industrial policies.

- To attract and link multinational corporations (MNCs), investment policies may help reduce regulatory or procedural burdens for foreign investors, provide public goods within special economic zones, or use investment incentives to tilt MNCs' decisions to locate to a new country. In other cases, investment promotion agencies can showcase a country's comparative advantages and help facilitate entry.

- Policy makers can also help domestic firms internationalize and integrate into GVCs by supporting their engagement with MNCs through investment, partnerships, or trade. Successful support programs tend to combine information provision (to increase exposure), matchmaking (to overcome coordination failures), and temporary subsidies (to compensate for expected social benefits from these interactions).

- There is no "blueprint" for strengthening GVC participation. Reforms should be implemented as coherent packages rather than as individual, one-off policies that are likely to have only a marginal effect. A successful reform package requires a sustained, coordinated, and long-term approach based on the design of incentive mechanisms that are tailored to the specific needs of countries, revealed and latent comparative advantages of firms, and value chains in question.

- The best approaches help to improve firm performance without "picking winners." Through GVCs, firms in developing countries enter foreign markets at lower costs, benefit from specialization in niche tasks, and gain access to larger markets for their output. Such specialization is often the result of a country's long-term involvement in a specific sector that takes advantage of and builds on the country's unique combination of factor endowments and firm capacity.

How investment policies can help global value chain participation

In the past five decades, governments, in many cases, have played key roles in promoting global value chain (GVC) participation. Governments shape key elements of GVC through their macroeconomic policies, trade agreements, infrastructure building, and human capital development. In some cases, governments have played a more direct role, in what some describe as "soft" or "light-handed" industrial policies (Harrison and Rodríguez-Clare 2010; Taglioni and Winkler 2016). These descriptors refer to government policy making at the micro level, aimed at solving market failures caused by externalities, imperfect information, and coordination problems. These policies could act either as catalysts, as shown in the East Asian "miracle" countries (Birdsall et al. 1993; Wade 1990), or as inhibitors, as in Latin America's experience with import substitution (Gerber 2007).

Policies that help attract foreign direct investment (FDI) and that link multinational corporations (MNCs) to domestic firms can do much to stimulate GVC participation and upgrading. As shown in previous chapters, FDI is a key driver in developing countries' GVC participation. MNCs can help countries reshape their comparative advantages and enter new GVCs or move up in existing GVCs (Freund and Moran 2017; Freund and Pierola 2015). Their productivity can also spill over to domestic firms, and they can help such firms internationalize (as described in chapter 3).[1]

To attract FDI, policy makers seek to improve and showcase their country's comparative advantages to MNCs. As illustrated in chapter 2, MNCs may offshore their production to exploit differences in factor costs across countries. Geographic proximity to major markets, availability of cheap labor, local industry agglomeration, supportive business environments, good infrastructure, and open trade and investment policies are all common determinants of where MNCs choose to expand their FDI and trade.

FIGURE 4.1 **Investment policy instruments to integrate countries into global value chains**

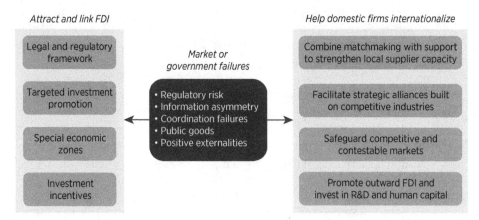

Source: World Bank elaborations of the literature.
Note: FDI = foreign direct investment; R&D = research and development.

Investment policies aim to solve specific market or government failures aligned with these determinants (figure 4.1). To bring in FDI, policy makers may focus on regulatory reforms to reduce restrictions or procedural burdens for investors. They also may aim to provide public goods (such as high-quality infrastructure) to MNCs within a special economic zone (SEZ). In other cases, foreign investors may simply be made aware of a country's endowments by the country's investment promotion agencies (IPAs). A government can also use investment incentives to entice MNCs to resettle in a country by reducing the MNCs' tax burdens.

Government policies can also help domestic firms internationalize and upgrade by learning from their engagement with foreign firms. As shown in chapter 3, increased exposure to foreign firms (such as MNCs) can raise domestic firms' productivity and help them obtain the production capabilities and foreign market knowledge needed to compete internationally. Governments are willing to invest their resources to stimulate such positive externalities. However, domestic firms' efforts to internationalize may be held back by low exposure to MNCs and global markets and by the firms' own limited production capacity (figure 4.1). Integrated support programs combining information provision (to increase exposure), matchmaking (to overcome coordination failures), and temporary subsidies (to compensate MNCs for the expected social benefits of these interactions) are tailored to promote learning from international firms by encouraging interaction.

Foreign direct investment policy and promotion

Necessary conditions

To attract FDI, governments need to meet a set of necessary minimum conditions. The 2019 World Bank Global Investment Competitiveness (GIC) Survey of the locational decision-making factors of 2,500 MNCs shows that political stability, macroeconomic stability, an enabling legal and regulatory environment, and local talent and skills are the top four considerations in foreign investors' decision-making processes (figure 4.2). Physical infrastructure and the ability to export also rank highly. Basic technical capabilities for the GVC segments in the FDI host country are also important and are reflected in the availability of talent and skills, supply chain coordination, and local input sourcing from capable suppliers. Without these necessary conditions, a country is unlikely to participate in GVCs. In all five qualitative case studies included in part II of this report (chapters 6 to 10), the factors mentioned were present and were deemed crucial for MNCs to include the studied countries in their long lists of potential locations. A large body of literature and survey results confirms that governments need to address these minimum conditions to be considered attractive investment destinations and to attract opportunities for local firms to enter GVCs (see Crescenzi, Harman, and Arnold [2019] for an overview of this literature).

Meeting the necessary macroeconomic, infrastructure, and endowment conditions is often not sufficient to attract FDI. Depending on the type of GVC and the specific GVC segment a government seeks to enter, the government may discover that it needs to use more specific policy instruments to attract and leverage the intended FDI (Moran 2014).

FIGURE 4.2 Factors that are critically important or important to multinational corporations' locational decisions

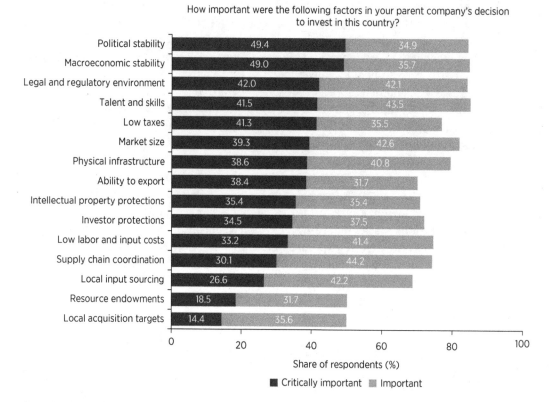

How important were the following factors in your parent company's decision to invest in this country?

Factor	Critically important	Important
Political stability	49.4	34.9
Macroeconomic stability	49.0	35.7
Legal and regulatory environment	42.0	42.1
Talent and skills	41.5	43.5
Low taxes	41.3	35.5
Market size	39.3	42.6
Physical infrastructure	38.6	40.8
Ability to export	38.4	31.7
Intellectual property protections	35.4	35.4
Investor protections	34.5	37.5
Low labor and input costs	33.2	41.4
Supply chain coordination	30.1	44.2
Local input sourcing	26.6	42.2
Resource endowments	18.5	31.7
Local acquisition targets	14.4	35.6

Share of respondents (%)

■ Critically important ■ Important

Source: World Bank 2020.

Among the various FDI policy instruments, four are most commonly used:

1. An enabling legal and regulatory framework for FDI

2. Targeted investment promotion

3. Special economic zones

4. Investment incentives

An enabling legal and regulatory environment for foreign direct investment

Creating a transparent and predictable regulatory environment is crucial to attracting FDI and entering into GVCs. A large body of research suggests that the quality of a country's legal and regulatory environment is positively associated with its inward FDI (see, for example, Akame, Ekwelle, and Njei 2016; Buchanan, Le, and Rishi 2012; Gani 2007; Globerman and Shapiro 2002; Stein and Daude 2007; Vogiatzoglou 2016; Wei 2000; Wernick, Haar, and Singh 2009). Evidence from investor surveys reinforces that a supportive business climate is among the top priorities for foreign investors (figure 4.2).

The 2019 GIC Survey, which focused on investors' decisions to enter a set of 10 middle-income countries,[2] finds similar results: the countries' legal and regulatory environments ranked as the investors' third priority, after political and macroeconomic stability (Kusek, Saurav, and Kuo 2020). Notably, most large firms—those with more than 250 employees—rank the legal and regulatory environment as their top investment consideration, whereas smaller firms consider it only their fourth most important criterion. These differences may be driven by investment restrictions that apply only to larger firms or by the greater regulatory scrutiny that large firms tend to experience (Kusek, Saurav, and Kuo 2020). Larger firms also play disproportionately important roles in GVCs and contribute more to employment growth in their host countries.

Foreign investors are affected by a wide range of laws and regulations. Which types of laws are most important to them depends on the country context as well as on the investors' motivations. For example, MNCs that primarily seek access to natural resources, such as those in extractive industries, care mainly about access to land and to those resources, whereas market-seeking FDI tends to prioritize the size and purchasing power of the domestic market. Efficiency-seeking FDI, which includes most noncommodity GVC investment, focuses on factors that affect production and trade costs (World Bank 2020). Creating a legal and regulatory framework that attracts FDI and enables GVC entry thus ultimately requires a country- and sector-specific analysis of impediments to investor entry and operation.[3]

Entry barriers can inhibit FDI, and removing them is pivotal to GVC integration. Most of the literature confirms that statutory entry barriers to FDI, such as prohibitions on FDI in certain sectors, foreign equity ceilings, screening mechanisms, and restrictions on foreign managerial personnel or board members, can significantly inhibit FDI. Other legal entry barriers include minimum investment requirements, performance requirements, restrictions on land ownership, reciprocity requirements, restrictions on capital transfers, and any other form of discrimination between different types of foreign investors or between foreign and domestic investors.

A study by the Organisation for Economic Co-operation and Development (OECD) covering 60 advanced and developing countries over the period 1997–2016 shows that liberalizing FDI restrictions by about 10 percent, as measured by the OECD FDI Regulatory Restrictiveness Index,[4] could increase inward FDI stocks by an average of 2.1 percent (Mistura and Roulet 2019). The study also shows that this effect is greater for FDI in service sectors but that even manufacturing sectors—which are typically open to FDI—are negatively affected by countries' overall restrictiveness. Other studies confirm these findings, including in developing countries. De la Medina Soto and Ghossein (2013) find a positive correlation between average openness to foreign equity investment across sectors and per capita FDI inflows across 103 economies. Arnold et al. (2016) find that the liberalization of India's service sectors in the 1990s significantly increased the country's inflow of services FDI. And, notably, export-oriented FDI is particularly affected by entry barriers because there is no strong pull factor drawing foreign investors into any particular country (Kusek and Silva 2018). If foreign investors are restricted or deterred from entering a host country in the first place, few of the policy instruments discussed in this chapter can be applied.

Once the sectors seeking FDI have been liberalized on a nondiscriminatory basis, the next steps include streamlining business establishment procedures, such as the processes to obtain licensing, work permits, and visas. In the context of GVC integration, the World Bank Doing Business Index's "trading across borders" indicator, which measures the number of documents, the cost, and the time necessary to export from and import into a country, is particularly relevant. Governments also need to focus on de facto barriers to entry, such as lack of transparency and regulatory uncertainty, that arise from weak governance.

Investment approval or screening procedures should also be minimized and, where present, be nondiscriminatory. Such approval and screening mechanisms have gained prominence in recent years, following a general global trend toward increased protectionism in investment and trade policies. Some countries have also increased their scrutiny of foreign takeovers of strategic assets and technology companies (UNIDO 2018). Screening processes, especially when applied in discriminatory ways, are a significant deterrent to FDI. This effect is especially strong for service sectors and for efficiency-seeking investment, which is more mobile than other types of FDI and can choose host countries with simpler and more favorable business environments (Mistura and Roulet 2019). Although, in principle, governments use screening mechanisms as legitimate tools for pursuing economic objectives, deficiencies in the design of these mechanisms may impose significant burdens on investors without advancing the intended objectives. Even if the mechanisms are well designed, poor or discretionary administration of them may increase costs and uncertainty for investors without achieving the desired benefits.

Countries should limit approval or screening mechanisms to only the handful of sectors that can genuinely be considered "strategic" or "sensitive." These concepts (strategic, sensitive, and so on) should be defined in ways that are clear and differentiated but not too broad or all-encompassing. The screening processes should be made transparent and efficient, including by using objective criteria to screen projects, providing a recourse mechanism for investors whose applications are denied, and establishing negative lists and standard operating procedures for the agencies conducting the screenings or reviews. In addition, a risk-based approach to screening can allow the government to identify and focus its efforts on high-risk investment projects. Risks could be categorized according to the sensitivity of sectors or industries or, more generally, in accordance with health and safety, environment, and public security risks (or other criteria, according to public policy considerations).

Furthermore, governments should minimize regulatory risk to enhance investor confidence. Regulatory risk, a type of political risk,[5] is a government failure that arises when investors are subject to uncertainty because of government conduct. It may take the form of a lack of transparency, sudden changes in laws or regulations, breaches of contract, or expropriation, among others (Hebous, Kher, and Tran 2020). Regulatory risk is decreased when a country's legal system reduces the potential for unexpected losses caused by uncertainty and arbitrary government conduct and thus increases investor confidence. Hebous, Kher, and Tran (2020) use a new global data set of more than 14,000 parent companies investing in nearly 28,000 new and expanding FDI projects across 168 host countries and find that lowering regulatory risk increases FDI flows (figure 4.3). In fact, the study suggests that the effect of reducing regulatory risk on FDI is even greater than the effect of increasing trade openness. A 1-percentage-point reduction in regulatory risk boosts the likelihood of an investor entering or expanding its operations in a host country by as much as 2 percentage points. In contrast, a 1-percentage-point increase in the host country's ratio of trade to gross domestic product (GDP) boosts the likelihood of entry by no more than 0.6 of a percentage point.

FIGURE 4.3 Regulatory risk and foreign direct investment inflows

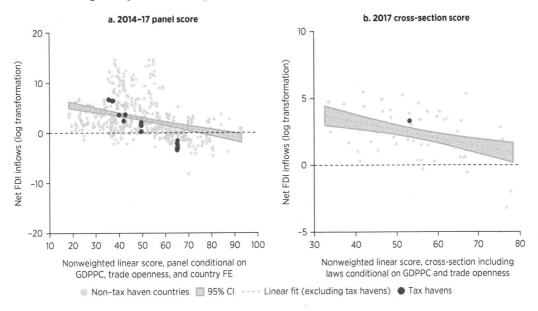

Source: Hebous, Kher, and Tran 2020.
Note: CI = confidence interval; FDI = foreign direct investment; FE = fixed effects; GDPPC = gross domestic product per capita.

Just as important, reducing regulatory risk is critical to retaining existing investors. Results from the *Global Investment Competitiveness Report 2019/2020* show the high frequency with which investors face these types of risks as well as investors' reactions to them (Hebous, Kher, and Tran 2020). The most common types of political risk caused about one in four investors to withdraw an existing investment or cancel a planned investment. In more severe cases, the negative effects on FDI were even stronger (Kusek and Silva 2018). Retaining investment is particularly important in the context of GVC upgrading through MNC-supplier linkages and spillovers. The longer FDI projects remain in a country, the more they tend to evolve and expand, increasing the possibilities for linkages and diversification into other connected sectors.

Investor confidence can be strengthened by improving a country's legal framework for investor protection, including by adopting international investment agreements (IIAs). Under such "investor protection guarantees," governments offer protections against adverse government conduct, including legal provisions against direct and indirect expropriation and guarantees of the investors' ability to transfer funds into and out of the country in convertible currency in a timely manner.[6] Such guarantees can be included in a country's domestic legal framework, such as in an investment code, or in IIAs, which include bilateral investment treaties (BITs) and investment chapters in preferential trade agreements (PTAs). Although empirical evidence about the relationship between IIAs and FDI flows is inconclusive (see box 4.1), survey data indicate the importance of investor protection guarantees as well as IIAs to foreign investors, particularly export-oriented ones (Kusek and Silva 2018). Honduras's experience entering the textile and apparel GVC further shows the importance of signing PTAs and BITs to attract FDI (see chapter 7 of this report).

BOX 4.1 The role of international agreements in attracting foreign direct investment

International trade and investment agreements have become increasingly prevalent around the world (figure B4.1.1 and table B4.1.1). These agreements shape trade and investment relations among member and nonmember economies. For example, the European Union's Single Market has been crucial to the high degree of integration in Eastern Europe (Brenton, Di Mauro, and Lücke 1999). Similarly, the North American Free Trade Agreement has encouraged trade and foreign direct investment (FDI) flows between the United States, Canada, and Mexico (MacDermott 2007).

FIGURE B4.1.1 Number of preferential trade agreements, 1948–2020

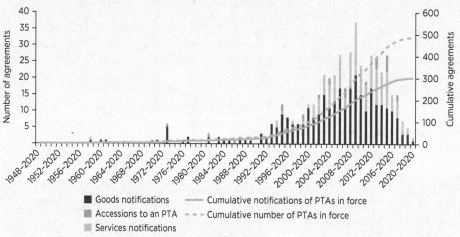

Source: World Bank calculations using World Trade Organization data.
Note: PTA = preferential trade agreement.

The relationship between international agreements, global value chains (GVCs), and FDI is affected by many factors; and there is no clear correlation between a region's number of trade and investment agreements and its regional value chain participation (see table B4.1.1). For example, the Middle East and North Africa region has the second-highest average number of bilateral investment treaties (BITs) per country, but its regional FDI stock is smaller than that of Europe and Central Asia, East Asia and Pacific, or Latin America and the Caribbean.

Agreements on trade and investment are generally associated with increases in trade and FDI flows, yet the findings depend on the scope of the provisions and on the context. In principle, BITs increase FDI by substituting for improved investment climate or democratic institutions (Arias, Hollyer, and Rosendorff 2017; Bhandari and Yang 2019). The effect of the BITs is strongest when FDI relies on strong contracts between firms and states (Danzman 2016).

Osnago, Rocha, and Ruta (2018) find that signing deeper preferential trade agreements (which go beyond traditional market access issues and include disciplines such as investment, competition policy, and harmonization of product regulations) can further increase the flows of vertical FDI between countries. BITs with stronger international dispute settlement provisions also prove to be associated with higher FDI flows (Frenkel and Walter 2018).

Continued on next page ›

BOX 4.1 The role of international agreements in attracting foreign direct investment *(continued)*

TABLE B4.1.1 International investment treaties and value chain and foreign direct investment network values, by region

Region	BITs Total	BITs In force	TIPs Total	TIPs In force	Regional value chain network (2019, US$, billion)	Regional FDI network (2017, US$, billion)
EAP	20	17	10	9	34.8	80.2
ECA	48	43	38	30	46.8	107.1
LAC	14	11	11	9	1.0	8
MENA	46	33	12	9	0.4	3.8
NA	26	25	30	23	n.a.	n.a.
SA	16	13	5	4	n.a.	n.a.
SSA	15	7	8	6	0.1	1.4

Source: World Bank calculations based on United Nations Conference on Trade and Development data.
Note: Because of the small number of countries in NA and SA, no values are estimated for the regional value chain or FDI networks. See chapter 1 for more details on the regional global value chain and FDI networks. BIT = bilateral investment treaty; EAP = East Asia and Pacific; ECA = Europe and Central Asia; FDI = foreign direct investment; LAC = Latin America and the Caribbean; MENA = Middle East and North Africa; NA = North America; n.a. = not applicable; SA = South Asia; SSA = Sub-Saharan Africa; TIP = treaty with investment provisions.

The effectiveness of BITs in encouraging bilateral FDI flows increases with the difference in GDP and GDP per capita between the source and host countries. BITs only have strong, significant positive effects where no FDI relationship was present or where an existing FDI relationship was disintegrating (Falvey and Foster-McGregor 2018). BITs mitigate the higher uncertainty and transaction costs associated with investing in far-away, unfamiliar markets (Gomez-Mera and Varela 2017).

Finally, the effect of international agreements on GVC participation and FDI flows also varies across sectors. Deep trade agreements seem to be particularly relevant for GVC integration in high-value-added industries, which are usually services industries characterized by nontangible activities (Laget et al. 2018). Colen, Persyn, and Guariso (2016) further find that BITs are most successful in attracting FDI in sectors with higher sunk costs, including utilities, real estate, banking, and mining.

Note: More detail on provisions that could make BITs more effective in attracting FDI can be found in Berger et al. (2013); Buthe and Milner (2014); Danzman (2016); Frenkel and Walter (2018); Lukoianova (2018); and Osnago, Rocha, and Ruta (2018).

Governments should also provide foreign investors with effective mechanisms for recourse if grievances or disputes arise. As a starting point, governments should strengthen their domestic judicial systems, such as by creating specialized commercial courts, stipulating time periods for judicial processes, and implementing case management systems (Hebous, Kher, and Tran 2020). In addition, access should be given to a wide range of dispute settlement mechanisms, including state-to-state as well as investor-to-state arbitration (UNCTAD 2019a). To retain and expand investment, governments should also introduce early-warning and tracking mechanisms to identify and resolve investor issues arising from government conduct. Enhanced legal frameworks for investor protection can greatly mitigate regulatory risk, but these laws and regulations are often insufficiently implemented, making countries' overall investment climates unpredictable and unstable. After ensuring the predictability of government behavior by offering investment protections and guarantees, governments can minimize regulatory risk at the source by addressing grievances early and effectively (World Bank Group 2019).

Last, investor confidence can be boosted by providing transparency regarding the content of laws and regulations as well as the process of making them. Improving transparency and reducing regulators' room for discretionary behavior can make a country's business environment more predictable and less risky for investors. Governments in developing countries can strengthen transparency by consulting systematically with the private sector and with other stakeholders. They can also provide accessible regulatory information, create business-to-government feedback loops to verify the effective implementation of regulations, and introduce rules-based indicators to prevent opportunities for discretionary behavior (Hebous, Kher, and Tran 2020).

Targeted promotion of inward foreign direct investment

Proactive efforts to attract and facilitate foreign investment can help overcome problems of imperfect information and information asymmetries among potential investors. Capital markets, especially those involving cross-border elements, often exhibit market failures in the form of transaction costs, imperfect information, and information asymmetries (Greenwald and Stiglitz 1986; Williamson 1975; Williamson 1986). Foreign investors often have large informational disadvantages relative to domestic investors (Mariotti and Piscitello 1995), resulting in mismatches between investors' location choices and host countries' comparative advantages. IPAs can use targeted information provision, outreach campaigns, and preestablishment support services to help foreign firms overcome information asymmetries and to demonstrate their countries' competitiveness in specific sectors. Information asymmetries are especially pronounced for firms that invest in previously nonexistent sectors (the so-called first-mover firms) (Moran 2014), so investment promotion programs are particularly relevant when IPAs are establishing a country's first linkage with a specific GVC (Crescenzi, Harman, and Arnold 2019).

Empirical evidence shows the positive effects IPAs can have on attracting FDI (Heilbron and Kronfol 2020). Several studies indicate that IPAs increase FDI inflows to their home economies (Cho 2003; Crescenzi, Di Cataldo, and Giua 2019; Morriset and Andrews-Johnson 2004; Pietersen and Bezuidenhout 2015), and some estimate the magnitude of this increase to be as large as 30–45 percent (Morrisset and Andrews-Johnson 2004, based on a global survey of IPAs across 58 countries in 2001). The quality of an IPA is pivotal to attracting more FDI (figure 4.4). Harding and Javorcik (2011) use a global survey of 124 countries together with US FDI data and find that investment promotion led to 155 percent higher FDI inflows and 58 percent greater employment in targeted sectors compared with nontargeted sectors. Studies find that IPAs are most effective in developing countries subject to high information asymmetries, challenging regulatory environments, and greater cultural

FIGURE 4.4 **Investment promotion agency quality and foreign direct investment inflows**

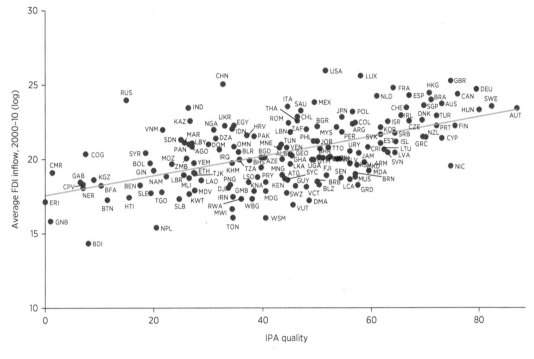

Source: Harding and Javorcik 2012.
Note: The IPA quality rating is based on the World Bank's Global Investment Promotion Benchmarking (GIPB) series. The figure shows the average results of GIPB scores from the 2006, 2009, and 2012 GIPB series. FDI = foreign direct investment; IPA = investment promotion agency.

distance from potential investors (Harding and Javorcik 2011, 2012). IPAs can also be highly cost-effective: one study shows that each US$1 spent on investment promotion yields US$189 in FDI inflows and that spending a relatively modest US$78 on investment promotion creates one additional job in the promoted sectors (Harding and Javorcik 2011).

Targeted investment promotion strategies can help countries attract high-quality investment, enter GVCs, and thereby stimulate economic upgrading and transformation. Costa Rica's IPA, for example, was instrumental in attracting Intel to the country in 1996, which stimulated FDI inflows, GVC integration, and exports. It also helped diversify the country's exports from mostly fruit commodities into advanced manufacturing (Nelson 2005, 2010; Spar 1998). In Malaysia, proactive investment promotion with high-level political support in the 1970s helped attract a number of foreign investors who jump-started Malaysia's electrical and electronics industry (see chapter 8 of this report). Similarly, in Morocco, investment promotion followed by demonstration effects from early anchor investors (including Boeing in 2002 and Renault-Nissan in 2012) played a key role in changing the country's export profile (Freund and Moran 2017). In all three countries, proactive, targeted investment promotion by strong IPAs contributed to attracting a few large, export-oriented MNCs, which in turn helped these countries integrate into new GVCs. Crucially, attracting high-profile first movers in each case generated a strong signaling effect that drew a cluster of follower firms that proved instrumental to subsequent GVC upgrading.[7]

Although more countries are now establishing IPAs, many of these IPAs are struggling to reach their full potential. Heilbron and Kronfol (2020) find that, although IPAs are expanding their annual budgets, staffing, and number of offices abroad, many of their operational characteristics remain the same. This finding suggests that these IPAs are not sufficiently responsive to emerging global trends and technologies. Also, troublingly, most IPAs either stagnated or deteriorated from 2006 to 2012 in their ability to respond to investor inquiries. Common challenges that prevent IPAs from performing better are inadequate institutional coordination, an overly wide range of mandates, uneven service coverage, and inadequate sector prioritization and focus (Heilbron and Kronfol 2020).

When setting up a new IPA or seeking to improve an existing one, a government should ensure that the agency is clearly focused on its target segments. To be most effective given limited resources, IPAs should focus their proactive promotion efforts and high-level service offerings on a few segments in which their country is competitive (Heilbron and Aranda-Larrey 2020; Heilbron and Kronfol 2020). In particular, many countries' IPAs are targeting entire sectors,[8] but GVC mapping (see the relevant section later in this chapter) would allow these agencies to target specific GVC segments in which their countries have revealed comparative advantages. In Malaysia, for example, the government adopted an "ecosystem approach" in 2012 under which it continuously mapped and analyzed the ecosystem of the Malaysian electrical and electronics industry. On the basis of these analyses, the agency focused on promoting specific high-value activities that were in line with Malaysia's comparative advantage, such as integrated circuit design (see chapter 8 of this report).

IPAs should also have sufficient high-level political support, institutional and financial autonomy, and capable staff to carry out their missions. High-level political support is essential to successful investment promotion because it gives IPAs the mandate and ability to better coordinate across ministries and stakeholders, to mobilize them to ensure that essential public goods are provided, and to address critical constraints. For example, Malaysia's case highlights how high-level political support was essential to establishing the infrastructure necessary to attract global lead firms (see chapter 8 of this report). In addition, IPAs need to have sufficient institutional and financial autonomy to implement their strategic plans and avoid political interference. They also need to be able to employ an appropriate staff, including employees with a mix of public and private sector experience and who have sufficient language skills and international experience to interact effectively with potential investors (Heilbron and Kronfol 2020).

Finally, IPAs should concentrate on investment promotion services rather than taking on regulatory responsibilities. IPAs should focus on four types of services that are particularly important: marketing, information, assistance, and advocacy. Adding other functions could impair the IPA's core function. As a general rule, IPAs should not engage in small and medium enterprise development, administration of incentives, screening or approval of investment projects, issuance of noninvestment licenses or permits, or management of state land or assets. Outward FDI and export promotion should in most cases also be handled by a separate unit (Heilbron and Whyte 2019).

Special economic zones

SEZs aim to overcome barriers to investment existing in a country's wider economy. SEZs are demarcated geographic areas with special regulatory regimes—most often customs and fiscal rules, but in some cases rules around foreign ownership or access to land—that are distinct from the rest of an economy. They often feature dedicated support services to ensure that investors face minimal disruption to their supply chains (World Bank 2020). Developing countries most commonly establish SEZs to link into labor-intensive manufacturing GVCs to kick-start industrialization (FIAS 2008). In transition economies, industry-specialized and innovation-driven zones (such as science parks) are most common; in developed countries, the majority of these zones are pure free-trade zones focused on facilitating trade logistics (UNCTAD 2019b).

A commonly used place-based policy tool, SEZs generally provide three types of benefits compared with what firms normally receive in areas outside the zones. These benefits include (a) infrastructure (such as serviced land, factory shells, and utilites), (b) tax incentives (including access to imported inputs free of tariffs and duties and reduced or eliminated corporate income and value added taxes), and (c) regulatory simplification (such as streamlined regulatory procedures, investor aftercare, and efficient customs administration). Because in many developing countries public infrastructure is undersupplied by the private sector and highly expensive to construct, these countries' governments may create public goods by directly investing in a specific location's infrastructure or by stimulating infrastructure investments there by foreign or domestic firms. Additionally, SEZ-specific regulatory simplification may address government failures, such as cumbersome or discretionary regulatory burdens that investors would face outside of these zones. These benefits may reduce the costs to produce and trade and thereby stimulate positive externalities for the host economy. However, the effectiveness of the various types of SEZ-specific benefits varies. Infrastructure provision and regulatory simplification tend to be the most important factors in making SEZs effective, whereas the effects of tax incentives are mixed (see box 4.2). In addition, SEZs can be used as "testing grounds" for new economic policies and approches, as they are in China and other East Asian economies (Zeng 2011).[9]

The global record on SEZs has been mixed. In some parts of the world, the SEZ model has delivered spectacularly, playing a catalytic role in growth and structural transformation (World Bank 2020). China; the Republic of Korea; Malaysia; Taiwan, China; and Singapore, among other Asian economies, managed to use SEZs as platforms for developing export-oriented manufacturing (Jeong and Zeng 2016; see also chapter 8 of this report). In the Middle East and North Africa, countries such as the Arab Republic of Egypt, Morocco, and the United Arab Emirates have used SEZs to catalyze the diversification of their exports. And a number of Latin American countries, including the Dominican Republic, El Salvador, and Honduras, have used free zones ("maquiladoras") to take advantage of preferential access to US markets and establish large-scale manufacturing sectors (see chapter 7 of this report).

However, SEZ programs in other regions did not yield the expected results. In some countries, such as India, Namibia, and Nigeria, SEZs either have failed to attract investors or have attracted investors that took advantage of the associated tax breaks without delivering substantial employment or export gains (World Bank 2020). Especially

BOX 4.2 Provisions of special economic zones and their effectiveness

- *Infrastructure and utilities.* Special economic zones (SEZs) may help address production challenges in a country by providing land and access to reliable and cheap utilities, such as water and electricity. Other facilities provided in SEZs may include prefabricated factory units and warehouses. Infrastructure and utility provision are found to be strongly correlated with increased foreign direct investment (FDI) and exports (Dollar, Hallward-Driemeier, and Mengistae 2004; Portugal-Perez and Wilson 2010) and with employment (Aggarwal 2005). They were also the most important determinant of effectiveness for a sample of SEZs across six African countries (Farole 2011a). Additionally, SEZs allow governments to improve their returns to infrastructure and utility provision by concentrating their investment in small, targeted areas (UNIDO 2009).

- *Regulatory simplification and investor aftercare.* Firms operating in SEZs may be given preferential regulatory services and better investment aftercare. These benefits, such as one-stop centers that enable firms to spend less time registering or obtaining permits, reduce the cost of doing business. One-stop centers may also have important indirect effects: firms can raise any specific problems there, access information about other (not SEZ-specific) government benefits, and obtain more timely access to information on new laws and regulations. However, not all one-stop centers are associated with better SEZ outcomes. Ineffective implementation sometimes prevents these centers from speeding up business registration or simplifying regulatory compliance (Farole 2011a). SEZs may further ease border regulations through trade facilitation schemes. Such interventions lower customs clearance times and reduce trade costs. There are strong empirical links between transportation and trade facilitation and export outcomes (Djankov, Freund, and Pham 2006; Dollar, Hallward-Driemeier, and Mengistae 2004; Freund and Rocha 2010; Portugal-Perez and Wilson 2010).

- *Tax incentives.* SEZs can attract new firms through designated tax incentives (such as tax holidays and rate reductions). The literature finds mixed results for these efforts. Although investors often lobby governments for additional tax incentives, providing such support might not translate into the governments' desired outcomes. A range of empirical studies on tax incentives suggests that they have little impact on attracting FDI (Bobonis and Shatz 2007; Wei 2000). Similarly, Farole (2011a) finds that the use of corporate tax holidays had no significant effect on the ability of African SEZs to attract FDI, improve exports, or increase employment. On the contrary, tax holidays may exacerbate economic distortions and lead to lower welfare as a result of the revenue lost (Kline and Moretti 2014). Successful SEZs (in China, Mauritius, and Vietnam, for instance) are increasingly removing such fiscal incentives and integrating their zones' tax regimes with those of their national economies (Farole 2011a; Zeng 2015).

Source: Adapted from Steenbergen and Javorcik 2017.

in Sub-Saharan Africa, few SEZs have had a transformative impact; their exports and employment generation lag behind those of zones on other continents (Farole 2011b). Although this effect may partly be caused by the broader structural economic challenges in Africa, including higher transportation and labor costs, Farole (2011b) shows that African SEZs often fail to provide sufficiently favorable business environments. A study of 13 African SEZs by Zeng (2020) shows that the market's demand factor and zone-level governance are also critical to a zone's success. Even for zones in the same country that face the same legal and business environment, the zones with stronger business orientation and higher implementation capacity tend to perform better.

Policy makers should design SEZs in such a way as to remove binding investment constraints and strengthen the sectors in which a country has comparative advantages. SEZs are no end in themselves, but they may be useful if multiple investment constraints apply within a country and alternative investment promotion is difficult to implement, as is often the case in low-income countries (UNCTAD 2019b). SEZs should therefore be designed in close consultation with investors and other relevant stakeholders and tailored to address specific constraints on investment. In that sense, they may act as shortcuts to policy reforms or infrastructure investments that would otherwise take many years to achieve (World Bank 2020).

SEZs can also play an important role in prioritizing infrastructure investments that can help reduce the production and trading costs of existing domestic industries, which will help them grow and establish the economies of scale needed to compete regionally (Farole 2011a). However, SEZs are too often used to strengthen sectors in which a country has no comparative advantage. For example, a number of resource-intensive countries (such as Ghana, Kuwait, and Nigeria) failed to develop manufacturing-oriented SEZs because they did not have the competitively priced labor or efficient infrastructure needed to support such activities (World Bank 2020). Governments should also refrain from using SEZs as explicit regional development programs; rather, they should let market mechanisms decide the zones' locations. In Honduras, for example, the government's attempt to designate specific areas as SEZs backfired, and FDI came only when its geographic restrictions were lifted (see chapter 7 of this report). There must always be commercial rationales for SEZs.

Special attention should be given to linking SEZs to the rest of their countries' economies and to helping firms establish innovation clusters. SEZs are often criticized for their typical focus on low-value-added activities and exports and their enclave-like nature (FIAS 2008). Countries that have successfully used SEZs to spur industrial development and upgrading have focused on establishing the conditions to foster ongoing exchange and technology transfer between the domestic economy and foreign investors located in the SEZs (Farole 2011b). These conditions include investments by domestic firms in the zones, forward and backward linkages, and movement of labor. This aspect of SEZ management also requires broader policy programs, especially enterprise and skills development policies, that foster domestic productive capacity (see the next section on domestic firm internationalization policies for details). Trade restrictions with non-SEZ firms (including those arising from customs regulations) should also be eliminated (Farole 2011b). And, just as important, SEZs should focus on creating clusters of firms participating in particular GVCs, which can help those firms innovate over time. The Malaysia case study in this report (chapter 8) shows the power that SEZs can have when they do so. In contrast, the Honduras case study (chapter 7) shows how, without continuous adaption, SEZs may limit a country to engaging in one narrow segment of a GVC.

To further allow the host country's whole economy to benefit, good practices from successful SEZs should be replicated in the rest of the economy to maximize positive spillovers. A review of the World Bank's lending portfolio in SEZs revealed that, in the absence of wider reforms, benefits arising from SEZs tend to remain within the zones themselves, with little spilling over to the wider economy (World Bank Group 2017).

Investment incentives

Governments use investment incentives to attract foreign firms and encourage specific behavior. Many governments offer tax concessions intended to steer investment into preferred sectors or specific regions or to enhance the investment's development effects (James 2014). However, tax incentives come at the expense of forgone revenue and should be seen as a type of government subsidy or a form of state-directed "investment" in a company's future. Tax incentives are justified only if they generate positive externalities that compensate for their present social costs (Harrison and Rodríguez-Clare 2010; Margalioth 2003; Wade 1990).

Tax incentives are often used to meet two types of objectives (figure 4.5):

1. *Locational incentives* hope to generate positive externalities by attracting MNCs that will provide new GVC opportunities and raise domestic firms' productivity and sector competitiveness. Because FDI is highly mobile across countries, attracting MNCs may require offering reduced tax rates or other incentives. This is a classic case in which incentives can lead to net social benefits (Margalioth 2003).

2. *Behavioral incentives* aim to generate positive externalities by stimulating specific firm behavior (such as innovation) that will yield high social benefits. Temporary support can help improve firms' long-term productivity. For such interventions to enhance welfare, they must pass two tests: the supported firms should eventually be able to survive international competition without the incentives, and the expected future benefits should compensate for the present subsidy costs. In practice, it is extremely hard to identify firms that would exhibit such spillovers if supported, let alone to identify the incentives that would pass a cost-benefit assessment (Harrison and Rodríguez-Clare 2010).

Developing countries are increasingly using tax incentives as part of their industrialization strategies. Andersen, Kett, and von Uexkull (2018) find that, for the period

FIGURE 4.5 Locational and behavioral incentives have different aims and expected benefits

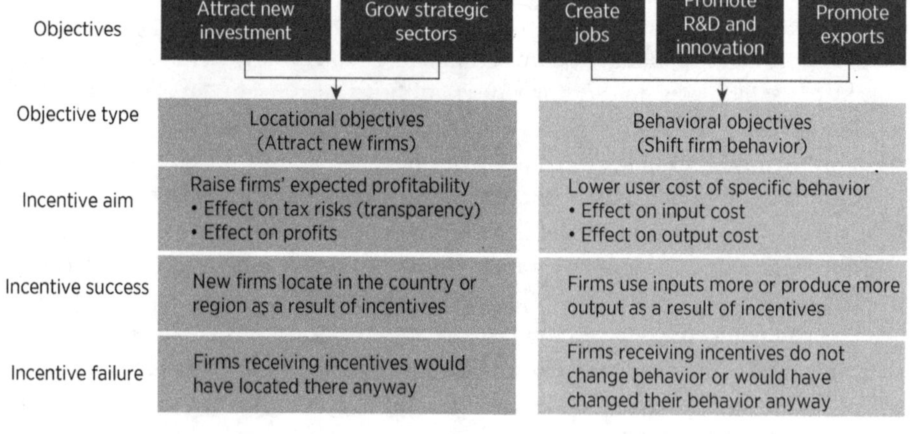

	Locational objectives (Attract new firms)	Behavioral objectives (Shift firm behavior)
Objectives	Attract new investment / Grow strategic sectors	Create jobs / Promote R&D and innovation / Promote exports
Objective type	Locational objectives (Attract new firms)	Behavioral objectives (Shift firm behavior)
Incentive aim	Raise firms' expected profitability • Effect on tax risks (transparency) • Effect on profits	Lower user cost of specific behavior • Effect on input cost • Effect on output cost
Incentive success	New firms locate in the country or region as a result of incentives	Firms use inputs more or produce more output as a result of incentives
Incentive failure	Firms receiving incentives would have located there anyway	Firms receiving incentives do not change behavior or would have changed their behavior anyway

Source: Kronfol and Steenbergen 2020.
Note: R&D = research and development.

2009–15, 46 percent of developing countries either reduced their corporate income tax rates or introduced new tax incentives. Incentives are particularly common in the construction, information technology and electronics, and machinery and equipment sectors. Among developing countries, tax holidays are the most widely used instruments (used in 77 percent of cases) and are often conditioned on a firm's locating in a SEZ or another specially designated area. Tax allowances are less common, offered by only 16 percent of developing countries.

Overall, there is a trend toward lower corporate taxation of foreign firms, emphasizing the risk of tax competition and a "race to the bottom." Indeed, Kronfol and Steenbergen (2020) find a strong, negative relationship between the generosity of countries' corporate tax incentives and corporate tax revenue as a share of GDP. A likely reason for this finding is that tax incentives often go not only to new firms in priority sectors but also to existing firms, eroding the country's corporate tax base. Strategies existing firms can use to take advantage of these tax incentives include round-tripping (creating an artificial new firm to qualify for the incentives) and transfer pricing (shifting intercompany assets to lower-tax locations) (Zolt 2013).

Evidence on the effectiveness of locational incentives to attract FDI is mixed. Although studies find a negative correlation between high corporate tax rates and FDI entry (see Bellak, Leibrecht, and Damijan 2009; Bénassy-Quéré, Fontagné, and Lahrèche-Révil 2005; Büttner et al. 2008; Desai, Foley, and Hines 2006), evidence on the impact of tax incentives is limited, and several studies find that they have little to no effect at the aggregate level (see Allen et al. 2001; James 2014; Klemm and Vasn Parys 2012; Van Parys 2012; Van Parys and James 2010). Data from the 2019 GIC survey confirms that other variables, such as political stability, regulatory quality, and market size, are generally considered more important by investors than tax rates and incentives. Incentives are both the most prevalent and the most valued in sectors dominated by export-oriented manufacturing (Andersen, Kett, and von Uexkull 2018; Kusek and Silva 2018).[10] However, when investor motivation is based on less mobile factors (such as natural resources or domestic markets), incentives are often redundant (Andersen, Kett, and von Uexkull 2018).

The effectiveness of locational incentives also depends strongly on country-level characteristics. Tax incentives are more effective in countries with better infrastructure, reasonable transportation costs, and a policy framework favoring investment (Bellak, Leibrecht, and Damijan 2009; Kinda 2014). In fact, tax incentives have been shown to be eight times more effective in attracting FDI in countries with good investment climates than in those with worse climates (James 2014). Other country-level factors, such as political stability, regulatory quality, and market opportunities, are more critical to investors' initial location considerations than are tax rates and incentives (UNIDO 2011; World Bank Group 2019). In general, a low tax burden cannot compensate for a weak or unattractive FDI environment (Göndör and Nistor 2012). However, for suitable locations, incentives can play a role in the final stage of the site selection process, in which investors decide between shortlisted locations and often waver between similar options (Freund and Moran 2017; World Bank 2018). Several of the case studies in part II of this report (chapters 6 to 11) illustrate this point (particularly those on Honduras, Malaysia, and Mauritius). Locational incentives helped attract foreign investors to these countries, but they could only do so because the countries had strong foundations for investment in place.

Behavioral incentives may be used to induce investors to pursue various types of behaviors, including research and development (R&D), innovation, and workforce training. The literature shows a positive association between tax incentives and R&D intensity (Busom, Corchuelo, and Martínez-Ros 2012). Tax credits seem to have the most impact on larger firms without financing constraints, whereas direct grants are most effective at influencing small and medium enterprises and firms with no previous R&D experience (Correa, Andres, and Borja-Vega 2013; Correa and Guceri 2013). As for incentives related to workforce training, a mix of tax incentives and grants targeted to specific groups of enterprises or employees appears to be more appropriate than a single incentive for a large number of companies (Müller and Behringer 2012). Malaysia's experience shows how R&D grants and workforce training incentives can help stimulate firms to undertake higher-value-added activities in a country (see chapter 8 of this report).

Different approaches to tax incentives may be warranted in different countries, depending on their investment climates. In countries with poor investment climates, it may be best to streamline tax incentives to protect the countries' tax bases. Tax revenues can instead be directed toward helping reduce firms' costs of doing business (such as through public investment in infrastructure and utilities). In countries with better investment climates, tax incentives should be targeted toward high-potential investors who are likely to both be influenced by these instruments and contribute to the countries' economic development objectives. Determining the appropriate targets for these incentives requires an understanding of their costs and benefits.[11]

To strengthen a country's investment incentive regime, it is important to consider the design, transparency, and administration of the incentives. Figure 4.6 presents a framework for strengthening investment regimes that is based on six steps and criteria. The specific and measurable policy goals to be pursued through the incentives should serve as the starting point. Next, countries should reflect on the targets of the incentives and ensure that the selection criteria are objective and tied to the policy goals. Third, countries should consider which instruments (such as tax credits, investment allowances, or R&D grants) are most conducive to achieving the policy goals. To ensure that the regime is as cost-effective as possible, firms receiving incentives should be subject to regular review and rigorous monitoring, and effective safeguards should be put in place to provide sunset clauses for any ongoing incentives.

FIGURE 4.6 Framework for strengthening a country's investment incentive regime

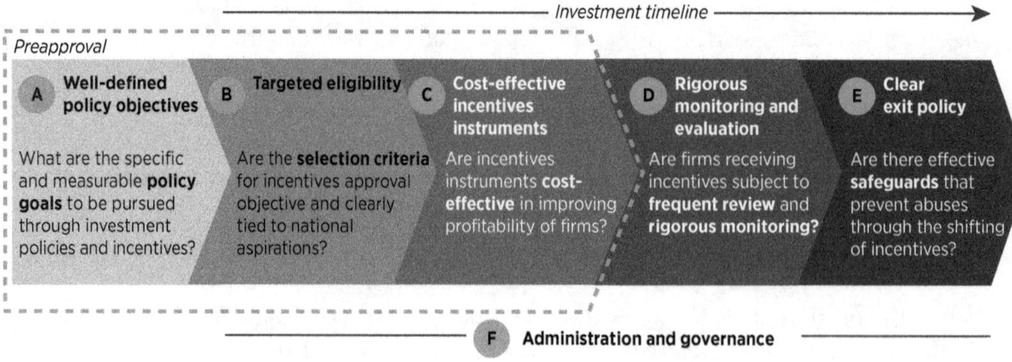

Source: World Bank, forthcoming.

Finally, countries must ensure effective administration and maintain a transparent, rules-based legal and governing system to underpin these incentives.

Domestic firm internationalization policy

Domestic firm internationalization policy is another critical means for stimulating GVC participation and ensuring that the benefits of GVCs are extended to local firms (see chapter 3). Governments can further strengthen the role that domestic firms play within GVCs and assist them in upgrading to higher-value-added activities using the following four policy instruments:

1. Combining matchmaking with support to strengthen local supplier capacity
2. Facilitating strategic alliances built on competitive industries
3. Safeguarding competitive and contestable markets
4. Removing restrictions on outward FDI and investing in R&D and human capital

Combining matchmaking with support to strengthen local supplier capacity

Firms' potential to establish linkages is typically restricted by two types of market failures: information asymmetries and coordination failures. Information asymmetries may arise because newly established MNCs face high search and screening costs because they lack sufficient information on local suppliers and their capabilities. And, on the supply side, local firms often struggle to understand what opportunities are available, who to contact in pursuit of them, and what requirements and standards need to be met to qualify as a supplier for MNCs. The second type of market failure, coordination failures, may restrict the quality of domestic suppliers. MNCs operate in competitive global markets, requiring their inputs and suppliers to meet quality, cost, and timeliness criteria. Local firms often do not meet these minimum requirements, but they are reluctant to bear the costs of upgrading their production capabilities (such as in management, skills, or technology) without a supplier contract.

MNCs and supplier firms dedicate much effort to establishing their supply dynamics, which can be transformational for both those firms and their host countries. MNCs often assign "talent scouts" to search for potential suppliers and apply detailed screening procedures to identify the most suitable domestic firms (World Bank 2018). They need to engage in these costly procedures in part because the market does not provide sufficient information for them to identify the right domestic firms to source from (Jordaan, Douw, and Qiang 2020). Large fixed costs are also associated with switching suppliers, including the support, training, and certification that new suppliers will need before they can produce inputs that meet global standards (see chapter 3 of this report). However, when such linkages happen, they can do much to facilitate GVC participation (see chapter 6 of this report).

To promote linkages between MNCs and domestic firms, host governments have implemented a variety of policies. The effectiveness of these policies often depends largely on the governments' ability to address information asymmetries and coordination failures.

Local content requirements are generally ineffective and counterproductive at stimulating supply linkages. Historically, countries have aimed to boost the development of local firms through laws and regulations that required that a certain percentage of goods used by MNCs operating in the country be purchased from domestic firms. Such policies were generally unsuccessful, in part because they were difficult and costly to enforce: firms could easily circumvent such measures through creative accounting practices or deceptive statistics (Sutton 2014).[12] In addition, these policies do not address either of the constraints on local sourcing (information asymmetries or coordination failures). Instead, they force producers to use higher-cost and lower-quality domestic inputs, creating market inefficiencies that may reduce the overall productivity and competitiveness of the country's export sector (Spray 2017). Thus, counterproductively, these policies can discourage foreign investment in the host country and raise costs for local consumers (Johnson 2013). A study of the Russian Federation's heavy vehicles sector confirms the distortive effects and costs that such policies can have for both producers and consumers (Deringer et al. 2018).

Information campaigns are an important, low-cost intervention that can help spread knowledge between MNCs and local suppliers. To deal with the problems caused by asymmetric information on suppliers, databases containing production and financial information about domestic firms could reduce the information constraints and search costs faced by MNCs when identifying and matching with local suppliers. In addition, governments could create qualification or certification programs to help preselect the domestic firms that are most likely to operate effectively as suppliers (Moran 2014). These selection criteria may serve as important signals about domestic firms to MNCs (Jordaan, Douw, and Qiang 2020).

Governments can further support local suppliers' upgrading by aligning public and private standards. Firms often incur multiple burdensome certification procedures or design numerous production processes for the same product to comply with conflicting standards. Simplifying and publishing national production standards, aligning them with international quality standards and the general requirements of MNCs, and producing guidelines that illustrate how to meet these standards can go a long way toward creating clarity for local suppliers (Cusolito, Safadi, and Taglioni 2016).

Supplier development programs (SDPs) that combine matchmaking with proactive support to help local suppliers upgrade can be transformative, though costly. These programs address information asymmetries by arranging special matchmaking events at which local suppliers and MNCs can explore possible partnerships. These programs can then work together with the MNCs to develop appropriate training and capacity-building programs so that the local suppliers can produce the necessary inputs at the required quality standards in return for supply contracts (Steenbergen and Sutton 2017). These programs can be highly transformational for suppliers. For example, in Costa Rica, such a program significantly raised firm sales and productivity (Alfaro-Ureña, Manelici, and Vasquez 2019). In Chile, a program combining matchmaking services with subsidized credit was found to significantly increase sales, employment, and the sustainability of participating small and medium enterprises (Arraiz, Henriquez, and Stucchi 2013). A Czech SDP was found to increase sales for about one-third of all participating firms, and it helped one-fifth of the firms initiate exports or obtain contracts for higher-value-added content (Mariscal and Taglioni 2017). However, SDPs are often very expensive, and they require significant capacity to design and implement. They are thus often relatively small, which can limit their

BOX 4.3 **Lessons learned from five supplier development programs**

A study of five supplier development programs (SDPs) confirms the importance of facilitating linkages, strengthening the supply capacity of local companies, and using targeted incentives to encourage skills upgrading. Heher (2020) reviews five historical SDPs that have all been deemed successful: those of the Czech Republic, Ireland, Malaysia, Singapore, and Thailand. Although these programs differed in their approaches and country contexts, they all showed that developing supply linkages requires a long-term view, with both policy commitment to addressing specific market failures and, at the same time, the flexibility to adapt to new opportunities and challenges along the way.

These five cases confirm the importance of focusing such programs on changing the demand side rather than imposing local content on unwilling multinational corporations (MNCs). Changing the demand side requires a thorough and realistic understanding of MNCs' business needs and requirements. Thus, it is advisable to integrate MNCs into the governance structure of SDPs or to have the international private sector either closely advise or even run certain linking initiatives (as was done in the Czech Republic's and Malaysia's programs, respectively). Because trust and information gaps are often problems for these initiatives, at least initially, involving MNCs in them as partners from the beginning is crucial. Countries that passed laws requiring investors to use local goods or services in host-country operations often undermined their own long-term competitiveness. These requirements tended to increase the cost or lower the quality of production in those countries, deterring exactly the investors that the governments wanted to attract: those who would bring capital, technology, and jobs to the host countries.

Strengthening the supply capacity of local companies is, in most cases, the key challenge to developing foreign direct investment (FDI) linkages. Thus, improving those firms' competitiveness and productivity should be at the core of the programs. Because market failures play out at the firm level, increasing productivity is the ultimate goal of most SDPs (Cusolito and Maloney 2018). A firm's potential to increase its productivity should be a key criterion in selecting domestic firms to participate. Thus, it is necessary to appreciate that supplier capacity development, in contrast to more broad-based small and medium enterprise development, should focus on firms that are close to meeting MNCs' supplier criteria or capable of becoming long-term partners of MNCs (such as for design or research and development [R&D] activities). Although the five programs examined in Heher (2020) differed in the levels of targeting and support they gave, most of them either started out providing tailored support or adapted to focus on meeting specific MNC production criteria. In Ireland, Malaysia, and Thailand, skills upgrading was particularly important (in areas ranging from technical skills in production processes to management competencies).

Many of these programs applied targeted incentives for skills upgrading and supplier engagement. Broad tax incentives impose a significant fiscal cost, and emerging evidence supports targeted approaches over broad incentives. For example, incentives focused on training and skills, R&D, high-tech and higher-value-added production, and local sourcing have been successfully applied in Malaysia and Singapore to strengthen the technology and skills acquisition of local firms (OECD 2018).

SDPs touch upon multiple important thematic areas and require a committed and coordinated institutional landscape. The various examples given in Heher (2020) show different institutional setups, but what they have in common are relatively well-funded mandates (which are based on widely communicated policy agendas) and high-level political buy-in. Although several institutions had roles to play in promoting linkages between these countries' local firms and MNCs, these programs always involved national focal points for both foreign and domestic firms. It was also key that these programs could coordinate policies and interventions through an entity that guided the policy agenda, such as a ministry of industry. Such an entity can bring together several thematic areas, including cluster policies, industrial ecosystem development, and standards, and promote access to financial services and education policies that focus on technical and managerial skills.

Source: World Bank adaptation of Heher 2020.
Note: More details on using incentives to establish supply linkages can be found in Sabha, Liu, and Douw (2020).

transformative potential (Farole and Winkler 2014). Box 4.3 provides more lessons from a study of five SDPs (Heher 2020).

Facilitating strategic alliances built on competitive industries

Several potential market and government failures warrant policy makers' attention when supporting strategic alliances. The first challenge may come from positive externalities. MNCs may be reluctant to engage in new alliances (such as joint ventures) for fear of leaking trade secrets to domestic firms (Jiang et al. 2018). As with MNC-supplier linkages, these alliances can be prone to information asymmetries, in which firms may not know each other's capacities, or to coordination failures, in which firms are reluctant to invest in the short term to realize a future partnership (UNCTAD 2011). Certain well-intentioned policies meant to stimulate alliances, such as joint venture requirements, may actually increase the cost of investment in a country and scare off potential investors, thus limiting the opportunities for domestic firms to collaborate with MNCs (UNCTAD 2011).

The most promising alliance-promoting approaches often build on the strengths of an existing, high-performing industry and use a facilitative process to stimulate strategic alliances between local firms and MNCs. Governments can promote strategic alliances by facilitating the process of forming them (such as by providing all necessary information to establish them, temporary support for them, and light-touch regulation to address any underlying market failures). However, the decisions to form such alliances still ultimately depend on two firms possessing fundamentally complementary interests. For that reason, these approaches tend to be most effective when used to stimulate existing, high-performing industries to improve their performance and link them more closely with higher-value GVCs. Governments could then use a combination of facilitation and incentives to encourage partnerships via contracts or equity stakes and to generate positive knowledge spillovers for local firms and industries. (One such program, which took place in Mauritius's tourism industry, is described in chapter 9 of this report.)

Joint venture requirements often have counterproductive results and lead to fewer opportunities for strategic alliances. Some developing countries have established policies that require MNCs, in exchange for market access, to transfer knowledge or technology into the country by forming joint ventures with domestic firms. Under such quid pro quo policies, MNCs often face restrictions by which foreign ownership of any local firm is capped at less than 50 percent (Jiang et al. 2018). The most well-known example of such a policy comes from China, which adopted such restrictions in several strategic industries[13] with the aim of helping domestic producers learn from their foreign partners and eventually grow into worthy competitors in the international market (Bai et al. 2019). Evidence shows that these policies did lead to technology transfers, both to the joint venture and to the Chinese partner firm, and helped raise the average quality of the industries (Bai et al. 2019; Jiang et al. 2018). However, it was only because of China's very large domestic market, which most developing countries do not have, that MNCs were willing to put up with these restrictions so they could enter China's priority sectors. Indeed, many investors considered the technology transfer requirement a critical barrier that dissuaded them from investing in China.[14]

Jiang et al. (2018) also find that technology spillovers were largest in sectors that were more open, and positive technology externalities were dampened in industries with many prohibitions on types of foreign investment. The 2020 pledge by the Chinese government to remove its foreign ownership restrictions and specific requirements for some sectors is thus expected to have profound impacts on these industries. Liberalizing these sectors could give MNCs stronger incentives to bring their most advanced technology to the Chinese market by allowing them to better guard it (Bai et al. 2019). Hence, even countries that have the bargaining power necessary to impose investment or performance requirements are still likely to find them counterproductive, leading to reduced FDI inflows, fewer opportunities for strategic alliances, and, ultimately, less knowledge transferred between firms.

A clear and stable legal and regulatory framework would also help promote alliances, in part because it would offer an important locational determinant for FDI. Commercial and contract laws are particularly important because many alliances between MNCs and local firms are essentially contract based. Among other things, business parties need to know what domestic rules govern their alliances, the extent to which the country's regulations constrain contractual discretion, whether the parties can choose the law of a third country or international arbitration to apply to their contracts, what the consequences would be of a breach of contract, what procedures would apply in the event of a dispute, and how a judicial decision or arbitration award could be enforced (UNCTAD 2011).

Specific laws that govern particular types of alliances (such as franchising or licensing) are equally important. Laws concerning intellectual property are particularly important for equity-based alliances, including joint ventures (UNCTAD 2011). However, identifying the relevant laws and regulations can be complicated, because many countries do not have specific rules for each type of alliance and instead apply general contract laws along with other types of legislation.[15] In such situations, ensuring a transparent and coherent legal framework becomes paramount. Other measures, such as simplifying the administrative steps needed to set up a new business (including a joint venture) or adopting communication campaigns to inform businesses of existing regulations, can further support such alliances (UNCTAD 2011).

IPAs can also support strategic alliances through information and matchmaking campaigns. Similar to how they support MNC-supplier linkages, IPAs can support alliances by providing information and facilitating projects. For example, they can host investment fairs to promote franchising and management contract opportunities. Broader matchmaking programs (comparable to supplier development programs) have also been used by IPAs to stimulate joint ventures (UNCTAD 2011). In some cases, an IPA may suggest a strategic alliance with a local partner as a way to help an MNC access scarce resources or overcome existing bureaucratic hurdles. In these cases, IPAs serve a joint role by facilitating FDI while working to maximize domestic spillovers (de Caldas Lima 2008).

In many cases, legal reforms and IPA support are combined with more proactive measures that help prepare local firms for strategic alliances. These measures include a range of policies and activities, such as entrepreneurship policies, skills policies, technological training, and measures to ease financial access. The overall form this assistance takes depends on the type of alliance. UNCTAD (2011) finds that local entrepreneurship programs are often linked to franchising, project negotiations are used to support management contracts, and skills development and technological training, along with fiscal and financial subsidies, are most used to promote joint ventures. Examples of such programs abound. For example, the government of Malaysia has introduced franchising-specific legislation and used various agencies to launch information campaigns and offer financial support to local firms that set up franchises of MNCs.[16] Similarly, the governments of Brazil and the Philippines use a combination of skills and language training and tax incentives to assist any joint ventures between local firms and MNCs to galvanize their call center industries. To best ensure that such capacity-building strategies are successful, local firms must be made aware of them and focus on the MNCs they aim to partner with (UNCTAD 2011).

Safeguarding competitive and contestable markets

In many cases, the entry of FDI into a country increases the contestability of national markets and improves competition. However, FDI can also increase market concentration. As described in chapter 2, MNCs apply a range of strategies to increase their market power in GVCs. They may indulge in anticompetitive behavior, such as abusing their dominant position to prey upon their competitors or suppliers or colluding with other producers of the same product. Although global markets are by definition more contestable than segmented national markets (because producers from around the world can participate in them), MNCs can still acquire a dominant position in selected production processes in a country at the expense of local competitors or supplier firms (for details, see chapter 2.) It may thus be important to monitor a country's MNCs for potentially anticompetitive practices. The relatively large size and productivity of these firms compared with domestic firms makes them more able to engage in predatory pricing (to drive local competitors out of business) or to acquire domestic competitors, in both cases reducing competition and dissuading new entry into the market (UNCTAD 1997).

Both equity and nonequity strategic alliances can result in anticompetitive behavior. One main way in which competition law and FDI interact is when foreign entry is accomplished through a merger, acquisition, or joint venture with significant impact on the host country's market (including the creation or strengthening of a dominant position). Policy makers need to carefully consider the trade-offs between the benefits associated with new FDI, on one hand, and the reduction of economic welfare caused by that FDI's anticompetitive effects, on the other (UNCTAD 1997). In addition, specific contractual provisions in nonequity strategic alliances, such as exclusive dealing obligations, territorial constraints, or resale price maintenance, may also raise competition concerns. All of these provisions enable one party (such as an MNC) to use its market power to the detriment of competitors or local suppliers (UNCTAD 2011).

A strong legal framework and a competent and effective competition enforcement agency are critical to safeguarding competitive and contestable markets. A strong legal framework and competition law become increasingly necessary as FDI is liberalized to ensure that former statutory obstacles to contestability are not replaced by firms' anticompetitive practices (as described in the previous paragraph), thus negating the benefits of liberalization (Goldman, Kissack, and Witterrick 1997; UNCTAD 1997; World Bank and OECD 2017). Such regulations should aim to remove anticompetitive sectoral regulations and to eliminate government interventions that encourage collusive outcomes (such as price controls) or discriminate among firms (such as state aid). Also necessary is a competent and effective competition enforcement agency with broad powers to investigate firm behavior, including the authority to analyze the competitive effects of the entry and operations of foreign investors. This agency should focus on preventing or dismantling cartel agreements that may affect the cost of or access to key inputs or final products, preventing anticompetitive mergers, strengthening the host country's antitrust framework, and controlling state aid to ensure competitive neutrality (World Bank and OECD 2017).

Policy makers can further help strengthen the bargaining position of domestic firms. MNCs provide essential technology and global market access and therefore often hold stronger bargaining positions (in supplier linkages and strategic alliances) than their local counterparts. Thus, to ensure that MNC–local firm partnerships persist over time, it is important for local partners to build on their strengths and to maintain or increase their relevance within the partnership (see chapter 3). Governments can also help strengthen the bargaining positions of domestic firms to ensure that both contracting parties fairly share the partnership's risk and to prevent the arrangement from confining the local firm to low-value-added activities. They can provide local partners with legal protection by mandating precontractual requirements on the MNC's part.[17] In addition, public agencies can offer advice to local partners on topics such as how to negotiate contracts or how to form equity-based alliances. Agencies can also publish relevant materials such as negotiating guidelines, checklists of issues to be considered in negotiations, codes of conduct, model contracts, or benchmark prices for the relevant products and services. Finally, supporting collective bargaining, including the formation of domestic producers' associations, can help counterbalance MNCs' negotiating power (UNCTAD 2011).

Promoting outward foreign direct investment and investing in research and development and human capital

As explained in chapter 3 of this report, the most productive and capital-rich local firms in an economy may be able to enter GVCs by engaging in outward foreign direct investment (OFDI)—in other words, by becoming MNCs themselves. To help these firms do so, policy makers may need to remove regulatory restrictions, help reduce information asymmetries, and adopt complementary measures to maximize the benefits of this OFDI for the home economy. Examples from Korea, China, and Singapore suggest that an approach combining targeted information provision, local capacity building, market access support, access to finance, and strategic planning assistance can contribute significantly to strengthening firm performance and stimulating domestic firms' roles within global production networks. (See chapter 10 of this report for details on the examples of Korea and China, and see Perea and Stephenson [2018] for details on Singapore's.)

The most common restriction on OFDI is government-operated capital controls on outward investment. Although OFDI offers promising opportunities for both the firms engaging in it and their source countries, many governments still restrict it. According to the International Monetary Fund's Annual Report on Exchange Arrangements and Exchange Restrictions database, 86 out of 192 countries had controls in place on outward direct investment in 2018 (IMF 2019). These controls are most common in developing countries; 58 percent of such countries still control outward direct investment, whereas only 21 percent of high-income countries do so. Such controls have traditionally been used to achieve macroeconomic objectives (such as financial stability). However, the efficacy of capital controls in achieving such goals has been questioned, and such restrictions may hold back firms' OFDI potential (Perea and Stephenson 2018).

Outward investment promotion agencies, which perform a function for OFDI analogous to what regular IPAs do to promote investment within a country, can use foreign relations (at times, in partnership with overseas embassies) to help local firms develop knowledge connections and access foreign markets. These initiatives help firms because such relationships may spur them to take a more long-term view of FDI, helping to strengthen nascent sectors in the country that may become more strategically important over time (Crescenzi, Di Cataldo, and Giua 2019). An example of this strategy comes from Korea, whose Korea Overseas Company Information System runs several websites with OFDI information and provides consulting services for Korean firms looking to invest abroad (Kim and Rhee 2009). In addition, its Korea Overseas Company Assistance Center helps Korean firms collect information on financing and possible business sites (Nicolas, Thomsen, and Bang 2013).

In some cases, outward investment promotion agencies provide more direct support through financial and fiscal measures aimed to compensate for the positive externalities associated with OFDI and with GVC participation more broadly. China, for example, has recently adopted many such policies. It supports OFDI by providing low lending rates, flexible terms for projects, and fast regulatory approval. It also provides credit support and financial assistance both to large-scale business groups that possess sufficient capital, technology, management skill, and branding for priority OFDI projects and to outward investors who want to build foreign R&D centers on China's behalf (CDB and EXIM 2006; China, MOFCOM 2014). Chinese outward investors are also compensated for several types of political risk (including expropriation, restrictions on the transfer and conversion of funds, damage caused by war, inability to operate because of war, and breach of contractual undertakings) through government-offered insurance (Sauvant and Chen 2013).

Investments in R&D and human capital, and policies to promote them, would make OFDI strategies more effective. Firms need to have a specific strength to engage successfully in OFDI, whether it be a brand, a technology, or a specific managerial or organizational capability (Antràs and Yeaple 2014). Investing in domestic firms' technology, innovation, and human capital is therefore an important way to ensure their upgrading.

Policies to promote in-house R&D collaboration between large local firms and universities were found to help increase the probability of outward investment in India (Thomas and Narayanan 2017). China also accompanied its OFDI strategy with a push toward technological innovation. It adopted more than 170 policies to stimulate innovation using a wide range of instruments: fiscal incentives, grants, loan guarantees, vouchers, equity, public procurement, technology extension services, incubators, accelerators, competitive grants and prizes, science and technology parks, and collaboration and networks. Tax incentives account for about half of the value of China's total support for OFDI (OECD 2017). In addition, lack of access to finance seems to be a main market failure that policy makers should address to stimulate innovation (see chapter 10 of this report).

To complement any R&D spending, governments should invest in human capital, especially in science and technology skills. Competing in knowledge-intensive GVCs requires strengthening the overall technical foundations of the society. Evidence of this effect can be found in dedicated projects in Korea, India, China, and Singapore that helped train the next generation of high-skilled workers and scientists. In China, the number of science and engineering students pursuing bachelor's degrees increased rapidly to almost 1.5 million in 2014, more than the combined number in the United States and eight countries in the European Union.[18] This increase was partially realized by providing students with grants and scholarships to receive education, training, and experiences at Western and Japanese universities and research institutions (see chapter 10 of this report).

Strategy and approaches for global value chain integration

An integrated, sector-based strategy

Successful integration of low-income countries into GVCs requires coherent packages of reforms. The previous sections present a range of investment policies at governments' disposal. Individually, such policies are likely to have only a marginal effect on a country's GVC participation; each one can only partially address existing market or government failures. However, these policies are highly complementary, so a combined approach could be greatly influential in shaping the behavior of both MNCs and domestic firms (Akileswaran, Calabrese, and Said 2018). Such a strategy would require a sustained, coordinated, and long-term approach based on incentive mechanisms tailored to the specific needs of the country, types of firms, and value chains in question (Cusolito, Safadi, and Taglioni 2016).

From an investment perspective, the most effective approach to stimulating and supporting GVC integration is to mix horizontal measures to strengthen the business enabling environment with a targeted vertical method for sector promotion (Felipe 2015). This approach includes providing a strong general environment for investment by lowering the costs faced by any investors, making the investment process easier, and providing the right infrastructure to support it (Rodrik 2004). Though important, such horizontal measures alone are often insufficient to overcome the market failures that hold back private sector investment in a country (Stiglitz and Norman 2015). To complement them, governments that have managed to significantly scale up GVC participation have also played a more direct role through "soft" or "light-handed" industrial policy at the micro level (Harrison and Rodríguez-Clare 2010; Taglioni and Winkler 2016) to address various sectors' particular market failures.

Using this sector-based approach can help those in charge prioritize among the many different policy instruments and stakeholders involved. Because of the variety of challenges faced by sectors (and thus the variety of interventions needed to address them), this approach requires amending a range of policies that cut across many different ministries, including investment policy, trade policy, public infrastructure, and skills training (World Bank 2020). However, policy makers cannot address all problems at once. Coordination across ministries is difficult, especially given the limits to political capital and institutional capacity often faced by senior policy makers. Setting a few promising value chains as policy anchors makes it easier to communicate priorities and thus to provide a clear sense of direction for the many stakeholders in the effort—in both the public and the private sectors—to rally around. It also helps governments maintain a coherent thread running through their priorities: from the effort's overall vision, to sector-level plans, to subsector plans, to plans for particular value chains, and, finally, to specific flagship regulations, policies, and projects (Akileswaran, Calabrese, and Said 2018).

Although many developing countries approve of sector-based approaches to stimulating economic development, many fall short when they attempt them because of inconsistent and incomplete implementation. Countries often outline the sectors to be developed in many policy and strategy documents. However, these documents often identify different sectors as priorities, with a country's medium-term strategies, national industrial policy, and export promotion policy all differing in their priority sectors. An even starker difference may be found in countries' actual investment regulation and tariff policies, which rarely reflect national strategic considerations and are typically oriented toward purely horizontal purposes or short-term interests (te Velde et al. 2018). These discrepancies generate confusion and hinder coordinated use of scarce government resources, limiting the strategies' overall effectiveness (Akileswaran, Calabrese, and Said 2018).

To illustrate the power of an integrated, sector-based strategy, box 4.4 discusses Rwanda's National Coffee Strategy. This strategy helped transform Rwanda's coffee sector by liberalizing the coffee industry, actively attracting foreign investors to establish the infrastructure necessary to produce and export coffee, and shifting farmers from producing ordinary coffee to producing "fully washed" coffee. As a result, Rwanda's coffee export value increased by almost 500 percent in a little more than a decade.

Global value chain segment mapping to help shape sector-based strategies

A country's GVC strategies should be based on its comparative advantages and its firms' capabilities. The choice of sector is crucial to any sector-based strategy. However, such strategies are not about "picking winners." GVCs make it possible for firms in developing countries to enter foreign markets at lower costs, benefit from specialization in niche tasks, and gain access to larger markets for their output (World Bank 2020). Such specialization is often the result of a country's long-term involvement in a specific sector that takes advantage of and builds on the country's unique combination of factor endowments and firm capacity. Countries tend to upgrade into products that are comparable to the goods they are currently specialized in, and they rarely jump into an entirely new sector (Hidalgo et al. 2007). Because of the evolutionary nature of GVC participation, initial success in one GVC niche can induce rapid growth in adjacent segments (Whittaker et al. 2010). Thus, sector-based strategies should also build on countries' existing revealed comparative advantages.

Firm capacity constraints also matter, including the ability of firms to innovate and adopt new technologies, their management and organization, and their capacity to tap

BOX 4.4 How an integrated, sector-based strategy helped transform Rwanda's coffee sector

In the late 1990s, Rwanda's coffee sector was in a dire state. The sector was closely controlled by the government, with a single coffee price on the basis of volume dictated for the entire season. Two export trading companies dominated the industry: one government owned and one privately owned. Together, they accounted for over 65 percent of total coffee exports (Behuria and Goodfellow 2016). Low market competition depressed farm gate prices for coffee cherries. Farmers had no incentive to upgrade to higher-value coffee processing techniques. As investment fell in the coffee industry, existing coffee tree stocks aged, soil fertility declined, and insect and fungal diseases affected crops. By 2000, Rwanda's coffee production had declined in volume, and 90 percent of Rwanda's coffee harvest was classified as low-quality, "ordinary" coffee.

To break out of this low quantity–low quality trap, the country adopted a National Coffee Strategy in 2002. A key objective of the strategy was to increase the share of high-quality ("fully washed") coffee produced. To encourage farmers to upgrade their production processes, the government shifted the basis of coffee bean pricing from volume to quality. The government also sought additional foreign investment for coffee-washing stations through targeted investment promotion and special incentives for the coffee industry. Furthermore, it accelerated the sector's rate of liberalization, passing additional legislation to provide legal structure and protections for cooperatives in the agriculture sector to encourage domestic investment.

The effect of this strategy on Rwanda's participation in the coffee global value chain has been significant. The strategy's focus on quality and higher-value-added products was the main reason why Rwandan coffee exports increased from US$14.5 million in 2002 to US$69 million in 2018 (figure B4.4.1).

This strategy helped transform Rwanda's coffee sector by stimulating production of fully-washed specialty coffee. In its first decade, Rwanda attracted more than US$70 million in foreign direct investment (FDI) into the sector. Foreign firms invested heavily in washing stations and expanded the value chain for fully washed specialty coffee. During this process, the technical capacity of farmers and operators of coffee-washing stations was upgraded: the number of washing stations increased from 2 in 2002 to more than 250 in 2015 (figure B4.4.2), providing additional opportunities for value addition. In addition, the number of licensed coffee

FIGURE B4.4.1 **Rwandan coffee export values and volumes, 1996–2018**

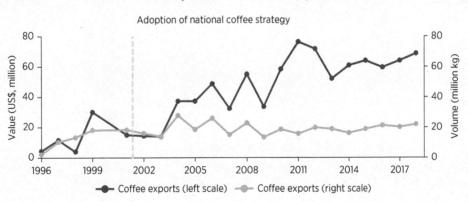

Source: World Bank adaptations of Morjaria and Steenbergen 2017 and United Nations Comtrade data.

Continued on next page ›

BOX 4.4 **How an integrated, sector-based strategy helped transform Rwanda's coffee sector** *(continued)*

exporters in the country also increased to 86 in 2017 and the market power of the top actors was substantially reduced. This change increased market contestability for coffee cherries, which, along with the rise in quality, raised the average domestic farm gate price from around 50 Rwanda francs per kilogram in 2002 to 250 Rwanda francs per kilogram in 2015. The share of fully washed coffee in the country's coffee exports rose from less than 1 percent in 2002 to 50 percent in 2015 (figure B4.4.3).

FIGURE B4.4.2 **Rwandan coffee exports, by coffee type, 2002–15**

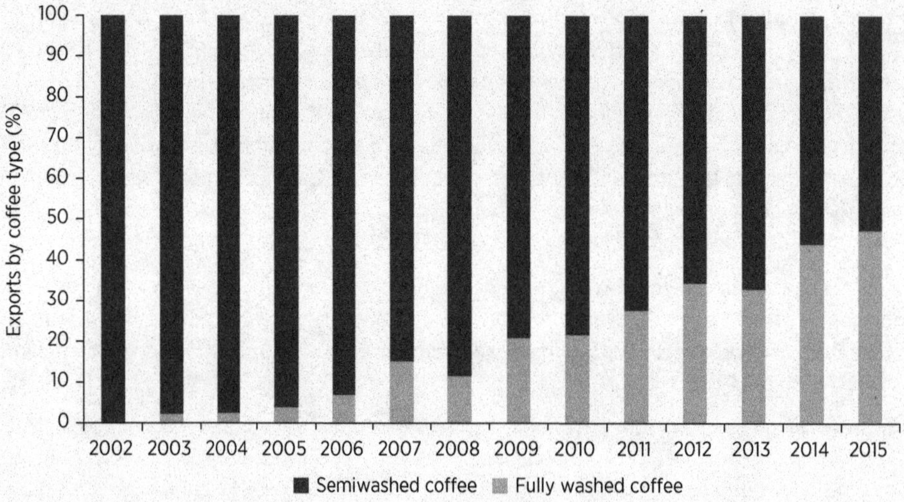

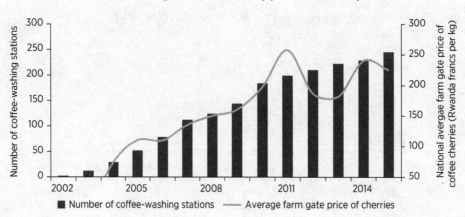

Source: Morjaria and Steenbergen 2017.

FIGURE B4.4.3 **Coffee-washing stations and cherry prices in Rwanda, 2002–15**

Source: Morjaria and Steenbergen 2017.

into relevant networks (Bloom and Van Reenen 2010; Cusolito, Safadi, and Taglioni 2016). As noted by Cusolito, Safadi, and Taglioni (2016, 97) "[f]or the [sector] to thrive from the country's participation in GVCs, appropriate policy frameworks are needed that allow countries and firms to capitalize on their existing productive capacities and create spillover benefits from foreign investment, knowledge, and innovations."

GVC segment mapping is an important tool to help identify firm-level constraints and guide policy makers in shaping their strategies. Such mapping can be conducted in several ways, relying on various combinations of benchmarking and stakeholder consultations, conceptual maps, and data-driven analysis. A brief overview of these tools is given in box 4.5.

Approaches for leveraging foreign investment to integrate into global value chains

In shaping a sector-based GVC integration strategy, governments can combine and emphasize different investment policy tools. As illustrated earlier in this chapter, particular investment policies aim to solve specific market or government failures related to MNCs' expansion of FDI within a country or domestic firms' engagement with foreign firms. Depending on the type of GVC segment and the country's endowments, business environment, and firm capacity, a government may choose to combine and emphasize various investment policy tools to make its GVC strategy as effective as possible.

This report identifies several successful examples of governments leveraging FDI to motivate GVC participation and upgrading. Its broad review of government responses to strengthen GVC participation makes clear that there is no blueprint for doing so: different countries have adopted different approaches to attracting and leveraging FDI according to their own comparative advantages and target GVCs. However, some successful examples have been identified in which governments used FDI to integrate their countries into GVCs (figure 4.7).[19] Each of these cases demonstrates a different strategic approach in which a government applied a set of interministerial policies to improve the country's investment climate, link up with global lead firms, and reduce the cost of producing and trading products in a selected GVC sector or segment. These strategic approaches are described briefly in box 4.6; chapters 6 to 11 of this report provide more detail.

The type of approach a country chooses to boost GVC participation is based in part on its income level. As shown in figure 4.7, there is a link between the prevalence of certain strategies and countries' income levels. This effect may stem from how, from left to right, the sectors become more complex and increasingly demanding of the domestic firms that participate in their GVCs. Sectoral complexity and firm capability are both correlated with income level: the economies of low-income countries tend to be more agricultural or commodity-based; middle-income countries often specialize in manufacturing; and higher-income countries tend to specialize in services (Bloom and Van Reenen 2010; McMillan, Rodrik, and Verduzco-Gallo 2014). This trend can partially explain why different approaches come about in different countries.

A GVC's characteristics may also help illustrate which approaches would be more or less conducive to stimulating GVC integration.[20] Countries use different strategies and approaches to enter into different GVC sectors and archetypes. Some of this variation can be explained by the characteristics of and the cost

BOX 4.5 **The importance of global value chain segment mapping in shaping a sector-based strategy**

To develop a global value chain (GVC) strategy, it is important to start by diagnosing which stakeholders are involved in the value chain, where they are located, and what specific comparative and competitive advantages they have for engaging in their segments (Crescenzi, Harman, and Arnold 2019; De Backer and Miroudot 2013; Frederick 2016). It also helps to "unpack" a specific sector by considering the business functions along its supply chain, such as research and development (R&D), procurement, production, marketing, and customer service. Countries tend to specialize in specific business functions rather than specific industries, such as assembly operations for China or business services for India (De Backer and Miroudot 2013). At times, this specialization may even entail breaking down a value chain into a set of tasks. These tasks can be outsourced, and their offshoring becomes "trade in tasks" (Grossman and Rossi-Hansberg 2008). Countries may therefore choose to stimulate GVC participation by specializing in a set bundle of tasks, each involving its own specific lead firms, production requirements, and trade needs.

GVC segment mapping combines benchmarking and stakeholder consultation to assess competitiveness and identify binding constraints. Any GVC strategy should be based on a good understanding of a country's comparative advantages and firm capabilities as well as on existing policy bottlenecks and market failures that constrain firm performance (Crescenzi, Harman, and Arnold 2019). To obtain this understanding, the GVC can be mapped across the life of its product (for example, from R&D through raw material sourcing, production, and delivery to product disposal). Time and cost levels can be recorded and benchmarked against those of global competitors to identify areas in which the sector and its firms are falling behind. In-depth consultations with companies, industry associations, and government ministries can then provide a comprehensive picture of any major bottlenecks that may explain the presence of high time and cost requirements across segments (Hallaert and Munro 2009; WTO 2006). (Issues discussed in these consultations may include physical infrastructure, logistics and customs procedures, barriers to trade, standards and testing for product quality, other supporting services, investment climate issues [such as policy or regulatory impediments or administrative requirements], and the availability and cost of finance and skilled labor [WTO 2006].)

This exercise will help countries understand how they want to engage with a particular GVC, whether by building it up, embedding it deeper into their economies, or reshaping their actions along it (Crescenzi, Harman, and Arnold 2019). On the basis of this analysis, policy makers may decide whether to engage with and strengthen the country's participation in existing segments along the value chain or encourage firms to focus on new segments (Bailey, Pitelis, and Tomlinson 2018; Crescenzi, Harman, and Arnold 2019). Policy makers should also be aware that value chains can fragment, and thus they should be careful not to leave a country stuck in any narrow segment that provides limited chances for technological upgrading (Venables 1999). This mapping exercise can also contribute to an identification and positioning process that helps a country develop a specific brand by which to position itself as successful and unique from other countries (Konzelmann, Fovargue-Davies, and Wilkinson 2018).

Conceptual GVC maps offer a useful starting point for these exercises. (Many such maps draw on the work of Duke University's Global Value Chains Center.) These maps can show an entire GVC and identify the roles played by domestic firms within it. For example, figure B4.5.1 provides a conceptual map of Kenya's role in the horticulture GVC. It gives an overview of the five different stages of production, the roles played by various firms (such as farms, packhouses, processing companies, and supermarkets), and examples of lead firms that play dominant roles within this process domestically and abroad. From this map, policy makers can consider whether any part of the value chain has any major policy bottlenecks and use this information to inform their sector strategy.

Continued on next page ›

BOX 4.5 The importance of global value chain segment mapping in shaping a sector-based strategy *(continued)*

FIGURE B4.5.1 **Conceptual mapping of Kenya's involvement in the horticulture global value chain**

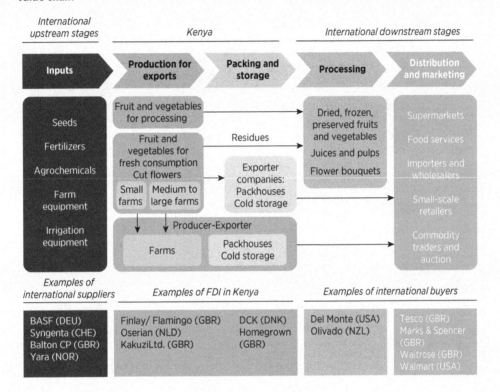

Source: Adapted from Fernandez-Stark, Bamber, and Gereffi 2011 and UNCTAD 2009; see also chapter 6 of this report.
Note: FDI = foreign direct investment.

To complement these maps, firm- and transaction-level data can be used to map out the domestic part of a GVC (a recent innovation). This process provides details on the domestic firms engaged in exports and maps out the domestic part of their supply chains. For example, figure B4.5.2 shows Rwanda's garment and leather value chain. From this map, it becomes clear that the industry is dominated by a small number of foreign-owned firms that source dyes, textiles, and machinery from at least three tiers of domestic suppliers while importing chemicals and machines from hundreds of firms around the world. This mapping approach can show which types of firms are engaging in GVCs as exporters and as suppliers (according to their ownership, size, and location). As such, it provides insights into the wide network of GVC actors that may be less easily observable with traditional stakeholder analysis (such as second-tier suppliers). This technique may assist in developing a GVC strategy, and it can also be used to monitor the strategy's overall progress. One downside of this approach, however, is that no data are available for firms not based within the country, so only the part of the GVC taking place within the country is observable.

Continued on next page ›

BOX 4.5 **The importance of global value chain segment mapping in shaping a sector-based strategy** *(continued)*

FIGURE B4.5.2 **Firm-level mapping of Rwanda's textiles, apparel, and leather value chain**

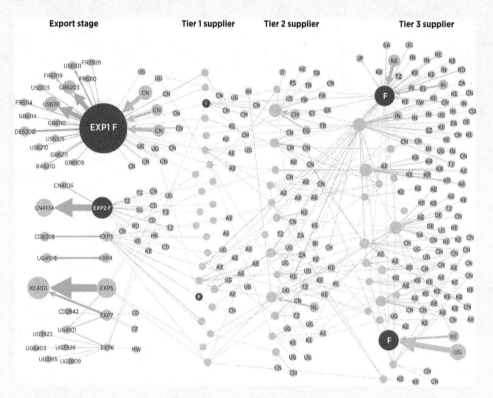

Source: World Bank calculations based on firm-to-firm value added tax data; see chapter 11 of this report.
Notes: Exports are denoted with green arrows; orange arrows represent imports. Each node represents a firm. Foreign-owned firms are dark blue, and domestic firms are light blue. The thickness of the edges between the nodes is proportional to the transaction amount between the two respective firms, and the size of each node represents the node's weighted degree in the network.

drivers for GVCs' production inputs and their implications for market and government failures (see figure 4.8, which provides some examples for illustrative purposes). One GVC segment may have multiple characteristics that would require more than one approach (for example, the characteristics of electronics GVCs lend themselves well to both targeted investment promotion and facilitation of strategic alliances).

Strengthening MNC-supplier linkages can be especially effective at boosting GVCs that are simple and require inputs that can be supplied at arm's length but that also need to meet stringent requirements set by global lead firms. Such GVCs include

BOX 4.6 Strategic approaches used to leverage foreign direct investment to integrate into global value chains

- *Using linkages between multinational corporations (MNCs) and suppliers to help local firms meet global product standards.* In many cases, the fastest way to integrate existing local firms into global value chains (GVCs) is to create pathways into international markets for them. Supplier linkages to foreign firms help local firms meet global product standards by stimulating the three L's: linking (providing local firms with supply channels and necessary information on global standards), learning (supporting them as they train to meet those standards), and labeling (facilitating the process of certifying their ability to meet the standards). Examples of this strategy are found in Rwanda's coffee industry (box 4.4) and Kenya's horticulture industry (see chapter 6 of this report).

- *Investing in special economic zones and using trade and investment agreements to attract export-processing foreign direct investment (FDI).* Another approach to jump-starting GVC participation is to attract export-oriented MNCs into a country. To lower operating and trading costs for such firms, governments can concentrate scarce public funding on building up certain areas (known as SEZs) with higher-quality infrastructure, flexible labor laws, and lower tax rates. To complement these efforts, governments can use bilateral investment treaties and trade agreements to lower investors' risks and trade costs for low-cost, low-margin export processing. Examples of this approach were identified in Honduras's textile and garment industry (see chapter 7 of this report) as well as in many other countries, including in Ethiopia (Oqubay 2015).

- *Using targeted investment promotion, incentives, and facilitation to attract global lead firms.* A government may also target specific global lead firms in a select GVC and assign a proactive investment promotion agency to attract them to the country. The government can also offer these MNCs temporary tax incentives and firm-specific support (such as vocational training, purpose-built infrastructure, and customs support) to entice them to come and to compensate for any temporary disruption to their supply chains caused by the move. Such lead firms are expected to help establish a new GVC cluster in the country that will help upgrade domestic suppliers and attract additional FDI over time. This approach is most commonly associated with the electronics industries in Malaysia (which used it to attract FDI from AMD, Hewlett-Packard, and Intel, among other firms; see chapter 8 of this report) and Costa Rica (which used it to attract Intel) (Freund and Moran 2017).

- *Partnering with foreign firms to help expand and upgrade an existing, viable industry.* Another approach aims to expand and upgrade an existing, viable industry into a higher-value GVC segment. Local firms may seek out partnerships with foreign firms to access their technology, international brands, product development capacity, and managerial techniques. At the same time, MNCs may wish to partner with local firms to gain access to their complementary capacities and knowledge of the domestic market. Facilitating such collaborations (through joint ventures, franchising, or licensing) can help a country's existing industries shift into higher-value tasks and segments within their GVCs. Notable examples of this approach are found in Mauritius's tourism industry (see chapter 9 of this report) as well as in India's recent shift from business processing to financial technology (Fernandez-Stark, Bamber, and Gereffi 2011).

- *Promoting outward FDI and invest in human capital and research and development to help domestic firms develop and compete globally.* A final approach is for large, competitive domestic firms to develop their own global production and sales networks by investing overseas. Governments may support this development by building human capital and helping firms to invest in research and development. Outward FDI can be stimulated by liberalizing outward investment regulation and through proactive promotion using a combination of financial and fiscal measures, information provision, development assistance programs, and international investment agreements. Prominent examples of this approach are found in the Republic of Korea, India, and China related to the digital economy (see chapter 10 of this report).

FIGURE 4.7 **Strategic approaches used to leverage foreign direct investment to integrate into global value chains**

Strategic approach	Use MNC-supplier linkages to help local firms meet global product standards	Invest in SEZs, and use investment and trade agreements to attract export-processing FDI	Use targeted investment promotion, incentives, and facilitation to attract global lead firms	Partner with foreign firms to help expand and upgrade an existing, viable industry	Promote outward FDI and invest in human capital and R&D capacity to help domestic firms develop and compete globally
Examples	Rwanda (coffee) Kenya (horticulture)	Honduras (textiles) Ethiopia (textiles)	Malaysia (electronics) Costa Rica (electronics)	Mauritius (tourism) India (BPO to fintech)	Korea Rep., India, and China (digital economy)

Lower-income countries → Higher-income countries

Prevalence of use, based on country's income level

Source: World Bank elaborations of the literature.
Note: BPO = business process outsourcing; FDI = foreign direct investment; fintech = financial technology; MNC = multinational corporation; R&D = research and development; SEZ = special economic zone.

FIGURE 4.8 **Common approach for leveraging FDI, by GVC characteristic and archetype**

GVC characteristics	Examples of GVCs	Common approach for leveraging FDI
GVCs with simpler inputs that can be supplied at arm's length but need to meet stringent global requirements set by lead firms.	Coffee (commodities) and horticulture (regional processing)	Use MNC supply linkages to help local firms meet global product standards
GVCs with many low-margin, distributed suppliers with highly competitive production and trade costs to supply global MNCs.	Textiles (labor-intensive goods)	Invest in SEZs, and use investment or trade agreements to attract export-processing FDI
GVCs dominated by a few global lead firms with expansive supply networks and distinct requirements to avoid supply chain disruptions.	Electronics (knowledge-intensive goods)	Use targeted investment promotion, incentives, and facilitation to attract global lead firms
GVCs that rely on intangible assets (brands, management practices, production techniques, and the like) that can be codified or protected (for example, via licensing).	Tourism (labor-intensive services), Electronics (knowledge-intensive goods)	Leverage foreign firms to help expand and upgrade an existing, viable industry
GVCs that rely on intangible assets (for example, intellectual property) that are highly specialized and difficult to protect from competitors.	Software (knowledge-intensive services)	Promote outward FDI and invest in human capital and R&D to help domestic firms develop and compete globally

Source: World Bank elaborations of the literature and chapters 6 to 11 of this report.
Note: FDI = foreign direct investment; MNC = multinational corporation; R&D = research and development; SEZ = special economic zone.

regional processing (including horticulture, as shown in chapter 6 of this report) and commodities (including Rwanda's coffee sector, discussed in box 4.4).

Investing in SEZs and making investment and trade agreements may be important for GVCs with large numbers of distributed suppliers that earn thin margins and supply a few global MNCs. Such firms often must be able to achieve highly competitive production and trade costs. Their efforts can be supported by investing in infrastructure in a concentrated region (a SEZ) and by reducing investor risks and trade barriers via international investment and trade agreements. Some labor-intensive goods GVCs exemplify these characteristics (such as textiles and apparel, as shown in chapter 7 of this report).

Targeted investment promotion, incentives, and facilitation can be influential in GVCs that are dominated by a few global lead firms with substantial need to avoid supply chain disruptions. MNCs may be drawn into a country via targeted campaigns by IPAs, temporary subsidies (such as tax incentives, vocational training, and the construction of special infrastructure) to compensate for relocation costs, and facilitation to limit any disruption caused by public regulation. Some knowledge-intensive goods GVCs include such powerful lead firms (including electronics, as shown in chapter 8 of this report).

Leveraging foreign firms to help expand and upgrade an existing industry can be particularly useful in GVCs that rely on intangible assets used by MNCs (such as special production techniques, brands, or management practices) that can be codified or protected (such as by licensing agreements). Policy makers can help local firms move into higher-value GVC positions by acquiring such technology through strategic alliances with MNCs. Examples of this strategy are common in knowledge-intensive goods GVCs (such as electronics, as shown in chapter 8 of this report) and labor-intensive services GVCs (such as tourism, as shown in chapter 9 of this report).

Promoting OFDI to help domestic firms develop and compete globally is especially important in GVCs that rely on specialized types of intellectual property at risk of leaking to competitors. MNCs may be less willing to share such technology through partnerships. Instead, domestic firms may have to directly invest in R&D or obtain foreign technology via acquisitions to develop and compete globally. Examples of this strategy are common in knowledge-intensive goods GVCs (such as high-end electronics production) and knowledge-intensive services GVCs (such as software), as shown in the case study on the digital economy (chapter 10 of this report).

This chapter presents a range of policy instruments and strategies to illustrate how policy makers can stimulate GVC participation and upgrading. These successful examples included here and in part II (chapters 6 to 11) of this report can inspire policy makers as they work to identify which set of interministerial policy instruments will best improve the business environment of their target GVC sector or segment, help attract global lead firms, and enhance domestic firms' competitiveness within that sector or segment.

Notes

1. For examples of these effects, see Arnold and Javorcik (2009), Bajgar and Javorcik (2020), Buelens and Tirpak (2017), Djankov and Hoekman (2000), Javorcik (2004), Javorcik and Li (2013), and Newman et al. (2016).
2. The 10 countries were Brazil, China, India, Indonesia, Malaysia, Mexico, Nigeria, Thailand, Turkey, and Vietnam.
3. Such analysis should include laws on property rights, land ownership, trade, taxes, competition, and other topics.
4. For details on the OECD FDI Regulatory Restrictiveness Index, see Kalinova, Palerm, and Thomsen (2010).
5. Political risk encompasses a wide range of issues related to government conduct, from the threat of political violence and geopolitical tensions to the chance of outright expropriation to more subtle forms of pressure, including confiscatory taxation, corruption, or economic constraints such as exchange rate controls. In sum, political risk is the risk that the host government will violate the terms of its implicit contract with an investor to not impede the investor's efforts (Graham, Johnston, and Kingsley 2016).
6. For an overview of investor protection guarantees, see chapter 5 in World Bank (2010).
7. Importantly, attracting these lead firms was possible only because of the countries' strong commitments to macroeconomic stability, skills development, and infrastructure provision. To minimize disruption to MNCs' global production networks, information about investment conditions was backed up by public-private vocational training partnerships and infrastructure reforms (Freund and Moran 2017).
8. IPAs often try to achieve too much. A 2017 World Bank global survey of IPAs found that 84 percent of IPAs listed five or more "priority" sectors for investment promotion (Heilbron and Kronfol 2020).
9. The successful Shenzhen SEZ in China is an example of one such reform-oriented SEZ.
10. Studies supporting this finding include Hebous, Kher, and Tran (2020); James (2014); and Overesch and Wamser (2008).
11. See Kronfol and Steenbergen (2020) for various methods of conducting cost-benefit analysis of incentives.
12. An example of this type of policy and its detrimental effect can be found in Latin America's automotive industry (Sutton 2014).
13. These industries include aircraft, automobiles, finance, higher education, pharmaceuticals, and shipbuilding (Jiang et al. 2018).
14. According to the China Business Climate Survey Report conducted by the American Chamber of Commerce in China (AmCham 2017), 21 percent of the 434 companies surveyed faced pressure to transfer technology upon entering the Chinese market. Such pressure was most often felt in strategically important industries such as aerospace (44 percent) and chemicals (41 percent).
15. Many areas of the law may come into play regarding these alliances, such as intellectual property (for licensing or franchising), competition, consumer protection, employment, and environmental protection.
16. For details on this effort, see its website: http://www.ifranchisemalaysia.com.
17. The most common such obligation is for the MNC to provide precontractual disclosure of all relevant information (including business experience, past or pending litigation, financial statements, contract fees, and the firm's existing network of alliances). Some countries have detailed lists of required information (including China, France, Japan, Mexico, and the United States), whereas others rely on general principles (such as the United Kingdom) or case law (such as Germany) (UNCTAD 2011).
18. The eight European Union countries with the highest number of science and engineering bachelor's degrees in 2014 were the United Kingdom, Germany, France, Poland, Italy, Spain, Romania, and the Netherlands.

19. These examples of strategic approaches are meant to be illustrative, and they are by no means the only ways to combine investment policies to stimulate GVC participation.
20. These patterns are drawn from the case studies and findings from internalization theory, imperfect contracting theory, and property rights theory (Benito, Petersen, and Welch 2019; Gereffi, Humphrey, and Sturgeon 2005; UNCTAD 2020) as well as from global sectoral data. See chapters 2 and 3 for more details on how GVC characteristics affect MNC strategies and domestic firm internalization.

References

Aggarwal, A. 2005. "Performance of Export Processing Zones: A Comparative Analysis of India, Sri Lanka and Bangladesh." Indian Council for Research on International Economic Relations (ICRIER), New Delhi.

Akame, A. J., M. E. Ekwelle, and G. N. Njei. 2016. "The Impact of Business Climate on Foreign Direct Investment in the CEMAC Region." *Journal of Economics and Sustainable Development* 7 (22): 66–74.

Akileswaran, K., L. Calabrese, and J. Said. 2018. "Missing Links for Economic Transformation: Securing Policy Coherence in Eastern Africa." Tony Blair Institute for Global Change and Overseas Development Institute, London.

Alfaro-Ureña, A., I. Manelici, and J. P. Vasquez. 2019. "The Effects of Joining Multinational Supply Chains: New Evidence from Firm-to-Firm Linkages." Working Paper. https://papers .ssrn.com/sol3/papers.cfm?abstract_id=3376129.

Allen, N. J., J. Morisset, N. Pirnia, and L. T. Wells, Jr. 2001. "Using Tax Incentives to Compete for Foreign Investment: Are They Worth the Costs?" Foreign Investment Advisory Service Occasional Paper 15, World Bank, Washington, DC.

AmCham China (The American Chamber of Commerce in the People's Republic of China). 2017. "2018 China Business Climate Survey Report." AmCham China, Beijing. https:// www.bain.com/contentassets/68e8c134156642daa510fb7498586943/bain20report_2018 _china_business_climate_survey_report.pdf.

Andersen, Maria R., Benjamin R. Kett, and Erik von Uexkull. 2018. "Corporate Tax Incentives and FDI in Developing Countries." In *Global Investment Competitiveness Report 2017/2018: Foreign Investor Perspectives and Policy Implications*. Washington, DC: World Bank.

Antràs, P., and S. R. Yeaple. 2014. "Multinational Firms and the Structure of International Trade." In *Handbook of International Economics*, Vol. 4, edited by G. Gopinath, E. Helpman, and K. Rogoff, 55–130. Oxford, U.K.: North-Holland.

Arias, E., J. R. Hollyer, and B. P. Rosendorff. 2018. "Cooperative Autocracies: Leader Survival, Creditworthiness, and Bilateral Investment Treaties." *American Journal of Political Science* 62 (4): 905–21.

Arnold, Jens Matthias, Beata S. Javorcik, Molly Lipscomb, and Aaditya Mattoo. 2016. "Services Reform and Manufacturing Performance: Evidence from India." *Economic Journal* 126 (590): 1–39.

Arnold, Jens Matthias, and Beata S. Javorcik. 2009. "Gifted Kids or Pushy Parents? Foreign Direct Investment and Plant Productivity in Indonesia." *Journal of International Economics* 79 (1): 42–53.

Arraiz, Irani, Francisca Henriquez, and Rodolfo Stucchi. 2013. "Supplier Development Programs and Firm Performance: Evidence from Chile." *Small Business Economics* 41 (1): 277–93.

Bai, J., P. Barwick, S. Cao, and S. Li. 2019. "Quid Pro Quo, Knowledge Spillover and Industrial Quality Upgrading." CID Working Paper 368, Center for International Development, Harvard University, Cambridge, MA.

Bailey, D., C. Pitelis, and P. Tomlinson. 2018. "A Place-Based Development Regional Industrial Strategy for Sustainable Capture of Co-created Value." *Cambridge Journal of Economics* 42 (6): 1521–42.

Bajgar, Matej, and Beata Javorcik. 2020. "Climbing the Rungs of the Quality Ladder: FDI and Domestic Exporters in Romania." *Economic Journal* 130 (628): 937–55.

Behuria, Pritish, and Tom Goodfellow. 2016. "Political Settlement and 'Deals Environment' in Rwanda: Unpacking Two Decades of Economic Growth." ESID Working Paper 57, Effective States and Inclusive Development Research Center, Manchester, U.K.

Bellak, Christian, Markus Leibrecht, and Joze P. Damijan. 2009. "Infrastructure Endowment and Corporate Income Taxes as Determinants of Foreign Direct Investment in Central and Eastern European Countries." *World Economy* 32 (2): 267–90.

Bénassy-Quéré, A., L. Fontagné, and A. Lahrèche-Révil. 2005. "How Does FDI React to Corporate Taxation?" *International Tax and Public Finance* 12: 583–603.

Benito, G. R., B. Petersen, and L. S. Welch. 2019. "The Global Value Chain and Internalization Theory." *Journal of International Business Studies* 50 (8): 1414–23.

Berger, Axel, Matthias Busse, Peter Nunnenkamp, and Martin Roy. 2013. "Do Trade and Investment Agreements Lead to More FDI? Accounting for Key Provisions inside the Black Box." *International Economics and Economic Policy* 10 (2): 247–75.

Bhandari, Abhit, and Joonseok Yang. 2019. "An Unintentional Substitute for Democracy: Bilateral Investment Treaties and U.S. Firms' Investment in Developing Countries." Unpublished working paper. https://static1.squarespace.com/static/5ade668fb27e39802ce49e40/t/5df8019ca6d1327327e7c668/1576534428778/BhandariYang_BIT.pdf.

Birdsall, Nancy M., Jose Edgardo L. Campos, Chang-Shik Kim, W. Max Corden, Lawrence MacDonald (editor), Howard Pack, John Page, Richard Sabor, and Joseph E. Stiglitz. 1993. *The East Asian Miracle: Economic Growth and Public Policy: Main Report.* A World Bank Policy Research Report. Washington, DC: World Bank. http://documents.worldbank.org/curated/en/975081468244550798/Main-report.

Bloom, Nicholas, and John Van Reenen. 2010. "Why Do Management Practices Differ across Firms and Countries?" *Journal of Economic Perspectives* 24 (1): 203–24.

Bobonis, G., and H. Shatz. 2007. "Agglomeration, Adjustment, and State Policies in the Location of Foreign Direct Investment in the United States." *Review of Economics and Statistics* 89 (1): 30–43.

Brenton, Paul, Francesca Di Mauro, and Matthias Lücke. 1999. "Economic Integration and FDI: An Empirical Analysis of Foreign Investment in the EU and in Central and Eastern Europe." *Empirica* 26 (2): 95–121.

Buchanan, Bonnie, Quan V. Le, and Meenakshi Rishi. 2012. "Foreign Direct Investment and Institutional Quality: Some Empirical Evidence." *International Review of Financial Analysis* 21 (C): 81–89.

Buelens, C., and M. Tirpák. 2017. "Reading the Footprints: How Foreign Investors Shape Countries' Participation in Global Value Chains." *Comparative Economic Studies* 59 (4): 561–84.

Buthe, T., and H. V. Milner. 2014. "Foreign Direct Investment and Institutional Diversity in Trade Agreements: Credibility, Commitment, and Economic Flows in the Developing World, 1971–2007." *World Politics* 66 (1): 88–122.

Busom, Isabel, Beatriz Corchuelo, and Ester Martínez-Ros. 2012. "Tax Incentives or Subsidies for R&D?" MERIT Working Paper 2012-056, United Nations University–Maastricht Economic and Social Research Institute on Innovation and Technology.

Büttner, Thiess, Michael Overesch, Ulrich Schreiber, and Georg Wamser. 2008. "The Impact of Thin-Capitalization Rules on Multinationals' Financing and Investment Decisions." Discussion Paper Series 1: Economic Studies No. 03/2008, Deutsche Bundesbank, Frankfurt am Main. https://EconPapers.repec.org/RePEc:zbw:bubdp1:7114.

CDB (China Development Bank) and EXIM (Export-Import Bank of the United States). 2006. CDB and EXIM Enhance their Financial and Insurance Support for Key Investment Projects Overseas Encouraged by the State [CDB 2006 No. 11 Order]. Beijing: CDB and EXIM.

China, MOFCOM (Ministry of Commerce of China). 2014. "Administrative Measures for Overseas Investment." MOFCOM, Beijing. http://english.mofcom.gov.cn/article/policyrelease/aaa/.

China, MOFCOM (Ministry of Commerce of China). 2020. "Global Investment and Cooperation Information Service System." http://femhzs.mofcom.gov.cn/fecpmvc/pages /fem/CorpJWList.html.

Cho, J. 2003. "Foreign Direct Investment: Determinants, Trends in Flows and Promotion Policies." In *Investment Promotion and Enterprise Development Bulletin for Asia and the Pacific*, 99–112. United Nations.

Colen, Liesbeth, Damiaan Persyn, and Andrea Guariso. 2016. "Bilateral Investment Treaties and FDI: Does the Sector Matter?" *World Development* 83 (July): 193–206.

Correa, Paulo, Luis Andres, and Christian Borja-Vega. 2013. "The Impact of Government Support on Firm R&D Investments: A Meta-analysis." Policy Research Working Paper 6532, World Bank, Washington, DC.

Correa, Paulo G., and Irem Guceri. 2013. "Tax Incentives for Research and Development." Innovation, Technology and Entrepreneurship Policy Note 4, World Bank, Washington, DC.

Crescenzi, Riccardo, Marco Di Cataldo, and Mara Giua. 2019. "FDI Inflows in Europe: Does Investment Promotion Work?" Working Paper 10/2019, Institute of Global Affairs, London School of Economics and Political Science.

Crescenzi, Riccardo, Oliver Harman, and David Arnold. 2019. "Move On Up! Building, Embedding and Reshaping Global Value Chains through Investment Flows: Insights for Regional Innovation Policies." Background paper for OECD/EC Workshop Series "Broadening Innovation Policy: New Insights for Regions and Cities," September 21, 2018, Paris.

Cusolito, Ana Paula, and William F. Maloney. 2018. *Productivity Revisited: Shifting Paradigms in Analysis and Policy*. Washington, DC: World Bank.

Cusolito, Ana Paula, Raed Safadi, and Daria Taglioni. 2016. *Inclusive Global Value Chains: Policy Options for Small and Medium Enterprises and Low-Income Countries*. Directions in Development Series. Washington, DC: World Bank.

Danzman, Sarah Bauerle. 2016. "Contracting with Whom? The Differential Effects of Investment Treaties on FDI." *International Interactions* 42 (3): 452–78.

De Backer, Koen, and Sébastien Miroudot. 2013. "Mapping Global Value Chains." OECD Trade Policy Paper 159, OECD Publishing, Paris.

de Caldas Lima, J. M. 2008. *Patterns of Internationalization for Developing Country Enterprises: Alliances and Joint Ventures*. Vienna: United Nations Industrial Development Organization.

De la Medina Soto, Christian, and Tania M. Ghossein. 2013. "Starting a Foreign Investment across Sectors." Policy Research Working Paper 6707, World Bank, Washington, DC.

Deringer, Hanna, Fredrik Erixon, Philipp Lamprecht, and Erik Van der Marel. 2018. "The Economic Impact of Local Content Requirements: A Case Study of Heavy Vehicles." ECIPE Occasional Paper 1/2018, European Centre for International Political Economy, Brussels.

Desai, Mihir A., C. Fritz Foley, and James Hines. 2006. "Capital Controls, Liberalizations, and Foreign Direct Investment." *Review of Financial Studies* 19 (4): 1433–64.

Djankov, S., C. Freund, and C. S. Pham. 2006. "Trading on Time." Policy Research Working Paper 3909, World Bank, Washington, DC.

Djankov, Simeon, and Bernard Hoekman. 2000. "Foreign Investment and Productivity Growth in Czech Enterprises." *World Bank Economic Review* 14 (1): 49–64.

Dollar, D., M. Hallward-Driemeier, and T. Mengistae. 2004. "Investment Climate and International Integration." Policy Research Working Paper 3323, World Bank, Washington, DC.

Falvey, Rod, and Neil Foster-McGregor. 2018. "On the Relationship between the Breadth of Preferential Trading Arrangements and Trade Flows." *World Economy* 41 (4): 1088–110.

Farole, T. 2011a. *Special Economic Zones in Africa: Comparing Performance and Learning from Global Experiences*. Washington, DC: World Bank.

Farole, T. 2011b. "Special Economic Zones: What Have We Learned?" Economic Premise Note 64, World Bank, Washington, DC.

Farole, T., and D. Winkler, eds. 2014. *Making Foreign Direct Investment Work for Sub-Saharan Africa: Local Spillovers and Competitiveness in Global Value Chains*. Washington, DC: World Bank.

Felipe, Jesus. 2015. "Development and Modern Industrial Policy in Practice: Issues and Country Experiences." Asian Development Bank, Manila.

Fernandez-Stark, K., P. Bamber, and G. Gereffi. 2011. "The Offshore Services Value Chain: Upgrading Trajectories in Developing Countries." *International Journal of Technological Learning, Innovation and Development* 4 (1): 206–34.

FIAS (Foreign Investment Climate Advisory Service). 2008. "Special Economic Zones. Performance, Lessons Learned, and Implications for Zone Development." World Bank, Washington, DC.

Frederick, S. 2016. "GVCs: Concept & Tools." Global Value Chains Initiative, Duke University, Durham, NC. https://globalvaluechains.org/concept-tools.

Frenkel, Michael, and B. Walter. 2018. "Do Bilateral Investment Treaties Attract Foreign Direct Investment? The Role of International Dispute Settlement Provisions." *World Economy* 42 (5): 1316–42.

Freund, C., and T. Moran. 2017. "Multinational Investors as Export Superstars: How Emerging-Market Governments Can Reshape Comparative Advantage." PIIE Working Paper 17-1, Peterson Institute for International Economics, Washington, DC.

Freund, Caroline, and Martha Denisse Pierola. 2015. "Export Superstars." *Review of Economics and Statistics* 97 (5): 1023–32.

Freund, C. L., and N. Rocha. 2010. "What Constrains Africa's Exports?" Policy Research Working Paper 5184, World Bank, Washington, DC.

Gani, Azmat. 2007. "Governance and Foreign Direct Investment Links: Evidence from Panel Data Estimations." *Applied Economics Letters* 14: 753–56.

Gerber, James B. 2007. "Import Substitution Industrialization." Chapter 41 in *Handbook on International Trade Policy*, edited by William A. Kerr and James D. Gaisford. Cheltenham, U.K.: Edward Elgar Publishing.

Gereffi, G., J. Humphrey, and T. Sturgeon. 2005. "The Governance of Global Value Chains." *Review of International Political Economy* 12 (1): 78–104.

Globerman, Steven, and Daniel Shapiro. 2002. "Global Foreign Direct Investment Flows: The Role of Governance Infrastructure." *World Development* 30 (11): 1899–919.

Goldman, C. S., J. T. Kissack, and C. L. Witterick. 1997. "The Transition from Closed to Open Economy: The Role of Competition Policy." *International Business Lawyer* 25 (10): 451–52.

Gomez-Mera, Laura, and Gonzalo J. Varela. 2017. "A BIT Far? Geography, International Economic Agreements, and Foreign Direct Investment: Evidence from Emerging Markets." Policy Research Working Paper 8185, World Bank, Washington, DC.

Göndör, Mihaela, and Paula Nistor. 2012. "Does High Corporate Tax Rates Attract Foreign Direct Investment?" *Ovidius University Annals, Economic Sciences Series* XII (1): 1433–38.

Graham, Benjamin A. T., Noel P. Johnston, and Allison F. Kingsley. 2018. "Even Constrained Governments Take." *Journal of Conflict Resolution* 62 (8): 1784–813.

Greenwald, Bruce C., and Joseph E. Stiglitz. 1986. "Externalities in Economies with Imperfect Information and Incomplete Markets." *Quarterly Journal of Economics* 101 (2): 229–64.

Grossman, G. M., and E. Rossi-Hansberg. 2008. "Trading Tasks: A Simple Theory of Offshoring." *American Economic Review* 98 (5): 1978–97.

Hallaert, Jean-Jacques, and Laura Munro. 2009. "Binding Constraints to Trade Expansion: Aid for Trade Objectives and Diagnostics Tools." OECD Trade Policy Working Paper 94, Organisation for Economic Co-operation and Development, Paris.

Harding, Torfinn, and Beata Javorcik. 2011. "Roll Out the Red Carpet and They Will Come: Investment Promotion and FDI Inflows." *Economic Journal* 121 (18): 1445–76.

Harding, Torfinn, and Beata Javorcik. 2012. "Investment Promotion and FDI Inflows: Quality Matters." Department of Economics Discussion Paper 612 (June), University of Oxford, Oxford, U.K.

Harrison, Ann, and Andrés Rodríguez-Clare. 2010. "Trade, Foreign Investment, and Industrial Policy for Developing Countries." Chapter 63 in *Handbook of Development Economics*, Vol. 5, edited by Dani Rodrik and Mark Rosenzweig, 4039–214. Oxford, U.K.: Elsevier.

Hebous, Sarah, Priyanka Kher, and Trang Thu Tran. 2020. "Regulatory Risk and FDI." In *Global Investment Competitiveness Report 2019/2020: Rebuilding Investor Confidence in Times of Uncertainty.* Washington, DC: World Bank Group.

Heher, Ulla. 2020. "FDI Linkages Development: International Experience." Background paper, "Expanding FDI Localization and Linkages in the Russian Federation: Perspectives of Firms and Lessons from Global Experience." World Bank, Washington, DC.

Heilbron, Armando, and Yago Aranda-Larrey. 2020. "Strengthening Service Delivery of Investment Promotion Agencies: The Comprehensive Investor Services Framework." In Focus Note, World Bank, Washington, DC.

Heilbron, Armando, and Hania Kronfol. 2020. "Increasing the Development Impact of Investment Promotion Agencies." In *Global Investment Competitiveness Report 2019/2020: Rebuilding Investor Confidence in Times of Uncertainty.* Washington, DC: World Bank Group.

Heilbron, Armando, and R. Whyte. 2019. "Institutions for Investment: Establishing a High-Performing Institutional Framework for Foreign Direct Investment." In Focus Note, World Bank, Washington, DC.

Hidalgo, Cesar, Bailey Klinger, Albert-Laszlo Barabasi, and Ricardo Hausmann. 2007. "The Product Space Conditions the Development of Nations." *Science* 317 (5837): 482–87.

IMF (International Monetary Fund). 2019. *Annual Report on Exchange Arrangements and Exchange Restrictions 2018.* Washington, DC: IMF.

James, Sebastian. 2014. "Tax and Non-Tax Incentives and Investments: Evidence and Policy Implications." Investment Climate Advisory Service, World Bank, Washington, DC.

Javorcik, Beata S. 2004. "Does Foreign Direct Investment Increase the Productivity of Domestic Firms? In Search of Spillovers through Backward Linkages." *American Economic Review* 94 (3): 605–27.

Javorcik, Beata, and Yue Li. 2013. "Do the Biggest Aisles Serve a Brighter Future? Global Retail Chains and Their Implications for Romania." *Journal of International Economics* 90 (2): 348–63.

Jeong, Hyung-Gon, and Douglas Zhihua Zeng. 2016. "Promoting Dynamic & Innovative Growth in Asia: The Cases of Special Economic Zones and Business Hubs." KIEP Research Paper Policy Analysis 16-01, Korea Institute for International Economic Policy, Sejong.

Jiang, K., W. Keller, L. D. Qiu, and W. Ridley. 2018. "International Joint Ventures and Internal vs. External Technology Transfer: Evidence from China." NBER Working Paper 24455, National Bureau of Economic Research, Cambridge, MA.

Johnson, O. 2013. "Exploring the Effectiveness of Local Content Requirements in Promoting Solar PV Manufacturing in India." DIE Discussion Paper 11/2013, German Development Institute, Bonn.

Jordaan, J., W. Douw, and C. Z. Qiang. 2020. "Foreign Direct Investment, Backward Linkages, and Productivity Spillovers." In Focus Note, World Bank, Washington, DC.

Kalinova, B., A. Palerm, and S. Thomsen. 2010. "OECD's FDI Restrictiveness Index: 2010 Update." OECD Working Papers on International Investment, No. 2010/3, OECD Investment Division, Organisation for Economic Co-operation and Development.

Kim, June-Dong, and In-Soo Rang. 1997. "Outward FDI and Exports: The Case of South Korea and Japan." *Journal of Asian Economics* 8 (1): 39–50.

Kim, Jungmin, and Dong Kee Rhee. 2009. "Trends and Determinants of Korean Outward FDI." *Copenhagen Journal of Asian Studies* 27 (1): 126–54.

Kinda, Tidiane. 2014. "The Quest for Non-Resource-Based FDI: Do Taxes Matter?" IMF Working Paper 14/15, International Monetary Fund, Washington, DC.

Klemm, A., and S. Van Parys. 2012. "Empirical Evidence on the Effects of Tax Incentives." *International Tax and Public Finance* 19 (3): 393–423.

Kline, P., and E. Moretti. 2014. "People, Places, and Public Policy: Some Simple Welfare Economics of Local Economic Development Programs." *Annual Review of Economics* 6: 629–62.

Konzelmann, S., M. Fovargue-Davies, and F. Wilkinson. 2018. "Britain's Industrial Evolution: The Structuring Role of Economic Theory." *Journal of Economic Issues* 52 (1): 1–30.

Kronfol, Hania, and Victor Steenbergen. 2020. "Evaluating the Costs and Benefits of Corporate Tax Incentives: Methodological Approaches and Policy Considerations." In Focus Note, World Bank, Washington, DC.

Kusek, Peter, Abhishek Saurav, and Ryan Kuo. 2020. "Outlook and Priorities for Foreign Investors in Developing Countries: Findings from the 2019 Global Investment Competitiveness Survey in 10 Middle-Income Countries." In *Global Investment Competitiveness Report 2019/2020: Rebuilding Investor Confidence in Times of Uncertainty*. Washington, DC: World Bank Group.

Kusek, Peter, and Andrea Silva. 2018. "What Matters to Investors in Developing Countries: Findings from the Global Investment Competitiveness Survey." In *Global Investment Competitiveness Report 2017/2018: Foreign Investor Perspectives and Policy Implications*, 19–50. Washington, DC: World Bank.

Laget, E., A. Osnago, N. Rocha, and M. Ruta. 2018. "Deep Trade Agreements and Global Value Chains." Policy Research Working Paper 8491, World Bank, Washington, DC.

Lawrence, R. Z. 1996. *Regionalism, Multilateralism and Deeper Integration*. Washington, DC: Brookings Institution.

Lukoianova, Tatiana. 2018. "The Signaling Role of BIT Stringency for Facilitating FDI." *Academy of Management*, February 23, 2018. https://doi.org/10.5465/ambpp.2013.104.

MacDermott, Raymond. 2007. "Regional Trade Agreement and Foreign Direct Investment." *North American Journal of Economics and Finance* 18 (1): 107–16.

Margalioth, Y. 2003. "Tax Competition, Foreign Direct Investments and Growth: Using the Tax System to Promote Developing Countries." *Virginia Tax Review* 23: 161.

Mariotti, S., and L. Piscitello. 1995. "Information Costs and Location of FDIs within the Host Country: Empirical Evidence from Italy." *Journal of International Business Studies* 26: 815–41.

Mariscal, A., and D. Taglioni. 2017. "GVCs as a Source of Firm Capabilities." Unpublished, World Bank, Washington, DC.

Mattoo, A., A. Mulabdic, and M. Ruta. 2017. "Deep Trade Agreements as Public Goods." VoxEU.org, October 12, 2017. https://voxeu.org/article/trade-effects-deep-agreements.

McMillan, M., D. Rodrik, and I. Verduzco-Gallo. 2014. "Globalization, Structural Change, and Productivity Growth, with an Update on Africa." *World Development* 63: 11–32.

Mistura, F., and C. Roulet. 2019. *The Determinants of Foreign Direct Investment: Do Statutory Restrictions Matter?* OECD Working Papers on International Investment. Paris: Organisation for Economic Co-operation and Development.

Moran, T. 2014. "Foreign Investment and Supply Chains in Emerging Markets: Recurring Problems and Demonstrated Solutions." PIIE Working Paper 14-12, Peterson Institute for International Economics, Washington, DC.

Morisset, Jacques, and Kelly Andrews-Johnson. 2004. *The Effectiveness of Promotion Agencies at Attracting Foreign Direct Investment*. FIAS Occasional Paper 16. Washington, DC: World Bank.

Morjaria, A., and V. Steenbergen. 2017. "Understanding Constraints to Value Addition in Rwanda's Coffee Sector." IGC Policy Brief, International Growth Centre, London.

Müller, N., and F. Behringer. 2012. "Subsidies and Levies as Policy Instruments to Encourage Employer-Provided Training." OECD Education Working Paper, Organisation for Economic Co-operation and Development, Paris.

Nelson, Roy C. 2005. "Competing for Foreign Direct Investment: Efforts to Promote Nontraditional FDI in Costa Rica, Brazil, and Chile." *Studies in Comparative International Development* 40 (3): 3–28.

Nelson, Roy C. 2010. *Harnessing Globalization: The Promotion of Nontraditional Foreign Direct Investment in Latin America*. University Park, PA: Pennsylvania State University Press.

Newman, Carol, John Page, John Rand, Abebe Shimeles, Mans Soderbom, and Finn Tarp. 2016. *Made in Africa: Learning to Compete in Industry*. Washington, DC: Brookings Institution.

Nicolas, F., S. Thomsen, and M. H. Bang. 2013. "Lessons from Investment Policy Reform in Korea." OECD Working Papers on International Investment, OECD Publishing, Paris. http://dx.doi.org/10.1787/5k4376zqcpf1-en.

OECD (Organisation for Economic Co-operation and Development). 2017. "China Economic Survey 2017." OECD Publishing, Paris.

OECD (Organisation for Economic Co-operation and Development). 2018. *OECD Investment Policy Reviews: Southeast Asia 2018*. Paris: OECD Secretariat.

Oqubay, Arkebe. 2015. *Made in Africa: Industrial Policy in Ethiopia*. Oxford, U.K.: Oxford University Press.

Osnago, L. E., A. N. Rocha, and M. Ruta. 2018. "Deep Trade Agreements and Global Value Chains." Policy Research Working Paper 8491, World Bank, Washington, DC.

Overesch, M., and G. Wamser. 2008. "Who Cares about Corporate Taxation? Asymmetric Tax Effects on Outbound FDI." IFO Working Papers 59, IFO Institute for Economic Research, University of Munich.

Perea, Jose Ramon, and Matthew Stephenson. 2018. "Outward FDI from Developing Countries." In *Global Investment Competitiveness Report 2017/2018: Foreign Investor Perspectives and Policy Implications*, 101–34. Washington, DC: World Bank Group.

Pietersen, Pontévechio Hawarden, and Henri Bezuidenhout. 2015. "South African IPAs Attracting FDI: Investment Promotion Strategies." *Journal of Applied Business Research* 31 (3).

Portugal-Perez, A., and J. Wilson. 2010. "Export Performance and Trade Facilitation Reform: Hard and Soft Infrastructure." Policy Research Working Paper 5261, World Bank, Washington, DC.

Rodrik, Dani. 2004. "Industrial Policy for the Twenty-First Century." Working paper, Harvard University, Cambridge, MA. https://drodrik.scholar.harvard.edu/files/dani-rodrik/files/industrial-policy-twenty-first-century.pdf.

Sabha, Yassin, Yan Liu, and Willem Douw. 2020. "Investment Linkages and Incentives: Promoting Technology Transfer and Productivity Spillovers from Foreign Direct Investment (FDI)." In Focus Note, World Bank, Washington, DC.

Sauvant, Karl P., and Victor Zitian Chen. 2013. "China's Regulatory Framework for Outward Foreign Direct Investment." *China Economic Journal* 7 (1): 141–63.

Spar, D. 1998. *Attracting High Technology Investment: Intel's Costa Rican Plant*. Washington, DC: World Bank.

Spray, John. 2017. "Exports and Promoting Backward Linkages: Ideas and Lessons for the Made in Rwanda Policy." IGC Policy Brief 38412, International Growth Centre, London.

Steenbergen, V., and B. Javorcik. 2017. "Analyzing the Impact of the Kigali Special Economic Zone on Firm Behavior." IGC Working Paper F-38419-RWA-1, International Growth Centre, London.

Steenbergen, V., and J. Sutton. 2017. "Establishing a Local Content Unit for Rwanda." IGC Policy Note, International Growth Centre, London.

Stein, Ernesto, and Christian Daude. 2007. "Longitude Matters: Time Zones and the Location of Foreign Direct Investment." *Journal of International Economics* 71 (1): 96–112.

Stiglitz, J., and A. Norman, eds. 2015. *Industrial Policy and Economic Transformation in Africa*. New York: Columbia University Press.

Sutton, J. 2014. *An Enterprise Map of Mozambique*. London: International Growth Centre.

Taglioni, Daria, and Deborah Winkler. 2016. *Making Global Value Chains Work for Development*. Washington, DC: World Bank.

te Velde, Dirk Willem, Neil Balchin, Karishma Banga, and Sonia Hoque. 2018. "Manufacturing in Africa: Factors for Success." Paper prepared for Supporting Economic Transformation's Second Africa Transformation Forum, Accra, Ghana, June.

Thomas, R., and K. Narayanan. 2017. "Determinants of Outward Foreign Direct Investment: A Study of Indian Manufacturing Firms." *Transnational Corporations* 24 (1): 9–26.

UNCTAD (United Nations Conference on Trade and Development). 1997. *World Investment Report 1997: Transnational Corporations, Market Structure and Competition Policy*. New York and Geneva: United Nations.

UNCTAD (United Nations Conference on Trade and Development). 2011. *World Investment Report 2011: Non-equity Modes of International Production and Development*. Geneva: United Nations.

UNCTAD (United Nations Conference on Trade and Development). 2019a. "Reforming Investment Dispute Settlement: A Stocktaking." IIA Issues Note 1, UNCTAD, Geneva.

UNCTAD (United Nations Conference on Trade and Development). 2019b. *World Investment Report 2019: Special Economic Zones*. Geneva: United Nations.

UNCTAD (United Nations Conference on Trade and Development). 2020. *World Investment Report 2020: International Production beyond the Pandemic.* Geneva: United Nations.

UNIDO (United Nations Industrial Development Organization). 2009. *Industrial Development Report 2009: Breaking In and Moving Up: New Industrial Challenges for the Bottom Billion and the Middle-Income Countries.* Vienna: UNIDO.

UNIDO (United Nations Industrial Development Organization). 2011. *Africa Investor Report: Towards Evidence-Based Investment Promotion Strategies.* Geneva: UNIDO.

UNIDO (United Nations Industrial Development Organization). 2018. "Global Value Chains and Industrial Development: Lessons from China, South-East and South Asia." UNIDO, Vienna.

Van Parys, Stefan. 2012. "The Effectiveness of Tax Incentives in Attracting Investment: Evidence from Developing Countries." *Reflets et perspectives de la vie économique* 2012 (3): 129–41.

Van Parys, Stefan, and Sebastian James. 2010. "The Effectiveness of Tax Incentives in Attracting Investment: Panel Data Evidence from the CFA Franc Zone." *International Tax and Public Finance* 17 (4): 400–29.

Venables, A. 1999. "Fragmentation and Multinational Production." *European Economic Review* 43 (4): 935–45.

Vogiatzoglou, Klimis. 2016. "Ease of Doing Business and FDI Inflows in ASEAN." *Journal of Southeast Asian Economies* 33 (3): 343–63.

Wade, Robert. 1990. *Governing the Market: Economic Theory and the Role of Government in East Asian Industrialization.* Princeton, NJ: Princeton University Press.

Wei, S.-J. 2000. "How Taxing Is Corruption on International Investors?" *Review of Economics and Statistics* 82 (1): 1–11.

Wernick, David A., Jerry Haar, and Shane Singh. 2009. "Do Governing Institutions Affect Foreign Direct Investment Inflows? New Evidence from Emerging Economies." *International Journal of Economics and Business Research* 1 (3): 317–32.

Whittaker, D. H., T. Zhu, T. Sturgeon, M. H. Tsai, and T. Okita. 2010. "Compressed Development." *Studies in Comparative International Development* 45: 439–467.

Williamson, Oliver E. 1975. *Markets and Hierarchies: Analysis and Antitrust Implications: A Study in the Economics of Internal Organization.* Hoboken, NJ: The Free Press.

Williamson, Stephen D. 1986. "Costly Monitoring, Financial Intermediation, and Equilibrium Credit Rationing." *Journal of Monetary Economics* 18 (2): 159–79.

World Bank. 2010. *Investment Law Reform: A Handbook for Development Practitioners.* Washington, DC: World Bank.

World Bank. 2018. *Global Investment Competitiveness Report 2017/2018: Foreign Investor Perspectives and Policy Implications.* Washington, DC: World Bank.

World Bank. 2020. *World Development Report 2020: Trading for Development in the Age of Global Value Chains.* Washington, DC: World Bank.

World Bank. Forthcoming. *A Unified Framework for Strengthening a Country's Investment Incentive Regime.* Washington, DC: World Bank.

World Bank and OECD (Organisation for Economic Co-operation and Development). 2017. *A Step Ahead: Competition Policy for Shared Prosperity and Inclusive Growth.* Washington, DC: World Bank.

World Bank Group. 2017. "Special Economic Zones: An Operational Review of Their Impacts." Competitive Industries and Innovation Program, World Bank, Washington, DC.

World Bank Group. 2019. "Retention and Expansion of Foreign Direct Investment: Political Risk and Policy Responses." World Bank Group, Washington, DC. http://documents.worldbank.org/curated/en/387801576142339003/Political-Risk-and-Policy-Responses.

WTO (World Trade Organization). 2006. "Recommendations of the Task Force on Aid for Trade." Document WT/AFT/1, WTO, Geneva.

Zeng, Douglas Zhihua. 2011. "How Do Special Economic Zones and Industrial Clusters Drive China's Rapid Development?" Policy Research Working Paper 5583, World Bank, Washington, DC.

Zeng, Douglas Zhihua. 2015. "Global Experiences with Special Economic Zones: Focus on China and Africa." Policy Research Working Paper 7240, World Bank, Washington, DC.

Zeng, Douglas Zhihua. 2020. "Special Economic Zones in Sub-Saharan Africa: What Drives Their Mixed Performance?" In *The Oxford Handbook of Industrial Hubs and Economic Development*, edited by Arkebe Oqubay and Justin Yifu Lin, 607–22. Oxford, U.K.: Oxford University Press.

Zolt, E. M. 2013. "Tax Incentives and Tax Base Protection Issues." Papers on Selected Topics in Protecting the Tax Base of Developing Countries Draft Paper 3, United Nations, New York.

Chapter 5

Global Value Chains in the Time of COVID-19 (Coronavirus)

Key findings

- The COVID-19 (coronavirus) pandemic brought unprecedented challenges to global value chains (GVCs) worldwide, with global trade projected to fall by 9.5 percent and foreign direct investment (FDI) by 42 percent in 2020. This stark drop in FDI and trade reflected the confluence of pandemic-induced supply and demand shocks with geopolitical and policy uncertainties.

- Most of the underlying trends in GVC development, such as the increasing focus on supply chain resilience and digitalization, began before the outbreak. However, the urgency and magnitude of these shifts have markedly increased. The search for diversification, resilience, and sustainability is happening for both economic and political reasons. Financial incentives, as well as considerations of national security and environmental sustainability, may affect the geographic configuration of some GVCs and locational decisions within them.

- It is, however, premature to conclude that firms should or will shift gears from "just-in-time" GVCs to "just-in-case" GVCs. Shorter GVCs and localized production are not necessarily less vulnerable to shocks. Supplier diversification and relocation can be costly and impractical for highly complex products. And holding more inventory and building redundant capacity could create inefficiencies in many industries.

- GVCs have proven their resilience during the pandemic, faciliating efficient production and timely delivery even when demand surged for certain goods and services. An extensive supply chain network with diversified and geographically dispersed suppliers can adjust better and contribute to a firm's speedy recovery. GVCs should be viewed as the solution in the pandemic rather than the problem.

- GVCs are always evolving, and opportunities belong to the firms that become more efficient and agile. COVID-19 response measures will not suddenly solve the global economy's preexisting structural issues, but developing countries should use the crisis as a stress test to prioritize reforms that improve their investment competitiveness in certain GVC segments and support robust economic recovery.

- The pandemic has further revealed the complex interdependence of firms and economies around the world. Tackling the complex challenges presented by the COVID-19 crisis will require global collaboration and coordination. Once again, the times are testing global leaders and policy makers. They must resist the lure of protectionist policies and work together to secure the hard-earned gains derived from GVCs.

Impact of COVID-19 (coronavirus) on foreign direct investment and global value chains

The COVID-19 (coronavirus) pandemic presented unprecedented shocks to the global economy, and particularly to global value chains (GVCs). The pandemic itself is still unfolding, as infections subside in certain regions and surge in others (figure 5.1). Its precise impact on businesses across regions and sectors continues to evolve, and its ultimate implications may take years to unfold. Nevertheless, emerging data can already provide evidence on the pandemic's distressing impact on GVC activity in the immediate term as well as on the adjustments businesses are making to their operations to cope with the new disruptions and business challenges.

Overall impact

The COVID-19 pandemic has posed unprecedented challenges to GVCs. Global trade is projected to fall by 9.5 percent in 2020, a 10.6-percentage-point decrease from 2019 (World Bank 2021). Indeed, stark drops in trade are already evident in recent data: merchandise trade is estimated to have fallen by 5 percent and 27 percent, respectively, in the first and second quarters of 2020 (UNCTAD 2020a). Although trade is expected to recover in 2021, the timing of this recovery depends on the duration of the outbreak and the effectiveness of policy responses to it (WTO 2020).

COVID-19's impact on foreign direct investment (FDI) has already been stark, and it may persist longer than the impact on trade. FDI, which was already in decline before the pandemic, fell by 42 percent in 2020 (UNCTAD 2021). The pandemic's

FIGURE 5.1 **Regions' shares of new COVID-19 (coronavirus) cases by month, January–December 2020**

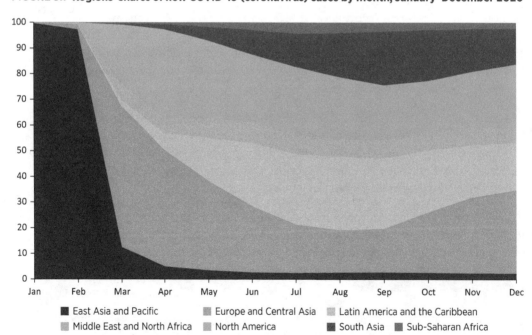

Source: World Bank calculations based on data from Our World in Data (https://ourworldindata.org/coronavirus).

immediate impact on FDI stemmed from a reduction in reinvested earnings as multinational companies' affiliates experienced large drops in profits. Equity capital flows also shrank as companies put new investment projects on hold amid travel bans, demand contractions, a liquidity crunch, and increased uncertainty. The pandemic affected all types of investment: greenfield investment projects announcements were down by 35 percent, cross-border merger and acquisition (M&A) fell by 10 percent, and new international project finance deals were 2 percent lower in 2020 compared with 2019 (UNCTAD 2021). Although profits and reinvestment of earnings will increase as the pandemic subsides, investor confidence (and, by extension, new greenfield and M&A projects) may take longer to recover. This slow recovery may bring long-term consequences for host economies, given FDI's role in development finance, knowledge transfers, and economic transformation.

The stark fall in trade and FDI in the early months of the pandemic reflected the confluence of pandemic-induced supply and demand shocks and policy and geopolitical uncertainty (figure 5.2).

Supply shocks have resulted from shutdowns in production and related disruptions to input supplies and supply chains. Lockdowns imposed by governments have led many businesses to close their operations, causing serious disruptions. Even where shutdowns are only partial, shifts to remote work, the health impacts of the virus on workers, and modifications to production lines to improve safety have decreased productivity and the labor supply at some firms. Finally, even where production has not been affected, the rapid reduction in air traffic has decreased belly cargo capacity (the space under the main deck of an aircraft where cargo is stowed), which accounts for roughly half of global air cargo capacity (World Bank 2020b). Production and logistics disruptions have also translated to lower trade volumes because producers either cannot meet or cannot ship global orders. And, where operations of multinational corporation (MNC) affiliates have been disrupted, drops in production have also decreased FDI by lowering profits and thus reinvested earnings.

These impacts extend beyond regions and firms that have been forced to shut down because of the integrated nature of GVCs: downstream producers of firms that

FIGURE 5.2 **Impact of COVID-19 (coronavirus) on global value chains**

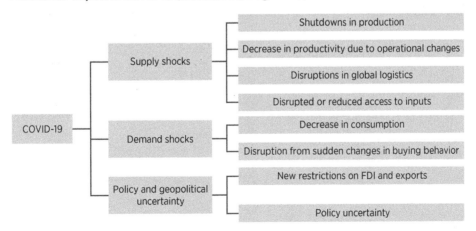

Source: World Bank 2020d.
Note: FDI = foreign direct investment.

have been shut down have faced input shortages and delays, especially if they rely on just-in-time deliveries, and have been unable to identify new suppliers to fill their gaps (Baldwin and Tomiura 2020; Qiang et al. 2020). As a result, about three-quarters of MNCs operating in low- and middle-income countries were already reporting decreases in worker productivity and supply chain reliability by the first quarter of 2020, and these impacts are expected to worsen over time (Saurav et al. 2020a). These domino effects have led to further decreases in trade (by reducing output) and FDI (by reducing profits) that have cascaded through GVCs.

The pandemic has also reduced demand for many goods and services. Both practical barriers to consumption, such as store closures, and declines in disposable income and consumer confidence have led to reductions in spending (Baldwin and di Mauro 2020). In June 2020, for example, 40 percent of consumers in the United States reported becoming more mindful of where they spent their money as a result of the pandemic.[1] As with supply shocks, these impacts transcend sectoral and geographic borders. Reductions in end-consumer demand translate into reduced demand for intermediate inputs and raw materials, leading to cancelled or reduced orders (Teodoro and Rodriguez 2020). In the context of GVCs, lower demand directly leads to reduced production, sales, and profits—and therefore reduced reinvestment FDI— at MNCs affiliates. In addition, lower business confidence caused by low demand leads to delays or cancellations of new FDI projects.

Governments have adopted various policies in response to the crisis. Several countries have stepped up their policies to support GVCs, including by providing tax relief to companies involved in GVCs. Map 5.1 shows preliminary evidence that 50 out of 51 countries analyzed have relaxed their business taxes (on value added, sales, payroll, or corporate income) in response to COVID-19. This aid came most often as either tax

MAP 5.1 Business tax reforms adopted during COVID-19 (coronavirus)

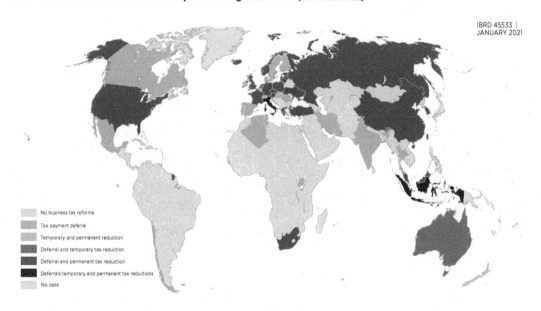

IBRD 45533 |
JANUARY 2021

No business tax reforms
Tax payment deferral
Temporary and permanent reduction
Deferral and temporary tax reduction
Deferral and permanent tax reduction
Deferrals temporary and permanent tax reductions
No data

Source: World Bank calculations based on Kronfol and Chan, forthcoming.
Note: Updated on June 30, 2020. The business taxes analyzed are value added taxes, sales taxes, payroll taxes, and corporate income taxes.

payment deferrals (22 countries) or permanent tax reductions (23 countries). Similarly, many investment promotion agencies (IPAs) have adopted investment retention initiatives. These initiatives include expediting foreign exchange approvals and advocating for urgent government actions to solve these companies' grievances more systematically and in ways that would benefit other, similar investors. Some countries are also allowing companies in export-oriented industrial parks to supply locally and are facilitating MNCs' expansion into new production lines as part of the countries' strategic reorientation to in-demand products and services in light of COVID-19.[2]

In contrast, other countries have introduced more restrictive investment and export measures in light of the pandemic. FDI restrictions were already increasing before the pandemic because of alleged national security considerations (World Economic Forum 2020b). Common pandemic-related restrictions include new screening legislation to prevent foreign acquisitions in strategically important sectors (UNCTAD 2020a) and export bans on goods such as medical equipment. Such measures hamper GVC activity by directly restricting trade and cross-border investment. Map 5.2 provides a preliminary analysis of investment regulation during COVID-19. Out of 42 countries included, only 8 have eased their investment regulations, 29 have tightened their regulations, and 5 have enacted both types of measures (map 5.2). Even where restrictions have not yet been introduced, uncertainty regarding the future course of government policies can hold back investment decisions.

Impact differentials across sectors

The pandemic has depressed GVC activities in different sectors to varying degrees. Although declines are evident across nearly all sectors, certain sectors have experienced

MAP 5.2 Easing and restricting investment regulation around the world during COVID-19 (coronavirus)

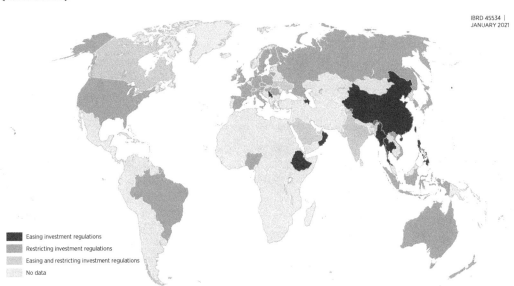

IBRD 45534 |
JANUARY 2021

- ■ Easing investment regulations
- ■ Restricting investment regulations
- ■ Easing and restricting investment regulations
- □ No data

Source: World Bank calculations using Forneris and de Bonneval, forthcoming.
Note: Updated January 13, 2021.

more severe supply disruptions or bigger drops in demand than others. From a supply perspective, sectors whose supply chains are more concentrated in areas heavily afflicted by the pandemic and those whose supply chains are longer or more complex have felt greater supply chain pressure. For example, during the early stages of the pandemic, the textile sector faced severe disruptions as critical raw materials factories in China shut down (Aung and Paul 2020). On the demand side, the direct effect of lockdowns and travel bans has been greater for sectors that rely on in-person spending, such as hotels and accommodations (Gourinchas et al. 2020). In contrast, the medical and health sector experienced steep surges in demand in the early phases of the pandemic. In addition, certain sectors, such as energy and financial services, are more procyclical than others, making them more vulnerable to the general decline in economic activity caused by the pandemic. As a result, sector performance has varied with regard to greenfield FDI and cross-border M&A (figure 5.3).

Unsurprisingly, sectors related to tourism and food service have faced particularly sharp declines. Travel bans have forced many tour operators to suspend or drastically curtail their operations, and the decline in consumer confidence and buying power has decreased demand even where travel is allowed. As a result, according to the Financial Times's fDi Markets and Thomson Reuters data, greenfield FDI projects in the hotel and restaurant sectors are down 69 percent in 2020 compared to 2019, while cross-border M&A transaction value in the sector is down about 51 percent. Similarly, trade in services related to travel and transportation is down sharply. In Mauritius, for instance, the number of international tourist arrivals in March 2020 was less than half the level in March 2019, although the country has had very few confirmed COVID-19 cases. As the virus quickly spread around the world and governments implemented stringent restrictions on international travel, the number of

FIGURE 5.3 Change in greenfield foreign direct investment announcement values and cross-border merger and acquisition transaction values, 2020 vs. 2019

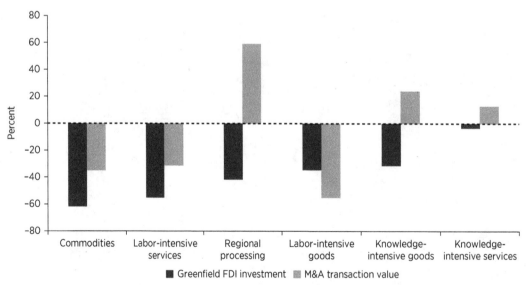

Source: World Bank calculations based on data from fDi Markets and Thomson Reuters.
Note: This figure compares the value of greenfield FDI project announcements and cross-border M&A transaction values in 2020 (whole year) with 2019. FDI = foreign direct investment; M&A = merger and acquisition.

arrivals plummeted further in April and remained near zero throughout the rest of 2020 (see chapter 9 of this report).

Commodity sectors—especially energy—have also been hit hard by the pandemic. Countries in full lockdown have experienced an average 25 percent decline in energy demand, and even countries that never closed or have reopened have cut back on energy use because of lower economic activity (International Energy Agency 2020). In turn, this drop in demand has adversely affected earnings and future investment prospects for the energy sector. The global market capitalization of energy companies fell by more than one-third from January to June 2020. Many other commodity sectors have experienced similar hits because they are also procyclical, although not necessarily to the same degree as the energy sector.[3] For FDI, greenfield project announcement values and cross-border M&A transaction values for deals related to commodity sectors declined by 62 percent and 35 percent, respectively, in 2020 relative to 2019 (figure 5.3). Trade in fuels and lubricants was also down sharply year over year (table 5.1).

Various subsectors of manufacturing—covering both labor- and knowledge-intensive goods—have also disproportionately suffered from the pandemic-induced economic crisis. Supply chain disruptions across GVCs, factory closures, drops in demand caused by store closings (for many labor-intensive goods, such as apparel), and drops in consumer confidence (for many knowledge-intensive consumer durables, such as automobiles) have affected the sales, profits, and investment prospects of many manufacturing firms (International Labour Organization 2020). Compared with 2019, the total value of greenfield FDI project announcements for labor-intensive and knowledge-intensive goods dropped by 35 percent and 31 percent, respectively. Similarly, cross-border M&A transaction values for labor-intensive goods have declined by 55 percent; knowledge-intensive goods, in contrast, have seen a 24 percent increase (figure 5.3). These impacts on manufacturing are reflected in how trade in transportation equipment has fallen even more than trade in most other sectors (table 5.1).

In contrast, certain knowledge-intensive service sectors have been more resilient, although their performance has generally declined as well. Demand for some software products has risen because of COVID-19 because many firms have switched to remote work and virtual meetings, customers have adopted or increased their use of digital entertainment and information technologies at home in lieu of going out, and school courses have gone online. As early as March 2020, Microsoft reported a 40 percent increase in users for its online collaboration software (Wakabayashi et al. 2020). Morgan Stanley Capital International's global index for information technology stocks actually increased 12 percent from January to June 2020, and trade in information and communication technology services has increased year over year as well. Greenfield FDI for knowledge-intensive services declined only slightly, by 3 percent, in 2020. This decline is smaller than that of other sectors, although the sector is still underperforming. M&A activity in this sector recorded a 13 percent growth (figure 5.3).

Sectors corresponding to consumer staples—notably food and beverages—have also been relatively resilient, although they have still faced some disruptions. Although a large part of the population has stayed indoors amid the crisis, food and beverage supply chains have continued to function mostly unhindered. Demand for essential products has remained relatively stable despite extended lead times and higher prices. Consumer staple sectors also tend to have more localized supply chains than other goods (that is, food value chains are often national or regional rather

TABLE 5.1 China, European Union, Japan, and the United States exports and imports, by detailed end use, March–May 2020

	Exports (year-over-year % change)			Imports (year-over-year % change)		
	March	April	May	March	April	May
Capital						
Capital goods	−9.7	−6.2	−10.0	−4.4	−4.6	−6.3
Transport equipment	−30.4	−54.3	−63.3	−30.9	−58.6	−71.4
Intermediate						
Food and beverages	7.7	8.6	3.7	7.2	−1.1	12.3
Industrial supplies	0.7	−8.7	−16.8	−0.4	−7.9	−10.8
Fuels and lubricants	−0.5	−33.4	−44.0	−22.3	−49.3	−58.4
Capital goods	−8.5	−11.4	−18.7	2.0	−7.5	−13.3
Transport equipment	−11.5	−40.2	−46.0	−10.4	−38.6	−48.7
Consumption						
Food and beverages	2.7	−2.6	−11.5	11.7	−0.1	−3.0
Transport equipment	−34.2	−40.5	−19.4	−12.1	−30.7	−19.6
Consumer goods	−6.7	−11.3	−6.5	−3.4	−9.8	−13.4
Not classified						
Food and beverages	−6.9	−17.8	−20.5	0.1	−15.5	−27.4
Fuels and lubricants	−14.5	−42.4	−67.2	−33.1	−63.2	−59.5
Transport equipment	−16.7	−65.2	−62.0	−6.5	−53.3	−69.7
Goods	−13.5	−31.0	−45.1	−5.0	−17.2	−38.5
Total	−7.0	−16.9	−22.4	−5.6	−18.4	−23.7

Source: World Bank estimates using official data from China, Eurostat, Japan, and the United States.
Note: Trade flows for the European Union (EU) include only extra-EU trade because of data availability. End-use categories are based on United Nations Broad Economic Categories (Rev 4).

than global). Thus, sectors corresponding to consumer staples have experienced lower-than-average stock market index declines as well as lower declines in FDI and trade activities. Greenfield FDI in food and beverages dropped by 13 percent in 2020, whereas M&A transaction value quadrupled.

Firms' responses to the disruption

Impacts on global value chain firms

Ultimately, the adverse effects of the COVID-19 pandemic on GVCs translate into impacts on the firms involved in GVCs, which range from MNCs and other large corporations to small local suppliers and customers. Emerging data illustrate the stark impact of the pandemic on the large firms and MNCs that anchor many GVCs. The earnings per share of the S&P 500 companies in the fourth quarter of 2020 have climbed to US$33 from US$12 in the first quarter of 2020, but that figure is still lower than their earnings per share in the fourth quarter of 2019.[4] A survey by the World Bank Group of MNC affiliates in low- and middle-income countries found similar results: two-thirds of respondents had experienced drops in their net income and revenue, among other adverse impacts, in the third quarter of 2020 compared with the same period in 2019 (figure 5.4).

Supply chain disruptions stand out as particularly important challenges for multinationals in the early phase of the pandemic. Of the MNC affiliates surveyed by the World Bank, 77 percent reported a decrease in the reliability of their supply chains in middle- and low-income countries in the second quarter of 2020, but the share of firms had dropped to 41 percent in the third quarter of 2020 (figure 5.4). Country-level surveys echo this trend: among large and medium-size firms in China, about 20 percent reported experiencing supply chain pressures (UNDP 2020). In another survey conducted in mid-February among the 169 member firms of the American Chamber of Commerce in China, 30 percent of respondents reported local supply chain disruptions (in China) and 17 percent reported global supply chain disruptions (AmCham China 2020). In the United States, about 30 percent of large firms reported supply chain impacts (JUST Capital 2020). A survey of chief financial officers of UK businesses, conducted in April 2020, showed that about half of their firms had

FIGURE 5.4 Impact of COVID-19 (coronavirus) on multinational corporations' affiliates, July–December 2020

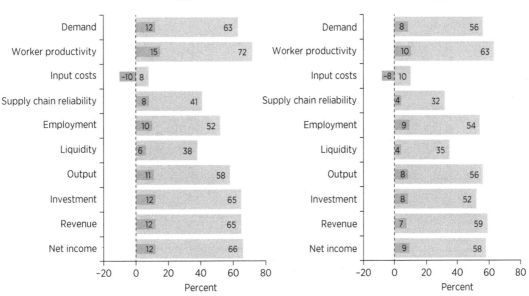

a. Experiences, July–September 2020
"From July to September 2020, what was your company's performance in your host country compared with the same period in 2019?"
N = 305

b. Expectations, October–December 2020
"From October to December 2020, what expectations do you have for your company's performance in your host country compared with the same period in 2019?"
N = 305

Share of MNCs reporting adverse impacts   Average adverse impact across MNCs

Source: Saurav et al. 2020b (November 2020).
Note: MNCs = multinational corporations.

suffered from supply chain disruptions and a quarter of their firms were experiencing disruptions to at least 25 percent of the inputs they buy, including service inputs. Supply disruption was well correlated with expected sales impacts, suggesting that supply disruptions constrain output (Bloom, Bunn, et al. 2020).

In turn, suppliers to MNCs, many of whom are small or medium enterprises (SMEs), are facing the most pressure. They are an integral part of GVCs and are exposed to ripple effects from both demand and supply shocks. A survey of Bangladeshi garment suppliers, for example, reveals how they have been affected in three phases of the pandemic and through various channels. In phase 1, Wuhan's lockdown reduced their access to raw materials (fabrics). About 90 percent of suppliers reported delayed shipments and higher prices for raw materials. In phase 2, as the pandemic began to hit buyers' bottom lines, 80 percent of suppliers began to face delays in payments of more than 10 days. And, in phase 3, the scourge of COVID-19 led buyers to cancel orders either in progress or completed, leaving suppliers in dire financial conditions. These firms, integrated into GVCs, are normally the most productive ones in their sector. However, in the wake of COVID-19, they are also likely to be more exposed to shocks. Losing this part of the Bangladeshi economy would slow the country's recovery and depress overall productivity.

The aforementioned impacts are alarming because SMEs are more financially fragile than larger firms and may lack the capacity to adjust their business models in light of the COVID-19 pandemic. The pandemic has thus far exacerbated preexisting credit and liquidity constraints among SMEs. For example, in Uganda, about 70 percent of surveyed firms reported a decline in access to credit, with 34 percent experiencing a decline of more than 50 percent (Lakuma and Sunday 2020). Furthermore, SMEs may not be able to afford preventive health measures such as offering hand sanitizer and distributing personal protective equipment to employees and customers.

Immediate response during the crisis

Firms have taken various measures to survive the crisis, such as furloughing employees, repurposing production lines, and adopting new technologies. Some of these measures were taken immediately at the start of the outbreak to keep businesses afloat, whereas other measures are intertwined with long-term megatrends and will take time to materialize.

Shrinking market demand and disruptions to supply chains push firms to aggressively reduce their expenditures. Some of their cost-cutting measures include freezing hiring, ending travel, tightening management of discretionary costs, and reducing their numbers of contractors. According to the JUST Capital corporate response tracker,[5] among the largest firms in the United States, the most common cost-cutting measure has been pay cuts taken by top executives (28 percent), followed by furloughing (25 percent) and laying off workers (11 percent). Even in countries where salary reductions or freezes are not normally allowed, such as Italy, companies were given special permission to reduce working hours and pay while nonessential business is suspended.

To mitigate the pandemic's adverse impacts, suppliers to MNCs, especially SMEs, are adopting all possible measures to cut labor costs. In Uganda, a significant percentage of manufacturing businesses have laid off employees, and 40 percent of them have reduced their numbers of employees by more than half (Lakuma and Sunday 2020). In South Africa, more than 40 percent of SMEs have already reduced capacity, laid off employees, or suspect they will need to lay off employees. In Bangladesh, at least 1.2 million garment workers have been furloughed because of order cancellations. Many suppliers in Bangladesh, Cambodia, and Myanmar have suspended work without paying workers for orders already completed because some MNCs, operating in survival mode, have not been paying their suppliers. This nonpayment has added to the gloomy prospects for employment in many developing countries, which may take years to recover from this crisis.

Many MNCs are also trimming their product offerings or rationalizing their SKUs (stock-keeping units, numbers that each represent a unique item). For example, Coca-Cola is ruthlessly prioritizing core SKUs to drive efficiency in its supply chains and streamline operations for retail customers. Procter & Gamble also narrowed its production focus to core SKUs to ensure supply flow despite an influx of demand (Cosgrove 2020). However, cost-cutting is less likely to occur in areas that are perceived to be critical to sustaining growth in the midst of the pandemic, such as digital transformation, customer experience management, and cybersecurity (Edwards 2020). In contrast to the cuts they've made to labor costs, firms are seizing the opportunity to roll out new technologies in these areas and to speed up their digital transformations.

Several businesses, across industries and countries, are repurposing their production lines and research and development (R&D) capabilities to supply critical materials for the fight against COVID-19 or are pivoting to new ways to generate revenue. For example, textile companies are switching their production lines from making garments to making hygienic masks and medical robes, cosmetics companies are making hand sanitizer, hotels have become quarantine centers, distilleries are creating disinfecting alcohol, and automotive companies are evaluating their options to produce urgently needed medical devices such as ventilators. Repurposing can simultaneously serve the greater good, help businesses keep their production lines up and running in times of low demand, generate moderate revenue, and positively affect businesses' reputations. In several cases, MNCs are leveraging their existing supplier bases to avoid lengthy qualification and onboarding processes and to maintain those suppliers' jobs (Betti and Heizmann 2020).

MNC support to suppliers is another critical way to create resilient production networks. MNCs increasingly recognize that their suppliers are their intricately linked partners. Thus, some MNCs (such as global garment retailers [Hughes 2020] and Boeing [Cameron 2020]) have accelerated payments to suppliers for goods that either have been produced or are in the process of being produced. MNCs have also helped suppliers adapt their production processes to the post–COVID-19 world. For example, Apple is helping its partners redesign and reconfigure their factory floorplans to maximize their workers' personal space (Gurman 2020). Evidence suggests that strengthening these long-term relationships is associated with more rapid recovery (Jain, Girotra, and Netessine 2016).

Megatrends and firms' medium- to long-term responses

In the medium to long term, firms' responses to the COVID-19 pandemic will take into consideration the megatrends that are either already altering the GVC landscape or emerging on the horizon. The pandemic has accelerated some preexisting trends and has triggered new changes. Disruptive technologies and policy uncertainty are among the most important of these megatrends, and they could profoundly influence the world's globalization trajectory.

Technology

The extraordinary advancement of technology is the ultimate enabler and driver of GVC expansion. Technologies have created new stages of production and have affected the distribution of value added in GVCs. New technologies have enabled more asset-light forms of investment; they have also changed production lengths in both directions and increased the market power of MNCs.

COVID-19 has been an unexpected catalyst for technology adoption across the world. When the outbreak and lockdown measures snarled GVCs, firms realized the importance of value chain visibility and risk management, as they have in previous crises. Because of this heightened understanding, 88 percent of MNCs surveyed by the World Bank in the fourth quarter of 2020 reported increasing their use of digital supply chain management technologies (Saurav et al. 2021). In an example from an earlier crisis, Toyota undertook a massive effort to build a risk-proof supply chain after the 2011 Japanese earthquake. As the founder of lean inventory management and just-in-time delivery systems, Toyota had stretched its supply chain thin before the crisis to maximize efficiency and reduce waste in storage and handling. However, because many of its components were single sourced, the 2011 earthquake and tsunami caused widespread parts shortages that persisted for several months. As a result, Toyota had to dramatically throttle production. To minimize supply chain risks in the future, Toyota developed its RESCUE (REinforce Supply Chain Under Emergency) system by establishing a database of supplier information that identified the vulnerabilities and parts information of more than 650,000 supplier sites. This supplier mapping effort allowed Toyota to track components and replace them easily during the COVID-19 outbreak. COVID-19 has boosted demand for this sort of end-to-end visibility, and big data, Internet of Things devices, and artificial intelligence will be increasingly deployed to help firms achieve greater efficiency, minimize waste, and enhance their robustness.

The pandemic also drove a rapid migration to online settings across every domain, and many of those changes are here to stay. At present, most firms have to serve their customers through online channels and allow employees to work remotely whenever possible, which has created a boom for video conferencing, online shopping, contactless payment, and delivery services. According to a survey by Adobe, COVID-19 spurred a spike in e-commerce in the United States: total online spending in May 2020 hit $82.5 billion, a 77 percent jump compared with the previous year (Koetsier 2020). A McKinsey survey of more than 20,000 European consumers in May 2020 found that digital adoption[6] in Europe jumped from 81 percent to 95 percent because of the COVID-19 crisis—a rise that would have taken two to three years in most industries at prepandemic growth rates (Fernandez, Jenkins, and Vieira 2020). And, all around the world, grocery stores have shifted to online ordering and delivery as their primary business, schools have pivoted to online learning and digital classrooms, doctors are providing telemedicine, and banks have made the transition to remote sales. Some of these shifts in the ways people live and work are likely to stay: firms are embracing the digital transformation as a core component of their competitiveness, and the rise of e-commerce and platform firms has allowed people to transact directly with one another, brought down prices, and increased match quality.

The COVID-19 lockdowns have also increased interest in robotics adoption. Although many firms have frozen their budgets, automation is the one place where some are increasing spending. The outbreak has had a severe impact on manufacturers' operations because factory work cannot be performed remotely. Plant shutdowns and the consequent labor shortages have rippled through industries from food processing to automotive manufacturing. Firms are increasingly looking to robotics to augment locked-down employees, support health and safety measures, and tap into new opportunities or salvage their operations. The biggest US meat company by sales, Tyson Foods, is speeding up its shift from human to robot meat cutters. Pilgrim's Pride Corp., the second-largest US chicken processor, now sees its deboning machines trail humans by only 1.0–1.5 percent in meat yield per chicken (Bunge and Newman 2020). However, robots still have a long way to go before they can match human dexterity and experience.

In service sectors, Walmart is now using robots to scrub its floors, and McDonald's has been testing robots as cooks and servers. In warehouses, such as those operated by Amazon and Walmart, robots were already used to improve efficiency. COVID-19 has both companies looking to increase their use of robots in sorting, shipping, and packing (Thomas 2020). YouTube is having machines do more content moderation (YouTube Team 2020). AMP Robotics, a US-based robotics company, has seen a significant increase in orders for its robots that use artificial intelligence to sift through recycled material and weed out trash (Corkery and Gelles 2020). And UVD Robots, a Danish manufacturer of ultraviolet light–disinfection robots, shipped hundreds of its machines to hospitals in China and Europe as demand for cleaning and sanitizing robots soared during the pandemic (Thomas 2020). With minimal human involvement, automation can achieve greater accuracy, improved efficiency, and higher productivity at many tasks. However, this development may dislocate certain jobs and pose additional challenges to the future of work.

Additive manufacturing and 3D (three-dimensional) printing also saw accelerated adoption because of the pandemic. 3D printing enables on-demand solutions for a wide spectrum of needs, ranging from personal protection equipment to medical devices and isolation wards. For example, an Italian engineering company, Isinnova, came up with a 3D-printable mask connector design to manufacture masks; 3D printing was also used to produce emergency respiration devices, testing swabs, and so on (Choong et al. 2020). The versatility and agility of 3D printing could bring a revolution to traditional manufacturing in the coming years and become a novel solution to the supply chain challenges faced by businesses today.

Increasing market power

Across the globe, corporate market power has increased noticeably over the past several decades. De Loecker and Eeckhout (2018) analyzed the evolution of markups over the past four decades using data from more than 70,000 firms in 134 countries.

Their research shows that the average global markup has increased from close to 1.1 in 1980 to 1.6 in 2016. Markups have risen the most in North America and Europe and the least in emerging economies in Latin America and Asia.

Technology has been a major force behind the rising market power of superstar firms. Innovation is getting more expensive, whereas returns to research are diminishing (Bloom, Jones, et al. 2020). Often, only large corporations can afford the exorbitant costs of conducting R&D that pushes the frontier of knowledge. In the meantime, digital technologies inherently favor incumbents and first movers, allowing big companies to seize market share from smaller ones and entrench their dominance. The rise in business lobbying and campaign finance contributions has also contributed to this market power effect (Philippon 2019).

COVID-19 could cause a further rise in corporations' market power because large corporations are in the best position to withstand the economic downturn and deploy new technologies. History suggests that economic slowdowns widen existing divisions between companies (Aviva Investors 2020). In the past three recessions, the share prices of US firms in the top quartile across 10 sectors rose by an average of 6 percent whereas the share prices of those in the bottom quartile fell by 44 percent. The same divergence has been evident since the start of the COVID-19 outbreak. Moreover, there has already been a wave of business bankruptcies (Mathurin, Aliaj, and Fontanella-Khan 2020) and permanent closures since the pandemic began, and the wave is expected to grow in the following months. Increasing corporate market power could lower consumer well-being, decrease demand for labor, and dampen investment in capital, eventually distorting the distribution of economic rents and discouraging innovation.

Policy uncertainty and geopolitical risks

Economic nationalism was the new norm even before the COVID-19 crisis, and it has gained further momentum since the outbreak began. Defensive nationalism—closing borders, building walls, imposing tariffs, and cutting back on migration—was a defining feature of the past decade as countries retreated into their national silos (Bush 2020). Such protectionist policies began in developed economies, stemming from their domestic backdrops of rising inequality and political polarization. An analysis of the policy platforms of the largest political parties in the Group of Twenty countries found that these parties have increasingly emphasized policies that stress national sovereignty, reject multilateralism, and seek to advance national interests at the expense of foreign interests (De Bolle and Zettelmeyer 2019). The trade frictions between China and the United States further escalated global uncertainty: global supply chains are at risk as the world's two biggest economies threaten to decouple.

The pandemic has reinforced recent trends toward restrictive investment and trade policies and economic nationalism. Concerned about the undervaluation of critical national assets and opportunistic acquisition by foreign investors during the pandemic, many countries have already adopted more stringent approaches to screening foreign investment to protect domestic businesses and industrial actors (see map 5.2). Of the 42 countries included in map 5.2, 34 have taken measures to tighten their investment regulations. The most common measure was increasing screening (29 countries), followed by restrictions on hiring foreign workers (7 countries), and tightening regulations on land ownership (1 country) (figure 5.5, panel a). Some countries are also emphasizing self-reliance and taking an inward-looking stance on both economic and foreign policy (Baldwin and Evenett 2020). As a result, the Global Economic Policy Uncertainty Index reached a historical peak in March 2020 (figure 5.5, panel b).

Policy uncertainty is detrimental to trade and is even more so to investment. A rise in policy uncertainty has confounded the already uncertain situation caused by COVID-19. The inability to estimate the probability of future events increases general uncertainty, which suppresses firms' hiring and R&D, delays investment and new business formation, and postpones households' consumption of durables. All these effects aggravate the devastating impact of the outbreak and delay economic recovery.

Sustainability

GVCs are a mixed blessing for the environment (World Bank 2020c). Whereas GVCs expand the scale of economic activity, alter the composition of economic activity, and bring about changes in production techniques that may have a positive effect on the environment (Grossman and Krueger 1991), hyperspecialization and agglomeration of economic activities could negatively affect the environment and health in regions specializing in pollution-heavy industries (Bombardini and Li 2020). Companies might deliberately migrate to jurisdictions where environmental regulations are lax. The composition effect is ambiguous.

Sustainability will play a bigger role in influencing the future development of GVCs. The COVID-19 crisis has raised critical awareness of the links between nature, health, and sustainable development. Recent climate change policies and green deals now being adopted in major constituencies and trading blocs will have a much more fundamental impact on the way firms operate (UNCTAD 2020b). A recent World Bank Group IPA survey also shows that two-thirds of the countries include green investment as a priority segment in their investment promotion strategies (Sanchiz and Omic 2020). The same report reveals that 60 percent of IPAs evaluate environmental

FIGURE 5.5 Rising policy uncertainty

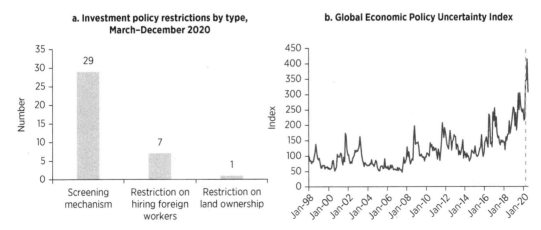

Sources: Panel a, World Bank calculations using Forneris and de Bonneval, forthcoming; panel b, Global Economic Policy Uncertainty Index (https://www.policyuncertainty.com/index.html).
Note: Panel a was updated on January 18, 2021.

and social impacts of investment projects they work with. Increased caution and scrutiny from regulatory authorities, consumers, investors, business partners, insurers, banks, and financial markets could all push firms to be more environmentally responsible and identify synergies between sustainability and business rationale.

A rising number of MNCs have already pledged to work only with suppliers that adhere to their social and environmental standards (Villena and Gioia 2020). This trend is likely to continue and accelerate, though it is important to recognize the costs associated with building up green production networks and develop collective approaches to address externalities and share the costs and responsibilities. By transforming private sector activity through sustainable investment, countries can accelerate recovery and stimulate resilient growth.

Global value chain adjustments

Economists and policy makers have drawn various conclusions about the performance of cross-border supply chains during COVID-19. Does the evidence so far support the reconfiguration of supply chains? Will nearshoring or reshoring take place? Will GVCs be regionalized? Has globalization gone too far?

GVC disruptions caused by crises are not new, and previous lessons suggest that an extensive supply chain network could contribute to a firm's speedy recovery. The 2008 global financial crisis, the 2011 Japanese earthquake, and the 2011 Chao Phraya River floods in Thailand each tested firms' ability to cope with value chain disruptions and in many ways made GVCs more resilient. A global pandemic is different from a financial crisis or a natural disaster, but some lessons from previous crises are still relevant to the present scenario (box 5.1).

Diversification of suppliers has always been a key strategy of MNCs to mitigate their risks and increase their bargaining power. Firms that have diversified suppliers and geographically dispersed production networks can adjust their production when a disaster occurs in one place. For example, Apple has long maintained a supply chain strategy of using multiple suppliers for the same component wherever possible (AICD 2015). For instance, in 2016 it sourced 70 percent of its cellular modems for iPhones from Qualcomm and the remaining 30 percent from Intel (Tayal 2017). And, when COVID-19 hit East Asia and the Pacific in February 2020, Samsung switched part of its smartphone production from the Republic of Korea to Vietnam, where it operates other factories (Song 2020). Supply chain diversification also allows for greater flexibility, enabling MNCs to respond to changing market trends and provide higher-quality service. Working with a diverse range of suppliers can also introduce innovation and creative approaches from outside the MNCs' thinking. By geographically broadening their supplier bases, MNCs are more likely to cut production costs by offering more competitive wages at the local level and more likely to better serve local customers by tailoring products to their demands.

The COVID-19 outbreak has highlighted the importance of supply chain robustness and resilience and reopened the debate on reshoring, nearshoring, and GVC regionalization. On one hand, some economists foresee more unexpected shocks and argue for a rethinking of GVC strategies, with an emphasis on holding more inventory, diversifying suppliers, and shortening supply chains (Javorcik 2020). The World Economic Forum (2020a) has recommended that firms "aggressively evaluate

BOX 5.1 Global value chain disruptions: Lessons from the 2011 Japanese earthquake

On March 11, 2011, Japan's northeastern shore was struck by a 9.0 magnitude earthquake, often referred to as the Great East Japan Earthquake. It was the most powerful earthquake ever recorded in Japan. The total economic cost of the quake was estimated by the World Bank to be US$235 billion, making it one of the costliest natural disasters in history. About 24,000 people were recorded dead, injured, or missing, and more than a million buildings were damaged to some extent. The devastating impact of the earthquake and the tsunami it caused was compounded by a subsequent accident at the Fukushima nuclear reactors, which in turn caused evacuations and radioactive contamination, and by continuing aftershocks and widespread infrastructure damage, including to transportation, electricity, telecommunications, and water infrastructure.

Although the physical shock of the Great East Japan Earthquake was confined to Japan's northeastern coastal areas, the earthquake wrought great economic damage on the whole country and even the rest of the world (Behravesh 2011; Rosenbush 2011; Zarathustra 2011). Although the four affected prefectures accounted for only 4.7 percent of total Japanese output (Carvalho et al. 2016), the shock to a small subset of firms was propagated and amplified throughout the economy via a network of input-output links, resulting in significant economic costs for other parts of Japan (Acemoglu, Akcigit, and Kerr 2015; Barrot and Sauvagnat 2016; Carvalho et al. 2016). When a firm that is connected in a production network reduces its output because of an idiosyncratic shock, its upstream or downstream firms might be influenced as well through their supplier-customer relationships (Acemoglu, Akcigit, and Kerr 2015). For example, Toyota and Honda had to suspend production in the United States because of the disruption to their supply chains in the disaster-stricken areas. Approximately 90 percent of Japan's output loss caused by the earthquake resulted from indirect effects through the supply chain network rather than from direct effects caused by the natural disaster (Tokui, Kawasaki, and Miyagawa 2017).

Nevertheless, Todo, Nakajima, and Matous (2015) argue that extensive supply chain networks could also help firms quicken their recovery from destruction. Firms with such connections are more likely to receive support from their suppliers and clients during the recovery, and supply chain networks provide information and input sharing that firms can use to replace their damaged property (as well as overall benefits from agglomeration). Econometric analysis by Todo, Nakajima, and Matous (2015) shows that affected firms connected with networks outside of the areas that received impacts were more likely to resume production in the early stages of recovery, and networks within the affected areas contributed to firms' sales recovery in the medium term.

The Japanese earthquake also prompted domestic firms to offshore production to other countries. Using Japanese firm-level data from 2010 through 2013, Zhu, Ito, and Tomiura (2016) find that increases in offshoring after the earthquake were higher among manufacturing firms than among service firms. This effect could be explained by the fact that manufacturing firms often require the transportation of physical intermediates and were thus more likely to be influenced by the earthquake's disruption.

However, the earthquake's shock did not lead to significant reshoring, nearshoring, or diversification by foreign multinationals (Freund et al. 2020). Some major global importers of automotive components have moved away from Japan in favor of lower-cost suppliers in developing countries. There was, however, no evidence of supplier diversification across countries after the crisis—the Herfindahl-Hirschman index of input suppliers remained flat. The finding that the earthquake's shock led suppliers to switch rather than widen their sources may have occurred because few countries are capable of producing auto components and such production often requires relationship-specific investments.

near-shore options to shorten supply chains and increase proximity to customers." Some policy makers are even calling for their countries' manufacturers to bring their production back home. On the other hand, many business executives find that such prescriptions oversimplify the problem. These calls for reshoring may be just wishful thinking because doing so on a large scale would defy economic rationality (Freund 2020). A recent World Bank survey of MNCs found that 37 percent and 18 percent were diversifying their sourcing and production bases, respectively, in response to COVID-19, but only a relatively small portion (14 percent) planned to nearshore or reshore (Saurav et al. 2020a).

It might be premature to conclude that firms should shift gears from "just-in-time" to "just-in-case" GVCs. It is important to distinguish between the resilience and robustness of a supply chain, which require different strategies to promote (Miroudot 2020). Resilience is defined as the ability to return to normal operations within an acceptable period after a disruption. Robustness is the ability to maintain operations during a crisis (Brandon-Jones et al. 2014). For strategic industries, such as key medical supplies in the case of COVID-19, robustness is what matters. Building redundant capacity and diversifying suppliers are strategies for robustness.

For most other industries, resilience is more of a concern. Firms need to accept the risk that their supply chains can be disrupted and production can grind to a halt, and invest in reducing the time needed for recovery. Resilient firms try to mitigate risk when it happens, but they do not invest significantly in anticipating and avoiding every possible type of disruption. Some firms diversify their suppliers even before crises; others invest in long-term relationships with single suppliers instead of switching to other suppliers and incurring sunk costs, to facilitate more rapid recovery (Jain, Girotra, and Netessine 2016). Each of these findings also points to the fact that the effects of GVC reconfiguration would likely differ greatly depending on the characteristics of the firms' products and services.

Shorter supply chains and localized production are not necessarily less vulnerable to shocks. In a global pandemic, almost every economy is affected by both supply and demand shocks, although to different degrees. Consumers' fear of contagion and government restrictions on the movement of people hit labor-intensive services most severely, and these sectors' GVCs are among the shortest. Supply chain risks could stem from all kinds of sources, such as production accidents, natural disasters, health shocks, financial risks, exchange rate volatility, political instability, macroeconomic crises, cyberattacks, quality issues, or delivery failures. These risks could happen in any location, so reshoring or nearshoring is no guarantee of more robust supply chains.

Supplier diversification or relocation, however, can be costly, and it is not an option for highly complex products in the short term. As explained in chapter 2, it takes time to identify, qualify and build relationships with potential suppliers. Diversification is not feasible if the product supplied is highly specialized or unique. For some GVC-intensive industries, such as the automotive industry, highly sophisticated supply chains involve thousands of different components, some manufactured to extremely low tolerances, and diversifying into different suppliers would require impractical effort and cost (Beattie 2020).

Furthermore, traditional supply chains have transformed over time into supply networks. This configuration makes it difficult to relocate suppliers to another country.

Supply networks are so complex that building them somewhere else would incur substantial cost and take a long time—and thus risk the lead firm losing its competitive position. Even if production facilities can be relocated, a whole ecosystem of talent, good infrastructure, and nearby upstream and downstream industries would be required to scale up production in a new location (Qiang et al. 2020).

Finally, holding excess inventory and building redundant capacity would create inefficiencies and waste that would outweigh these measures' benefits for most firms. Although many firms boosted their inventories and stocked up on raw materials during the COVID-19 crisis, this development is unlikely to turn into a long-term trend. Profit-oriented companies can hardly hold excess inventory because doing so not only ties up capital but also requires managing this inventory, including warehousing it, maintaining it, and preventing damage or theft of it. In addition, many products can expire or become obsolete while they are stored in inventory. Extra inventory could also cause management lapses—production managers could resort to simply replacing a defective part without investigating the underlying problem and taking corrective actions. Toyota Motor Corporation has proved that reducing inventory improves quality (Sheffi 2020). As consumers increasingly demand newer, better products with faster delivery, and as firms face increasing pressure to price competitively, losing cost advantage could result in a firm's downfall.

The geopolitical situation and financial incentives offered by some governments, however, are tilting investors' locational decisions. US lawmakers and officials are crafting proposals to push US companies to move operations or key suppliers out of China by offering tax breaks, new rules, and carefully structured subsidies (Shalal, Alper, and Zengerle 2020). Japan has set aside a record US$2.2 billion support package to subsidize manufacturers to move their production out of China (Bloomberg 2020). Already, 87 companies have signed up to benefit from the first round of subsidies, with 57 companies receiving a total of US$535 million to open factories in Japan and 30 others being paid to expand production in Myanmar, Thailand, Vietnam, and other Southeast Asian countries (Denyer 2020). And Taiwan Semiconductor Manufacturing Company, the world's largest contract integrated circuit manufacturer, announced it will invest US$12 billion to build an advanced semiconductor fabrication plant in the US state of Arizona (TSMC 2020).

The extent to which firms will move their supply chains out of China remains to be seen. Recent cases of GVC relocation are not all pandemic-specific; rather, they are a result of tariffs, rising labor costs in China, and geopolitical risks. Surveys of firms' plans to leave China show mixed results. A survey of more than 3,000 companies released in February 2020 by Bank of America revealed that companies in 10 out of 12 sectors said they intended to shift at least a portion of their supply chains from their current locations (BofA Securities 2020). A Gartner survey of 260 supply chain leaders in February and March 2020 also found that one-third of the firms had either already moved sourcing and manufacturing activities out of China or planned to do so in the next two to three years (Gartner 2020).

In contrast, a joint survey by the American Chambers of Commerce and PricewaterhouseCoopers in March 2020 showed that most US firms in China had no plans to relocate production to other parts of the country or abroad (Goh 2020). Despite high tariffs and a looming threat of US-China decoupling, many firms may not pull out of China completely. China's economy has swiftly bounced back after the COVID-19 crisis, whereas many other economies are still mired in recession. The country is deeply embedded in GVCs and has grown into a sophisticated producer as well as a huge market. Both foreign and domestic firms have invested decades in building up entire ecosystems of suppliers in China that will not be easily replicated or replaced (Brown 2020). And businesses have invested in China both to source there and to sell there. Even if firms wish to relocate, the change will not come soon because cash-starved companies currently lack the funds to invest in new operations and because such strategic decisions require more deliberation.

Eventually, firms' supply chain strategies should adhere to the same principles as ever: assess risks and costs, take risk-based precautions, and build tools to enhance agility and flexibility. Mapping supply chains, investing in digital technologies to monitor risks and make timely adjustments, standardizing inputs to facilitate replacement, stockpiling strategically important inputs, building extra capacity (in low–risk tolerance businesses), and rationalizing production lines are all options. As business leaders struggle to guide their firms through the COVID-19 crisis and to plan for the long term, decisions from where to sell to how to manage supply chains will eventually hinge on business rationales as well as expectations about the future of globalization.

Implications for developing countries

Challenges and opportunities

The COVID-19 crisis and emerging megatrends pose new challenges and opportunities for developing countries. This pandemic has plunged the world into the worst recession since World War II. The World Bank's baseline forecast envisions a 5.2 percent contraction in global GDP in 2020, and the crisis will likely cause lasting scars to the global economy through subdued trade, investment, and mobility; erosion of human capital; heightened policy uncertainty; reduced innovation; and, more seriously, increasing inequality. Developing countries are especially vulnerable to these economic headwinds because of weak health care systems, dwindling remittances, and tight financial conditions amid mounting debt (World Bank 2020a). A substantial economic downturn would reverse years of progress toward development goals and tip tens of millions of people back into extreme poverty.

Meanwhile, potential GVC reconfigurations could create opportunities for some developing countries that are close to major markets and have both comparative advantages in relevant sectors and open and conducive business environments (IFC 2020). Nearshoring could benefit certain developing countries near major markets, but those countries would need to demonstrate their capability to meet MNCs' quality, speed, scale, and reliability requirements in the value chain segments they enter. Developing countries far away from consumer markets and those that fail to meet the minimum requirements for joining certain GVCs may stand to lose. GVCs are ever evolving, and opportunities belong to the firms that constantly adapt to become more efficient and resilient.

Optimists and pessimists are divided on what cutting-edge technologies may mean for developing countries, just as they are on technology's impact on employment and inequality. New technology is generally biased toward skills and other capabilities, which reduces the comparative advantage of low-income countries in traditional labor-intensive manufacturing activities. GVCs also make it harder for low-income countries to use their labor cost advantage to offset their technological disadvantage. New technologies therefore present a double blow to low-income countries (Rodrik 2018).

However, optimists believe that disruptive technologies create opportunities for low-income countries to leapfrog stages of development and catch up with more advanced economies. Latecomer countries can be in advantageous positions to embrace disruptive technologies because they are not locked into existing technologies (Mathews and Lee 2018). Mobile phones are a clear example of technology leapfrogging: they have given poor people in low-income countries access to long-distance communications without requiring costly investments in landlines and other infrastructure (Rodrik 2018). Technology is also a great equalizer that dramatically improves quality of life by removing barriers caused by a person's social characteristics, geographic location, or physical or sensory abilities (Kanevsky 2012). Digital technologies have allowed people from low-income countries to access information, goods, and services all over the world, creating more opportunities in education, health, and employment. For example, mobile banking has helped poor women in Kenya move out of subsistence agriculture into nonfarm businesses, providing a significant bump up the income ladder for those at the very bottom (Suri and Jack 2016). However, such ad hoc examples are not sufficient to generate meaningful long-term growth effects on low-income countries.

An increase in policy uncertainty, superpower frictions, and protectionism might be very destructive to many developing countries. Greater policy uncertainty deters new investment and rattles existing investors. A downward spiral of US-China relations would further push MNCs to either deeply localize their businesses or to withdraw to one of the two spheres. And nationalist policies could substantially dim developing countries' prospects of becoming new outsourcing or offshoring locations.

Policy implications

Policy makers need effective strategies to preserve and improve countries' investment climates through the COVID-19 pandemic and to expand the private sector's role in driving productive jobs and economic transformation.[7] The crisis is disrupting the pathways by which countries achieve productivity growth—and, by extension, job and wage growth—by threatening spatial integration (by disrupting international production), reallocation (by reducing competitive pressure), and technological upgrading (by reducing cross-border investment). However, the crisis also provides opportunities for deep structural change and for rebuilding old systems better than they were before.

In the postcrisis recovery stage, governments will have to deal with the immediate aftermath of the pandemic by focusing on long-term growth in a changed global economy. From an investment climate perspective, governments should review their FDI policies and promotion strategies, strengthen their countries' overall business environments, and promote robust competition to reallocate resources toward sectors and firms that will drive long-term employment and economic transformation. In most cases, countries' underlying bottlenecks to growth existed before the COVID-19 outbreak but have been amplified or accelerated by the crisis. However, the unique circumstances of the pandemic have provided many governments with unprecedented mandates for reform. Countries that manage to turn the crisis into an opportunity to undergo much-needed structural reforms (in areas such as climate change, business regulation, and gender equity) and to enact cutting-edge regulatory measures will see more resilient and sustainable recoveries. Along the way, governments should adjust their strategies to account for shifting postpandemic realities, such as changes to GVCs and the rise of the digital economy. Governments should also ensure a level playing field for all companies and should vigorously enforce competition law to defend competition in the markets both during and after the crisis.

Trends in GVC development push in different directions. As discussed in this chapter, it is still unclear whether COVID-19 will significantly change GVCs. Some economists foresee little significant change and predict that adjustments will be concentrated in health-related industries because the economic rationales for most GVCs continue to hold. Others believe that COVID-19 has become a wake-up call for a new risk-reward balance for GVCs (Baldwin and Evenett 2020) because pandemics, climate change, natural disasters, and human-caused crises may expose the world to more frequent shocks.

It is far too early to call the end of GVCs and globalization, as some are doing. The COVID-19 outbreak is a stress test for globalization. This pandemic has revealed the complex interdependence of economies around the world. For years to come, many will likely cite this crisis as one of the inflection points calling for a reevaluation of collective attitudes toward globalization. Protectionism and nationalism, like the world's other preexisting conditions, started before the COVID-19 crisis. It is not surprising to see heightened consideration of national security (in areas such as health, food, and information) and environmental sustainability in light of the outbreak. However, some of the new restrictions on investment and trade are not necessarily meant to increase productivity. Policy makers need to understand business rationales and how companies produce and trade goods and services, and these realities must guide policy deliberations.

Policy makers should pay attention to regional supply chains and to changes in sectoral dynamics to seize opportunities. Recent trade tensions between the United States and China had already prompted US firms to diversify their production facilities among other East Asian countries. Now, because of COVID-19, the push to diversify supply chains may intensify, and regional supply chains may gain more momentum. For example, Javorcik (2020) identifies the emerging competitive sectors in European and Central Asian countries that investors might consider if they decide to diversify away from their current China-based suppliers (figure 5.6). Hence, when updating their strategies, investment promotion agencies may choose to reemphasize the sports clothing sector, and Eastern European countries could look for new opportunities in the production of car parts. Policy makers may also respond to changes in sectoral dynamics, such as the rise in e-commerce and digital health services or the decline in fossil fuels (UNCTAD 2020b). Both types of changes may offer opportunities for developing countries according to their comparative advantages, and economic fundamentals will be increasingly important to attract FDI in a challenging context.

FIGURE 5.6 Which countries will take advantage of the diversification of global supply chains?

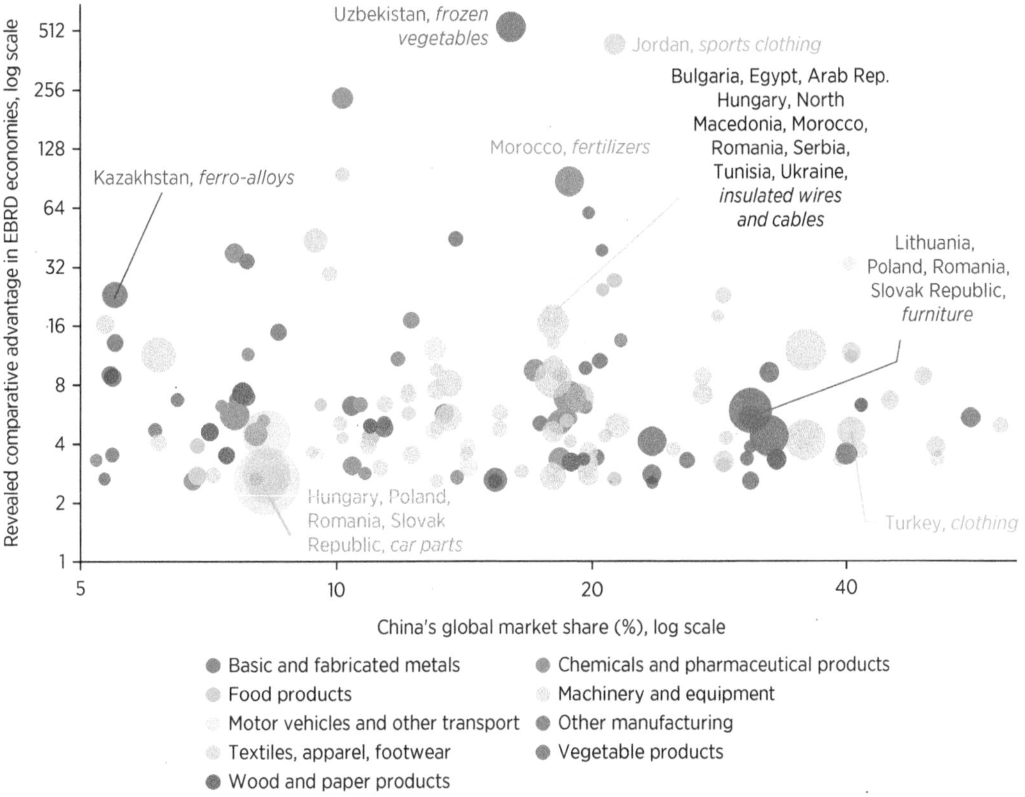

Source: Javorcik 2020.
Note: EBRD = European Bank for Reconstruction and Development.

Should new investment opportunities emerge, they will require new priorities for investment policies and investment promotion reforms. Policy makers should reflect on the market's possible shifts and let business realities guide their policy responses, building on economic fundamentals. These suggestions will entail realigning investment incentive regimes to the new national development priorities likely to emerge after COVID-19, such as job creation. Governments should also resist protectionist policies. And reforms are needed to ensure the limitation or phasing out of crisis-related investment screening and approval mechanisms to allow FDI to resume normal entry.

Tackling the complex challenges presented by the current global environment will require global leadership and cooperation. The pandemic has illustrated the shared public health and economic vulnerabilities that countries face. It has also highlighted the critical importance of exchanging data, sharing information on good practices, and strengthening collaboration. The magnitude and scale of the current crisis require policy makers to deploy their full arsenal of policy tools to improve business confidence and boost countries' investment competitiveness. An unprecedented synchronized and coordinated policy response was critical to containing the 2008 global financial crisis. Once again, the times are testing policy makers. They must rise to the occasion by showing global leadership and collaboration.

Notes

1. "COVID-19: Implications for business" (https://www.mckinsey.com/business-functions/marketing-and-sales/our-insights/survey-us-consumer-sentiment-during-the-coronavirus-crisis).
2. These countries include Ethiopia, Ghana, Ireland, and Saudi Arabia. See Qiang et al. (2020) for details.
3. The energy sector was also hit by disagreement among the Organization of the Petroleum Exporting Countries, the Russian Federation, and the United States about how to handle the pandemic-induced drop in demand.
4. These data can be explored at Ycharts (https://ycharts.com/indicators/sp_500_eps).
5. For more information, see "The COVID-19 Corporate Response Tracker: How America's Largest Employers Are Treating Stakeholders Amid the Coronavirus Crisis" (https://justcapital.com/reports/the-covid-19-corporate-response-tracker-how-americas-largest-employers-are-treating-stakeholders-amid-the-coronavirus-crisis/).
6. In this survey, "digital adoption" measures whether a respondent has used at least one digital service in at least one industry in the six months ending in May 2020. The industries asked about include banking, insurance, grocery, apparel, entertainment, social media, travel, telecommunications, utilities, and the public sector. Details are available at https://www.mckinsey.com/business-functions/mckinsey-digital/our-insights/europes-digital-migration-during-covid-19-getting-past-the-broad-trends-andaverages.
7. This section provides a summary of Qiang, Elgten, and Kuo (2020)and the overview in World Bank (2020b).

References

Acemoglu, Daron, Ufuk Akcigit, and William Kerr. 2015. "Networks and the Macroeconomy: An Empirical Exploration." NBER Working Paper 21344, National Bureau of Economic Research, Cambridge, MA.

AICD (Australian Institute of Company Directors). 2015. "A Case Study of Apple's Supply Chain." September 11, 2015. https://aicd.companydirectors.com.au/advocacy/governance-leadership-centre/governance-driving-performance/a-case-study-of-apples-supply-chain.

AmCham China (The American Chamber of Commerce in the People's Republic of China). 2020. "Supply Chain Challenges for US Companies in China." AmCham China, Beijing. https://www.amchamchina.org/press/supply-chain-challenges-for-us-companies-in-china/.

Aviva Investors. 2020. "Size Matters: Will COVID-19 Concentrate Corporate Power?" July 21, 2020. https://www.avivainvestors.com/en-us/views/aiq-investment-thinking/2020/04/will-covid-19-concentrate-corporate-power/.

Aung, T. T., and R. Paul. 2020. "Asia's Garment Industry Sees Lay-Offs, Factories Closing due to Coronavirus." Reuters, February 28, 2020. https://www.reuters.com/article/china-health-textiles/asias-garment-industry-sees-lay-offs-factories-closing-due-to-coronavirus-idUSL3N2AS1OE.

Baldwin, R., and B. W. di Mauro, eds. 2020. *Mitigating the COVID Economic Crisis: Act Fast and Do Whatever It Takes*. London: CEPR Press.

Baldwin, R., and S. J. Evenett, eds. 2020. *COVID-19 and Trade Policy: Why Turning Inward Won't Work*. London: CEPR Press.

Baldwin, R., and E. Tomiura. 2020. "Thinking Ahead about the Trade Impact of COVID-19." Chapter 5 in *Mitigating the COVID Economic Crisis: Act Fast and Do Whatever It Takes*, edited by R. Baldwin and B. W. di Mauro. London: CEPR Press.

Barrot, Jean-Noel, and Julien Sauvagnat. 2016. "Input Specificity and the Propagation of Idiosyncratic Shocks in Production Networks." *Quarterly Journal of Economics* 131 (3): 1543–92.

Beattie, Alan. 2020. "Be Wary of Scapegoating 'Just-in-Time' Supply Chains." *Financial Times*, May 28, 2020. https://www.ft.com/content/50618a30-809f-11ea-b0fb-13524ae1056b.

Behravesh, N. 2011. "Global Economic Impact of the Japanese Earthquake, Tsunami, and Nuclear Disaster." HIS Markit, March 16, 2011. http://www.ihs.com/products/global-insight/industry-economic-report.aspx?id=1065929196.

Betti, F., and T. Heizmann. 2020. "From Perfume to Hand Sanitizer, TVs to Face Masks: How Companies Are Changing Track to Fight COVID-19." World Economic Forum, March 24, 2020. https://www.weforum.org/agenda/2020/03/from-perfume-to-hand-sanitiser-tvs-to-face-masks-how-companies-are-changing-track-to-fight-covid-19/.

Bloom, Nicholas, Philip Bunn, Scarlet Chen, Paul Mizen, Gregory Thwaites, and Pawel Smietanka. 2020. "Coronavirus Expected to Reduce UK Firms' Sales by over 40% in Q2." VoxEU.org, May 20, 2020. https://voxeu.org/article/coronavirus-expected-reduce-uk-firms-sales-over-40-q2.

Bloom, Nicholas, Charles I. Jones, John Van Reenen, and Michael Webb. 2020. "Are Ideas Getting Harder to Find?" *American Economic Review* 110 (4): 1104–44.

Bloomberg. 2020. "Japan Sets Aside ¥243.5 Billion to Help Firms Shift Production out of China" *Japan Times*, April 9, 2020. https://www.japantimes.co.jp/news/2020/04/09/business/japan-sets-aside-%C2%A5243-5-billion-help-firms-shift-production-china/#.XsLiLmj0lPY.

BofA Securities. 2020. "Global Equity Strategy: Tectonic Shifts in Global Supply Chains." Redacted report. https://www.bofaml.com/content/dam/boamlimages/documents/articles/ID20_0147/Tectonic_Shifts_in_Global_Supply_Chains.pdf.

Bombardini, M., and B. Li. 2020. "Trade, Pollution and Mortality in China." *Journal of International Economics* 103321.

Brandon-Jones, E., B. Squire, C. W. Autry, and K. J. Petersen. 2014. "A Contingent Resource-Based Perspective of Supply Chain Resilience and Robustness." *Journal of Supply Chain Management* 50 (3): 55–73.

Brown, Sara. 2020. "Reshoring, Restructuring, and the Future of Supply Chains." *MIT Sloan School of Management* (blog), July 22, 2020. https://mitsloan.mit.edu/ideas-made-to-matter/reshoring-restructuring-and-future-supply-chains.

Bunge, Jacob, and Jesse Newman. 2020. "Tyson Turns to Robot Butchers, Spurred by Coronavirus Outbreaks." *Wall Street Journal*, July 9, 2020. https://www.wsj.com/articles/meatpackers-covid-safety-automation-robots-coronavirus-11594303535.

Bush, Stephen. 2020. "Gordon Brown: 'The Solution to this Crisis Is Still Global.'" *NewStatesman*, April 22, 2020. https://www.newstatesman.com/politics/uk/2020/04/gordon-brown-solution-crisis-still-global.

Cameron, Doug. 2020. "Boeing Offers More Support for MAX Suppliers." *Wall Street Journal*, February 23, 2020. https://www.wsj.com/articles/boeing-offers-more-support-for-max-suppliers-11582465420.

Carvalho, Vasco M., Makoto Nirei, Yukiko Saito, and Alireza Tahbaz-Salehi. 2016. "Supply Chain Disruptions: Evidence from the Great East Japan Earthquake." Working Paper No. 2017-01, Becker Friedman Institute for Research in Economics, University of Chicago.

Choong, Y. Y. C., H. W. Tan, D. C. Patel, W. T. N. Choong, C. H. Chen, H. Y. Low, M. J. Tan, C. D. Patel, and C. K. Chua. 2020. "The Global Rise of 3D Printing during the COVID-19 Pandemic." *Nature Reviews Materials* 5 (9): 637–39.

Corkery, Michael, and David Gelles. 2020. "Robots Welcome to Take Over, as Pandemic Accelerates Automation." *New York Times*, April 10, 2020. https://www.nytimes.com/2020/04/10/business/coronavirus-workplace-automation.html.

Cosgrove, Emma. 2020. "Coca-Cola, Mondelez Trim SKUs as CPGs Tackle Pandemic Stresses." Supply Chain Dive, June 2, 2020. https://www.supplychaindive.com/news/coronavirus-supply-chains-SKUs-pandemic-Mondelez-Procter-Gamble-Coca-Cola/579017/.

De Bolle, M., and J. Zettelmeyer. 2019. "Measuring the Rise of Economic Nationalism." PIIE Working Paper 19-15, Peterson Institute for International Economics, Washington, DC. https://www.piie.com/publications/working-papers/measuring-rise-economic-nationalism.

De Loecker, J., and J. Eeckhout. 2018. "Global Market Power." NBER Working Paper 24768, National Bureau of Economic Research, Cambridge, MA.

Denyer, Simon. 2020. "Japan Helps 87 Companies to Break from China after Pandemic Exposed Overreliance." *Washington Post*, July 21, 2020. https://www.washingtonpost.com /world/asia_pacific/japan-helps-87-companies-to-exit-china-after-pandemic-exposed -overreliance/2020/07/21/4889abd2-cb2f-11ea-99b0-8426e26d203b_story.html.

Edwards, Neil. 2020. "Two New COVID-19 Studies Reveal CFO's Focus on Workplace Reboot, Revenue, and Cost Cutting." *Forbes*, April 27, 2020. https://www.forbes. com/sites/neiledwards/2020/04/27/two-new-covid-19-studies-reveal-cfos-focus-on-work place-reboot-revenue-and-cost-cutting/#4b14221e65b6.

Fernandez, Santiago, Paul Jenkins, and Benjamin Vieira. 2020. "Europe's Digital Migration during COVID-19: Getting Past the Broad Trends and Averages." McKinsey Digital, July 24, 2020. https://www.mckinsey.com/business-functions/mckinsey-digital/our-insights /europes-digital-migration-during-covid-19-getting-past-the-broad-trends-and-averages.

Forneris, Xavier, and Philippe de Bonneval. Forthcoming. "FDI Entry Measures and COVID-19."

Forsthuber, O. G. F. 2020. "Globalization Comes to the Rescue: How Dependency Makes Us More Resilient." European Centre for International Political Economy, September 2020. https://ecipe.org/publications/globalization-makes-us-more-resilient/.

Freund, Caroline. 2020. "Governments Could Bring Supply Chains Home. It Would Defy Economic Rationality." *Barrons*, May 1, 2020. https://www.barrons.com/articles /will-supply-chains-come-home-after-the-coronavirus-recession-51588327200.

Freund, Caroline, Aaditya Mattoo, Alen Mulabdic, and Michele Ruta. 2020. "The Supply Chain Shock from COVID-19: Risks and Opportunities." In *COVID-19 in Developing Economies*, edited by Simeon Djankov and Ugo Panizza, 303–15. London: Centre for Economic Policy Research.

Gartner. 2020. "Gartner Survey Reveals 33% of Supply Chain Leaders Moved Business Out of China or Plan to by 2023." Press release, June 24, 2020. https://www.gartner.com/en /newsroom/press-releases/2020-06-24-gartner-survey-reveals-33-percent-of-supply-chain -leaders-moved-business-out-of-china-or-plan-to-by-2023.

Grossman, G. M., and A. B. Krueger. 1991. "Environmental Impacts of a North American Free Trade Agreement." Working Paper 3914, National Bureau of Economic Research, Cambridge, MA.

Goh, Brenda. 2020. "Most U.S. Firms Have No Plans to Leave China Due to Coronavirus: Survey." Reuters, April 16, 2020. https://www.reuters.com/article/us-health -coronavirus-china-business/most-u-s-firms-have-no-plans-to-leave-china-due-to -coronavirus-survey-idUSKBN21Z08K.

Gourinchas, P. O., Ş. Kalemli-Özcan, V. Penciakova, and N. Sander. 2020. "COVID-19 and SME Failures." NBER Working Paper 27877, National Bureau of Economic Research, Cambridge, MA.

Gurman, Mark. 2020. "Apple Helps Suppliers Reconfigure Factories to Limit COVID-19." Bloomberg, May 15, 2020. https://www.bloombergquint.com/business/apple-helps -suppliers-reconfigure-factories-to-limit-covid-19.

Hughes, Huw. 2020. "Marks & Spencer, H&M and Bestseller Detail Measures to Help Suppliers." Fashion United, April 24, 2020. https://fashionunited.com/news/business /marks-spencer-h-m-and-bestseller-detail-measures-to-help-suppliers/2020042433274.

IFC (International Finance Corporation). 2020. "When Trade Falls – Effects of COVID-19 and Outlook." Briefing Note, IFC, Washington, DC. https://www.ifc.org/wps /wcm/connect/78f10cad-7e00-440d-b6fd-da210e5a6d1e/IFC-Covid%26Trade-final-3 .pdf?MOD=AJPERES&CVID=nlC5u9P.

International Energy Agency. 2020. "Global Energy Review 2020: The Impacts of the Covid-19 Crisis on Global Energy Demand and CO_2 Emissions." International Energy Agency, Paris. https://www.iea.org/reports/global-energy-review-2020.

International Labour Organization. 2020. "COVID-19 and the Automotive Industry." ILO Brief, International Labour Organization, Geneva. https://www.ilo.org/sector/Resources/publica tions/WCMS_741343/lang--en/index.htm.

Jain, N., K. Girotra, and N. Netessine. 2016. "Recovering from Supply Interruptions: The Role of Sourcing Strategies." INSEAD Working Paper 2016/58/TOM, INSEAD, Fontainebleau.

Javorcik, Beata. 2020. "Global Supply Chains Will Not Be the Same in the Post-COVID-19 World." Chapter 8 in *COVID-19 and Trade Policy: Why Turning Inward Won't Work,* edited by R. Baldwin and B. W. di Mauro. London: CEPR Press.

JUST Capital. 2020. "The COVID-19 Corporate Response Tracker: How America's Largest Employers Are Treating Stakeholders amid the Coronavirus Crisis." JUST Report. https://justcapital.com/reports/the-covid-19-corporate-response-tracker-how-americas -largest-employers-are-treating-stakeholders-amid-the-coronavirus-crisis/.

Kanevsky, Dimitri. 2012. "Technology Change as the Great Equalizer." *The White House* (blog) May 7, 2012.https://obamawhitehouse.archives.gov/blog/2012/05/07 /technology-change-great-equalizer.

Koetsier, John. 2020. "COVID-19 Accelerated E-Commerce Growth '4 To 6 Years.'" *Forbes,* June 12, 2020. https://www.forbes.com/sites/johnkoetsier/2020/06/12/covid-19-accelerated-e-commerce-growth-4-to-6-years/#7859a26e600f.

Kronfol, Hania, and Nicholas James Chan. Forthcoming. "Business Tax Relief, Foreign Direct Investment and COVID-19."

Lakuma, Corti Paul, and Nathan Sunday. 2020. "Impact of COVID-19 on Micro, Small, and Medium Businesses in Uganda." *Africa in Focus* (blog), May 19, 2020. https://www.brookings .edu/blog/africa-in-focus/2020/05/19/impact-of-covid-19-on-micro-small-and-medium -businesses-in-uganda/.

Mathews, J., and K. Lee. 2018. "How Emerging Economies Can Take Advantage of the Fourth Industrial Revolution." World Economic Forum, January 11, 2018. https://www.weforum .org/agenda/2018/01/the-4th-industrial-revolution-is-a-window-of-opportunity-for -emerging-economies-to-advance-by-leapfrogging/.

Mathurin, P., O. Aliaj, and J. Fontanella-Khan. 2020. "Pandemic Triggers Wave of Billion-Dollar US Bankruptcies." *Financial Times*, August 21, 2020. https://www.ft.com /content/277dc354-a870-4160-9117-b5b0dece5360.

Miroudot, S. 2020. "Resilience versus Robustness in Global Value Chains: Some Policy Implications." VoxEU.org, June 18, 2020. https://voxeu.org/article/resilience -versus-robustness-global-value-chains.

Murray, Alan. 2020. "Fortune 500 CEO Survey: How Are America's Biggest Companies Dealing with the Coronavirus Pandemic?" *Fortune*, May 14, 2020. https://fortune .com/2020/05/14/fortune-500-ceo-survey-coronavirus-pandemic-predictions/.

Philippon, Thomas. 2019. *The Great Reversal: How America Gave Up on Free Markets.* Boston: Harvard University Press.

Qiang, Christine Zhenwei, Yue Li, Yan Liu, Monica Paganini, and Victor Steenbergen. 2020. "Foreign Direct Investment and Global Value Chains in the Wake of COVID-19: Lead Firms of GVC." *Private Sector Development Blog,* World Bank, May 21, 2020. https:// blogs.worldbank.org/psd/foreign-direct-investment-and-global-value-chains-wake -covid-19-lead-firms-gvc.

Rodrik Dani. 2018. "Will New Technology in Developing Countries Be a Help or a Hindrance?" World Economic Forum, October 9, 2018. https://www.weforum.org/agenda/2018/10 /will-new-technologies-help-or-harm-developing-countries/.

Rosenbush. R. 2011. "How Japan's Earthquake Will Impact the Global Economy." Institutional Investor, March 15, 2011. http://www.institutionalinvestor.com/article.aspx?articleID =2787087#.UQxtFo0gdHw.

Sanchiz, A., and A. Omic. 2020. *State of Investment Promotion Agencies: Evidence from WAIPA-WBG's Joint Global Survey*. Washington, DC: World Bank. Geneva: WAIPA (World Association of Investment Promotion Agencies).

Saurav, Abhishek, Peter Kusek, Ryan Kuo, and Brody Viney. 2020a. "The Impact of COVID-19 on Foreign Investors: Evidence from the Second Round of a Global Pulse Survey." *Private Sector Development Blog*, October 6, 2020. https://blogs.worldbank.org/psd /impact-covid-19-foreign-investors-evidence-second-round-global-pulse-survey.

Saurav, Abhishek, Peter Kusek, Ryan Kuo, and Brody Viney. 2020b. "The Impact of COVID-19 on Foreign Investors: Evidence from the Quarterly Global MNE Pulse Survey for the Third Quarter of 2020." World Bank, Washington, DC. https://openknowledge.worldbank

.org/bitstream/handle/10986/34924/The-Impact-of-COVID-19-on-Foreign-Investors -Evidence-from-the-Quarterly-Global-MNE-Pulse-Survey-for-the-Third-Quarter-of-2020 .pdf?sequence=1&isAllowed=y.

Saurav, Abhishek, Peter Kusek, Ryan Kuo, and Brody Viney. 2021. "The Impact of COVID-19 on Foreign Investors: Evidence from the Quarterly Global MNE Pulse Survey for the Fourth Quarter of 2020." World Bank, Washington, DC.

Shalal, Andrea, Alexandra Alper, and Patricia Zengerle. 2020. "U.S. Mulls Paying Companies, Tax Breaks to Pull Supply Chains from China." Reuters, May 18, 2020. https://www .reuters.com/article/us-usa-china-supply-chains/u-s-mulls-paying-companies-tax -breaks-to-pull-supply-chains-from-china-idUSKBN22U0FH.

Sheffi, Yossi. 2020. "Resilience through Redundancy." Chapter 10 in *The Resilient Enterprise: Overcoming Vulnerability for Competitive Advantage*. Cambridge, MA: MIT Press.

Song, Jung-a. 2020. "Samsung Shifts Some Smartphone Production to Vietnam due to Coronavirus." *Financial Times*, March 6, 2020. https://www.ft.com/content/79d80650-5f9d -11ea-b0ab-339c2307bcd4.

Suri, T., and W. Jack. 2016. "The Long-Run Poverty and Gender Impacts of Mobile Money." *Science* 354 (6317): 1288–92.

Tayal, Puja. 2017. "How Suppliers Are Reacting to Apple's Dual-Sourcing Strategy." Market Realist, June 2020. https://marketrealist.com/2017/06/how-suppliers-are-reacting-to-apples -dual-sourcing-strategy/.

Teodoro, A., and L. Rodriguez. 2020. "Textile and Garment Supply Chains in Times of COVID-19: Challenges for Developing Countries." *UNCTAD Transport and Trade Facilitation Newsletter* 53 (86).

Thomas, Zoe. 2020. "Coronavirus: Will COVID-19 Speed Up the Use of Robots to Replace Human Workers? BBC News, April 18, 2020. https://www.bbc.com/news/technology-52340651.

Todo, Yasuyuki, Kentaro Nakajima, and Petr Matous. 2015. "How Do Supply Chain Networks Affect the Resilience of Firms to Natural Disasters? Evidence from the Great East Japan Earthquake." *Journal of Regional Science* 55 (2): 209–29.

Tokui, J., K. Kawasaki, and T. Miyagawa. 2017. "The Economic Impact of Supply Chain Disruptions from the Great East-Japan Earthquake." *Japan and the World Economy* 41 (March): 59–70.

TSMC (Taiwan Semiconductor Manufacturing Company). 2020. "TSMC Announces Intention to Build and Operate an Advanced Semiconductor Fab in the United States." Press release, May 15, 2020. https://www.tsmc.com/tsmcdotcom/ PRListingNewsArchivesAction.do?action=detail&newsid=THGOANPGTH&language=E.

UNCTAD (United Nations Conference on Trade and Development). 2020a. "Investment Promotion Agencies: Striving to Overcome the COVID-19 Challenge." IPA Observer Special Issue 8, United Nations, Geneva.

UNCTAD (United Nations Conference on Trade and Development). 2020b. *World Investment Report 2020*. Geneva: United Nations. https://unctad.org/webflyer/world-investment-report-2020.

UNCTAD (United Nations Conference on Trade and Development). 2021. *Investment Trends Monitor*, Issue 38. United Nations, Geneva. https://unctad.org/system/files/official-document/ diaeiainf2021d1_en.pdf.

UNDP (United Nations Development Programme). 2020. "Assessment Report on Impact of COVID-19 Pandemic on Chinese Enterprises." United Nations Development Programme in China. https://www.undp.org/content/dam/china/docs/Publications/EN_Assessment%20 Report%20Impact%20of%20COVID-19%20Pandemic%20on%20Chinese%20 Enterprises.pdf.

Villena, V. H., and D. A. Gioia. 2020. "A More Sustainable Supply Chain." *Harvard Business Review*. https://hbr.org/2020/03/a-more-sustainable-supply-chain.

Wakabayashi, Daisuke, Jack Nicas, Steve Lohr, and Mike Isaac 2020. "Big Tech Could Emerge from Coronavirus Crisis Stronger Than Ever." *New York Times*, March 23, 2020. https://www. nytimes.com/2020/03/23/technology/coronavirus-facebook-amazon-youtube.html.

World Bank. 2020a. "The Global Economic Outlook During the COVID-19 Pandemic: A Changed World." News release, June 8, 2020. https://www.worldbank.org/en/news /feature/2020/06/08/the-global   -economic-outlook-during-the-covid-19-pandemic -a-changed-world.

World Bank. 2020b. *Global Investment Competitiveness Report 2019/2020: Rebuilding Investor Confidence in Times of Uncertainty*. Washington, DC: World Bank.

World Bank. 2020c. *World Development Report 2020: Trading for Development in the Age of Global Value Chains*. Washington, DC: World Bank.

World Bank. 2020d. "Supporting Businesses and Investors: A Phased Approach of Investment Climate Policy Responses to COVID-19." World Bank, Washington, DC. http://pubdocs .worldbank.org/en/683441596248620234/COVID-19-Investment-Climate-Policy-Measures -Phased-Approach-071520.pdf.

World Bank. 2021. *Global Economic Prospects*. Washington, DC: World Bank. https://www.world-bank.org/en/publication/global-economic-prospects.

World Economic Forum. 2020a. "Coronavirus Is Disrupting Global Value Chains. Here's How Companies Can Respond." World Economic Forum, February 27, 2020.

World Economic Forum. 2020b. "International Investment in the Age of Geopolitical Competition, Technological Change and Trade Confrontation." Briefing, World Economic Forum, Geneva. http://www3.weforum.org/docs/WEF_GFC_Investment_Scenarios_ Briefing_Paper.pdf.

WTO (World Trade Organization). 2020. "Trade Set to Plunge as COVID-19 Pandemic Upends Global Economy." Press release 855, April 8, 2020. https://www.wto.org/english/news_e /pres20_e/pr855_e.htm.

YouTube Team. 2020. "Protecting Our Extended Workforce and the Community." *YouTube Official Blog,* March 16, 2020. https://blog.youtube/news-and-events/protecting-our -extended-workforce-and.

Zarathustra, W. 2011. "The Impact of Japan's Earthquake on the Economy." Business Insider, March 14, 2011. https://www.businessinsider.com/the-impact-of-japan8217s -earthquake-on-the-economy-2011-3.

Zhu, Lianming, Koji Ito, and Eiichi Tomiura. 2016. "Global Sourcing in the Wake of Disaster: Evidence from the Great East Japan Earthquake." Discussion Paper 16089, Research Institute of Economy, Trade and Industry, Tokyo.

PART II

Introduction

Part II of this report consists of a range of case studies examining the experience of developing countries in leveraging foreign direct investment (FDI) to stimulate and facilitate global value chain (GVC) participation and upgrading. It includes both qualitative and quantitative case studies.

Qualitative case studies: Examples of approaches to foreign direct investment-led global value chain participation

Policy makers have a wide range of policy tools with which to stimulate GVC participation but often do not know how best to prioritize and sequence them. The 2020 World Development Report found that GVC participation is strongly determined by four elements: factor endowments (access to FDI, capital, labor, and skills), market size (for both inputs and sales), geography (proximity to and cost for trading with major production hubs), and institutions (including macroeconomic and political stability) (World Bank 2020). Each of these elements can be influenced in part by public policies. Yet, as illustrated in figure I.1, this leaves a wide range of possible areas in which policy makers can intervene. Addressing all or some of these policies simultaneously would be overwhelming for even the most capable governments. But guidance on how policy makers might choose to prioritize and sequence interventions to best facilitate GVC participation is limited.

There is no blueprint for strengthening GVC participation: countries have adopted different approaches to attracting FDI based on their comparative advantages and target GVCs. Strategies for integrating into GVCs often bundle policies to improve the business environment, link up with global lead firms, and make it less costly to produce and trade products for a selected GVC sector or segment. The type of strategy used is partly based on a country's income level. GVC characteristics may also help identify high-priority market or government failures, and therefore illustrate which strategy is most conducive to stimulating GVC participation.

The five qualitative case studies (chapters 6 to 10 of this report) identify several successful examples of governments implementing such strategies and policy packages for integrating their countries into GVCs. Through a literature review, five distinct approaches were identified through which countries managed to leverage FDI to stimulate GVC participation and upgrading. These cases were selected to illustrate these different approaches for five different GVC archetypes, and cover low-income, lower-middle-income, and upper-middle-income countries (figure I.2). Each case study describes the specific strategy and the mix of policy instruments used to strengthen that country's GVC participation by attracting FDI, helping domestic firms internationalize, or both.

FIGURE I.1 Examples of national policy to support global value chain participation

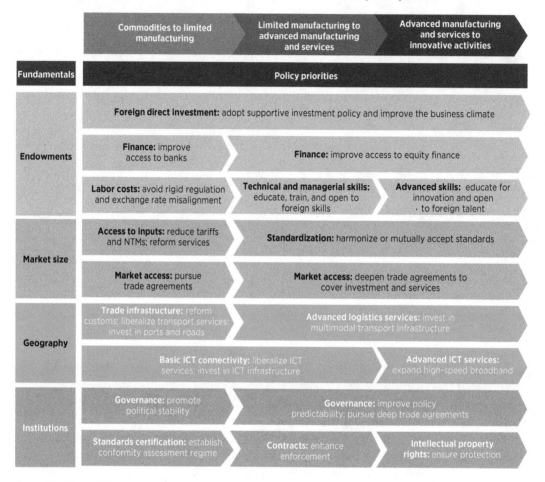

Source: World Bank 2020.
Note: ICT = information and communication technology; NTMs = nontariff measures.

- **Kenya** shows how pioneering foreign investment helped create a route to international markets for local firms in *horticulture*. Supplier relationships with multinational corporations (MNCs) exposed local firms to global product standards and certification and helped such firms master the required processes and technologies.

- **Honduras** used special economic zones and international trade and investment agreements to develop its *textile and apparel industry*. The combination of new infrastructure, regulatory flexibility, and lower trade costs helped boost investor confidence and attract export-processing FDI.

- **Malaysia** used targeted investment promotion, incentives, and facilitation to attract "superstar" firms and help jump-start its *electrical and electronics (E&E) industry*. Evolving linkages and incentive programs supported cluster development and a gradual shift toward higher-value-added activities.

- **Mauritius** shows how FDI liberalization and alliances with MNCs helped expand and upgrade its *tourism industry*. Local companies engaging in such partnerships

FIGURE I.2 Qualitative case studies included in the report and their strategic approaches

	Chapter 6: Kenya—Supplying to multinationals exposed local firms to international horticulture markets	Chapter 7: Honduras—Using maquilas and international agreements to boost the garment industry	Chapter 8: Malaysia—Attracting superstar firms in the electrical and electronics industry through investment promotion	Chapter 9: Mauritius—Partnering with foreign firms to upgrade the tourism industry	Chapter 10: Korea, India and China—Investing outward helped digital firms develop and complete
Case study					
Strategic approach	Use MNC-supplier linkages to help local firms meet global product standards	Invest in SEZs, and use trade and investment agreements to attract export-processing FDI	Use targeted investment promotion, incentives, and facilitation to attract global lead firms	Partner with foreign firms to help expand and upgrade an existing, viable industry	Promote outward FDI and invest in human capital and R&D to help domestic firms develop and compete globally

Lower-income countries ──────────── Prevalence of use, based on country's income level ──────────→ *Higher-income countries*

Source: World Bank elaborations on the literature and qualitative analysis.
Note: FDI = foreign direct investment; MNC = multinational corporation; R&D = research and development; SEZ = special economic zone.

acquired management expertise and new technology to strengthen their brand, diversify their products, and reach new export markets.

- **The Republic of Korea, India, and China** were able to integrate and upgrade in the *digital economy* GVC by combining outward foreign direct investment (OFDI) with investment in human capital and research and development (R&D). The availability of technical graduates and initial R&D investments were essential to establish domestic industries. Yet outward FDI helped leading domestic companies in these countries to acquire new technology, explore new markets, and compete internationally.

The discussion that follows briefly summarizes each case study; the case studies are presented in full in subsequent chapters.

Kenya (horticulture)

Kenya managed to promote horticulture exports in large part because pioneering FDI and foreign entrepreneurs jointly helped local farmers access the international market. They did so by fostering the three Ls: labeling (exposing firms to global product standards and certification), linking (developing lasting supply relationships with MNCs), and learning (helping firms master newly required processes and technologies). Initially, the Kenyan government was hands off, with limited policy intervention and an open FDI regime, but over time it established an enabling ecosystem of regulation, advocacy, and extension services.

FIGURE I.3 **Kenya's horticulture exports, 1976–2018**

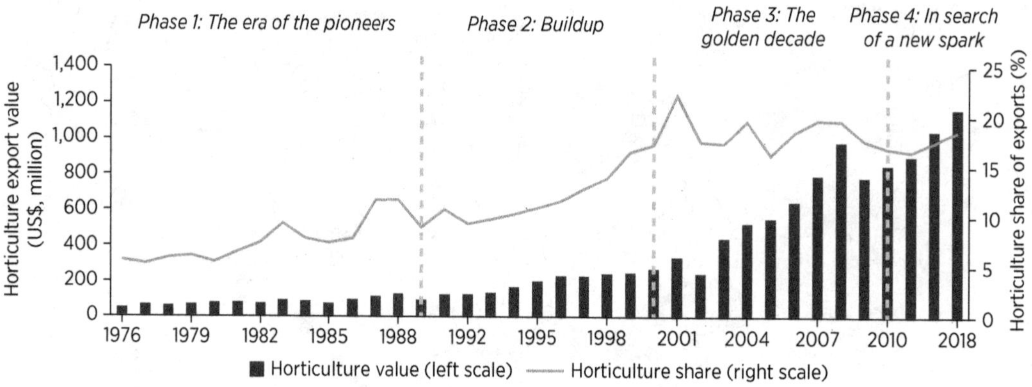

Source: World Bank calculations based on United Nations Comtrade data.

Kenya's horticulture exports underwent four main phases (figure I.3). Initial horticulture production (flowers, fruits, and vegetables) was driven by FDI from a handful of foreign entrepreneurs with strong ties to markets in Europe, often through kin connections (phase 1). A wave of economic liberalization and increase in global demand triggered more foreign firms to shift horticulture production to Kenya. To meet demand, these foreign firms introduced contract farming schemes with training programs to ensure smallholder farmers could produce to global product standards (phase 2). Following efforts in linking farmers, both large exporters and smallholder contract farmers increased their supply to European supermarkets and experienced a rapid surge in export growth for flowers, fruits, and vegetables (phase 3). In more recent years, the sector began maturing and exports are strong (up to almost US$1.2 billion in 2018). Yet the sector also faces new challenges from increasing regional competition, growing climate risks, and changing consumer preferences and is now in search of a new spark (phase 4).

Selected lessons from Kenya for other countries

• Targeted efforts to link smallholder farmers to exporters and buyers can help raise the performance of local firms through export participation. Local suppliers were able to leverage their FDI relationships to access new customers (often through referral) or new export markets. About 50 percent of Kenyan agricultural firms became exporters as a result of first supplying a foreign-owned firm in-country.

• Direct transfers of innovative knowledge can increase value chain participation. Although foreign capital was important in launching the sector, over time, exposure to foreign demand, expertise, and technology became more important.

- Governments can sometimes best support an emerging sector by adopting a relatively hands-off approach with limited sectoral regulation and a liberal approach to FDI. Government support is most helpful for solving market failures that impede the development of key infrastructure and for providing an ecosystem for regulation, advocacy, support for training (for example, extension services), and R&D (seed development, for instance).

Honduras (textiles and apparel)

Honduras used a combined approach of establishing special economic zones (SEZs) (*maquilas*) and signing international trade and investment agreements to attract FDI and integrate the country into the global textile and apparel market. Maquilas were established as geographically limited enclaves with dedicated infrastructure, mostly private administration, and generous fiscal incentives to attract FDI. Preferential trade and investment agreements helped lower the cost of importing raw materials, enabled duty-free exports to the US market, and reduced political risk for foreign investors by providing investor protection guarantees.

The rise of Honduras's textile and apparel sector followed three phases (figure I.4). In the first phase, Honduras established the maquila program, but FDI and exports were limited. Beginning in the late 1980s, several policies helped increase exports and later FDI (phase 2). These policies included legal changes to the maquiladora regime in 1987, allowing domestic investors to invest in SEZs across the country; the signing of several trade and investment agreements; and the provision of key infrastructure and engaging in export and investment promotion. From the early 2000s onward, changes in global GVC configurations, emerging competition from Asia, and external shocks such as the 2007–08 financial crisis led to stagnating exports and FDI flows and exposed Honduras's vulnerability to supply shocks (phase 3).

FIGURE I.4 Honduras's textile and apparel exports, 1965–2017

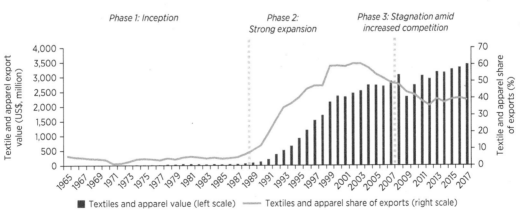

Source: World Bank calculations using United Nations Comtrade data.

Selected lessons from Honduras for other countries

- SEZs can be a catalyst for attracting FDI. The increased volume of FDI in the mid- to late 1990s was triggered by the establishment of these geographically limited areas with high-quality infrastructure, regulatory flexibility, and generous fiscal incentives. Participation by domestic investors may bring in additional funding and help accelerate the development of SEZs. Supplier linkages between foreign investors and domestic companies may bring additional benefits.

- The implementation of trade and investment agreements within SEZs can help improve the competitiveness of the country in labor-intensive goods. International agreements reduced trade costs and increased investor confidence, thereby stimulating investments and access to export markets.

- Although SEZs can help attract FDI, they also risk creating a dual economy. SEZ rules of origin may curtail the ability to increase local content production, and SEZ incentives often exclude small and medium enterprises. Although some backward linkages developed in Honduras, closer ties between zones and the rest of the economy were prevented by a tax on local inputs to be supplied to the zones, thus encouraging imports. Focus on the zones also prevented broader attention to reforming and upgrading the entire economy.

Malaysia (electrical and electronics)

Malaysia used targeted investment promotion and facilitation to attract global lead firms and help jump-start its E&E industry. Building on a strong foundation (low-cost

FIGURE I.5 Malaysia electrical and electronics exports, 1970–2017

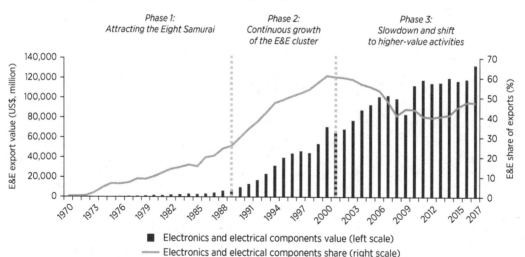

Source: World Bank calculations using United Nations Comtrade data.
Note: The "Eight Samurai" were Advanced Micro Devices (AMD), Clarion, Hewlett Packard (now Agilent Technologies), Hitachi Semiconductor (now Renesas), Intel, Litronix (now Osram Opto Semiconductors), National Semiconductor (now Fairchild Semiconductor), and Robert Bosch. E&E = electrical and electronics.

labor, basic technical capabilities, good English language skills, and political stability), Malaysia in the early 1970s combined active investment promotion, infrastructure provision, and incentives to attract a number of MNCs into its free trade zones. Successful linking programs and workforce development initiatives and evolving incentives programs supported the development of an E&E cluster in Penang and a gradual shift toward higher–value added activities.

Malaysia's E&E exports went through three main phases (figure I.5). In the early 1970s, proactive investment promotion with high-level political support and a competitive investment climate led to a few superstar firms locating in Malaysia, launching an incipient industry focused on labor-intensive, low-skilled production and assembly (phase 1). By the late 1980s, when a second wave of FDI entered the country, the E&E industry had become the largest generator of manufacturing employment, value-added activities, and exports in Malaysia, and an E&E cluster in Penang had formed. In the 1990s, the government strategy shifted toward developing supplier links, and about 2000 the E&E industry peaked in export and employment growth (phase 2). Subsequently, the emergence of China, the Philippines, and Vietnam as competitors began to take its toll, and several firms relocated out of Malaysia. At the same time, significant upgrading was achieved, facilitated by research grants to foreign companies and liberalization of visas for foreign professionals (phase 3).

Selected lessons from Malaysia for other countries

- If the minimum conditions for foreign investment are in place, active investment promotion can help attract superstar firms, which can jump-start the development of an industry. With an English-speaking, low-cost labor force complemented by the establishment of free trade zones and the provision of generous incentives, the foundation was in place in Malaysia in the 1970s.

- High-level political support and a solutions-oriented attitude by the government are critical for a successful investment promotion strategy. Information about investment conditions was backed up by a strong commitment to infrastructure provision and the removal of any disruptions to foreign investors' operations. This approach enjoyed high-level political support from the chief minister.

- Malaysia's experience also highlights the investment promotion benefits that can be derived from different levels of government complementing each other. In Malaysia, policy guidance at the federal level—in the form of planning and several incentive programs—was complemented by the proactive role of subnational agents who proved pivotal to attracting investors into the country.

- Incentives can be useful for attracting export-oriented FDI but need to be adjusted and eventually phased out with evolving development priorities. In the 1970s, incentives proved to be an important factor in attracting FDI to Malaysia into low-value-added, labor-intensive E&E GVC segments. In the early 1990s, both the tax holidays for pioneer industries and the investment tax allowance were made less generous, except for high-technology companies. After 1995, labor-intensive projects were no longer eligible for incentives and allowances unless they satisfied a set of narrow performance requirements.

Mauritius (tourism)

Mauritius leveraged FDI to significantly expand and upgrade its existing tourism industry. Liberalizing the tourism and aviation sectors and the creation of specific incentive schemes led to a surge in FDI inflows, a boom in the industry, and significant GVC upgrading. FDI helped diversify the tourism industry by creating new offerings such as golf tourism. Foreign-owned companies also offered training programs and helped domestic firms upgrade through transfer of skills, management expertise, and technology.

Mauritius's experience can be divided into three phases (figure I.6). In phase 1 (from the late 1970s to the early 2000s), Mauritius's tourism industry arose from investments in hotels by domestic sugarcane producers. The government facilitated the growth of a domestic tourism industry by providing basic infrastructure, ensuring air access through the national carrier, and marketing the country as an upscale tourism destination. FDI was permitted only in select segments (mainly hotels). Once the industry had become viable in the early 2000s, Mauritius opened up its economy in phase 2. FDI was liberalized and promoted, leading to a surge in FDI inflows. In phase 3, the sector matured, and domestic Mauritian companies have become outward investors to strengthen their brand and diversify their products. Both the opening of the economy and its outward expansion have significantly helped domestic firms upgrade, shifting to higher-value tourism and resulting in a steady increase in aggregate tourism exports.

Selected lessons from Mauritius for other countries

- A clear strategy is crucial to developing the tourism industry. Mauritius set out to become an upscale tourism destination in part by tightly regulating the industry (for example, by establishing a minimum number of rooms in hotels and minimum investment per room) and closely managing its growth. Initial control of the

FIGURE I.6 International tourism receipts in Mauritius, 1980–2018

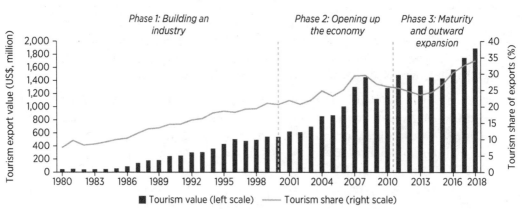

Source: World Bank calculations using United Nations Comtrade data.

industry further helped develop local small and medium enterprises. In contrast to many other countries, there is a significant local presence in large luxury hotels, and many five-star hotels in Mauritius are locally owned and managed.

• The role of MNCs will depend on country-specific circumstances. Mauritius had sufficient domestic capital available from the sugar industry to channel into the tourism industry. Other low-income countries may not have the necessary capital and may need to rely on MNC equity to get the tourism industry started.

• FDI in this case helped diversify the tourism industry, promoted the upgrading of existing players, and helped reach new export markets (foreign tourist locations). Domestic firms benefited from equity partnerships, management contracts, and franchising arrangements with MNCs. This interaction with MNCs led to the transfer of skills, management expertise, and technology, and helped the industry gain access to new customer groups through the MNCs' global networks.

The Republic of Korea, India, and China (digital economy)

The Republic of Korea, India, and China were able to integrate and upgrade in the digital economy GVC by combining outward foreign direct investment (OFDI) with investment in human capital and research and development (R&D). The availability of technical graduates and initial R&D investments were essential to establishing domestic industries. However, OFDI then helped their leading domestic companies acquire new technology, explore new markets, and compete internationally. Korea and China also invested determinedly in R&D and provided proactive government support for OFDI using a combination of financial and fiscal measures, provision of information, development assistance programs, and international investment agreements, in addition to the overall liberalization of OFDI regulations. India established software technology parks and provided software export credit and credit guarantees.

As a result of these interventions, some firms from Korea, India, and China managed to expand and have become significant players in different segments of the digital economy GVC. Korea specialized in ICT goods (such as semiconductors, wireless communication devices, flat panel displays, and consumer electronics), with such exports growing from US$2 billion in 1980 to almost US$190 billion in 2017 (figure I.7, panel a). India specialized mainly in ICT services (most notably business process management), increasing such exports from about US$50 million in the late 1980s to US$10 billion in 2000, rising to US$130 billion in 2017 (figure I.7, panel b). China is increasingly active in both ICT goods (personal computers, mobile phones, televisions, drones) and ICT services (financial technology, e-commerce, internet platforms, digital content). In 2004, China surpassed the United States as the world's leading ICT goods exporter, with US$240 billion in ICT goods exports, rising to US$820 billion in 2017. The country's ICT services exports have also grown continuously, rising from about US$59 billion in 2000 to US$130 billion in 2017 (figure I.7, panel c).

FIGURE I.7 **The exports of Korea, India, and China in the digital economy, 1980–2017**

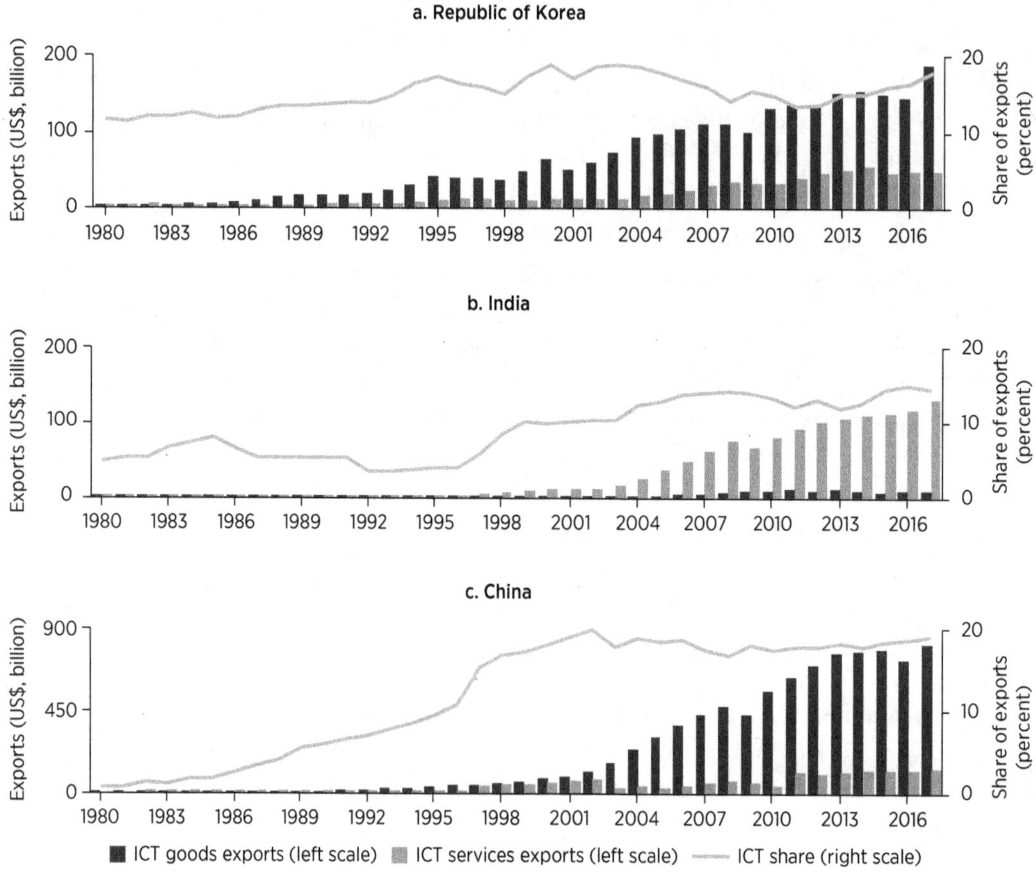

Source: World Bank calculations based on Atlas for Economic Complexity data.
Note: ICT goods are defined as standard international trade classification codes 75–77. ICT services include information technology and communication services. ICT = information and communication technology.

Selected lessons from Korea, India, and China for other countries

- To stimulate participation in the digital economy GVC, governments should first and foremost invest in their country's human capital. Investment in tertiary education in the areas of science, technology, engineering, and math is critical and will take time to bear fruit. The examples of Korea, India, and China show that such investment in building a large skills pool has, over time, established the foundation that gave domestic firms a competitive edge in this GVC.

- Proactive government support in R&D may also be needed to help domestic firms better understand and absorb existing technologies to engage in the digital economy. Through a wide array of policy instruments, particularly financial instruments, both Korea and China helped build the production and innovation capacity of local firms and enabled them to become leading R&D hubs. R&D also helps prepare more competitive firms to internationalize and become outward investors and MNCs themselves.

- OFDI is an internationalization channel for the most competitive domestic firms. All three countries demonstrate a strong, positive link between rising OFDI and exports of ICT goods and services. Leading domestic firms often chose to invest in high-income countries to acquire strategic assets such as R&D and proprietary technology, globally recognized brand names, and established customer networks and sales channels. In parallel, they also invested in developing countries to establish production facilities. Such OFDI thus helped the more productive domestic firms further develop their technological capabilities, expand their production networks and markets, and compete on a global scale.

- For governments seeking to stimulate OFDI, liberalizing outward investment regulations is an essential first step. In addition, as shown for Korea and China, OFDI can be supported using a combination of financial and fiscal measures, the provision of information, development assistance programs, and international investment agreements.

Quantitative case study: A comparative analysis of firm dynamics in global value chains

The quantitative case study presented in chapter 11 of this report aims to show how novel data sets and methodologies can be used to analyze the dynamics of MNCs and domestic firms across GVCs. By using country-, firm-, and transaction-level data sets, the study aims to provide important new findings that can help policy makers better understand the dynamics of firms within GVCs and help design better sector-industrial strategies and approaches to stimulate their GVC integration.

Rwanda (low income) and West-Bengal, India (lower-middle income), were selected because of their income levels and access to detailed firm- and transaction-level data sets that include firm ownership, trade, and linkages.[1] In both cases, FDI plays an important role in their GVC participation. Foreign firms are more likely to export and contribute a disproportionally higher share of exports. There is also a strong positive correlation at the sector level between FDI and that sector's export share, and at the firm level between being a foreign-owned firm and being an exporter.

Using firm- and transaction-level data, network analyses help illustrate interfirm relationships in selected value chains. This approach can show which types of firms (according to their ownership, size, and location) are engaging in GVCs as exporters and as suppliers. As such, it provides insights into the wide network of GVC actors, such as second-tier suppliers, that may be less easily observable with traditional stakeholder analysis. One downside to this approach, however, is that no data are available for firms not based within the country, so only the part of the GVC taking place within the country is observable. According to the network analyses, foreign firms in both case studies tend to be positioned at the end of domestic value chains because they are more likely to export. GVC participation across multiple sectors is dominated by a small number of foreign-owned firms.

The analysis also provides greater insights into how domestic firms and foreign firms interact in GVCs. Only the most productive firms manage to participate in GVCs. Three types of pathways are dominant in raising the probability that domestic firms will become direct exporters: MNC-supplier linkages, joint ventures between MNCs and domestic firms, and outward foreign investment. However, there are some important differences across GVCs. For example, whereas supply linkages appear most important in GVCs with higher product standards that require firm-level skills upgrading to accommodate (for example, in textiles, chemicals, and professional services), joint ventures are most important for sectors where local firms offer complementarities to foreign firms (such as speaking the local language or by being able to manage the complex, local regulatory environment. The overall difference in the *type* of firms that choose to export (direct GVC exporters, large firms diversifying into exports alongside domestic sales, or firms shifting from one export product into another) may further help shape the approaches to stimulating and facilitating GVC integration.

Note

1. A third planned case study, Turkey (higher-middle income), had to be dropped after COVID-19 (coronavirus) prevented access to its data laboratory.

Reference

World Bank. 2020. *World Development Report 2020: Trade for Development in the Age of Global Value Chains*. Washington, DC: World Bank.

Chapter 6

Kenya—Supplying to multinationals exposed local firms to international horticulture markets

ULLA HEHER AND VICTOR STEENBERGEN

Summary

This case study focuses on the rise of Kenya's horticulture industry, which illustrates how pioneering foreign investment helped create a route to international markets for local firms.

By providing access to foreign expertise, technology, and capital, foreign direct investment (FDI) was critical to launching Kenyan producers into the horticulture global value chain (GVC). Pioneering FDI and entrepreneurs of foreign origin living in Kenya (who had strong, often kinship connections to markets in Europe) ignited the growth of the sector. Subsequently, economies of scale made possible crucial investments in the local infrastructure and enabled commercial-scale production. Sourcing strategies along the value chain adapted over time to favor contract farming over original plantation production. Thus, FDI plays a less direct but no less important role in horticulture compared with other GVCs (Kaiser Associates Economic Development Partners 2014; Moran 2018). The sector's strong growth in the 1990s reflected the export push from foreign investors and the simultaneous demand pull from retailers in their home markets. Kenya's revealed comparative advantage in horticulture took off from there, and horticulture's share in the country's total exports doubled within a decade.

Linkages between domestic horticulture producers and the GVC's lead firms have increased Kenyan firms' competitiveness and supported their internationalization. Competing at the high-value end of the market requires firm-level sophistication. Changing consumer demand, constantly evolving food standards, and the just-in-time delivery required by perishable produce necessitates careful supply chain management and close cooperation with overseas clients (English, Jaffee, and Okello 2004). Global buyers abroad coordinate the sector's supply chain through preprogramming and standards-setting. Through contract-farming schemes with horticulture exporters, Kenyan farmers were encouraged to organize and upgrade their capabilities. As part of these contracts, lead producers provided necessary production inputs, training, and market information and access. Moreover, public-private models have delivered critical extension services and workforce training to Kenyan farmers (World Bank 2020). The gradual improvement of GVC suppliers also helped expand regional value chains in East Africa (Krishnan 2017).

Kenya's case reflects how GVC participation may contribute to economic upgrading in low-income countries and kick-start structural transformation. The knowledge and technology spillovers from Kenya's GVC participation set off a trajectory of economic upgrading that allowed the country to move from commodities to limited manufacturing between 1990 and 2015. GVC participation rose significantly in the agribusiness sector, by about 10 percent over this time frame (World Bank 2020). Kenya's horticulture GVC development is primarily a story of a dynamic private sector in which entrepreneurs and farmers innovated and took chances. The government at first played an ambiguous role in the process, but it gradually learned to be a facilitator (English, Jaffee, and Okello 2004).

The horticulture global value chain and Kenya's position in it

Agribusiness is the largest sector in Kenya's economy, and the sector has transformed considerably over the past several decades.[1] As of 2019, agricultural production generates 29 percent of Kenya's gross domestic product (GDP), provides nearly 60 percent of employment, and accounts for 57 percent of all exports; and downstream agriprocessing generates an additional (and comparatively low) 3.2 percent of GDP and 2.4 percent of employment (IFC 2019; Kenya HCD 2019). Horticulture, as a subsector of agriculture, comprises fruit and vegetables, fresh or processed, as well as cut flowers. Although tea is Kenya's single largest export product, horticulture products constitute about 20 percent of the country's exports, making it an important source of foreign exchange. Within horticulture, flowers are the biggest contributor, in both production and export share, followed by vegetables and fruit. The European Union is by far the most important export market for these products.

The structure of the horticulture GVC is highly product specific, but in general it comprises five segments (figure 6.1) (see Fernandez-Stark, Bamber, and Gereffi 2011; Kaiser Associates Economic Development Partners 2014; Otieno and Knorringa 2012; Whitaker and Kolavalli 2006). The following discussion describes this GVC from Kenya's perspective, highlighting the main difference between its major export product categories: floriculture (including cut flowers and bouquets) and fruits and vegetables (F&V). Kenya has focused mostly on primary agricultural products that pass through early forms of processing before arriving at the end consumer (Kaiser Associates Economic Development Partners 2014). Because many horticulture products are perishable, their GVCs require much coordination between all actors to ensure that products reach their destinations in good condition. Thus, logistics, transportation, and cold storage play key supporting roles in the GVC and have significant impacts on the products' value, as do the testing and grading of produce by regulatory bodies.

Investment in agribusiness GVCs allows participants to raise their productivity by adopting new knowledge, technology, and techniques. Linkages between foreign investors and local supply chains and labor markets are more prevalent in agriculture than in many other value chains, given the fundamental requirement of sourcing domestic agricultural products (Kaiser Associates Economic Development Partners 2014). However, significant differences exist between countries in value addition (especially that of processing and manufacturing), which is—as in other sectors' value chains—driven mainly by the sophistication of domestic firms and commercial-scale farms.

International investors participate at various points along the horticulture value chain in direct and indirect forms (UNCTAD 2009). In indirect nonequity participation (arm's length trade), farmers or firms in the host country produce according to the specifications of a foreign multinational corporation (MNC) involved in downstream or upstream activities. Coordination between these parties may be low or high, but it is grounded in compliance with standards. Direct nonequity participation is characterized by contract farming, in which host-country farmers or firms are tightly coordinated with and controlled by an MNC. Because of the more relational

FIGURE 6.1 **Illustration of Kenya's horticulture global value chain**

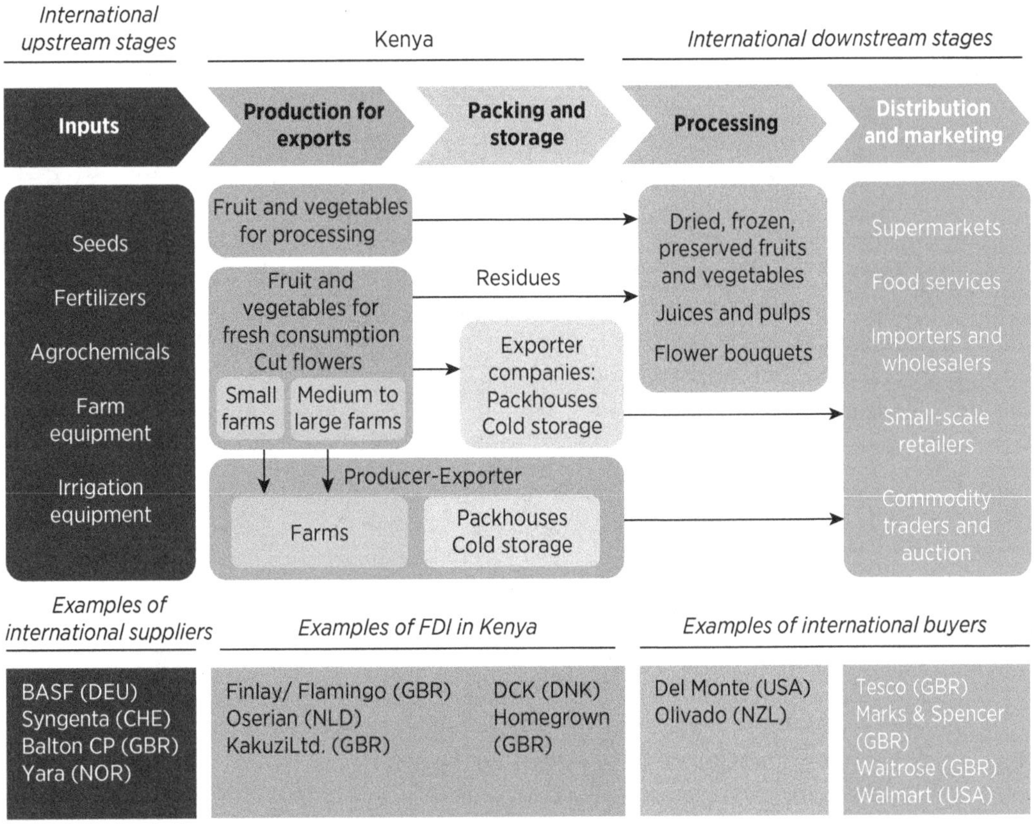

Source: Adapted from Fernandez-Stark, Bamber, and Gereffi 2011 and UNCTAD 2009.
Note: FDI = foreign direct investment.

and longer-term character of these contracts, the MNC is encouraged to support the farmers. A third type of participation, direct equity participation through FDI, fully internalizes coordination and control of transactions within the MNC. In the Kenyan horticulture GVC, this last form has been used most frequently in floriculture, which requires more up-front capital, involves specialized skills, and exports most of its production (Whitaker and Kolavalli 2006).

The horticulture GVC is driven and supervised by global buyers. International standards, codes of conduct, and certifications act as catalysts for knowledge transfer and as instruments governing the GVC. Lead firms, often international supermarkets, exert significant control over the entire value chain and dictate how output is produced, harvested, transported, processed, and stored. This control extends to the characteristics of products, including their quality, size, and exposure to pesticides, as well as the social and environmental conditions of cultivation and postharvest handling. Suppliers around the world are required to meet buyers' demands to maintain their access to export markets. In return, these buyers enable farmers to market their produce and provide support for logistics, finance, and capacity building to comply with traceability requirements and product standards.

Inputs

Global MNCs are the main providers of inputs to Kenya's horticulture GVCs. The large majority of these MNCs are headquartered in developed countries but are also present in Kenya.[2] The most important inputs are seeds, fertilizers, agrochemicals (pesticides), farm equipment, and irrigation equipment. The power of these global input suppliers over their buyers working in the production stage can be significant, especially when they control key technologies (UNCTAD 2009). As the scale of local production in Kenya has increased, most of the main input providers have opened outlets in the country. The local supply market is characterized by weak competition and is heavily influenced by government interventions, which often serve important social objectives but also create unintended, negative distortions (IFC 2019).

Production

The organization of the production segment varies considerably among horticulture products and according to their final markets. Producers range from smallholders to large farms that supply exporters to producer-exporters that also offer packing and storage for export. The last group is made up of commercial farms that manage groups of contract farmers in addition to their own plantations but also keep direct contracts with international buyers. For smallholders, the commercial farms are important partners that provide certification and export licenses that would otherwise require significant investment from each farmer (Otieno and Knorringa 2012). These firms also help by sharing market risk because failure to supply supermarkets with the required volumes comes with high fines (Kaiser Associates Economic Development Partners 2014). The technology and facilities needed to produce a product determine whether it is suitable for contract farming. For F&V exports (such as avocados, French beans, and mangoes), 70–80 percent of products are grown by smallholder farmers and the remainder is supplied by large, exporter-owned farms. This ratio is inverted in the flower segment (including cut flowers and foliage), in which about 80 percent of products are produced at a few large commercial farms, several of which are foreign owned. Furthermore, the final market's consumption requirements determine what standards need to be applied during the production of each product.

Packing and storage

Grading is central for exporting and making use of economies of scale critical at this stage. Before produce is packed and shipped, exporters sort it into multiple grades and sizes and organize it for residue testing by the Kenya Plant Health Inspectorate Service (KePHIS). Postharvest handling has a huge impact on the grade and price received by produce. The main handling activities undertaken, depending on the product, are washing, trimming, chopping, mixing, packing, and labeling. In floriculture, postharvest handling may also include the preparation of bouquets ready to be sold in supermarkets abroad, although most flowers from Kenya are still exported in bulk. Given the substantial capital investment needed for packing (including air-conditioning and ventilation systems, water purification, and blast coolers), it requires economies of scale and is carried out by large producer-exporters or by specialized export companies, which in Kenya are located near the international airport in Nairobi. Because of its GVC participation, Kenya today benefits from well-developed cold-chain logistics for imports and exports via both air and sea (IFC 2019).

Processing

The main value added the processing stage achieves is an increase of the product's shelf life. Processed goods include dried, frozen, and preserved produce as well as juices and pulps. Processing plants typically purchase F&V from producers and export their processed products under either their own brand or the buyer's brand (Fernandez-Stark, Bamber, and Gereffi 2011). Most of the handful of horticulture processing plants in Kenya are owned by MNCs. Two such companies are Del Monte (for canned pineapple), one of the largest food production companies worldwide and one that pioneered FDI in Kenya in the 1960s, and Olivado, a New Zealand firm that entered into a joint venture with a Kenyan partner in 2017 to process avocado oil.[3]

Distribution and marketing

Retailers dominate the distribution and marketing of horticultural goods. At this stage, efficient logistics are crucial. Key distribution channels include supermarkets, wholesalers, small-scale retailers, and food services. In floriculture, commodity traders and the Dutch auction are also used, though flowers and bouquets have increasingly been sold directly to retailers as well. Global buyers have the power to set strict process and product standards that producers must meet to engage in this value chain. Because of the perishability of most horticulture products, access to efficient and reliable logistics and transportation services is critical. As the scale of its exports increased, Kenya invested in the industry's infrastructure for logistics and storage, strengthened the country's airport facilities, and expanded space for air cargo (Azizi 2020). Domestic food retail in Kenya has been dominated by local supermarkets (such as Nakumatt, Uchumi, and Tuskys), some of which have also invested outward across East Africa. Since 2015, foreign retailers such as South Africa's Shoprite and France's Carrefour have also set up shop in Kenya.

The development of the horticulture value chain in Kenya and the role of foreign direct investment

The dynamics and structure of Kenya's horticulture GVC have evolved substantially over the past several decades (Humphrey, McCulloch, and Ota 2004). Today, the sector accounts for slightly less than US$1.2 billion in exports and represents an

FIGURE 6.2 **Kenya's horticulture export performance, 1976–2018**

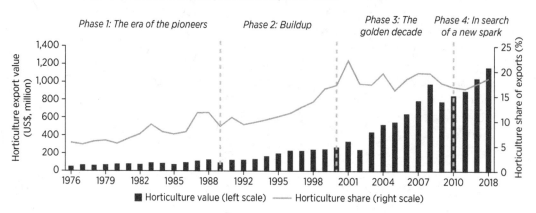

Source: World Bank calcualations based on United Nations Comtrade data.

important income stream for the country. The industry has evolved and upgraded and has become a highly sophisticated supplier of prepackaged, mostly unprocessed, "ready to eat" fruits and vegetables as well as of cut flowers. Horticulture has formed the most dynamic part of Kenya's agricultural trade because its products are typically of higher value. It also has enabled Kenya to diversify away from the country's stagnating traditional commodity exports (including coffee, tea, and sugar) (UNCTAD 2009).

Horticulture has a long tradition in Kenya. The roots of the sector were established before World War II. Independence in 1963 brought three reforms important to GVC participation: (a) a land reform that supported commercial farming by smallholders, (b) the establishment of a Horticultural Crops Development Authority (HCDA) to regulate the industry's quality and trade, and (c) an open investment climate to grow international investment in the horticulture sector (Minot and Ngigi 2004).

The broader development of Kenya's horticulture sector in the modern era can be divided into four main phases (figure 6.2). From 1970 to 1990, the sector was driven by a select group of pioneers. From 1990 to 2000, the industry started building up. A "golden decade" of rapid growth occurred from 2000 to 2010. And, since then, Kenyan horticulture has been in search of a new spark.

Phase 1: The era of the pioneers (1970–90)

Kenya's horticulture sector began with FDI into key segments, which drove export growth. By 1970, Del Monte had taken over a state-owned pineapple processing operation, a British investor had set up a new project to dehydrate vegetables for export, a Swiss company had developed a passion fruit–juice export business, and the Danish firm Dansk Chrysanthemum and Kultur (DCK) had invested in growing flowers (English, Jaffee, and Okello 2004). F&V exports rose on average by 8 percent per year in real terms during this period (Minot and Ngigi 2004). This trend was supported by falling commodity prices for coffee and tea, which encouraged farmers to diversify into crops that would generate more income. By the end of this period, Kenya was the main supplier of fresh and chilled vegetables to the European Union (Dolan, Humphrey, and Harris-Pascal 1999).

Kenya accessed new export markets by serving international customers at home and abroad. Demand for the country's exports grew further as an indirect effect of the expulsion of the South Asian community from Uganda under Idi Amin. Many of those expelled resettled in the United Kingdom, driving up demand for Asian vegetables. With a suitable climate for year-round supply and experience growing Asian vegetables for its own Asian community, Kenya was ready to meet that demand. Most important, social ties were established between Asian traders in London and in Nairobi, reducing the risks and transaction costs of expanding this trade route (Dijkstra 1997). The growth of tourism in Kenya helped as well because the cargo capacity of passenger jets was used to airfreight Kenyan produce to Europe and because the growth of hotels and restaurants in Kenya increased domestic demand for high-quality F&V.

Smallholder participation in F&V production increased during this period, but MNCs needed time to figure out how to best organize local farmers to ensure predictable supply. Over this period, the export volume provided by smallholders grew from about 20 percent of exports in the 1970s to 40–65 percent (mostly French beans, Asian vegetables, mangoes, avocados, and passion fruit) by 1990 (Jaffee and Masakure 2005). Export companies offered a reliable market to farmers' groups, which in return needed seeds and inputs on credit. In some cases, technological changes, increasing competition, and the unreliability of farmers' organizations encouraged commercial-scale operations, such as Del Monte, to integrate vertically and start production on their own farms.

In floriculture, the pioneering firm DCK was soon followed by several major investments in the sector. Generously supported by the Kenyan government and motivated by lower labor costs and longer growing seasons, DCK made a large-scale investment in Kenya in 1969, which it expanded in the following years (Whitaker and Kolavalli 2006). Despite frequent changes in ownership, DCK enjoyed considerable success and remains one of the major players in Kenya's flower industry. Other FDI came from the United States–based Yoder Bros. and from the Oserian Development Company, owned by a Dutch family in Kenya. The expatriate flower specialists brought in by foreign investors, together with Kenyans initially trained at the pioneering farms, founded several dozen spin-off joint ventures in the mid-1980s (English, Jaffee, and Okello 2004).

Unlike Kenya's traditional export commodities (tea, coffee, cotton, and tobacco), the country's horticulture sector received hardly any government attention at first (Bates 2005; Minot and Ngigi 2004). However, as commodity prices declined in the 1970s, Kenyan farmers were encouraged to produce higher-value-added crops to increase export earnings. In sharp contrast to the marketing boards for coffee and tea, which suffered from corruption and cronyism, the HCDA decided to leave marketing to the private sector and avoided involvement in price setting or monopoly creation for horticulture products (Tyce 2020). This hands-off approach immensely benefited the development of the sector. As the sector's economic success increased, the HCDA

TABLE 6.1 **Share of Kenya's horticultural exports by firm ownership, 1985–86**

Firm ownership	Fresh F&V	Cut flowers	Processed F&V	Combined
Foreign	0	58	91	54
Private, local	97	38	9	43
Kenyan-Asian	81	0	7	30
Kenyan-European	9	35	2	10
Kenyan	7	3	0	3
Local cooperative	0	1	0	1
Kenyan state	· 3	3	0	2
Total	100	100	100	100

Source: Jaffee 1992.
Note: F&V = fruits and vegetables.

gained political influence and resources, mostly from external donors, which it used to build horticulture-specific infrastructure (World Bank 1989).

Although the Kenyan government promoted "Kenyanization" during this period, it remained more open to FDI than many other African countries. After obtaining its political independence, Kenya sought economic independence from both Asian Kenyans (who at the time controlled much of the country's F&V exports) and European investors (who played a similarly dominant role in floriculture). The government redistributed land, restricted the hiring of non-Kenyans, and provided export promotion services, preferential access to air cargo, and credit schemes to black Kenyan firms (Jaffee 1992). Despite these efforts, the horticulture trade remained largely under the control of companies owned by foreigners and nonblack Kenyans (table 6.1) because recipients of state support often lacked the experience, knowledge, and interest in exporting horticulture products to establish a successful business (Azizi 2020).

Throughout this period, the pioneering FDI dominated the horticulture sector but created positive externalities. The sector also drew in new, large-scale FDI, supported by generous incentives and an open market. These investments produced important externalities, highlighted Kenya's comparative advantage in horticulture, and brought about several critical improvements in the country's infrastructure, labor force, and market development. By imitating the production, sales, and marketing processes of foreign investors, local firms sought to become more productive and competitive in export markets. For smallholders, the most direct benefit came from linking up with pioneering firms through subcontracting (Azizi 2020).

Phase 2: Buildup (1990–2000)

The liberalization of Kenya's trade policies and the adoption of market-friendly regulations attracted a second wave of FDI from 1990 to 2000. Political instability and an economic recession, including a heavy exchange rate devaluation in 1993, triggered a period of structural adjustment, which forced the Kenyan government to enact economic reforms in the 1990s. The government removed controls on foreign exchange, imports, and airfreight and established a more stable macroeconomic environment. Also, Kenya's trade policies evolved from import substitution toward a greater export orientation (Gertz 2008). Although the journey was by no means straightforward, by the end of this period, exports had grown and firms were better able to adapt to evolving market conditions and buyer standards (English, Jaffee, and Okello 2004). Many large and medium floriculture firms also shifted their production from established markets (Germany, the Netherlands, and the United Kingdom) to Kenya. This increase in demand triggered knock-on FDI by input suppliers for greenhouse facilities, seeds, and fertilizers (Azizi 2020). The inflow of foreign capital, technology, and knowledge also created incentives for local firms to invest in horticulture.

During this period, increasing competition in the global horticulture industry pushed Kenyan firms to reorient and upgrade. New sources of supply (such as the Arab Republic of Egypt and Morocco) cut into Kenya's market share for exports to Europe and drove down prices. The average unit values of bulk produce fell considerably (for example, the value of green beans fell by 15–25 percent between 1995 and 2001 [COLEACP 2001]). Thus, Kenyan producers were forced to adapt their business models. They successfully introduced new crops (such as peas) and added value by exporting semiprocessed products that were washed, cut, sliced, and packed ready for supermarket sale at the destination (including mixed salads and assortments of cut vegetables for stir-fries or dips). The low cost of labor for Kenyan packhouse workers compared with similar workers in Europe supported Kenya's competitiveness in this value chain segment. Jaffee and Masakure (2005) show that the typical net profit on "fine beans" shipped in bulk was 0–2 percent, compared with a profit of 12–14 percent on a tray of "stir-fry mix." Kenya's export values subsequently increased sharply. The need to bundle a greater variety of produce before shipping also reinforced contract farming schemes.

Although greater competition, not higher standards, initiated the upgrading process to achieve higher product values, Kenya also started to focus on the premium customer segment during this period. The UK market was already a prime destination for Kenyan exports, but the shifts in Kenya's product mix and targeted market segments reinforced that focus. Kenya gravitated toward markets where consumers were ready to pay a premium for higher value added and convenience. Meanwhile, Kenya's trade contracted in markets where price was the primary competitive criterion. This repositioning required the industry to compete in the market for high-quality products and to improve its systems for procurement (backward integration, product segmentation, extension services, and higher-intensity out-grower systems), quality assurance, and food safety management.

The growth of the horticulture industry led to the rise of business networks and an enabling ecosystem. The Kenya Flower Council (KFC) and Fresh Produce Exporters Association of Kenya (FPEAK) increased their power, ambition, and advocacy. These organizations pushed for the privatization of Kenya Airways by entering a strategic partnership with the airline KLM in 1996; once accomplished, this privatization decreased transportation costs and raised Kenyan competitiveness (Tyce 2020). Similarly, FPEAK effectively lobbied for the duty-free import of agricultural inputs and equipment as well as for exemptions for the horticulture sector to permit the free flow of resources, technology, and foreign technical experts (Whitaker and

Kolavalli 2006). As quality assurance gained importance, KePHIS was founded to establish a good reputation for the industry by introducing market-friendly regulation and stringent food safety management systems. The Kenyan government also assumed a more facilitative role in governing the sector, not least because horticulture helped offset the lost export earnings from traditional commodities.

The growing role of supermarkets in Europe changed the dynamics along the horticulture GVC (box 6.1). Increasingly, supermarket chains bypassed wholesalers to negotiate with and source directly from preferred exporters in Kenya, thereby creating a more direct link between consumer demand and producers. Kenyan commercial farms were able to take advantage of this shift, which required (a) process upgrading to meet standards, (b) product upgrading to sell semiprepared and prepacked produce, and (c) functional upgrading to integrate logistics, freight, and marketing. Supermarkets organized much of this new production; as stated by a former manager at Homegrown Ltd., one of the largest foreign horticultural exporters in Kenya, "Homegrown [rarely] grows anything unless a supermarket has programmed it" (Evans 1999).

The structural changes in Kenyan exports led to greater concentration and a decline in smallholder participation but also to better jobs and opportunities to form linkages. By 2000, seven firms controlled 75 percent of all Kenyan horticulture exports (Dolan and Humphrey 2004), and the export of flowers had been controlled by large producer-exporters from the start. Smallholder participation in UK supermarkets' value chains declined rapidly, from 50–55 percent in 1999 to less than 20 percent in 2001, as demand increased for more consistency in the supply, taste, and appearance of produce and for greater traceability and compliance with environmental and labor standards (Dolan and Humphrey 2000, 2004). The process upgrading and investment required to meet these new requirements were often beyond the reach of smallholders. However, because of new sales channels that arose in the growing regional trade for horticulture products, horticulture smallholders still earned more income than those in other sectors (Krishnan 2017).[4]

BOX 6.1 The rise of supermarkets in Africa

Since the 1990s, supermarkets have emerged as the key market channel for food retail sales in Africa and have transformed African horticulture. Within a decade, the average share of supermarkets in food retail increased to 50–60 percent (Reardon et al. 2003). At the same time, the continent's supermarket segment consolidated as large multinationals such as Walmart, Carrefour, Tesco, and Royal Ahold entered developing markets (Farole and Winkler 2014). Supermarkets' degree of control over their supply chains increased, and they began coordinating the value chain, from sourcing to production and distribution to retail, by pushing for standards certification and traceability.

Most supermarkets in Kenya have domestic, rather than foreign, roots. Larger Kenyan chains, such as Nakumatt,[a] Uchumi, Chandarana, and Tuskys, were followed by Naivas and Zucchini in the late 1990s, about the same time the country's horticulture exports began to grow dramatically (Krishnan 2017).

a. Nakumatt was Kenya's leading supermarket chain for decades. It sourced products from 1,500 suppliers, directly employed 6,720 workers, and generated turnover of roughly 1 percent of Kenya's gross domestic product. However, it filed for bankruptcy in 2017 because of overambitious expansion, the destruction of its flagship store during the 2013 terrorist attacks in Nairobi, and rampant theft of cash and stock at its stores (Golubski 2017).

The professionalization of production in the horticulture sector increased employment, particularly for women, who benefited from new permanent jobs at packhouses with higher wages and skill requirements (Fernandez-Stark, Bamber, and Gereffi 2011). Similarly, opportunities for linkages increased as large exporters expanded their contract farming arrangements. The need to provide a more diverse range of products, together with the severe fines imposed if exporters were unable to supply the quality and quantity of products promised to supermarkets, increased contracts for smallholders, who could supplement the exporters' products and share their risks (such as demand peaks and crop contagion). The largest exporters contracted with between 1,000 and 2,000 farmers, who benefited from the provision of inputs, training, finance, and help with quality assurance. The prerequisite conditions for contract farmers, in turn, were a certain scale, minimum quality certification, and formality as a crucial factor for enforcing contracts (Kaiser Associates Economic Development Partners 2014).

Rather than posing an insurmountable barrier to the Kenyan horticulture sector, the rise in competition and the rapid pace of standards introduction and product innovation that occurred during this period threw a lifeline to the sector, which it successfully grabbed. As freight and production costs increasingly undercut Kenya's ability to compete on price, Kenya entered the higher-value market segments of semiprocessed and packaged products, for which the competitive factors were value addition, convenience, safety, and traceability.

Phase 3: The golden decade (2000–10)

The structures and upgrading pathways put in place during the 1990s paid off. Kenyan horticulture recorded its strongest period of growth between 2001 and 2007, with fruit, vegetable, and flower exports all experiencing dramatic surges supported by strong global demand. "During those years, we could sell everything we put on the market," a manager from a lead exporter summarized. Exports in the F&V segment focused on semiprocessed products. In floriculture, the rise of supermarkets opened another sales channel apart from the Dutch auction, which had been the traditional trading hub for floral products, and allowed producers to diversify into packaging bouquets ready for sale, which requires more skill and adds more value (Azizi 2020; Whitaker and Kolavalli 2006).

Increasing competition among European supermarkets pushed much of the horticulture sector's packing and semiprocessing to developing countries. To cater to UK supermarkets during the 1990s, Kenyan exporters had already made significant investments in upgrading their packhouses; by the end of the 1990s, almost all Kenyan exporters had large packing facilities close to Kenya's international airport, from which the European market could be served within 24 to 48 hours. Also, more international investment in the sector followed, such as from Paragon Print and Packaging, the leading packaging manufacturer in the United Kingdom (Fernandez-Stark, Bamber, and Gereffi 2011).

The horticulture sector's ecosystem expanded, with a strong emphasis on increasing skills and certification (box 6.2). During this period, the horticulture industry came to require a higher level of skills and formal education than its workforce could attain at the time. Thus, Kenyan universities and education institutes launched degree programs in food science and processing technology. HCDA, KePHIS, and the Kenyan Agriculture Research Institute provided many industry participants with training and information on agriculture crops, pest control, and disease prevention as well as market intelligence. Industry associations (including the Chamber of Commerce, FPEAK, and the KFC) further supported their members by providing marketing advice and links to international buyers as well as by lobbying for favorable regulation and public investment in the development of the sector. To enhance inclusiveness, international donors started many programs to support the integration of Kenyan smallholders into GVCs and to train Kenya's workforce.[5]

A growing regional market in East Africa opened up yet more opportunities for Kenyan producers. The number of supermarket outlets in Kenya grew from approximately 60 in 2007 to 192 by 2014, and the revenue earned by the three largest supermarkets in Kenya increased by 43 percent between 2007 and 2014—a substantially faster growth rate than for the more saturated supermarket sector in Europe (Krishnan 2017). GVC suppliers thus began to participate in the expanding regional market, where they sell excess or rejected horticulture produce goods. What started as opportunistic participation by farmers soon became a strategy for diversifying their buyers and thus improving their bargaining positions and earning higher prices.

BOX 6.2 The centrality of standards: Global versus local, public versus private, and mandatory versus voluntary

European retailers created the Global Good Agricultural Practices in 1997, which Kenya localized in 2007 to decrease the complexity and cost of compliance for smallholders. These standards have come to govern quality, size, pesticide use, and residue limits as well as hygiene requirements for postharvest handling; they also require precise traceability of products. Global standards certification is a prerequisite for accessing export markets (Moran 2018). Because smallholders often reported difficulties in developing the necessary capabilities and affording the cost of certification, group certification was made possible for smallholders contracted with by larger producers. The Horticultural Crops Development Authority amended its standards to align with local conditions, and the Fresh Produce Exporters Association of Kenya supported smallholders with training on the Kenyan standards, which are enforced by domestic supermarkets and wholesalers (Fernandez-Stark, Bamber, and Gereffi 2011).

As sourcing has globalized and concerns over food safety have increased, private food standards have rapidly proliferated. These standards often complement, rather than displace, public standards; are more stringent and specific to individual buyers; and are frequently related to specific trademarks (such as fair trade). Although voluntary in principle, these standards are almost mandatory for commercial purposes because they are either required to access business opportunities or are otherwise beneficial to differentiate a producer's goods from those of competitors (Otieno and Knorringa 2012). Most standards for traceability, agricultural practices, environmental and social practices, and other factors are voluntary codes of conduct. Legally mandated standards are enforced through export markets' trade regulations; these standards include sanitary and phytosanitary measures as well as maximum residue limits. The rise in standards has led to a proliferation of certification, monitoring, and auditing bodies, resulting in higher costs for producers seeking certification (Evers et al. 2014).

As regional supermarkets established themselves, they came to depend on the better-quality produce from GVC suppliers. Thus, Kenya's GVC participation in supplying European supermarkets created positive spillovers in the development of the regional horticulture market. Export-quality produce compliant with international good agricultural practices, as well as new crop varieties, gradually infiltrated regional retail, raising regional standards and food safety.[6]

Increasing domestic policy instability and the global financial crisis brought an end to the golden era. Exports plunged in 2009 because of postelection violence, constitutional reform, and the global financial crisis, which caused high uncertainty among domestic and foreign investors. Following the period of strong growth, the government also decided to retract some incentives previously granted to horticultural producers, such as access to economic processing zones (areas that provide a special investment regime, including more lucrative incentives, to enhance commercial and industrial exports), and clamped down on tax evasion and questionable transfer pricing modalities (Tyce 2020). At the end of this period, there were about 1.5 million smallholder horticulture producers in Kenya, and they produced about 70 percent of F&V and 10 percent of flowers for export (Government of Kenya 2012). This statistic highlights the sector's importance for socioeconomic development in Kenya: about 5 million Kenyans depend directly or indirectly on horticulture for their livelihoods (Otieno and Knorringa 2012).

Phase 4: In search of a new spark (2010–today)

As Kenya's horticulture sector matures, the industry is looking for a new spark to underpin its future growth. From 2009 to 2013, the sector experienced reduced and more erratic growth. Although this decline in growth was caused in part by external events, domestic policy weaknesses revealed that the sector's previous success might have been more fragile than expected. Following the decision to decentralize the central government and empower local administration, local governments started imposing additional taxes and business license regulation on horticulture producers, often duplicating or even contradicting those of the central government. Between 2012 and 2013, the European Union intercepted several horticulture products from Kenya that did not meet its food safety standards, leading to full-scale bans on Kenyan imports (Koigi 2016; Muchira 2019; Waitathu 2014). These events helped new competitors such as Ethiopia, Nigeria, and Senegal to rise.

Even though effective public-private governance enabled the horticulture industry to recover at home and abroad, it needed a new vision. A new national standard (KS 1758) was introduced in 2015 as a prerequisite for firms to obtain export licenses. Also, the Kenya Horticultural Council, which included representatives from KFC, FPEAK, and HCDA, was founded to revive the public-private governance that had increasingly characterized Kenyan horticulture (Mwangi 2018). Although access to the European export market remains critical to the sector, part of the new vision is to promote access to new markets, reduce the sector's dependence on Europe, and realize trade agreements with China, the Russian Federation, other East Asian and Middle Eastern countries, and, most recently, the United States so that new trade and flight routes can be opened.

Process upgrading is still increasing yields in floriculture, but Kenyan F&V producers have seen their profitability suffer. Similar to the upgrading of F&V exports to semiprocessed fruit and vegetables in the 1990s, foreign-owned investors have been increasing the production of ready-for-sale flower bouquets in Kenyan operations. Although this shift in location increases costs for storage, freight, and handling and has required specialized training and investments in new assembly lines, it has paid off.[7] It opened new opportunities for local farmers to tap into the more concentrated export market for flowers because bouquets are supplemented with locally produced summer flowers that require less infrastructure and can be grown in rain-fed conditions by local firms. The F&V segment, in contrast, faces constraints to its market share despite substantial global opportunities. Its profitability has declined because of changes in demand and increased operating and transportation costs, all in the context of a very competitive retail market in Europe. Several prominent exporters have stopped operations in Kenya, most notably Finlay Horticulture, which grew fruit and vegetables, or have been forced into refinancing or joint venture investments to stay afloat (Fintrac Inc. 2014).

A shift toward climate-smart and technology-intensive horticulture is needed to improve Kenyan producers' yields, efficiency, and profitability. Dwindling productivity, low value addition compared with the scale of production, and high exposure to climate change risks resulted in Kenya losing competitiveness in the sector compared with its East African neighbors (IFC 2019). Crops such as mangoes have not yet lived up to their potential, largely because of weak farmer organization, poor postharvest handling (leading to losses of up to 40 percent of produce), and lack of capital investment. Because water shortages and rising temperatures are increasing operational costs, pushing smallholders out of the market, industry associations and donors have urged producers to more toward more sustainable and inclusive production. Additionally, following the success of the mobile money provider M-Pesa, Kenya became known as a leader in adapting modern technology to meet local needs, driven by dynamic entrepreneurs and market-based innovation. Applications of new technology range from providing farmers with weather updates, market data, and access to finance to driving logistical efficiencies and increasing traceability across the value chain. For example, agri-tech firms such as Twiga Foods and Apollo Agriculture have successfully introduced innovative business models in recent years.[8]

Despite the challenges it faces, horticulture remains a promising sector for Kenya's development. Fruits and vegetables have some of the highest multipliers for production, employment, and value added among agricultural commodities in Kenya, as shown by a study assessing the potential of different economic sectors to create wealth and employment (Boulanger et al. 2018).

Conclusion: Main lessons for other countries and outlook for Kenyan horticulture

In addition to a favorable climate, well-planned strategic investments, and political and economic stability at the time, Kenya's horticulture sector benefited from a first-mover advantage. Kenya's geographic location, fertile soils, and climate that permits a year-round growing season were unquestionable prerequisites for the development of the country's horticulture GVC. In the sector's initial days, growth relied on an enabling business environment and public-private cooperation that promoted investment in strategic infrastructure and the development of a supportive ecosystem for the sector. The government mostly refrained from intervening strongly in the market. Kenya was also the beneficiary of numerous private sector– and donor-funded projects over the past three decades that helped improve the country's logistics infrastructure, product quality, and horticulture skills. GVC entry is much more difficult for newcomers today because of consolidation and the adoption of rigorous standards within the horticulture GVC.

Although foreign capital was essential to launching Kenya's horticulture sector, over time the sector's exposure to foreign expertise and technology became more important. Remaining open to FDI and actively supporting pioneering investment has been critical. Kenya sent a strong market signal, attracting more domestic and foreign investment. Local producers took up the opportunities presented and absorbed the positive externalities and spillovers created by FDI, which transferred important technology, skills, and capital as well as the marketing and quality control expertise needed to penetrate international markets. As a manager from a leading multinational corporation confirmed, these demonstration and linkage effects were especially valued by local partners: "The … foreign players that entered the market and often partnered with locals in various ways brought not necessarily capital but access to technology, markets, and know-how, which was what local producers were after." Krishnan and Foster (2017) confirm that Kenyan farmers involved in GVCs are more likely to be involved in innovation, mostly because of direct transfers of knowledge linked to GVC participation.

Linking to global buyers has proved to be an excellent training ground in which local producers can meet standards and internationalize (box 6.3). This case study also highlights the importance of external retail demand and international standards in enabling local firms to accumulate not only production but also end-market capabilities. This effect became evident as the supermarket revolution provided Kenyan horticulture producers more independence from their previous sales channels, allowing them to build more direct relationships with global retailers. As a result, a new group of smaller local firms, often in niche segments, entered the GVC through subcontracting arrangements.

Also critical to the success of Kenyan horticulture have been the country's competitive ecosystem and a policy environment that encourages business initiative. Predictable and noninterventionist public governance has left investors confident that they can reap the benefits of their long-term investments. Additionally, the country's targeted efforts to link smallholder farmers to high-value urban and export markets have done much to reduce poverty. Because horticulture value chains require economies of scale, the right balance between promoting smallholders and developing large-scale and capital-intensive farms is paramount for competitiveness. This balance is usually best left to the private sector because horticulture products are too diverse, too risky, and too fast-changing for the public sector to effectively prescribe their production structures (Minot and Ngigi 2004). However, policy support has proven effective at (a) establishing high-quality research and extension services and institutions, (b) promoting standards and certification, and (c) facilitating access to finance (Kaiser Associates Economic Development Partners 2014). Also, credible national infrastructure for quality measurement that conducts audits, provides certification,

BOX 6.3 **The role of the three L's—labeling, linking, and learning—in firm internationalization**

Global value chain (GVC) participation fosters the internationalization of local firms through three channels: labeling, linking, and learning. Pietrobelli and Rabellotti (2011) find that GVC participation drives innovation in low-income countries by pushing firms to adhere to standards to access international markets. For example, farmers may adopt rainwater harvesting techniques to achieve environmental standards or adopt new seed varieties to ensure their produce is attractive to consumers abroad. This sort of "frugal" innovation is just as important to their livelihoods as disruptive mechanization technologies (Raina et al. 2009). As a local horticulture producer explained, "Product or process improvements trickle down as farmers observe what their neighbors are doing."

The Kenyan horticulture sector reflects the importance as well as the interconnectedness of these three channels (Krishnan and Foster 2017). *Labeling* refers to standards or certifications that codify market demand and focus upgrading efforts, and thus are key tools for improving productivity. *Linking*, defined as forming relationships between actors along the value chain, is especially important in the agriculture sector, in which local farmers are fundamental to foreign firms' operations. Trust, reflected in the longevity and strength of their relational ties, affects the intensity of their link. *Learning*, the acquisition, accumulation, and appropriation of tacit and explicit knowledge, forms an integral part of innovation and is determined by the way networks operate and interlink. Kenyan farmers linked to GVCs innovate more because they adhere to international labels, benefit from stronger linkages, and have access to more forms of learning (Krishnan and Foster 2017).

Foreign firms tend to support local farms via supply chain relationships, and labor market linkages diffuse new skills across networks. Survey results[a] show that nearly all foreign-owned agricultural investors help local firms by providing inputs and materials, advance payments, and support for quality assurance and standards adherence. Providing access to funding and financing, worker training, and help in identifying export opportunities is also relatively common in Kenya. This assistance helped local suppliers upgrade, and these suppliers were then able to leverage their FDI relationships to access new customers (often through referrals). In fact, about 50 percent of Kenyan firms indicate that they became exporters after first supplying a foreign-owned firm within the country. Also, individual employees who had worked for foreign companies in-country were more likely to start new operations. On average, 80 percent of Kenya's skilled staff today are local employees, which reflects the long tradition of the horticulture sector in the country. Furthermore, about 10 percent of all employees at Kenyan firms have previous experience with foreign operations (Kaiser Associates Economic Development Partners 2014).

Source: This analysis is based on a combination of literature reviews and interviews conducted by the authors between January and March 2020 with representatives of multinational corporations, domestic firms, and trade associations affiliated with the Kenyan horticultural industry, as well as government officials; the interviews are the source for direct quotations that are not otherwise attributed.

a. This survey, presented in Kaiser Associates Economic Development Partners (2014), reached out to foreign- and domestic-owned agricultural firms in Ghana, Kenya, Mozambique, and Vietnam.

and prevents diseases from spreading has been essential to establishing trust with international buyers and facilitating local upgrading.

The unprecedented disruptions of 2019–20 are forcing horticulture producers and the Kenyan government to reflect on the current state of the sector. Hobbled by the triple impact of flooding, locust infestations, and the COVID-19 (coronavirus)

BOX 6.4 Impact of COVID-19 (coronavirus) on Kenya's horticulture sector

Amid the initial economic shocks of the COVID-19 (coronavirus) pandemic, horticulture in Kenya has been resilient so far. At the onset of the pandemic, demand and consumption sharply decreased because of containment measures and supply chain disruptions. With inward- and outward-bound flights grounded, trade was paralyzed, and export sales eroded. Although the initial trade shock caused by the COVID-19 crisis looked dramatic at first (Roussi 2020), research by Mold and Mveyange (2020) reveals that domestic horticulture exports have actually performed extraordinarily well under the circumstances, showing incremental growth since 2019, while reexports and imports have been hit worse.

The strong export performance of tea and certain horticulture products underscores the diverse sectoral impacts of the COVID-19 crisis. Of Kenya's three largest export product categories, food and beverage exports increased while the others declined markedly (Smartfarmer Digital 2020). Kenya's coffee, tea, and fruits exports all grew in the second and third quarters of 2020 despite the pandemic. Tea exports grew nearly 40 percent and 20 percent in the second and third quarters of 2020, respectively, compared with the same period in 2019; and fruit exports more than doubled in the second quarter of 2020 (figure B6.4.1). In contrast, flowers, a luxury product, saw demand crash in the second quarter of 2020 as ceremonies such as weddings and funerals were restricted during lockdown. Cut flower exports almost halved in the second quarter of 2020 compared with the first quarter. As of May 2020, 30,000 temporary workers in this sector have been let go and 40,000 permanent workers have been furloughed (Pais, Jayaram, and van Wamelen 2020). However, cut flower exports rebounded in the third quarter as global mobility restrictions eased. The only major category that has not recovered since the pandemic began is vegetables.

FIGURE B6.4.1 Kenyan agricultural commodity exports, 2019–20

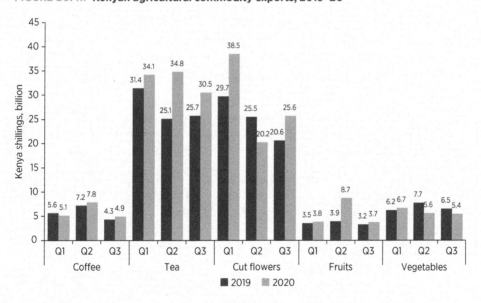

Source: World Bank calculations based on data from Kenya Central Bank data.

Continued on next page ›

BOX 6.4 Impact of COVID-19 on Kenya's horticulture sector *(continued)*

Although Kenyan businesses adapted quickly to the COVID-19 crisis with innovative solutions, the long-term impact of this complex crisis is hard to predict. Twiga Foods, for instance, responded with a new partnership with e-commerce platform Jumia to deliver bundles of fruits and vegetables directly to people's homes. This partnership provided higher-quality produce than local markets, but did so at lower prices than offered by supermarkets (Roussi 2020). In another example, Kenya Airways has converted grounded passenger planes into freighters to sustain exports of tea and horticulture (Kimuyu 2020). Kenyan producers have been quick to develop new markets, create new revenue streams and outlets for small farmers, and push the value chain to digitalize. However, the decline of capital and consumer goods imports might have a dampening effect on the sector's long-term growth. Should local producers manage to fill the void created by reduced imports, they could also help revitalize national and regional industrialization. With restrictions on movement, digital interaction between farmers and value chain partners has become more important than ever—and it could provide the "new spark" Kenya has been searching for to sustain its competitiveness in horticulture.

Note: Box reflects information as of October 2020.

pandemic (box 6.4), Kenya's horticulture industry is under pressure. As it rebounds, public and private actors should examine ways to ensure that the sector builds back stronger. Kenya's horticulture success relies on the country's land quality and structure, infrastructure and trading position, and capacity for innovation (IFC 2019). However, these advantages, and the benefits of GVC participation, are increasingly at risk because of regulatory, economic, and environmental challenges. The following are some proposals to policy makers:

- Address sector-specific barriers and draw in private investment by (a) improving competition in the input and transportation sectors; (b) realizing the value-addition potential of crops through better farmers' organizations, extension services, and research and development support; and (c) strengthening the environmental sustainability of horticulture production.

- Support firms' internationalization and participation in GVCs by (a) fostering firm productivity, standards compliance, and technology use; (b) facilitating market linkages and value chain finance and insurance; and (c) improving export promotion and product diversification.

- Facilitate FDI entry and partnerships by (a) reducing the risk and cost of doing business caused by policy unpredictability and the regulatory burden, (b) better aligning the country's FDI policy with its development goals, and (c) removing discrepancies in the regulatory and institutional framework.

Participation in the horticulture GVC has been important for Kenya's economic development. Through this participation, the country was able to increase its export performance as well as employment and income. Like most developing countries, Kenya has had more success with upgrading into the packing segment, but most processing remains outside of Kenya. As the horticulture GVC becomes increasingly saturated and market opportunities become less plentiful, Kenyan producers are under pressure to rethink their path to future growth and to develop a new vision for the future.

Notes

1. The analysis in this case study is based on a combination of literature reviews and interviews conducted by the authors between January and March 2020 with representatives of multinational corporations, domestic firms, and trade associations affiliated with the Kenyan horticultural industry, as well as government officials; the interviews are the source for all direct quotations included in this chapter that are not otherwise attributed.
2. The world's 25 largest agricultural input providers are based in developed countries. Eight of these firms are headquartered in the United States, three in Germany, and two each in Denmark, Japan, Norway, and Switzerland (UNCTAD 2009).
3. For more information on the Olivado partnership, see "Olivado in Kenya" (https://www .olivado.com/the-story/kenya).
4. According to McCulloch and Ota (2002) and Weinberger and Lumpkin (2007), net farm income among smallholder farmers that produced horticulture products for export has been four to five times higher per family member than among similar smallholders not producing horticulture products.
5. For information on one such program, funded by the United States Agency for International Development (USAID), see "Kenya Horticulture Competitiveness Project" (https://partnerships.usaid.gov/partnership/kenya-horticulture-competitiveness-project-khcp).
6. Krishnan (2017) shows that most farmers selling domestically still followed about 70 percent of the Global Good Agricultural Practices standards.
7. Interview with a production manager of a large foreign-owned horticulture exporter in March 2020.
8. For more information on these firms, see "AgriTech Startups in Nairobi" (https://tracxn.com/explore/AgriTech-Startups-in-Nairobi) and Apollo Agriculture (https://www.apolloagriculture.com/).

References

Azizi, Sameer Ahmad. 2020. "Kenyan-Owned Firms in the Floriculture Global Value Chain: A Multi-level Analysis of the Historical Development of Local Firms." CAE Working Paper 2020/2, Centre of African Economies, Roskilde University, Roskilde, Denmark.

Bates, Robert. 2005. *Beyond the Miracle of the Market: The Political Economy of Agrarian Development in Kenya.* Cambridge, U.K.: Cambridge University Press.

Boulanger, P., H. Dudu, E. Ferrari, A. J. Mainar Causapé, J. Balié, and L. Battaglia. 2018. *Policy Options to Support the Agriculture Sector Growth and Transformation Strategy in Kenya.* Luxembourg: Publications Office of the European Union.

COLEACP (Europe-Africa-Caribbean-Pacific Liaison Committee). 2001. "EU Imports of Fresh Fruit and Vegetables from 1994 to 2000". COLEACP Pesticides Initiative. Paris, France.

Dijkstra, T. 1997. *Trading the Fruits of the Land: Horticultural Marketing Channels in Kenya.* Aldershot, U.K.: Ashgate Press.

Dolan, C., and J. Humphrey. 2000. "Governance and Trade in Fresh Vegetables: The Impact of UK Supermarkets on the African Horticulture Industry." *Journal of Development Studies* 37 (2): 147–76.

Dolan, C., and J. Humphrey. 2004. "Changing Governance Patterns in the Trade in Fresh Vegetables between Africa and the United Kingdom." *Environment and Planning* 36 (3): 491–509.

Dolan, C., J. Humphrey, and C. Harris-Pascal. 1999. *Horticultural Commodity Chains: The Impact of the UK Market on the African Fresh Vegetable Industry.* Sussex, U.K.: Institute for Development Studies.

English, P., S. Jaffee, and J. Okello. 2004. "Exporting out of Africa – Kenya's Horticulture Success Story." Case study for Scaling Up Poverty Reduction: A Global Learning Process and Conference, Shanghai, May 25–27.

Evans, R. K. 1999. "From Small Farms to Supermarkets." Homegrown Ltd., Nairobi, Kenya.

Evers, B., M. Opondo, S. Barrientos, A. Krishnan, F. Amoding, and L. Ndlovu. 2014. "Global and Regional Supermarkets: Implications for Producers and Workers in Kenyan and Ugandan Horticulture." Working Paper 39, Capturing the Gains, University of Manchester, U.K.

Farole, T., and D. Winkler, eds. 2014. *Making Foreign Direct Investment Work for Sub-Saharan Africa: Local Spillovers and Competitiveness in Global Value Chains.* Washington, DC: World Bank.

Fernandez-Stark, K., P. Bamber, and G. Gereffi. 2011. "The Fruit and Vegetable Global Value Chain: Economic Upgrading and Workforce Development." Center on Globalization, Governance, and Competitiveness, Duke University, Durham, NC.

Fintrac Inc. 2014. "Global Competitiveness Study: Benchmarking Kenya's Horticulture Sector for Enhanced Export Competitiveness." Kenya Horticulture Competitiveness Project, United States Agency for International Development, Washington, DC.

Gertz, G. 2008. "Kenya's Trade Liberalization of the 1980s and 1990s: Policies, Impacts, and Implications." Background paper, "The Impact of the Doha Round on Kenya," Carnegie Endowment for International Peace, Washington, DC.

Golubski, Christine. 2017. "Africa in the News: Nakumatt's Bankruptcy Woes, Senegal's New Airport, and Cameroon's Growing Crisis." *Africa in Focus* (blog), December 8, 2017. https://www.brookings.edu/blog/africa-in-focus/2017/12/08/africa-in-the-news-nakumatts-bankruptcy-woes-senegals-new-airport-and-cameroons-growing-crisis/.

Government of Kenya. 2012. "National Horticulture Policy 2012." Government of Kenya, Nairobi, Kenya.

Humphrey, J., N. McCulloch, and M. Ota. 2004. "The Impact of European Market Changes on Employment in the Kenyan Horticulture Sector." *Journal of International Development* 16 (1): 63–80.

IFC (International Finance Corporation). 2019. *Creating Markets in Kenya: Unleashing Private Sector Dynamism to Achieve Full Potential.* Country Private Sector Diagnostic. Washington, DC: International Finance Corporation.

Jaffee, S. 1992. "How Private Enterprise Organized Agricultural Markets in Kenya." Policy Research Working Paper 823, World Bank, Washington, DC.

Jaffee, S., and O. Masakure. 2005. "Strategic Use of Private Standards to Enhance International Competitiveness: Vegetable Exports from Kenya and Elsewhere." *Food Policy* 30 (3): 316–33.

Kaiser Associates Economic Development Partners. 2014. "Sector Case Study Agribusiness." In *Making Foreign Direct Investment Work for Sub-Saharan Africa: Local Spillovers and Competitiveness in Global Value Chains,* edited by T. Farole and D. Winkler, 163–207. Washington, DC: World Bank Group.

Kenya HCD (Horticulture Crops Directorate). 2019. "Horticulture – Validated Report 2017–2018." Kenya Agriculture and Food Authority, Nairobi.

Kimuyu, Hilary. 2020. "Kenya: COVID-19: KQ Converts Passenger Planes into Cargo Freighters." AllAfrica, April 13, 2020. https://allafrica.com/stories/202004140083.html.

Koigi, Bob. 2016. "EU Policy on Kenyan Exports Creating a Local Health Crisis." Euractiv, December 12, 2016. https://www.euractiv.com/section/development-policy/news/eu-policy-on-kenyan-exports-creating-a-local-health-crisis/.

Krishnan, A. 2017. "The Origin and Expansion of Regional Value Chains: The Case of Kenyan Horticulture Global Networks." *Global Networks* 18 (2): 238–63.

Krishnan, Aarti, and Christopher Foster. 2017. "A Quantitative Approach to Innovation in Agricultural Value Chains: Evidence from Kenyan Horticulture." *European Journal of Development Research* 30 (1): 108–35.

McCulloch, N., and M. Ota. 2002. "Export Horticulture and Poverty in Kenya." IDS Working Paper 174, Institute of Development Studies, Brighton, U.K.

Minot, N., and M. Ngigi. 2004. "Are Horticultural Exports a Replicable Success Story? Evidence from Kenya and Côte d'Ivoire." EPTD Discussion Paper, International Food Policy Research Institute, Washington, DC.

Mold, A., and A. Mveyange. 2020. "The Impact of the COVID-19 Crisis on Trade. Recent Evidence from East Africa." Africa Growth Initiative Policy Brief, Brookings Institution,

Washington, DC. https://www.brookings.edu/wp-content/uploads/2020/07/EAC_COVID _Mold_Mveyange.pdf.

Moran, T. H. 2018. "FDI and Supply Chains in Horticulture (Vegetables, Fruits, and Flowers, Raw Packaged, Cut and Processed): Diversifying Exports and Reducing Poverty in Africa, Latin America, and Other Developing Economies." Working Paper 475, Center for Global Development, Washington, DC.

Muchira, Njiraini. 2019. "EU Steps Up Monitoring of Horticulture Imports." *The East African*, November 17, 2019. https://www.theeastafrican.co.ke/tea/business /eu-steps-up-monitoring-of-horticulture-imports-1431054.

Mwangi, N. 2018. "The Power to Flourish: Unearthing the Roots of Kenyan Flower Producers' Market Access Strategies." PhD thesis, Cambridge University.

Otieno, Gloria, and Peter Knorringa. 2012. "Localizing Global Standards. Illustrative Examples of Kenya's Horticulture Sector." In *Global Value Chains: Linking Local Producers from Developing Countries to International Markets*, edited by M. P. van Dijk and J. Trienekens, 119–36. Amsterdam: Amsterdam University Press.

Pais, Gillian, Kartik Jayaram, and Arend van Wamelen. 2020. "Safeguarding Africa's Food Systems through and beyond the Crisis." McKinsey & Company.

Pietrobelli, C., and R. Rabellotti. 2011. "Global Value Chains Meet Innovation Systems: Are There Learning Opportunities for Developing Countries?" *World Development* 39 (7): 1261–69.

Raina, R. S., K. J. Joseph, E. Haribabu, and R. Kumar. 2009. "Agricultural Innovation Systems and the Coevolution of Exclusion in India." Working Paper SIID-07/2009, Systems of Innovation for Inclusive Development Project.

Reardon, T., C. P. Timmer, C. B. Barrett, and J. Berdegué. 2003. "The Rise of Supermarkets in Africa, Asia and Latin America." *American Journal of Agricultural Economics* 85 (5): 1140–46.

Roussi, Antoaneta. 2020. "Kenya Farmers Face Uncertain Future as Covid-19 Cuts Exports to EU." *Financial Times*, June 4, 2020. https://www.ft.com/content /05284de8-c19f-46de-9fe7-482689be364b.

Smartfarmer Digital. 2020. "Good News for Flower and Horticulture Sectors." Smartfarmer Kenya, April 28, 2020. https://smartfarmerkenya.com/good-news-for-flower-and -horticulture-sectors/.

Tyce, M. 2020. "A 'Private-Sector Success Story'? Uncovering the Role of Politics and the State in Kenya's Horticultural Export Sector." *Journal of Development Studies* 56 (10): 1877–93.

UNCTAD (United Nations Conference on Trade and Development). 2009. *World Investment Report 2009: Transnational Corporations, Agricultural Production and Development*. Geneva: UNCTAD.

Waitathu, Nicholas. 2014. "Fresh Produce Farmers, Firms Banned from European Union." *The Standard*, August 12, 2014. https://www.standardmedia.co.ke/article/2000131207 /fresh-produce-farmers-firms-banned-from-european-union-market.

Weinberger, K., and T. A. Lumpkin. 2007. "Diversification into Horticulture and Poverty Reduction: A Research Agenda." *World Development* 35 (8): 1464–80.

Whitaker, M., and S. Kolavalli. 2006. "Floriculture in Kenya." In *Technology, Adaptation, and Exports: How Some Developing Countries Got It Right*, edited by V. Chandra, 335. Washington, DC: World Bank.

World Bank. 1989. *Successful Development in Africa: Case Studies of Projects, Programs, and Policies*. Washington, DC: World Bank.

World Bank. 2020. *World Development Report 2020: Trading for Development in the Age of Global Value Chains*. Washington, DC: World Bank.

Chapter 7

Honduras—Using maquilas and international agreements to boost the garment industry

MONICA PAGANINI AND VICTOR STEENBERGEN

Summary

This case study examines the role of foreign direct investment (FDI) in Honduras in the textile and apparel global value chain (GVC). The study shows how the Honduran government's establishment of special economic zones (SEZs) for export-oriented production, known as *maquilas*, and signing of preferential trade and investment agreements jointly helped attract foreign investment and led to the development of the Honduran textile and apparel industry. The Honduran SEZ program was formally established in 1976. After a slow start, it took off in the early 1990s as more foreign manufacturers moved their labor-intensive operations serving the US market to Honduras. The government established maquilas as geographically limited enclaves with dedicated infrastructure, streamlined public administration, and generous fiscal incentives to attract FDI. A series of trade and investment agreements helped lower the cost of importing raw materials and enabled duty-free exports to the US market for certain textile and apparel goods. As a result, this small Central American republic managed to become a leading exporter of textile and apparel products to the United States.

Honduras's role in the global textile and apparel value chain

The global textile and apparel value chain

The textile and apparel value chain is characterized by a highly globalized production and trade network.[1] The industry is identified as a buyer-driven value chain, a feature common in labor-intensive GVCs. Its lead firms tend to have extensive global sourcing capabilities and to perform the most valuable activities in the value chain themselves, and they are typically headquartered in the leading markets—Europe, Japan, and the United States. A complex network of contractors in developing countries carries out the production stages, making finished goods for foreign buyers, and the large retailers or marketers that order these goods supply their specifications (Fernandez-Stark, Frederick, and Gereffi 2011).

The textile and apparel GVC is also highly consumer driven. Given the global demand for textiles and the variety of specifications required by consumers (such as size, suitability for various occupations and types of weather, and cultural and personal preferences), along with the relatively low unit price of each garment, the industry is among the least concentrated. Global buyers decide what is to be produced, where, by whom, and at what price. Consequently, many lead firms have to rapidly adjust their production to meet consumer tastes, and they tend to outsource the manufacturing process to a global network of suppliers (Fernandez-Stark, Frederick, and Gereffi 2011).

Conventional textile manufacturing consists of a long process to convert natural fibers into useful products such as fabric, home textiles, and apparel. Technical textiles, made with the use of special finishing effects, require a process with yet more steps. The processing stages in textile manufacturing, from fiber production to finished fabrics, are continuously subject to enhancements in process control and evaluation.

The textile value chain comprises a number of networks and components, which can be organized into five main parts (figure 7.1). Its production process involves processing raw materials, creating components such as fabrics and textiles, producing apparel, exporting and logistics, and, finally, marketing the apparel. From an activities viewpoint, Honduran firms work primarily to assemble final products (cutting and sewing), with activities outside of manufacturing (design, branding, sourcing and logistics coordination, and sales and customer acquisition) performed elsewhere (Bamber and Frederick 2018). The different stages can be described as follows:

- *Input supply.* The product at this stage usually consists of various natural or artificial fibers (yarn or thread). These fibers may be processed or unprocessed. Most of the time, the raw material from which this fiber is made is a natural resource such as cotton, oil, or rubber.

- *Component network.* This stage involves the processing of the fibers. The product is manufactured mainly from imported components or raw materials. The main activities at this stage are spinning yarn, weaving, knitting, and finishing fabric.

FIGURE 7.1 The textile and apparel value chain

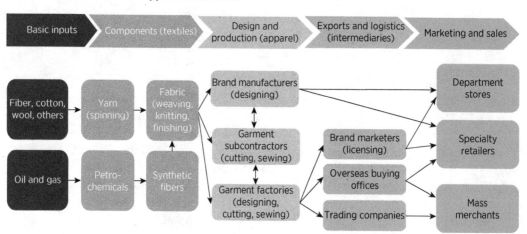

Source: World Bank elaboration of Frederick 2010, Gereffi and Frederick 2010, and Gereffi and Memedovic 2003.

- *Production network.* At this stage apparel manufacturers, such as garment factories or garment subcontractors, design, cut, and sew the fabrics produced.

- *Export networks and logistics.* Some garment firms sell their finished products directly to wholesalers (such as overseas buying offices or trading companies) or to retailers. In other cases, brand marketers collect final products and conduct quality inspections before selling the goods to department stores or retailers.

- *Marketing and services.* This final stage includes the marketing and retail sales of apparel products.

Lead firms in the contemporary textile and apparel GVC have significant market power. This power is reflected in their size (as measured by sales) and in the combination of high-value activities they carry out, including design, marketing, consumer services, and logistics.

Four types of lead firms dominate the value chain: mass merchants, specialty retailers, brand marketers, and brand manufacturers (Gereffi and Memedovic 2003). Each type of firm has its own brands and operates in its own part of the value chain (table 7.1). The retailer category is divided between mass merchants (such as Walmart) that sell a diverse array of products and specialty retailers (such as H&M) that sell only apparel items. Such companies do not own their manufacturing facilities; rather, they license final products with their own branding. Brand marketers (such as Nike) source their products through original equipment manufacturers or full-package producers. The buyer provides detailed garment specifications, and the supplier is responsible for acquiring the inputs and coordinating all parts of the production process: purchasing textiles, cutting pieces, assembling garments, washing and finishing them, and packaging and distributing them. Finally, brand manufacturers (such as Zara) are actively involved in manufacturing and directly coordinate the supply of intermediate inputs to their production networks (Gereffi and Frederick 2010).

Since the 2007 global financial crisis, top exporter countries in the textile and apparel GVC have begun to focus on their domestic markets to avoid the slowdown in global exports. This shift aims to accelerate the process of upgrading from assembly and full-package supply to original design manufacturing and

TABLE 7.1   **Brand types and lead firms**

Brand type	Lead firm type	Sample firms
Private label Firm owns or licenses branded products but does not own the manufacturing of these products.	**Mass merchant** Department stores that carry private labels or licensed brands that are available exclusively in their stores.	Marks & Spencer, Target, Tesco, Walmart
	Specialty retailer Retailers that develop labels that include their name.	Gap, H&M, Limited Brands, Next
National brand Firm develops labels that include its name.	**Brand marketer** Firms that own brand name but do not manufacture branded products ("manufacturers without factories"). Products are sold at a variety of retail outlets.	Diesel, Hugo Boss, Levi's, Nike
	Brand manufacturer Firms that own brand names and manufacturing. They typically coordinate a supply of intermediate inputs to their production networks to sell their products in the home or neighboring countries.	Fruit of the Loom, Zara

Source: Gereffi and Frederick 2010.

original brand manufacturing. Although many apparel manufacturers have quality management or ISO (International Organization for Standardization) 9000 standard certifications, the importance of product and process standards is comparatively low in this sector because apparel does not pose a significant health or safety risk to users (Bamber and Frederick 2018). The distribution of production networks and buyer-supplier relationships in this GVC has been driven by tariffs, trade and investment agreements, and government intervention in the textile and apparel supply chain. Import tariffs on apparel products are among the highest for all imported goods in key consuming markets such as Europe and the United States.

Honduras's participation in the textile and apparel value chain

Participation in the global textile and apparel value chain generally requires the presence of three factors: favorable trade and investment agreements, low-cost labor, and proximity to end markets (Keane and te Velde 2008). Building on these three factors through designated economic processing zones, locally referred to as maquilas, Honduras has been able to attract several large textile and apparel manufacturers into the country and has started participating in the value chain. Honduras fares well among the top 10 apparel suppliers to the United States. The apparel producers' cost in Honduras is US$2.78 per unit (measured in square meter equivalents), making it the fifth-cheapest supplier to the United States. Additionally, relative to its major competitors and neighbors (such as El Salvador and Guatemala), labor costs in Honduras remain competitive even with an increase of 7 percent in its minimum wage.

Honduras's participation in the textile and apparel GVC is concentrated in the components and production phases. The Honduran market for textiles is relatively small, and local companies have little expertise in branding, marketing, or retailing. Although the country's supply chain participation expanded over time (from basic sewing to cutting, dyeing and washing, trimming, finishing products, and producing fabrics and yarn), Honduras still relies mainly on low-cost labor working in the cutting and sewing stages of apparel production (Bamber and Frederick 2018). Despite some local production of fabrics, many firms rely on imported fabrics (often from the United States[2]) to produce apparel (Bilandzic et al. 2007). Most Honduran products are then exported on to lead firms (brand marketers, wholesalers, or retail companies) in Central America or the United States.

Honduras exports a wide range of textile and apparel products. The country is one of Latin America's leading exporters of textile products (including silk, wool, cotton, vegetable textile fibers, human-made filaments, wadding, carpets, special woven products, and textile fabrics). In 2017, Honduras exported about US$15 billion in apparel articles, split between general apparel, knitted wear, human-made filaments, and other types of textiles (figure 7.2). With regard to specific articles, Honduras is the top T-shirt exporter, the second-largest exporter of sweatshirts, and the fifth-largest exporter of cotton shirts to the United States (AHM 2018). Honduras is also the third-largest exporter of knitted garments to the United States, making it the largest exporter in this category after the "big two" clothing exporters, China and Vietnam. Knit T-shirts alone make up 16 percent of Honduras's total exports, exceeding the share of coffee, and knit sweaters make up 13 percent. Honduras's preferential

FIGURE 7.2 **Honduran textile and apparel exports, 1994–2017**

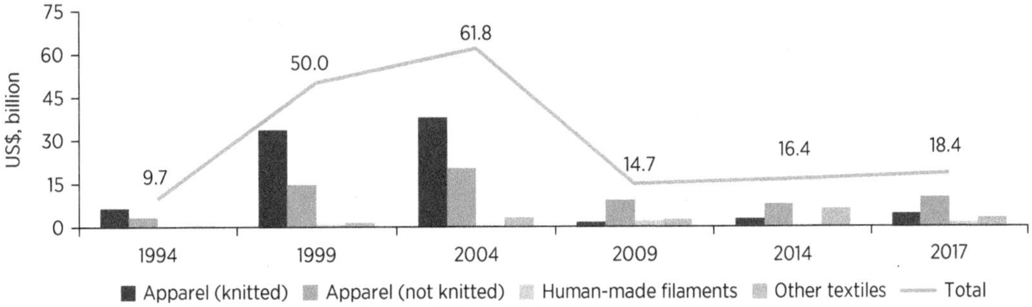

Source: World Bank elaborations on United Nations Comtrade data.

treatment by the United States has pushed the country to advance in the components and production phases of the textile value chain, making Honduran employees highly specialized in low-skilled activities, particularly sewing. However, the presence of large brands in the country has led it to expand into the exporting and marketing phases by implementing higher standards for employee work and for productivity, driving domestic innovation.

The textile and apparel industry constitutes an important part of the Honduran economy. In 2018, 127 textile and apparel firms were located in Honduras's maquilas, with an export volume of US$3.5 billion. Jointly, these firms made up 82.5 percent of maquila exports (Central Bank of Honduras 2018). Of this export volume, approximately US$660 million was exported to the United States. Many of these factories are subsidiaries of large US companies and supply high volumes of relatively simple inputs, with little value added locally. Maquilas overall account for more than 26 percent of Honduras's total manufacturing sector output and make up 4.4 percent of total gross domestic product (GDP) (Central Bank of Honduras 2018). The maquilas employ about 7,500 workers, or 30 percent of the labor force of the Honduran manufacturing industry (Central Bank of Honduras 2018).

Honduras's concentration in narrow segments of the textile and apparel GVC leaves the country vulnerable. The spread of the textile and apparel industry through Honduras's maquilas has brought many new opportunities and increased employment. However, the industry's dependence on imported inputs and its narrow concentration in the components and production phases have made the country susceptible to global supply shocks. This concentration is also gradually decreasing Honduras's general competitiveness and reducing its pool of investors. The low-skilled workforce available forces maquilas toward more traditional garment and assembly operations and prevents them from developing more sophisticated textile products. To further upgrade its activities in the textile and apparel GVC, Honduras needs to strengthen the quality of its workforce. It may also need to attract more investors in higher-value segments (such as design, marketing, consumer services, and logistics) to help further expand its economic activity into additional stages of the GVC.

The development of Honduras's textile and apparel industry

Honduras's involvement in the textile and apparel GVC can be divided into three phases (figure 7.3):

- *Phase 1: Inception* (mid-1960s to late 1980s). Honduras's textile and apparel industry entered the GVC when the country established its first maquilas and enacted its first investment laws in favor of export-oriented companies. This change attracted some FDI and allowed established export-oriented companies to develop further.

- *Phase 2: Strong expansion* (late 1980s to mid-2000s). A combination of a more active maquila industry, several trade and investment agreements, and fiscal incentives led to a large inflow of FDI. As a result, the textile and apparel industry grew rapidly and became the largest exporter and the largest manufacturing employer in Honduras.

- *Phase 3: Stagnation amid increased competition* (mid-2000s to today). Following the global financial crisis, both FDI inflows and the share of Honduran exports derived from textiles and apparel started to stagnate. Greater regional competition led to a further loss of competitiveness for Honduras's maquilas.

These three phases also show the important role that FDI inflows played in the export development of Honduras's textile and apparel industry (figure 7.4). During the inception phase, Honduras saw very limited inflows of FDI. However, in phase 2, overall FDI inflows increased from about 1.0 percent of GDP in 1988 to 8.7 percent in 2008. Following the financial crisis (phase 3), aggregate FDI inflows declined dramatically (to 3.4 percent in 2009). Although most FDI inflows

FIGURE 7.3 The three stages of Honduras's textile and apparel industry, 1965–2017

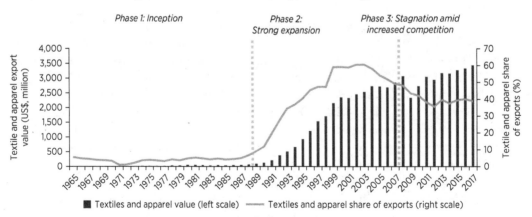

Source: World Bank elaborations on United Nations Comtrade data.
Note: Exports include textile fibers (SITC 26), yarn products (SITC 65), and apparel and clothing (SITC 84). SITC = Standard International Trade Classification.

FIGURE 7.4 **Total foreign direct investment flows into Honduras, 1970–2018**

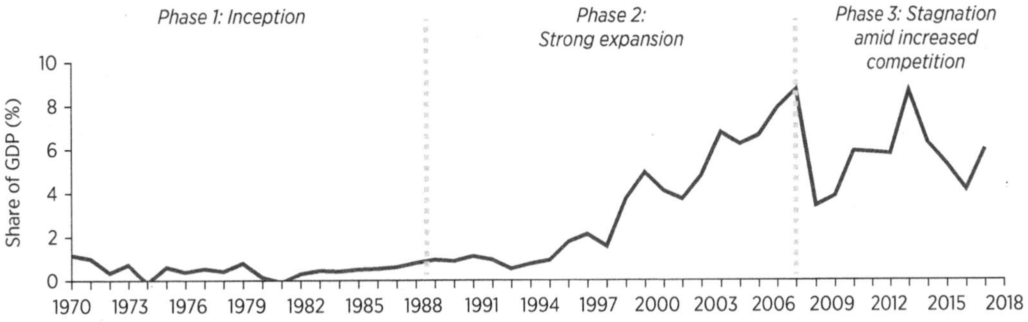

Source: World Bank elaboration on World Development Indicators data.
Note: Foreign direct investment includes many sectors other than textiles and apparel.

initially went to the maquilas, stagnation led to a decline in their share of FDI. In 2015, only US$160 million out of US$850 million in FDI (19 percent) flowed to the maquilas (WTO Secretariat 2016).

Phase 1: Inception (mid-1960s–late 1980s)

In 1976, the country established its first SEZ-maquila program with the First Free Zone Law. (Free zones are also known as ZOLIs, for *zonas libres*.) This law established dedicated infrastructure for the maquilas and ensured that they could streamline public administration and offer fiscal incentives to attract FDI and technology for labor-intensive and export-oriented production. Companies operating under the free zone status had to be involved in the mechanical, physical, or chemical processing of raw materials or semiprocessed or finished goods and export at least 95 percent of their annual output; in return, they were allowed several incentives (including exemption from the payment of duties, charges, and consular fees for a 15-year period).[3] The zone covered a publicly owned enclave near Puerto Cortés and was later extended in 1979 to include other counties (Amapala, Choloma, La Ceiba, Omoa, and Tela). The law distinguished between "industrial companies" and "commercial and trading companies." Free zone status was allowed only to the latter, which "primarily engaged in export activities" and allocated "no less than 50 percent of annual sales to export or re-export." Although this law was neutral as to the country of origin of investors, in practice only foreign investors received the incentives, whereas local companies were not allowed to operate within the zones (Farole and Akinci 2011).

A range of preferential trade and investment agreements further helped establish textile and apparel production in Honduras. In the early 1970s, Honduras signed the Multi Fibre Arrangement, which helped establish quotas and preferential tariffs on apparel and textile items imported from Honduras by Canada, the United States, and many European nations. Then, in 1984, the Caribbean Basin Initiative (CBI) came into effect. This initiative, a unilateral and temporary program initiated by the United

States, offered preferential market access to clothing and apparel exports from several countries in the Caribbean and Central America. Through this program, Honduran producers did not have to pay duties on reexported inputs, such as textiles and fabrics of US origin. This change enabled manufacturers to conduct the most labor-intensive operation along the value chain (sewing) in lower-cost countries without having to pay import duties. In 1984, Honduras also passed the Temporary Importation Regulations Law, which allowed export-oriented companies with operations outside the free zones to import machinery and equipment free of duties. Although this policy aimed mainly to create a domestic base of suppliers, most of its beneficiaries were larger, export-oriented foreign companies (Engman 2011).

About this time, Honduras also began to prioritize public infrastructure and investment promotion. The government invested heavily in infrastructure, especially in roads between the city of San Pedro Sula and the maquila (Puerto Cortés). In addition, a national export and investment promotion agency, the Foundation for Investment and Development of Exports, was established in 1984. This agency aimed to promote investment in Honduras, develop the country's export markets, and work closely with the government and other private organizations to improve the country's business climate. It also supported entrepreneurs by facilitating their investment and exports, accomplished by establishing export promotion offices in the United States to expand Honduran producers' networks and connect them with leading US-based textile companies.

Phase 2: Strong expansion (late 1980s–mid-2000s)

The main catalyst for FDI in Honduras's textile and apparel industry came in 1987: the establishment of export processing zones (EPZs).[4] In 1987, Honduras enacted the EPZ law (also known as the ZIP law, for *zonas industriales de procesamiento*), which allowed privately owned and managed SEZs to be established anywhere in the country. Within these SEZs, exporting firms enjoyed duty-free entry into US markets for certain manufactured goods assembled there (including textiles and apparel).[5] This measure allowed the agglomeration of investors to take place on the basis of market factors rather than only within publicly designated areas, and it enabled domestic investors to act as catalysts for FDI. Domestic investors provided the up-front investments to establish and operate these industrial parks, which then attracted foreign investors. During this time, the government proved to be a key facilitator of domestic investment in the maquilas by setting up a program in which it bought loans at a premium from domestic firms suffering from debt crises in exchange for agreements to invest in free zones and other infrastructure (Farole and Akinci 2011).

Maquilas further developed with the establishment of the Asociación Hondureña de Maquiladores (AHM) in 1991. The AHM was founded to assist and support private investors and shape the business environment to further attract FDI. It actively lobbied the government to provide greater regulatory flexibility for the private sector within the SEZs. The changes it brought about allowed zone operators to strengthen the investment climates in their zones by ensuring that SEZ firms faced limited regulatory burdens and minimal government interference. The AHM is an industry body; its members pay US$1,000 to apply to join, followed by a US$110 monthly fee. Along with providing statistics about the maquila industry, it has six main functions (Bilandzic et al. 2007; Viery 2014):

1. Promote and stimulate the maquila industry.
2. Propose and negotiate the formulation and execution of national policies.
3. Develop international market programs to increase development.
4. Propose incentives for the industry, such as administrative or credit-related incentives.
5. Assess and guide associates to ensure that their products and services meet market standards.
6. Sustain relationships with international institutions whose interests parallel the AHM's.

A continuing set of trade and investment agreements reduced Honduras's trade costs even more. Honduras signed several preferential trade agreements during this period with its largest trading partner, the United States. In 1990, the Caribbean Basin Economic Recovery Expansion Act made the incentives in the CBI permanent, thereby ensuring duty-free access to the US market for most Honduran goods. Another important step came in 1994, when Honduras joined the World Trade Organization (WTO). This move further reduced trade costs by allowing Honduran producers to enjoy most-favored nation treatment, thereby receiving the best trade terms given by its trading partner to the other 152 members of the WTO. Additionally, in 1995 Honduras signed a bilateral investment treaty with the United States that aimed to protect US investments and to assist Honduras in developing its private sector and building a business environment to attract FDI. About the same time, Honduras signed several bilateral investment treaties with China, European countries, the Republic of Korea, and countries in Latin America such as Chile, Cuba, and Ecuador. Two other important trade agreements were passed in 2000. In that year, the United States signed the Caribbean Basin Trade Partnership Act (CBTPA), which extended preferential tariff treatment to garments assembled from US fabric (which had been excluded from the CBI). This change allowed for duty-free exports to the United States of garments that were made using US yarns and fabrics, which encouraged Honduran companies to use more local content in their production and led to significant Honduran investment in textile mills. Finally, in 2005, a free trade agreement was signed between the United States and regional actors; the Dominican Republic–Central America Free Trade Agreement (CAFTA-DR) spurred significant investment from the United States into Honduras (Janesen et al 2007).[6] As a result of its preferential access to the US market via CAFTA-DR and the CBTPA, Honduras became the seventh-largest apparel exporter to the United States (Engman 2011).

The EPZ law, the AHM, and trade policy jointly triggered investment from local entrepreneurs to develop the industrial parks; and they helped catalyze inflows of foreign investment, especially from North American multinationals. Domestic investors jointly established 23 industrial parks in Honduras, located mainly in the north of the country, that hosted 225 maquila firms. In the early 1990s, more than 52 percent of FDI into Honduras went to the maquilas, which accounted for more than 44 percent of all national investment (AHM 2018). The EPZ law and the AHM also helped many new foreign companies settle in the country. By 1998, more than 60 percent of all apparel firms in Honduras were foreign owned, and most of them were from North America or Asia (table 7.2). The textile and apparel industry also accounted for the country's largest source of FDI, receiving almost 64 percent of total FDI in the manufacturing sector over the period 2004–07 (table 7.3).

This phase was marked by the continuous growth of exports in the maquilas and a boom in job creation. SEZ exports expanded quickly, rising by a factor of approximately 10 between 1993 and 2006 in US dollars (Engman 2011). This growth continued until the third phase began in 2007. During this time, Honduras's producers started to excel at producing small orders for expedient delivery to the US market, taking advantage of their proximity to the United States and the speed to market it enabled.[7] This proximity was a key comparative advantage, given the rapid shifts in

TABLE 7.2   **Apparel firms in Honduras's maquilas, by origin, 1998**

Origin	Number	Share (%)
Foreign owned	125	62
North American	75	37
Asian	50	25
Honduran	67	33
Other (including joint ventures)	11	5
Total	203	100

Source: IBP USA 2001.

TABLE 7.3   **Foreign direct investment in manufacturing activities, 2004–07**
(US$, million)

Activity	2004	2005	2006	2007	Average share, 2004–07 (%)
Textiles	92.2	76.3	127.3	197.6	63.7
Input services	20.7	22.9	32.0	20.0	12 3
Commerce	–3.3	8.0	16.3	5.8	3.5
Agriculture and fishery	7.7	7.8	8.2	4.3	3.6
Cardboard products	3.8	3.3	–9.1	1.9	0
Plastic products	0	0.6	0.4	0.1	0.1
Chemical products	0	2.7	0	0	0.3
Furniture and wood products	0.5	–0.4	0.5	–1.5	–0.1
Tobacco	22.4	53	–0.1	–3.6	3.1
Electronic components	28.7	65.3	2.3	–5.3	11.7
Other industry	2.2	3.9	6.9	0.2	1.7
Total	174.9	195.8	184.7	219.6	

Source: Central Bank of Honduras 2007.
Note: Negative numbers indicate disinvestments in a particular sector.

consumers' tastes as well as retailers' efforts to minimize the cost of their inventory. According to the AHM, Honduras was the fourth-largest supplier of clothing products to the United States (with 5.9 percent market share) and the world's largest importer of US yarn. Out of all maquila workers, 77 percent were employed in the textile and clothing sector; this increase in employment boosted female participation and benefited low-skilled workers in the SEZs (Walker and Michel 2019).

However, the maquila model also led to a widening divide between the economies of the SEZs and the rest of the country. Qualifying for SEZ status required a certain minimum level of investment, employment creation, and export orientation. Even though Honduran enterprises were not formally excluded from the SEZs, in practice most small and medium enterprises were unable to meet these minimum conditions (Hernandez Ore, Sousa, and Lopez 2015). As a result, only large investors were able to obtain the extensive fiscal benefits (often with no sunset clauses) associated with the SEZs. In addition, maquila firms were allowed to pay workers less than the national minimum wage. As a result, the average market wages were about 25 percent lower in the SEZs than in the rest of the country (237 Honduran limperas per month in the maquilas versus 318 Honduran limperas per month in the rest of Honduras) (Viery 2014).

Backward linkages were further constrained by the rules of origin set out in many trade agreements. For instance, the CBI's rule of origin allowed local producers to export only a limited number of products. SEZs also established perverse incentives to import goods rather than use local products because imports were exempt from customs taxes or value added taxes whereas the government imposed a 12 percent tax on domestically produced inputs used in the maquilas. This difference created unfair competition and widened the divide between the SEZs and the domestic economy.

Phase 3: Stagnation amid increasing competition (mid-2000s–today)

The Honduran textile and apparel industry entered a third phase in the mid-2000s, when the industry faced increased global competition. Three global dynamics increased Honduras's competition. First, China's accession to the WTO in 2001 led to a large drop in that country's trade costs with the United States and caused a surge in Chinese exports to the American market (Liu and Gu 2007). At the same time, WTO rules around discriminatory trade practices meant that the Honduran government was forced to phase out its fiscal incentives scheme. Second, a range of other Asian countries, including Bangladesh, Cambodia, and Vietnam, started competing in the North American apparel market, which resulted in a global decline in apparel prices. Third, retail-oriented branded apparel chains (such as Zara) gained market power, shifting their strategy to a "fast fashion" model in which the value chain was leveraged to produce trendy, fashion-oriented apparel at affordable prices. This shift increased the importance of lead times and quality and resulted in some reshoring of production from Honduras to the producers' countries (such as Spain, in the case of Zara).

The business environment in Honduras continued to lose competitiveness in this period because of several negative shocks. The global economic downturn hit Honduras at the end of 2008, leading to significant appreciation of the domestic

FIGURE 7.5 Apparel exports and world export share, Honduras, 1987–2017

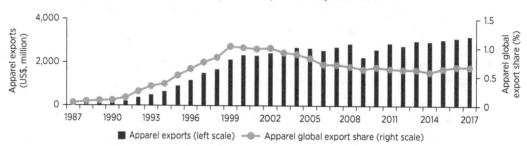

Source: World Bank elaborations on United Nations Comtrade data.
Note: Apparel is defined using Standard International Trade Classification 84 (apparel and clothing).

currency, the lempira, and affecting US sales of textiles and apparel—and thus most SEZ exports (figure 7.5). As a result, Honduras's global market share in apparel went from a high of 1.0 percent in the late 1990s to about 0.6 percent in 2017.[8] The downturn thus exacerbated the decline caused by Asian competition and the shift of US clothing assembly to Asia. These events exposed Honduras's vulnerability to global supply shocks and the country's dependence on imported inputs in light of its narrow concentration in the component and production phases. They also led to a significant drop in the number of employees at the maquilas, from 134,000 workers in 2007 to 100,000 workers in 2009 (Engman 2011). Many unemployed workers from the maquilas moved to the informal sector or left the country to seek employment in the United States.

During this period, Honduras initiated a range of interventions to help restore its economy. The Honduran constitution was amended, allowing for the creation of the State Secretariat for Economic Development, which replaced the State Secretariat for Industry and Trade, and established employment and economic development zones as administrative subdivisions in Honduran national territory. The country also entered into a wider selection of preferential trade and investment agreements with several Central American countries, Korea, Panama, and Peru. In addition, the National Investment Council was created as a public-private entity aiming to promote investment in several priority sectors, including textiles and apparel (WTO 2016).

Current challenges

Honduras still enjoys several advantages in textile and apparel production. Its maquilas currently see their success as based on a number of strengths:

- Proximity to the US southern and east coast markets

- Competitive labor costs and relatively high labor productivity compared with both neighboring countries and major exporting countries such as Bangladesh, China, and Vietnam (IFC, forthcoming)

- Preferential market access, secured by international trade and investment agreements such as CBTPA and CAFTA-DR

- Investment in port infrastructure that has led to efficient trade logistics[9]

- A critical mass of maquilas based around San Pedro Sula, forming clusters and economies of scale

- Several influential industrial families with long histories in textile and apparel production, leading to deep industrial knowledge and relational ties to global producers

However, the sector also faces several significant challenges. In the immediate term, the COVID-19 pandemic has had a major negative impact on the sector. The global shock caused by the pandemic initially led to a strong decline in Honduras's textile and apparel exports. However, the pandemic also brought new opportunities, most notably in the personal protective equipment (PPE) subsector. As a result, many apparel firms are adjusting their product portfolios to include more PPE production (box 7.1).

BOX 7.1 **The impact of COVID-19 (coronavirus) on Honduras's textile and apparel industry**

The COVID-19 (coronavirus) crisis has significantly affected the global textile and apparel industry. Because of the pandemic and the associated lockdowns, global demand for textiles and apparel has declined. This shift has forced many leading brands and retailers, including those that source significantly from Honduras, to cancel and delay orders. In addition, the sector faced several supply shocks when some global fabric suppliers initially closed their factories or reduced their suppliers, causing a ripple effect among the major apparel supplier countries. The resulting declines in worldwide apparel exports have been significant. According to the Office of Textiles and Apparel, US apparel imports from the world declined by 42.8 percent between March and May 2020.

In response to these developments, Honduras's textile and apparel exports declined rapidly. Honduras initially announced temporary factory closures. Many businesses eventually opened up again, but at severely reduced capacity. As one of the top 10 exporters of textiles and apparel to the United States, Honduras experienced a sharp initial decline in exports in April and May (figure B7.1.1). Production increased again from a low of US$19 million in April to US$247 million in October, reaching a level similar to that in 2019. However, in November Honduras adopted a second COVID-19 lockdown, which resulted in another considerable decline in exports compared with 2019.

However, the COVID-19 crisis also provided opportunities for apparel companies, most notably in the manufacture of personal protective equipment (PPE). Several factories have turned to producing PPE, especially masks and medical gowns, which has buffered the COVID-19 shock. Early in the pandemic, factories in Honduras were mandated by the government to produce 9 million masks for domestic use. An estimated 18 million masks have been produced so far, alongside a growing number of medical gowns.

Several companies have been able to use PPE production to increase their output. For example, Grupo Karim initially suffered a 12 percent reduction in orders because of the pandemic.

Continued on next page ›

BOX 7.1 **The impact of COVID-19 (coronavirus) on Honduras's textile and apparel industry** *(continued)*

FIGURE B7.1.1 **Honduran textile and apparel exports to the United States, 2019–20**

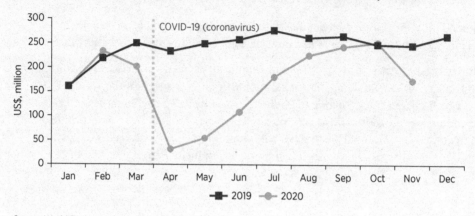

Source: World Bank calculations using United Nations Comtrade data.

However, it then gained new customers from the United States that sought PPE. The company secured orders from two large retailers, Staples and Kohl's, to supply masks. Similarly, the Kattan Group is aligning its production to a post-COVID-19 environment. It produces medical gowns, a business it has been able to expand because of increased demand in the United States. It has also begun making polypropylene gowns (which are easier to clean, a useful feature in a COVID-19 setting). The company recently signed a contract to supply 2 million gowns per month to a customer in the United States.

Honduras appears well placed to address opportunities to supply the US market with PPE. Although such orders account for a small percentage of their overall capacity, several apparel companies believe PPE will remain an important product for the foreseeable future. They also note that Honduras is well situated to serve the US market in general given its proximity and speed-to-market advantage. As a result, many apparel firms are readjusting their product portfolios to include more PPE in comparison with the traditional products that have been the sector's lifeblood.

Source: IFC, forthcoming (including interviews with Grupo Karim, EU Light Manufacturing, Elcatex [Elasticos Centroamericanos y Textiles], the Asociación Nacional de Industriales, and the Asociación Hondureña de Maquiladores).

The Honduran textile and apparel industry also faces some major challenges that need to be addressed in the medium term. Its dependence on imported inputs and its narrow concentration in the components and production phases have left the country vulnerable to global supply shocks, led to a gradual decline in general competitiveness, and reduced its pool of investors (Farole and Akinci 2011; USITC 2004). Honduras also needs to attract investors in higher-value segments, including design, marketing, consumer services, and logistics, to expand its economic activity to additional stages of the textile and apparel GVC.

Workforce training is needed beyond what is currently offered through the AHM and at the factory level. The maquilas still employ a very low-skilled workforce and remain focused on traditional garment and assembly operations, which prevents them from developing more sophisticated textile products. Under the AHM, some training has occurred.[10] More advanced training is also carried out by individual factories, with approximately 99 percent of the needed training delivered in-house. Nevertheless, as Honduras moves up the textile and apparel value chain to more advanced manufacturing processes, new training curricula—in soft skills such as professional, managerial, and technical skills—will be required (IFC, forthcoming).

Slow customs clearance is also cited as a continuing inhibitor of Honduras's participation in the textile and apparel GVC. Although Honduras's port is efficient, there are significant delays in customs in the broader region. These inefficiencies work against the speed-to-market advantage that Honduras enjoys with the United States. The Northern Triangle region of El Salvador, Guatemala, and Honduras needs to improve its customs administration through regional integration. Although Honduran customs has been integrated with that of El Salvador and Guatemala, this integration should be expanded to Nicaragua and other nearby countries. Companies also report that, although customs procedures at the regional borders are electronic in theory, in practice they are still paper based, which slows the clearance process (IFC, forthcoming).

Although the Honduran government has in recent years simplified the administrative procedures for establishing a company, bureaucratic red tape is still prevalent. According to the 2019 World Bank Doing Business Report (World Bank 2019), the average time required to start a business in Honduras is 13 days, and doing so requires 11 procedures. This measure also needs to be improved upon (IFC, forthcoming).

Furthermore, Honduras needs to reduce the cost and improve the reliability of its electricity service. At 15 US cents per kilowatt-hour on average, energy costs are high in Honduras. Given that energy costs represent approximately 10–15 percent of the average garment company's operating costs, this expense cuts into factories' cost competitiveness. Electricity distribution is also a problem, with much power lost from the grid. Frequent outages further increase costs and operating inefficiencies because of the need for backup generators. To fill the void in electricity provision, most companies also invest in their own supplemental energy, including by installing solar panels. In fact, Honduras has the most solar panels installed in Latin America. In some factories, 100 percent of roofs have solar installations (IFC, forthcoming). The Honduran government should liberalize the power sector to allow private competition to bring costs down.

Although the textile and apparel industry is a key priority for the Honduran government, it currently lacks a coherent strategic vision for the industry. Under the country development program known as Honduras 2020, Honduras is focusing on increasing annual exports to 7.4 billion Honduran limperas and adding 200,000 jobs within the country by 2020 (AHM 2018). Although the country's mix of apparel products continues to be dominated by knits, and cotton knits in particular, there has been a push in recent years to increase the production capacity for other fabrics, particularly woven textiles. To accomplish this shift, the AHM estimates that at least US$250 million in new investment will be needed in the coming years. In addition, the Honduran government is investing US$3.4 billion to develop its synthetics industry, partly by recruiting production technicians and by engaging in public-private partnerships with selected domestic and multinational companies to train their employees in synthetic production methods. However, the Honduras 2020 program does not set forth a road map for increasing the country's overall competitiveness. Likewise, the government's role in attracting new investment is seen as facilitating the industry's needs rather than driving the effort. The government could play a more prominent role in investment promotion, but it has been unable to do so effectively. As a result, the private sector is filling the void by organizing itself and by asking the government to play more of a role (IFC, forthcoming).

Finally, more should be done to use regional integration to stimulate growth within the textile and apparel sector. To further grow the industry, intraregional trade and customs integration is vital. The three Northern Triangle countries—El Salvador, Guatemala, and Honduras—make up the Central American Customs Union. This three-country bloc allows 95 percent of products manufactured within them to circulate duty free among the member countries. The union also establishes common taxes and broader crossing administration, which is meant to shorten bureaucratic processes and decrease transit times. Although the bloc has made progress, including in the digitalization of customs procedures, there is still work to be done: operators within the sector note inefficient regional customs as a continuing challenge. Regional integration should encourage the development of vertical value chains within Honduras as the global textile and apparel sector further consolidates and major US brands and retailers shorten their supply chains.

Conclusion

This case study shows how the government of Honduras's establishment of maquilas and signing of preferential trade and investment agreements jointly helped attract foreign investment and led to the development of Honduras's textile and apparel industry. This approach has increased Honduras's integration with international markets, taking advantage of its preferential market access to the United States, and brought about workforce development and linkage programs over time. With the establishment of the maquila program and SEZs, more and more foreign manufacturers were able to extend their labor-intensive operations into the US market by taking advantage of dedicated infrastructure, tailored fiscal incentives, and trade agreements that favored their entrance into the US market. Despite a turbulent political environment, this small Central American republic managed to become a leading exporter of clothing and apparel products to the United States.

Honduras has shown the importance of SEZs in catalyzing FDI. SEZs in Honduras have allowed domestic parties to invest and operate during all three phases of the industry's development. The SEZs have also provided resilient infrastructure and a generous incentives regime encouraging foreign investors to enter the country and focus on manufacturing activities. However, the SEZs have dissuaded firms from upgrading and have excluded small and medium enterprises from some of their incentives, shunting FDI into low-value-added functions in textile and apparel manufacturing because of Honduras's lack of workforce development. Honduras is still very concentrated in narrow segments of the textiles and apparel GVC, which leaves it vulnerable to shocks. Over the three phases of the industry's development, maquilas became more and more independent in importing fabrics. Also, the increasing number of maquilas in the country led Honduras to supply more of its own inputs. However, lacking the capacity to carry out the entire value chain, the country is very sensitive to competition and shifts in international trade and has not been able to attract a very diverse pool of investors. Honduras has scope to diversify within the textile GVC, particularly into the production of synthetic fabrics. Although the country has worked to make its textile industry more competitive, it cannot stop there; the global, rapidly changing economy requires firms to continually upgrade their skills and seek more sophisticated advantages.

An important lesson comes from the way the Honduran government shifted policies over the three phases of development to increase participation by the domestic private sector. When the main concern was to attract FDI, in the first phase, the country focused on maximizing linkages. In the second phase, the country boosted the benefits of existing FDI by increasing backward linkages. It was not until the third phase, after the signing of several international agreements and a range of negative macroeconomic events, that the domestic private sector saw an unprecedented loss of competitiveness.

One of the challenges facing Honduras is to develop a stronger strategy for upgrading. Although the maquilas still face several hurdles, the companies working in them need longer-term visions to exploit the country's competitive advantages at producing textiles and apparel. The AHM and the Honduran government should provide incentives to move these textile companies along the value chain. This shift could be achieved by improving managerial skills and increasing Honduran firms' presence in the parts of the value chain that add more value: design, production, branding, and retail. For instance, developing stronger linkages with Mexican suppliers or building strategic alliances with East Asian firms in the fast-fashion segment could strengthen the Honduran textile value chain.

SEZs have played a catalytic role in Honduras's industrialization, diversification, and trade integration, leaving the government to establish more comprehensive policy reform that could benefit all investors and entrepreneurs.

Notes

1. The analysis in this case study is based on a combination of literature reviews and interviews conducted by the authors between January and March 2020 with representatives of multinational corporations, domestic firms, and trade associations affiliated with the Honduran garment industry, as well as government officials.
2. Honduras is the top global buyer of yarn from the United States. Its purchases represent US$1 billion in imports, equivalent to 23 percent of the United States' total yarn sales (AHM 2018).

3. According to a modification made by government decree in 2020, this time period can, upon lapsing, be extended for an additional 10 years.
4. Export processing zones are a subtype of SEZs. They are thus referred to henceforth as SEZs.
5. Such companies were also exempt from all federal and municipal taxes as well as from any domestic duties and charges associated with trade, and no time limit was attached to these fiscal incentives. The law also extended fiscal incentives to real estate developers who invested in the physical infrastructure of these industrial parks.
6. Under the so-called yarn forward rule of origin, the agreement covers textile and apparel products made using US, Central American, or Dominican yarns and fabrics.
7. In addition to the country's proximity to the United States, Honduras has the best, most efficient, and largest deep-water port in Central America, Puerto Cortés. This port earned the US Customs-Trade Partnership Against Terrorism certification, which improved its security and reduced the likelihood that products sent from it would be examined at a US port of entry.
8. Still, Honduras remains among the top 10 exporters of apparel to the United States, accounting for about 3 percent of US apparel imports.
9. According to the IFC (forthcoming), Honduras has the best and most efficient port in Central America. Transit times of 48 to 72 hours to the United States and efficient processing through Honduras's major port ensure a significant competitive advantage in speed to market.
10. A training program called Procinco was established in 2004 to focus on four main training areas: productivity, health and safety, human resources, and legislation and compliance.

References

AHM (Asociación Hondureña de Maquiladores). 2018. "Memoria 2018." AHM, San Pedro Sula.

Bamber, P., and S. Frederick. 2018. "Central America in Manufacturing Global Value Chains (GVCs)." Global Value Chains Center, Duke University, Durham, NC.

Bilandzic, N., L. Feinzaig, D. Kafie, J. Neto, and L. Peia. 2007. "The Apparel Cluster in Honduras." Institute for Strategy and Competitiveness, Harvard Business School, Boston, MA.

Central Bank of Honduras. 2007. "Actividad Maquiladora en Honduras Ano 2006 y Expectativas Para El Ano 2007." Subgerencia de Estudios Economicos Tegucigalpa: Government of Honduras.

Central Bank of Honduras. 2018. Informe de Bienes para Transformacion y Actividades Conexas. Tegucigalpa: Government of Honduras.

Engman, M. 2011. "Case Studies of Special Economic Zones." In *Special Economic Zones: Progress, Emerging Challenges, and Future Directions*, edited by T. Farole, and G. Akinci, 47–68. Washington, DC: World Bank.

Farole, T., and G. Akinci, eds. 2011. *Special Economic Zones. Progress, Emerging Challenges, and Future Directions*. Directions in Development Series. Washington, DC: World Bank.

Fernandez-Stark, K., S. Frederick, and G. Gereffi. 2011. "The Apparel Global Value Chain." Center on Globalization, Governance, and Competitiveness, Duke University, Durham, NC.

Frederick, S. 2010. "Development and Application of a Value Chain Research Approach to Understand and Evaluate Internal and External Factors and Relationships Affecting Economic Competitiveness in the Textile Value Chain." PhD thesis, North Carolina State University, Raleigh, NC.

Gereffi, G., and S. Frederick. 2010. "The Global Apparel Value Chain, Trade and the Crisis. Challenges and Opportunities for Developing Countries." Policy Research Working Paper 5281, World Bank, Washington, DC.

Gereffi, G., and O. Memedovic. 2003. "The Global Apparel Value Chain: What Prospects for Upgrading by Developing Countries." Sectoral Studies Series, United Nations Industrial Development Organization, Vienna.

Hernandez Ore, Marco Antonio, L. Sousa, and J. Humberto Lopez. 2015. *Honduras: Unlocking Economic Potential for Greater Opportunities*. Systematic Country Diagnostic. Washington, DC: World Bank.

IBP USA. 2001. *Honduras: A Country Study Guide—Volume 1: Strategic Information and Developments*. Washington, DC: International Business Publications, Inc.

IFC (International Finance Corporation). Forthcoming. "Honduras Light Manufacturing Assessment." IFC, Washington, DC.

Jansen, Hans G.P., S. Morley, and G. Kessler, et al. 2007. "The Impact of the Central America Free Trade Agreement on the Central American Textile Maquila Industry." IFPRI Discussion Paper 720: International Food Policy Research Institute. https://www.ifpri.org/publication /impact-central-america-free-trade-agreement-central-american-textile-maquila-industry.

Keane, J., and D. W. te Velde. 2008. "The Role of Textile and Clothing Industries in Growth and Development Strategies." Overseas Development Institute, London.

Liu, PingQing, and Qiang Gu. 2007. "Present Position of China's Local Industrial Clusters (LICs) in the Global Value Chain (GVC): Apparel and Textile Industry Case Study." *Canadian Social Science* 3 (3): 11–19.

USITC (United States International Trade Commission). 2004. "Textiles and Apparel: Assessment of the Competitiveness of Certain Foreign Suppliers to the US Market." Investigation No. 332-448, USITC Publication 3671, USITC, Washington, DC.

Viery, A. 2014. "The Development of the Maquila Industry in Honduras: A Holistic Approach to the Industry's Effect on Women and Honduran Society." Syracuse University Honors Program Capstone Project. https://surface.syr.edu/cgi/viewcontent .cgi?article=1806&context=honors_capstone.

Walker, I., and V. Michel. 2019. "Honduras: Job Diagnostic." Jobs Series Issue No. 17, World Bank, Washington, DC.

World Bank. 2019. *Doing Business 2019: Training for Reform*. Washington, DC: World Bank.

WTO (World Trade Organization) Secretariat. 2016. "Trade Policy Review: Honduras." World Trade Organization, Geneva. https://www.wto.org/english/tratop_e/tpr_e/tp436_e.htm.

Chapter 8

Malaysia—Attracting superstar firms in the electrical and electronics industry through investment promotion

MAXIMILIAN PHILIP ELTGEN, YAN LIU, AND YEW KEAT CHONG

Summary

This case study shows how attracting foreign direct investment (FDI) through active investment promotion jump-started the development of Malaysia's electrical and electronics (E&E) industry, which, facilitated by workforce development and linking programs, significantly upgraded over time. In the early 1970s, proactive investment promotion with high-level political support, along with a competitive investment climate, led a few of the industry's "superstar" firms to locate in Malaysia. This move launched an incipient industry focused on labor-intensive, low-skilled production and assembly. Over the years, the multinational corporations (MNCs) operating in Malaysia gradually shifted into higher-value-added activities and developed local suppliers, and domestic companies emerged onto the scene. This process was supported by a number of government programs, including the provision of incentives, supplier development efforts, and workforce development initiatives. The creation of the Penang Skills Development Centre in 1989 stands out as an internationally recognized example of a tripartite, industry-led workforce development initiative involving the private sector, government, and academia. By looking at a 50-year process, this case study also provides insights into the effectiveness of distinct strategic approaches and policy tools for leveraging FDI at different phases of a country's development.

Malaysia's role in the electrical and electronics global value chain

The electrical and electronics global value chain

The E&E global value chain (GVC) comprises a number of electrical and electronic components, assembly processes, and distribution channels that serve a variety of end markets (see figure 8.1).[1,2] Broadly speaking, the GVC can be divided into five separate production stages:

1. *Inputs stage.* Depending on the component, different raw materials are used in production, such as silicon, plastic, or various metals or chemicals.

2. *Components stage*. This stage involves the production of (a) electronic components, which are elements with two or more leads or metallic pads intended to create an electronic circuit (such as semiconductors, active and passive integrated circuit [IC] components, and printed circuit boards), and (b) electrical components that transmit and distribute electric power (such as switchgear, transformers, and wires and cables).

3. *Subassemblies stage*. Depending on the final product, its components may go through several assembly stages. For example, electronic components such as circuit boards are often put into plastic or metal enclosures to form electronic subassemblies. Electrical subassemblies generate or store electric power.

4. *Final products and market segments*. The three principal end-market segments (also known as the three C's) are computers, consumer electronics, and communications and networking equipment. Other end markets include automobiles, medical equipment, aerospace and defense, and industrial equipment.

5. *Distribution and sales channels*. The final distribution and sales channels of E&E products depend on the stage of the value chain from which the products are sold, but

FIGURE 8.1 Electrical and electronics global value chain

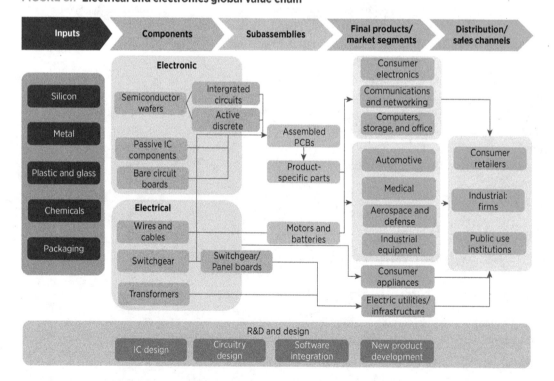

Source: Frederick and Gereffi 2016, 11. Reproduced with permission.
Note: IC = integrated circuit; PCBs = printed circuit boards; R&D = research and development.

in general the main distribution channel for consumer products is retailers, the main channel for industrial products is direct sales to firms, and the main channel for products with public use is sales to institutions.

There are also research and development (R&D) and design activities that add value outside of the manufacturing process, including IC design, circuitry design, software integration, and new product development.

The E&E GVC is characterized by rapid technological change, large investments in R&D, stringent quality standards, and value chain modularity. The emergence of information technology standards and related standards that spread across the world has allowed specifications for E&E products to be codified and transmitted across distances. Consequently, different stages in the GVC can easily be separated and performed by a variety of geographically dispersed actors, which has led to a high degree of offshoring (Frederick and Gereffi 2013).

The key actors in the E&E GVC are lead firms, contract manufacturers and tier 1 suppliers, and component semiconductor suppliers (Frederick and Gereffi 2016). The GVC's lead firms are engaged in the highest-value-added activities, such as R&D, marketing, branding, design, and new product development. Although some lead firms are still involved in production, many of their functions related to production and logistics have in recent years been outsourced to contract manufacturers (Sturgeon and Kawakami 2011). This change has led to the emergence of large supplier firms that are mainly engaged in production services (electronics manufacturing services) such as component purchasing, circuit board assembly, final product assembly, and testing. If they also engage in some design services, such firms are called original design manufacturers. These contract manufacturers often have their own global production networks; for example, many original design manufacturers are based in Taiwan, China, but perform manufacturing operations in mainland China (Frederick and Gereffi 2016).

The greatest share of value in this GVC is captured by lead firms and component suppliers with strong platform leadership (Sturgeon and Kawakami 2010). Lead firms have buying power through the orders they place with suppliers; this power is earned by technological leadership, large investments in brand development, and the financial risk these firms take on. Contract manufacturers, in contrast, generally capture a smaller share of value because their services are highly substitutable. Although they purchase many components, their buying power is weaker given that their purchases are made on behalf of their customers. In some industries, platform leaders (that is, companies that implant their technology in the products of other companies) play an important role, because they define the system architecture upon which other companies build (Frederick and Gereffi 2016).

The geographic distribution of the E&E GVC has, in recent years, shifted strongly toward Asia for both supply and demand. Although many lead firms in the GVC are still based in the European Union, Japan, or the United States, lead firms have also emerged in newly industrialized countries, such as in China (Huawei and Lenovo); the Republic of Korea (Samsung and LG); and Taiwan, China (Acer). China in particular has increasingly gained importance; in addition to those lead firms, it also hosts a large share of contract manufacturers and component suppliers. Other countries involved in these activities include Indonesia, Malaysia, the Philippines, Singapore, and most recently Thailand and Vietnam (Frederick and Gereffi 2016).

Malaysia's participation in the electrical and electronics global value chain

The E&E industry has played an important role in Malaysia's economy since the 1970s, and it continues to account for a large part of the country's exports. In 2019, Malaysia exported 372.67 billion Malaysian ringgit (RM) (about US$87 billion) in E&E products, which constituted 37.8 percent of its total exports and 44.7 percent of manufacturing exports (MIDA 2020). The country's major export destinations include China; the United States; Singapore; Hong Kong SAR, China; and Japan.

Components, in particular, electronic components, make up a large part of Malaysia's exports. In 2018, the country's E&E export composition was as follows: electronic components (57.2 percent), final electronic products (30.6 percent), final electrical products (6.4 percent), and electrical equipment (5.6 percent) (see figure 8.2). More than 80 percent of the electronic components exported were electronic ICs and micro assemblies. The final electronic products exported were in the following market categories: 42.8 percent computers, storage, and office equipment; 31.3 percent consumer electronics; 17.6 percent industrial equipment; and 8.2 percent medical devices. Although most of Malaysia's exports have grown steadily over the past 30 years, exports in some end markets (such as computers and consumer electronics) have been declining since 1999.

Globally, Malaysia is a significant player in E&E products, accounting for 2.8 percent of world E&E exports in 2018 (4.0 percent of world exports in E&E components and 2.0 percent of world exports in E&E final products and subassemblies) (see table 8.1). However, although Malaysia's exports have increased steeply overall, the country's shares in E&E exports for the East Asia and Pacific region and

FIGURE 8.2 Structure of Malaysia's electrical and electronics exports, 1990–2018

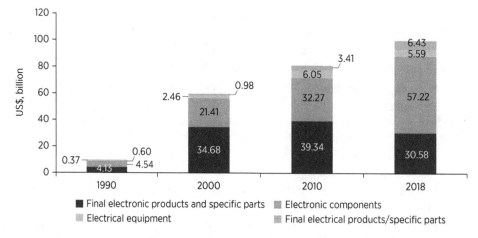

Source: United Nations Comtrade 2020.
Note: Electrical and electronics exports include the following Harmonized System codes: final electronic products or specific parts: 8469, 8470, 8471, 8472, 8473, 8517, 8518, 8519, 8520, 8521, 8522, 8525, 8526, 8527, 8528, 8529, 9006, 9009, 9012, 9014, 9016, 9018, 9019, 9021, 9022, 9024, 9027, 9028, 9029, 9030, 9032, and 950410; electronic components: 8524, 8532, 8533, 8540, 8541, and 8542; electrical equipment: 8501, 8502, 8503, 8504, 8505, 8506, 8535, 8536, 8537, 8538, 8544, 8545, 8546, 8547, and 8548; and final electrical products or specific parts: 732111, 732112, 732113, 841430, 841451, 8415, 8418, 842112, 842191, 842211, 8450, 8509, 8510, 8513, 8514, 8515, 8516, 8530, 8531, 8543, and 9405.

the world have declined over the past two decades (figure 8.3). The main reason for this decline has been a strong shift in both global and regional market share to China over the same period. Whereas in 2000 China's market share of E&E components was only 4 percent globally and 8 percent in the East Asia and Pacific region,

TABLE 8.1   Electrical and electronics exports and market share of select East Asian and Pacific countries, by value chain stage, 1990–2018

	Value (US$, billion)				CAGR (%)	World (EAP) market share (%)			
	1990	2000	2010	2018		1990	2000	2010	2018
E&E components									
Malaysia	5.14	23.87	38.33	62.80	9	7 (11)	5 (11)	4 (8)	4 (7)
China	—	18.18	144.98	249.51	22	0 (0)	4 (8)	16 (31)	17 (28)
Japan	26.27	72.94	88.06	77.35	4	35 (58)	14 (33)	10 (19)	5 (9)
Korea, Rep.	6.54	29.06	58.88	144.26	12	9 (14)	6 (13)	6 (13)	10 (16)
E&E final products and subassemblies									
Malaysia	4.50	35.67	42.75	37.00	8	3 (4)	4 (12)	3 (6)	2 (3)
China	—	50.64	446.97	694.88	26	0 (0)	6 (17)	31 (62)	34 (58)
Japan	67.72	39.16	60.55	50.31	−1	42 (65)	5 (13)	4 (8)	2 (4)
Korea, Rep.	10.54	89.39	66.01	59.55	6	7 (10)	11 (30)	5 (9)	3 (5)

Source: World Bank calculations based on United Nations Comtrade data, 2020.
Note: — = not available; CAGR = compound annual growth rate; E&E = electrical and electronics; EAP = East Asia and Pacific.

FIGURE 8.3   Malaysia's total electrical and electronics exports and its share in East Asia and Pacific and world exports, 1990–2018

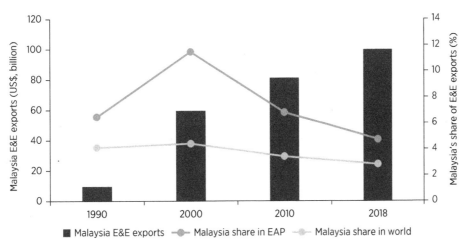

Source: United Nations Comtrade data, 2020.
Note: E&E = electrical and electronics; EAP = East Asia and Pacific.

its market share in the segment in 2018 was 17 percent globally and 28 percent in the region (table 8.1). For E&E final products and subassemblies, China's share of exports has grown even more.

Malaysian firms, both foreign and domestic, operate in different segments of the E&E GVC. Several companies are engaged in component manufacturing, especially wafer fabrication,[2] Others are more focused on assembly, packaging, and testing.[3] Some companies have also engaged in IC design and R&D.[4]

The development of Malaysia's electrical and electronics industry: The role of foreign direct investment

FDI has played a crucial role in the development of Malaysia's E&E industry. According to Malaysian Investment Development Authority (MIDA) estimates, by 2013, close to 85 percent of investments in Malaysia's E&E industry had been FDI (Frederick and Gereffi 2016). More recent data confirm this trend. Out of the RM 81.6 billion invested in Malaysia's E&E industry from 2013 to 2019, RM 74.1 billion (more than 90 percent) were FDI (MIDA 2020).

Malaysia's experience at leveraging FDI to enter into and upgrade within the E&E GVC can be divided into three phases (figure 8.4). From 1970 to the late 1980s (phase 1), Malaysia successfully attracted export-oriented FDI from superstar firms, developing an incipient industry focused on low-skilled components and parts assembly. From the late 1980s to the early 2000s (phase 2), Malaysia's E&E industry became the country's largest generator of manufacturing employment, value-added activities, and exports. Large new FDI inflows were drawn from East Asia, E&E clusters were developed, the first movers upgraded their production capacities, local supplier linkages were created, and domestic firms began to emerge. In the early 2000s, however, growth in exports and employment slowed down, marking the beginning of phase 3. During that phase, the size of Malaysian manufacturing activities decreased as competitors emerged (such as China and Vietnam), but engineering and design activities expanded as existing firms moved new activities into Malaysia. Some domestic firms began to internationalize, and pockets of the industry moved into higher-value-added segments of the GVC.

Phase 1: Early 1970s to late 1980s

The E&E industry in Malaysia had its beginnings in 1972, when the state government of Penang, by actively promoting and creating a favorable climate for investment, managed to attract the first group of foreign investors to the industry. Against a background of 15 percent unemployment in Penang in 1969, then–Chief Minister Dr. Lim Chong Eu created the Penang Development Corporation as the state's investment promotion agency. Subsequently, corporation officials, with high-level political support from Dr. Lim, proactively visited flagship firms abroad to persuade them to locate facilities in Malaysia. They found success: in 1972, eight foreign firms—called the "Eight Samurai"—decided to invest in Malaysia (Hai 2013).[5]

FIGURE 8.4 Malaysia electrical and electronics exports, 1970–2017

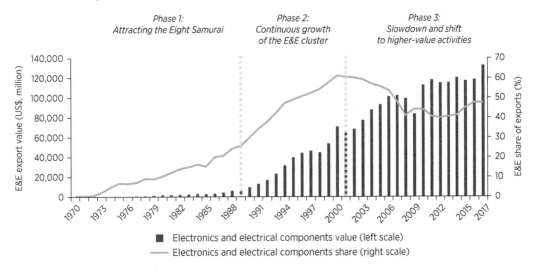

Source: World Bank calculations using Atlas of Economic Complexity Data.
Note: The Eight Samurai were Advanced Micro Devices (AMD), Clarion, Hewlett Packard (now Agilent Technologies), Hitachi Semiconductor (now Renesas), Intel, Litronix (now Osram Opto Semiconductors), National Semiconductor (now Fairchild Semiconductor), and Robert Bosch. E&E = electrical and electronics.

To attract foreign investors, Malaysia needed to create a competitive investment climate. Under the umbrella of the Second Malaysia Plan of 1971–75, Malaysia began to shift its economic strategy from promoting import substitution to encouraging export-oriented manufacturing. To attract FDI, the country established free trade zones, most notably the Penang Bayan Lepas industrial parks, and licensed manufacturing warehouses[6] to provide foreign investors with the infrastructure they needed as well as incentives to invest. Such incentives included income tax holidays for up to eight years under "pioneer" status, investment tax credits of up to 40 percent, and export incentives (Rasiah 2015). In addition, under the Second Malaysia Plan, tariff-free operations were offered (Malaysia, Office of the Prime Minister 1971). The E&E industry was also explicitly excluded from requirements to employ *bumiputera* (the indigenous people of Malaysia).

Malaysia was attractive to MNCs in the first phase of development both for structural reasons and because of government policies. Foreign investors found the main reasons to invest to be the availability of low-cost labor with basic technical and English language capabilities, ease of doing business, political stability, tax incentives, active investment promotion, and—especially for reinvestments—strong government support. According to a former executive of one of the Eight Samurai interviewed for this report, "the Government had been doing a remarkable job in supporting foreign investors—every little problem was sought to be immediately resolved, and the Government did not only have an open ear, but actively visited foreign investors to hear about their problems. Every Thursday at 7pm, Chief Minister Lim met with MNC CEOs to discuss and solve the most recent issues." Many of these actions were tailored to individual companies and focused on limiting any disruptions to their GVCs (Freund and Moran 2017). Although Malaysian workers' English language capabilities were not seen as essential, technical capabilities played an important role. According to an industry veteran interviewed for this report, "then Intel CEO Andy Grove made the decision to invest in Malaysia when having a meal in a Chinese restaurant. Mr. Grove saw a 5 percent service charge, and was very impressed when the waiter could calculate that charge in a matter of seconds." With regard to investment promotion, a clear value proposition, persistence (in the form of multiple visits to certain investors), and high-level government support (from Dr. Lim) were seen as particularly convincing.

In the initial years, GVC upgrading and the creation of local supplier linkages were limited. The first round of investment was in low-value-added parts of the GVC, such as low-skilled component manufacturing or parts assembly (for products such as printed circuit boards), basic consumer product manufacturing and assembly, and simple product testing. In the 1970s and 1980s, forward linkages were basically nonexistent; all output of the semiconductor corporations was exported (Rasiah 1988). Indeed, firms investing in free trade zones or licensed manufacturing warehouses were required to export 100 percent of their production. Backward linkages were also scarce—according to a MIDA survey, in 1981 only 1 percent of inputs to semiconductor firms were supplied by local supporting firms, although by 1986 several firms in Penang reported using more than 6 percent local inputs. The materials supplied locally were mainly unrelated to production, such as papers, boxes, and office furniture (Rasiah 1988). However, these initial FDI inflows helped Malaysia integrate into the E&E GVC, brought Malaysia to the attention of other investors, and set the foundation for further development. By attracting FDI, the Malaysian government achieved its main goal of generating employment—the unemployment rate in Penang fell from 15 percent in the late 1960s to 4 percent in 1980 (Rasiah 2015). Remarkably, 80 percent of employees in the semiconductor industry were female (Rasiah 1988). Additionally, attracting that first set of foreign investors encouraged other investors to follow and proved to be the starting point for development of an E&E cluster. According to a former MNC executive interviewed for this report, "the Eight Samurai coming to Malaysia proved to be the 'tipping point' for more investors to follow in due course." In 1981, 80 percent of companies in the E&E industry were owned by foreign investors (Rasiah 1988).

Phase 2: Late 1980s to early 2000s

The second phase in the development of Malaysia's E&E industry was marked by continuous growth in E&E exports, employment, and FDI inflows as well as the development of supplier linkages. On the back of a commodities crisis in the mid-1980s that led to the consolidation of the industry, the late 1980s saw a new wave of FDI entering Malaysia, which prompted recovery. By then, the E&E industry had become the country's largest generator of manufacturing employment, value-added activities, and exports, and an E&E cluster had formed in Penang. In the 1990s, supplier linkages were developed, although functional upgrading was limited. In about 2000, the E&E industry peaked in export and employment growth—after that, the emergence of competitors such as China, the Philippines, and Vietnam began to take its toll, and several firms relocated out of Malaysia (Kharas, Zeufack, and Majeed 2010).

The second large wave of FDI into Malaysia's E&E industry, in the late 1980s, came mainly from East Asian MNCs (from Hong Kong SAR, China; Japan; Korea; Singapore; and Taiwan, China). The main reasons these firms relocated from their home countries or economies were a strong appreciation of the yen, won, new Taiwan dollar, and Singapore dollar and the loss of Generalized System of Preferences beneficiary status for Hong Kong SAR, China; Korea; Singapore; and Taiwan, China (Rasiah 2015). FDI flows into Malaysia continued in the 1990s—the industry attracted an average of RM 3.31 billion per year between 1991 and 1999. In six of those nine years, according to MIDA, this FDI made up more than 80 percent of total capital investment in Malaysia (Ismail 2001). During this phase, investors chose Malaysia as an FDI destination primarily because of the country's existing ecosystem of firms, adaptable workforce, and investment incentives. For example, when an IC-manufacturing MNC interviewed for this case study considered moving to Malaysia in the early 1990s, "the choice had been between Suzhou (China), Singapore, Bada Valley (Indonesia), and Penang. Ultimately, we chose Penang because it had an entire ecosystem in place, and we had strong confidence in the people on the ground, a decision we haven't regretted for a single day." In 1986, the Malaysian government introduced new incentives to invest, most notably an investment tax allowance of up to 100 percent for qualifying capital expenditures incurred within five years of the project's date of approval (MIDA 2010). However, in the early 1990s both the pioneer companies' tax holidays and this investment tax allowance were made less generous (except for high-technology companies). After 1995, labor-intensive projects were no longer eligible for promotion incentives unless they were located in certain areas or satisfied other narrow conditions (OECD 2013). Malaysian policy makers thus increasingly began to focus their investment promotion efforts on high-value-added activities in the E&E GVC.

Through this influx of new FDI and the development of existing FDI, Malaysia's E&E industry began to mature: new processes and functions were introduced, and its exporters entered new markets. Following the crisis in the mid-1980s, many firms began to focus on raising their productivity. Cutting-edge process control technologies such as just-in-time manufacturing, quality control circles, integrated materials resource planning, and statistical processes were introduced (Rasiah 2015). Firms also began to switch from simple hand assembly to automated assembly and to some extent to process design and production design as well as supply chain management, especially among affiliates of multinational investors (Moran 2014). The 1990s saw firms entering the computer products market and increasing their presence in the consumer products market; exports in these two segments rose significantly.

The Malaysian government, during phase 2, focused mainly on fostering upgrading, workforce development, linkages, and economic clustering, as was formulated in the Action Plan for Industrial Technology Development (in 1990) and the Second Industrial Master Plan (in 1996). Several policy actions were taken, such as the establishment of the Human Resource Development Fund in 1992. Manufacturing firms with more than 50 employees were required to contribute 2 percent of their payroll to this fund, from which approved training expenses could be claimed (Rasiah 2015). Also, the Malaysian Technology Development

Corporation, a venture capital organization for the industry, was created in 1992. In 1993, the Malaysian Institute of Microelectronics Systems was corporatized. As a result, the government-owned wafer fabrication firms Silterra and 1st Silicon were established (Rasiah 2015). However, despite these initiatives, economic upgrading in the 1990s remained within lower-value-added activities. This focus changed only with the Industrial Master Plan 3 of 2006, which introduced research grants for foreign investors.

The government of Malaysia also began several successful linkage programs during this phase. The Vendor Development Program, launched in 1992 for the electronics sector, had limited success, primarily because of the limited capacity of the local small and medium enterprises (SMEs) selected to participate. At first, only suppliers owned by bumiputera were eligible to join. However, later versions of the program with less restrictive requirements proved more effective, underscoring the need to select participants for such programs with the capacity to produce high-quality products (UNCTAD 2011). Subsequent programs, such as the Industrial Linkage Program (launched in 1996) and the Global Supplier Program (launched in 2000) yielded better results because they gave MNCs a larger role in supplier selection and provided complementary support for SMEs to access finance, build their capabilities, and expand into new markets.[7] These programs influenced some firms, such as Intel, in their decisions to develop local SMEs as suppliers (OECD 2018; OECD Investment Committee 2005).

These national activities were effectively supplemented by state-level initiatives, especially in Penang. In particular, the Penang Skills Development Centre (PSDC), a tripartite, industry-led initiative involving the state government, the private sector, and academia, is an internationally recognized example of workforce development that proved instrumental to further developing Penang's E&E industry (see box 8.1). In many stakeholder interviews, the PSDC was mentioned as a prime example of the culture of Penang in the 1990s, in which various firms and the state government came together to exchange experiences, hold workshops and conferences, and learn from each other. According to an industry veteran, Penang is "the only place in the world where competition meets in a friendly manner."

With the help of these government programs, the E&E industry in the 1990s saw significant development of backward linkages with local suppliers, although not all of those suppliers were owned by Malaysians. In Penang, MNCs' share of procurement from local sources rose from 10 percent in the mid-1980s to 46 percent in 1996 (UNCTAD 2011), although this rise was uneven among industry segments. In 1998, the local sourcing rates of 10 major firms in Penang were found to be 40–50 percent for consumer electronics, 20–40 percent for other electronic components, 13–60 percent for computers, and 4–10 percent for semiconductor components (Best and Rasiah 2003). However, although many of these suppliers were located in Malaysia, a significantly smaller percentage were Malaysian-owned (Yean and Siang 2011). In fact, much of the technology deepening that occurred during this period took place within MNCs. This differs from the development experiences of Korea and Taiwan, China, where the percentages of locally owned firms were higher (Yean and Siang 2011). Many MNCs in Malaysia established their own

BOX 8.1 **Penang Skills Development Centre**

The Penang Skills Development Centre (PSDC) is frequently referenced and studied as a successful model for skills upgrading (OECD 2013; OECD and UNIDO 2019; UNCTAD 2011). Established in 1989, it was the first tripartite, industry-led skills training and education center in Malaysia. Initially, it concentrated on vocational training in electrical engineering and electronics to help the country advance into the production of standardized components. Subsequently, it ventured into higher-value-added products and components (such as those in the semiconductor, information technology, audio visual, and digital camera sectors). From 2000 onward, it continued along its upgrading path, adding programs in the life sciences, biotechnology, pharmaceuticals, and medical devices.

Since its inception, the PSDC has grown to become the leading vocational learning institution in the country. Its management board continues to be staffed by multinational corporation (MNC) representatives to induce a demand-led focus in its training curricula. Membership on this board rose from 25 MNCs and 6 local supplier firms in 1989 to 56 MNCs and 52 supplier firms in 2005. Over a period of 30 years, the PSDC has trained more than 233,000 participants through more than 10,000 courses, pioneered local industry development initiatives, and provided input on and assisted in the formulation of national policies pertaining to human capital development. To ensure that its vocational training programs stay abreast of industry trends, the PSDC has created several partnerships with universities in Australia, Germany, Malaysia, and the United Kingdom. Over the years, its focus has shifted from workforce transformation aimed at specific professions toward more broadly upgrading skill sets.

The PSDC's contributions to supplier development inspired the federal-level Global Supplier Program, which also supported customized small and medium enterprise training based on MNC criteria (and used the center as one of its registered training centers).

Sources: Interviews with relevant stakeholders conducted in February 2020; UNCTAD 2011.

suppliers, but others did train local firms to gradually take on more and more complex tasks (box 8.2).

Although Malaysian government programs to create linkages were generally successful, linkage creation also occurred outside official policy initiatives. The main drivers of this development were arguably MNCs. As exporters competing globally, Malaysia's MNCs were forced during this period to adopt new technologies, such as just-in-time manufacturing, that required them to source in close proximity to their production facilities (Rasiah 2015).

Spillovers from MNC operations in Malaysia can be observed in the form of former MNC employees establishing supplier firms. Such firms include Carsem, Eng Teknologi, Globetronics Technology, Unico Holdings, Unisem, and ViTrox (UNCTAD 2011). Some of the executives interviewed for this case study stressed that their experience working for MNCs in Malaysia had been essential to their success in creating their own companies by teaching the executives about modern management techniques and helping them build networks of contacts. According to the chief executive officer of a leading Malaysian company, "the experience of working more than

BOX 8.2 Intel in Malaysia

Intel's experience in Malaysia is a good example of firm-level upgrading. Following its first investment in an assembly plant in Penang in 1972 (100 million Malaysian ringgit [RM]), Intel gradually expand-ed its operations in the country: in 1978 it operated a test plant, and in 1990 it moved into product design and development. In 1996, the company opened its first plant, in Kulim engaged in system manufacturing, which evolved into a board design center and an assembly test plant in 1999. In 2000, it further located shared services and in 2017 programmable solutions to Penang. Over the years, Intel has invested more than RM 22 billion in Malaysia, and it now employs 10,800 workers involved in ad-vanced manufacturing and research and development, as well as in software development, product design marketing, and other local and global shared services. It also spends RM 1 billion each year with local suppliers and has registered 460 patents generated by Malaysian engineers.

Facilitated by the Malaysian government, Intel was also successful in developing local suppliers. It was one of the founders of the Penang Skills Development Centre and extensively used and contributed to its services. It also relied on tax incentives and financial support such as the Global Supplier Program to develop its network of Malaysian suppliers. Intel saw these initiatives as benefiting multinational corporations as well as small and medium enterprises by shifting the production of low-level compo-nents to dependable local firms, allowing the transnational corporations to concentrate on upgrading and developing new technologies. Intel has helped develop a number of successful Malaysian small and medium enterprises, such as Eng Teknologi, Globetronics Technology, LKT Engineering, Metfab Engineering, Polytool Technologies, Prodelcon, Rapid Synergy, and Seng Choon Engineering.

Source: This analysis is based on interviews conducted by the authors between January and March 2020 with representatives of multinational corporations, domestic firms, and trade associations affiliated with the Malaysian electronics industry, as well as government officials, and UNCTAD 2011.

15 years for an MNC taught me an entrepreneurial spirit [and] the necessity of open communication, trust, and respect, as well as that institutions are governed by sys-tems, not by people, which I successfully implemented in my company." As seen in Malaysia, MNCs may even encourage their staff to form supplier firms and may help nurture those companies as they develop and subsequently expand. From an MNC's perspective, there are mutual benefits in contracting out to former employees rather than taking chances on unknown firms.

Phase 3: Early 2000s to today

The current phase in the development of Malaysia's E&E industry is characterized by a decline in growth rates, a move toward higher-value-added activities, and a structural shift from personal computers (PCs) and parts to semiconductors. After 2000, the E&E industry's growth in exports, employment, and contribution to gross domestic product all slowed down. Although E&E exports still grew from about US$48 billion in 2000 to US$82 billion in 2018, Malaysia's share of the East Asia and Pacific region's exports, as well as the country's share of world exports, has been declining since 2000 (according to United Nations Comtrade data from 2020; see also figure 8.3). To a large extent, this decline can be explained by the emergence of competitors such as China and Vietnam. From the early 2000s until the 2008 financial crisis, Malaysia's

E&E industry was driven mainly by products and services related to PCs and their parts (such as testing and assembly for ICs and manufacturing of components). Subsequently, Malaysia was affected by the structural shift in consumer preferences from PCs to smartphones and tablets. This shift slowed the country's recovery from the crisis and led Malaysian firms to diversify away from the PCs and parts segment into other segments such as automotive semiconductors and cloud computing semiconductors (Bank Negara Malaysia 2016).

Although FDI inflows have been consistent throughout this period, the government's strategy for attracting FDI has become more targeted. Between 2013 and 2018, FDI inflows held steady at about RM 8 billion to RM 10 billion per year (MIDA 2020). According to both state and national investment promotion agencies, investment promotion has become more targeted, featuring active promotion efforts on the basis of the desirability of a specific project for the Malaysian economy. In 2012, MIDA adopted an "ecosystem approach" under which it continuously maps and analyzes the ecosystem of the Malaysian E&E industry. On the basis of this analysis, it focuses on promoting specific activities that are scarce, such as R&D and IC design. From 2000 onward, the government has also offered customized incentives (both fiscal and financial) for investment perceived as high quality and in sectors deemed strategic. Incentives have been tied less to economic performance metrics (such as exports) and more to innovation and responsible business conduct: training workers, conducting R&D, and protecting the environment (OECD 2013; Thomsen 2004). In addition, the government has focused on stimulating investment into less developed areas. For example, the Northern Corridor Economic Region was created to foster economic development in the states of Kedah, Perak, Perlis, and Pulau Pinang (Kharas, Zeufack, and Majeed 2010).

Significant upgrading has been achieved during this period by providing foreign firms with research grants and by liberalizing the import of foreign professionals. With its 2006 Third Industrial Master Plan, the Malaysian government built upon the previous master plans by targeting the E&E industry for further upgrading. Most notably, the plan provided for up-front research grants for foreign investors. Such grants had previously been confined to the government-owned firms Silterra and 1st Silicon. In 2006, Penang was approved for Multimedia Super Corridor status, which allowed firms in Penang to import human capital for their operations. As a direct result of these policies, a number of firms moved wafer fabrication, IC design, and R&D operations to Malaysia—the number of semiconductor firms performing these functions in Malaysia rose from 0 in 1999 to 11 in 2014 (Rasiah 2015). In addition, the number of patents registered in the United States by semiconductor firms from Malaysia rose significantly, from 7 patents in the period 1980–2005 to 309 in 2006–11 (Rasiah 2015). However, this upgrading occurred only in pockets of the industry, and it was concentrated among a small number of firms.

Phase 3 of the development of Malaysia's E&E industry also saw firms enter into new market segments. From 2000 to 2018, exports rose significantly in the industrial equipment and medical device component segments. This increase can be explained by a surge in global demand for these products as well as Malaysia's existing strength in other segments of the E&E GVC. The government also provided an impetus for the industry to venture into new segments, especially in the downstream sector, by implementing the E&E 2.0 initiative in 2013. This initiative was the second phase of the industry's modernization program under the country's Economic Transformation Program. It focused on 20 new entry point projects clustered into five key areas: manufacturing services and design, advanced materials, industrial and integrated electronics, wafer technology, and advanced assembly. Also, under the Eleventh Malaysia Plan (2016–20), medical devices were identified as a sector with high potential for growth. Malaysia has in recent years become a hub for medical device exports, which involve an ecosystem of more than 200 firms (Bernama 2018). Exports of E&E-related medical devices thus increased as a part of the country's overall surge in medical device exports.

Successful Malaysian companies have begun to engage in SME development initiatives of their own. One example of such an initiative is the Penang Automation Cluster, which seeks to develop the local supply ecosystem in Penang (box 8.3). Although some SMEs have become exporting superstars, others are struggling to develop. Notably, some incentives in place may discourage foreign investors from increasing their local sourcing, such as exemptions from customs duties and sales taxes on imports without corresponding exemptions from local sales and service taxes when buying from local suppliers (World Bank Group 2020).

The transformation of production through the Fourth Industrial Revolution is widely regarded as the biggest opportunity for Malaysia to further develop its E&E industry. According to stakeholder interviews, Malaysian firms are seen to have special potential to advance in equipment technology and electronics manufacturing services. To promote Malaysia's role in the shift toward new technologies, in 2018 the government passed the National Industry 4.0 Policy (MITI 2018).[8] Further strategic decisions on how to promote the industry are expected in the Industrial Master Plan 4, scheduled to be released by the Ministry of International Trade and Industry in the fourth quarter of 2020.

BOX 8.3 Penang Automation Cluster

The Penang Automation Cluster (PAC) is an example of a small and medium enterprise development program created by successful Malaysian companies. Established in 2017 as a joint venture between three domestic companies (ViTrox Corporation, Pentamaster Technology, and Walta Engineering), PAC aims to build and manage the local supply chain ecosystem to support large local companies and multinational corporations. PAC is the first small and medium enterprise precision metal fabrication or automation cluster in Malaysia, and serves as a one-stop metal component supply chain hub. Its objective is to support and enhance the development of the existing supply chain ecosystem of industries and services in Penang, primarily those in semiconductor, electrical and electronics, medical devices, light-emitting diodes, and avionics segments. In addition to creating jobs, PAC also provides employees with the opportunity to attend German Dual Vocational Training.

Source: This analysis is based on a combination of interviews conducted by the authors between January and March 2020 with representatives of multinational corporations, domestic firms, and trade associations affiliated with the Malaysian electronics industry, as well as government officials, and the PAC website (http://pa-cluster.com/).

Current challenges

Although Malaysia's E&E industry has developed significantly since its inception, it currently faces several challenges that are impeding further upgrading. Both private sector and public sector actors see a lack of talent as the overarching challenge hampering the development of the sector. A significant proportion of firms reports difficulties in finding domestic talent with the advanced technical, entrepreneurial, communication, and job-specific skills required to propel the E&E industry forward. It is therefore not surprising that electrical, electronic, and mechanical engineers, whose talents and skills are the most sought after in the E&E sector, have been listed on Malaysia's Critical Occupations List[9] for five consecutive years since 2015, indicating continuing talent shortages in these critical occupations (CSC 2020). Compounding domestic talent constraints is the problem of highly skilled Malaysians migrating to other countries. This migration has been significant and geographically concentrated (the most common destinations are Australia, Singapore, the United Kingdom, and the United States), and it has a strong ethnic dimension. The key factors that motivate Malaysians to move abroad include differences in earning potential, career prospects, and quality of life and perceptions of social injustice in Malaysia (World Bank 2011). Insufficient R&D spending and a lack of local "superstar" firms compared with competitors like China, Korea, and Taiwan, China, are also seen as factors holding back development. On the investment front, although Malaysia's business investment in R&D as a share of gross domestic product has increased in recent years, it has remained lower than those of aspirational comparators such as the Czech Republic, Poland, and Turkey. The COVID-19 (coronavirus) pandemic led to a decline in Malaysia's E&E exports in early 2020, but from May onward exports largely recovered thanks to favorable government measures and the overall resilience of the global E&E GVC. In the medium to long term, the global pandemic and the ongoing trade tensions between China and the United States are widely seen as opportunities for Malaysia to further increase its E&E exports and attract investors diversifying away from China (box 8.4).

BOX 8.4 The COVID-19 (coronavirus) pandemic's impact on Malaysia's electrical and electronics exports

Malaysia's electrical and electronics (E&E) exports were first negatively affected by the COVID-19 (coronavirus) pandemic at the beginning of 2020. From January to February 2020, E&E exports declined by 20 percent, caused by a cyclical slowdown in the global technology cycle and by the sector being closely integrated into China-centric production networks (World Bank 2020). As a result of Chinese offices and factories closing, Malaysian companies relying on Chinese products experienced supply chain disruptions, especially in raw materials sourcing, assembly, testing, and shipping. In particular, contract manufacturers and electronics manufacturing services were affected (Teng 2020).

The experience of Pentamaster, a Penang-based automation manufacturing and technology solutions provider, illustrates the issues Malaysian companies were facing. One-fifth of Pentamaster's

Continued on next page ›

BOX 8.4 **The COVID-19 (coronavirus) pandemic's impact on Malaysia's electrical and electronics exports** *(continued)*

FIGURE B8.4.1 **Malaysia electrical and electronics exports, January 2019–September 2020**

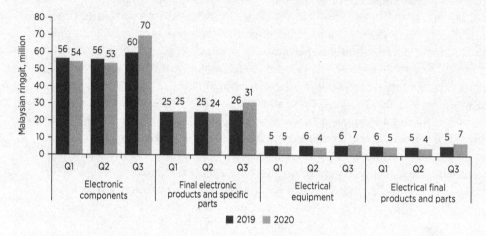

Source: World Bank calculations based on Department of Statistics Malaysia (2020) Malaysia External Trade Statistics Online (METS Online), https://metsonline.stats.gov.my/.

components and parts are directly and indirectly sourced from China. In an interview in March 2020, Pentamaster cofounder and chairman, Chuah Choon Bin, acknowledged that "over the past one month, certain parts and components that we want to buy have been affected. When we called the suppliers, there was no response. Some of them told us that they do not know when they can supply to us" (Teng 2020). In addition, project delivery was delayed. Pentamaster's chairman added, "We sell machines to China. When the machines were sent there, we were not able to send our people to install and set them up. That affects our machine and project delivery" (Teng 2020).

In March and April, exports further declined, mainly because of supply disruptions in Malaysia. As the outbreak in Malaysia became widespread with higher community transmission, the government on March 16 announced a four-week movement control order (MCO), which included general prohibitions of mass gatherings, restrictions on travel, and closures of schools, universities, and government and private premises except those involved in essential services (Teng 2020). This order was extended a number of times, until from May onward businesses were allowed to gradually reopen under severe restrictions. Some companies in the E&E industry received approval to operate during all phases of the MCO because they were deemed essential in helping fight COVID-19, but this approval often only extended to 50 percent of the workforce (Hamdan 2020), so supply was affected.

From May 2020 onward, Malaysia's E&E exports have exhibited a strong upward trajectory. On the demand side, the industry profited from the overall resilience of the global E&E value chain, in which demand (even for nonessential products) never halted completely (OECD 2020). On the supply side, the partial allowance to operate during the MCO and the reopening from May onward supported Malaysia's E&E industry, as did other government measures such as interest rate cuts, economic stimulus packages, and the Short-Term Economic Recovery Plan (Hamdan 2020). Notably, the recovery has extended to all segments of the GVC, with the rebound being particularly strong in the third quarter of 2020 in comparison with 2019 (figure B8.4.1). Notably, medical device exports increased

Continued on next page ›

BOX 8.4 **The COVID-19 (coronavirus) pandemic's impact on Malaysia's electrical and electronics exports** *(continued)*

considerably, from 0.2 percent of Malaysia's total E&E exports in December 2019 to 2.9 percent in September 2020.

In the medium to long term, Malaysian policy makers have a positive outlook for the country's E&E industry. The ongoing global pandemic is expected to increase demand for devices that enable remote work, virtual learning, or e-commerce (Bernama 2020). Additionally, Malaysia will seek to benefit from firms looking to diversify their production away from China because of COVID-19–related risks and trade tensions with the United States. According to Malaysia's Ministry of International Trade and Industry, "many (firms) view that Malaysia can be a new alternative center for Asia, having the advantage [of] a strong E&E base, [a] good supporting local engineering cluster, and [a] talent base" (Reuters 2020).

Source: This analysis is based on a combination of literature reviews and interviews conducted by the authors between January and March 2020 with representatives of multinational corporations, domestic firms, and trade associations affiliated with the Malaysian electronics industry, as well as government officials.

Conclusion

Malaysia's experience shows how attracting a few superstar firms using active investment promotion can jump-start the development of an industry if the minimum conditions for foreign investment are in place. With an English-speaking, low-cost labor force complemented by the establishment of free trade zones and licensed manufacturing warehouses and the provision of generous investment incentives, Malaysia in the 1970s had the foundation in place to attract foreign investors. Through aggressive investment promotion with high-level political support, Malaysia succeeded in leveraging these advantages to attract FDI and thereby launch the development of its E&E industry. Crucial in this regard were a solutions-oriented attitude by the government and reassurances by higher political authorities to MNCs of the ability to seamlessly integrate into GVCs (Freund and Moran 2017). Information about investment conditions had to be backed up by a strong commitment to infrastructure reforms and the removal of any disruptions to foreign investors' operations, which could only be credibly provided by high-level political authorities, such as Penang's chief minister.

The information gap between foreign investors and potential host countries may be smaller in today's world, but recent research shows that investment promotion with high-level political support can still play a critical role in attracting FDI (Heilbron and Kronfol 2020). Other countries (for example, Thailand and Vietnam) show that it is still possible to enter the E&E GVC, but Malaysia's experience also shows that development of an industry by attracting FDI is easiest at inflection points, that is, at a point where internal and external conditions overlap. Although the Malaysian government's actions were crucial, the country also profited from the general trend at the time of developed countries' firms moving their labor-intensive manufacturing and assembly parts of their business outside their home countries.

Incentives proved key to attracting FDI and upgrading along the E&E GVC, but their role changed over time. In the 1970s, incentives were an important factor in Malaysia's attracting FDI into low-value-added, labor-intensive segments of the E&E GVC. However, although locational incentives can be useful when attracting efficiency-seeking FDI, governments may need to realign these incentives when development priorities shift, as did Malaysia's. In the early 1990s, both the tax holidays for the pioneer firms and the investment tax allowance were made less generous except for high-technology companies. After 1995, labor-intensive projects were no longer eligible for promotion incentives unless they were located in certain areas or satisfied other narrow conditions. Over time, Malaysia's policy focus shifted toward using behavioral incentives to stimulate linkages and inducing foreign firms to locate high-value-added R&D activities in Malaysia. The tax and financial incentives to both MNCs and SMEs as part of the linkage programs lowered the costs of linking for both sets of participants, thereby facilitating the creation of linkages. And the R&D grants that were extended to foreign companies from the mid-2000s onward (which had previously been limited to domestic companies) played an important role in convincing MNCs to move R&D activities into Malaysia.

The development of Malaysia's E&E industry also provides several lessons on the stimulation of supplier linkages. The different degrees of success of the various linkage programs (the Vendor Development Program, the Industrial Linkages Program, and the Global Supplier Program) show that it is important, when promoting linkages, that MNC representatives select the content of their specific training programs and that participants are chosen on the basis of the MNCs' criteria. Incentives to participate should be targeted at both MNCs and SMEs. Also, even with these programs, many local linkages in Malaysia occurred because the country's MNCs were forced by external pressures (such as the global trend toward just-in-time delivery in the 1980s) to source in close proximity to their production facilities. The track record of supplier development programs in Malaysia also shows that these programs are highly contingent on continuous human capital development. The PSDC is a good example of how this development can happen as a collaborative effort between the private sector, the government, and academia.

One of Malaysia's challenges has been to attract the highest-value-adding activities, such as frontier R&D and marketing, to the country. The country's recent experience has shown the importance of providing R&D grants to foreign companies to entice them to upgrade their functions in-country. However, so far none of Malaysia's MNCs has brought frontier R&D (for example, R&D related to miniaturization or the enlargement of the wafer diameter of semiconductor chips) into the country (Rasiah 2015). Although human capital development and grants may induce firms to locate some R&D activities in a country, the final stage of development often requires the development of homegrown lead firms. Ultimately, most of the value in the E&E GVC is captured by lead firms, and foreign MNCs can be expected to keep the highest-value-added functions in their home countries. Arguably, one of the reasons why countries and economies such as China, Korea, and Taiwan, China, have been so successful in capturing high-value activities in the E&E GVC is that they have been able to develop their own lead firms. Other reasons may include less severe brain drain and stronger linkages between their universities and industry.

Malaysia's experience also highlights the benefits that can be derived from different levels of government exercising complementary functions. In Malaysia, policy guidance at the federal level, in the form of planning and several incentive programs, was complemented by the proactive role of subnational agents, who proved pivotal in attracting investors into the country. Globally, subnational actors are growing in prominence: when promoting investment, subnational governments seek to leverage their deep knowledge of the local business environment and its value propositions to investors as well as their strong ties to local agencies that are more heavily involved in the day-to-day operational needs and issues of investors (Heilbron and Kronfol 2020). Although subnational agencies can have unique roles in a country's institutional framework for investment policy, it is essential that their tasks are clearly allocated and that effective collaboration mechanisms are in place to ensure complementarity between the different levels of government (Heilbron and Kronfol 2020).

One last lesson from the Malaysian experience is that strategies and policies should be adapted to the country's and the industry's specific phases of development. In the 1970s and 1980s, the focus of Malaysian policy makers with regard to the E&E industry was primarily on attracting FDI to create jobs. Beginning in the late 1980s, their focus gradually shifted toward the creation of linkages to maximize the benefits of existing FDI. A country's strategies and policies should always be based on its phase of development and the phase of development of the industry in question. Such a phased approach can help developing countries focus their resources on their most pressing needs while also keeping a long-term perspective. Malaysia's experience also shows that different structural characteristics and policy tools are important to attracting FDI at different phases of development. Whereas investment incentives had greater relevance when Malaysia was attracting FDI in the first phase of developing its E&E industry, they became less important in later phases, and Malaysia reacted by tailoring its incentives more and more toward special policy initiatives. In contrast, human capital was not as important in the early phases of the industry's development, but it became more important later on, when Malaysia was trying to attract highest-value-added activities such as R&D.

Notes

1. The analysis in this case study is based on a combination of literature reviews and interviews conducted by the authors between January and March 2020 with representatives of multinational corporations, domestic firms, and trade associations affiliated with the Malaysian electronics industry, as well as government officials; the interviews are the source for all direct quotations included in this chapter that are not otherwise attributed.
2. Examples include SilTerra and MIMOS (majority domestically owned) as well as Infineon, OSRAM, ON Semiconductor, and SunEdison (majority foreign owned).
3. Examples include Carsem, Aemulus, Unisem, Inari, and Globetronics (majority domestically owned) as well as Intel, Infineon, Texas Instruments, AMD, ASE Group, and Amkor (majority foreign owned).
4. Examples include ViTrox, Symmid, Key ASIC, and Oppstar (majority domestically owned) as well as Intel, UST Global, Whizz Systems, and Phison (majority foreign owned).
5. The Eight Samurai were Advanced Micro Devices (AMD), Clarion, Hewlett Packard (now Agilent Technologies), Hitachi Semiconductor (now Renesas), Intel, Litronix (now Osram

Opto Semiconductors), National Semiconductor (now Fairchild Semiconductor), and Robert Bosch.

6. The institution of licensed manufacturing warehouses was established under the provisions of section 65/65A of the Customs Act of 1967. A licensed manufacturing warehouse is a manufacturing unit (factory) granted to any person for warehousing and manufacturing approved products on the same premise. It is intended to cater primarily to export-oriented industries. Exemption from customs duties is given to all raw materials and components used directly in the manufacturing of approved products, from the initial stage of manufacturing until the finished products are packed and readied for export.

7. The Industrial Linkage Program seeks to build linkages by offering tax incentives for SME suppliers producing eligible products to improve their capacities as well as for MNCs that incur costs to help their suppliers upgrade, such as costs for training, product development and testing, and factory auditing. The Global Supplier Program covers 80 percent of SMEs' fees for courses at registered training providers, and it provides MNCs with financial and organizational support for sending specialists to local firms for upgrading purposes (UNCTAD 2011).

8. The National Industry 4.0 Policy aims to drive digital transformation of the manufacturing sector and related service sectors in Malaysia. It calls for tax incentives, efficient digital infrastructure, a regulatory framework to increase industry adoption of new technologies, investment in future skilled labor, and increased access to smart technologies.

9. This list is published annually by Malaysia's Critical Skills Monitoring Committee to identify shortages of labor in occupations associated with the country's growing knowledge-based economy.

References

Bank Negara Malaysia. 2016. "Bank Negara Malaysia Annual Report 2015." Bank Negara Malaysia, Kuala Lumpur.

Bernama. 2018. "Exports of Made-in-Malaysia Medical Devices Expected to Cross RM23b in 2019." Malaysiakini, December 6, 2018. https://www.malaysiakini.com/news/454998.

Bernama. 2020. "Malaysia Remains Competitive amid COVID-19 Pandemic – MIDA." June 17, 2020. https://www.mida.gov.my/mida-news/malaysia-remains-competitive-amid-covid-19-pandemic-mida/.

Best, M. H., and R. Rasiah. 2003. "Malaysian Electronics: At the Crossroads." Programme Development and Technical Cooperation Division, United Nations Industrial Development Organization, Vienna.

CSC (Critical Skills Monitoring Committee). 2020. "Critical Occupations List 2019/2020: Technical Report." Talent Corporation Malaysia, Kuala Lumpur.

Frederick, S., and G. Gereffi. 2013. "Costa Rica in the Electronics Global Value Chain." Center on Globalization, Governance & Competitiveness, Duke University, Durham, NC.

Frederick, S., and G. Gereffi. 2016. "The Philippines in the Electronics and Electrical Global Value Chain." Center on Globalization, Governance & Competitiveness, Duke University, Durham, NC.

Freund, C., and T. Moran. 2017. "Multinational Investors as Export Superstars: How Emerging-Market Governments Can Reshape Comparative Advantage." PIIE Working Paper 17-1, Peterson Institute for International Economics, Washington, DC.

Hai, Dato' Wong Siew. 2013. "The Malaysian Electrical & Electronics (E&E) Industry – At an Inflexion Point." *Jurutera* 2013 (7): 6–9.

Hamdan, Muhammed Ahmad. 2020. "E&E Sector Poised to Remain Firm Thanks to Govt Proactive Measures, Says MIDA." The Edge Markets, June 4, 2020. https://www.theedgemarkets.com/article/ee-sector-poised-remain-firm-thanks-govt-proactive-measures-says-mida.

Heilbron, Armando, and Hania Kronfol. 2020. "Increasing the Development Impact of Investment Promotion Agencies." In *Global Investment Competitiveness Report 2019/2020: Rebuilding Investor Confidence in Times of Uncertainty*. Washington, DC: World Bank Group.

Ismail, M. N. 2001. "Foreign Direct Investments and Development: The Malaysian Electronics Sector." CMI Working Paper 2001:4, Chr. Michelsen Institute, Bergen.

Kharas, H., A. Zeufack, and H. Majeed. 2010. *Cities, People & the Economy: A Study on Positioning Penang*. Kuala Lumpur: Khazanah Nasional Berhad and World Bank.

Malaysia, Office of the Prime Minister. 1971. *The Second Malaysia Plan 1971-1975*. Kuala Lumpur: Government Printers. https://www.pmo.gov.my/dokumenattached/RMK/RMK2.pdf.

MIDA (Malaysian Investment Development Authority). 2010. "Malaysia's Experience: Reform of Investment Incentives." MIDA, Kuala Lumpur. https://www.tepav.org.tr/upload/files/haber/1285937305-6.Country_Experience___Malasia__INDUSTRIAL_POLICY_1__edited_090910.pdf.

MIDA (Malaysian Investment Development Authority). 2020. "Malaysia Investment Performance Report 2019." MIDA, Kuala Lumpur. https://www.mida.gov.my/home/administrator/system_files/modules/photo/uploads/20200421151258_MIDA%20IPR%202019%20fullbook_FINAL.pdf.

MITI (Ministry of International Trade and Industry). 2018. "Industry4WRD: National Policy on Industry 4.0." MITI, Kuala Lumpur. https://www.miti.gov.my/miti/resources/STA%20Folder/PDF%20file/Industry4WRD_-_National_Policy_on_Industry_4.0_.pdf.

Moran, T. 2014. "Foreign Investment and Supply Chains in Emerging Markets: Recurring Problems and Demonstrated Solutions." PIIE Working Paper 14-12, Peterson Institute for International Economics, Washington, DC.

OECD (Organisation for Economic Co-operation and Development). 2013. *OECD Investment Policy Reviews: Malaysia 2013*. Paris: OECD Publishing.

OECD (Organisation for Economic Co-operation and Development). 2018. *OECD Investment Policy Reviews: Southeast Asia 2018*. Paris: OECD Publishing.

OECD (Organisation for Economic Co-operation and Development). 2020. "COVID-19 and Global Value Chains: Policy Options to Build More Resilient Production Networks." OECD Publishing, Paris.

OECD (Organisation for Economic Co-operation and Development) and UNIDO (United Nations Industrial Development Organization). 2019. "Integrating Southeast Asian SMEs in Global Value Chains: Enabling Linkages with Foreign Investors." OECD and UNIDO.

OECD (Organisation for Economic Co-operation and Development) Investment Committee. 2005. "Encouraging Linkages between Small and Medium-Sized Companies and Multinational Enterprises." OECD, Paris. http://www.oecd.org/daf/inv/investmentfordevelopment/35795105.pdf.

Rasiah, R. 1988. "The Semiconductor Industry in Penang: Implications for the New International Division of Labour Theories." *Journal of Contemporary Asia* 18 (1): 44–65.

Rasiah, R. 2015. "The Industrial Policy Experience of the Electronics Industry in Malaysia." In *The Practice of Industrial Policy Government—Business Coordination in Africa and East Asia*, edited by John Page and Finn Tarp, 123–44. Oxford, U.K.: Oxford University Press.

Reuters. 2020. "Malaysia Says Tech Firms, Hit by Pandemic and Trade War, Keen to Move to Country." Reuters, June 5, 2020. https://www.reuters.com/article/us-health-coronavirus-malaysia-investmen/malaysia-says-tech-firms-hit-by-pandemic-and-trade-war-keen-to-move-to-country-idUSKBN23C1K7.

Sturgeon, T., and M. Kawakami. 2010. "Global Value Chains in the Electronics Industry: Was the Crisis a Window of Opportunity for Developing Countries?" In *Global Value Chains in a Postcrisis World: A Development Perspective*, edited by Olivier Cattaneo, Gary Gereffi, and Cornelia Staritz, 245–301. Washington, DC: World Bank.

Sturgeon, T., and M. Kawakami. 2011. "Global Value Chains in the Electronics Industry: Characteristics, Crisis, and Upgrading Opportunities for Firms from Developing Countries." *International Journal of Technological Learning, Innovation and Development* 4 (1): 120–47.

Teng, Liew Jia. 2020. "The State of the Nation: Malaysian Manufacturers Feeling the Chill from China's Cold." The Edge Markets, March 6, 2020. https://www.theedgemarkets.com/article/state-nation-malaysian-manufacturers-feeling-chill-chinas-cold.

Thomsen, S. 2004, "Investment Incentives and FDI in Selected ASEAN Countries." In *International Investment Perspectives 2004*. Paris: OECD Publishing.

UNCTAD (United Nations Conference on Trade and Development). 2011. *Best Practices in Investment for Development: How to Create and Benefit from FDI-SME Linkages—Lessons from Malaysia and Singapore*. Investment Advisory Series B, No. 4. Geneva: United Nations.

World Bank. 2011. "Brain Drain." *Malaysia Economic Monitor* (April). World Bank, Washington, DC.

World Bank. 2020. "East Asia and Pacific in the Time of COVID-19." *World Bank East Asia and Pacific Economic Update* (April). World Bank, Washington, DC.

World Bank Group. 2020. "2019 Investment Policy and Regulatory Review: Malaysia." World Bank Group, Washington, DC. http://documents.worldbank.org/curated/en/952491586324182535/Malaysia-2019-Investment-Policy-and-Regulatory-Review.

Yean, T. S., and L. C. Siang. 2011. "Foreign Direct Investment and Spillovers in Malaysia." In *Foreign Direct Investments in Asia*, edited by Chalongphob Sussangkarn, Yung Chul Park, and Sung Jin Kang, 71–103. New York: Routledge.

Chapter 9

Mauritius—Partnering with foreign firms to upgrade the tourism industry

MAXIMILIAN PHILIP ELTGEN AND VICTOR STEENBERGEN

Summary

The Mauritius case study shows how foreign direct investment (FDI) can be leveraged to build on and upgrade an existing viable industry. In the late 1970s, Mauritius began to develop its tourism industry by encouraging the accumulation of capital into the industry through the provision of incentives. By providing basic infrastructure; ensuring air access through the national carrier, Air Mauritius; and actively marketing the country as an upscale tourism destination, the government facilitated the growth of a mainly domestic industry. At the time FDI was permitted and encouraged only in select segments (mainly hotels). Once the industry had become viable in the early 2000s, FDI was gradually liberalized and encouraged (through investment promotion), which led to a surge in FDI inflows, a boom in the industry, and significant global value chain (GVC) upgrading. The case study also highlights the important role that nonequity modes (NEMs) of production, such as management contracts (hotels) or franchising arrangements (restaurants and car rentals), can play in accessing skills, management expertise, and technology. Such arrangements have been important throughout the development of Mauritius's tourism industry. By looking at a 50-year process, the case study provides insights into the effectiveness of distinct strategic approaches and policy tools for leveraging FDI at different phases of development.

Mauritius's role in the tourism global value chain

The tourism global value chain

Tourism is an important driver of economic growth around the world.[1] In 2018, tourism supported an estimated 123 million jobs (3.8 percent of global employment) and generated US$8.8 trillion in direct revenue (3.2 percent of global gross domestic product [GDP]). The total contribution of tourism to GDP (including wider effects from investment, the supply chain, and induced income impact) was US$8.8 billion (10.4 percent of global GDP) (WTTC 2019).

Developing countries are playing an increasingly prominent role in the tourism industry. In 2018, 45.6 percent of international tourist arrivals and 35.4 percent of tourism receipts accrued to emerging economies (UNWTO 2019). Because tourism is employment-intensive and often has linkages to many other parts of the economy, it directly contributes to poverty reduction. For many developing countries, tourism is one of the main sources of foreign exchange income and a major component of exports, creating much-needed employment and development opportunities (UNCTAD 2007).

Conceptualizing the tourism industry from a GVC perspective provides insights into the main actors and their relationships, different value creation processes, and upgrading pathways. Figure 9.1 shows the tourism GVC as a sequence of direct flows of money from consumers to service providers along different distribution channels. There are three types of actors in the tourism GVC: consumers, intermediaries, and service providers (Daly and Guinn 2016). There are also three main distribution channels:

1. *Direct booking channel.* Through this channel, consumers bypass distribution intermediaries and book directly with service providers such as airlines and hotels.

2. *Online package channel.* Online portals and travel agencies such as Expedia, Priceline, and booking.com have grown in prominence in recent years. These online portals offer many of the same services as in-person travel agencies. In some cases, they work together with the global distribution system. The global distribution system provides a shared platform for information regarding airline, hotel, and tour scheduling, including prices, which allows travel agents to reserve and book directly in real time.

FIGURE 9.1 **The tourism global value chain**

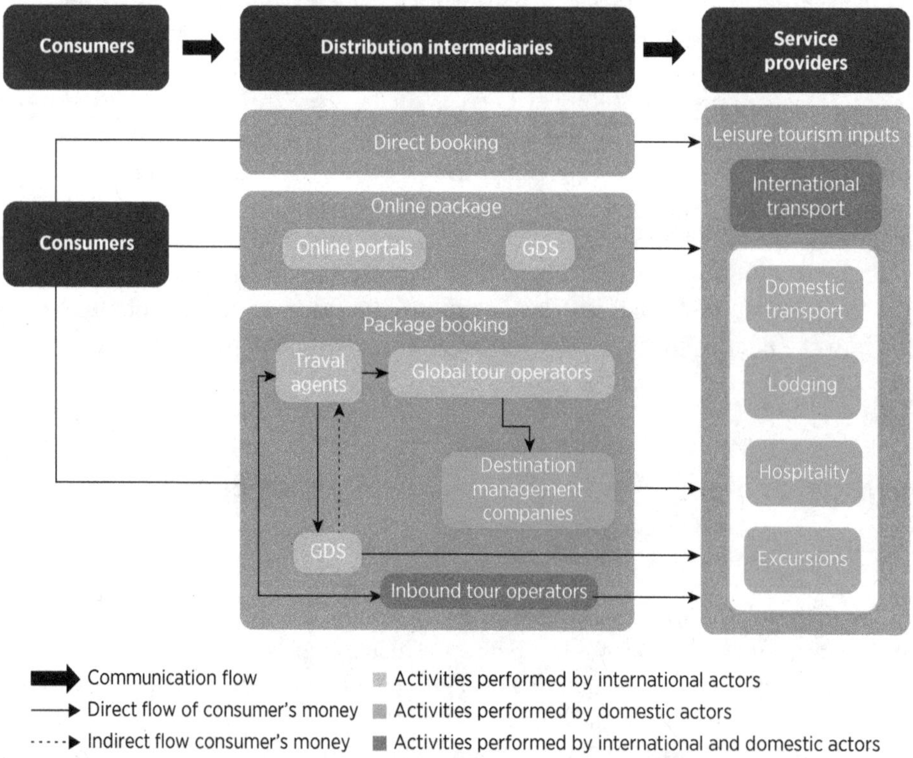

Source: Duke Global Value Chains Center, in Daly and Guinn 2016.
Note: GDS = global distribution system (coordinating online portals).

3. *Package booking channel.* Traditionally, this has been the main distribution channel for many countries. It involves a number of different distribution intermediaries:

- *Travel agents* often act as retailers selling already assembled tours but may also work with the global distribution system to sell individual services or with inbound tour operators or destination management companies (DMCs).

- *Global tour operators* purchase services from individual providers and assemble them into products, which are most often sold through travel agents. Some large companies have vertically integrated and sell directly to consumers.

- *Destination management companies* work closely with global tour operators to purchase local services for the operator's offering, given that DMCs often have better knowledge of the local product. They may also support the management of consumers in the inbound country.

- *Inbound tour operators* perform similar services to DMCs but focus on direct sales to customers in the inbound country.

The lead firms in the leisure tourism GVC are international airline carriers, cruise lines, global tour operators, online travel agencies, and multinational hotel brands (Christian et al. 2011). These firms often play a key role though marketing campaigns and close contact with consumers and capture much of the value created in the GVC. Global tour operators and online travel agencies may have profit margins of more than 20 percent as opposed to about 10–20 percent for DMCs or travel agents (Daly and Guinn 2016).

Mauritius's participation in the tourism global value chain

The tourism industry has played an important role in Mauritius's economy since the late 1970s and continues to account for a large part of the country's exports. International tourism receipts have grown steadily from as low as US$9.7 million in the 1970s to US$2.16 billion in 2018, constituting 34 percent of the country's total exports. Direct employment in the tourism industry exceeds 73,600, up from about 20,700 in 2002 (Statistics Mauritius 2017; UNCTAD 2008). As of 2019, the industry accounted for 12.8 percent of total employment in Mauritius (Statistics Mauritius, in AHRIM 2019).

The number of tourism arrivals has also risen steadily, from an average of 120,000 a year in the 1980s to 1.4 million in 2018 (UNWTO 2020) (figure 9.2). As has traditionally been the case, the majority of tourists in 2018 were from European countries, mostly from France (20.4 percent of arrivals), the United Kingdom (10.9 percent), and Germany (9.5 percent). Regional tourism has also been important for Mauritius since the 1990s; in 2018, 9.9 percent of tourists came from Réunion and 9.2 percent from South Africa. However, other regional sources of tourists (for example, the Comoros, Kenya, the Seychelles, and Zimbabwe) have not contributed significantly to arrivals. Among the new markets that have been growing and that are explicitly targeted by tourism promotion are India (6.1 percent of arrivals in 2018) and China (4.7 percent) (AHRIM 2019). Almost all tourists (97.2 percent) arrive via air transport. According to a survey of inbound tourism, in 2018 the main purpose of visit was holiday (79.3 percent), followed by honeymoon (13.1 percent), business (2.7 percent), and visiting friends and relatives (1.4 percent) (Statistics Mauritius 2018). The purpose of visits has remained virtually constant over time.

Mauritius today boasts a comprehensive ecosystem of actors directly operating in the tourism industry. As of March 2019, 2,846 entities are directly licensed with the Mauritius Tourism Authority (figure 9.3). About 66 percent of available rooms are hotel rooms, but in recent years nonhotel accommodation has been growing faster than hotel accommodation (8.9 percent compared with 2.0 percent average growth over the period 2009–19).

Distribution channels in Mauritius are slowly beginning to change. Package booking through tour operators is still the most important distribution channel, especially for traditional markets such as France and Germany. New markets such as China, by

FIGURE 9.2 Number of international tourism arrivals in Mauritius, 1982–2018

Arrivals
1,600,000
1,400,000
1,200,000
1,000,000
800,000
600,000
400,000
200,000
0
1982
1985
1988
1991
1994
1997
2000
2003
2006
2009
2012
2015
2018

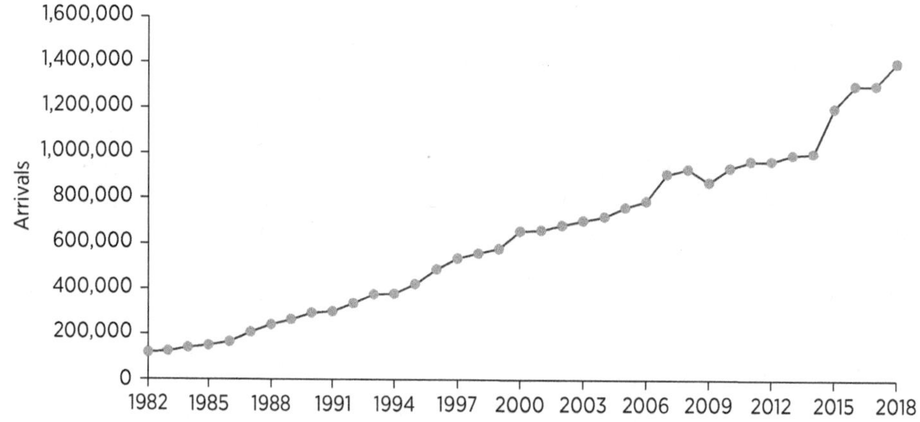

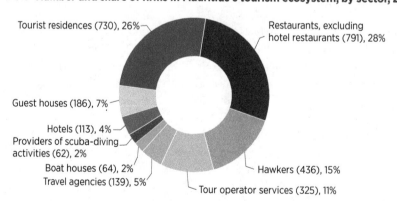

Sources: Statistics Mauritius data; World Bank World Development Indicators.

FIGURE 9.3 Number and share of firms in Mauritius's tourism ecosystem, by sector, 2019

Tourist residences (730), 26%
Restaurants, excluding hotel restaurants (791), 28%
Guest houses (186), 7%
Hotels (113), 4%
Providers of scuba-diving activities (62), 2%
Boat houses (64), 2%
Travel agencies (139), 5%
Hawkers (436), 15%
Tour operator services (325), 11%

Source: AHRIM 2019.

contrast, are almost entirely dominated by online travel agencies, according to interviews with hotel group executives. Direct online booking is also becoming more and more important.

In recent years, the type of products tourists demand has also shifted. Tourists in Mauritius traditionally booked half-board (which includes pension, breakfast, and dinner) or bed and breakfast. However, according to interviews with stakeholders conducted for this case study, tourists have switched to requesting all-inclusive packages, following a global trend. The largest proportion of meal arrangements in 2015 was half-board (48 percent), but the largest proportion in 2018 was all inclusive (42 percent) (Statistics Mauritius 2015, 2018). As a result, it has become more difficult for hotels to profit from selling beverages, which had often been a significant part of revenue. Spending outside of the hotels has also been depressed as a result.

The development of Mauritius's tourism industry: The role of foreign direct investment

Mauritius's experience in leveraging FDI to enter and upgrade in the tourism GVC can be divided into three phases. In phase 1 (late 1970s to early 2000s), Mauritius's tourism industry grew mainly by relying on domestic capital that was channeled from the sugar sector to the tourism industry. The government of Mauritius supported this process by providing a number of incentives, and further helped generate tourism demand by active marketing and by creating the state carrier, Air Mauritius, to ensure air connectivity. Multinational corporations (MNCs) played a less significant role during that phase. FDI in the narrow sense was restricted in most segments of the economy; as a consequence, the only foreign investors were a number of hotels. At the same time, other actors played a role through NEMs, which were allowed. NEMs are arrangements in which an MNC may have significant de facto control or influence over a local investor or local enterprise even without an equity stake, including through management contracts, leasing, or franchising (UNCTAD 2007). In the first phase, most foreign restaurant and car rental chains were present through franchises. Throughout this phase, Mauritius saw steady growth in exports, from US$42 million in 1980 to US$542 million in 2000 (figure 9.4).

In phase 2 (early 2000s to late 2000s), FDI in the form of direct capital flows became important. Gradual liberalization and the creation of specific programs to attract foreign investors into real estate and resort development led to significant FDI inflows from the mid-2000s onward (see figure 9.5; notably, NEMs such as franchising and management contracts do not appear in official FDI data). Other tourism segments such as tour operators also gradually began to be liberalized. As a result, exports almost doubled between 2000 and 2010 (US$542 million to US$1.29 billion).

From the late 2000s onward (phase 3), FDI and exports continued to grow. NEMs, especially hotel management contracts, played an increasing role; and domestic hotel groups also began to become outward investors, which helped further upgrading.

FIGURE 9.4 **International tourism receipts in Mauritius, 1980–2018**

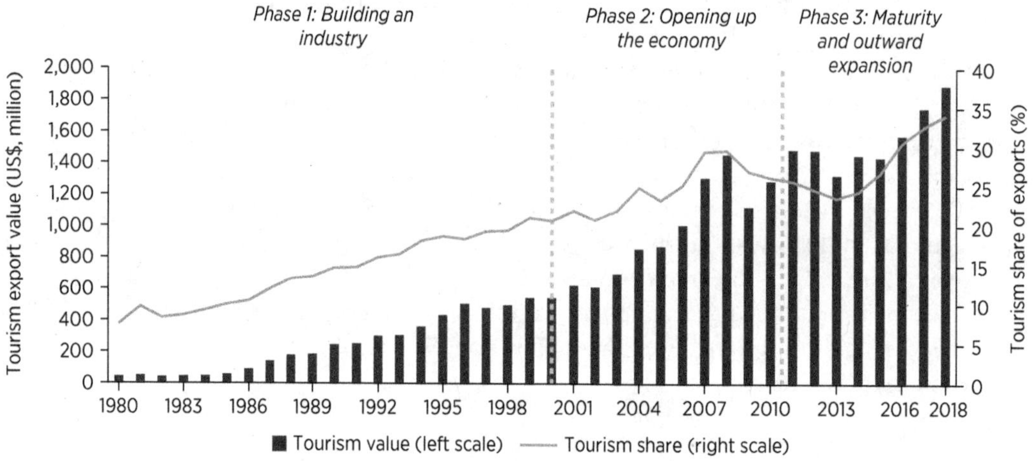

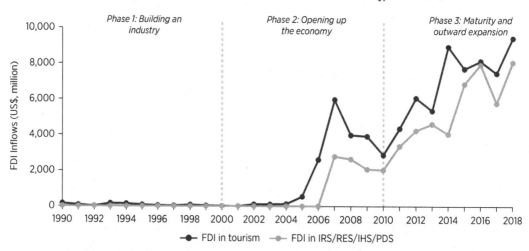

Source: World Bank calculations based on United Nations Comtrade data.

FIGURE 9.5 **Inward foreign direct investment flows in the tourism industry, 1990–2018**

Sources: Bank of Mauritius Monthly Statistical Bulletins, various issues; WTO 1995, 2001, 2008, 2014.
Note: From 1994 to 2006, the Bank of Mauritius in its sector-specific FDI data included a specific "tourism" category. From 2007 onward, to categorize FDI inflows, the government of Mauritius has used the International Standard Industrial Classification, which does not list tourism as a category, so the category "accommodation and food services" is used as a proxy for FDI in tourism. More detailed tourism FDI comes from four government schemes (IRS, RES, IHS, and PDS). FDI in travel agencies or tour operators is not included. FDI data for 2018 are preliminary estimates. FDI = foreign direct investment; IHS = Invest-Hotel Scheme; IRS = Investment Resort Scheme; RES = Real Estate Scheme; PDS = Property Development Scheme (which replaced the IRS and RES in 2015).

Phase 1: Building an industry (late 1970s–early 2000s)

Tourism in Mauritius had its beginnings in the late 1970s, when domestic investors began to invest in the industry. In the 1960s and 1970s, Mauritius was predominantly an agricultural economy, with only minor economic activity in manufacturing and tourism. In the early 1970s, there was only one hotel in Mauritius, mainly catering to the crew of Air Mauritius. When a large boom in the sugar cane market led to a surge in domestic capital, the owners decided to invest into other industries, especially textiles and tourism (Cattaneo 2009). In the 1980s, the global sugar market had changed and countries such as Brazil were on the rise. To diversify away from sugar, the private sector in Mauritius, together with the government, focused on export diversification. Because a few small hotels were doing well, the decision was made to strengthen the tourism industry.

The shift toward tourism was strongly supported by the Mauritian government. In addition to providing a stable and secure business environment, the government offered a number of incentives. Under the 1974 Development Incentives Act, which also applied to hotel development, tax relief was granted to investment projects for a period of 10 years. In addition, a number of items were exempt from customs duty. In 1982, the Mauritian government set up two programs to specifically provide incentives for the development and management of hotels: the Hotel Management Scheme and the Hotel Development Scheme. Under both programs, the corporate tax rate was lowered (to 15 percent instead of the statutory 30 percent) and dividends received by shareholders were exempt from income tax for 10 years. Approved hotels under the Hotel Development Scheme were granted a Hotel Development Certificate, which permitted a one-time exemption of customs duties on the importation of equipment. Holders of such certificates were also eligible for subsidized loans from the Development Bank of Mauritius. According to an industry veteran interviewed for this case study, "these loans had been extremely important in the 1980s and 1990s for stimulating hotel construction. Subsidized loans had interest rates as low as 8-9%, which were significantly cheaper than the 22% market rates at the time." Other tourism industry segments were also supported, including tour operators, car rental agencies, and first-class restaurants (WTO 1995); and labor market regulations were relaxed to enable foreign labor to be imported (Zafar 2011).

From the beginning, the government of Mauritius's strategy was clear: to promote the development of upscale tourism. Because of limited space on the island, ecological concerns, a "dislike for mass tourism and high-rise building" (Zafar 2011, 101), and the identification of tourism as a niche, the government decided to develop an industry targeting wealthy individuals from developed countries, particularly France, Germany, and the United Kingdom.

To ensure the positioning of Mauritius as an upscale tourism destination, the government tightly regulated the industry and managed its growth. With the 1989 hotel regulations, several important conditions were established (UNCTAD 2008):

- The maximum number of rooms per hotel was limited to 200.

- Hotel projects had to be financed by at least 40 percent equity.

- Investment per room was to be at least 4.5 million Mauritian rupees (MUR).

- For coastal hotels, the promoter had to have at least 4 acres of land; foreign-owned coastal hotels were required to lease land, at least 10 acres per project, from the government.

In the 1980s, government control also extended to the amount of foreign ownership in the economy—most segments of the tourism industry were closed to FDI. Full foreign ownership of new hotel developments was permitted only for hotels of more than 100 rooms; foreign participation was limited to 49 percent for hotels with fewer rooms. In addition, a minimum capital investment requirement for foreign-owned hotels of MUR 10 million (US$400,000) applied (UNCTAD 2001). Under the 1975 Non-Citizen Property Restrictions Act, foreigners were allowed to buy property only with approval from the Prime Minister's Office, and foreign-owned coastal hotels had to lease land from the government (WTO 1995), also subject to approval. Foreign participation in restaurants was limited to 49 percent, and only where investment exceeded MUR 10 million, which would be a rare occurrence (WTO 1995). No foreign investment was permitted in travel agencies, tour operators, tourist guides, car rental agencies, and yacht charters. Equity participation in duty-free shops by foreigners was limited to 30 percent. Foreign travel agencies arranging for services in Mauritius had to work through an agent established in Mauritius. Establishing a travel agency also required clearance from a designated committee chaired by the Minister of Tourism, Leisure and External Communications (WTO 1995).

To attract a sufficient number of upscale tourists, the government actively promoted Mauritius as a tourism destination. With high-level engagement, notably by the politician Gaëtan Duval, Mauritius pioneered "celebrity marketing," which was seen as the ideal way to promote Mauritius as a luxury destination. In 1996 the Mauritius Tourism Promotion Authority was established to provide a more formalized tourism promotion framework. With offices in several countries, its function is to promote Mauritius abroad as a tourist destination by conducting advertising campaigns, participating in tourism fairs, and organizing promotional campaigns and activities in Mauritius and abroad.

In the early stages, one essential factor facilitating tourism in Mauritius was the state-owned carrier, Air Mauritius. Together with Air France and the British Overseas Airways Corporation (BOAC), the government of Mauritius in 1967 created the airline. Several industry veterans interviewed for this case study highlighted Air Mauritius as key to enabling rising numbers of tourists to Mauritius, particularly because it would continue to schedule flights in the off season, when other airlines would not fly.

Mauritius's air access policy in the 1980s and 1990s was driven by the dual objectives of protecting Air Mauritius as the flag carrier and attracting up-market tourists (WTO 2001). The strategy was characterized by maintenance of single-designation clauses in air service agreements (one airline per route to Mauritius); double-approval fare systems that entitled the government to control fares; restrictions with respect to capacity and frequencies; reluctance to exchange fifth freedom rights; a noncharter policy (with some exceptions); modest liberalization efforts, only in a regional context; and no full privatization (WTO 2001). This restrictive policy was largely supported by both the government and the private sector to maintain high prices and thereby to prevent mass tourism (Page 1999). Notably, although protecting Air Mauritius may initially have been an effective way to facilitate tourism, keeping these protections in place over decades may have eventually been detrimental to the development of Mauritius's air connectivity overall (see section on current challenges).

MNCs in the 1980s and 1990s mainly played a role through the technological know-how and access to markets that they brought rather than because of capital inflows. The only segment of the tourism industry in which FDI in a narrow sense was significant was in hotels; in 2001, about 40 percent of larger hotels (more than 100 rooms) were foreign owned (UNCTAD 2001). In other segments, MNCs were present through NEMs. Most major restaurants and car rental chains were represented through franchises (UNCTAD 2001). A number of stakeholder interviews highlighted that global hotel chains contributed significantly in bringing more tourists to Mauritius. In particular, attracting ClubMed and Maritim, the first two hotel chains that came to Mauritius in the late 1970s, helped put Mauritius on the map for tourists from Europe.

As a result of the government-led, private sector–driven initiatives, Mauritius's tourism industry began to boom. The number of tourists rose from 75,000 in 1975 to 656,000 in 2000, and the contribution to GDP increased from 1.6 percent in 1976 to 7.4 percent in 2000 (UNCTAD 2008). Several domestic hotel groups, such as Beachcomber, Constance, and Sun Resorts, emerged and dominated the industry. In 1999, the largest hotel chain in Mauritius was entirely Mauritian owned, and the second largest was 82 percent Mauritian owned (Page 1999).

Linkages with other sectors of the economy were limited to select food items and maintenance services. Facilitated by duty-free concessions, most furniture and construction materials were imported. Local products that were used had frequently only received final processing in Mauritius (Page 1999). Meat (except beef), fish, and a few vegetables tended to be sourced locally, but other food items, including fruits, were mainly imported. Services supporting the tourism industry, such as the maintenance of equipment, vehicles, and refrigerators, were mostly contracted out to local firms (UNCTAD 2008).

Interviews conducted for this case study suggest that these local sourcing dynamics have not changed significantly through the present, which is not surprising for a small island nation. Government support, according to the interviews, is focused on promoting the development of specific industries; for example, subsidies and grants are given to local fishermen as well as for small and medium enterprise development. However, the promotion of supplier linkages seems to be largely limited to informal encouragement of hotel groups to source locally and contribute to the community. Several hotels interviewed had specific programs in place to source with the local community, for example, to promote Creole food in the hotel restaurants or to work with young composers and musicians to perform on the hotel site.

Phase 2: Opening up the economy (early 2000s–late 2000s)

Having built a sizable tourism industry in the 1980s and 1990s under a regime of close control, the Mauritian government in the 2000s began liberalizing and actively promoting FDI to further develop the industry. The Board of Investment (replaced in 2017 by the Economic Development Board, EDB) was created in 2000 to serve as an investment promotion agency, signaling a stronger emphasis on FDI to develop the Mauritian economy. Beginning in 2002, the government of Mauritius introduced a number of incentive schemes that allowed foreign citizens and companies to acquire different types of immovable property (see box 9.1). These schemes were the main impetus for a strong increase in FDI inflows from the mid-2000s onward (see figure 9.5) and contributed to diversifying Mauritius's leisure tourism industry. Foreign investors such as Four Seasons and ClubMed began to use the incentive programs to develop large hotel complexes, of which single units were sold to high–net worth individuals.

BOX 9.1 **Key incentive programs for developing the accommodation sector**

In the 2000s, three schemes were introduced that allowed foreign citizens and companies to purchase real estate property:

1. *Invest-Hotel Scheme* (IHS), 2002. The IHS allowed hotel developers to finance the development of a hotel project by selling villas, suites, rooms, or other components that form part of the hotel complex to individual buyers, including to noncitizens and foreign companies. The buyer of a unit entered into a lease agreement by which the property was leased back to the seller. For the acquisition of a stand-alone villa, the minimum investment requirement was US$500,000; otherwise there was no minimum requirement. The scheme was applicable for both freehold and leasehold (state) land.

2. *Integrated Resort Scheme* (IRS), 2002. The IRS was introduced to attract high–net worth noncitizens to Mauritius by allowing them to acquire resort and residential property. Under the scheme, no authorization from the Prime Minister's office was required for the acquisition of immovable property by noncitizens or companies registered as foreign companies. Beginning in 2007, several conditions were imposed: a minimum size of more than 10 hectares of the integrated resort development area, a social contribution of 200,000 Mauritian rupees (approximately US$6,700) per residential property, and a minimum investment requirement of US$500,000. Resident status was granted to noncitizens acquiring the property.

3. *Real Estate Scheme* (RES), 2007. The RES was introduced as an extension of the IRS for small landowners. It provided for the development of residential units of international standing on freehold land of at least one arpent (about an acre) but not more than 10 hectares (23.69 arpents); commercial facilities and leisure amenities attached to the residential units; and day-to-day management services to the residents, such as security, maintenance, gardening, solid waste disposal, and household services. Unlike the IRS, the RES imposed neither a minimum purchase fee on a residential plot nor the payment of a social contribution. Also, no residence permit was attached to the purchase.

In 2015, the IRS and RES were consolidated under the Property Development Scheme, which aligned the servicing fees and put a stronger emphasis on the social contribution of each unit toward social amenities and community development that have to be provided to qualify for the scheme (EDB 2019).

Sources: OECD 2014; WTO 2008.

Often, these units were then rented out by the hotel group on behalf of the owners. In several cases, resorts were constructed within the country (instead of on the coastline) and thus provided a different offering to tourists, including novelties such as golf courses that attracted tourists from East Asia.

In the mid-2000s, the government of Mauritius also began to liberalize other segments of the tourism industry. Since 2006, foreign equity restrictions on restaurants and on hotels with fewer than 100 rooms have no longer applied. Investment in the pleasure craft sector was authorized subject to an initial investment of MUR 10 million and the originality of the project proposal (WTO 2008). In 2012, restrictions on foreign investment in car rental, travel agency, and tour operator services were removed to enable a bilateral investment treaty with the United States to be signed (WTO 2014). Economy-wide, investment screening was removed, and the acquisition of property was conditioned on approval from the Board of Investment for business purposes instead of requiring prime minister approval (WTO 2014). Although equity restrictions have largely been removed, there may be other conditions depending on the activity.

Liberalization led to significant firm-level upgrading. Based on stakeholder interviews, there have been several cases in which local companies acquired by MNCs benefited from the transfer of skills, management expertise, training programs, and local staff opportunities (for firm examples, see box 9.2).

To further support an increase in tourists, the government of Mauritius in 2005 began to gradually liberalize its air access policy. There has been a shift from single or dual designation to multiple designation regimes in Mauritius's bilateral air service arrangements. Many newly signed bilateral agreements in force provide for the fifth freedom traffic rights. Mauritius has also been moving away from its policy of only allowing scheduled flights. It is open to allowing, on a case-by-case basis, charter and

---

BOX 9.2 **How foreign acquisitions help upgrade domestic firms**

The acquisition of a local destination management company (DMC) by a global tour operator serves as a good example of firm-level benefits of foreign direct investment. After having been a local supplier for the global tour operator for several years, in the mid-2000s the multinational corporation (MNC) decided to purchase 51 percent of the equity of the DMC. According to a DMC executive, the MNC was looking for a company that could be "the eyes and ears for the MNC on the ground." Through vertical integration, the MNC sought to capture different components of the value chain and thus gain a competitive advantage over online travel agents such as booking.com.

For the DMC, acquisition by the MNC has resulted in significant growth. The number of employees has grown from 140 at the time of acquisition to 270 in 2020. It also brought significant intangible benefits. According to a DMC executive, "management by the global tour operator keeps us on the edge and instills a mindset of excellence. The acquisition brought strategic thinking, and helped to align technology, finance processes and service delivery; ultimately, it made the staff and the service delivery better. Had the MNC not bought us, we would not have had these consequences."

Benefits extend beyond the DMC. The DMC owns a large fleet of vehicles but also uses subcontractors to serve its clients; as of 2020, the DMC works with 57 subcontractors. There have been several cases in which drivers who worked directly for the DMC became their own business owners, now working as subcontractors.

Another example is the acquisition of a domestic construction company by a multinational engineering services firm. According to an executive, "becoming part of the multinational group has enabled us to have access to global skills. If there is a specific issue for which we lack expertise, we can ask anyone in the global intranet to solve problems that we have; for example, we have the possibility to call an acoustic engineer, of which there are few in Mauritius. Being part of the group is thus a differentiator for our clients. In addition, we can now offer opportunities for our staff to work on global projects in other countries, and we also have access to training opportunities offered by the group, which serves as a nonfinancial bonus for our workers."

Source: This analysis is based on a combination of literature reviews and interviews conducted by the authors between January and March 2020 with representatives of multinational corporations, domestic firms, and trade associations affiliated with the Mauritian tourism industry, as well as government officials; the interviews are the source for all direct quotations that are not otherwise attributed.

special flights on routes that are not being served by airlines operating scheduled air services. The shift in policy can be explained by other countries progressing toward an open skies policy, as well as the reduction in airfares to many competing destinations (to Southeast Asia, for instance) (Cattaneo 2007). Notably, Air Mauritius continues to be majority owned by the Mauritian government, which may have negatively affected the development of air connectivity.

Incentives that had been granted to developers of hotels were progressively withdrawn. The Development Incentives Act, which had granted tax relief to tourism enterprises for a period of 10 years, was repealed in 2000. In 2006, the Hotel Management Scheme, which had stimulated investment in the hotel industry since 1982 (WTO 2008), was also cancelled. These changes can be seen as an overall change in strategy turning away from granting numerous incentives toward having a low-tax regime and targeted promotion of projects (WTO 2008).

In addition to opening up, the government of Mauritius in the 2000s also emphasized regulation and, under the heading of "democratization of the economy," sought to ensure that its benefits were distributed equitably. In 2002, the Mauritius Tourism Authority was established, with the main function of promoting the sustainable development of the tourism industry. It establishes codes of practice and standards, and monitors compliance. All tourist establishments must obtain a tourist enterprise license from the Tourism Authority before beginning operations (WTO 2008). In addition, an environmental protection fee of 0.75 percent was levied on the monthly turnover of hotels and boarding houses, and several funds were set up to increase the welfare of employees and promote community development.

An important facilitating factor for a thriving tourism industry has been workforce development programs, particularly for the hospitality industry. The Hotel School of Mauritius had been set up to prepare potential employees for the tourism sector, particularly for work in hotels. The University of Technology, Mauritius, and the University of Mauritius complemented the Hotel School by offering academic courses leading to undergraduate and postgraduate degrees in tourism, marketing, and hospitality management. By the mid-2000s, the Hotel School produced about 250 graduates per year, and the universities about 100 graduates (UNCTAD 2008). The government of Mauritius actively supported workforce development through a scheme whereby hotels received a 60 percent refund of the expenses for approved training through the Hotel School of Mauritius and the Mauritius Qualifications Authority (UNCTAD 2008). In addition, many hotels also trained their employees internally.

However, training programs were not sufficient to fulfill the needs of a rapidly growing industry, and they also provide evidence of the difficulty of requalifying workers for the tourism industry. Despite being able to provide training to a significant number of workers, the tourism industry was still constrained by labor shortages, especially in skilled labor such as middle management and skilled specialists (chefs and bar staff) (Cattaneo 2007). Under a pilot program, the government provided a two-month wage subsidy for workers from the textile sector who took up jobs with on-the-job training in the hotel sector. Few workers were kept on after the subsidy ended, however, often because of their age and relatively low level of skills (the majority had only primary school education) (Cattaneo 2007). As a result, the government decided to promote general training programs rather than subsidy schemes.

The experience shows how challenging the requalification of unskilled workers for the tourism industry may be (Cattaneo 2007).

Phase 3: Expanding abroad and adapting to digitalization (late 2000s–today)

Following a period of liberalization, Mauritius's tourism industry has grown further. International tourism receipts, the number of tourist arrivals, employment in the tourism industry, and FDI flows have all increased (see figures 9.4 and 9.5).

As a result of the growth of the industry, domestic companies have, since the mid-2000s, begun to emerge as outward investors. In the 1990s outward FDI (OFDI) had been limited, but a clear increase can be observed beginning in 2003 (figure 9.6). In addition, several hotel groups interviewed for this study indicated that they used management contracts to manage properties abroad, a situation that does not appear in the official FDI data. The significant increase in tourism OFDI can possibly be explained by the development of core competencies and know-how in hotel management by Mauritian companies (UNCTAD 2001). Geographic proximity has also been a factor. Most tourism OFDI has gone to Réunion, the Comoros, Maldives, and the Seychelles (UNCTAD 2008). Domestic firms interviewed for this case study indicated that OFDI helped them expand and diversify, build a brand, and gain the ability to offer regional package tours.

OFDI in Mauritius has not been subject to restrictions but has instead been supported by the government through information sharing, incentives, and international agreements. In 1994, the government formalized its policy of having no official foreign exchange controls (Nkuna 2017). In 1998, it set up the Regional Development Certificate Scheme, which provides a number of fiscal incentives to firms that hold at least a 35 percent share in an approved regional development project, including

FIGURE 9.6 Outward foreign direct investment flows in tourism, 1990–2018

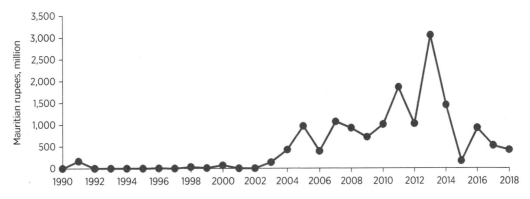

Sources: Bank of Mauritius Monthly Statistical Bulletins, various issues; WTO 1995, 2001, 2008, 2014.
Note: From 1990 to 2006, the Bank of Mauritius in its sector-specific FDI data included a specific "tourism" category. From 2007 onward, to categorize FDI inflows, the government of Mauritius has used the International Standard Industrial Classification, which does not list tourism as a category. For the purposes of this study, the category accommodation and food services is used as a proxy for FDI in tourism from 2007 onward. It includes the provision of short-stay accommodation for visitors and other travelers and the provision of complete meals and drinks fit for immediate consumption. FDI data for 2018 are preliminary estimates. FDI = foreign direct investment.

several provisions for investment relief and allowances, a 15 percent corporate tax, and no tax on dividends (IBP USA 2012). Since 2012, the Board of Investment (now the EDB) has been operating an Africa Center of Excellence dedicated to facilitating investment from Mauritius into Africa. It acts as a repository of business information for Mauritian entrepreneurs about investment opportunities in different sectors in Africa (US Department of State 2019). In addition, the government of Mauritius has signed a number of bilateral investment treaties with African states to protect its investments abroad.

One of the most significant shifts in Mauritius's tourism industry in recent years has been in the type of distribution channels used to sell tourism services, influenced by the digitalization of tourism. Digital technologies and platforms are disrupting the way the tourism sector operates from end to end—affecting the way destinations facilitate tourism, develop products, gather data, access markets, and attract visitors (Bakker and Twining-Ward 2018). As a result, hotel groups interviewed for this case study see a significant rise in bookings through online travel agencies (partially from Chinese tourists) and direct booking. These new channels offer opportunities for hotels to increase their profit margins by omitting intermediaries. Although many hotel groups still work closely together with tour operators, because of long-term business relationships or because there is the danger of losing business by turning away, they are also strategically realigning. There seems to be a clear understanding that to do so they must have a strong brand, because ultimately brands attract customers who book directly with hotels. Different strategies can be observed in this regard (box 9.3).

Digitalization is also altering the tourism accommodation landscape in Mauritius by facilitating peer-to-peer (P2P) accommodation. Increasingly, private rooms, bungalows, or villas on Property Development Scheme or Invest-Hotel Scheme property are offered for rent on platforms such as Airbnb. Some stakeholders interviewed for this case study raised concerns that such accommodation may be unlicensed; may not have the required level of service, guest protection features, insurance, security, and so on; and may prejudice Mauritius's reputation as an upscale tourist destination. Others saw the emergence of P2P accommodation as welcome competition and an opportunity to diversify Mauritius's tourism landscape.

The rise in P2P accommodation is a global trend and provides both challenges and opportunities. Before COVID-19 (coronavirus), the projected annual growth rate for global P2P accommodation was estimated at 31 percent between 2013 and 2025, six times the growth rate of traditional bed-and-breakfasts and hostels (Bakker and Twining-Ward 2018). Many countries are facing challenges similar to those in Mauritius, and country-specific government interventions and standards are necessary to achieve sustainable P2P accommodation. The World Bank Group's report "Tourism and the Sharing Economy" presents recommendations for policy makers in Mauritius and in other countries seeking to regulate P2P accommodation (Bakker and Twining-Ward 2018).

In recent years, Mauritius has also begun to diversify its tourism industry away from leisure tourism to other types of tourism, especially to business tourism and medical tourism. In particular, the meetings, incentives, conferences, and events (MICE) market promises not only to grow the number of tourists but also to complement traditional leisure tourism by increasing the average occupancy rate of hotels. However, stakeholders interviewed for this case study generally agreed that

BOX 9.3 Strategic alignment with online booking: The role of brands

Because of the increased role of online distribution channels, domestic firms in Mauritius are focusing more and more on the role of brands when developing their strategies. A strong global brand and marketing strategy is seen as essential to compete for customers who have a variety of options when coming to Mauritius and, when comparing different offers on online platforms, often tend to decide on the basis of brand recognition.

One strategy for domestic hotel groups is to develop their own brand. To be competitive, one of the domestic hotel groups interviewed decided in the early 2010s to build its own brand under which all hotels owned and managed by the group would be marketed. The company invested heavily in training and marketing to successfully rebrand and created several additional products to enhance brand recognition, such as a coffee chain and branded mattresses. To increase the number of direct customers, which results in a higher margin, the company has focused extensively on its online presence by making its website user friendly and used online advertisements and social media to build a larger customer base. As a result, 25 percent of customers now book directly on the website, 30 percent through online travel agencies, and only 30 percent through tour operators—significantly less compared with other hotel groups. Through management contracts, the company leverages its brand abroad.

Another strategy is to partner with a multinational corporation (MNC) to leverage the MNC's brand. A second domestic hotel group interviewed also acknowledged the increased importance of brands but came to the conclusion that it did not possess the necessary capital, human resources, and expertise to build its own brand. According to an executive, "it is very difficult to survive in today's world in the luxury segment without brand equity, both to get the rate right and to get the occupancy. At the same time, it is also very difficult for a local firm to build that brand and to manage it successfully." Instead, this hotel group chose to partner with and learn from existing brands under varying arrangements; in some cases, the MNC acquired a minority interest in the hotel project and in other cases a pure management contract arrangement was used. From the domestic group's perspective, a minority interest by the MNC is preferred; such an interest helps to align interests under a pure management contract because the MNC may be focused more on developing its own brand than on acting in the shareholder's interests. With the help of the MNC, the domestic group has focused on developing an online travel agency strategy and extending its digital marketing. It now possesses its own team that works on a web strategy for leveraging social media and bloggers. In addition, working with the MNCs made it possible to attract different types of customers and learn about distribution channels other than tour operators; for example, one of the partner brands was particularly savvy in attracting high-net worth Chinese customers, whereas the hotel group had previously mainly attracted middle-class customers.

Source: This analysis is based on a combination of literature reviews and interviews conducted by the authors between January and March 2020 with representatives of multinational corporations, domestic firms, and trade associations affiliated with the Mauritian tourism industry, as well as government officials; the interviews are the source for all direct quotations that are not otherwise attributed.

Mauritius's potential for the business tourism sector is still largely untapped, making up only 3.8 percent of total tourist numbers in 2018 (AHRIM 2019). To further promote MICE tourism, the EDB recently created a targeted VAT Refund Scheme (EDB 2020b). Efforts have also been made to develop Mauritius as a destination for medical tourism by granting specific incentives (EDB 2020a). However, private sector stakeholder perceptions are that medical tourism is likely to remain a niche market, mainly because of higher costs in comparison with competitors.

Current challenges

The most significant challenges that Mauritius's tourism industry is currently facing are related to COVID-19. Strict lockdown measures and travel restrictions issued at the beginning of 2020 led to a severe decline in tourism arrivals and tourism earnings. To mitigate adverse impacts on the industry, the government of Mauritius implemented measures to provide relief to firms operating in the industry and to save jobs. The crisis has also had considerable impacts on Air Mauritius (box 9.4).

Mauritius is also increasingly facing competition as a tourist destination. According to stakeholder interviews, other regional players such as Maldives, the Seychelles, and Sri Lanka, as well as destinations in Southeast Asia, have become strong competitors. For many European tourists, airfares to Southeast Asia are much cheaper in comparison, and countries in that region are catching up in their tourism offerings. According to one industry veteran, "the problem is that Mauritius is no longer a 5-star destination. The average daily spending is 120 euros, much less than in the Maldives (270), the Seychelles (180), and also Sri Lanka (160)." A problem in that regard is the shift toward all-inclusive packages, which reduce the amount spent per tourist, as well as a lack of diversification. As another industry veteran states, "the problem is the lack of viable tourist products. We have built a hotel industry, not a tourism industry—outside of hotels, there is not much to do. Especially new customer groups such as millennials expect more cultural experiences; sun-sea-sand for them is an insufficient attraction." There is consensus about the need to diversify into other types of tourism and within leisure tourism, for example, by providing more evening programs and in-country activities. At the same time, a strategic decision will have to be made on whether to remain in or return to the upscale segment, or whether a turn toward a more mass-market approach is acceptable. This strategy also raises the question of air access, with many stakeholders calling for full liberalization of air access, similar to Maldives's open-sky policy, and privatization of Air Mauritius.

The hotel industry is currently confronting a skills gap. Several hotel managers report a lack of skilled domestic workers, causing a need to rely on foreign workers. However, it is difficult to attract sufficiently skilled foreign workers, so that service quality and hospitality, which had originally been Mauritius's key strengths, suffer as a consequence. The skills gap is explained mainly by a cultural change in society regarding working in the tourism industry (now considered less attractive) and the fact that many potential hotel employees are poached by cruise ships, which often offer three times the salary. The government is working with the private sector to fill this gap through several initiatives, but with varied success. Every employer is required to pay a 1.5 percent training levy to a National Training Fund, which funds programs to train youth and encourage women to go back to work, among other goals. However, according to AHRIM, the beneficiary numbers are often not attained and few employers participate (AHRIM 2019). One successful initiative that several hotels mentioned is the National Skills Development Program, announced in the

BOX 9.4 The impact of COVID-19 (coronavirus) on Mauritius's tourism exports

At the beginning of 2020, strict lockdown measures and travel restrictions to combat the COVID-19 (coronavirus) pandemic led to strong declines in tourism arrivals and tourism earnings for Mauritius. In January 2020, the government of Mauritius began screening arrivals and enforcing mandatory quarantine on visitors from high-risk countries. When, on March 18, 2020, the first three cases of COVID-19 were detected, the government in the following days responded with a series of stringent lockdown measures, including closing down schools, supermarkets, and shops, as well as imposing travel restrictions (Jeeneea and Sukon 2020). By swiftly implementing one of the most stringent government responses globally (Hale et al. 2020), Mauritius was successful in limiting the COVID-19 outbreak. As of September 2020, the measures had limited the number of cases to 356 and the number of COVID-19-related deaths to 10.[a] At the same time, Mauritius's economy, especially its tourism industry, had been strongly affected. The number of tourism arrivals and earnings began to plummet in February 2020 as a result of screenings of visitors from high-risk countries and a decrease in demand resulting in cancellations (figure B9.4.1). Beginning in March, travel restrictions led to the number of arrivals eventually falling to near zero until August. After that, arrivals rose again to reach about 1,000 per month through the end of the year. According to Statistics Mauritius, closed borders will likely result in the tourism industry's output shrinking by 70 percent compared with a year earlier. The closed borders have also significantly affected Air Mauritius, which had already been struggling with its finances in previous years. In April 2020, Air Mauritius entered into voluntary administration to avoid going bankrupt and has received government support (Bloom 2020). Overall, the country's economy is expected to contract by 13 percent in 2020 (Bhuckory 2020).

FIGURE B9.4.1 **Mauritius international tourism arrivals and earnings, July 2019–December 2020**

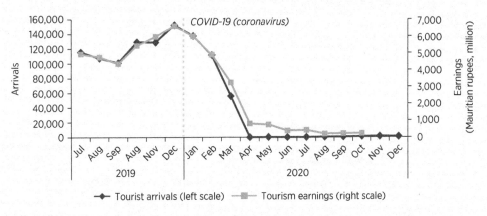

Source: Bank of Mauritius (http://statsmauritius.govmu.org/English/Publications/Pages/Monthly-Tourist-Arrival.aspx).

To mitigate the adverse impact on the country's tourism industry, the government of Mauritius implemented a number of measures to provide relief to tourism operators and save jobs. In addition to economy-wide stimulus and relief measures, such as debt moratoriums and tax payment deferrals, tourism-specific measures were implemented to help operators in the industry. These measures include exemptions from the payment of fees for tourism licenses for a period of two years, suspension of the 0.85 percent environmental protection fee, reductions of the training levy by 0.5 percentage point, waivers for rental payments on state lands for the upcoming financial year, and

Continued on next page ›

BOX 9.4 The impact of COVID-19 (coronavirus) on Mauritius's tourism exports (*continued*)

allowing companies operating under the Deferred Duty and Tax Scheme as well as the Mauritius Duty Free Paradise to sell products on the local market upon payment of the taxes (Government of Mauritius 2020b). To safeguard employment, the government is supporting the tourism industry through the Wage Assistance Scheme and the Self-Employed Assistance Scheme. Through the end of July, about 2 billion Mauritian rupees had been disbursed to more than 39,000 tourism employees under the Wage Assistance Scheme and approximately 26 million Mauritian rupees to about 1,500 Mauritians under the Self-Employed Assistance Scheme (Government of Mauritius 2020a). According to the Mauritian Treasury, both programs will be maintained for the duration of the travel restrictions (Bhuckory 2020). In addition, the Bank of Mauritius has set up the Mauritius Investment Corporation, which will invest in large and medium-sized enterprises having a minimum annual turnover of 100 million Mauritian rupees to mitigate the impacts of the crisis and thus may have a lasting impact on the structure of the tourism industry (Bhuckory 2020).

To help the tourism industry recover, the government of Mauritius announced a staged reopening as well as a rebranding. In September, the government announced a phased easing of travel restrictions beginning in October 2020 under strict conditions, including testing before arrival and a 14-day quarantine in Mauritius (MTPA 2020). These safety measures are also part of a rebranding effort that, according to Mauritius's Minister of Tourism, will focus strongly on presenting Mauritius as a COVID-19-free destination with robust health protocols in place. To that end, the government in November 2020 launched a new long-term visa (Premium Visa) to meet demand from digital nomads, remote workers, and retirees who seek to relocate to the COVID-19-secure island (MTPA 2020).

a. See the Mauritius Ministry of Health and Wellness's web page, "COVID-19 Coronavirus à Maurice" (https://covid19.mu/).

2016/17 budget. It enlists 4,000 unemployed youth ages 16–35 with a Higher School Certificate (secondary education) for training in sector-specific training centers and places them with companies under a full government-paid stipend.[2]

Next to the effects of COVID-19, the biggest medium- to long-term challenge for Mauritius's tourism industry is climate change. Mauritius's ecosystem presents key vulnerabilities to its tourism industry, which may be harmed by other sectors in the country. For example, a recent spill of 1,000 tonnes of fuel oil caused by the bulk carrier MV Wakashio running aground on a coral reef on July 25, 2020, adds to concerns about littering and ocean pollution that threaten the sustainability of Mauritius's tourism industry (British Broadcasting Corporation 2020). Similarly, rising sea levels are threatening to erode Mauritius's coasts and beaches, which are the basis of its tourism industry. According to the executive of an engineering services firm, "with the current development, there likely won't be any more beach resorts in 50 years time. While it may be possible to stabilize the shores for 4-5 years, it will be very difficult to do so for decades." As a member of the United Nations Framework Convention on Climate Change (UNFCCC 2015) and the Paris Agreement, Mauritius engages in finding multilateral solutions to address climate change. In its Third National Communication to the UNFCCC (UNEP 2019), Mauritius identifies tourism as a sector vulnerable to climate change and outlines various climate change–related impacts observed in the coastal areas. However, stakeholders describe the current regulatory climate for beach reshoring as very difficult, and policy solutions as not effectively implemented. As a local tourism expert stated, "there is a need for an integrated strategy and clearer legal framework for environmental protection to avoid coastal erosion. One cannot rely on private actors only, since many non-hotels are not able to pay for the coastal restoration."

Conclusion

Mauritius's experience shows how FDI can be leveraged to significantly upgrade and grow an existing industry. Once a viable tourism industry had been created by the early 2000s, liberalization of the tourism and aviation sectors and the creation of specific incentive schemes led to a surge in FDI inflows, to a boom in the industry, and to significant GVC upgrading. FDI helped diversify the tourism industry by creating new offerings such as golf tourism and led to the upgrading of existing players. Several formerly domestic firms indicated that they had strongly benefited from an acquisition or partnership through transfer of skills, management expertise and technology, the availability of training programs, and opportunities for local staff to develop.

The case study also highlights the important role that MNCs can play in GVC upgrading through NEMS. Through management contracts (hotels) or franchising arrangements (restaurants and car rentals) with MNCs, domestic companies in Mauritius have learned, among other things, about building and managing a global brand and how to leverage digitalization skills that they have subsequently been able to successfully apply in other operations. Domestically owned hotel groups have also been able to use management contracts with international hotel brands to gain access to new customer groups through the MNCs' global networks.

Mauritius's experience shows that it is crucial to have a clear strategy for developing a tourism industry and to coordinate different policy areas accordingly. Beginning in the 1980s, the government of Mauritius explicitly set out to become an upscale tourism destination. To achieve that goal, the government engaged in "celebrity marketing" and charged expensive airfares through Air Mauritius to target wealthy individuals and create an image of luxury and exclusivity. In addition, it tightly regulated the industry (for example, minimum number of rooms in hotels and minimum investment per room) and closely managed its growth—not only to prevent mass tourism but also to not lose acceptance within society and prevent adverse impacts on the environment and local communities.

At the same time, the case study raises the question of whether initially restricting FDI is conducive to the development of a country's tourism industry. For Mauritius, the experience is mixed. Close control of the industry through targeted opening to FDI and strong reliance on NEMs enabled high value capture by domestic enterprises. In contrast to many other countries, it also led to a significant local presence in large luxury hotels—many of the five-star hotels in Mauritius are locally owned and managed. This strong domestic presence was possible only because of existing capital available from the sugar industry conglomerates, which also became the main benefactors of an emerging tourism industry.

Globally, country experiences vary. There are a number of examples similar to Mauritius's where countries, at least initially, developed their tourism industry primarily with local capital and local expertise, including India, the Republic of Korea, and Mexico (UNCTAD 2007). India, for example, generally did not allow equity investments or management contracts, but limited MNC relations to franchising and marketing agreements. In Indonesia and in the Philippines, ad hoc technical service agreements were often preferred to equity involvement or medium- to long-term management contracts (UNCTAD 2007). Other countries, such as the Dominican Republic, have developed their tourism industries using FDI from the beginning (UNCTAD 2007). From the 1980s onward, there has been a trend toward liberalization so that, as early as 2006, tourism was one of the most liberalized sectors in developing countries, including in many of the examples listed above (UNCTAD 2007).

Policy makers need to take into account a number of factors when determining whether to rely on FDI to kick-start the development of a new industry. One of these factors is the availability of the necessary absorptive and productive capacity that would allow them to effectively leverage FDI. Without this capacity, there is the danger of creating enclaves, with little or no interaction with the local economy (UNCTAD 2007). Availability of capital also plays a role. Whereas Mauritius had sufficient domestic capital available from the sugar industry that could be channeled to tourism, other countries, especially developing countries, may not have the capital required and thus would have to rely on MNC equity involvement to get the tourism industry started.

The case study also provides mixed findings on the appropriate role of governments in supporting a national airline carrier. Mauritius provided considerable financial support and legal protection to establish Air Mauritius as a flag carrier. Although these protections may have initially led to some successes in facilitating tourism, keeping these protections in place over decades may have eventually held back the development of Mauritius's air connectivity. More recently, Air Mauritius has been pushed into voluntary administration because several years of struggling finances and COVID-19 have moved it close to bankruptcy. Increasingly, evidence suggests that small, state-owned flag carriers tend to drain state funds, are not sustainable, and hinder the sector's development. An open system with competition will best ensure that services are provided. To stimulate servicing for socially desirable but less sustainable routes, subsidies can be used that are transparently granted after a competitive bidding process. Government intervention and ownership of assets should occur only in expensive infrastructure projects that by their nature are monopolies, not in service provision (Bofinger 2017).

Lessons can also be learned from Mauritius's experience in stimulating GVC upgrading through workforce development. With the aim of filling a perennial skills gap in Mauritius's tourism industry, the government has experimented with several subsidy schemes to retrain workers from other sectors or to employ specific target groups, such as women, the unemployed, and others, with varied success. Programs that were successful seem to have focused on younger people with higher education. The programs also included training by training centers in addition to on-the-job experience, highlighting the importance of having a higher-level education for being able to successfully work in the tourism industry, and it shows that the requalification of unskilled workers may be challenging.

Finally, the case study highlights the trend toward digitalization of tourism. The experience of Mauritian hotel groups shows that a slow shift from using tourist operators as the main distribution channel toward online platforms and direct bookings makes it important to have a recognized brand. To react to this trend, Mauritian hotel groups have focused either on building a new global brand, including through acquiring or managing hotels abroad, or on leveraging a global MNC brand through a management agreement. This shift in distribution channels, especially toward direct booking, presents opportunities for local companies to increase profits by cutting out the middlemen in the value creation process. Anecdotal evidence suggests that other countries in the region, especially Maldives, have already profited from this shift by successfully marketing themselves as tourism destinations using social media.

Notes

1. The analysis in this case study is based on a combination of literature reviews and interviews conducted by the authors between January and March 2020 with representatives of multinational corporations, domestic firms, and trade associations affiliated with the Mauritian tourism industry, as well as government officials; the interviews are the source for all direct quotations included in this chapter that are not otherwise attributed.
2. See the Human Resource Development Council's web page, "About NSDP"(https://nsdp .hrdc.mu/index.php/about).

References

AHRIM (Association des Hoteliers et Restaurateurs Ile Maurice). 2019. "2018/19 Annual Report." AHRIM, Port Louis.

Bakker, Martine Hendrica Elize, and Louise D. Twining-Ward. 2018. "Tourism and the Sharing Economy: Policy & Potential of Sustainable Peer-to-Peer Accommodation." World Bank Group, Washington, DC.

Bhuckory, Kamlesh. 2020. "Mauritius Says It Spent $265 Million on Virus Wage Assistance." Bloomberg, July 18, 2020. https://www.bloomberg.com/news/articles/2020-07-18 /mauritius-says-it-spent-265-million-on-virus-wage-assistance.

Bloom, Laura Begley. 2020. "You Won't Believe How Many Airlines Haven't Survived Coronavirus. How Does It Affect You?" *Forbes*, June 27, 2020. https://www.forbes.com/sites/ laurabegleybloom/2020/06/27/airlines-coronavirus-travel-bankruptcy/.

Bofinger, H. C. 2017. "Air Transport in Africa: A Portrait of Capacity and Competition in Various Market Segments." WIDER Working Paper 2017/36, UNU-WIDER, Helsinki.

British Broadcasting Corporation News. 2020. "Mauritius Oil Spill: Wrecked MV Wakashio Breaks Up." August 16, 2020. https://www.bbc.com/news/world-africa-53797009.

Cattaneo, O. 2007. "Promoting Diversification and Exports in the Tourism Sector—Lessons from Mauritius, Zambia and Nigeria." In World Bank workshop on Export Growth and Diversification: Proactive Policies in the Export Cycle, World Bank, Washington, DC.

Cattaneo, O. 2009. "Tourism as a Strategy to Diversify Exports: Lessons from Mauritius." In *Breaking into New Markets: Emerging Lessons for Export Diversification*, edited by Richard Newfarmer, William Shaw, and Peter Walkenhorst, 183–96. Washington, DC: World Bank.

Christian, M., K. Fernandez-Stark, G. Ahmed, and G. Gereffi. 2011. "The Tourism Global Value Chain: Economic Upgrading and Workforce Development." In *Skills for Upgrading, Workforce Development and Global Value Chains in Developing Countries*, edited by G. Gereffi,

K. Fernandez-Stark, and P. Psilos, 276–80. Center on Globalization, Governance, and Competitiveness, Duke University, Durham, NC.

Daly, J., and A. Guinn. 2016. "Primates and Beyond: Tourism Value Chains in East Africa." Duke Center on Globalization, Governance, Competitiveness, Duke University, Durham, NC.

EDB (Economic Development Board) Mauritius. 2019. "The Property Development Scheme (PDS): Guidelines." EDB, Port Louis. http://www.edbmauritius.com/media/2526/guidelines-pds_-august-2019.pdf.

EDB (Economic Development Board) Mauritius. 2020a. "Attractiveness for Mauritius as a Medical Hub." EDB, Port Louis. http://www.edbmauritius.com/opportunities/healthcare/attractiveness-for-mauritius-as-a-medical-hub/.

EDB (Economic Development Board) Mauritius. 2020b. VAT Refund Scheme – MICE, Event Registration. https://www.edbmauritius.org/schemes/vat-refund-scheme-meetings-incentives-conventions-and-exhibitions-mice/.

Government of Mauritius. 2020a. "Government Committed to Rethink Mauritian Tourism and Its Future, States DPM Obeegadoo." Government Information Service, August 18, 2020. http://www.govmu.org/English/News/Pages/Government-committed-to-rethink-Mauritian-tourism-and-its-future,-states-DPM-Obeegadoo.aspx.

Government of Mauritius. 2020b. "The Strategy of the Tourism Industry Reviewed in the Wake of COVID-19 Challenges." Government Information Service, June 16, 2020. http://www.govmu.org/English/News/Pages/The-strategy-of-the-tourism-industry-reviewed-in-the-wake-of-COVID-19-challenges.aspx.

Hale, T., N. Angrist, B. Kira, A. Petherick, T. Philips, and S. Webster. 2020. "Variation in Government Responses to COVID-19." BSG Working Paper 2020/032, Blavatnik School of Government, University of Oxford.

IBP USA. 2012. *Mauritius Business Law Handbook – Volume 1: Strategic Information and Basic Laws.* International Business Publications.

Jeeneea, Ramanand, and Kaviraj Sharma Sukon. 2020. "The Mauritian Response to COVID-19: Rapid Bold Actions in the Right Direction." VoxEU.org, May 9, 2020. https://voxeu.org/article/mauritian-response-covid-19.

MTPA (Mauritius Tourism Promotion Authority). 2020. "Quarantine Procedures Following Easing of Travel Restrictions." Fact sheet, MTPA, Port Louis. https://www.mymauritius.travel/sites/default/files/wakashio/8sept/BookingPlatform18092020.pdf.

Nkuna, Onelie. 2017. "Intra-Regional Foreign Direct Investment in SADC: South Africa and Mauritius Outward Foreign Direct Investment." AERC Research Paper 341, African Economic Research Consortium, Nairobi.

OECD (Organisation for Economic Co-operation and Development). 2014. *OECD Investment Policy Reviews: Mauritius 2014.* Paris: OECD Publishing. https://doi.org/10.1787/9789264212619-en.

Page, S. 1999. "Tourism and Development: The Evidence from Mauritius, South Africa and Zimbabwe." Unpublished report prepared for the Overseas Development Institute, London.

Statistics Mauritius. 2015. "Survey of Inbound Tourism 2015." Statistics Mauritius, Ministry of Finance and Economic Development, Port Louis. https://statsmauritius.govmu.org/Documents/Census_and_Surveys/Surveys/Tourism/2015/SIT_Yr15.pdf.

Statistics Mauritius. 2017. "The Tourism Satellite Account (TSA)." Statistics Mauritius, Ministry of Finance and Economic Development, Port Louis. https://statsmauritius.govmu.org/Documents/Statistics/By_Subject/Tourism/SIT/TSA_Report_Yr17.pdf.

Statistics Mauritius. 2018. "Survey of Inbound Tourism, Year 2018." Statistics Mauritius, Ministry of Finance and Economic Development, Port Louis. https://statsmauritius.govmu.org/Documents/Census_and_Surveys/Surveys/Tourism/2018/SIT_Yr18.pdf.

UNCTAD (United Nations Conference on Trade and Development). 2001. "Investment Policy Review Mauritius." UNCTAD/ITE/IPC/Misc. New York and Geneva, United Nations.

UNCTAD (United Nations Conference on Trade and Development). 2007. *FDI in Tourism: The Development Dimension.* Geneva: United Nations.

UNCTAD (United Nations Conference on Trade and Development). 2008. *FDI and Tourism: The Development Dimension – East and Southern Africa.* Geneva: United Nations.

UNEP (United Nations Environment Programme). 2019. "Overview and Hotspots Analysis of the Tourism Value Chain in Mauritius." UNEP, Nairobi.

UNFCCC (United Nations Framework Convention on Climate Change). 2015. "Paris Agreement." United Nations. https://unfccc.int/sites/default/files/english_paris_agreement.pdf.

UNWTO (United Nations World Tourism Organization). 2019. *International Tourism Highlights, 2019 Edition*. Madrid: UNWTO.

UNWTO (United Nations World Tourism Organization). 2020. "Yearbook of Tourism Statistics." Compendium of Tourism Statistics and Data files. UNWTO, Madrid.

US Department of State. 2019. "2019 Investment Climate Statements: Mauritius." US Department of State, Washington, DC. https://www.state.gov/reports/2019-investment-climate-statements/mauritius/.

WTO (World Trade Organization). 1995. "Trade Policy Review Mauritius." WT/TPR/S/5, WTO, Geneva.

WTO (World Trade Organization). 2001. "Trade Policy Review Mauritius." WT/TPR/S/90, WTO, Geneva.

WTO (World Trade Organization). 2008. "Trade Policy Review Mauritius." WT/TPR/S/198/Rev.1, WTO, Geneva.

WTO (World Trade Organization). 2014. "Trade Policy Review Mauritius." WT/TPR/S/304, WTO, Geneva.

WTTC (World Travel and Tourism Council). 2019. "Travel and Tourism: Economic Impact 2019—World." WTTC, London.

Zafar, A. 2011. "Mauritius: An Economic Success Story." In *Yes Africa Can: Success Stories from a Dynamic Continent*, edited by Punam Chuhan-Pole and Manka Angwafo, 91–106. Washington, DC: World Bank.

Chapter 10

Korea, India, and China—Investing outward helped digital firms develop and compete globally

MAXIMILIAN PHILIP ELTGEN, YAN LIU, AND
VICTOR STEENBERGEN

Summary

This case study highlights the integration and upgrading in the digital economy global value chain (GVC) in three countries—the Republic of Korea, India, and China. It shows that two elements are critical to a country's participation in the high-value-added segments of the digital economy GVC: outward foreign direct investment (OFDI) and human capital and research and development (R&D) capacity. First, all three countries tapped into their own large pools of graduates in science, technology, engineering, and math (STEM) areas and successfully established domestic industries. Then leading domestic companies, pushed by competitive pressure from foreign investors when inward FDI was liberalized, invested overseas to explore new markets and compete internationally. Korea and China also invested determinedly in R&D and provided proactive government support for OFDI using a combination of financial and fiscal measures, provision of information, development assistance programs, and international investment agreements, in addition to the overall liberalization of OFDI regulations. India established software technology parks and provided software export credit and credit guarantees. Some firms from Korea, India, and China managed to expand and have become significant players in certain segments of the digital economy GVC.

The digital economy global value chain

Introduction to the digital economy global value chain

There is no universally accepted definition of the digital economy. However, a general distinction is made between narrow and broad definitions of the term. Narrow definitions refer only to the information and communication technology (ICT) sector, which includes telecommunications, the internet, information technology (IT) services, computer hardware, and software (Zhang and Chen 2019). The broad definitions refer to the digital economy as "the entirety of sectors that operate using Internet Protocol–enabled communications and networks," irrespective of which network they use and for what purpose (Lovelock 2018, 6).

For this case study, the digital economy is conceptualized as a GVC made up of various production segments that enable firms to store, collect, interpret, organize, transmit, and exchange data (figure 10.1). The firms in this GVC can be broadly divided into ICT goods firms and ICT services firms. Three main market segments make up the ICT goods part of the digital economy GVC: servers, IT components, and IT devices. ICT services include software, IT services, and telecommunications and infrastructure services (Frederick, Bamber, and Cho 2018). Such ICT services also include four digital services segments: internet platforms, e-commerce, digital content, and digital solutions (UNCTAD 2017).

Some companies that have integrated themselves into the digital economy GVC were established decades ago as electronics hardware or operating software firms. To upgrade within the GVC, these firms needed to build their digital portfolios of intellectual property and domain expertise. They grew organically by spending relatively high shares of their revenue on R&D (PwC 2018). Mergers and acquisitions and investment in start-ups (venture capital investment) are also common growth methods (Frederick, Bamber, and Cho 2018).

However, the digital economy GVC is mainly characterized by new types of firms and new sources of revenue. The agents of change are a combination of start-ups that provide new digital technologies, suppliers that embrace new opportunities to move up the value chain, and customers who are not just on the receiving end of a product or service but actively co-creating it (UNCTAD 2017). Revenue sources, especially in the consumer segments, are often closely tied to advertising. For example, Google and

FIGURE 10.1 The digital economy global value chain

	Role	Broad segment	Specific segment	Firm examples
ICT Goods	Data storage	Servers	Data storage hardware	HPE, Inc., IBM, Inc.
		IT components (chips, sensors)	IC firms (fab and fabless)	Intel, Inc., Qualcomm, Inc., Samsung, Inc.
	Local data collection and use	IT devices (computers, phones)	Electronics manufacturing	Apple, Inc., Dell, Inc., Lenovo, Inc., Samsung, Inc.
		Operating software	Software (operating)	Apple, Inc., Microsoft, Inc.
		Application software	Software	Citrix, Salesforce, SAP, SAS
ICT Services	Data services (data interpretation, organization, management and transmission)	IT services	IT consulting, BPS, BPO	Accenture, Inc., IBM, Inc., Infosys, Ltd.
		Database software	Data storage software (middleware)	GE, Inc., Oracle, Inc., Siemens, Inc.
		Telecommunications	Internet service providers	AT&T, Inc., Huawei, Inc., Verizon, Inc.
	Digital services (electronic delivery of information across multiple platforms and devices)	Internet platforms	Search engines, social networks	Facebook, Inc., Google, Inc., Tencent, Inc.
		Digital solutions	E-payments, cloud (IaaS, PaaS)	AWS, Inc., Google, Inc., Microsoft, Inc., PayPal, Inc.
		E-commerce	Internet retailers, other e-commerce	Amazon, Inc., Alibaba, Inc., TripAdvisor, Inc.
		Digital content	Digital media, games, information, and data	HBO, Inc., Netflix, Inc., Tencent, Inc.

Sources: Adapted from Frederick, Bamber, and Cho (2018) and UNCTAD (2017).
Note: BPS = business process solutions; BPO = business process outsourcing; IaaS = Infrastructure as a Service; IC = integrated circuit; ICT = information an communication technology; PaaS = Platform as a Service.

Facebook earn most of their revenue from targeted advertising using user-created data (83 percent and 99 percent, respectively) (Wallach 2020).

The United States is the dominant player in the digital economy GVC. Of the top 100 digital multinational corporations (MNCs) by sales or operating revenues, two-thirds are US firms, 23 are European, and 4 are Japanese (UNCTAD 2017). For ICT MNCs, the picture is more heterogeneous: whereas the United States leads with 21, a larger number of firms are from East Asia: Japan (15); Taiwan, China (14); China (6); India (5); and Korea (4) (UNCTAD 2017).

The roles of Korea, India, and China in the digital economy global value chain

Korea is a leading player in the ICT hardware segment of the digital economy GVC, focusing on four key activities. The first is semiconductors, which accounted for 7.8 percent of its gross domestic product (GDP) and 17.3 percent of its exports in 2019.[1] Korea is home to Samsung Electronics and SK hynix; these two companies held 73 percent of the global dynamic random-access memory and 44 percent of the NAND flash memory markets (US ITA 2020). The second relates to wireless communications devices, for which Samsung Electronics and LG Electronics hold 13.3 percent and 8.7 percent of global 5G patents, respectively, making Korea the top country in 5G patents (Statista 2020). Third is flat panel displays, with LG Display alone enjoying a global market share of 27 percent in 2019 (Statista 2020). The fourth sector is consumer electronics. Korea is a global leader in televisions, handsets, and other consumer electronics components through Samsung Electronics, LG Electronics, and LG Display.

India is a leading player in the IT services segment of the digital economy GVC. In fiscal year 2019/20, India's IT and business process management (BPM) industry revenue was about US$191 billion, about 7.4 percent of India's GDP. More than 77 percent of the revenues derived from export (US$141 billion), accounting for 55 percent of global BPM market share (IBEF 2021). India's BPM industry is expected to grow to between US$205 billion and US$250 billion by 2025 according to McKinsey Global Institute estimates (MGI 2019b). In recent years, India has also become an important center for the industrial internet of things (IIoT).[2] All major global industrial firms with IIoT platforms are present in India and collaborating with major Indian IT firms to build applications for their platforms (Frederick, Bamber, and Cho 2018).

China is a leading player across a range of segments of the digital economy GVC. The first is ICT hardware. China accounts for 32 percent of global ICT goods exports (Zhang and Chen 2019). It produces 90 percent of the global supply of personal computers, 90 percent of mobile phones, and 70 percent of televisions (MGI 2019a). In recent years, China has also become a leader in drone manufacturing. Dajiang, one of China's leading companies in the industry, accounts for 50 percent of the drone market in North America (Zhang and Chen 2019). The second segment is financial technology, in which China accounts for more than 70 percent of global valuations. Alipay and WeChat Pay, two popular third-party payment applications, are increasingly expanding overseas and are now accepted at physical retailers in 28 countries (Zhang and Chen 2019). A third area relates to e-commerce. China accounts for more than 40 percent of the global e-commerce market, up from 1 percent about a decade ago. Some Chinese e-commerce companies, especially Alibaba, are venturing abroad (MGI 2017). The fourth area involves internet platforms and digital content. Although most of China's digital content firms are still domestically oriented, a small number have become global lead firms, such as Tencent in the video game industry (Casanova and Miroux 2019). The video platform TikTok has become one of the most popular social media applications in the world, reaching more than 2 billion downloads as of April 2020 (Leskin 2020).

The development of Korea's digital economy global value chain

Korea's early electronics industry developed in the 1960s and 1970s through a combination of proactive government support and partnerships with foreign firms (Lim 2016). During this period, the major products Korea produced included consumer products and the localization of noncore components. Total ICT goods exports increased from US$3.5 million in 1966 to US$1.8 billion in 1979.

Starting in the 1980s, the country's priorities shifted from consumer electronics to the ICT sector. The government dramatically scaled up innovation capacity for ICT by investing 3 percent of Korea Telecom's revenues in R&D. It provided key infrastructure for informatization and e-government, and worked with the private sector to identify and promote new engines of growth. As a result, Korea developed an early lead in key digital infrastructure, developing a digital switching system in 1982 and 64K digital random-access memory in 1983 (third in the world, after the United States and Japan). Korean firms diversified their products and developed core components and materials. They continued to pursue a fast follower-innovator strategy and aggressively invested in R&D and volume production.

Joint efforts by the government and the private sector helped elevate Korea's electronics industry to world-class status by investing in core competencies and quality improvement. During this phase, ICT goods exports grew from US$2 billion in 1980 to almost US$190 billion in 2017. The country's ICT services exports also expanded rapidly, rising from US$3 billion to US$10 billion between 1980 and 2000, and then to almost US$50 billion by 2017. Combining goods and services, ICT exports grew from 11 percent of Korea's total exports in 1980 to 18 percent in 2017 (figure 10.2).

Building human capital and research and development capacity

A focus on higher education was an important pillar of Korea's rise in the digital economy, with considerable investment in human capital development by the Korean government. Korean households simultaneously devoted much of their resources to education, thereby fueling a drastic expansion in school enrollment. The country's tertiary gross enrollment ratio increased from less than 7 percent in 1971 to 95 percent by 2015, and the number of students in higher education jumped from 201,000 to 3.3 million over the same period (Mani and Trines 2018; UIS 2021).

As soon as Korea formulated its electronics industry promotion strategy in 1968, the government also began establishing and reinforcing electronics-related departments

FIGURE 10.2 The Republic of Korea's information and communication technology goods and services exports

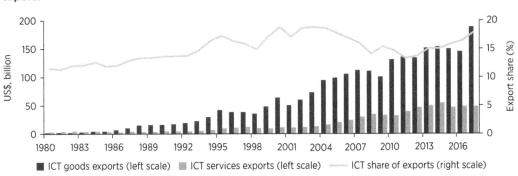

Source: World Bank calculations based on Atlas for Economic Complexity data.
Note: ICT goods are defined as Standard International Trade Classification codes 75–77. ICT services include information technology and communication services. ICT = information and communication technology.

at universities. The Korea Advanced Institute of Science was created in 1973 to produce top-quality scientists and engineers. The government also enacted the Support of Specific Research Institutes Act, under which it provided public funding to specific research institutes and joint management bodies. These institutes and joint management bodies were, in turn, required to give priority to R&D and technical support requests from the government.

Korea also established industry-specific research institutes to drive innovation in the electronics industry. The Korea Electronics Technology Institute, the Korea Electric Research and Testing Institute, and the Korea Electronics and Telecommunications Research Institute were established in 1976. The Korea Electronics Technology Institute greatly expanded R&D activities in computer and semiconductor fields, and the other two organizations made significant contributions to the development of electronic communications equipment (Lim 2016).

The Korean government urged the country's large industrial groups, known as *chaebols*, to invest heavily in R&D with a focus on applied technologies, while shielding them from competition by restricting FDI inflows in the early stages of development (Dayton 2020; Nicolas, Thomsen, and Bang 2013). Chaebols such as Samsung Electronics and LG Electronics engaged in numerous corporate-academic collaborations to conduct cutting-edge research and apply frontier knowledge in their products. As a result, Korea's R&D expenditure as a share of GDP was 4.8 percent in 2018, second only to Israel at 4.9 percent.[3] This expenditure was also exceptionally high relative to the country's income level. Korea's systematic attention to and high spending on R&D has been a crucial factor in creating an innovative economy and enabling its success in the electronics industry (Dayton 2020).

The role of outward foreign direct investment

Korea's policy approach to OFDI has evolved strategically over time, reflecting the needs of its economy at different stages of development. The export boom in the

1980s encouraged OFDI liberalization, but active OFDI promotion only began in the 1990s. Korea's membership in the Organisation for Economic Co-operation and Development in 1996 prompted free capital movements and led to liberalization of both inbound and outbound FDI. In the late 1990s, the Korean government began to actively promote OFDI, with even more proactive policies following the global financial crisis of the late 2000s. The government provides three types of OFDI support: financial support, information provision, and overseas investment services:

1. *Financial support* is mainly provided by the Export-Import Bank of Korea through loans to firms investing abroad. The loans cover up to 80 percent of total capital invested abroad (or 90 percent for small and medium enterprises). The Korea Export Insurance Corporation provides export credit insurance and helps firms abroad that suffer from expropriation, war, breach of contract, and risk associated with remittance transactions.

2. *Information provision* comes from the Ministry of Economy and Finance, which runs an overseas direct investment information network website and provides information on host countries' FDI procedures and investment-related features and on Korean overseas companies. The Ministry of Economy and Finance and the Korea Overseas Investment Information System also run several websites to share OFDI information and provide consulting services for Korean firms interested in investing abroad (Kim and Rhee 2009).

3. *Overseas investment services* come from the Korea Trade-Investment Promotion Agency (KOTRA). KOTRA provides comprehensive supportive services; it helps Korean firms expand their business in overseas markets, spreads foreign market information, and offers business consulting services. The government also encourages cooperation among Korean firms to form Korean business associations abroad and to build regional co-logistics centers to be shared among Korean firms (Nicolas, Thomsen, and Bang 2013).

Korean firms invested abroad for a variety of reasons. Firms faced a saturated domestic market and intense competition in industries such as electrical appliances, which placed pressure on firms to go abroad for higher profits. Firms report that OFDI was preferred over exports to reduce transaction costs in foreign markets (Kim and Rhee 2009). In addition, operating closer to overseas customers was seen to help firms respond quickly to consumer needs and to access design facilities. For example, Samsung Electronics built design centers in China, Italy, Japan, the United Kingdom, and the United States to cater to local market tastes. Finally, concerns about increasing labor costs at home led some Korean firms to invest abroad (Fung, Garcia-Herrero, and Siu 2009; Nicolas 2003).

As a result of both government support and business need, Korea's total stock of OFDI grew rapidly, from US$25 billion in 2000 to US$384 billion in 2018 (figure 10.3, panel a). A sizable share of this OFDI is in ICT goods, ICT services, and scientific R&D—growing from US$43 billion in 2014 to US$73 billion in 2018. The majority of OFDI is in ICT goods, but a growing share is in ICT services (figure 10.3, panel b). Overall, OFDI played a crucial role in Korea's advancement in the digital economy GVC (Nicolas 2003).

FIGURE 10.3 **Outward foreign direct investment in the Republic of Korea**

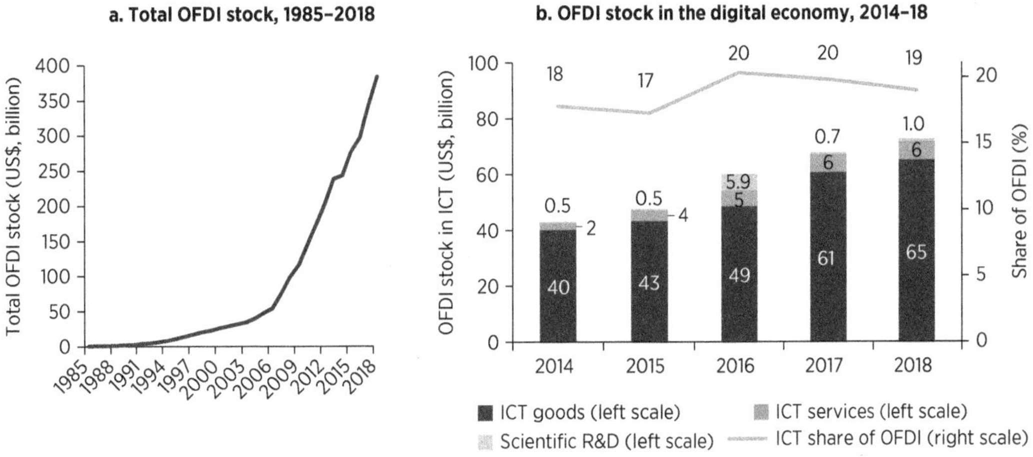

Source: World Bank calculations using Organisation for Economic Co-operation and Development foreign direct investment statistics.
Note: ICT = information and communication technology; OFDI = outward foreign direct investment; R&D = research and development.

The development of India's digital economy global value chain

The rise of India's ICT sector is generally considered to have started in 1988, when the government established software technology parks in 39 locations. At each park the government provided IT and telecommunications infrastructure, tax benefits, and satellite uplinks, as well as import certifications and market analysis to foreign investors (Couto and Fernandez-Stark 2019). After India's 1991 balance of payments crisis, the government abolished industrial licensing, removed entry barriers, created exemptions from corporate taxes, liberalized trade, and devalued the rupee, among other measures. In addition, software exports by MNCs registered with the Department of Electronics were provided with export promotion benefits, such as export shipment credit and credit guarantees, similar to those given to manufacturing exporters (Kathuria 2010).

India's integration into the digital economy GVC accelerated in the 1990s when the country began to provide simple IT support services to global clients, particularly in the United States. From about US$50 million in exports in the late 1980s, the industry grew by 50–60 percent annually in the mid- and late 1990s (Bhatnagar 2006), reaching US$10 billion in 2000. Since then, growth has been even more pronounced, shooting up to US$130 billion in 2017. At the same time, ICT goods exports increased, rising from US$1 billion in 2000 to US$9 billion in 2017. In total, exports from the digital economy sectors grew from less than 5 percent of India's total exports in the 1980s to about 15 percent in 2017 (figure 10.4).

Years of significant investment in IT higher education have endowed India with a large number of well-trained, low-cost, English-speaking software professionals.

FIGURE 10.4 India's information and communication technology goods and services exports

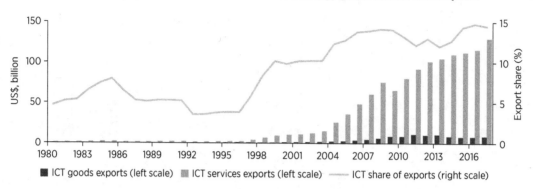

Source: World Bank calculations based on Atlas for Economic Complexity data.
Note: ICT goods are defined as Standard International Trade Classification codes 75–77. ICT services include information technology and communication services. ICT = information and communication technology.

This cadre of professionals proved highly opportune when the IT boom in the late 1990s resulted in a huge shortage of suitable personnel, which had been exacerbated by the Y2K problem.[4] India's software engineers were thus available on short notice to execute short-term projects and lower-end jobs such as coding and data conversion (Fernandez-Stark, Bamber, and Gereffi 2011).

As a result, MNCs were eager to set up IT, BPM, and R&D centers in India, which in turn benefited local companies through linkages and spillovers (Couto and Fernandez-Stark 2019). Driven by high-quality talent, synergies with traditional sourcing operations in the area, and lower operating costs, India's IT services sector emerged as one of the leading global players across all segments in the late 2000s.

In addition, a number of Indian IT professionals who had worked in the United States returned to India, bringing with them managerial expertise and good business connections, and successfully created their own IT firms. These firms have evolved into India's well-known leading firms such as TCS, Infosys, and Wipro (Fernandez-Stark, Bamber, and Gereffi 2011). Notably, foreign ownership of software operations in India was quite small—in 2010, fewer than one-fifth of Indian software companies were majority foreign-owned (Kathuria 2010).

Having developed experience in dealing with complex IT systems, several Indian companies became internationally competitive and opened offices abroad, offering a wider range of services, such as executing large and complex projects involving integration, IT strategy, and end-to-end solutions (Jalote and Natarajan 2019). Leading firms, now MNCs themselves, were quick to realize that demand for low-end services had limited value added; they thus diversified into other domains such as insurance, finance, and customer support, as well as R&D offshoring (Couto and Fernandez-Stark 2019).

In recent years, India has become a hub for technologies related to IIoT and Industry 4.0. More than 1,250 global companies have set up their own centers across all industries, and are starting to drive digital engineering work from their Indian development centers (Jalote and Natarajan 2019). The country is home to the largest IIoT labs for several firms outside of their home countries, including Siemens, SAP, and Bosch (Frederick, Bamber, and Cho 2018). For example, Bosch has 15,500 R&D

associates in India, which makes it the largest R&D campus outside of Germany, with 22 percent of its R&D employee count; the campus is focused on developing data mining and software solutions (Bosch 2019).

Building human capital and research and development capacity

Beginning in the 1960s, the Indian government's public investments in technical education provided the foundation for the growth of the IT industry. In collaboration with leading universities in the United States, the government created a series of elite institutes for higher education in engineering and management, which proved pivotal in developing a large, well-trained pool of engineers and management personnel. In addition, the government eased policies regarding the ability to establish private education institutions to help fill the skills gap. It also helped create and expand computer science departments in existing engineering colleges and introduced quality-control systems for engineering colleges and other IT-training institutions (Bhatnagar 2006).

By 1997 India had set up more than 600 institutions for degree qualification in engineering and another 1,135 institutions granting engineering diplomas. By 1999 the higher technical education system produced more than 250,000 scientists and technologists a year, including more than 10,000 doctorates awarded in various disciplines (Kumar 2014).

The Indian government also facilitated India's brain gain during the 2000s. Expatriates who had been living in the United Kingdom and the United States were returning to India, attracted by high salaries and entrepreneurship opportunities, but only enabled by the lifting of restrictions related to visas, investment, and the purchase of property by Indian nationals who were citizens of other countries (Couto and Fernandez-Stark 2019).

R&D has been gaining in importance to India's participation in the digital economy GVC as the country continues to upgrade and compete in knowledge-intensive services. R&D expenditure by both private Indian firms and the government has traditionally been low in India compared with other countries, and has been dominated by the government (Kumar 2014). As of 2018, Japan's and China's R&D spending of 3.3 percent and 2.2 percent of GDP clearly outranked India's 0.6 percent. This spending difference can be at least partly explained by the country's service focus, as opposed to a product focus, which would require greater investment in R&D (Bhatnagar 2006).

However, although the relatively low investment in R&D was not a significant impediment early on, the IT industry's shift toward the adoption of new technologies such as artificial intelligence, automation, and cloud computing, among others, is making R&D an increasingly important factor for the competitiveness of Indian firms (CTIER 2016). Because of India's comparatively low public R&D spending, the country will continue to rely on foreign R&D for the bulk of cutting-edge innovation, given the gap between indigenous and multinational innovation (Branstetter, Glennon, and Jensen 2019).

The role of OFDI

Starting in 1992, India's government gradually liberalized its formerly restrictive OFDI policy regime, with the aim of achieving technological upgrading and internationalization of leading Indian companies (Pedersen 2010). Liberalization measures included instituting automatic approval procedures, removing the prohibition on majority ownership of foreign entities, and gradually increasing the amount of OFDI allowed under the automatic route to 100 percent of a company's net worth in 2004 and subsequently to 400 percent today (Kathuria 2010). All of these measures, coupled with the opening up of and hence the increased competition in Indian domestic markets,[5] as well as the liberalization of trade and investment regimes in overseas markets, led Indian firms to expand abroad (Sauvant and Pradhan 2010).

OFDI from India increased significantly after 2000 (figure 10.5, panel a). ICT companies took a strong lead in OFDI after having developed competitive advantages such as the knowledge and skills gained as an outsourcing destination for several years and the exposure to intense competition. OFDI in ICT increased steeply, from US$743 million in 1990–99 to US$10.1 billion in 2000–09, which further rose to US$43.6 billion, or 26 percent of the total India OFDI, in the following five-year period (figure 10.5, panel b). This performance marks the industry as the most globalized and internationalized sector in India (Pradhan 2017).

OFDI has allowed Indian IT firms to access new markets, skills, and technologies, and to enlarge the global scale and scope of their operations. Indian companies predominantly established greenfield subsidiaries in other countries to provide services on site closer to the customer and to seek out new business opportunities (Couto and Fernandez-Stark 2019). In addition, Indian firms had also been aggressively acquiring overseas strategic assets (Pradhan 2007). For example, Wipro in 2007 acquired the US-based business process outsourcing company Infocrossing for US$600 million, one of the largest acquisitions by an Indian company in the United States at the time, to obtain Infocrossing's five data centers in the United States to be able to become a full-service company (Ruet 2010).

FIGURE 10.5 Outward foreign direct investment in India, 1980–2014

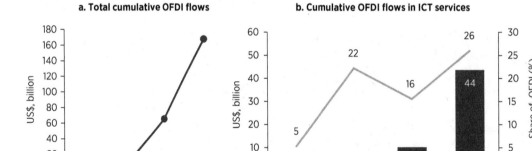

Source: World Bank calculations based on Pradhan 2017.
Note: ICT services include information technology and communication services. ICT = information and communication technology; OFDI = outward foreign direct investment.

The majority of overseas investments by Indian IT services companies were in developed countries (close to 70 percent), with the United Kingdom and the United States being the two major hosts (Pradhan 2007). Because of the nature of software—requiring effective integration between different types of services and involving trade secrecy and protected data—almost all investments were majority owned (Pradhan 2007).

More recently, Indian IT companies have been investing in new technologies to expand to new lines of business and to new markets. Based on CBInsights' analysis of 51 acquisitions by major Indian IT companies between 2012 and 2017, acquisitions are particularly prominent in companies working in data management (18 percent), the internet of things (10 percent), cybersecurity (10 percent), artificial intelligence (8 percent), and payment and invoicing (6 percent) (CBInsights 2017). Indian companies tend to acquire rather than make venture capital investments, with the exception of Wipro and Infosys, which, in addition to making acquisitions, have also been active venture capital investors and built their own corporate venture capital arms (Frederick, Bamber, and Cho 2018).

The development of China's digital economy global value chain

China's journey entering and upgrading in the digital economy GVC began in the 1980s, when it successfully attracted export-oriented FDI through incentives and infrastructure provision, often using special economic zones. This strategy allowed it to develop a competitive ICT hardware industry focused on low-skilled and low-value-added components and parts assembly (Ning 2009). The technology, knowledge, and market access that foreign MNCs brought to China, with the assistance of government policies, helped upgrade the competitiveness of domestic firms by transferring technology through joint ventures, forward and backward linkages, spillovers, competition effects, industrial structure expansion, and labor spin-offs (Chen 2018).

Since the early 2000s China has extended its status as the global leader in select segments of the ICT hardware industry, especially in the computer and peripheral equipment segment and the communication equipment segment. In 2004, China surpassed the United States as the world's leading ICT goods exporter, with US$240 billion in ICT goods exports. In recent years, ICT goods exports have continued to expand, rising to US$820 billion in 2017 (figure 10.6).

During this time, China also developed the world's largest telecommunications market, which, unlike the country's ICT hardware industry, was dominated by state-owned enterprises (WTO Secretariat 2006). Other segments of China's digital economy remained small and focused on the domestic market, but as time went on their growth rates picked up. China's software industry, which barely existed before the 1990s, exhibited a steady 30 percent growth rate from 1992 to 2000. However, unlike Europe, India, and the United States, China developed only a limited range of IT service providers during this period (WTO Secretariat 2006). E-commerce in China took off in 1999 as a wave of dot-com start-ups went public on the NASDAQ stock exchange (Qiang 2007). The country's ICT services exports have also grown continuously, rising

FIGURE 10.6 China's information and communication technology goods and services exports

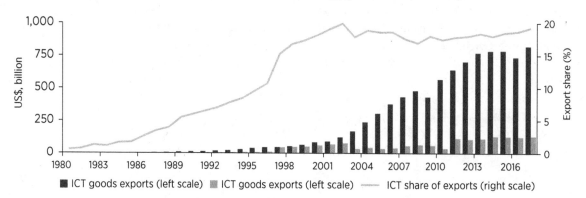

Source: World Bank calculations based on Atlas for Economic Complexity data.

Note: ICT goods are defined as Standard International Trade Classification codes 75–77. ICT services include information technology and communication services. ICT = information and communication technology.

from about US$59 billion in 2000 to US$130 billion in 2017. Concurrently, China saw a significant rise in ICT exports, growing from less than 1 percent in the 1980s to 11 percent in 1996, and still rising at almost 20 percent of total Chinese exports (figure 10.6).

The rise of China's digital economy firms can be explained by both structural and policy factors. The relevant structural factors include China's market size (McCarthy 2020), growth in digital adoption, inefficiencies in traditional sectors (MGI 2017), and strong manufacturing base. Chinese policy makers at various levels of government have adopted a combination of measures aimed at supporting its domestic digital firms. On the one hand, Chinese authorities gave domestic digital firms space to experiment and innovate in its large domestic market under low levels of regulation (MGI 2017), learning and upgrading their capacity gradually before they could compete at the frontier. On the other hand, foreign firms are perceived to have disadvantages in China, including limited market access, insufficient intellectual property protection and enforcement, internet control and censorship, and subsidies for Chinese firms (Ferracane and Lee-Makiyama 2017; USTR 2018). Although this protection provided domestic firms with a first-mover advantage, it may have been counterproductive. Jiang et al. (2018), for example, find that Chinese technology spillovers were largest in sectors that were more open, and positive technology externalities were dampened in industries with many prohibitions on types of foreign investment.

Building human capital and research and development capacity

Building on earlier reforms, in the mid-2000s the Chinese government, using a wide array of policy instruments, set out to build an enterprise-centered technology innovation system that would make China one of the world's leading R&D hubs.

Under the 2006 Medium- to Long-Term Plan for the Development of Science and Technology, Chinese policy makers set out to (a) build an innovating-based economy by fostering indigenous innovation capacity, (b) foster an enterprise-centered technology innovation system and enhance the innovation capabilities of Chinese firms, and (c) achieve major breakthroughs in targeted strategic areas of technological development and basic research (OECD 2007). The plan committed China to achieving four broad objectives by 2020: allocating 2.5 percent of GDP to R&D, sourcing 60 percent of growth from the contribution of scientific and technological progress, basing 70 percent of production on homegrown technologies, and raising the share of strategic and emerging industries to 15 percent of GDP (Chen and Naughton 2016).

To further these objectives, the Chinese government has introduced more than 170 policies supporting science, technology, and innovation (STI) since 2011. These policies span socioeconomic objectives (productivity, diversification, human capital, entrepreneurship, and inclusion) and STI objectives (research excellence, technology transfer, and R&D and non-R&D innovation). They also use a wide range of instruments, including fiscal incentives, grants, loan guarantees, vouchers, equity, public procurement, technology extension services, incubators, accelerators, competitive grants and prizes, science and technology parks, and collaboration networks. The approach seems to favor financial instruments over regulatory, advisory, and other types of support, suggesting that the main market failure that the authorities seek to address is the lack of funding and access to finance. The Chinese government's volume of support for business R&D is close to the Organisation for Economic Co-operation and Development median, much higher than what China's level of income would suggest. Tax incentives account for about half of the total value of the support (OECD 2017).

Complementing China's large and growing expenditure on R&D are investments in the development of human resources in science and technology. Students in science and engineering (S&E) account for about half of all bachelor's degrees awarded in China, and in 2014 Chinese S&E graduates numbered almost 1.5 million—more than the combined total of S&E graduates in the United States and the eight European Union countries with the highest number of S&E bachelor and doctoral degrees awarded that year. In addition, more than 3,000 of these graduates received doctorates, more than in the United States and three times more than in India. Training at western and Japanese research institutions, and the connections forged there, have contributed greatly to the quality of China's research human capital. Today, China is a global innovation hub, boasting among the world's highest numbers for STI spending and patent applications (World Bank Group 2020).

These advances helped enable Chinese firms to become outward investors in the first place, and they also enabled Chinese firms and the Chinese economy more broadly to benefit from OFDI, as several studies have confirmed (Huang and Zhang 2017; Li et al. 2016).

The role of outward foreign direct investment

In the 1980s and 1990s, OFDI played a limited role in the development of China's digital economy. Until the mid-1980s, only state-owned enterprises were allowed to invest abroad, and case-by-case approval was required for all investment. The government then partially extended the right to apply for permission to invest abroad (OECD 2008). Until the late 1990s, however, controls on financial outflows remained tight in response to the state's losses from speculative investments in real estate and stock markets in the early 1990s, and to prevent capital flight during the East Asian financial crisis (Wang and Gao 2019). China's average total OFDI flows from 1992 to 1999 remained low at US$2.7 billion (Wang and Gao 2019).

In 2000, the Chinese government began to embrace the liberalization and promotion of outward investment as a development strategy. With the 10th Five-Year Plan on Economic and Social Development, China formalized its "Going Out" strategy, listing OFDI as one of the four key thrusts that would enable the Chinese economy "to adjust itself to the globalization trend" (Sauvant and Chen 2013). In a number of subsequent pronouncements and policy documents, the government further elaborated this strategy and repurposed its OFDI policy and regulatory frameworks in light of two objectives: to help Chinese firms become more competitive internationally, and to assist the country in its development efforts by using OFDI to achieve economic restructuring. In pursuit of these objectives, China's regulatory framework for OFDI has moved "from restricting, to facilitating, to supporting, and finally to encouraging OFDI" (Sauvant and Chen 2013, 1).

Following its "Going Out" strategy, China has incrementally streamlined and liberalized its OFDI regulations. It gradually simplified approval procedures and documentation requirements, decentralized authority from national regulators to their provincial counterparts (MOFCOM 2004; NDRC 2004), and gradually loosened restrictions on the use of foreign exchange for OFDI. To that end, the government abolished compulsory repatriation of overseas profits, and in 2006 eliminated the long-imposed quota of US$5 billion per year on foreign exchange allocated to OFDI (OECD 2008). Importantly, under the 2014 Catalogue of Investment Projects Subject to the Approval of Government, the general framework for OFDI was changed from an approval-based system to a recording system (World Bank Group 2020). In that same year, the regulatory framework for OFDI matured to embrace corporate social responsibility when investing abroad, such as minimizing the environmental and social impacts of investment on host economies (Perea and Stephenson 2018).

In addition to liberalizing its OFDI regulations, the Chinese government has directly supported and encouraged OFDI. Sauvant and Chen (2013) identify five ways in which the Chinese government supports OFDI (box 10.1).

OFDI flows from China rose from less than US$2 billion in 2000 to US$146 billion in 2015. In 2016, Chinese OFDI flows reached two milestones: they became the second highest in the world, after those from the United States, and they overtook FDI flows into China for the first time (Perea and Stephenson 2018). The digital economy makes up an important share of the total increase in OFDI. Manufacturing OFDI (led by ICT-related products) rose from US$2 billion in 2005 to US$30 billion in 2017 (figure 10.7, panel a). Similarly, OFDI for ICT services and R&D grew from less than US$30 million in 2005 to a high of US$23 billion in 2016 (figure 10.7, panel b). Not only has OFDI in ICT goods and services expanded rapidly, but it has also exceeded 20 percent of total OFDI every year since 2015 (sum of panels a and b in figure 10.7).

Government support proved to be an important factor in China's rising OFDI flows. In a 2011 survey of Chinese outward investors conducted by the China Council for the Promotion of International Trade, 55 percent of firms identified China's "Going Out"

BOX 10.1 **Chinese government support for outward foreign direct investment**

The Chinese government supports outward foreign direct investment (OFDI) through a number of measures:

- *Financial and fiscal measures.* The Export-Import Bank of China and other state-owned commercial banks support OFDI by offering low lending rates, flexible terms, and a fast approval process for OFDI projects. In 2003, a Special Fund of Lending for Investment Overseas was established to extend special financial services (including discounted lending rates) to large-scale business groups possessing sufficient capital, technology, management skills, and brands to invest abroad (CDB and EXIM 2006). Another fund established by the Chinese Ministry of Finance and the Ministry of Commerce (MOFCOM) provides direct subsidies to OFDI projects that, among other criteria, build foreign research and development centers (Ministry of Finance and MOFCOM 2012). A number of tax incentives to support OFDI were granted by the State Taxation Administration, including a special corporate income tax rate for high-technology enterprises (reduced from 25 percent to 15 percent) (STA 2011). In addition, a new foreign exchange policy was introduced in 2011 that allows Chinese firms to directly use yuan to invest abroad if certain conditions are met (PBC 2011).

- *Provision of information.* MOFCOM, the National Development and Reform Commission, and the Ministry of Foreign Affairs jointly publish an annual OFDI Guidebook that lists current investment opportunities by country, industry, and project. MOFCOM also provides information through its global commercial consulate offices and offers services such as the collection of information and statistics and decision-making support (MOFCOM 2020).

- *Development assistance programs.* Since 2006, the Chinese government has assisted in the construction of foreign economic and trade cooperation zones. These zones are designed to provide developed infrastructure to the firms operating within them, and they are mostly focused on export processing and scientific and technological projects.

- *International investment agreements (IIAs).* Since China began its IIA program in 1982, the country has signed more IIAs (146) than any other country except Germany (which has signed 201).[a] During this time, China's approach toward IIAs has undergone significant shifts. In its IIAs signed from 1982 to 1998, China limited substantive protections and access to investor-state dispute resolution, reflecting China's status during that time as a predominantly capital-importing country (Sauvant and Nolan 2015). In its IIAs signed between 1998 and 2008, China's consent to arbitration was often broadened given that its interest in protecting its investments abroad had increased (Sauvant and Nolan 2015). In IIAs signed subsequently, China developed a more balanced approach, both tightening admissibility requirements for investors' claims and increasing levels of substantive investment protection. The country's focus became to ensure that Chinese state-owned enterprises' investments were protected while also allowing sufficient regulatory flexibility (Sauvant and Nolan 2015).

- *Political risk insurance.* Chinese outward investors, and the institutions that finance their investment, may receive investment protection from the China Export & Credit Insurance Corporation (Sinosure). Sinosure offers insurance against the loss of capital and earnings abroad caused by several types of political risk, including expropriation, restrictions on the transfer and conversion of funds, damage from war, inability to operate because of war, and breach of contract.

Source: Based on Sauvant and Chen 2013 and Sauvant and Nolan 2015.
a. UNCTAD (United Nations Conference on Trade and Development), 2020, Investment Policy Hub (https://investmentpolicy.unctad.org).

FIGURE 10.7 Outward foreign investment in China, 2005–18

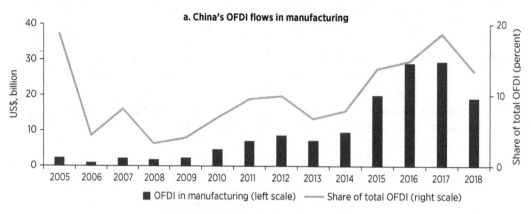

a. China's OFDI flows in manufacturing

■ OFDI in manufacturing (left scale)   —— Share of total OFDI (right scale)

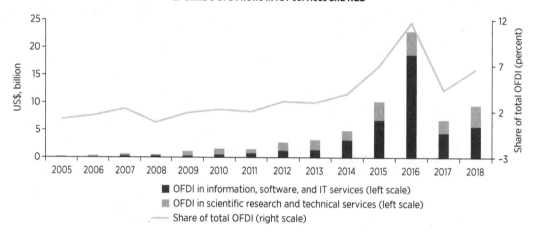

b. China's OFDI flows in ICT services and R&D

■ OFDI in information, software, and IT services (left scale)
■ OFDI in scientific research and technical services (left scale)
----- Share of total OFDI (right scale)

Source: Statistical Bulletin of China's Outward Foreign Direct Investment (several editions, 2006–18) (http://cdi.cnki.net/Titles/SingleNJ?NJCode=N2017120333).
Note: ICT = information and communication technology; IT = information technology; OFDI = outward foreign direct investment; R&D = research and development.

strategy as an important or very important factor in their decisions to invest abroad; in fact, they considered it more important than almost all other factors influencing OFDI decision-making (CCPIT 2012). A large majority, 74 percent, of respondents said that they had benefited from the government's OFDI policies. Moreover, a substantial amount of OFDI was financed by the government. Gallagher and Irwin (2014) estimate the total amount of OFDI financing provided by the China Development Bank and the Export-Import Bank of China at US$140 billion from 2002 to 2012, amounting to at least 30 percent of China's total OFDI.

OFDI has allowed Chinese firms to enter and upgrade in various segments of the digital economy GVC. It has also contributed to structural changes in China's economy through its home-country effects. Both outward investors and other firms in the digital sector have benefited from OFDI through a number of channels, including direct knowledge transfers (of technology, production techniques, and management skills), indirect knowledge transfers from related firms (including reverse spillover effects from developed to developing markets), labor mobility, competition effects, and scale and scope effects. A number of studies find positive home-country effects in economy-wide productivity (Zhao, Liu, and Zhao 2010), growth (Liu and Lu 2011), employment (Cozza, Rabellotti, and Sanfilippo 2015), exports (Wang and Zhang 2010), and innovation (Chen, Li, and Shapiro 2012; Chen and Tang 2014; Fu, Hou, and Liu 2018; Li et al. 2016; Mao and Xu 2014).

A comparison of the three countries

This case study highlights the critical role of human capital—building absorptive capacity and indigenous innovation—in entering and upgrading along the digital economy GVC. The digital economy is one of the most knowledge-intensive sectors and is therefore greatly dependent on the level of technological capabilities. Investment in higher education in the STEM areas is critical. The examples of Korea, India, and China show that such investment in building a large skills pool is strategic, establishes the foundation, and helps give domestic firms a competitive edge in this GVC.

The three countries also seem to have motivated actors and technologies from both domestic and foreign markets to innovate in specific segments in the digital economy GVC. Although there are many commonalities in the three countries' experiences (for example, using inward FDI to jumpstart the industry, liberalizing OFDI to help leading domestic firms internationalize, and investing in human capital), distinct features shaped each country's path (table 10.1). Korea and China adopted more selective inward FDI policies and engaged in proactive OFDI promotion, whereas the Indian government was more hands-off with regard to OFDI. Korea spent most aggressively on R&D and achieved leading positions in several ICT goods segments. China also has relatively high R&D expenditure and is becoming a top player in multiple segments in both ICT goods and services. India currently invests less in R&D, partly because it specializes in ICT services that are less technology intensive, such as business process management. These differing experiences show again that the usefulness of the various approaches is partly based on GVC characteristics and partly on the general capacity that exists within local firms.

Conclusion

For countries aiming to stimulate their participation in the digital economy GVC, this case study suggests that governments should first and foremost invest in their country's human capital. The digital economy is one of the most knowledge-intensive sectors and is therefore greatly dependent on technological skills. Investment in tertiary education in the STEM areas is critical and will take time. The examples of Korea, India, and China show that such investment in building a large skills pool has, over time, established the knowledge skills foundation that gave domestic firms a competitive edge in this GVC.

TABLE 10.1   Comparison of the three countries' approaches

	Republic of Korea	India	China
Leading GVC segments	ICT goods (semiconductors, wireless communication devices, flat panel displays, consumer electronics)	ICT services (business process management)	Both ICT goods (personal computers, mobile phones, televisions, drones) and ICT services (fintech, e-commerce, internet platforms, digital content)
Building human capital	• Large public and private investments heavily expanded the tertiary education enrollment rate • Government established various electronics-related departments at universities • Creation of multiple scientific research institutions focused on ICT goods– and ICT services–related R&D	• Public investment in technical education since the 1960s • Creation of a series of elite institutes for higher education and management together with leading US universities • Relaxed regulations on private education institutions to fill the skills gap • Expanded computer science departments in universities • Introduced IT training institutions	• Large investments in the development of human resources in science and technology • Half of all bachelor's degrees in China awarded to students in science and engineering
R&D investment	• Government urged *chaebols* to invest heavily in R&D in ICT goods • Chaebols engaged in numerous corporate-academic collaborations and invested in advanced countries to obtain cutting-edge technologies • Second-highest R&D expenditure relative to GDP (4.8%) in the world	• Relatively low R&D investment (0.6% of GDP) • R&D dominated by government • Low R&D partly because of its services focus, which requires less investment in R&D than do ICT goods	• Established various research institutions since the 1950s • Adopted a wide range of policies to support science, technology, and innovation, including fiscal incentives, grants, loan guarantees, vouchers, equity, public procurement, science and technology parks, and collaboration networks • Relatively high R&D expenditure as a share of GDP (2.2%)
Inward FDI policies	• Selective promotion of inward FDI as part of overall industrial policy • Restricted FDI inflows in ICT goods initially to protect domestic firms • FDI not major engine of ICT goods industry but helped strengthen local firms' technological capacity	• The Liberalization, Privatization, and Globalization reforms in 1991 opened Indian economy to FDI • IT, BPO, computer software and hardware, telecommunications were top FDI-receiving sectors • Inward FDI instrumental in developing India's ICT services industry	• Liberalized FDI regulations since 1980s • Selective promotion of FDI in manufacturing and export-oriented industries • Large influx of FDI since the 1980s helped China develop a competitive ICT goods industry
Outward FDI policies	Proactive government promotion of OFDI since 1990s, with a range of financial support measures, information provision, and overseas investment services	Relatively hands-off, gradually liberalized OFDI policies since 1992 to help technological upgrading and domestic firms' internationalization	Liberalized OFDI in 2000, and encouraged OFDI through financial and fiscal measures, provision of information, development assistance programs, international investment agreements, and political risk insurance

Source: World Bank.
Note: BPO = business process outsourcing; FDI = foreign direct investment; fintech = financial technology; GVC = global value chain; ICT = information and communication technology; IT = information technology; OFDI = outward foreign direct investment; R&D = research and development.

Proactive government support in R&D may also be needed to help domestic firms develop the necessary technology to engage in the digital economy. Through a wide array of policy instruments, particularly financial instruments, both Korea and China helped build the production and innovation capacity of local firms and enabled them to become leading R&D hubs. These support measures initially helped young digital economy firms better understand and absorb existing technologies in their sector. Over time, such R&D efforts also prepared the more competitive domestic firms to internationalize and make the transition into outward investors and MNCs themselves.[6]

This case study further shows that OFDI is an internationalization channel for the most competitive domestic firms. All three countries demonstrate a strong, positive link between rising OFDI and exports of ICT goods and services. Leading domestic firms chose to invest overseas (often in high-income countries using mergers and acquisitions and venture capital) to acquire strategic assets such as R&D and proprietary technology, globally recognized brand names, and established customer networks and sales channels. In parallel, they also invested in developing countries (commonly via greenfield FDI) to establish production facilities. Korean firms, for example, invested heavily in the United States to obtain advanced technology, and invested in low-cost countries to manufacture and sell their products (Kim, Driffield, and Love 2018). This approach helped the more productive domestic firms further develop their technological capabilities, expand their production networks and markets, and compete on a global scale.

For governments seeking to stimulate OFDI, liberalizing outward investment regulations is an essential first step. In all three countries, a boom in outward investment was preceded by the liberalization of OFDI rules. Yet, according to the International Monetary Fund's Annual Report on Exchange Arrangements and Exchange Restrictions database, 86 out of 192 countries had controls in place on OFDI in 2018 (IMF 2019). These controls are most commonplace in developing countries—58 percent of developing countries still control OFDI, whereas only 21 percent of high-income countries do so.

In addition, as shown for Korea and China, OFDI can be supported using a combination of financial and fiscal measures, the provision of information, development assistance programs, and international investment agreements. This combined approach of investing in building human capital, R&D, and supporting OFDI has helped Korea, India, and China become leading players in segments of the digital economy GVC.

Finally, similar to the other case studies in this report, the three countries' experiences also highlight the crucial role of inward FDI and more broadly the interactions with MNCs. In all three cases, MNCs were attracted by a number of tools, including the provision of infrastructure and incentives (for example, software technology parks in India). Technology, know-how, and market access that foreign MNCs brought to the three countries helped upgrade the competitiveness of domestic firms. The domestic firms then developed and accumulated knowledge about foreign markets and built networks and linkages before venturing abroad. Moreover, the types of investments the countries attracted in the digital economy GVC progressed over time from low-value-added goods production to high-value-added services and R&D, often performed in collaboration with local firms or research institutes.

Notes

1. Ministry of Trade, Industry and Energy, https://www.trade.gov/country-commercial-guides/south-korea-information-and-communication-technology.
2. IIoT refers to the use of smart sensors attached to physical devices and real-time analytics to enhance manufacturing and industrial processes. IIoT falls across a number of segments of the digital economy GVC, including components, software, cloud systems, and IT services.
3. Based on World Bank World Development Indicators.
4. The Y2K problem was a computer flaw, or bug, that may have caused problems when dealing with dates beyond December 31, 1999. Global demand for IT professionals increased because of the need to remedy this issue.
5. The measures included removal of the restrictions on the growth of firms (such as the Foreign Exchange Regulation Act), the removal of the licensing regime, the dismantling of product reservation systems for publicly owned and small and medium enterprises, facilitation measures for foreign firms, and a massive reduction in import duties (Pradhan and Sauvant 2010).
6. The *World Development Report* (World Bank 2020) similarly emphasizes the importance of investment in R&D and human capital as a prerequisite for participation in knowledge-intensive GVCs such as the digital economy.

References

Bosch. 2019. "2019 Annual Report: Innovation for Times of Transition." Bosch, Stuttgart, Germany. https://assets.bosch.com/media/global/bosch_group/our_figures/pdf/bosch-annual-report-2019.pdf.

Bhatnagar, S. 2006. "India's Software Industry." In *Technology, Adaptation, and Exports: How Some Developing Countries Got It Right*, edited by V. Chandra, 54–56. Washington, DC: World Bank.

Branstetter, L. G., B. Glennon, and J. B. Jensen. 2019. "The IT Revolution and the Globalization of R&D." NBER Working Paper 24707, National Bureau of Economic Research, Cambridge, MA. https://www.journals.uchicago.edu/doi/pdf/10.1086/699931.

Casanova, L., and A. Miroux. 2019. "Tencent: An Innovative Tech Giant." In *The Era of Chinese Multinationals: Competing for Global Dominance*, 179–202. London: Academic Press.

CBInsights. 2017. "India's IT Giants Are Investing and Acquiring to Catch up with Trends in Cloud, AI, and Automation." CBInsights Research Briefs. https://www.cbinsights.com/research/india-it-investments-acquisitions/.

CCPIT (China Council for the Promotion of International Trade). 2012. "Survey on Chinese Enterprises' Outbound Investment and Operation." CCPIT, Beijing. http://www.ccpit.org/docs/2012-08-03/2012_haiwaitouzi_diaochabaogao.pdf.

CDB (China Development Bank) and EXIM (Export-Import Bank of China). 2006. "CDB and EXIM Enhance Their Financial and Insurance Support for Key Investment Projects Overseas Encouraged by the State." CDB 2006 No. 11 Order, CDB and EXIM, Beijing.

Chen, C. 2018. "The Liberalization of FDI Policies and the Impacts of FDI on China's Economic Development." In *China's 40 Years of Reform and Development: 1978–2018*, edited by Ross Garnaut, Ligang Song, and Cai Fang, 595–618. Canberra: Australian National University Press.

Chen, L., and B. Naughton. 2016. "An Institutionalized Policy-Making Mechanism: China's Return to Techno-Industrial Policy." *Research Policy* 45 (10): 2138–52.

Chen, V. Z., J. Li, and D. M. Shapiro. 2012. "International Reverse Spillover Effects on Parent Firms: Evidences from Emerging Market MNEs in Developed Markets." *European Management Journal* 30 (3): 204–18.

Chen, W., and H. Tang. 2014. "The Dragon Is Flying West: Micro-Level Evidence of Chinese Outward Direct Investment." *Asian Development Review* 31 (2): 109–40.

Couto, V., and K. Fernandez-Stark. 2019. "Pakistan in the Offshore Services Global Value Chain." Duke University Global Value Chains Center, Durham, NC. https://gvcc.duke.edu/wp-content/uploads/PakistanOffshoreServicesGVC.pdf.

Cozza, C., R. Rabellotti, and M. Sanfilippo. 2015. "The Impact of Outward FDI on the Performance of Chinese Firms." *China Economic Review* 36 (December): 42–57.

CTIER (Centre for Technology Innovation and Economic Research). 2016. "Indian IT Industry: Future Competitiveness Demands Increased R&D Spending." CTIER Brief 02, CTIER, Maharashtra, India. http://www.ctier.org/pdf-event/2016-10-CTIER-Brief-IT%20Industry.pdf.

Dayton, L. 2020. "How South Korea Made Itself a Global Innovation Leader." *Nature* 581: S54–S57.

Fernandez-Stark, K., P. Bamber, and G. Gereffi. 2011. "The Offshore Services Value Chain: Upgrading Trajectories in Developing Countries." *International Journal of Technological Learning, Innovation and Development* 4 (1–3): 206–34.

Ferracane, M. F., and H. Lee-Makiyama. 2017. "China's Technology Protectionism and Its Non-Negotiable Rationales." ECIPE Trade Working Paper 2/2017, European Centre for International Political Economy, Brussels.

Frederick, S., P. Bamber, and J. Cho. 2018. "The Digital Economy, Global Value Chains and Asia." Joint report, Duke University Global Value Chains Center and Korea Institute for Industrial Economics and Trade, Durham NC. https://gvcc.duke.edu/wp-content/uploads/DigitalEconomyGVCsAsia2018.pdf.

Fu, X., J. Hou, and X. Liu. 2018. "Unpacking the Relationship between Outward Direct Investment and Innovation Performance: Evidence from Chinese Firms." *World Development* 102: 111–23.

Fung, K. C., A. Garcia-Herrero, and A. Siu. 2009. "A Comparative Empirical Examination of Outward Foreign Direct Investment from Four Asian Economies: People's Republic of China; Japan; Republic of Korea; and Taipei, China." *Asian Development Review* 26 (2): 86–101.

Gallagher, K. P., and A. Irwin. 2014. "Exporting National Champions: China's Outward Foreign Direct Investment Finance in Comparative Perspective." *China & World Economy* 22 (6): 1–21.

Huang, Y., and Y. Zhang. 2017. "How Does Outward Foreign Direct Investment Enhance Firm Productivity? A Heterogeneous Empirical Analysis from Chinese Manufacturing." *China Economic Review* 44 (July): 1–15.

IBEF (India Brand Equity Foundation). 2021. "IT & BPM Industry in India." https://www.ibef.org/industry/information-technology-india.aspx.

IMF (International Monetary Fund). 2019. *Annual Report on Exchange Arrangements and Exchange Restrictions 2018.* Washington, DC: International Monetary Fund. https://www.imf.org/en/Publications/Annual-Report-on-Exchange-Arrangements-and-Exchange-Restrictions/Issues/2019/04/24/Annual-Report-on-Exchange-Arrangements-and-Exchange-Restrictions-2018-46162.

Jalote, P., and P. Natarajan. 2019. "The Growth and Evolution of India's Software Industry." *Communications of the ACM* 62 (11): 64–69.

Jiang, K., W. Keller, L. D. Qiu, and W. Ridley. 2018. "International Joint Ventures and Internal vs. External Technology Transfer: Evidence from China." NBER Working Paper 24455, National Bureau of Economic Research, Cambridge, MA.

Kathuria, V. 2010. "Outward Investment by Indian Pharmaceutical and Software Multinational Enterprises: Are the Factors Different?" In *The Rise of Indian Multinationals,* edited by Jaya Prakash Pradhan, Karl P. Sauvant, Ayesha Chatterjee, and Brian Harley, 167–85. New York: Palgrave Macmillan.

Kim, J., and D. K. Rhee. 2009. "Trends and Determinants of Korean Outward FDI." *Copenhagen Journal of Asian Studies* 27 (1): 126–54.

Kim, J.-Y., N. Driffield, and J. H. Love. 2018. "The Location of Technology Sourcing FDI: South Korean Investment in the US." Paper presented at the 6th Copenhagen Conference on "Emerging Multinationals: Outward Investment from Emerging Economies." Copenhagen, Denmark, October 11–12.

Kumar, N. 2014. "National Innovation Systems and the Indian Software Industry Development." In *Innovation in India: Combining Economic Growth with Inclusive Development*, edited by S. Ramani, 143–85. Cambridge: Cambridge University Press. doi:10.1017/CBO9781139794640.006.

Leskin, P. 2020. "TikTok Surpasses 2 Billion Downloads and Sets a Record for App Installs in a Single Quarter." Business Insider, April 30, 2020. https://www.businessinsider.com/tiktok-app-2-billion-downloads-record-setting-q1-sensor-tower-2020-4?r=DE&IR=T.

Li, J., R. Strange, L. Ning, and D. Sutherland. 2016. "Outward Foreign Direct Investment and Domestic Innovation Performance: Evidence from China." *International Business Review 25* (5): 1010–19.

Lim, W. 2016. *The Development of Korea's Electronics Industry during Its Formative Years (1966–1979)*. Sejong, Korea: KDI School of Public Policy and Management, Ministry of Strategy and Finance.

Liu, H., and J. Lu. 2011. "The Home-Employment Effect of FDI from Developing Countries: In the Case of China." *Journal of Chinese Economic and Foreign Trade Studies* 4 (3): 173–82.

Lovelock, P. 2018. "Framing Policies for the Digital Economy: Towards Policy Frameworks in the Asia-Pacific." UNDP Global Centre for Public Service Excellence, Singapore.

Mani, D., and S. Trines. 2018. "Education in South Korea," World Education News + Review (WENR), October 16, 2018. https://wenr.wes.org/2018/10/education-in-south-korea.

Mao, Q. L., and J. Y. Xu. 2014. "Effects of China's Outward FDI on Employees' Income: An Empirical Study Based on Propensity Score Matching." *Journal of International Trade* 11.

McCarthy, Niall. 2020. "98% of Chinese Internet Users Are Mobile." Statista, August 24, 2020. https://www.statista.com/chart/15202/the-number-of-internet-users-in-china/.

MGI (McKinsey Global Institute). 2017. "Digital China: Powering the Economy to Global Competitiveness." McKinsey & Company.

MGI (McKinsey Global Institute). 2019a. "China and the World: Inside the Dynamics of a Changing Relationship." McKinsey & Company.

MGI (McKinsey Global Institute). 2019b. "Digital India: Technology to Transform a Connected Nation." McKinsey Global Institute. https://www.mckinsey.com/~/media/McKinsey/Business%20Functions/McKinsey%20Digital/Our%20Insights/Digital%20India%20Technology%20to%20transform%20a%20connected%20nation/MGI-Digital-India-Report-April-2019.pdf.

Ministry of Finance and MOFCOM (Ministry of Commerce of China). 2012. "Announcement for Application for 2012 Special Fund of International Economic and Technological Cooperation." Ministry of Finance and MOFCOM, Beijing. http://www.mofcom.gov.cn/aarticle/cwgongzuo/huiyjl/201207/20120708225224.html.

MOFCOM (Ministry of Commerce of China). 2004. "Provisions on the Examination and Approval of Investment to Run Enterprises Abroad." MOFCOM, Beijing. http://www.asianlii.org/cn/legis/cen/laws/poteaaoitrea831/.

MOFCOM (Ministry of Commerce of China). 2020. "Global Investment and Cooperation Information Service System." MOFCOM, Beijing. http://femhzs.mofcom.gov.cn/fecpmvc/pages/fem/CorpJWList.html.

NDRC (National Development and Reform Commission). 2004. "Interim Administrative Measures for Approving Investment Projects Overseas." NDRC, Beijing.

Nicolas, F. 2003. "FDI as a Factor of Economic Restructuring: The Case of South Korea." In *International Trade, Capital Flows and Economic Development in East Asia: The Challenge in the 21st Century*, edited by A. Bende-Nabende. London: Ashgate.

Nicolas, F., S. Thomsen, and M. H. Bang. 2013. "Lessons from Investment Policy Reform in Korea." Working Paper on International Investment 2013/02, OECD Publishing, Paris. http://dx.doi.org/10.1787/5k4376zqcpf1-en.

Ning, L. 2009. "China's Leadership in the World ICT Industry: A Successful Story of Its 'Attracting-in' and 'Walking-out' Strategy for the Development of High-Tech Industries?" *Pacific Affairs* 82 (1): 67–91.

OECD (Organisation for Economic Co-operation and Development). 2007. "OECD Reviews of Innovation Policy: China." Synthesis Report, OECD Publishing, Paris.

OECD (Organisation for Economic Co-operation and Development). 2008. *OECD Investment Policy Reviews—China 2008: Encouraging Responsible Business Conduct.* Paris: OECD Publishing.

OECD (Organisation for Economic Co-operation and Development). 2017. *OECD Economic Surveys: China.* Paris: OECD Publishing.

PBC (People's Bank of China). 2011. "Interim Administrative Measures on Investment Overseas Settlement Accounts in Renminbi [PBC 2011 No. 1 Order]." PBC, Beijing.

Pedersen, J. D. 2010. "Political Factors behind the Rise of Indian Multinational Enterprises: An Essay in Political Economy." In *The Rise of Indian Multinationals*, edited by Jaya Prakash Pradhan, Karl P. Sauvant, Ayesha Chatterjee, and Brian Harley, 57–77. New York: Palgrave Macmillan.

Perea, J. R., and M. Stephenson. 2018. "Outward FDI from Developing Countries." In *Global Investment Competitiveness Report 2017/2018: Foreign Investor Perspectives and Policy Implications*, 101–34. Washington, DC: World Bank Group.

Pradhan, J. P. 2007. "National Innovation System and the Emergence of Indian Information and Software Technology Multinationals." ISID Working Paper 2007/09, Institute for Studies in Industrial Development, New Delhi. https://papers.ssrn.com/sol3/papers .cfm?abstract_id=1515648.

Pradhan, J. P. 2017. "Indian Outward FDI: A Review of Recent Developments." *Transnational Corporations* 24 (2): 43–70. doi:10.18356/32864c71-en.

Pradhan, J. P., and K. P. Sauvant. 2010. "Introduction: The Rise of Indian Multinational Enterprises: Revisiting Key Issues." In *The Rise of Indian Multinationals*, edited by Jaya Prakash Pradhan, Karl P. Sauvant, Ayesha Chatterjee, and Brian Harley, 1–23. New York: Palgrave Macmillan.

PwC (PricewaterhouseCoopers). 2018. "The 2017 Global Innovation 1000 Study: Investigating Trends at the World's 1000 Largest Corporate R&D Spenders." PwC.

Qiang, C. Z.-W. 2007. *China's Information Revolution: Managing the Economic and Social Transformation.* Washington, DC: World Bank.

Ruet, J. 2010. "When a Great Industry Globalizes: Indian Conglomerates Pioneering New Trends in Industrial Globalization." In *The Rise of Indian Multinationals*, edited by Jaya Prakash Pradhan, Karl P. Sauvant, Ayesha Chatterjee, and Brian Harley, 79–110. New York: Palgrave Macmillan.

Sauvant, K. P., and V. Z. Chen. 2013. "China's Outward Foreign Direct Investment: Salient Features, Drivers and Its Institutional Framework." Unpublished. https://papers.ssrn.com/ sol3/papers.cfm?abstract_id=3217852.

Sauvant, K. P., and M. D. Nolan. 2015. "China's Outward Foreign Direct Investment and International Investment Law." *Journal of International Economic Law* 18 (4): 893–934.

STA (State Taxation Administration). 2011. "Circular on the Reduction and Exemption of Revenues from Oil and Gas Extraction Projects Overseas by Chinese Enterprises." STA 2011 No. 23 Order, STA, Beijing.

Statista. 2020. "LG Display Panels Global Market Share 2013–2019." https://www.statista.com/ statistics/679773/lg-display-panel-market-share-south-korea/.

UIS (UNESCO Institute for Statistics). 2021. UNESCO Institute for Statistics, Data Centre. http:// data.uis.unesco.org/.

UNCTAD (United Nations Conference on Trade and Development). 2017. *World Investment Report 2017: Investment and the Digital Economy.* Geneva: United Nations.

US ITA (United States International Trade Administration). 2020. "South Korea – Country Commercial Guide: Information and Communication Technology." US ITA, Department of Commerce, Washington, DC. https://www.trade.gov/country-commercial-guides/ south-korea-information-and-communication-technology.

USTR (United States Office of the US Trade Representative). 2018. "Findings of the Investigation into China's Acts, Policies and Practices Related to Technology Transfer, Intellectual Property, and Innovation Under Section 301 of the Trade Act of 1974." USTR, Washington, DC.

Wallach, Omri. 2020. "How Big Tech Makes Their Billions." Visual Capitalist, July 6, 2020. https://www.visualcapitalist.com/how-big-tech-makes-their-billions-2020/.

Wang, B., and K. Gao. 2019. "Forty Years Development of China's Outward Foreign Direct Investment: Retrospect and the Challenges Ahead." *China & World Economy* 27 (3): 1–24.

Wang, G. Z., and Y. Zhang. 2010. "Research on the Impact of Outward Foreign Direct Investment on Trade Competitiveness." Paper prepared for 2010 International Conference on Machine Learning and Cybernetics, July 11–14.

World Bank. 2020. *World Development Report 2020: Trade for Development in the Age of Global Value Chains*. Washington, DC: World Bank.

World Bank Group. 2020. "Promoting Innovation in China: Lessons from International Good Practice." FCI Insight, World Bank Group, Washington, DC. http://documents1.worldbank.org/curated/en/571611587708038991/pdf/Promoting-Innovation-in-China-Lessons-from-International-Good-Practice.pdf.

WTO (World Trade Organization) Secretariat. 2006. "Trade Policy Review – Report by the Secretariat: People's Republic of China." WT/TPR/S/161/Rev.1, WTO, Geneva.

Zhang, L., and S. Chen. 2019. "China's Digital Economy: Opportunities and Risks." Working Paper 19/16, International Monetary Fund, Washington, DC.

Zhao, Wei, Ling Liu, and Ting Zhao. 2010. "The Contribution of Outward Direct Investment to Productivity Changes within China, 1991–2007." *Journal of International Management* 16 (2): 2121–30.

Chapter 11

Rwanda and West Bengal, India—A comparative analysis of firm dynamics in global value chains

YAN LIU AND VICTOR STEENBERGEN

Summary

This case study investigates the role of foreign direct investment (FDI) in the global value chain (GVC) participation of Rwanda and West Bengal, India. It analyzes the dynamics of multinational corporations (MNCs) and domestic firms across different GVC archetypes. The chapter first shows the current GVC participation and FDI performance of Rwanda and West Bengal, India. Next, it sets out the various approaches used in this chapter. Subsequently, it briefly explores the relationship between FDI inflows and GVC participation. It then considers the position and role of MNCs in production networks across different GVCs. Finally, it explores the firm characteristics that may predict domestic firms' GVC participation and considers how GVC participation affects firm performance.

Current global value chain participation and foreign direct investment performance of Rwanda and West Bengal

This study focuses on a single sector in each of the six GVC archetypes for both countries based on the size and importance of sectors in each country's economy. Table 11.1 shows focus sectors for each country and each archetype. The services sectors in West Bengal are not considered because data were unavailable.

Rwanda's global value chain and foreign direct investment performance

Using Rwandan customs data, figure 11.1 shows the contribution of the exporting firms in the four goods sectors to Rwanda's total export volume over the period 2008–17. As is evident from this illustration, firms in the four focus sectors in goods GVCs contribute significantly to Rwanda's export basket, with commodities (coffee and tea) being the largest foreign exchange earner in Rwanda's goods export portfolio. In 2017, the four goods GVCs together accounted for roughly one-third of total exports. Whereas agriprocessed goods as well as textiles, apparel, and leather have been a part of Rwanda's export mix for many years, the exporting of pharmaceuticals and chemicals is a relatively new occurrence.

Tourism makes up close to half of all services exports using the set of firms in the data set. Tourism exports in 2017 were higher than textiles, apparel, and leather; processed foods;

TABLE 11.1 **Focus sectors for Rwanda and West Bengal, India, across global value chain archetypes**

GVC archetype	Focus sectors for Rwanda	Focus sectors for West Bengal
Commodity	Coffee and tea	Tea, rice, and oil seeds
Regional processing	Food products	Food products
Labor-intensive goods	Textiles, apparel, and leather	Textiles, apparel, and leather
Knowledge-intensive goods	Chemicals	Chemicals
Labor-intensive services	Tourism	—
Knowledge-intensive services	Professional services	—

Source: World Bank.
Note: GVC = global value chain; — = not available.

FIGURE 11.1 **The contribution of global value chain archetypes to Rwanda's exports, 2008–17**

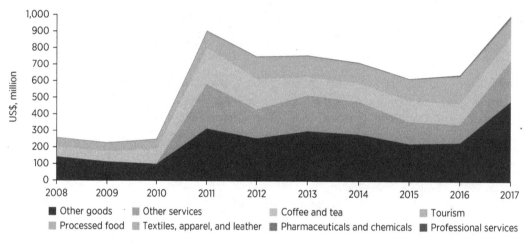

Source: World Bank calculations based on Rwandan customs data and value added tax data.
Note: Export flows behind the global value chain archetypes are limited to those by firms that exported at least 0.5 percent of all exports of a global value chain sector in any given year. US$ values are in constant 2014 values. Most "Other goods" exports are in mining (including cassiterite, wolfram, coltan, and gold). Most "Other services" exports are in wholesale and retail trade.

and pharmaceutical exports combined. Professional services made up only about 1 percent of total services exports in 2017. Most of the "other" services exports are in wholesale and retail trade.

FDI stock in Rwanda increased steadily from 2011 through 2017. In 2011, FDI in Rwanda equated to about US$495 million, or 7.5 percent of gross domestic product (GDP). By 2017, this figure had increased to almost US$1.8 billion, or about 20 percent of GDP. The chapter uses data on announced investments by foreign-owned firms (in million US dollars and cumulative over the study period 2011–17) to provide a breakdown of FDI by the six focus sectors and "other" sectors (figure 11.2). The six focus sectors accounted for 72 percent of the total value of FDI announced in Rwanda. Coffee and tea and professional services received the highest FDI inflows. The services sectors attracted relatively less FDI than each of the four goods sectors included in this study, which is especially noteworthy given that tourism is one of Rwanda's most important exports.

FIGURE 11.2 **Announced foreign direct investment, cumulative 2011–17 (share of total foreign direct investment)**

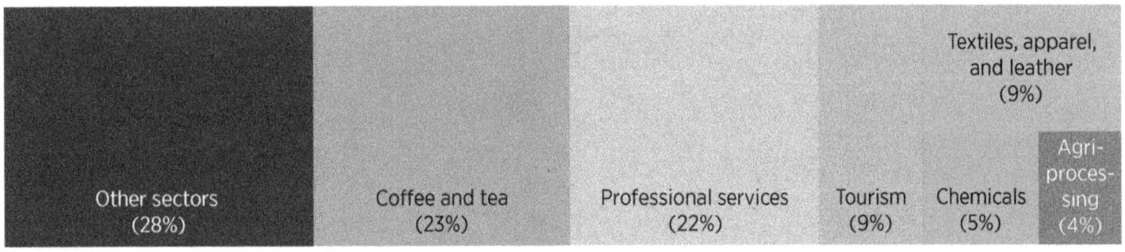

Source: World Bank illustration based on Rwanda Development Board investment announcements.
Note: Announced investments by firms usually cover several years of planned investments. "Other sectors" mainly include energy and mining.

West Bengal's global value chain and foreign direct investment performance

West Bengal,[1] located on the east coast of India, is one of the country's leading exporters of leather goods, tea, and rice. Despite its proximity to East and Southeast Asian economies, West Bengal's overall GVC participation and FDI inflows are limited. West Bengal had the sixth-highest state domestic product (SDP) in 2017/18; its SDP accounted for 5.67 percent of India's total GDP, but its exports represented only 3 percent of India's total exports in 2017/18. Total exports from West Bengal have stagnated in recent years: exports reached a peak of more than US$10 billion in 2013/14, then slumped to US$7.47 billion in 2015/16. Its exports stood at US$9.15 billion in 2017/18, a level lower than five years before. West Bengal's share of India's exports also declined from 3.2 percent to 3.0 percent.

West Bengal's stagnant exports may reflect a shift away from manufacturing and toward services since the early 1980s. The share of manufacturing in SDP has declined from 22 percent in 1980 to less than 10 percent in 2010. Agriculture's share in SDP has also shown a relative decline, dropping from 30 percent in 1980 to 24 percent in 2010 (Pal 2013).

Using data from West Bengal's major ports, table 11.2 shows that the four goods sectors made up more than 40 percent of West Bengal's total exports in 2018. The textiles, apparel, and leather segment has the highest share of exports among the four focus sectors (17 percent), followed by agricultural goods[2] (11 percent), food products (9 percent), and chemicals (5 percent). Other sectors are mainly basic commodities such as iron and steel, aluminum, gold, and petroleum products.[3]

West Bengal has performed relatively poorly in attracting FDI. Figure 11.3 shows the overall value of West Bengal's FDI inflows, together with its relative share of India's FDI and India's GDP. With the exception of 2015, West Bengal's FDI inflows never exceeded US$500 million. It is capturing only 1–2 percent of India's total FDI inflows (despite making up about 6 percent of India's GDP). Its performance also seems to be deteriorating over time, given that it accounted for only 0.2 percent and 0.5 percent of India's total FDI inflows in 2016 and 2017, respectively. No data are available on sectoral FDI inflows.

TABLE 11.2   **The contribution of global value chain archetypes to West Bengal's goods exports, 2018**

Sectors	US$, million	Share %
Focus sectors	4,996	41.6
Agricultural goods	1,275	10.6
Food products	1,078	9.0
Textiles, apparel, and leather	2,081	17.3
Chemicals and chemical products	563	4.7
Other sectors	7,007	58.4
Other agricultural goods	105	0.9
Other basic commodities	5,188	43.2
Other manufacturing	1,714	14.3
Total	12,003	100.0

Source: World Bank calculations using Directorate General of Commercial Intelligence and Statistics data for 2018 for all West Bengali ports (Ghajadanga, Petrapole, Mani Kanchan, Hili, TT Shed, Singabad, Chengrabandha, Ranaghat, Kollam Port, Kolkata Sea, Kolkata Air, Falta, Mohedipur).

FIGURE 11.3   **West Bengal's total foreign direct investment inflows and relative share of India's foreign direct investment, 2011–17**

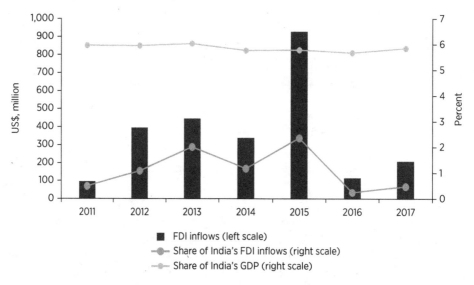

FDI inflows (left scale)
Share of India's FDI inflows (right scale)
Share of India's GDP (right scale)

Source: World Bank calculations based on Reserve Bank of India region-based statements.
Note: FDI = foreign direct investment.

Firm-level data also show limited MNCs in West Bengal's productive sector. Figure 11.4 illustrates the number of publicly listed MNCs in West Bengal, and their percentage shares across sectors. The total has increased over time, growing from 188 in 2011/12, to 194 in 2013/14, and 205 in 2015/16. Yet, of those, just 20 percent (about 40 MNCs) are in the four selected sectors. Most MNCs in these sectors are in chemical products (11 percent); followed by textiles, apparel, and leather (5 percent); agricultural goods (4 percent); and food products (2 percent). Overall, these MNCs are very likely to be exporters: in aggregate between 50 percent and 60 percent of

FIGURE 11.4 **Average number and sectoral share of multinational corporations, 2011–16**

Chemical products (21), 11%

Textiles, apparel, leather (9), 5%

Agri-cultural goods (8), 4%

Other sectors (163), 79%

Food products (3), 2%

Source: World Bank calculations using Orbis database and value added tax data.
Note: Multinational corporations include foreign-owned firms, joint ventures, and domestic firms with overseas affiliates.

all MNCs export in GVC sectors. Other sectors are more domestically oriented, with about one-third of MNCs exporting.

Analyzing the dynamics between firms and global value chain participation—data and methodology

Many studies on GVCs ignore the roles of individual firms in global production networks. A firm participates in a GVC if it produces at least one stage in the value chain (Antràs 2020). GVC participation, however, is often defined at the country-industry level using world input-output tables (see chapter 1). This perspective ignores the roles of individual firms in global production networks. Even studies that consider firm-level GVC participation often limit their definition of participation to only firms that both import and export (Antràs 2020; Johnson 2018; and the Organisation for Economic Co-operation and Development's Analytical Activities of MNEs (multinational enterprises)" database). However, GVC participation does not always require that a firm directly export goods or services. Instead, firms may be integrated into GVCs indirectly by producing and supplying intermediates to exporting firms or by offshoring part of their production facilities (Cusolito, Safadi, and Taglioni 2016). Therefore, to get the most accurate representation of GVC participation, it is important to consider the wide variety of firms engaged in global production networks.

This study combines novel data sets and methodologies to analyze the dynamics of MNCs and domestic firms across different GVC archetypes. The data sets and methods vary in Rwanda and West Bengal, which are covered separately.

Rwanda

Data. The data set for Rwanda includes firm registration data, firm corporate income tax data, firm customs data, and firm-to-firm transactions data from 2008 to 2017. The rich data sets allow identification of exporters in each focus sector, firm ownership status (domestic or foreign), firm age, employment, industry, financials, imports and exports, and interfirm linkages.

Identifying exporters in each focus sector. Using transactions-level customs data on Rwanda's exports, firms in the four goods value chains (coffee and tea; processed foods; textiles, apparel, and leather; and chemicals) are identified through the Harmonized System (HS) codes in export transactions.[4] Because only large formal firms that are likely to participate in GVCs are of interest, the data are restricted to firms that account for more than 0.5 percent of total exports of their respective GVCs. Because the customs data capture only goods exports, different identifying criteria are used for tourism and professional services. For tourism, all firms that self-register as "hotels" or "travel agents" in their annual corporate income tax returns are included.[5] For firms active in professional services, all companies that report being active in International Standard Industrial Classification activities M (Professional, Scientific and Technical Activities) or J (Information or Communication) and that at the same time report nonzero exports in their monthly value added tax (VAT) declarations are included.

Network analysis of production networks. Network analysis is used to visualize GVCs at the firm level. This is a challenging task because all firms are interconnected through myriad transactions every day. Including all firm-to-firm linkages does not help provide an understanding of the key players and structure of the value chain. Conceptual mapping of selected value chains by industry experts is therefore used, and only key input suppliers are included for each value chain. For the ease of visualization and interpretation, data from 2017—the latest year for which data are available—are used.

First, the largest exporters for each focus sector based on customs data are identified. The network graphs (figures B11.1.1 and B11.2.1 in boxes 11.1 and 11.2) show the combination of destination country and HS 4-digit product code for top exporters. VAT data at the transaction level are used to identify tier 1 domestic suppliers of top exporters, and to trace them back to tier 2 and tier 3 suppliers. Only domestic suppliers that manufacture or sell key inputs for the focus sector are kept. Customs data are then used to show import suppliers for each relevant HS 4-digit product for top exporters and their tier 1 to tier 3 suppliers.

Sector- and firm-level regressions. The relationship between FDI and exports at the sector level, that is, the intraindustry effect of FDI on exports, is also considered. Formally, specifications of the following kind are estimated:

$$ExportShare_{st} = \beta_0 + \beta_1 \, \boldsymbol{FDI}_{st} + \omega_s + \mu_t + \varepsilon_{st},$$ (11.1)

where *ExportShare*$_{st}$ is the share of a sector's *s* output exported in year *t*, mirroring a sector's participation in (and reliance on) global market opportunities. **FDI**$_{st}$ corresponds to one of four different proxy measures to consider the prevalence of FDI in a sector: the number of MNCs in a sector, the share of total domestic purchases of a sector made by MNCs in the sector, the share of total output of a sector generated by MNCs, and the share of a sector's total employment provided by MNCs. The terms ω_s and μ_t correspond to sector and year fixed effects, and ε_{st} captures other, unobserved characteristics at the sector level. Standard errors are clustered at the sector level in all estimations.

The analysis also considers how different firm types affect a firm's relationship with GVCs, and specifically its probability of becoming a direct exporter itself. Formally, the following specification is estimated:

$$\Pr(Exporter)_{ist} = \beta_0 + \beta_1 \, \textbf{FirmType}_{ist} + \omega_s + \mu_t + \varepsilon_{st}, \tag{11.2}$$

where $\Pr(Exporter)_{ist}$ is the probability that a firm *i* in sector s in year *t* has a positive export volume. **FirmType**$_{ist}$ corresponds to different firm characteristics that may explain GVC participation. These characteristics are either the firm's status as supplier to exporters or firm ownership (joint venture [JV] or foreign-owned firm). The terms ω_s and μ_t correspond to sector and year fixed effects, and ε_{st} captures other, unobserved characteristics at the sector level. Standard errors are clustered at the sector level in all estimations.

GVC participation event study.   To study how GVC participation affects firm behavior, a simple event study is used that compares firms that started participating in GVCs with those that did not in the years preceding and following their GVC participation. The sample is first restricted to only those firms that are in the data set for at least six years (two years preceding GVC participation, the year GVC participation began, and three years following). Then, for the control group, only firms in the similar subsector are included. Unfortunately, each subsector cannot be observed directly, so the analysis instead relies on an aggregate set of "business activities" in which the exporting firms operate. Next, comparable age is used as the other main comparator. Simple descriptive statistics are then used to compare the behavior of GVC exporting firms *preceding* and *following* GVC participation. A number of key variables are presented and the analysis captures the difference in value with a domestic firm in the same sector of similar age.

West Bengal

Data.   The data sets for West Bengal are more restricted than those for Rwanda and are mainly based on three types of VAT data. First, firm VAT registration data include information for 14 business types[6] and the description and amount of the top three commodities sold by the firm. Second, firm VAT declaration data hold information on each firm's purchases (imported or purchased locally), total sales, and their total VAT. Third, firm VAT transaction data contain information on the total amount a supplier sold to a purchaser each year, and the overall taxes paid on these purchases. Finally, the

Orbis database is merged with West Bengal firm VAT registration data by firm name to identify foreign-owned firms, JVs, and domestic firms with foreign affiliates.

Identifying exporters in each focus sector.   As a first step toward identifying the exporting firms across the four selected focus sectors, the names of all reported commodities were cleaned and a fuzzy matching algorithm was used to identify their closest matching HS commodity code (HS2, HS4, or HS6). Using several rounds of cleaning, matching, manual checks for accuracy, and finally manual lookups for remaining items, 1,394 out of 1,423 unique commodities (98 percent) were matched to a specific HS code. Across each commodity, the corresponding HS2 code was used as the basis for identifying focus sectors.

Next, total exports were identified by using the discrepancy between a firm's reported total sales and the VAT duty on its sales (because VAT is charged on domestic sales but not on exported goods). For this step, the total expected VAT from the firm's top three commodities was estimated by multiplying the amount sold by the commodity-specific VAT rate.[7] Next, the resulting amount was compared with the actual VAT reported for the firm's top three commodities. The assumption is then made that this difference is entirely due to exports, and that goods are exported proportional to total sales. Firms that meet three criteria are considered main exporters in the respective focus sector in a given year: the firm operates in the focus sector, has nonzero exports in a given year, and exports at least 0.5 percent of that sector's total annual exports.

Sector- and firm-level regressions.   Data constraints prevented a sectoral analysis of FDI and exports in West Bengal. However, an analysis was conducted of how different firm types affect a firm's relationship with GVCs, and specifically the firm's probability of becoming a direct exporter itself, following the same specification set out in equation (11.2). The only difference is that for firm ownership status the data show whether firms are JVs or foreign-owned firms or if a domestic firm has a foreign affiliate.

Network analysis of production networks.   For each product, the analysis starts with the top exporting firms and traces back to their three tiers of suppliers. First, key products in the four sectors of interest are selected, and exporters in the respective sector are identified on the basis of main commodities reported by firms. The analysis then focuses on the top 10 firms by estimated export value. Because of the scarcity of MNCs, firms are included if they are MNCs and among the top 20 exporters. VAT data are used at the transaction level to identify tier 1 local suppliers of top exporters, and then to trace back to tier 2 and tier 3 suppliers. Only domestic suppliers that manufacture or sell key inputs for the selected final product are kept. For tier 2 and tier 3 suppliers, the sample is limited to manufacturing or two-way trading firms to avoid noise from small retailers.

GVC participation event study.   To study how GVC participation affects firm behavior, a simple event study is used that compares firms that started participating in GVCs with those that did not in the years preceding and following their GVC participation. Unfortunately, only three time periods are available (2011/12, 2013/14, and 2015/16) each with a yearly gap in between them. For that reason, the sample is restricted to those firms that did not export in the first year but started exporting in the middle year. For the control group, firms in the same subsector that did not export during the entire period are included. Simple descriptive statistics are then used to compare the behavior of GVC exporting firms *preceding* and *following* initial GVC participation. A number of key variables are presented and the difference in value with a domestic firm in the same sector is captured.

General limitations and caveats

Because of limitations in the data sets, this approach has certain caveats, especially in the West Bengal analysis. The analysis is only descriptive in both cases and, although suggestive, cannot establish a direct causal relationship between FDI and GVC participation, or GVC participation and firm performance.

Global firm-to-firm value chains and the full production stages cannot be mapped out because the data sets are confined to a certain country or state. In the West Bengal case, both exporting status and exports value are based on discrepancies between a firm's reported total sales for the top three commodities and the actual VAT duty. Firms often sell a range of products; the discrepancy could be the result of sales of other products not reported. Moreover, the analysis assumes that firms export the same proportion of all of the top three commodities, which will certainly not be true. "Import" has a slightly different meaning in the West Bengal case than is typical because a firm is deemed to be an importer if it purchases from suppliers in other states of India or abroad. There is no way to determine whether a firm is purchasing from other states of India or from foreign countries. In addition, reliance on the Orbis database to identify firm ownership means that only large companies are identified, which is another reason the analysis finds very few MNCs in West Bengal.

Finally, to compare firms' market power and profitability, the analysis assumes a firm's total purchases are equal to material costs and subtracts that from total sales to get gross profits. Gross profits are then divided by total sales to get gross margin. This method causes distortions in firms' profitability because firms also purchase capital goods and non-production-related goods and services.

The effect of aggregate foreign direct investment inflows on global value chain participation

A key question of interest in this study is whether FDI inflows foster GVC participation in Rwanda and West Bengal. The relationship between FDI and exports at the sectoral level is explored.[8] Table 11.3 presents estimation results for the specification in equation (11.2) using an ordinary least squares regression with sector and year fixed effects for Rwanda.[9]

There is a positive and statistically significant relationship between number of MNCs in a sector and the share of output that is exported in the sector. Entry of an additional MNC into a sector is associated with an increase in that sector's export share by about 0.7 percentage point on average (column (1) of table 11.3). Similarly,

TABLE 11.3   The effect of foreign direct investment on a sector's participation in global markets in Rwanda

FDI variables	Share of output exported by sector			
	(1)	(2)	(3)	(4)
Number of MNCs in sector	0.00679*			
	(0.00404)			
Share of sector's local purchases by MNCs		0.00007		
		(0.000756)		
Share of sector's total output by MNCs			0.00193*	
			(0.00100)	
Share of sector's total employment by MNCs				0.00154*
				(0.000926)
Observations	1,123	1,123	1,123	1,123
R-squared	0.762	0.761	0.767	0.765
Sector fixed effects	Yes	Yes	Yes	Yes
Year fixed effects	Yes	Yes	Yes	Yes

Source: World Bank.
Note: Standard errors in parentheses. Standard errors are clustered at the sector ("main activity") level. Included sectors are manufacturing and services sectors following Reyes (2018). Foreign-owned firms are included in the calculation of export shares. FDI = foreign direct investment; MNC = multinational corporation. *** $p<0.01$, ** $p<0.05$, * $p<0.1$.

as evident from columns (3) and (4) of table 11.3, an increase in MNCs' share of output or employment is associated with a 0.2-percentage-point increase of a sector's export share on average. The point estimate on the effect of a sector's local purchases on participation in global markets is small and estimated imprecisely. However, the positive association between FDI and a sector's exports seems to be driven by the MNCs themselves rather than by domestic firm spillovers. No significant effect is found of foreign investment on the export share of domestic firms (see Steenbergen and Liu et al. 2021 for details), suggesting that most of the exporting is conducted by MNCs themselves.

Although data constraints prevented a sectoral analysis of FDI and exports in West Bengal, in both Rwanda and West Bengal a strong positive correlation was identified at the firm level between being a foreign-owned firm and being an exporter (see figure 11.7 later in this chapter).

The role of multinational corporations in production networks

This study uses network analysis and descriptive statistics to offer a snapshot of production networks and the role of MNCs in selected value chains in Rwanda and West Bengal. It highlights the positions of MNCs in the production networks and compares the length and complexity of production networks and exporters' market power across different GVCs.

The position and role of multinational corporations

Longer and more complex GVCs tend to have more foreign firms and two-way trading firms.[10] This composition could be the result of both government policies and MNCs' competitive positioning. Two-way trading firms make up only 15 percent of total trading firms but contribute more than 80 percent of total trade in many countries (World Bank 2020). Empirical evidence also shows two-way traders are less likely to lose their exporting status (Díaz-Mora, Córcoles, and Gandoy 2015).

Visualizations of production networks are shown in box 11.1 for the textiles, apparel, and leather GVC in Rwanda and in box 11.2 for the chemicals and pharmaceuticals GVC in West Bengal. In both cases, the important role that foreign firms play in a country's GVC participation is illustrated. Foreign firms were more likely to be positioned at the end of domestic value chains because they are more likely to export and account for a disproportionately high share of total exports. This analysis can show which types of firms are engaging in GVCs as exporters and as suppliers (according to their ownership, size, and location). As such, it provides insights into the wide network of GVC actors that may be less easily observable using traditional stakeholder analysis (such as tier 2 suppliers). One downside of this approach, however, is that no data are available for firms not based within the country, so only the part of the GVC taking place within the country is observable.

Length and complexity of production networks

Another important dimension within GVCs is production length, which is defined as the number of firms (including cross-border intrafirm trade) a product or service must go through before reaching final demand (see chapter 2 of this book; Fally 2012; Wang et al. 2017). Production length captures the complexity and coordination intensity of GVCs. Complex products and services tend to go through more firms, requiring more specialization and coordination along the chain, thereby creating more opportunities for knowledge spillovers. Theoretically, production length can be measured as the sum of firm-to-firm links. Practically, however, firms can source the same input from multiple suppliers, so to calculate the precise production length on the basis of firm linkages data alone is impossible.

In both Rwanda's and West Bengal's cases, firms are engaged in only a few segments of the supply chain, so not all stages of production can be observed to estimate production length. Thus, some tentative indicators are used to compare production length across archetypes: In Rwanda, number of imported product types (type is defined as HS6 code) and number of key input suppliers for export firms are used. In West Bengal, the average number of suppliers at each stage is used. The rationale for these proxies is that complex products require more types of inputs, more suppliers, and higher degrees of specialization.

Production length is shortest in professional services and longest in the textiles, apparel, and leather value chain in Rwanda (table 11.4). Textiles, apparel, and leather and chemicals also have the highest number of tier 1 suppliers in West Bengal

BOX 11.1 The textiles, apparel, and leather value chain in Rwanda

Rwanda's textiles, apparel, and leather exports totaled US$8 million in 2017. This exercise focuses on the top seven exporters for which data are available: one large garment exporter, one bag exporter, and five leather exporters (figure B11.1.1). Key inputs for the garment and leather value chain include yarn, fabrics, coloring matter, and textile and sewing machinery. The top garment and top leather exporter are both foreign owned. There are two foreign wholesalers among tier 1 suppliers, and two foreign-owned chemical firms among tier 3 suppliers. Unlike the coffee and tea value chain, many domestic suppliers import key inputs directly because the garment and leather sector requires more kinds of inputs, many of which are less available in Rwanda. The top garment exporter sells coats, T-shirts, and pullovers to Europe and the United States; it imports a wide range of inputs (including woven fabrics, yarn, synthetic fibers, sewing threads, buttons, glues, sewing machines, and labels) from China and fabrics from Uganda; and it sources other materials from local suppliers.

Production length in the textiles, apparel, and leather value chain is long (see chapter 2 of this report), but this fact is not directly obvious from figure B11.1.1 because the figure captures only three tiers of domestic suppliers. More important, the full production length of the textiles, apparel, and leather value chain cannot be observed because Rwandan firms do not carry out all the production stages by themselves—most of the raw materials and intermediate inputs are imported. Foreign-owned exporters also enjoy some market power over their domestic suppliers because they provide key inputs and source only relatively simple and standard inputs from local suppliers.

FIGURE B11.1.1 Textiles, apparel, and leather value chain in Rwanda

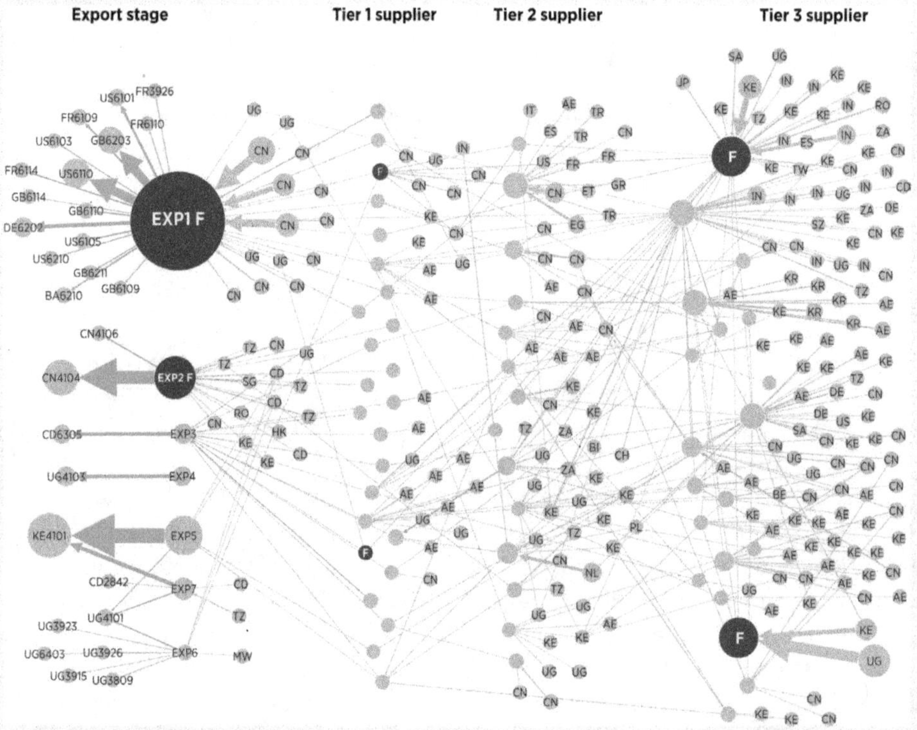

Source: World Bank calculations based on firm-to-firm value added tax data in 2017.
Note: Exports are denoted by green arrows; orange arrows represent imports. Each node represents a firm. Foreign-owned firms are dark blue, and domestic firms are light blue. The thickness of the edges between the nodes is proportional to the transaction amount between the two respective firms, and the size of each node represents the node's weighted degree in the network.

BOX 11.2 The chemicals and pharmaceuticals value chain in West Bengal, India

West Bengal is home to some of India's oldest and most successful chemical and pharmaceutical firms. Figure B11.2.1 shows the top 10 chemical product exporters. These firms produce a wide range of products, including industrial raw materials, fertilizers and pesticides, gases, washing detergent, chemicals, and medicines. Nine of the ten firms also import inputs from other states or foreign countries. Two exporters are multinational corporations (MNCs): exporter 6 is an Indian-owned multinational that sells fertilizers and pesticides; exporter 20 is a foreign firm producing rare gases. MNCs are present in all three tiers of suppliers, though MNCs are not the largest firms by sales. Unlike the textiles, apparel, and leather value chain, in which connections between tier 2 and tier 3 suppliers become sparse, tier 2 suppliers in the chemicals and pharmaceuticals value chain have far more tier 3 suppliers, and connections remain dense. The inputs provided by each tier of suppliers are also very diverse and include scientific equipment, metals, petroleum products, acids, oxides, carbonates and bicarbonates, adhesives, polyvinyl chloride goods, rubber and plastic, and pollution control equipment.

FIGURE B11.2.1 Chemicals and pharmaceuticals value chain in West Bengal

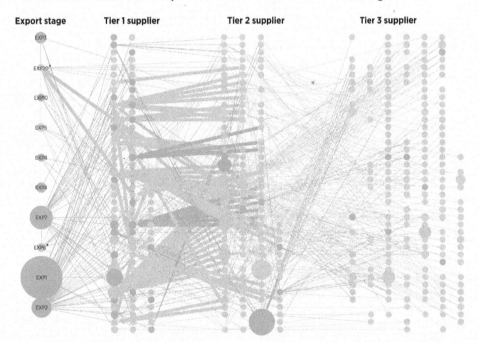

Source: World Bank calculations based on firm-to-firm value added tax data in 2015/16.
Note: Each node represents a firm. Foreign-owned firms are orange, and domestic firms are blue. Green nodes represent firms that both export and import. The thickness of the edges between the nodes is proportional to the transaction amount between the two respective firms, and the size of each node represents the node's weighted degree in the network. Multinational corporations that are also two-way traders are highlighted with an asterisk.

TABLE 11.4 **Length and complexity of global value chains across archetypes in Rwanda, 2017**

Focus sector	Average number of import types	Maximum number of import types	Typical imports	Average in-degree of exporters
Coffee and tea	0.63	4	Fertilizers; hand tools used in agriculture; agricultural machinery	3.4
Agriprocessing	1.38	10	Oil seeds; cereal groats; sugars; bakery and food and drink preparation machinery	4.4
Textiles, apparel, and leather	8.57	37	Tanning substance; raw hides and skins; clothing accessories; textile machinery; sewing machines; glues; acids; fabrics; sewing thread; yarn; twine; pigments; labels; buttons	9.1
Chemicals	19.50	30	Ammonia; iron, titanium, lead oxides; alcohols; acids; organic compounds; hydrogen peroxide; hydrocarbons; dyes; laboratory machinery and equipment; optical instruments and apparatus	19.5
Tourism	4.16	47	Mattresses; bed linen; rugs; lamps; curtains; furniture; soaps; ovens; cookers; glassware; chairs; seats; tricycles	2.6
Professional services	0	0	n.a.	2.0

Source: World Bank calculations.
Note: Type of imports is defined by number of different Harmonized System 6-digit products. "In-degree" measures how many incoming links a node has in a network, which indicates how many suppliers an exporter has in this case study. n.a. = not applicable.

(table 11.5). Production length based on micro measures is largely consistent with macro measures: goods-producing value chains have longer production lengths than services, and production length increases from commodities to knowledge-intensive goods. Supplier diversification is ubiquitous in all selected GVCs, though suppliers seem to be most diversified in the upstream coffee and tea value chain in Rwanda and in prepared food in West Bengal, where there can be dozens of suppliers for the same input. Generally, firms source the same input only from a few suppliers because identifying qualified suppliers and maintaining the relationship can be costly.

Market power of exporters and multinational corporations

To assess exporters' market power in Rwanda, this analysis compares total sales and gross margin between lead firms and their suppliers to show their power asymmetry.[11] In Rwanda, the coffee and tea value chain[12] sheds some light on power asymmetry between exporters and suppliers: the median business income for coffee and tea exporters is 6,138 million Rwanda francs (RF), but only 250 million RF for tier 1 suppliers; exporters also capture most of the value added along the chain (table 11.6). Median gross profit as a share of sales is 0.28 for exporters, 0.14 for tier 1 suppliers, and only 0.06 for tier 2 suppliers, which is consistent with the literature that exporting firms are more productive than firms serving only domestic markets.

Market power could not be fully compared across archetypes in Rwanda because such a comparison requires a large sample of key input suppliers (which is unavailable

TABLE 11.5 **Length and complexity of global value chains across archetypes in West Bengal, India, 2015/16**

Focus sector	Average number of tier 1 suppliers	Average number of tier 2 suppliers	Average number of tier 3 suppliers	Typical inputs sourced from local suppliers
Tea, rice	5.20	2.73	0.85	Agricultural inputs, machinery for tea industry, fertilizers, tools, chemicals
Prepared food	11.78	3.08	0.83	Animal or vegetable fats and oils, spices, chemicals, machinery for food and food processing
Textiles, apparel, and leather	14.40	1.92	1.86	Textile, yarn, fabrics, sewing thread, sewing machine, button, hides and skins, tailoring material, needle, textile machinery, labels, chemicals
Chemicals and pharmaceuticals	11.80	1.56	2.62	Organic chemicals, inorganic chemicals, metals, minerals, optical equipment, weighing machines

Source: World Bank calculations using value added tax data in West Bengal.

TABLE 11.6 **Power asymmetry across global value chain archetypes in Rwanda, 2017**

Focus sector	MNC contribution		Median sales (Rwanda francs, million)		Median gross margin (%)		
	Percentage of exporters	Percentage of exports	Exporters	Tier 1 suppliers	Exporters	Tier 1 suppliers	Tier 2 suppliers
Coffee and tea	31.3	46.0	6,138	250	28	14	6
Agriprocessing	25.0	76.3	921	1,029	10	10	7
Textiles, apparel, and leather	28.6	61.9	1,183	341	11	13	15
Chemicals	0.0	0.0	75	8,320	—	28	25
Tourism	5.3	6.2	658	366	70	49	—
Professional services	0.0	0.0	49	431	—	—	—

Source: World Bank calculations based on Rwanda firm-level data.
Note: Sales in million Rwanda francs captures a subset of high-value global value chain exporting firms for 2017 only, and so differs slightly from the descriptive statistics. — = not available; MNC = multinational corporation.

because Rwanda relies heavily on imports for most key inputs). It also requires data on lead firms' financial performance outside the country, which are also not present for this study. In addition, meaningful conclusions on exporters' market power in West Bengal could not be drawn because of data limitations.

The internationalization of domestic firms

To extend the productive benefits from GVC participation to the wider economy, local firms must also be integrated into these same global production networks. Integration can happen either by *supplying* exporters or by *becoming* direct exporters.

Rwandan firms' GVC participation is presented in table 11.7, which shows that the degree of GVC participation is relatively low across all GVCs (most firms are nonsupplier, nonexporting domestic firms). Overall, the largest number of GVC exporting firms are in tourism and professional services. Agriprocessing has the highest number of active MNCs, followed by coffee and tea and chemicals. The overall number of formal suppliers[13] differs significantly, with large numbers in chemicals and textiles, apparel, and leather. In contrast, coffee and tea and tourism see a relatively small number of large suppliers.[14]

TABLE 11.7   **Rwanda: The number of firms across global value chains—domestic, multinational corporations, and suppliers, 2008–17**

		Number of firms		
Focus sector	All firms[a]	Suppliers to exporting firms[b]	Exporting firms (domestic)	Exporting firms (MNCs)[c]
Coffee and tea	902	40	41	6
Agriprocessing (food)	16,007	1,004	32	7
Textiles, apparel, and leather	4,992	224	37	2
Chemicals	13,941	1,299	42	5
Tourism (hotels and tour operators)	385	22	78	3
Professional services	8,675	535	60	2

Source: World Bank calculations.
Note: MNC = multinational corporation.
a. Each sector cannot be observed directly, so instead the full number of firms for an aggregate set of "business activities" in which the global value chain exporting firms operate is reported.
b. Suppliers to exporting firms are restricted to nonexporters.
c. MNCs include both fully foreign-owned firms and joint ventures.

TABLE 11.8   **West Bengal: The number of firms across global value chains—domestic, multinational corporations, and suppliers, 2015/16**

		Number of firms		
Focus sector	All firms[a]	Suppliers to exporting firms[b]	Exporting firms (domestic)	Exporting firms (MNCs)[c]
Agricultural goods	2,408	354	36	4
Food products	7,409	160	31	2
Textiles, apparel, and leather	11,170	617	43	6
Chemical products	13,072	683	20	9
Total	34,059	1,814	130	21

Source: World Bank calculations.
Note: MNC = multinational corporation.
a. Each sector cannot be observed directly, so instead the full number of firms for an aggregate set of "business activities" in which the global value chain exporting firms operate is reported.
b. Suppliers to exporting firms are restricted to nonexporters.
c. MNCs include foreign-owned firms, joint ventures, and domestic firms with foreign affiliates (outward foreign direct investment).

Table 11.8 provides a breakdown of West Bengal's firm participation in GVCs, again showing a relatively low share of GVC participation across firms. Overall, the largest number of exporting firms is in textiles, apparel, and leather. The chemical products industry has the largest number of suppliers to exporting firms. In contrast, food products and agricultural goods have a relatively small number of exporters or suppliers.

In both Rwanda and West Bengal, GVC participants tend to be the most productive firms. Rwanda's distribution of output per worker by firm type is presented in figure 11.5, which shows that for merchandise goods domestic firms are the least productive, followed by GVC suppliers and GVC exporters (domestic), whereas GVC exporters (MNCs) are the most productive on average. For services, the difference between domestic firms and domestic GVC exporters is not as pronounced.[15] However, we still see that GVC suppliers and GVC exporters run by MNCs are much more productive than domestic firms (their overall distribution lies to the right). In West Bengal, two productivity metrics were considered: gross profits and profit margins (figure 11.6).[16] Both panels show that domestic firms tend to be less profitable, both in absolute terms and as a share of their overall sales. The next most profitable are suppliers to domestic exporters and domestic exporters, whose gross profits closely overlap. However, suppliers have lower average profit margins. Exporting MNCs are

FIGURE 11.5 **Productivity distribution of Rwanda's firms in goods and services, domestic firms, suppliers, and exporters, 2008–17**

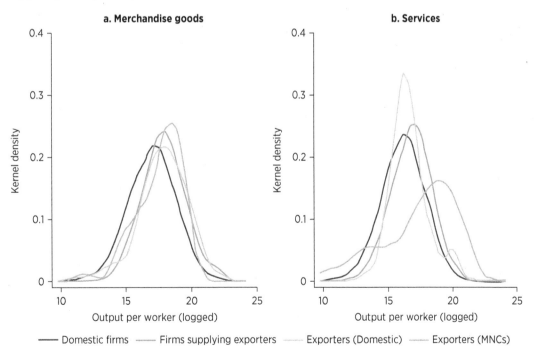

Source: World Bank calculations.
Note: Merchandise goods includes coffee and tea; agriprocessing; textiles, apparel, and leather; and chemicals. Services includes tourism and professional services. GVC = global value chain; MNC = multinational corporation.

FIGURE 11.6 **Productivity distribution of West Bengal's firms in goods, 2011–15**

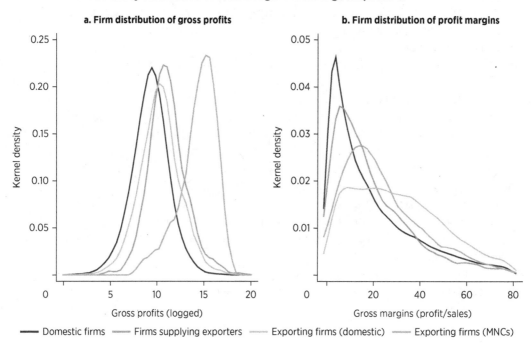

Source: World Bank calculations.
Note: Suppliers to exporting firms are restricted to nonexporters; MNCs include foreign-owned firms, joint ventures, and domestic firms with outward foreign investment. Sectors include agricultural goods; food products; textiles, apparel, and leather; and chemicals. GVC = global value chain; MNC = multinational corporation.

both considerably more profitable and most likely to have high profit margins. Hence, the most productive firms tend to become exporting firms.[17]

Pathways for internationalization

As shown in chapter 3, firms have three different pathways for internationalization: MNC-supplier linkages, JVs between MNCs and domestic firms, and outward investment by domestic firms. Results from both areas (figure 11.7) suggest that all pathways of entry into GVCs raise the probability that a firm will become a direct exporter. The more closely domestic firms interact with international firms, the more likely they will start exporting. As such, investment-based GVC participation (JVs and outward FDI) is a stronger predictor than supplier links of becoming an exporter. In many cases, domestic firms were also found to engage in more than one pathway to GVC entry (for example, supplying some MNCs while engaged in a joint JV with another MNC).

In both Rwanda and West Bengal, the importance of supply linkages differs across GVC types. In Rwanda, supply linkages are most conducive to internationalization in more-complex GVCs. The importance of supply linkages is largest in more-complex GVCs that may embody some relational ties, including in textiles, apparel, and leather; chemicals; and professional services, providing firms with an opportunity to produce to higher product standards. In contrast, there is less opportunity to move into GVCs for relatively simple inputs such as coffee and tea

FIGURE 11.7 The comparative impact of different types of global value chain participation on the probability of a firm becoming a direct exporter in select value chains

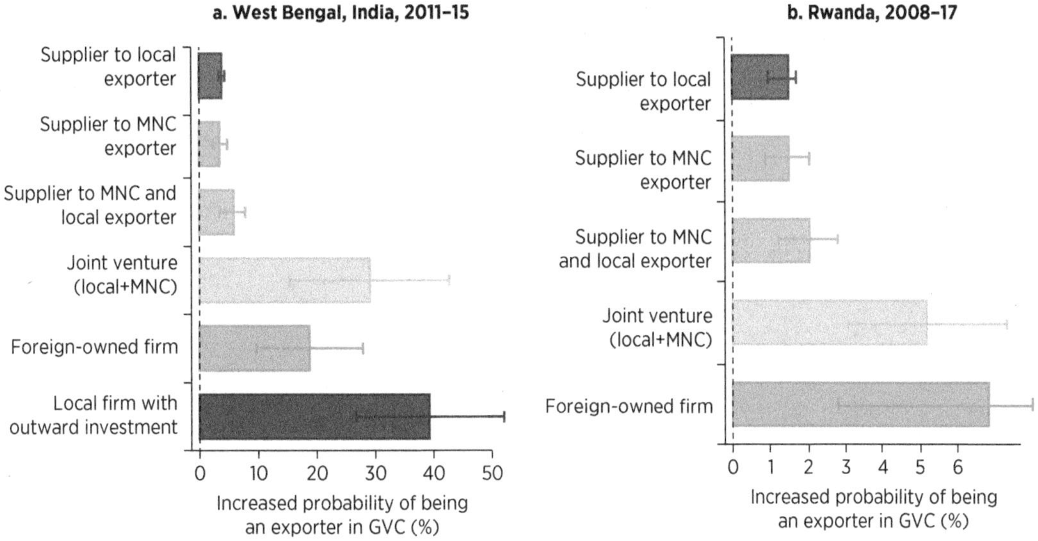

Source: World Bank calculations.
Note: West Bengal's foreign firms were identified using Orbis data only, and therefore represent only a small number of large, publicly listed firms in the region. The ownership of Rwandan firms was determined using data from the national investment promotion agency (the Rwanda Development Board). All regressions include sector and year fixed effects and robust standard errors. Joint ventures are defined as any firms in which a foreign partner has an equity stake of between 10 and 50 percent. Foreign-owned firms are firms in which a foreign partner has an equity stake of 51 percent or more. Local with outward investment firms are defined as firms that are headquartered in the country and have one or more foreign subsidiaries. GVC = global value chain; MNC = multinational corporation.

and agriprocessing. For West Bengal, being a supplier for food product exporters is associated with the greatest likelihood that the firm itself will become an exporter. The effect of supply linkages is smallest in the textiles, apparel, and leather and chemical products sectors. This difference could possibly be explained by the total number of export suppliers in each sector. There are relatively few firms supplying food products, so each supplier may provide a broader range of inputs for a specific exporter (relational sourcing). In contrast, there are many more firms supplying exporters in textiles, apparel, and leather and chemical products, indicating a situation in which many small firms sell individual inputs (spot sourcing) rather than a few firms supplying a range of inputs for a specific exporter (relational sourcing). Another possibility is that firms in food products and agriculture source more goods locally, whereas the other sectors are more import dependent.[18]

Foreign ownership tends to predict being an exporter across most GVC archetypes. In both Rwanda and West Bengal, foreign-owned firms were considerably more likely to be exporters across GVC archetypes. In West Bengal, domestic firms with outward investment were even more likely to be exporters. JVs, however, were more varied. JVs were most likely to occur in sectors in which foreign and domestic firms complement each other. In Rwanda, for example, JVs are significant predictors for becoming GVCs in only two sectors—agriprocessing and professional services. Both may be examples of sectors in which Rwandan firms offer key complementarities to foreign firms either by engaging with suppliers who speak only the local language (agriprocessing) or by being able to manage a complex regulatory environment (professional services).

The effect of global value chain participation on firm behavior

Finally, this chapter considers how GVC participation affects firm behavior by making use of a simple event study that compares firms in the years preceding and following their initial participation in GVCs (see chapter 3 for details).

The analysis first considers the ways in which firms become direct exporters (figure 11.8). Three distinct dynamics are identified: diversifying into exports, shifting into different export sectors, and starting as exporters.

FIGURE 11.8 **The three main ways in which firms become direct exporters in Rwanda and West Bengal, India**

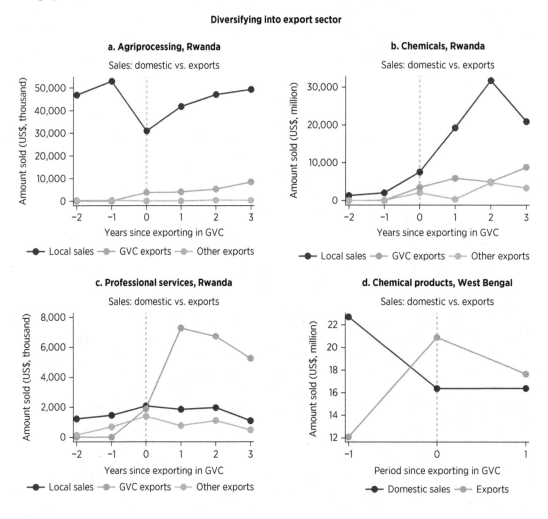

Diversifying into export sector

a. Agriprocessing, Rwanda

b. Chemicals, Rwanda

c. Professional services, Rwanda

d. Chemical products, West Bengal

Continued on next page >

FIGURE 11.8 The three main ways in which firms become direct exporters in Rwanda and West Bengal
(continued)

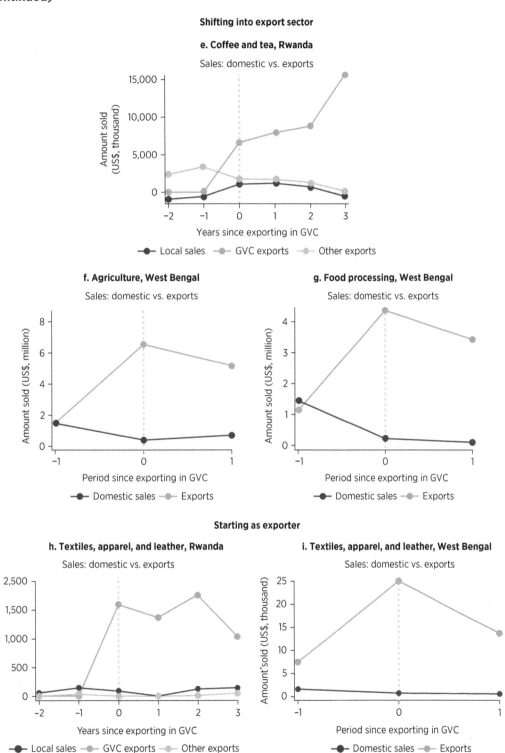

Shifting into export sector

e. Coffee and tea, Rwanda

Sales: domestic vs. exports

Local sales — *GVC exports* — *Other exports*

f. Agriculture, West Bengal

Sales: domestic vs. exports

Domestic sales — *Exports*

g. Food processing, West Bengal

Sales: domestic vs. exports

Domestic sales — *Exports*

Starting as exporter

h. Textiles, apparel, and leather, Rwanda

Sales: domestic vs. exports

Local sales — *GVC exports* — *Other exports*

i. Textiles, apparel, and leather, West Bengal

Sales: domestic vs. exports

Domestic sales — *Exports*

Source: World Bank calculations.
Note: For West Bengal's "Period since exporting," −1 = 2011/12, 0 = 2013/14, 1 = 2015/16. GVC = global value chain.

1. *Diversifying into exports.* The most common way in which domestic firms enter into GVCs appears to be for large, domestic firms to gradually expand into exports alongside their domestic operation. This is the case in Rwanda for exporters in agriprocessing, chemicals, and professional services, and for chemical products in West Bengal. These firms were able to both grow exports and maintain sizable domestic sales. In this case, sourcing dynamics appear relatively unaffected.

2. *Shifting into the export sector.* Another option is for a firm to move from one market into another (either by pivoting production or operating as a trader of a specific commodity). This option seems to be the dominant modality for exporters in coffee and tea in Rwanda and for agricultural goods and food processing in West Bengal. For such firms, domestic sales were initially significant, but then the increase in exports was accompanied by a decline in domestic production. Interestingly, these firms all tended to have strong domestic sourcing before becoming exporters; their sourcing amounts subsequently increased, but most of their sourcing continued to come from domestic purchases.

3. *Starting as an export-only company.* For textiles, apparel, and leather, much of the industry is fully oriented toward the export market, and for that reason many exporting firms in this sector focus entirely on exporting. These firms have specialized in exports since their establishment. For these firms, overall sales were close to zero before entering GVCs, and production is mostly geared toward exports. Almost all the inputs for this sector appear to be imported, with limited local sourcing (further supporting the evidence in the previous section for why supply linkages appear less conducive to internationalization in this sector).

Evidence for firms' improvements in competitiveness after beginning to participate in GVCs was also found. In both the Rwanda study and the West Bengal study, firms that started exporting for international markets often grew and became more productive (figures 11.4 and 11.5). They also became more dependent on more-complex imports either directly preceding or following their internationalization, suggesting that they were sourcing capital equipment rather than raw inputs (figure 11.9, top row). GVC participation also has a significant effect on firms' employment dynamics, often leading to a steep rise in employment (figure 11.9, bottom row). Similar findings were identified in West Bengal. Overall, these dynamics suggest that recently internationalized firms tend to upgrade their essential production capabilities (for example, their capital, skill, and research and development intensity) to meet more demanding global product requirements.

Conclusion

This case study uses novel data sets and methodologies to provide new insights into firm-level dynamics across GVCs. The analysis finds that, in both Rwanda and West Bengal, FDI plays an important role in GVC participation. Foreign firms are more

FIGURE 11.9 **The effect of global value chain participation (direct exporting) on firm imports and employment in Rwanda, 2008–17**

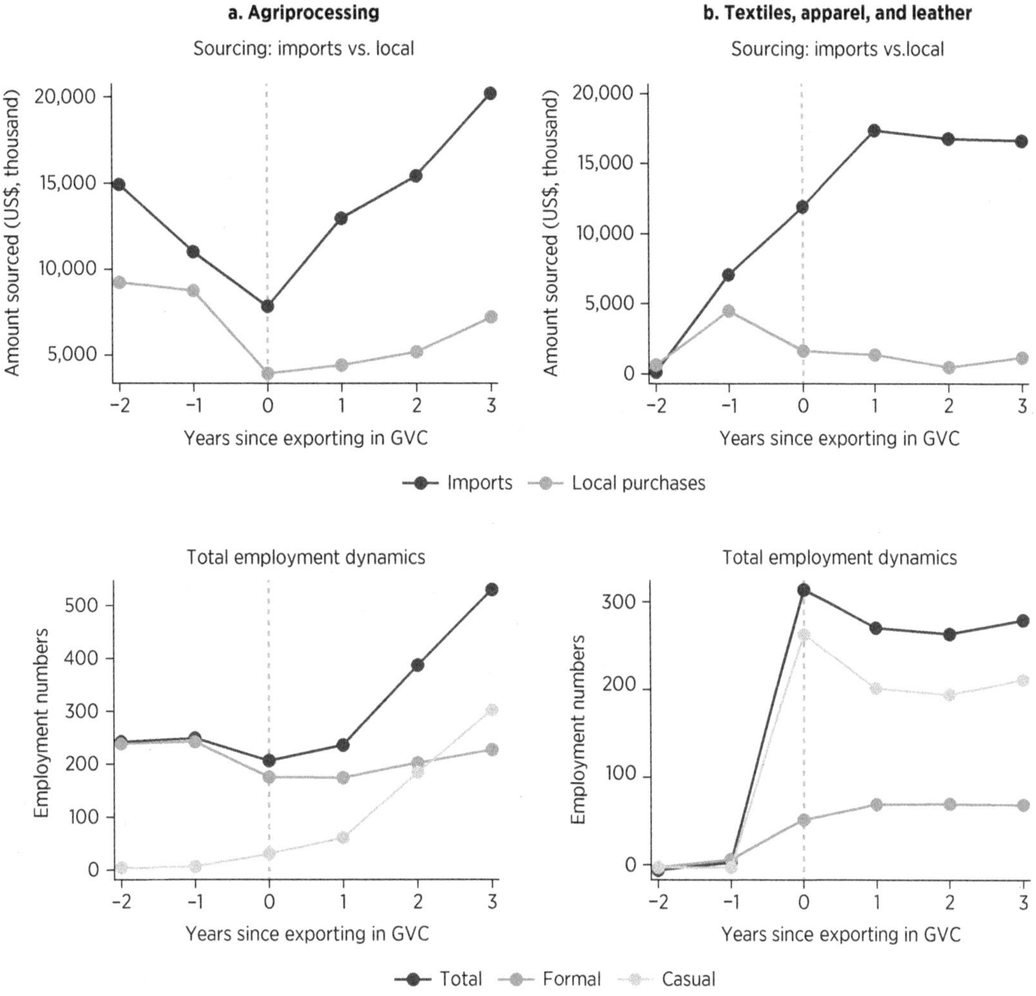

a. Agriprocessing

Sourcing: imports vs. local

b. Textiles, apparel, and leather

Sourcing: imports vs. local

- Imports   - Local purchases

Total employment dynamics

Total employment dynamics

- Total   - Formal   - Casual

Source: World Bank calculations.
Note: GVC = global value chain.

likely to export and contribute a disproportionally high share of exports, and regression analysis suggests FDI is positively correlated with a sector's export share.

Using firm- and transaction-level data, network analysis helps illustrate interfirm relationships in selected value chains. The network analysis shows that foreign firms tend to be positioned at the end of domestic value chains, given that they are more likely to export. Network analysis further suggests that GVC participation across multiple sectors is dominated by a small number of foreign-owned firms. This approach can show which types of firms are engaging in GVCs as exporters and as suppliers (according to their ownership, size, and location). As such, it provides insights into the wide network of GVC actors that may be less easily observable with traditional stakeholder analysis (such as tier 2 suppliers). This technique may assist in developing a GVC strategy, and it can also be used to monitor the strategy's overall progress. One downside of this approach, however, is that no data are available for firms not based within the country, so only the part of the GVC taking place within the country is observable.

The analysis indicates that participation in GVCs tends to be restricted to the most productive firms. Three types of pathways are dominant in raising the probability that domestic firms will become direct exporters: MNC-supplier linkages, JVs between MNCs and domestic firms, and outward foreign investment. However, some important differences across GVCs are found, depending on the sector, that any GVC strategy should accommodate. For example, whereas supply linkages appear most important in GVCs with higher product standards that require firm-level skills upgrading to accommodate (for example, in textiles, apparel, and leather; chemicals; and professional services), JVs are most important for sectors in which domestic firms offer complementarities to foreign firms, either by engaging with suppliers who speak only the local language (agriprocessing) or by being able to manage a complex regulatory environment (professional services). The overall difference in *type* of firms that choose to export (direct GVC exporters, large firms diversifying into exports alongside domestic sales, or firms shifting from one export product to another) may further help shape approaches to stimulating GVC participation.

This chapter demonstrates how researchers can make use of novel firm- and transaction-level data sets to provide greater insights into a country's GVC participation. Although this approach is not without limitations, consistent use of such analysis may provide important new findings that can help policy makers better understand the dynamics of firms within GVCs and help design better sector-industrial strategies to stimulate their GVC participation.

Notes

1. West Bengal has a population of about 100 million and ranks as the sixth-highest contributor to India's GDP. Its GDP per capita stands at US$1,500 in 2018/19 (Reserve Bank of India 2020, https://m.rbi.org.in/Scripts/PublicationsView.aspx?id=20004). The state shares international borders with Bangladesh to the east and Nepal and Bhutan to the north, and it is the gateway to the northeastern part of India.
2. Agricultural goods exports are particularly concentrated in two products, rice and tea, which make up 4.4 percent and 3.3 percent of all exports, respectively.
3. Part of the export of basic commodities may include products that are produced elsewhere in India and exported via West Bengal, or that are imported into the state and reexported to neighboring countries. The Directorate General of Commercial Intelligence and Statistics data do not separate out such products.
4. For example, to identify Rwandan firms that are part of the commodities (coffee and tea) global value chain, those firms that export goods listed under HS headings 0901 and 0902 are included. If a firm exports multiple products, the firm is assigned to the GVC in which it is most engaged. A table presenting all criteria used to identify firms active in the six GVC archetypes considered is available in Steenbergen et al. (2021).

5. The simplifying assumption that all of hotel and tour operator services are exported is applied.

6. The business types are Manufacturer, Distributor, Agency, Wholesaler, Retailer, Auctioneer, Works Contractor, Transferor of Right to Use Goods, Hire Purchaser, Hotelier, Club, Importer, Exporter, and Others.

7. West Bengal has four rates across commodities: 0, 1.0, 5.0, and 14.5 percent.

8. When calculating the dependent variable (the share of a sector's output that is exported), the exercise also includes the contribution of foreign-owned firms themselves, which is important because MNCs are known to be large, positive outliers with regard to exporting.

9. In line with Reyes (2018) only sectors in manufacturing and services are included in the sample.

10. Two-way trading firms in this study are defined as firms that both import and export in the same year.

11. Although the use of price markups was initially planned, it was ultimately dropped given challenges in the available data and difficulty in estimating markups accurately.

12. The coffee and tea value chain might be the only representative value chain because the numbers of firms in other value chains are too small to draw any meaningful conclusions on market power.

13. This group includes only firms that are registered to pay VATs (so only medium and large firms), which likely excludes key informal providers such as coffee-washing stations for coffee GVCs or food suppliers for hotels.

14. The limited number of suppliers in tourism is partly a result of the limited data that classify any larger hotel or tour operator as a direct exporter.

15. This is partly because tourism sales to foreigners (exports) and sales to Rwandans (domestic sales) cannot be differentiated and thus all income is treated as exports. For professional services, GVC firms are found to be considerably more productive than domestic firms.

16. Ideally, total factor productivity or output per worker would have been examined, but this was not possible with the available data.

17. Reverse causality is also a possibility, whereby firms that supply GVCs or start exporting become more productive, so that their productivity is improved (Alfaro-Ureña, Manelici, and Vasquez 2019).

18. For more details, see Steenbergen et al. (2021).

References

Alfaro-Ureña, A., I. Manelici, and J. P. Vasquez. 2019. "The Effects of Joining Multinational Supply Chains: New Evidence from Firm-to-Firm Linkages." Working Paper. https://papers.ssrn.com/sol3/papers.cfm?abstract_id=3376129.

Antràs, P. 2020. "Conceptual Aspects of Global Value Chains." Background paper, *World Development Report 2020: Trading for Development in the Age of Global Value Chains*, World Bank, Washington, DC.

Cusolito, Ana Paula, Raed Safadi, and Daria Taglioni. 2016. *Inclusive Global Value Chains: Policy Options for Small and Medium Enterprises and Low-Income Countries*. Directions in Development Series. Washington, DC: World Bank.

Díaz-Mora, Carmen, David Córcoles, and Rosario Gandoy. "Exit from Exporting: Does Being a Two-Way Trader Matter?" *Economics: The Open-Access, Open-Assessment E-Journal* 9 (2015–20): 1–27.

Fally, Thibault. 2012. "Production Staging: Measurement and Facts." University of Colorado, Boulder, CO.

Johnson, Robert C. 2018. "Measuring Global Value Chains." *Annual Review of Economics* 10 (August): 207–36.

Pal, Parthapratim. 2013. "Pattern of International Trade through West Bengal: Some Evidence from Port-Level Data." Report WPS 737, Indian Institute of Management, Calcutta.

Reyes, Jose Daniel. 2018. "Effects of FDI on High-Growth Firms in Developing Countries." Chapter 2 in *Global Investment Competitiveness Report 2017–2018*. Washington, DC: World Bank.

Steenbergen, Victor, Yan Liu, Anna Twum, and Jakob Rauschendorfer. 2021. *The Role of Foreign and Domestic Investors in Rwanda's Participation in Global Value Chains*. Washington, DC: World Bank.

Wang, Z., S. J. Wei, X. Yu, and K. Zhu. 2017. "Characterizing Global Value Chains: Production Length and Upstreamness." NBER Working Paper 23261, National Bureau of Economic Research, Cambridge, MA.

World Bank. 2020. *World Development Report 2020: Trading for Development in the Age of Global Value Chains*. Washington, DC: World Bank.